Controversies in
American Public Policy

Controversies in American Public Policy

John A. Hird

University of Massachusetts at Amherst

ST. MARTIN'S PRESS

New York

Executive editor: Don Reisman
Manager, publishing services: Emily Berleth
Publishing services associate: Kalea Chapman
Project management: Till & Till, Inc.
Production supervisor: Joe Ford

Library of Congress Catalog Card Number: 94-65225

Manufactured in the United States of America.
98765
fedcba

For information, write:
St. Martin's Press, Inc.
175 Fifth Avenue
New York, NY 10010

ISBN: 0-312-10407-3

Acknowledgments

It is a violation of the law to reproduce these selections by any means whatsoever without the written permission of the copyright holder

"America's Public Schools: Choice Is a Panacea." Copyright © 1990 The Brookings Institution. Reprinted with permission from *The Brookings Review*, Summer 1990.

"The Great School Sell-Off." Copyright © 1993, New Prospect Inc. Reprinted with permission from *The American Prospect*, Winter 1993.

"Jobs for the Welfare Poor: Work Requirements Can Overcome the Barriers." Reprinted with permission from *Policy Review*, Winter 1990.

"Punishing the Poor, Again: The Fraud of Workfare." Copyright © 1993 The Nation Company, Inc. Reprinted with permission from *The Nation*, May 24, 1993.

"How Privatization Incentives Can Revive Inner-City Housing." Reprinted with permission from *National Forum*, Spring 1990.

"From 'Projects' to Communities: How to Redeem Public Housing." Copyright © 1992, New Prospect Inc. Reprinted with permission from *The American Prospect*, Summer 1992.

"Teaching Children about AIDS." Copyright © 1987 Issues in Science and Technology. Reprinted with permission from *Issues in Science and Technology*, Fall 1987.

"The Failure of AIDS-Prevention Education." Copyright © 1988 by National Affairs, Inc. Reprinted with permission from *The Public Interest*, Summer 1988, pp. 3–31.

"Canada's Health-Care System: A Model for the United States?" Copyright © 1991, Current History, Inc. Reprinted with permission from *Current History* magazine, December 1991.

"The Canadian Model: Could It Work Here?" Reprinted with permission from author and *Vital Speeches of the Day*. © 1989, William E. Goodman, M.D. All rights reserved. This piece originated as a speech to the Association of American Physicians and Surgeons, was published in book form by the A.A.P.S., and was subsequently reprinted in *Vital Speeches of the Day*, February 15, 1990.

"A Healthier Approach to Health Care." Copyright © 1991 National Academy of Sciences, Washington, DC. Reprinted with permission from *Issues in Science and Technology*, Winter 1991, pp. 59–65.

Acknowledgments and copyrights are continued at the back of the book on page 480, which constitutes an extension of the copyright page.

for Sharon

PREFACE

This book grew out of a series of public policy debates in an undergraduate course in public policy that I have taught at the University of Massachusetts at Amherst for the past six years. As anyone who teaches public policy or any related courses knows, there are dozens of ways to design such a course. I wanted the course to achieve several objectives: to assess substantive public policy issues, to convey the ethical and ideological underpinnings of policy disputes, to explain the rudiments of policy analysis, and, most important, to get students actively engaged in discussing and thinking critically about what they consider to be "good" public policy. It seemed to me that a debate format could best achieve these objectives and would complement traditional lectures more effectively.

Students in my public policy class now debate more than a dozen issues during the course of a semester, with three or four students on either side of each policy debate. Debate topics range from "Should drugs be legalized?" to "Should the United States promote free-trade policies?" to "Would school choice improve the quality of education?" After both debate teams present their arguments, a question-and-answer and discussion session involving the entire class follows (the other members of the class are required to write two-page memos advocating one position or the other). These discussions serve several purposes: to allow the entire class to become involved in the debate and to question and challenge the debaters, to clarify ambiguous or confusing points, to sharpen the discussion on key subjects, to convey the complexity of policy issues, to show that there are more than two sides to each issue, and to make connections to other public policy issues and perspectives. Judged by student reactions during the debates—and the occasional spillover of discussion into the hall after class—the debate format has been quite successful.

Besides teaching, this book is motivated by a number of public policy concerns. The first is the perception on the part of some (perhaps most prominently Ross Perot) that simple solutions to public policy problems are attainable if only experts would get together and hash out the issues. As the positions on numerous and important public policy issues in this book show, experts can and do disagree vehemently over the proper course of public policy. Policy solutions are not simple and involve more than reconciling technical issues for which experts' advice is especially valuable; indeed, there is rarely any solution at all. Furthermore, public policy debates involve divergent issues and agendas, complicated technical issues, confusing (and not always public) forms of communication, and political actors with varied motivations, not to mention different views of what constitutes the public interest. All of these factors complicate efforts to "do the right thing," or even to identify what the right thing is.

Another motivation for this book is to show that resolving policy problems involves more than eliminating pork-barrel politics or the influence of special interests and that policy problems stem from deeper sources than the assumption that politicians are bought and paid for by big money interests (*Mr. Smith Goes to Washington* notwithstanding). It appears, using as one piece of evidence the movement for congressional term limits, that many Americans believe that if we replace the "scoundrels" in Washington with a new batch of representatives, public policy will be greatly improved. To be sure, special interests have disproportionate influence, and there are certain benefits from new faces in Washington, but it is important to recognize that "special interests" include groups whose missions have broad support, such as the American Association for Retired Persons (among the elderly), Greenpeace (among environmentalists), the National Rifle Association (among gun owners), Common Cause (among campaign finance reform supporters), and many others. Many citizens underestimate the degree to which legislators take their cues from voter opinion (and not just from lobbyists) and overestimate the degree to which money influences public policy decisions (in contrast to elections).

Finally, I wanted to produce a book that focused on the substance of politics rather than on the horse race of political campaign coverage and scandals that seem to dominate headline stories. While the sport of politics can be entertaining, it seems important not to lose sight of the fact that public policy decisions are what elected representatives are sent to state and national capitals for in the first place. The book therefore attempts to provide the means necessary for citizens to learn about the substance of politics and perhaps even to view politics—the struggle to define and resolve competing interests—in a more favorable light.

There are several ways for instructors to use this book in class. The first is to arrange in-class debates, in which two teams of students present their arguments on each side of the question in front of the class. A second would be to use these readings to illustrate different policy perspectives in order to provide a foundation for class discussions of substantive policy issues. The book could also be used to complement large lectures in American Government or Public Policy with smaller discussions focusing on the substance of government. Most instructors probably will not draw on all seventeen debates in the book, but there are enough debates and sufficient variety to satisfy the specific interests of most instructors.

A few caveats are in order. First, there are (obviously) more than two sides to these debates; I attempt only to supply major arguments and encourage instructors and students to fill in other more radical or moderate positions. Second, there are many other debates that could have been included in this book, but finding articles of sufficiently high quality on either side of a specific debate question proved difficult in some cases. Further, the book's organization into sections on economic policy, social policy, international policy, and rights and regulations is somewhat arbitrary, since nearly all of the debate topics involve several categories to some degree; other organizing principles can be substituted for course use, such as by level of government involved (state, local, national, or international). Instructors are encouraged to point out linkages among these debate topics; a useful discussion point is to ask students to identify some important ones, such as between immigration and affirmative action, enterprise zones and public housing, and national health insurance and welfare policy, among others.

I would like to acknowledge the significant contributions of several people who made this book possible, particularly those of Craig Farringer, Michael Reese, and Sharon Tracey. I would also like to thank my colleague Jerry Mileur and the reviewers for St. Martin's Press, whose suggestions for organizing the book and choosing selections improved the manuscript immensely: Michael B. Berkman, Pennsylvania State University; N. Joseph Cayer, Arizona State University; Clarke Cochran, Texas Tech University; Jerry Johnson, Montana State University; and Anne Khademian, University of Wisconsin. I am also grateful for the generous financial assistance of the Massachusetts Institute for Social and Economic Research at the University of Massachusetts at Amherst and for the help of Kelly Spang and Tara Hood in assembling the final product.

John A. Hird
Amherst, Massachusetts

CONTENTS

PART I
SOCIAL POLICY   1

1. **Education Policy:** *"Would 'School Choice' Improve
   the Quality of U.S. Education?"*   3
   YES *John E. Chubb and Terry M. Moe* "America's Public
          Schools: Choice *Is* a Panacea"   7

   NO *Peter Schrag* "The Great School Sell-Off"   20

   Discussion Questions   30
   Additional Readings   31

2. **Welfare Policy:** *"Should Welfare Recipients Be
   Required to Work in Exchange for AFDC and Other
   Transfer Payments?"*   33
   YES *Lawrence M. Mead* "Jobs for the Welfare Poor:
          Work Requirements Can Overcome the Barriers"   37

   NO *Richard A. Cloward and Frances Fox Piven* "Punishing
          the Poor, Again: The Fraud of Workfare"   54

   Discussion Questions   58
   Additional Readings   59

3. **Privatization and Public Housing Policy:** *"Should Public
   Housing Be Sold to Tenants or Otherwise Privatized?"*   61
   YES *Stuart M. Butler* "How Privatization Incentives Can
          Revive Inner-City Housing"   66

   NO *John Atlas and Peter Dreier* "From 'Projects' to
          Communities: How to Redeem Public Housing"   71

   Discussion Questions   84
   Additional Readings   84

4. **AIDS Policy:** *"Does AIDS-Prevention Education Work?"*   87
   YES *C. Everett Koop* "Teaching Children about AIDS"   92

   NO *William E. Dannemeyer and Michael G. Franc* "The
          Failure of AIDS-Prevention Education"   97

   Discussion Questions   108
   Additional Readings   108

5. **National Health Insurance:** *"Should the United States Adopt a Single-Payer System of National Health Insurance?"* 111
YES *Theodore R. Marmor* "Canada's Health-Care System: A Model for the United States?" 114

NO *William E. Goodman* "The Canadian Model: Could It Work Here?" 124

Discussion Questions 133
Additional Readings 134

6. **State Health Care Policy:** *"Should Other States Follow the 'Oregon Plan' in Rationing Health Care under the Federal Medicaid Program?"* 137
YES *John Kitzhaber* "A Healthier Approach to Health Care" 140

NO *Robert H. Brook and Kathleen N. Lohr* "Will We Need to Ration Effective Health Care?" 149

Discussion Questions 156
Additional Readings 157

**PART II
ECONOMIC POLICY** 159

7. **Industrial Policy:** *"Should the Federal Government Play a Greater Role in Promoting Specific Industries or Technologies?"* 161
YES *James Fallows* "Looking at the Sun" 163

NO *Karl Zinsmeister* "MITI Mouse: Japan's Industrial Policy Doesn't Work" 185

Discussion Questions 198
Additional Readings 198

8. **Energy Policy:** *"Should the United States Have a National Energy Policy?* 201
YES *Christopher Flavin* "Beyond the Gulf Crisis: An Energy Strategy for the '90s" 207

NO *Irwin Stelzer* "National Energy Planning Redux" 216

Discussion Questions 225
Additional Readings 225

9. **Budgetary Policy:** *"Should Balancing the Budget Be a Major Federal Priority?"* 227
YES *Charles L. Schultze* "Of Wolves, Termites, and Pussycats or, Why We Should Worry about the Budget Deficit" 231

NO *Robert Eisner* "Our Real Deficits"   242
Discussion Questions   250
Additional Readings   250

10. **Urban Policy:** *"Are Enterprise Zones Effective Tools
    in Developing Inner Cities?"*   253
    YES *Jack Kemp* "Tackling Poverty: Market-Based Policies
        to Empower the Poor"   256

    NO *Sar A. Levitan and Elizabeth I. Miller* "Enterprise Zones
       Are No Solution for Our Blighted Areas"   263
    Discussion Questions   270
    Additional Readings   270

PART III
INTERNATIONAL POLICY   271

11. **International Trade Policy:** *"Should the Federal
    Government Vigorously Pursue International
    Free-Trade Policies?"*   273
    YES *Robert E. Litan and Peter O. Suchman* "U.S. Trade
        Policy at a Crossroad"   278

    NO *Robert Kuttner* "Managed Trade and Economic
       Sovereignty"   291
    Discussion Questions   307
    Additional Readings   307

12. **Immigration Policy:** *"Should the United States Allow
    Substantial Increases in Immigration?"*   309
    YES *Julian L. Simon* "The Case for Greatly Increased
        Immigration"   313

    NO *Vernon M. Briggs Jr.* "Immigration Policy: Political
       or Economic?"   325
    Discussion Questions   336
    Additional Readings   337

13. **International Environmental Policy:** *"Should the United
    States Take Immediate Action to Address the Threat
    from Global Warming?"*   339
    YES *Claudine Schneider* "Preventing Climate Change"   343

    NO *Jeffrey Salmon* "Greenhouse Anxiety"   353
    Discussion Questions   359
    Additional Readings   360

PART IV
RIGHTS AND REGULATIONS 361

14. **Affirmative Action/Equal Opportunity:** *"Is Affirmative Action an Effective Means to Advance the Interests of Minorities?"* 363
    YES *Stanley Fish* "Reverse Racism or How the Pot Got to Call the Kettle Black" 368

    NO *Shelby Steele* "A Negative Vote on Affirmative Action" 375

    Discussion Questions 380
    Additional Readings 381

15. **Drug Policy:** *"Should Drugs Be Legalized?"* 383
    YES *Ethan A. Nadelmann* "The Case for Legalization" 388

    NO *James Q. Wilson* "Against the Legalization of Drugs" 411

    Discussion Questions 429
    Additional Readings 430

16. **Gun Control:** *"Should the Sale of Handguns Be More Strictly Controlled?"* 431
    YES *William Greider* "A Pistol-Whipped Nation" 436

    NO *David B. Kopel* "Hold Your Fire: Gun Control Won't Stop Rising Violence" 441

    Discussion Questions 453
    Additional Readings 453

17. **Abortion Policy:** *"Should the Federal Government Provide Funding for Abortions through Medicaid?"* 455
    YES *Senators Robert W. Packwood and William D. Hathaway and Representatives Patricia Schroeder and Daniel Flood* 460

    NO *Representatives Robert E. Bauman, Henry J. Hyde, and Ron Paul* 471

    Discussion Questions 478
    Additional Readings 479

About the Author 481

PART I
SOCIAL POLICY

1
EDUCATION POLICY

"Would 'School Choice' Improve the Quality of U.S. Education?"

Education, by one definition "learning what you didn't know you didn't know," is one of the most important public functions in the United States. The United States educates nearly 50 million students in grades K–12 and another 13 million in colleges and universities. Although elementary and secondary education policy in the United States is the product of influences from federal, state, and local governments, it is unusual among major public functions in that it is dominated by local interests and funding. With more than 15,000 school districts, states and localities spend more than $300 billion annually on education, 80 percent of it on elementary and secondary education. Most funding for elementary and secondary education is derived from local property taxes, and over half of state and local government employment is devoted to education (including higher education).[1] In contrast, the federal government generally plays a relatively minor role, spending approximately $50 billion annually in elementary and secondary education. On the whole, approximately 92 percent of spending on elementary and secondary education is from public sources.

The United States spends a larger portion of its Gross Domestic Product on higher education than any other industrialized country,* and a higher proportion of U.S. students attends postsecondary schools than in other industrialized nations.† The federal role in higher education is far greater, however, accounting for 59 percent of all federal educational expenditures. Indeed, when federal research funding is included, the federal government spends more on higher education than elementary and secondary combined. Further, while most spending at the elementary and secondary levels is public, for higher education the share dips to 36 percent. Therefore, elementary and secondary education tends to be publicly funded from state and local sources, while higher education relies much more heavily on federal and private sources of funding.

The United States education system has produced some impressive achievements over the past several decades. The percentage of individuals

---

* This amount dwarfs the proportion spent in other industrialized countries (Canada is next with 1.8 percent of its GDP, Japan spends 1.0 percent, Germany and the United Kingdom spend 0.9 percent, and France 0.7 percent) (*Statistical Abstract of the United States, 1992*).

† More than 5 percent of the U.S. population is enrolled in higher education, compared with just 2.5 percent in Germany, 2.3 percent in France, 1.9 percent in Japan, and 1.8 percent in the United Kingdom. Ibid.

(twenty-five years and older) with four or more years of college education increased sharply from 7.7 percent in 1960 to more than 21 percent by 1992; the portion of individuals with less than twelve years of schooling has plummeted from 59 percent to 21 percent over the same period; and the percentage of high school dropouts has fallen slightly from 12.2 percent in 1970 to 10.5 percent in 1991.[2] U.S. higher education continues to attract hundreds of thousands of foreign students from around the world. Education has, of course, provided significant benefits that cannot be quantified, such as assimilating immigrants into American customs and culture, promoting civic mindedness, and improving employment skills.

Despite important progress, primary and secondary education has been faulted for the declining educational achievements of today's students, both compared with past test scores and in comparison with the abilities of students in other countries (particularly those with whom the United States competes economically). Test scores, while surely imperfect measures of learning, indicate declines in achievement in both verbal and mathematical ability over the past several decades. Average combined SAT scores fell from 958 in 1967 to 902 by 1994.[3] Similar declines were experienced in individual math and verbal scores, by both males and females. While some of the declines have begun to be reversed, there is concern not only with how well students stack up with previous generations, but also with students in other industrialized nations. Recent comparisons show that U.S. students routinely score low in geography, science, and mathematics compared with students from other wealthy nations, fueling added fears for the economic as well as the educational health of the nation.*

These problems have drawn attention to numerous educational reforms. Although the symptoms are apparent, there is little agreement about the most important causes. Some fault the inequity in educational preparation, varying with economic status and geographic differences. School spending varies widely across states and communities. New Jersey, with the nation's highest per-pupil expenditures ($9,429) in 1994, spent nearly three times as much per student as Utah, the lowest.[4] This disparity partly reflects purchasing power (a dollar buys more in Utah than in New Jersey), partly the relative incomes of different states, and partly the emphasis voters place on educational spending. (Average spending does not necessarily correlate with improved average performance, however; Utah students scored 174 points higher on average SAT scores than their New Jersey counterparts in 1994.) States vary in educational achievement as well. For example, high school graduation rates in the District of Columbia were under 60 percent, while Minnesota, North Dakota, Iowa, Wisconsin, and several others boasted graduation rates in excess of 85 percent.[5] Moreover, spending within states varies

---

* Colleges and universities have come under criticism as well. A recent report called undergraduate education in the United States "little more than secondary school material—warmed over and reoffered at much higher expenses." Reported in William H. Honan, "Report Says Colleges Are Failing to Educate," *New York Times* (December 5, 1993), p. 46.

considerably as well, largely because school spending is strongly tied to a community's property tax receipts; because tax receipts in poorer districts fall behind those of wealthier ones, school funding and other public services are short-changed. Some have argued that this vicious circle (where poor districts beget underfunded schools, leading to reduced economic opportunities for the residents, and leading back to poor districts) unfairly disadvantages some, especially the poor and minorities. This has led courts in more than two dozen states to order changes in state school financing, generally in ways that move away from the strong link between property taxes and school funding levels.

Some critics fault bureaucratic licensing requirements that prohibit competition among teachers; others fault a tenure system that they believe encourages mediocrity and indolence; others decry a curriculum too far removed from "reading, writing, and arithmetic"; others fault excessively bureaucratic school systems that strangle teacher initiative, and so on. While criticisms are legion, systematic reform proposals—such as magnet schools, raising teacher salaries, and extending the school year—often require funds that many localities cannot or do not want to supply. Further, efforts to delink property taxes and school spending are sure to meet substantial political resistance. For mobile or affluent families, school quality is an important criterion for deciding where to live, and families pay a premium in terms of housing prices for living in a town with excellent schools (since funding is tied to local property taxes). Therefore, decoupling school spending and property taxes will mean substantial wealth transfers from areas with high per-pupil spending to those with lower educational spending. The inability of state legislatures to reconcile these political differences has meant that courts have had to impose school finance reforms on states.

One of the most important challenges to educational policy in the United States has come from advocates of "school choice." Economist Milton Friedman provided the intellectual foundation for school choice by advocating a system of vouchers to be given to students, redeemable at the school of their choice.* Choice systems vary considerably in their specifics, but the underlying principle is to allow students to select which school they will attend. This choice may be limited to the several schools in a district, or it may include any school within the region or state. (Presumably there would be de facto geographic limits given commuting costs and times.) Supporters argue that a system that forces schools to compete with one another for students will foster improved education. Two of the most prominent supporters, John Chubb of the Brookings Institution and Terry Moe of Stanford University, argue that a system of school choice will solve the fundamental problem faced by the educational system because it will replace the existing bureau-

---

* A proposal to provide vouchers to all California students lost overwhelmingly in a state-wide referendum in 1993, but the issue is sure to recur there and elsewhere as states grapple with school financing alternatives.

cratic governing institutions with a system of market controls, which will force schools to be well organized. They argue that school organization is the primary determinant of school effectiveness and that the present system of democratic accountability has resulted in an educational bureaucracy that has forced schools to organize in an ineffective manner. By abandoning democratic accountability and bureaucratic control, a system of school choice will give schools both the autonomy and the incentive to organize in the most effective way possible. Peter Schrag, an editor at the *Sacramento Bee*, agrees that bureaucratic control of schools should be abandoned in favor of autonomous, cooperative school management, but he argues that there is little evidence that a system of school choice will accomplish this goal. The danger of a system of school choice, he argues, is that it would undermine the public spirit and faith in governmental control that are essential for effective school reforms while at the same time encourage a misplaced faith in abstract notions of market competition and institutional reform. The authors amplify these points in their articles below.

Endnotes

1. Federal Reserve Bank of Cleveland, *Economic Trends* (October 1993), p. 11.
2. U.S. Department of Commerce, Bureau of the Census, *Statistical Abstract of the United States, 1993* (Washington, D.C.: U.S. Government Printing Office, 1993).
3. "Study Says Small Schools Are Key to Learning," *New York Times* (September 21, 1994), p. B12.
4. Ibid.
5. Ibid.

YES

America's Public Schools: Choice *Is* a Panacea

John E. Chubb and Terry M. Moe

For America's public schools, the last decade has been the worst of times and the best of times. Never before have the public schools been subjected to such savage criticism for failing to meet the nation's educational needs—yet never before have governments been so aggressively dedicated to studying the schools' problems and finding the resources for solving them.

The signs of poor performance were there for all to see during the 1970s. Test scores headed downward year after year. Large numbers of teenagers continued to drop out of school. Drugs and violence poisoned the learning environment. In math and science, two areas crucial to the nation's success in the world economy, American students fell far behind their counterparts in virtually every other industrialized country. Something was clearly wrong.

During the 1980s a growing sense of crisis fueled a powerful movement for educational change, and the nation's political institutions responded with aggressive reforms. State after state increased spending on schools, imposed tougher requirements, introduced more rigorous testing, and strengthened teacher certification and training. And, as the decade came to an end, creative experiments of various forms—from school-based management to magnet schools—were being launched around the nation.

We think these reforms are destined to fail. They simply do not get to the root of the problem. The fundamental causes of poor academic performance are not to be found in the schools, but rather in the institutions by which the schools have traditionally been governed. Reformers fail by automatically relying on these institutions to solve the problem—when the institutions are the problem.

The key to better schools, therefore, is institutional reform. What we propose is a new system of public education that eliminates most political and bureaucratic control over the schools and relies instead on indirect control through markets and parental choice. These new institutions naturally function to promote and nurture the kinds of effective schools that reformers have wanted all along.

SCHOOLS AND INSTITUTIONS

Three basic questions lie at the heart of our analysis. What is the relationship between school organization and student achievement? What are the conditions that promote or inhibit desirable forms of organization? And how are these conditions affected by their institutional settings?

Our perspective on school organization and student achievement is in agreement with the most basic claims and findings of the "effective schools" literature, which served as the analytical base of the education reform movement throughout the 1980s. We believe, as most others do, that how much students learn is not determined simply by their aptitude or family background—although, as we show, these are certainly influential—but also by how effectively schools are organized. By our estimates, the typical high school student tends to learn considerably more, comparable to at least an extra year's worth of study, when he or she attends a high school that is effectively organized rather than one that is not.

Generally speaking, effective schools—be they public or private—have the kinds of organizational characteristics that the mainstream literature would lead one to expect: strong leadership, clear and ambitious goals, strong academic programs, teacher professionalism, shared influence, and staff harmony, among other things. These are best understood as integral parts of a coherent syndrome of organization. When this syndrome is viewed as a functioning whole, moreover, it seems to capture the essential features of what people normally mean by a team—principals and teachers working together, cooperatively and informally, in pursuit of a common mission.

How do these kinds of schools develop and take root? Here again, our own perspective dovetails with a central theme of educational analysis and criticism: the dysfunctions of bureaucracy, the value of autonomy, and the inherent tension between the two in American public education. Bureaucracy vitiates the most basic requirements of effective organization. It imposes goals, structures, and requirements that tell principals and teachers what to do and how to do it—denying them not only the discretion they need to exercise their expertise and professional judgment but also the flexibility they need to develop and operate as teams. The key to effective education rests with unleashing the productive potential already present in the schools and their personnel. It rests with granting them the autonomy to do what they do best. As our study of American high schools documents, the freer schools are from external control the more likely they are to have effective organizations.

Only at this late stage of the game do we begin to part company with the mainstream. While most observers can agree that the public schools have become too bureaucratic and would benefit from substantial grants of autonomy, it is also the standard view that this transformation can be achieved within the prevailing framework of democratic control. The implicit assumption is that, although political institutions have acted in the past to bureaucratize, they can now be counted upon to reverse course, grant the schools autonomy, and support and nurture this new population of autonomous schools. Such an assumption, however, is not based on a systematic understanding of how these institutions operate and what their consequences are for schools.

POLITICAL INSTITUTIONS

Democratic governance of the schools is built around the imposition of higher-order values through public authority. As long as that authority exists and is available for use, public officials will come under intense pressure from social groups of all political stripes to use it. And when they do use it, they cannot blithely assume that their favored policies will be faithfully implemented by the heterogeneous population of principals and teachers below—whose own values and professional views may be quite different from those being imposed. Public officials have little choice but to rely on formal rules and regulations that tell these people what to do and hold them accountable for doing it.

These pressures for bureaucracy are so substantial in themselves that real school autonomy has little chance to take root throughout the system. But they are not the only pressures for bureaucracy. They are compounded by the political uncertainty inherent in all democratic politics: those who exercise public authority know that other actors with different interests may gain authority in the future and subvert the policies they worked so hard to put in place. This knowledge gives them additional incentive to embed their policies in protective bureaucratic arrangements—arrangements that reduce the discretion of schools and formally insulate them from the dangers of politics.

These pressures, arising from the basic properties of democratic control, are compounded yet again by another special feature of the public sector. Its institutions provide a regulated, politically sensitive setting conducive to the power of unions, and unions protect the interests of their members through formal constraints on the governance and operation of schools—constraints that strike directly at the schools' capacity to build well-functioning teams based on informal cooperation.

The major participants in democratic governance—including the unions—complain that the schools are too bureaucratic. And they mean what they say. But they are the ones who bureaucratized the schools in the past, and they will continue to do so, even as they tout the great advantages of autonomy and professionalism. The incentives to bureaucratize the schools are built into the system.

MARKET INSTITUTIONS

This kind of behavior is not something that Americans simply have to accept, like death and taxes. People who make decisions about education would behave differently if their institutions were different. The most relevant and telling comparison is to markets, since it is through democratic control and markets that American society makes most of its choices on matters of public importance, including education. Public schools are subject to direct control through politics. But not all schools are controlled in this way. Private schools—representing about a fourth of all schools—are subject to indirect control through markets.

What difference does it make? Our analysis suggests that the difference is considerable and that it arises from the most fundamental properties that distinguish the two systems. A market system is not built to enable the imposition of higher-order values on the schools, nor is it driven by a democratic struggle to exercise public authority. Instead, the authority to make educational choices is radically decentralized to those most immediately involved. Schools compete for the support of parents and students, and parents and students are free to choose among schools. The system is built on decentralization, competition, and choice.

Although schools operating under a market system are free to organize any way they want, bureaucratization tends to be an unattractive way to go. Part of the reason is that virtually everything about good education—from the knowledge and talents necessary to produce it, to what it looks like when it is produced—defies formal measurement through the standardized categories of bureaucracy.

The more basic point, however, is that bureaucratic control and its clumsy efforts to measure the unmeasurable are simply *unnecessary* for schools whose primary concern is to please their clients. To do this, they need to perform as effectively as possible, which leads them, given the bottom-heavy technology of education, to favor decentralized forms of organization that take full advantage of strong leadership, teacher professionalism, discretionary judgment, informal cooperation, and teams. They also need to ensure that they provide the kinds of services parents and students want and that they have the capacity to cater and adjust to their clients' specialized needs and interests, which this same syndrome of effective organization allows them to do exceedingly well.

Schools that operate in an environment of competition and choice thus have strong incentives to move toward the kinds of "effective-school" organizations that academics and reformers would like to impose on the public schools. Of course, not all schools in the market will respond equally well to these incentives. But those that falter will find it more difficult to attract support, and they will tend to be weeded out in favor of schools that are better organized. This process of natural selection complements the incentives of the marketplace in propelling and supporting a population of autonomous, effectively organized schools.

INSTITUTIONAL CONSEQUENCES

No institutional system can be expected to work perfectly under real-world conditions. Just as democratic institutions cannot offer perfect representation or perfect implementation of public policy, so markets cannot offer perfect competition or perfect choice. But these imperfections, which are invariably the favorite targets of each system's critics, tend to divert attention from what is most crucial to an understanding of schools: as institutional systems, democratic control and market control are strikingly different in their fundamental properties. As a result, each system structures individual and social choices about education very differently, and each has very different consequences for the organization and performance of schools. Each system puts its own indelible stamp on the schools that emerge and operate within it.

What the analysis in our book suggests, in the most practical terms, is that American society offers two basic paths to the emergence of effective schools. The first is through markets, which scarcely operate in the public sector, but which act on private schools to discourage bureaucracy and promote desirable forms of organization through the natural dynamics of competition and choice.

The second path is through "special circumstances"—homogeneous environments free of problems—which, in minimizing the three types of political pressures just discussed, prompt democratic governing institutions to impose less bureaucracy than they otherwise would. Private schools therefore tend to be effectively organized because of the way their system naturally works. When public schools happen to be effectively organized, it is in spite of their system—they are the lucky ones with peculiarly nice environments.

As we show in our book, the power of these institutional forces is graphically reflected in our sample of American high schools. Having cast our net widely to allow for a full range of noninstitutional factors that might reasonably be suspected of influencing school autonomy, we found that virtually all of them fall by the wayside. The extent to which a school is granted the autonomy it needs to develop a more effective organization is overwhelmingly determined by its sectoral location and the niceness of its institutional environment.

Viewed as a whole, then, our effort to take institutions into account builds systematically on mainstream ideas and findings but, in the end, puts a very different slant on things. We agree that effective organization is a major determinant of student achievement. We also agree that schools perform better the more autonomous they are and the less encumbered they are by bureaucracy. But we do not agree that this knowledge about the proximate causes of effective performance can be used to engineer better schools through democratic control. Reformers are right about where they want to go, but their institutions cannot get them there.

The way to get schools with effective organizations is not to insist that democratic institutions should do what they are incapable of doing. Nor is it to assume that the better public schools, the lucky ones with nice environments, can serve as organizational models for the rest. Their luck is not transferable. The way to get effective schools is to recognize that the problem of ineffective performance is really a deep-seated institutional problem that arises from the most fundamental properties of democratic control.

The most sensible approach to genuine education reform is therefore to move toward a true institutional solution—a different set of institutional arrangements that actively promotes and nurtures the kinds of schools people want. The market alternative then becomes particularly attractive, for it provides a setting in which these organizations take root and flourish. That is where "choice" comes in.

EDUCATIONAL CHOICE

It is fashionable these days to say that choice is "not a panacea." Taken literally, that is obviously true. There are no panaceas in social policy. But the message this aphorism really means to get across is that choice is just one of many reforms with something to contribute. School-based management is another. So are teacher empowerment and professionalism, better training programs, stricter accountability, and bigger budgets. These and other types of reforms all bolster school effectiveness in their own distinctive ways—so the reasoning goes—and the best, most aggressive, most comprehensive approach to trans-forming the public school system is therefore one that wisely combines them into a multifaceted reformist package.

Without being too literal about it, we think reformers would do well to entertain the notion that choice *is* a panacea. Of all the sundry education reforms that attract attention, only choice has the capacity to address the basic institutional problem plaguing America's schools. The other reforms are all system-preserving. The schools remain subordinates in the structure of public authority—and they remain bureaucratic.

In principle, choice offers a clear, sharp break from the institutional past. In practice, however, it has been forced into the same mold with all the other reforms. It has been embraced half-heartedly and in bits and pieces—for example, through magnet schools and limited open enrollment plans. It has served as a means of granting parents and students a few additional options or of giving schools modest incentives to compete. These are popular moves that can be accomplished without changing the existing system in any funda-mental way. But by treating choice like other system-preserving reforms that presumably make democratic control work better, reformers completely miss what choice is all about.

Choice is not like the other reforms and should not be combined with them. Choice is a self-contained reform with its own rationale and justification. It has the capacity *all by itself* to bring about the kind of transformation that reformers have been seeking to engineer for years in myriad other ways. Indeed, if choice is to work to greatest advantage, it must be adopted *without* these other reforms, since they are predicated on democratic control and are imple-mented by bureaucratic means. The whole point of a thoroughgoing system of choice is to free the schools from these disabling constraints by sweeping away the old institutions and replacing them with new ones. Taken seriously, choice is not a system-preserving reform. It is a revolutionary reform that introduces a new system of public education.

A PROPOSAL FOR REAL REFORM

The following outline describes a choice system that we think is equipped to do the job. Offering our own proposal allows us to illustrate in some detail what a full-blown choice system might look like, as well as to note some of the policy decisions that must be made in building one. More important, it allows us to suggest what our institutional theory of schools actually entails for educational reform.

Our guiding principle in the design of a choice system is this: public authority must be put to use in creating a system that is almost entirely beyond the reach of public authority. Because states have primary responsibility for American public education, we think the best way to achieve significant, enduring reform is for states to take the initiative in withdrawing authority from existing institutions and vesting it directly in the schools, parents, and students. This restructuring cannot be construed as an exercise in delegation. As long as authority remains "available" at higher levels within state government, it will eventually be used to control the schools. As far as possible, all higher-level authority must be eliminated.

What we propose, more specifically, is that state leaders create a new system of public education with the following properties.

The Supply of Schools

The state will be responsible for setting criteria that define what constitutes a "public school" under the new system. These criteria should be minimal, roughly corresponding to the criteria many states now use in accrediting private schools—graduation requirements, health and safety requirements, and teacher certification requirements. Any educational group or organization that applies to the state and meets these minimal criteria must then be chartered as a public school and granted the right to accept students and receive public money.

Existing private schools will be among those eligible to participate. Their participation should be encouraged, because they constitute a supply of already effective schools. Our own preference would be to include religious schools too, as long as their sectarian functions can be kept clearly separate from their educational functions. Private schools that do participate will thereby become public schools, as such schools are defined under the new choice system.

School districts can continue running their present schools, assuming those schools meet state criteria. But districts will have authority over only their own schools and not over any of the others that may be chartered by the state.

Funding

The state will set up a Choice Office in each district, which, among other things, will maintain a record of all school-age children and the level of funding—the "scholarship" amounts—associated with each child. This office will directly compensate schools based on the specific children they enroll. Public money will flow from funding sources (federal, state, and district governments) to the Choice Office and then to schools. At no point will it go to parents or students.

The state must pay to support its own Choice Office in each district. Districts may retain as much of their current governing apparatus as they wish—superintendents, school boards, central offices, and all their staff. But they have to pay for them entirely out of the revenue they derive from the scholarships of those children who voluntarily choose to attend district-run schools. Aside from the governance of these schools, which no one need attend, districts will be little more than taxing jurisdictions that allow citizens to make a collective determination about how large their children's scholarships will be.

As it does now, the state will have the right to specify how much, or by what formula, each district must contribute for each child. Our preference is for an equalization approach that requires wealthier districts to contribute more per child than poor districts do and that guarantees an adequate financial foundation to students in all districts. The state's contribution can then be calibrated to bring total spending per child up to whatever dollar amount seems desirable, under an equalization scheme, that would mean a larger state contribution in poor districts than in wealthy ones.

While parents and students should be given as much flexibility as possible, we think it is unwise to allow them to supplement their scholarship amounts with personal funds. Such "add-ons" threaten to produce too many disparities and inequalities within the public system, and many citizens would regard them as unfair and burdensome.

Complete equalization, on the other hand, strikes us as too stifling and restrictive. A reasonable trade-off is to allow collective add-ons, much as the current system does. The citizens of each district can be given the freedom to decide whether they want to spend more per child than the state requires them to spend. They can then determine how important education is to them and how much they are willing to tax themselves for it. As a result, children from different districts may have different-sized scholarships.

Scholarships may also vary within any given district, and we strongly think that they should. Some students have very special educational needs—arising from economic deprivation, physical handicaps, language difficulties, emotional problems, and other disadvantages—that can be met effectively only through costly specialized programs. State and federal programs already appropriate public money to address these problems. Our suggestion is that these funds should take the form of add-ons to student scholarships. At-risk students would then be empowered with bigger scholarships than the others, making them attractive clients to all schools—and stimulating the emergence of new specialty schools.

Choice among Schools

Each student will be free to attend any public school in the state, regardless of district, with the student's scholarship—consisting of federal, state, and local contributions—flowing to the school of choice. In practice most students will probably choose schools in reasonable proximity to their homes. But districts will have no claim on their own residents.

To the extent that tax revenues allow, every effort will be made to provide transportation for students who need it. This provision is important to help open up as many alternatives as possible to all students, especially the poor and those in rural areas.

To assist parents and students in choosing among schools, the state will provide a Parent Information Center within its local Choice Office. This center will collect comprehensive information on each school in the district, and its parent liaisons will meet personally with parents in helping them judge which schools best meet their children's needs. The emphasis here will be on personal contact and involvement. Parents will be required to visit the center at least once, and encouraged to do so often. Meetings will be arranged at all schools so that parents can see firsthand what their choices are.

The Parent Information Center will handle the applications process in a simple fashion. Once parents and students decide which schools they prefer, they will fill out applications to each, with parent liaisons available to give advice and assistance and to fill out the applications themselves (if necessary). All applications will be submitted to the Center, which in turn will send them out to the schools.

Schools will make their own admissions decisions, subject only to nondiscrimination requirements. This step is absolutely crucial. Schools must be able to define their own missions and build their own programs in their own ways, and they cannot do that if their student population is thrust on them by outsiders.

Schools must be free to admit as many or as few students as they want, based on whatever criteria they think relevant—intelligence, interest, motivation, special needs—and they must be free to exercise their own, informal judgments about individual applicants.

Schools will set their own "tuitions." They may choose to do so explicitly, say, by publicly announcing the minimum scholarship they are willing to accept. They may also do it implicitly by allowing anyone to apply for admission and simply making selections, knowing in advance what each applicant's scholarship amount is. In either case, schools are free to admit students with different-sized scholarships, and they are free to keep the entire scholarship that accompanies each student they have admitted. That gives all schools incentives to attract students with special needs, since these children will have the largest scholarships. It also gives schools incentives to attract students from districts with high base-level scholarships. But no school need restrict itself to students with special needs, nor to students from a single district.

The application process must take place within a framework that guarantees each student a school, as well as a fair shot at getting into the school he or she most wants. That framework, however, should impose only the most minimal restrictions on the schools.

We suggest something like the following. The Parent Information Center will be responsible for seeing that parents and students are informed, that they have visited the schools that interest them, and that all applications are submitted by a given date. Schools will then be required to make their admissions decisions within a set time, and students who are accepted into more than one school will be required to select one as their final choice. Students who are not accepted anywhere, as well as schools that have yet to attract as many students as they want, will participate in a second round of applications, which will work the same way.

After this second round, some students may remain without schools. At this point, parent liaisons will take informal action to try to match up these students with appropriate schools. If any students still remain unassigned, a special safety-net procedure—a lottery, for example—will be invoked to ensure that each is assigned to a specific school.

As long as they are not "arbitrary and capricious," schools must also be free to expel students or deny them readmission when, based on their own experience and standards, they believe the situation warrants it. This authority is essential if schools are to define and control their own organizations, and it gives students a strong incentive to live up to their side of the educational "contract."

Governance and Organization

Each school must be granted sole authority to determine its own governing structure. A school may be run entirely by teachers or even a union. It may vest all power in a principal. It may be built around committees that guarantee representation to the principal, teachers, parents, students, and members of the community. Or it may do something completely different.

The state must refrain from imposing *any* structures or requirements that specify how authority is to be exercised within individual schools. This includes the district-run schools: the state must not impose any governing apparatus on them either. These schools, however, are subordinate units within district government—they are already embedded in a larger organization—and it is the district authorities, not the schools, that have the legal right to determine how they will be governed.

More generally, the state will do nothing to tell the schools how they must be internally organized to do their work. The state will not set requirements for career ladders, advisory committees, textbook selection, in-service training, preparation time, homework, or anything else. Each school will be organized and operated as it sees fit.

Statewide tenure laws will be eliminated, allowing each school to decide for itself whether or not to adopt a tenure policy and what the specifics of that policy will be. This change is essential if schools are to have the flexibility they need to build well-functioning teams. Some schools may not offer tenure at all, relying on pay and working conditions to attract the kinds of teachers they want, while others may offer tenure as a supplementary means of compensating and retaining their best teachers.

Teachers, meantime, may demand tenure in their negotiations (individual or collective) with schools. And, as in private colleges and universities, the best teachers are well positioned to get it, since their services will be valued by any number of other schools. School districts may continue to offer districtwide tenure, along with transfer rights, seniority preference, and whatever other personnel policies they have offered in the past. But these policies apply only to district-run schools and the teachers who work in them.

Teachers will continue to have a right to join unions and engage in collective bargaining, but the legally prescribed bargaining unit will be the individual school or, as in the case of the district government, the larger organization that runs the school. If teachers in a given school want to join a union or, having done so, want to exact financial or structural concessions, that is up to them. But they cannot commit teachers in other schools, unless they are in other district-run schools, to the same things, and they must suffer the consequences if their victories put them at a competitive disadvantage in supplying quality education.

The state will continue to certify teachers, but requirements will be minimal, corresponding to those that many states have historically applied to private schools. In our view, individuals should be certified to teach if they have a bachelor's degree and if their personal history reveals no obvious problems. Whether they are truly good teachers will be determined in practice, as schools decide whom to hire, observe their own teachers in action over an extended period of time, and make decisions regarding merit, promotion, and dismissal.

The schools may, as a matter of strategy, choose to pay attention to certain formal indicators of past or future performance, among them: a master's degree, completion of a voluntary teacher certification program at an education school, or voluntary certification by a national board. Some schools may choose to require one or more of these, or perhaps to reward them in various ways. But that is up to the schools, which will be able to look anywhere for good teachers in a now much larger and more dynamic market.

The state will hold the schools accountable for meeting certain procedural requirements. It will ensure that schools continue to meet the criteria set out in their charters, that they adhere to nondiscrimination laws in admissions and other matters, and that they collect and make available to the public, through the Parent Information Center, information on their mission, their staff and course offerings, standardized test scores (which we would make optional), parent and student satisfaction, staff opinions, and anything else that would promote informed choice among parents and students.

The state will not hold the schools accountable for student achievement or other dimensions that call for assessments of the quality of school performance. When it comes to performance, schools will be held accountable from below, by parents and students who directly experience their services and are free to choose. The state will play a crucial supporting role here in monitoring the full and honest disclosure of information by the schools—but it will be only a supporting role.

CHOICE AS A PUBLIC SYSTEM

This proposal calls for fundamental changes in the structure of American public education. Stereotypes aside, however, these changes have nothing to do with "privatizing" the nation's schools. The choice system we outline would be a truly public system—and a democratic one.

We are proposing that the state put its democratic authority to use in creating a new institutional framework. The design and legitimation of this framework would be a democratic act of the most basic sort. It would be a social decision, made through the usual processes of democratic governance, by which the people and their representatives specify the structure of a new system of public education.

This framework, as we set it out, is quite flexible and admits of substantial variation on important issues, all of them matters of public policy to be decided by representative government. Public officials and their constituents would be free to take their own approaches to taxation, equalization, treatment of religious schools, additional funding for disadvantaged students, parent add-ons, and other controversial issues of public concern, thus designing choice systems to reflect the unique conditions, preferences, and political forces of their own states.

Once this structural framework is democratically determined, moreover, governments would continue to play important roles within it. State officials and agencies would remain pivotal to the success of public education and to its ongoing operation. They would provide funding, approve applications for new schools, orchestrate and oversee the choice process, elicit full information about schools, provide transportation to students, monitor schools for adherence to the law, and (if they want) design and administer tests of student performance. School districts, meantime, would continue as local taxing jurisdictions, and they would have the option of continuing to operate their own system of schools.

The crucial difference is that direct democratic control of the schools—the very *capacity* for control, not simply its exercise—would essentially be eliminated. Most of those who previously held authority over the schools would have their authority permanently withdrawn, and that authority would be vested in schools, parents, and students. Schools would be legally autonomous: free to govern themselves as they want, specify their own goals and programs and methods, design their own organizations, select their own student bodies, and make their own personnel decisions. Parents and students would be legally empowered to choose among alternative schools, aided by institutions designed to promote active involvement, well-informed decisions, and fair treatment.

DEMOCRACY AND EDUCATIONAL PROGRESS

We do not expect everyone to accept the argument we have made here. In fact, we expect most of those who speak with authority on educational matters, leaders and academics within the educational community, to reject it. But we will regard our effort as a success if it directs attention to America's institutions of democratic control and provokes serious debate about their consequences for the nation's public schools. Whether or not our own conclusions are right, the fact is that these issues are truly basic to an understanding of schools, and they have so far played no part in the national debate. If educational reform is to have any chance at all of succeeding, that has to change.

In the meantime, we can only believe that the current "revolution" in public education will prove a disappointment. It might have succeeded had it actually been a revolution, but it was not and was never intended to be, despite the lofty rhetoric. Revolutions replace old institutions with new ones. The 1980s reform movement never seriously thought about the old institutions and certainly never considered them part of the problem. They were, as they had always been, part of the solution—and, for that matter, part of the definition of what democracy and public education are all about.

This identification has never been valid. Nothing in the concept of democracy requires that schools be subject to direct control by school boards, superintendents, central offices, departments of education, and other arms of government. Nor does anything in the concept of public education require that schools be governed in this way. There are many paths to democracy and public education. The path America has been trodding for the past half-century is exacting a heavy price—one the nation and its children can ill afford to bear, and need not. It is time, we think, to get to the root of the problem.

NO

The Great School Sell-Off

Peter Schrag

Long before Bill Clinton appeared on the presidential horizon, he had, as governor of Arkansas, established himself as one of a half-dozen national leaders in the public school reform movement of the 1980s. The movement was determinedly bipartisan, pragmatic, and nonideological. In addition to Clinton, it included Republican governors Thomas Kean of New Jersey and Lamar Alexander of Tennessee, as well as independent California State School Superintendent Bill Honig. These reformers sought, and generally achieved, tougher graduation requirements; more rigorous curricula and textbooks; competency tests for both students and teachers; merit pay or other incentives for outstanding teachers; longer school days and school years; and better funding for K–12 schools almost everywhere.

But before the decade was over, a combination of recession, budget cuts, impatience, and political expediency helped start a deep and very ideological current running in the opposite direction—a retreat from public education. With a lot of cheerleading from George Bush, the self-proclaimed education president, more people began to ask just what the country had bought with its school reform dollars. The greater the belief that the Germans and Japanese were beating us in the global economy, the greater the influence of international test results showing American students scoring behind their foreign counterparts. As a result, the encouraging returns from the reforms of the 1980s—they were not great, as we shall see, but they were hardly negligible—were ignored. The schools, according to the conventional wisdom, were simply failing, and stronger medicine was required.

For the Bush administration, a growing number of conservative scholars and businesspeople, and the religious right, that medicine was vouchers—tax-supported "scholarships" allowing parents to send their children to any school, public or private, in an educational free market. School choice was also one of the few issues that could replace Communism in linking the Republican Party's suburban conservatives with free-market libertarians and Christian-right fundamentalists.

THE CHOICE BANDWAGON

The idea is hardly new. Milton Friedman first proposed vouchers more than 30 years ago. In the 1960s, it was taken up by liberal reformers such as Christopher Jencks and Henry M. Levin and by academics such as John E. Coons and Stephen D. Sugarman at Berkeley. In the 1980s, Ronald Reagan occasionally talked about private school tuition tax credits but paired the idea so closely with school prayer and even creationism that it looked more like an ideological crumb for Christian fundamentalists than a serious policy.

Bush had come to office declaring the country couldn't afford vouchers for private schools. But by 1991 the idea had become the centerpiece of his education policy, with the support of respected activists like the Department of Education's Alexander, former Xerox chairman David Kearns, and educational historian Diane Ravitch.

A further event that gave choice intellectual respectability was the 1990 publication by the Brookings Institution, home of Democratic brains-in-exile, of John E. Chubb and Terry M. Moe's *Politics, Markets, and America's Schools*. The book argues not only that the reforms of the 1980s were inadequate but that such reforms couldn't succeed as long as schools were run by school boards, superintendents, central offices, and departments of education—what the authors disparagingly call "direct democratic control." The only way to escape that, Chubb and Moe assert, is by letting parents choose among self-governing schools, public or private, with state tax money following their children to the schools they select, thereby building into schools a market incentive to offer better service. The authors are uncompromising. "Without being too literal about it, we think that reformers would do well to entertain the notion that choice *is* a panacea. . . . Choice is not like other reforms and should not be combined with them as part of a reformist strategy. . . . It has the capacity *all by itself* to bring about the kind of transformation that, for years, reformers have been seeking to engineer in myriad other ways" (italics original).

Bush's one foray into a voucher plan was his call early in 1992 for a trial federal "scholarship" program that would give 500,000 middle- and low-income students $1,000 apiece to use in any educational setting. It was dead on arrival in Congress, and given Clinton's support for public education, it will likely never be heard from again. Equally significant, on the same day Clinton was elected, Colorado voters by a two-to-one margin rejected a state-wide voucher proposal that would have given every parent a $2,500 "scholarship" to pay tuition in any private or parochial school in the state—or even to pay for home schooling.

Nonetheless, the broader idea of school choice is probably here to stay: The question is whether it will be limited to the public system—or part of an open market system where virtually any provider, public or private, could participate. The Gallup Poll has traced a steady increase in support among Americans for some version of parental choice; as usual, the detailed responses (public versus private, for example) depend on how the questions are asked. In principle, Bill Clinton supports choice, the American Federation of Teachers supports choice, the Catholic Bishops support choice, the Houston Republicans support choice. There are choice experiments in Cambridge, Massachusetts, Milwaukee, Minneapolis, Indianapolis, and other cities, and while their results to date are both small and ambiguous, that hasn't slowed the movement.

California residents will vote in the June 1994 primary on a broad voucher plan that includes all schools. Despite its obvious flaws, the accumulating fiscal and social troubles of the schools give it an increasingly good chance of passing.

If the plan is defeated, it's likely to take all of the enormous financial and political power of the California Teachers Association to do so. (As this was being written, there was a possibility that California Governor Pete Wilson would set a special election before 1994, in order to move it from a primary election at which he himself might be challenged by the kind of right-wing Republican who would gain from the turnout of fundamentalist Christians come to support the voucher.) Perhaps more indicative yet, Chris Whittle, whose commercial in-school TV news program, Channel 1, reaches 8 million teenagers (far more than watch all three network news programs combined) is planning to create a national chain of 1,000 private schools called the Edison Project by the end of the decade. Whittle may be betting wrong, but it's hard to imagine that he expects to succeed without help from vouchers.

The issue, then, is not whether, but which kind. Will choice be limited to the public system—with sensitivity for diversity and equal opportunity as well as academic quality—or will it be privatized, divisive, and indifferent to the commonweal? There is fairly broad agreement, though hardly unanimity, that as part of a scheme of other reforms—increased school site control in particular—choice within the public system has possibilities. However, these possibilities, in turn, depend in considerable part on whether Clinton can reverse the moral and social priorities of the past decade and halt the loss of faith in community that has done so much to drive the rising interest in vouchers.

TARNISHED MYTHS

Of all the sectors of American life, none seems so driven by the myth of a lost golden age as education—time and other details unspecified—when all children went to nice bright schools, sat in orderly rows before dedicated teachers, learned what they had to know (by first learning "the basics") and then graduated, every one of them, to become productive citizens.

Just to say that, of course, is to expose its absurdity. Until the 1950s, U.S. schools were never expected to succeed with all children. Some attended only five or six months a year and quit after the fourth or fifth grade; many more left after the eighth grade to enter an economy that had plenty of unskilled and semi-skilled jobs. Schools, accordingly, were judged not by their failures—by dropout rates (a phrase that did not exist fifty years ago) or by how many did not go to college or fell below some standard test score—but by their successes. Blacks rarely figured into the education calculus at all.

One might even say that the golden age myth is itself a piece of vestigial racism—those nice orderly classrooms were predominantly, if not totally, white—but it's also important in explaining our pervasive discontent with the schools and the calls for radical "restructuring" that are based on it. No nation, Henry Commager once wrote, demands as much of its schools—expects them not only to teach reading and writing, but patriotism, morality, the evils of alcohol and tobacco (to which we have now added the dangers of drugs and AIDS), not to mention driver education, good citizenship, racial tolerance, self-esteem, and a hundred other things. And never have the schools been required to do it with a population as diverse—not to say troubled—as the schools do now. In 1970, one child in seven fell below the poverty line; now it's closer to one in five, and in the elementary grades it's closer to one in four. In 1970, 15 percent of the nation's school-age population was nonwhite; now it's well over 20 percent. In states like California, where whites are now a minority of the public school enrollment, one child in four is on welfare; one in four comes from a home where English is not the primary language. Los Angeles, the country's second largest school system, now enrolls children speaking some 80 different languages. Of the 185,000 new children who entered the state's schools in fall 1992, less than half came from homes where the primary language is English.

The facile response to such data is that American schools have always absorbed huge numbers of immigrants—Germans, Swedes, Italians, Poles, Russians, Greeks. But never have they been expected to do it as completely and against such great odds. Today there is a much smaller market for unskilled dropouts—quite the contrary in this global economy—and thus no significant possibility that the schools can forget about their failures, much less threaten to boot them out as they could a half century ago.

That's not to say that criticism of American public schools is unfounded. Many schools are mindless; many districts are paralyzed by self-serving bureaucracies; many teachers, a lot of whom came from the lowest ranks of their college classes, do as much to sabotage curiosity and thinking as they do to encourage them. Nothing that follows should be taken as an indication that things are fine in American education. But many of the common assumptions about educational performance are wrong.

Dropouts. If one adds those who have graduated from high school (about 75 percent) and those who have a high school equivalency diploma, roughly 90 percent of young Americans are now high school graduates, the highest percentage in history. Over 20 percent are college graduates. The percentage who drop out of high school continues to decline—and that includes all races except perhaps first-generation Hispanic immigrants, who often leave for extended returns to the old country.

Academic Achievement in the "Basics." According to the National Assessment of Education Progress, much of the decline of the 1970s, though not all, was offset by progress in the 1980s. Black students, while not yet on a par with whites in math and reading, made substantial gains through the 1970s and the 1980s.

Average SAT Scores. Although they sank badly in the 1970s, scholastic aptitude test scores started to come back in the 1980s, particularly in math. This rebound came despite the substantial increase in the percentage of high school graduates (and thus the number of students not in the top ranks of their classes) who now take SATs. The number of students taking more intense academic programs in secondary school, like honors courses, advanced placement courses, and more serious math and science courses, has risen substantially in the past decade.

College Graduation Rates. Roughly 26 percent of all U.S. twenty-two-year-olds obtained a bachelor's degree in 1987, according to the National Center for Education Statistics, substantially more than in Japan (21 percent), Germany (13 percent), the UK or France (14 percent each). Similarly, we outrank other major nations in the percentage of twenty-two-year-olds getting a bachelor's degree in science and engineering. And since the institutions from which they graduate continue to draw hundreds of thousands of foreign students—we are far and away the world's leading exporter of education—the complaints about curricular inadequacy need a lot of qualification.

Collectively, the data are nothing to cheer about. A lot of students don't know in what century the Civil War took place or on what continent to find Ethiopia. American thirteen-year-olds rank at or near the bottom in most international measures of math and science proficiency. The comparisons may be somewhat misleading since most of those countries begin specialized education at age fourteen, placing more emphasis on high test performance in the earlier grades, and since some teach geometry to thirteen-year-olds (usually taught to American children at fourteen or fifteen). At the same time, however, even after the reforms of the 1980s, U.S. students appear to do less homework and have less demanded of them, either by schools or parents, than their foreign peers.

It's hard to know how much of that can be controlled by the school and how much comes from our indifferent intellectual atmosphere. Given the enormous changes in the demographics of American schools and considering the idiot culture in which our students live most of the day, it's surprising the schools have done as well as they have.

TICKET TO RIDE

It's precisely the demographic and social factors that are driving some middle-class Americans to buy their way out of the system. Some parents honestly perceive schools to be unsafe; the schools can't deal with the diversity of cultures; the systems are distracted by the avalanche of personal and social problems that students bring and that no other institution addresses.

More and more voters are not parents, and more parents are not voters. That's one of the reasons support for public education is eroding. In 1970, white school children, who, of course, bring the most electoral clout, were fully 21 percent of the total population. In 1990, twenty years beyond the end of the baby boom, white school children were 14 percent of the population. In the suburbs, where parents are concentrated and have political clout, communities still provide lavish support for schools, but increasingly they become islands of exception.

Those groups who vote in high numbers, older people in particular, tend not to have children in the schools, while Americans who have more children in the schools have fewer votes per child and often don't exercise them. California's Proposition 13, which was passed in 1978 and which set the tone for much of U.S. social policy in the past decade, was largely a revolt of elderly people against high property taxes at the expense of local services for children: schools, parks, libraries. (This year, about 20 percent of California voters were parents of school children, roughly half of what it was a generation ago.) Even now, when local districts attempt to pass school bonds in California, they often exempt property owned by people over sixty-five from the additional taxes.

The middle class, of course, is not alone in looking for escape or in supporting vouchers. The Catholic church, whose remaining inner-city parochial schools are struggling to survive, has been seeking government help for years. And so have many inner-city black parents who desperately want some escape from the brutal schools their children are forced to attend. With a modest voucher, they could afford to attend those parochial schools; as a result, inner-city parents lead the polls in their support for vouchers. There's also support from the parents of Christian fundamentalist school children. But it's unlikely that vouchers would enjoy their widespread attention without considerable middle-class support.

For the conservatives who are now its greatest champions, choice may well have an additional use. If the problem are the schools and not children, no one has to concern himself too much about nutrition, health and day care, decent housing, or the children's issue in general. The *Wall Street Journal* editorial page, among others, is fond of quoting UNESCO data showing that the United States spends more per child on schools than most other modern nations. But the *Journal* fails to acknowledge the universal day care in France, the German social welfare system, the homogeneity of Japanese society, or the universal health care and generous other benefits that nearly all those countries provide—social programs that relieve the burdens on schools. The blessings that the market is supposed to bestow on the schools tend to drive the rest of the problem into obscurity. If the good people can get away from the nasty kids, however defined, the conditions that shape those children's lives become practically, politically, and morally invisible.

REFORM SCHOOL BOYS

Terry Moe, who teaches political science at Stanford and is a senior fellow at Brookings, says that the school market is like any other—he recently compared it to the market for candy bars. People shop around, choose what's best for them, and thus drive all competitors to improve their products. But there's no empirical evidence of that. In a study of the one public-private plan (Milwaukee's) now in operation, the Carnegie Foundation found that while the small number of students who have been enabled to leave the public schools "feel pleased with the decision they have made," more than 40 percent of those who left the public schools in 1991–92 for a private school didn't return to the private school in 1992–93. More important, there was "no evidence . . . that the participating students made significant academic advances or that either the public or the private schools have been revitalized by the transfers."

Overall, Carnegie found, as have others, that "choice is a wholly unrealistic proposal for literally millions of children (because) there simply is no other school within easy reach or, if there is, the alternative school may be no better than the one close by."

Nor, despite their intimidating statistical analysis, do the theoretical arguments in Chubb and Moe's book hold up. Those arguments attempt to define what are "effective" public schools in terms of student achievement and to prove they are like private schools—relatively autonomous. By that, Chubb and Moe mean they are free of downtown bureaucracies and thus have "clear goals . . . ambitious academic programs, strong educational leadership." But the difficulty of distinguishing correlation from cause seems overwhelming: Does the heavy hand of bureaucracy generate school failure or is it itself the result of failure? Is the "autonomy" that Chubb and Moe associate with effective schools and all the good feelings among teachers and principals that come with it the cause of student success or itself a result of students affluent, smart, or motivated enough to make such autonomy possible?

Chubb and Moe's measure of student achievement fails to separate out such things as student ability, motivation, parental resources (including predisposition to academic achievement), as well as the general noise of the surrounding culture. Even as Chubb and Moe seek to link private sector schools with autonomy and effective organization, they fail to cite any correlation between private control and achievement. In an essay in the *Yale Law Journal* (October 1991), James Liebman even suggests that it may be precisely because parents of children in private and suburban schools have so little choice—they are already at the top of the heap and thus have to fight to protect the quality of those schools—that their schools are so effective. In a real market system, where schools are free to choose and expel students on any basis except perhaps race, the effective choice may not be so much the parent's as the school's.

The voucher movement is silent about society's interest in common schooling. In the West and Southwest, where the only semblance of community is the shopping mall, the freeway, and the radio talk show, the public school is virtually the last institution that spans the entire community, bringing together not only children but their parents and often their neighbors in a common enterprise. Public schools embody the idea of community itself—the democratic ideals of a common culture that assimilates and integrates diversity even as it celebrates it. That's not an ideal that, however short of realization, can be casually abandoned.

What of children of parents who can't negotiate the market or are not interested in their schooling at all? What of the need, especially now, to acculturate immigrants? What of racial integration and understanding? One of the great ironies is to hear people like former education secretary William Bennett, who became apoplectic when Stanford University added a few nonwestern writers and a few women to its western civilization course a few years ago, defend a choice system that would feed tax money to Moonie schools, to the flat earth society, to African nationalists (the Louis Farrakhan school?), or indeed any other cultural separatist who could attract a few suckers.

Coons and Sugarman worry—with good reason—that unless voucher regulations are carefully written, the affluent will use them to supplement private school tuition while the poor will be stuck with whatever schooling the voucher will provide. While that could be fixed by limiting vouchers to schools that charge no more than the voucher is worth (which is what Chubb and Moe and Coons and Sugarman propose), no plan yet overcomes other problems in an unregulated market: that racial and ethnic segregation would rise, or that some parents would not be able to find a school that will take their children. The advocates of the California voucher argue that since they propose "scholarships" averaging only about half of what existing public schools spend per pupil, vouchers, if widely used, could save money. But since no plan that's made it to the ballot significantly limits how or where vouchers can be used, vouchers will not only become tuition supplements for private school parents but also an inducement to those schools to raise their tuition.

Nor is it likely that any radically different voucher plan would go very far. Any plan that is too restrictive about how and where a voucher can be used would immediately lose its parochial and fundamentalist school constituency; any plan that's too costly will look too blatantly like a raid on the treasury. Both the Colorado and California plans provide roughly $2,500, about half what the public schools spend. That's enough for a parish elementary school but no more than a third of the tuition at a good private day school and not remotely enough to educate a handicapped child or any other child with special needs.

Chubb and Moe would provide "add-ons" for such children, as well as a whole range of other "special educational needs . . . arising from economic deprivation, physical handicaps, language difficulties, emotional problems," all of it to be determined and refereed by an oxymoronic "choice office" in each district. In addition, there would be an array of other bureaucracies—to inform parents of their options, to place children who aren't accepted by any school (which, of course, conflicts with their insistence that all schools be autonomous regarding admissions and expulsions), to organize transportation, and to monitor compliance with the health, safety, and credentialing regulations that they seem to favor. That may not restore all of the old school bureaucracy, but the groups that have put vouchers on the ballot say they'll tolerate no such restrictions. As a "market," what this most resembles is our two-tier medical system, with the assigned-risk schools the corollary of the emergency room at the county hospital.

THE MARKET CANARD

The more the system becomes a "market," the more the child and her parents become customers rather than citizens. In the existing system, the public schools have to register every child who lives in the appropriate attendance area. With an unrestricted voucher plan and deregulated schools, nobody has to take (or notice) anybody. The voucherites are designing a system that will allow more people to buy their way out but that will lock the children from whom they're trying to escape not just into their third-class schools, or out of schools altogether, but into civic and political invisibility.

Voucher advocates are probably correct when they suggest that just the possibility of choice will begin to challenge arrogant school bureaucracies and unions. For example, while per-pupil funding in California has sharply declined relative to the national average (from fifth among the states in 1965 to roughly fortieth in 1992), teacher salaries there have remained among the highest. The give, needless to say, has been in the quality of the program. Can anyone think of a better formula for driving people to the exits?

The voucher movement has already created a willingness in the public school establishment to consider far more flexible arrangements. California's legislature in fall 1992 authorized the creation of 100 charter schools—all free from most existing curricular requirements, all liberated from most teacher contract restrictions and credentialing requirements—that might never have been approved were it not for the voucher proposal on the 1994 ballot. Meanwhile, countless districts around the country are trying to decentralize school control, to create schools within schools, to give parents and teachers more local control and accountability, and, recognizing that different kids have different interests and different learning styles, to allow parents and children more choice among the schools. But vouchers are the ultimate weapon, and if the threat is ever carried out, it may well be impossible to restore the traditional common school. One can hear some future politician saying, "What, you want socialized education?"

Many of the reform plans of the past decade, of course, have run afoul of the same school boards, unions, and bureaucracies. But if the failures justify any head-on fight, it's a fight to liberate the local schools from the stultifying power of those organizations, not to launch a frontal attack on the principle of the common school. In some cases, that fight has been slow, in part because school boards, downtown bureaucracies, and state credentialing agencies are reluctant to yield authority; in part because various groups of ideological snoops and true believers demand an inventory of everything that's said or read or done inside the schoolhouse (*Catcher in the Rye*? Witches? Birth Control? Secular Humanism?); and in part because some state and local teacher organizations continue to insist that teacher contracts be modeled on those of industrial unions, with their tight work rules, their resistance to pay differentials, their rigid seniority system, and their refusal to participate in peer review or in anything else that could be regarded as management decisions. In Los Angeles last year, teachers, protesting threatened pay reductions, refused to appear for back-to-school nights. In other districts, teachers refused to write recommendations for students applying to college.

But the voices at the top are beginning to send different signals. Albert Shanker, the president of the American Federation of Teachers, has long been a vigorous force for reform (including public school choice) and for the creation of what he long ago called world-class academic standards. Keith Geiger, who heads the National Education Association, may be showing similar flexibility.

Just as important, there are signs that teachers are driving their schools, and often their whole school systems, to greater flexibility and school-site innovation and accountability. Frank Newman, who heads the Education Commission of the States, says school boards now seem to be more of a drag on innovation and flexibility than any of the other major players in American education.

None of that should suggest that all institutional barriers against change are gone. But neither is there anything that so far justifies the far more radical attempt to finance a general breakout from (and breakup of) the public system.

REAL REFORM

Perhaps the greatest irony of the voucher movement is that even as it pretends to be concerned with individuals, it so thoroughly focuses on abstractions: the market, competition, the schools as institutions. But if one looks at real schools or real children, it's clear that the solutions, like the problems, are far more complicated and qualified. There are no panaceas here. The research is not even clear on how much difference money, class size, or the school them-selves make. Still, there are a number of emerging conclusions.

The most successful schools are those with a clear sense of mission and shared values—schools that foster cooperative rather than bureaucratic rela-tionships. That suggests that more school site control is preferable to more control by downtown bureaucrats and that more diversity and choice are preferable to a single model. Choice within the public system therefore makes sense, but as the Carnegie study points out, probably only as part of a plan of broader reforms; only if the schools are able to create sufficiently compelling programs; only if there is enough reliable information and quality control so that the choices can be made intelligently; and only if there are relevant pro-grams even for marginal students.

One of the most interesting and celebrated of the public school choice programs now in operation—East Harlem's—didn't begin with choice at all. It began with attempts within a few schools to create distinctive and attractive programs—a performing arts school, among others, a math–science school, a bilingual school, a "bridge" school for tough-to-teach kids. Once these schools were established, choice was necessary to allow the children to opt for those programs. The voucherite faith has it the other way: that once there is a market, other reforms will automatically follow.

But there is no real reason to believe that. If there is any moral justification anywhere for limited vouchers, it's in the inner-city. But the better alternative is to give parents a greater voice and to make the necessary social investment—in health, in training parents to teach their preschool kids (the model is an Israeli program that Hillary Clinton brought to Arkansas), and in school–industry apprenticeship programs. The point is that real reform, particularly in the cities, requires precisely the kind of broad social concern that vouchers and an educational free market would allow the country to avoid. To address that concern, federal education policy in the next couple of years probably ought not focus on schools at all but on children. Maureen DiMarco, California secretary of education and social services, has urged that if there is more money for children, most of it should go not to the schools but to health (especially prenatal care and nutrition), Head Start, day care, counseling, housing, and recreation. Though extreme, such a focus reflects a justified sense that the needs are more urgent in, and that the money can be spent more effectively on, children's social services and parent training than on an educational system whose reform depends primarily on the states and local communities.

That's not to say the schools are well funded; many are not. But any additional money for schools (most of it no doubt state money) should be disbursed only with a quid pro quo—in curricular changes, school-site control, accountability for teachers and parents, and, where real options justify it, public school choice. Without these, little will change. Surely Bill Clinton, who was the driving force behind the school reforms in Arkansas, understands that as well as anyone. The essence of school reform during the 1980s, from Arkansas and Mississippi to New Jersey and California, was its ability to use additional funding to buy those higher standards for teachers, even a few halting steps toward merit pay, as well as tougher graduation requirements and other re-forms—trading some flexibility from the unions and the bureaucrats for greater tax support. The reforms fell short largely in their failure to get enough reform for their additional tax dollars.

National performance-based testing can help. If done right—if we measure higher-order skills such as problem solving, historical analysis, as well as writing and other creative work (all of which, of course, is expensive)—it may do more to generate a realistic appreciation of how the nation's schools are doing and how every particular school is doing against Shanker's world standard. It certainly could shake up those very satisfied parents; and it could shake up school boards, legislatures, and perhaps teachers colleges as well.

In the final analysis, however, the most important thing a Clinton administra-tion—or any national administration—could do now for schools is to re-energize general confidence in government, in community, and in the efficacy of public service. Private school vouchers, after all, are not much more than the educational version of privatization in a dozen other areas. If the idea is driven by a desire to escape from the latter day (mostly social) problems of the schools, it can also be dampened by renewed confidence in government's interest in, and ability to deal with, those problems. For the most part, schools are local and state concerns anyway—the federal government funds no more than 6 percent of the total enterprise, less than it did when Reagan came to office in 1980. Though that federal contribution should be raised, what Washington mainly can do is set the climate. And in the past decade, the climate has been awful.

DISCUSSION QUESTIONS

1. Some have argued that weaknesses in the public school system can be explained largely by inequities and/or deficiencies in school funding. How

do these two articles address such an argument? Which arguments do you find most convincing?

2. Each of these articles contains an implicit notion of what goals we should set and what results we should ask of a system of public education. What are these competing notions? In what ways do you see them as adequate or inadequate?

3. What role do you think public education should play in a democracy? Do the arguments in either of the articles provide a policy proposal that would help the school system play the role that you think it should?

4. Chubb and Moe refer to parents and students as "clients" of schools. Does this accurately capture the relationship that should exist between students and schools?

5. What role should the federal government have in formulating and enacting an education policy?

6. Should the federal government be more actively involved in elementary and secondary education policy, or should that role be largely retained by states and localities?

7. A 1993 ballot initiative in California to give parents vouchers worth $2,600 for each child they send to a private school was soundly defeated. What is the difference between a voucher system and a "school choice" system? What are the relative advantages and disadvantages of each?

ADDITIONAL READINGS

Bierlein, Louann A. *Controversial Issues in Educational Policy* (Newbury Park, Calif.: Sage Publications, 1993).

Chubb, John E., and Terry M. Moe. *Politics, Markets, and America's Schools* (Washington, D.C.: Brookings Institution, 1990).

Clune, William H., and John F. Witte, eds. *Choice and Control in American Education* (London: Falmer, 1990).

Corson, Ross. "Choice Ironies: Open Enrollment in Minnesota." *The American Prospect* (Fall 1990).

Elmore, Richard F., and Associates. *Restructuring Schools: The Next Generation of Educational Reform* (San Francisco: Jossey-Bass, 1990).

Fliegel, Seymour. *Miracle in East Harlem: The Fight for Choice in Public Education* (New York: Times Books, 1993).

Guthrie, James W., Walter I. Garms, and Lawrence C. Pierce. *School Finance and Education Policy: Enhancing Educational Efficiency, Equality, and Choice*, 2d ed. (Englewood Cliffs, N.J.: Prentice-Hall, 1988).

Honig, Bill. "Why Privatizing Public Education Is a Bad Idea." *Brookings Review* (Winter 1990/91).

Howe, Harold. *Thinking About Our Kids* (New York: Free Press, 1993).

Kirp, David. "What School Choice Really Means." *The Atlantic Monthly* (November 1992).

Kozol, Jonathan. *Savage Inequalities: Children in America's Schools* (New York: Crown Publishers, 1991).

Lieberman, Myron. *Public Education: An Autopsy* (Cambridge, Mass.: Harvard University Press, 1993).

Quade, Quentin L. "School Reform: Toward Parental Choice." *Wisconsin Interest* (Summer/Fall 1992).

Rothstein, Richard. "The Myth of Public School Failure." *The American Prospect* (Spring 1993).

Wells, Amy Stewart. *Time to Choose: America at the Crossroads of School Choice Policy* (New York: Hill and Wang, 1993).

2
WELFARE POLICY

"Should Welfare Recipients Be Required to Work in Exchange for AFDC and Other Transfer Payments?"

James Baldwin once wrote that "money, it turned out, was exactly like sex; you thought of nothing else if you didn't have it and thought of other things if you did." But George Wiley's statement to the Democratic platform committee in 1968 in Chicago—"the basic cure for poverty is money"—is no longer the truism it once appeared to be. Attempts at alleviating poverty through cash transfers (such as the negative income tax—where a "negative income tax" or payments to individuals vary in proportion to income) floundered politically in the 1970s and appear to run counter to the preferences of many to provide those in poverty with shelter, food, and other essential *goods* rather than cash. To the contrary, today's debate about welfare policy is dominated less by how much money should be provided to the poor, but rather if and how welfare policies cause "dependency," "cultures of poverty," and the "underclass," and how welfare reforms may attenuate or eliminate these alleged effects.

Broadly defined, the welfare system in the United States is oriented mostly as social insurance against old-age poverty, loss of employment, and the inability to finance medical costs. Social insurance expenditures—the largest programs being Social Security, Medicare, workers' compensation, and unemployment insurance—comprise the bulk of social welfare expenditures, approximately $500 billion annually (including federal, state, and local contributions), and are not for the most part means-tested. Means-tested benefits (those based on income or other individual or family characteristics) amount to over $200 billion annually, including Medicaid, Aid to Families with Dependent Children (AFDC), Supplemental Security Income (SSI) for the blind, disabled, and aged, foods stamps, public housing and education assistance, and many others. About three-fourths of means-tested antipoverty expenditures in the United States do not give cash assistance to the poor, but rather provide food, housing, medical care, education, job training, energy assistance, and other in-kind benefits. The largest portion of mean-tested expenditures provides medical care for the poor, mostly through Medicaid. The largest means-tested cash assistance program for the poor is AFDC, the program synonymous for many with "welfare," with annual costs of approximately $25 billion (roughly half of it federal), or less than 1 percent of federal outlays and under 2 percent of all federal social welfare spending.[1] (The federal contribution to SSI is greater than to AFDC, although AFDC is larger when federal, state, and local contributions are totaled.)

Much of the impetus for welfare spending in the United States began with President Franklin Roosevelt's 1937 observation that "I see one-third of a nation ill-housed, ill-clad, ill-nourished." Designed as a social safety net, Social Security, Aid to Dependent Children (later AFDC), and unemployment insurance were launched. Although these are now expensive programs (particularly Social Security), one study notes that "between 1933 and 1940, more public money was spent creating jobs for the unemployed in public employment programs [like the Works Progress Administration and the Civilian Conservation Corps] than on all other forms of public assistance and social insurance combined," although job programs were phased out during World War II.[2] President Johnson's Great Society programs expanded the welfare state by adding Medicare, Medicaid, and food stamps (SSI began in 1974), although AFDC was scarcely touched. The number of AFDC recipients did increase substantially, however, through the efforts of the new Community Action programs to inform the eligible poor that they qualified for welfare benefits. Real (inflation-adjusted) AFDC expenditures tripled between 1965 and 1973, but since then have leveled off and even declined slightly.

The most significant increases in aid to the poor have come from increased expenditures for food stamps (which plateaued around 1980) and particularly Medicaid, which along with other health care expenditures has risen far more rapidly than inflation (SSI has risen only slightly in real terms since 1974). When all social welfare expenditures are counted together (Social Security, Medicare, food stamps, etc.), however, they have more than quadrupled in real terms between 1965 and today.[3] They now represent over half of the federal budget, compared with less than a third of much smaller federal budgets in the mid-1960s. The great increase in social welfare expenditures since the 1960s has not been driven by AFDC, but by the far more inclusive and larger programs like Social Security and medical care provided by Medicare and Medicaid. Although begun initially as a program to reduce old-age poverty, Social Security is now by far the largest cash assistance program, larger than all means-tested programs put together. While both taxpayers and recipients generally regard Social Security as a pension program—where one's benefits are tied to one's contributions—in reality it acts as supplemental income to the elderly regardless of income. It has been estimated that Social Security benefits received by retirees are two to five times greater than their payroll contributions (plus employer contributions) accumulated with interest over their lifetimes. Put another way, based on current Social Security benefit payments, one's prior payroll contributions are exhausted after only a few years of retirement.

There is considerable disagreement over what these vast social welfare expenditures—many not targeted to the poor—have actually accomplished. On one end, conservatives like Charles Murray contend that far from reducing poverty and dependence, welfare programs like AFDC have worsened the situation by, for example, providing financial incentives for single-parent families. This "cycle of dependency" is, from this view, the direct result of welfare programs. Indeed, the number of single-parent families on welfare assistance has increased substantially since the early 1970s, as has the incidence of children (particularly minorities) living in poverty. Other conservatives have complained of excessive waste in welfare programs, such as President Reagan's frequent references to "welfare queens" bilking the public coffers. Commentators on the political left, like professors Frances Piven and Richard Cloward, have argued instead that welfare programs are mere financial palliatives to prevent social unrest, representing political control over the poor, but were never truly intended to eliminate poverty. Moderates, like Theodore Marmor, Jerry Mashaw, and Philip Harvey, argue that the welfare state has been much more successful than critics give it credit for in eliminating poverty, although paradoxically through programs that are not directed at the poor (such as Social Security). While some gains have been made in reducing poverty in the United States, particularly among the elderly whose poverty rates are substantially below those of the nation as a whole, stubborn problems like unemployment among African-American male youths, the number of children living in poverty, poor educational achievements, and the general inability of welfare programs to deal effectively with the "underclass" remain. Some have argued that because poverty is mostly the result of unemployment, jobs or at least job training is the best route to combating persistent poverty.

The general gloomy public assessment of what welfare policy has achieved is also partly attributable to stagnant economic conditions since the early 1970s. For example, real median family income is no greater now than in 1972, and national unemployment rates have risen from 3–4 percent from 1966–1969 to over 6 percent in the early 1990s. (Unemployment rates for minorities are frequently more than twice the rate for whites.) There has been little reduction in poverty rates since the late 1960s (the poverty rate has hovered between 11 and 15 percent since the mid-1960s and is now closer to 15 percent), and for children the rate has consistently been higher, at around 20 percent and over 40 percent for African-American children. While some modest improvements have been achieved, the intractability of poverty is reflected in one researcher's statement, "If you had told me in 1963 or 1973 that we'd be arguing, in 1993, whether poor people are marginally better off, I would have been incredulous."[4] This has led liberals like professors Theda Skocpol and William Julius Wilson to argue that antipoverty programs targeted only to the poor or minorities are destined to fail politically and that only through broad inclusive programs like Social Security can poverty be overcome.

The most significant reform to AFDC since 1935 is the Family Support Act of 1988, intended to remove single mothers from welfare rolls both through providing additional support (such as child care subsidies) and work requirements. While the impact of the Family Support Act will not be understood for several more years, some experts caution against undue optimism that it will significantly reduce poverty. Sociologist Christopher Jencks argues that it will not move the nation's 3.7 million welfare families off of welfare because "single mothers do not turn to welfare because they are pathologically dependent on handouts or unusually reluctant to work—they do so because they cannot get jobs that pay better than welfare."[5] Nevertheless, expectations were high both that its changes would bolster political support for this new type of antipoverty program that combines assistance with work responsibilities and that the lives of certain groups of individuals would be improved, such as poor two-parent families and some working poor. But the most significant component, known as "workfare," has been the subject of considerable debate. Political scientist Lawrence Mead argues below that because poverty and unemployment are strongly linked, workfare programs for able-bodied adults appropriately require obligations of welfare recipients and can lessen problems of dependency. Professors Richard Cloward and Frances Piven argue that there are huge political and economic obstacles to finding work for millions of unemployed and underemployed workers and that it is degrading to require welfare recipients to find work when unemployment is high and wages low for unskilled workers. Their extended arguments follow.

Endnotes

1. Theodore R. Marmor, Jerry L. Mashaw, and Philip L. Harvey, *America's Misunderstood Welfare State* (New York: Basic Books, 1990), p. 85.
2. Ibid., p. 35.
3. Ibid.
4. Peter Gottschalk, quoted in Robert Pear, "Poverty 1993: Bigger, Deeper, Younger, Getting Worse," *New York Times* (October 10, 1993), p. E5.
5. Christopher Jencks, *Rethinking Social Policy* (Cambridge, Mass.: Harvard University Press, 1992), p. 204.

YES

Jobs for the Welfare Poor: Work Requirements Can Overcome the Barriers

Lawrence M. Mead

Work for welfare recipients has suddenly become a hot topic in Washington. Politicians say they want to place more dependent adults in training or employment programs. Some even claim we can turn welfare into "workfare," as President Nixon promised when he proposed his own ill-fated welfare reform nearly 20 years ago. The idea is popular, as the public has long wanted recipients to do more to help themselves.

The workfare debate has been brewing for several years. In 1981, Congress, under prodding from the Reagan administration, allowed states for the first time to introduce serious work requirements in Aid to Families with Dependent Children (AFDC), the main federal welfare program. Then, two years ago, President Reagan announced a further effort to reform welfare, leading to a flurry of work-oriented proposals from groups on the left and right.

A White House task force led by Charles Hobbs produced "Up From Dependency," a proposal for wider experimentation, including work initiatives, at the state and local levels. The administration also proposed Greater Opportunities through Work (GROW), which would define more AFDC recipients as employable (particularly by including mothers of preschool children) and would, over several years, require states to involve the great majority of these clients in school or work programs. The main features of the Hobbs and GROW plans have since been incorporated in HR 3200, a proposal by House Republicans drafted by Hank Brown and Bob Michel. The emphasis in all these plans is on stiffening work requirements. Funding for work programs would be increased slightly, if at all.

Democratic plans, however, have downplayed requirements in favor of greater spending. In the House, a bill largely drafted by Thomas Downey and supported by party leaders (HR 1720, recently renumbered HR 3644) was passed December 16, 1987, on a largely party-line vote. In the Senate, Daniel Patrick Moynihan of the Finance Committee has produced S-1511. Both bills would increase welfare benefits as well as spend more on child-care and job training services. But neither would effectively strengthen the requirements for work bearing on recipients or states. Indeed, both would restrict some "workfare" programs that states already have in effect. These bills would, if enacted, effectively revive the overblown, but voluntary, employment of programs of the 1970s. Since the administration opposes these plans, the odds currently favor no reform or a compromise bill that would make only marginal changes.

Liberal reformers presume that welfare recipients fail to work because they face special "barriers," notably a lack of jobs, child-care, and training opportunities. If government provided more of these things, liberals assert, welfare work levels would rise. That is a misconception. Research has shown that the presumed impediments rarely keep people from working, at least in low-skilled, low-paid jobs. The main reason for nonwork, rather, is the reluctance of many recipients to take such jobs. The main task of welfare work policy is to overcome that reluctance. While this probably requires some new services, it above all requires more clear-cut *requirements* that recipients work in return for benefits. Those who favor increased benefits are seeking not so much to promote work as to advance the traditional liberal interest in social equality.

Reform, to be effective, must abandon the illusion that work is impossible for the poor. The major obstacles to welfare employment lie in the minds of the poor, and in the permissive attitudes of federal legislators. Welfare policymakers must believe what the facts show—work can be required of the majority of adult recipients.

NONWORK AND DEPENDENCY

The work issue has come to the fore for a good reason: Nonwork is the immediate cause of much poverty and dependency today. There is still a tendency to see the poor simply as victims entitled to government redress. That view is most plausible for the elderly and disabled poor, whom society does not expect to work. But, it is implausible for families headed by able-bodied people of working age, whom society does expect to work.

This article focuses primarily on working-age adults; I do not suggest that children, the elderly, or the disabled should work. I also recognize that much of poverty is transient, and that half of all welfare cases leave the rolls in under two years. I am speaking here mainly of the long-term cases, and especially about the welfare mothers and absent fathers whose reluctance to work helps create entrenched dependency.

Among the working-age poor, poverty usually arises, at least initially, because the adults involved do not work normal hours. Of the heads of poor households in 1984, only 17 percent worked full-time, while 51 percent did not work at all.

In a world where most people still have to labor for a living, it is hardly surprising that *how much* one works often makes the difference between poverty and sufficiency. In 1986, fewer than 4 percent of families whose heads worked full-time were poor. The rate jumped to 20 percent for heads working part-time, and to 24 percent for heads not working at all. Among female-headed families, the comparable figures were 10, 48, and 56 percent, an even steeper gradient. As Mary Jo Bane and David Ellwood have shown, about half of all spells of poverty begin through a drop in family earnings, and 75% of them end through an increase in earnings.

Most families go on welfare because of the breakup or nonmarriage of parents, but nonwork often keeps them there. Very few adults work while they are on welfare. Only about 6 percent of AFDC families had earnings in May 1982, though a higher proportion do sometime during a year. Work is least common for the long-term dependent; after two years on the rolls, fewer than 5 percent of mothers leave because of work or reasons other than remarriage.

For most women who head families, work is quite simply the difference between going on welfare and avoiding it. Two-thirds of female family heads who do not work are on welfare, while only 7 percent of those who work full-time are. A fifth or more of welfare mothers also leave the rolls through work, a route second in importance only to marriage.

Those who doubt the efficacy of work in combating poverty point to the working, not the nonworking, poor. It is true that most poor families have some earnings, yet remain needy. But few of these families have members working full-time. Many more people are poor for lack of work than despite work. Moreover, for the vast majority of workers, poverty is uncommon or transient. Fewer than 3 percent of able-bodied, working-age adults lived in poor households with any earnings in 1970, and only 15 percent of these—or 0.3 percent of all working-age adults—were also poor in 1980.

To work substantial hours and still be poor, one must usually combine low wages with a large nonworking family. It is true that almost a third of all jobs do not pay enough to keep a four-person family out of poverty, but that assumes that only one parent works, even though both parents in most families work. In fact, since so many families have more than one worker, fewer than a fifth of workers who work at or below the minimum wage actually live in poor families. In general, low wages cause economic *inequality*, not poverty. Low working hours are a much more common cause of poverty and dependency.

A generation ago, many more of the poor were working. In 1959, 32 percent of the heads of poor families were working full-time, and only 31 percent did not work at all. Many more workers simply could not get above the poverty line then because of low wages or racial discrimination. Moreover, many more of them were elderly and disabled. It was easier to argue that the poor were "deserving," the victims of adverse conditions over which they had no control.

Since then, formalized racial discrimination has ended, and economic growth has carried most adults and their families above the poverty line—provided they are working. The main problem for the remaining poor adults is that they do not work steadily. That has shifted the debate about the reasons for poverty. Before, nonwork was only one of several causes. Now, it is itself the main mystery to be explained, as it so often leads directly to poverty, especially for welfare families.

The policy debate about how to overcome poverty has also shifted from benefit levels to employment strategies. Policymakers recognize that to reduce nonwork would reduce dependency among people of working age. But should programs to that end focus on "barriers" to employment or on work obligations? Liberals focus on lack of jobs, child-care, and training.

THE JOBS DEBATE

The main argument for a job shortage has always been the high unemployment of the last two decades. The overall jobless rate touched 10 percent in 1982–83, and much higher rates are routinely recorded for the groups most likely to be poor and dependent—minorities, women, and youth. Many take this as *prima facie* evidence that enough jobs must be lacking for all who seek them.

Job pessimists say social trends have overcrowded the labor market. The economy of the 1970s and early 1980s was prone to recession, yet it also had to absorb an enormous glut of new workers. The huge baby-boom generation came of age, and more women sought employment than ever before. As a result, between 1970 and 1985 the labor force—those working or seeking work—grew by an astounding 38 percent. Apparently, a tepid economy could not keep pace. Job-seekers outnumbered jobs. In the scramble for employment, the poor and dependent inevitably lost out.

But this account is outdated. Unemployment has fallen to 6 percent or below. Whatever its troubles, the economy has created jobs on a scale never before seen. From 1970 to 1985, total employment grew by 28 million jobs, or 35 percent, almost enough to match the growing labor force. Since the end of the 1981–82 recession, job growth has considerably outpaced the entry of new workers, which is slowing down with the "baby bust" that followed the baby boom.

Some critics say the new employment is no more than a symptom of the "deindustrialization of America." Many of the new jobs pay less than traditional manufacturing jobs. Many are part-time. They tend to fall in the service sector, which includes work in restaurants, hotels, conventions and entertainment, the maintenance of buildings and equipment, and other support services for business. It is easy to dismiss such jobs as marginal. But what unionized steel and auto workers used to make is not a realistic income standard now that our economy faces stiff foreign competition.

Even if a decline in job quality has occurred, it could not explain nonwork. For, in the face of lower wages, one might expect people to work *more* rather than less in order to maintain their incomes. That is what most Americans have done. During the 1970s, growth in real wages stagnated. Many housewives responded by seeking work for the first time. Many men took extra jobs. Average working hours rose. Only among poor and dependent people was there, in general, a flat or negative response. Work levels of welfare recipients rose hardly at all, even though benefits fell in real terms due to inflation. Poor blacks did not share in the great economic strides made by the black middle class during this period. Black men as a group reduced their labor force participation rate from 77 percent in 1970 to 71 percent in 1985, much more than whites.

Some might say that recipients fail to accept low-paid employment because they have the alternative of welfare. In other words, jobs must pay more than welfare does before it is worthwhile to take them. But this argument presupposes falsely that recipients have to leave welfare if they work. Actually, of mothers entering work in the typical AFDC work program, about half still receive some assistance. Because of this supplementation, welfare mothers should actually be freer to take low-paid jobs than many other people. Welfare and work are mutually exclusive only for unemployed fathers (whom states may choose to cover under AFDC), who may not work more than 100 hours a month without losing AFDC eligibility. But they represent only a small part of the employable caseload.

JOBLESSNESS IN A LABOR SHORTAGE

Across most of the low-skilled labor market, there is now a manifest labor shortage. Low-skilled jobs have become particularly hard to fill in suburban areas, where some employers have taken to transporting labor from inner-city areas at their own expense. Many are being forced to pay well above the minimum wage even for unskilled work. The presence of 7 million or more illegal immigrants in the country, mostly in urban areas, is testimony that at least menial jobs must exist in many cities as well. Without the illegals, many restaurant and laundry owners say they simply could not operate, because most citizens will not accept "dirty work."

To argue that sufficient job opportunities are unavailable today, one must contend that the poor are somehow walled off from the opportunities that do clearly exist. One such argument maintains that the labor market is "dual" or "segmented." Access to the preferred jobs is allegedly controlled by government, large firms, and nonprofit institutions, which hire on the basis of externals such as race or educational credentials, not actual ability, and thus choose mainly the better-off. The poor are relegated to menial or service-sector jobs that are transient and poorly paid. Actually, research has not demonstrated that labor markets treat the low-skilled unfairly. In fact, as shown by the University of Michigan panel study of income dynamics, blacks and the low-skilled, as well as whites and the better-off, experience considerable economic mobility over time, both up and down the economic ladder.

Another version is that there is a "mismatch" between most available jobs and the location or skills of the poor. As John Kasarda has shown, much employment has migrated to the U.S. Sunbelt or even overseas from the Eastern and Midwestern cities where most poor and dependent people live. Employment opportunities have also moved from inner cities to the suburbs, where urban job-seekers have great difficulty reaching jobs because of inadequate public transportation and costly housing. These shifts have been most pronounced among manufacturing employers whose jobs—manual but well-paid—offered the best opportunity to low-skilled workers. Of course, a "high-tech" economy based on finance, information, and computing has grown up in many central cities. But high-tech work, so the argument goes, demands employees with strong communication or technical skills, while most poor adults have only limited education.

William Julius Wilson claims such shifts go far to explain the extraordinary dysfunctions found in the inner city. In *The Truly Disadvantaged* (University of Chicago Press, 1987), he argues that old-fashioned racial discrimination has receded, but he attributes much of the urban social breakdown to a changing economy that has denied previously available opportunity to poor black men.

JOB EXPECTATIONS MISMATCH

One trouble with the "mismatch theory" is that employment today does not usually require advanced skills. Not everybody in the "high-tech" economy is a financier or a computer programmer. Though fields like these are fastest growing, the most hiring in the future, as in the past, will be for low- and medium-skilled workers, such as secretaries, janitors, retail clerks, and truck drivers. New York City is a center of the "information economy," but in 1981, 57 percent of its employment required only a high school diploma or less. That is a decline of only 1 percent since 1972.

The notion of a spatial mismatch in the labor market has been undercut by studies of Chicago by David Ellwood, and of Los Angeles by Jonathan Leonard, showing that the need of inner-city blacks to commute to jobs in the suburbs is only a minor reason for their unusually high unemployment. Even when poor blacks live as close to jobs as white or Hispanic workers, many fewer of them work. It is also doubtful that the black poor are as concentrated or as isolated from the rest of society as Wilson suggests. According to recent research by Mary Jo Bane and Paul Jargowsky, that problem seems acute only in a few large cities, especially New York and Chicago.

Although cases of long-term joblessness attract the most attention, most of the unemployed remain out of work only briefly. More have quit their jobs or just entered or reentered the labor force than have been "thrown out" of work. This pattern of turnover, rather than steady work, is most pronounced for minorities, women, and youth, the groups with the highest unemployment. White, male, and older workers tend to hold the same jobs longer.

Surveys have shown that most unemployed are jobless not because they cannot find any work, but because of the expectations they have about wages and working conditions. According to a Labor Department survey done in 1976, the average jobless person wants a 7 percent *raise* to go back to work, and his demands drop below his previous wage only after almost a year out of work. Most unemployed are also unwilling to move or commute more than 20 miles to reach new jobs. One may remain unemployed by the official definition even if one's expectations from the job market are totally unrealistic. It is thus wrong to take the presence of unemployment as proof that jobs are lacking.

Surveys focused specifically on the poor and dependent find much the same. Among poor adults, only 40 percent of those working less than full-time give inability to find work as the main reason, and only 11 percent of those not working at all do so. For poor blacks the comparable figures are 45 and 16 percent. Other constraints, including health problems and housekeeping responsibilities, are important, especially for nonworkers. Inner-city black youth regularly record unemployment rates over 40 percent, yet 71 percent say they can find a minimum-wage job fairly easily.

The adverse trends cited by Wilson and others have depressed the quality of jobs much more clearly than the number of jobs. In most areas jobs of some kind are commonly available, even to the low-skilled. Jobs are often *available* but *unacceptable* to job-hunters, both rich and poor.

Liberal reformers also say that welfare mothers face special difficulties in working. After all, AFDC was first instituted in 1935 on the supposition that mothers heading families were unemployable. They were supposed to stay home and raise their children. If we now demand that they work, government must first guarantee them child-care.

But the surge of women into jobs has changed social norms. Welfare mothers can no longer be seen as unemployable now that more than half of female family heads with children under 18 are working, nearly three-quarters of them full-time. For divorced and separated mothers like those on AFDC, the working proportion is nearly two-thirds. Welfare mothers are distinctly out of step. Only about 15 percent of them worked in the 13 years prior to the 1981 cuts in AFDC eligibility, which removed most working mothers from the rolls. This was so even though the mothers were often more employable during that period—younger, better-educated, and with fewer children (over 70 percent now have only one or two).

While children certainly make work difficult for mothers, they are not the hard-and-fast barrier that is often supposed. In fact, as high a proportion of single mothers work as do single women without children. Even young children are not prohibitive. Welfare mothers with pre-school children may be no less likely to work their way off the rolls than those with older children, and two-thirds of mothers who leave welfare this way still have children at home.

Working mothers certainly need child-care, but they seldom rely on organized facilities such as government child-care centers. Only 9 percent of primary child-care arrangements by working parents involved day-care centers or nursery schools in 1984–85. Even for the most dependent group, single mothers with children under 5, it was only 27 percent. Overwhelmingly, the parents rely on less formal arrangements, chiefly care by friends or relatives, either in their own homes or that of the caretaker.

Apparently, they arrange care fairly easily, as fewer than 6 percent of working mothers in a given month lose time on the job because of problems with their child-care arrangements. In only 10 percent of cases is the availability of care critical to a mother seeking work; finding the right job is much more important.

Child-care advocates claim that the parents would use more center care if it were available. But most mothers prefer informal arrangements, probably because they have more control over them. When government has offered free care in centers as part of social experiments, it has sometimes gone untaken. Informal care is also much less costly than center care, which must satisfy elaborate government staffing and licensing rules.

There appears, in fact, to be little unmet need for child-care. That is why proposals for a national day-care program covering the general population have always failed. Of course, government must *pay* for care for welfare mothers if it wants them to work. It already does this, usually by adjusting the mother's grant, while they are on welfare. More funding for transitional care after they leave welfare may be needed. But government need not provide the care in its own facilities.

TRAINING OVERSOLD

Finally, liberal reformers say that adult recipients can be expected to work only if they first receive training to raise their skills and earnings. Otherwise, they will fail to get jobs or, if they do get them, will not earn enough to get off welfare or out of poverty. That is the rationale behind the heavy emphasis on training in the Democratic reform plans.

The benefits of training have been deduced from evaluations of some of the post-1981 work programs by the Manpower Demonstration Research Corporation (MDRC). These suggest that well-run training and jobs programs for recipients have the potential to raise their income by as much as 25 percent, as well as reduce dependency.

But training is easily oversold. The earnings gains in even the best training programs are limited, seldom enough to get welfare families entirely out of poverty or off welfare. Furthermore, "training" can be a misnomer, as few programs raise the skills of adults on welfare, most of whom have shown little ability to learn in school. The main impact of training programs is not on job quality but on motivation—on causing the clients to work *more hours* in the rudimentary jobs they are already able to get.

The best training programs tend to be highly authoritative, aimed at impressing on clients a responsibility to work at whatever job they can get. Nondirective programs can actually *depress* work effort, as clients embark on unrealistic training programs for "better" jobs at the expense of immediate employment. Welfare employment programs have made that mistake in the past. They overinvested in training, only to see very few trainees go to work in available jobs. The current liberal reform proposals would repeat that error.

Nor is training usually necessary for work. In fact, welfare mothers average 2.6 years of work experience since they left school. Many work "off-the-books" while they are on welfare, a dodge that work requirements help to detect. Their problem is seldom that they are literally unemployable but rather that they do not work *consistently*.

This is not to say that work is easy for welfare mothers, or for anyone. Serious effort is required to find a job and to arrange one's private life for work. But these burdens do not seem notably greater for the poor and dependent than they are for other low-skilled people. What liberal reformers call "barriers" are mostly the ordinary demands of employment—demands that most working Americans cope with every day. Welfare adults face serious difficulties landing well-paid jobs, but not low-paid ones. Moreover, if the benefits provided in liberal reform bills were really necessary to employment, how do so many other low-skilled workers do without them? ·

Government could perhaps overwhelm these so-called barriers with benefits, guaranteeing jobs, child-care, and training especially for the poor and dependent. But to do that would be unfair to the many other Americans who already work in menial jobs without special assistance. It would also be ineffective in integrating the poor, because they would not earn the respect of others. Work where government bears all the burdens without holding the employee accountable for performance is not really work. It is simply another form of welfare.

THE PSYCHOLOGY OF NONWORK

To explain nonwork, therefore, it is more promising to look inside the poor than outside—to the mentality of those who have difficulty working. There have been three main psychological theories of nonwork.

The most common, but the least plausible, is that welfare recipients are deterred from working by the "disincentives" inherent in welfare itself. If they take a job, their earnings are normally deducted from their welfare grants, leaving them no better off than before. Why then should they work? Some conservatives find the deterrent prohibitive. They conclude that the poor will work only if welfare for the able-bodied is abolished. Liberals, instead, say the problem can be overcome with "work incentives," a policy of deducting only part of earnings from the grant, restoring at least some payoff to work. On this logic, Congress in 1967 allowed AFDC recipients to keep about a third of any earnings, in hopes that more of them would work.

However, research has failed to discover more than a weak connection between welfare benefits levels and work effort by recipients. Ellwood and Bane find that welfare disincentives have more impact on the structure of welfare families, by promoting divorce and especially by causing young unwed mothers to leave home and set up their own households. Work levels on welfare did not rise after work incentives were instituted, nor when real benefits fell during the 1970s. The main effect of incentives has been to expand eligibility for welfare and hence costs, by allowing more working people to get on the rolls despite their earnings. For these reasons, in 1981 a disappointed Congress withdrew most of the AFDC work incentive it had granted in 1967.

One might still argue that the mere presence of welfare depresses work levels below what they would otherwise be. But in a world where welfare already exists, variations in benefits and incentives have little further effect.

The disincentives theory is also implausible because of its economic logic. It assumes that the nonworking poor are rational in the economist's sense, that they calculate what will serve their pecuniary advantage and then act accordingly. But the mentality of most long-term poor people today is decidedly *non*-economic. Behaviors such as illegitimacy or crime may satisfy impulses, but they are not rational in any longer-run sense. Similarly, there is no way that nonwork can rationally be regarded as self-serving—especially given the very real opportunities that exist in this country, even for the poor. If the poor were as sensitive to economic payoffs as the disincentives theory supposes, they would seldom be poor in the first place.

A more persuasive theory is that nonwork is political. Perhaps nonworkers are not acting to maximize their incomes. They are protesting, by refusing to work, against the unattractive jobs the economy offers them. They demand that government force employers to pay them more or provide "better" jobs in government itself. To make that point, they will decline to work even though this is personally costly to them. Nonwork, in this view, is analogous to a strike for better wages and working conditions.

This interpretation fits the behavior of many nonworking men, especially ghetto youth. Members of this group do tend to see demands that they accept menial jobs as a denial of rights, a form of racial subjugation. They often resist direction by the staff of training programs, one reason they usually benefit less from training than do women. Black youth often refuse jobs that pay them less than white youth, even if this means they remain unemployed. Some welfare mothers say they should not have to take menial jobs, for example as domestics. They demand jobs with better pay and career prospects. Such feelings were aggressively voiced by the welfare rights movement of the 1960s.

The problem with this view is that political action is supposed to be proud, open, and collective in nature. Nonwork seldom is. Rather, it is individual, secretive, and frequently ashamed. Studies of the poor do not suggest that they are rebellious. Most, in fact, are deferential to all mainstream mores—to the despair of those who would see them as a revolutionary class. Most clients in workfare programs actually respond *positively* to the experience of being required to work, not negatively as they would if they truly rejected work. The majority accept the requirement as fair, and they feel they are contributing to society. They do not share the view, propagated by advocate groups, that workfare is negative and punitive, intended only to drive needy people off the rolls.

CULTURE OF POVERTY

The difficulty with both the economic and political theories of nonwork is that they assume that behavior corresponds to considered intentions. If the poor do not work, then they must not want to. The third and most plausible theory, especially for welfare mothers, may be called the "culture of poverty" theory, which says that aspirations can be radically inconsistent with behaviors. Thus the poor *want* to work and achieve other orthodox values but feel *unable* to do so because of forces beyond their control. They would like to observe strictures such as obedience to law, but feel they cannot in the circumstances they face. Social norms are held as *aspirations*, but not as *obligations* binding on actual behavior.

The tragedy of low-income life is that a pathological culture in which the poor participate often overrides their good intentions. Parents want their children to avoid trouble but lose control of them to a street life of hustling and crime. Children want to succeed but lack the discipline to get through school. Girls want to marry and escape poverty but succumb to pregnancy and welfare. Youths want to "make it," but can earn the money they want only by selling drugs.

Specifically, the poor are as eager to work as the better-off, but the strength of this desire appears to be unrelated to their work behavior. Whether they actually work depends, rather, on whether they believe they *can* work and *must* work. If they have successfully held jobs in the past and/or accept low-level positions to begin with, they will probably know they *can* work. If they have not become dependent on welfare or illegal sources of income, they probably will accept that they *must* work in order to survive. But simply the desire for employment is insufficient to make a person work. For those who do not accept these attitudes, work remains an aspiration, neither achievable nor required.

Disadvantaged clients in work programs often will accept work only if government first assumes most of the burdens of achieving it. They demand that the program arrange child-care and transportation, provide training, and, above all, guarantee attractive jobs in advance. To do these things does increase their interest in work, because they now feel they are "succeeding." But government cannot afford these burdens. And even if it could, guaranteed "employment" would not really be work, because it would not impose any real responsibility on the client. Work that is only a benefit, not an obligation, is welfare in disguise. The "welfare mentality" that expects everything from government is itself a barrier to employment, greater than any practical impediment the needy face.

The federal government learned this lesson during the 1970s, when it tried to provide government jobs for the poor on a large scale. As many as 750,000 positions a year were funded under the Comprehensive Employment and Training Act (CETA). This "public service employment" (PSE) was supposed to allow disadvantaged workers to experience "success" in relatively comfortable, well-paid jobs arranged by government in local agencies. It was hoped that they would grow more accustomed to work and then make the transition to regular employment.

But few did. After their CETA jobs ended, most clients went on unemployment or welfare, entered another training program, or left the labor force rather than take a regular job. In 1977, only 22 percent of disadvantaged PSE clients "graduated" from the program, less than half of them for unsubsidized jobs, and most of those, like the PSE positions themselves, were in the public sector. The hitch was that the private jobs these workers could command offered them nothing like the pay and security they had known in government.

Real work will always be tougher than a guaranteed job. That disappointment as well as other controversies—particularly the diversion of slots to support regular municipal employees—persuaded Congress to kill PSE in 1981.

At the core of the culture of poverty is the conviction that one is not responsible for one's fate, what psychologists call inefficacy. The long-term poor tend to feel that success or failure depends, not on their own efforts, or lack thereof, but on arbitrary forces beyond their control. If they fail in school or on the job, for example, they are more likely than the better-off to attribute it to the undeserved hostility of teachers or supervisors, or to racial discrimination, even if personal behavior is really to blame.

Inefficacy seems to be the result primarily of weak socialization. Due to erratic parenting, many poor children fail to internalize goals such as work and self-reliance with enough force to feel them as obligations—partly because the parents have often been unable to control their own lives. Welfare mothers who are dependent a long time often grew up in female-headed families; and youth who do not work often come from families living on welfare or in public housing.

These psychological theories, and especially culture of poverty, illuminate the real character of the work problem. Few poor adults, outside the disabled, are literally unemployable, but a great many have problems of work discipline. They find work with little more trouble than other people, but they have a great deal more trouble keeping it. They quit low-paid jobs rather than sticking with them long enough to earn raises and qualifications for better positions. The problem is partly rejection of the available jobs, but mostly an inability to *commit* to them. The long-term poor never get their feet on the bottom of the economic ladder, and thus never climb it.

Federal policies to promote work have succeeded when work discipline could be taken for granted. Measures to manage the business cycle and promote economic growth have expanded employment for all workers, rich and poor. Civil rights enforcement put an end to overt discrimination against minority workers, leading to rapid growth of the black middle class. Opportunity is all that is needed to overcome poverty when workers are committed, and that includes most adults of every race.

WHY WORK MUST BE REQUIRED

But work policies fail when discipline cannot be assumed. Employment programs aimed specifically at the poor and disadvantaged have shown little impact, mainly because they asked, and got, little commitment from their clients. The error of federal incentives, training, and jobs programs was that they offered only benefits in one form or another, without firm work requirements. All attempted, one way or another, to raise wages per working hours, as if low wages were the major cause of poverty. None directly confronted the greater problem—the low number of hours the poor work. All assumed that benefits of some sort could entice the jobless poor to work more. All assumed that opportunity was the main problem, instead of motivation.

Unfortunately, that assumption is invalid. The long-term poor seem to be a remarkably *un*responsive group. Their work levels have remained low for a generation, in good times and bad, in the face of a succession of programs meant to inspire or reward work. In fact, the opportunities and incentives the poor have to get ahead are already great, as shown by the recent success of Asian immigrants. No government benefit could add to the opportunity very much. There is now no reason to suppose that any reform that only changes incentives will get much response.

None of the work benefits directly mandated higher work levels. None set any standards for work effort. No training or jobs program required that clients be working, or have worked, in existing jobs in order to qualify for benefits. Accordingly, the programs operated more as substitutes for work than as preparations for it. By entering them, clients could avoid coming to terms with the low-skilled jobs that were all they could usually get, even after training. "Employment" programs thus undercut rather than affirmed the work norm.

Reluctantly, policymakers have begun to accept that work must be enforced as are other civilities such as obedience to the law or tax payment. Work serves important social values, particularly provision of higher income and social integration. So dependent adults should be required to work, even if—due to other income from families or programs—their immediate preferences are otherwise. Rather than be offered further opportunities and rewards for working, they should simply be *required* to work in return for the income they are already getting. They should face the demands for performance, for reciprocity, that nondependent Americans face every day.

Requirements approach the work problem as one of enforcement rather than barriers. Whereas the barriers theory says the poor are blocked from work and need greater freedom, the enforcement theory says they are in some ways too free. The solution to the work problem lies in *obligation*, not in freedom.

Requirements suit the irresolute mentality of the poor. They *want* to work but feel they *cannot*. Enforcement operates to close the gap between the work norm and actual behavior, and changes work from an aspiration to an obligation. It places the employable poor in a structure, combining supports and requirements, where they find they must do what they always wanted, which is to work.

Over the last 20 years, work tests have developed haltingly in the main welfare program, AFDC, and Food Stamps. Essentially, these requirements allowed welfare departments to refer employable recipients to work programs after 1967, and required them to do so after 1971. The work agency linked to AFDC was the Work Incentive (WIN) program, instituted in 1967 and still the most common welfare work program nationwide.

But only a minority of the clients referred had to participate actively in WIN, and those that did were usually required only to look for work, not actually work. Most WIN programs "creamed," or concentrated their attention on the most placeable of the employable clients, effectively exempting the rest.

CURRENT PROPOSALS

Besides costs, the main issue in the current reform debate is whether to force state programs to serve a broader slice of employable caseload, instead of "creaming." Current federal law sets a minimum participation rate of only 15 percent of the employable clients. The Republican reform proposals would raise that to 60 percent or more over several years. The Democratic proposals would delete even the 15 percent floor.

The Republicans are on the right track. Tougher participation requirements would sharply raise work levels among the poor, probably more than any other policy tried to date. We know from the WIN experience that the proportion of clients entering jobs is principally determined by the percentage who are obligated to participate actively in the program. The successful WIN programs make participation and work, rather than nonwork, the norm for their caseloads.

In the states that have replaced WIN, the main way the new programs differ is that they raise the participation rate, typically to about half. They seem to have achieved higher earnings and welfare servings than WIN as a result.

The Republican House proposal (HR 3200) gives priority to raising participation and thus would have much greater impact on work effort than the benefit-oriented Democratic bill (HR 3644). According to estimates from the Congressional Budget Office, the Brown/Michel proposal would cost only $1.1 billion in additional spending over 5 years, but would raise participation in work programs by 935,000 clients and cause 50,000 families to leave welfare mostly through work. The low cost is largely due to the savings from lower welfare spending, which almost cover the expense of added services. In contrast, the Downey bill would spend an additional $5.5 billion, chiefly for benefit expansions, but would raise participation by only 210,000 clients and would cause only 15,000 families to leave welfare. Clearly, the Republican and not the Democratic plan would make more welfare people independent, but even more important, would cause those remaining on welfare to undertake more effort to help themselves. Together, those shifts would go far toward changing the entitlement nature of welfare.

The rationale for workfare is simply that it has drawn more response from the dependent than any other measure. It has raised actual work effort, where benefits expanded only opportunities. Poor adults seem to respond more strongly to public authority than they ever did to incentives. The effect is especially great while clients are actually in the program, but some of it persists afterwards, showing up as higher earnings months later. That achievement outweighs the economic gains of the programs, as it suggests how the welfare work problem might finally be solved.

An effective welfare reform should define welfare mothers as employable when their youngest children are three or older, rather than six as now mandated. But above all it should require that higher proportions of the employable recipients, however defined, be genuinely working, looking for work, or training as a condition of eligibility for welfare. For teen-aged mothers, the obligation would be to stay in school until graduation. I would set an initial participation target of 50 percent, phased in over several years, and then see if higher levels were feasible. Child-care would be financed, but mothers would be required to arrange their own unless they could show that this was impossible. Some training would be included, but it would be confined to clients who were working, at least part-time, or who had a recent work record. Workfare policy should rely on government employment only when job search efforts in the private sector proved fruitless. Any government workfare jobs should have clear-cut performance standards, for which the workfare employees are held accountable.

DISDAIN FOR "DIRTY WORK"

Why, then, do liberals resist mandating higher participation levels? In part, no doubt, because the idea of serious work requirements strikes many as coercive. It also cuts against the pork-barrel proclivities of federal politics. Federal politicians would much rather give deserving groups good things than tell them how to behave. Until recently, even conservative politicians shared that attitude. They simply wanted fewer benefits than liberals. They counted on the private sector to enforce social mores such as the desire to work. Only the sharpening of the social problem has forced both sides to confront the need for functioning standards within welfare.

Liberals, in addition, resist accepting that the poor should be held responsible in any sense for their behavior. For a generation, they have defined the poor as victims. They assigned the responsibility for change entirely to government. Workfare, however, would share that onus between the poor adult and government. The two would work together to overcome dependency, the one by working more, the other by providing necessary support services. There seems no other way to change the dysfunctional patterns that now create poverty. Yet for welfare advocates, whose identity is wrapped up in claim-making, even a division of responsibility is anathema. Pressures from these groups explain why the Democratic plans give only lip service to requirements.

Greater than these difficulties, however, is the fact that the jobs commonly available to the poor are usually not very nice. For most recipients, relatively "dirty work" is the only realistic alternative to welfare. They must work in unappealing jobs, or not at all. No government policy can improve that choice very much. If training or government jobs could somehow qualify the poor for "better" positions, a policy requiring work would be less contentious. But they can do this only for a few. Work policy cannot be based on that hope, or higher work levels will never be achieved.

Most conservatives would accept those alternatives and enforce work. Most liberals reject them as a Hobson's choice. They want the poor to work—but only in "good" jobs. Their upset is that "dirty work" would not advance the goal of equality as they understand it—a more equal distribution of income and status in the United States. Low-paid jobs are enough to lift most families off welfare and out of poverty, if all adults work; but they would not assure middle-class incomes. Even if working, many of today's poor, like yesterday's, would have to wait for "success" in their children's lives rather than their own.

Concretely, the issue often comes down to whether the *first* job that recipients take must be a good one. Conservatives tend to say not. They accept that entry-level jobs are usually low-paid. The unskilled should take such jobs to accumulate a work record, after which they can qualify for "better" positions. Meanwhile, they can count on supplementation from welfare or other family members. This is acceptable because most workers in entry-level jobs are young. But advocate groups demand that available jobs be good enough to take the family off welfare and out of poverty immediately. Mainstream income cannot require any apprenticeship. Better to be idle and dependent than working-poor. For them, the low-paying, first job is as much of a "barrier" to employment as if no jobs existed at all.

The drive for equality shapes the positions liberals take even on issues of fact. Many, for instance, concede tacitly that jobs of a menial kind are usually accessible to the poor. They question, rather, whether "good," "decent," or "meaningful" jobs are available—a very different thing. By fudging whether they mean jobs or good jobs, they often avoid facing up to the evidence that work is already widely available. Bradley Schiller has written, for example, that to overcome poverty, government must assure "an abundance of jobs—jobs that provide decent wages and advancement opportunity," as if these were the same thing. Such comments suggest that the real dispute in work policy is about equality, not opportunity.

Some also disagree that the performance of work programs would improve if participation rates were raised. Perhaps earnings gains would deteriorate, as there would be more clients to serve for a given funding. This would force programs to place more recipients in available jobs, spend less on training them, and thus reduce the earnings gains each could make. But this assumes that the impact of programs is assessed *per individual*, as in the MDRC evaluations of the recent work programs, which assume the liberal criterion that the main purpose of work policy is to raise the income of clients. If, on the contrary, it is to enforce the work obligation for the benefit of society, then aggregate measures, such as total job entries and welfare savings, become more important. These are the measures that respond especially to higher participation.

A concern for equality in this economic sense blinds liberals to the true nature of the work problem and its solution. Their analysis and recommendations are predominantly concerned with things that affect relative incomes among those who are working; they downplay the problem of those who are not working. Few of the things that affect equality in their sense also affect nonwork. The alleged barriers facing the poor primarily limit the quality of jobs they can get, not their ability to work at all. The benefits liberals would provide through welfare reform would raise the incomes of recipients willing to participate, but would not make more participate.

The work problem *is* a problem of participation, not of equality. The great question is how to get more of the employable poor to participate in the economy, in any kind of job, not how to improve those jobs. Only after they were working could the concerns of liberals become relevant. For it is *working* people that government would help by raising job quality, and who also have the greatest power to help themselves. Liberals and conservatives can dispute whether working people really need help from government. They ought to agree that dependent adults should at least become workers.

I do not mean that conservative welfare reformers are indifferent to equality. They simply have a different meaning of it. To them, it means, not primarily equal status and income, but *equal citizenship*. To be equal in America means to possess the same essential rights *and* obligations as other people. That entails some entitlements to a minimum income and other social protections, but it also requires a capacity for essential civil duties, such as working, speaking English, and obeying the law. This meaning, rather than the liberal one, is the one most Americans share.

Work policies have gained momentum, in the end, because increasing numbers of Americans, and their leaders, no longer believe that simply to transfer entitlements to the poor serves equality in this sense. We must require equal obligations of the poor as well as assure them equal rights if they are to be truly integrated. To do that should be the purpose of welfare reform.

NO

Punishing the Poor, Again: The Fraud of Workfare

Richard A. Cloward and Frances Fox Piven

During the presidential campaign, Bill Clinton repeatedly promised to "reform" the welfare system. Polls showed it was his most popular issue, and it continues to be a sure-fire applause-getter in speeches. But since the cheering stopped, Clinton has moved slowly. The next step will be the appointment of a commission and hearings. Nevertheless, the general direction Clinton intends to take is well known: Some job training, more workfare, new sanctions and an effort to cut women off the rolls after two years.

Such proposals reflect a rising tide of antiwelfare rhetoric, whose basic argument is that people receiving public assistance become trapped in a "cycle of dependency." Thus, Senator Daniel Patrick Moynihan grandiosely proclaims in the press that "just as unemployment was the defining issue of industrialism, dependency is becoming the defining issue of postindustrial society." Conservative political scientist Lawrence Mead warns that "dependency" signals "the end of the Western tradition." The national press announces that dependency has reached epidemic proportions. According to these accounts, rising unemployment, declining wage levels and disappearing fringe benefits need not concern anyone. "The old issues were economic and structural," Mead says, and "the new ones are social and personal."

To cope with these new issues, the critics urge that women on welfare be put to work. Near-miraculous social and cultural transformations are predicted once welfare mothers are shifted into the labor market. Cohesion will be restored to family and community, crime and other aberrant behaviors will disappear and poverty will decline. Mickey Kaus, who advocates replacing welfare with a W.P.A.-style jobs program, invokes a grand historical parallel: "Underclass culture can't survive the end of welfare any more than feudal culture could survive the advent of capitalism."

But there is no economically and politically practical way to replace welfare with work at a time when the labor market is saturated with people looking for jobs. Unemployment averaged 4.5 percent in the 1950s, 4.7 percent in the 1960s, 6.1 percent in the 1970s and 7.2 percent in the 1980s, and job prospects look no better in the 1990s. The labor market is flooded with immigrants from Asia and Latin America, and growing numbers of women have taken jobs to shore up family income as wages decline. Confronted with an increasingly globalized economy, corporations are shedding workers or closing domestic plants and opening new ones in Third World countries with cheap labor. Meanwhile, defense industries are making huge work-force cuts.

Moreover, employers are increasingly offering "contingent work"—part-time, temporary and poorly paid. Some 30 million people—over a quarter of the U.S. labor force—are employed in such jobs. A substantial proportion of them would prefer permanent, full-time job but cannot find them. Contingent workers are six times more likely than full-time workers to receive the minimum wage, and they are much less likely to receive health and pension benefits.

Because most mothers who receive Aid to Families with Dependent Children are unskilled, they can command only the lowest wages and thus cannot adequately support their families, a problem that will grow worse as wages continue to decline. According to the Census Bureau, 14.4 million year-round, full-time workers 16 years of age or older (18 percent of the total) had annual earnings below the poverty level in 1990, up from 10.3 million (14.6 percent) in 1984 and 6.6 million (12.3 percent) in 1974. There is no reason to think that A.F.D.C. mothers can become "self-sufficient" when growing millions of currently employed workers cannot. In a study of the finances of welfare families, sociologists Christopher Jencks and Kathryn Edin found that "single mothers do not turn to welfare because they are pathologically dependent on handouts or unusually reluctant to work—they do so because they cannot get jobs that pay better than welfare."

Research on workfare programs bears this out. Sociologists Fred Block and John Noakes concluded that participants typically cannot find jobs that pay more than welfare. Reviewing the research in the field, the Center on Budget and Policy Priorities found that—highly publicized stories of individual successes notwithstanding—only a handful of people in workfare programs achieved "a stable source of employment that provides enough income for a decent standard of living (at least above the poverty line) and job-related benefits that adequately cover medical needs." Still another general survey, this one sponsored by the Brookings Institution, reports that none of the programs succeed in raising earnings of welfare mothers more than $2,000 above grant levels. Political scientists John E. Schwarz and Thomas J. Volgy write in their book *The Forgotten Americans*, "No matter how much we may wish it otherwise, workfare cannot be an effective solution" because "low-wage employment riddles the economy." They note that in 1989 one in seven year-round full-time jobs, or 11 million, paid less than $11,500, which was roughly $2,000 below the official poverty line for a family of four.

The situation is actually much worse. When the poverty line was first calculated in the 1960s, the average family spent one-third of its income on food, and the poverty line was set at three times food costs, adjusted for family size. But by 1990, food costs had dropped to one-sixth of the average family budget because the price of other components—such as housing and medical costs—had inflated at far higher rates. If the 1991 official poverty line of $13,920 for a family of four had been recalculated to reflect changes in real costs, it would have been set at about 155 percent of the official rate, or $21,600. That is more than twice the $8,840 annual earnings of a full-time worker receiving the minimum wage of $4.25 per hour.

Another reason to be skeptical about welfare-to-work programs is that, although they are promoted as economy measures, they would in fact be very expensive if implemented widely. Federal and state expenditures for A.F.D.C. now run about $20 billion, supplemented by another $10 billion in food stamp costs for welfare families. Administrative costs alone would overshadow any savings from successful job placements. And to this must be added the much larger costs of government-subsidized child care and health care—essential to mothers going off welfare, since the private market is curtailing such benefits for newly hired workers. Economists James Medoff estimates that the proportion of new hires who receive health benefits dropped from 23 percent to 15 percent during the past decade. Christopher Jencks estimates that A.F.D.C. mothers working at the minimum wage would have to be given "free medical care and at least $5,000 worth of other resources every year to supplement their wages," at a cost of up to $50 billion, a quixotic sum that Congress is unlikely to appropriate. Mickey Kaus offers a similar estimate of the cost of his recommendation for a mandatory jobs program for the poor. Congress is certainly not unmindful of these costs, as it shows by its endless squabbling over whether health and day care benefits should be given to working recipients at all.

Given these constraints, the results of existing workfare programs are predictable enough. Studies show that a substantial proportion of welfare recipients who find jobs end up reapplying for welfare because they cannot survive on their earnings, even with welfare supplements, and because temporary child care and Medicaid supports run out, or because of periodic crises such as layoffs or illness in the family. Nevertheless, the charade goes on, as experts and politicians promise to put an end to welfare "dependency." None of it makes pragmatic sense.

Other professed goals of these work programs are equally irrational, such as the unsubstantiated assertions that putting welfare recipients to work would transform family structure, community life and the so-called "culture of poverty." Kaus insists that "replacing welfare with work can be expected to transform the entire culture of poverty," including family patterns, because "it's doubtful" that working women would "be willing to share their hard-earned paychecks with non-working men the way they might have been willing to share their welfare checks." Therefore, "the natural incentives toward the formation of two-parent families will reassert themselves." But Kaus presents no data to support the assumption that the source of a woman's income influences marriage or living arrangements. In our judgment, marriage rates might indeed increase if jobs paying adequate wages and benefits were available to men, as well as to women on welfare who choose to work, but that outcome seems entirely unlikely in view of current economic trends.

It is also doubtful that putting poor women to work would improve the care and socialization of children, as Kaus claims. "If a mother has to set her alarm clock, she's likely to teach her children to set their alarm clocks as well," he says, thus trivializing the real activities of most of these women. Many A.F.D.C. mothers get their children up every morning and, because of the dangers of the streets, escort them to school, walk them home and keep them in their apartments until the next morning. Forcing these overburdened women to work would add a market job to the already exhausting job of maintaining a home without sufficient funds or services while living in dangerous and disorganized neighborhoods.

Putting welfare recipients to work is advertised as the way to reverse the deterioration of community life. This is hardly a new idea. The minutes of a meeting of academics, intellectuals and administrators in New York City after Richard Nixon's 1968 presidential election reported a consensus that the rising welfare rolls accompanied by spreading urban riots and other manifestations of civil disorder proved that "the social fabric . . . is coming to pieces. It isn't just 'strained' and it isn't just 'frayed'; but like a sheet of rotten canvas, it is beginning to rip. . . ." Converting A.F.D.C. to a workfare system was the remedy; work would restore the social fabric.

More likely, removing women from their homes and communities would shred the social fabric even more. Putting mothers to work would deprive the poor community of its most stable element—the women who, for example, have mounted campaigns to drive drug dealers from their housing projects and neighborhoods. Sally Hernandez-Piñero, chairwoman of the New York City Housing Authority, emphasized the important social role played by the approximately 65,000 women raising children alone in the New York City projects: "Anyone with even a nodding acquaintance with these women knows them for what they are, the sanity of the poor community, resourceful survivors of abandonment, slander and brutality. . . . In many poor communities, they are the only signatures on the social contract, the glue that keeps our communities from spinning out of control."

None of the critics convincingly explain why these women would contribute more to their communities by taking jobs flipping hamburgers. Nor do they explain why it would not be better public policy to shore up income supports (the real value of A.F.D.C. benefits has fallen by 43 percent since the early 1970s, and by 27 percent if food stamps are figured in) and social supports for women who are struggling to care for children under the junglelike conditions of urban poverty. Instead, the family and community work performed by these women—like the family and community work of women in general—is consistently ignored or devalued.

Feminists are not exactly rallying to the defense of their poorest sisters, perhaps because the issue of work provokes such strong feeling. Many welfare mothers do want to work, and they should have the chance, together with training and supportive benefits, such as day care and health care, as well as adequate wages and supplemental welfare payments. Under such conditions, many would take jobs, and coercion would be unnecessary. Realistically, however, such opportunities are not on the reform agenda. It is the charade of work that is on the agenda.

Despite workfare's record of failure, an aura of optimism still permeates the literature on welfare reform. Many experts are convinced that most welfare mothers can achieve self-sufficiency through work and that benign consequences for family and community will ensue. The key to eventual success, they say, is to find the proper mix of programs targeted at those who can best benefit from them. As theories and policies proliferate—none of them gaining ascendance for long, since none of them succeed in practice—the search goes on for new strategies, or a mix of strategies, that will produce the desired outcomes. As sociologist Sanford Schram points out, these initiatives serve "symbolic purposes at the expense of substantive benefits."

Politicians understand the value of this symbolism, however, and rush to divert voter discontent over rising unemployment and falling wage levels by focusing on "welfare reform," knowing that welfare mothers, a majority of whom are black and Hispanic, make convenient scapegoats. Welfare is thus defined as a major national domestic problem—bad for the country and bad for the poor. It drains public budgets and reduces work effort. Allowing poor mothers to opt out of paid work saps their initiative and induces disabling psychological and cultural patterns that entrench their incapacity for work all the more. Deepening poverty ostensibly follows. As Lawrence Mead puts it, the new inequality in the United States can be traced to the "nonworking poor."

Not only are better-off people encouraged to blame the poor for their own troubles but the rituals that degrade welfare recipients reaffirm the imperative of work at a time when wages are down, working conditions worse and jobs less secure. Kaus writes that while we cannot promise the poor who work that "they'll be rich, or even comfortably well-off" (and, he might have added, we cannot even promise them a living wage), "we can promise them *respect*" because they "would have the tangible honor society reserves for workers." The charade of work enforcement reform should thus be understood as a symbolic crusade directed at the working poor rather than at those on relief, and the moral conveyed is the shame of the dole and the virtue of labor, no matter the job and no matter the pay.

One thing seems clear: If Clinton and Congress actually adopt the proposed two-year cutoff of benefits in the current labor market, they will soon find themselves debating whether women unable to make it in the marketplace should be readmitted to the rolls. (During the 1992 presidential campaign, Clinton claimed that 17,000 Arkansas residents had been successfully moved off the A.F.D.C. and food stamp rolls under a state jobs program between 1989 and 1992, but the administrator of the program subsequently acknowledged that "many people returned to welfare during that period.") If they are not, the streets would soon fill with homeless women and children, and the venerable body of theory and historical research that attributes riots and political disorder to economic insecurity would once again be put to the test. It is hard to believe that national politicians will take that risk.

DISCUSSION QUESTIONS

1. Poverty statistics do not commonly include in-kind assistance like food stamps, Medicaid, etc. What is the appropriate definition of who is poor?

2. What obligations do Americans have to the poor, and do the obligations vary with the definition of the poor?
3. In what ways may welfare assistance (such as AFDC) be considered degrading to recipients? Is the same true of Social Security benefits? Why or why not?
4. Should assistance be tied to obligations (like workfare), or should assistance be coupled with other enabling provisions, such as day care, that would allow welfare recipients to work?
5. One argument, most often made by economists, holds that cash assistance is preferable to in-kind grants (e.g., public housing or food stamps). The reason is that recipients clearly prefer to have the cash value of in-kind benefits (recipients would prefer $50 in cash rather than $50 worth of food stamps) and that the cost to the government is equivalent. (Actually, the government cost would probably decrease because the administrative costs of sending out checks rather than monitoring food stamp use, ensuring that food stamps are printed, etc., would be eliminated.) Therefore, cash is preferred by recipients and donors are no worse off, so a "Pareto superior" position is achieved. (An opposing view is taken by Steven Kelman, referenced below.) Do you think that the poor are entitled to cash payments or, instead, assistance in-kind?
6. Should AFDC payments vary considerably from state to state (as they do now), or should there be a national standard benefit level (one that could vary with the cost of living)?
7. Should Social Security benefits be means-tested?
8. Should antipoverty programs be targeted to specific groups, or are they more effective when the programs are all-inclusive entitlements?

ADDITIONAL READINGS

Besley, Timothy, and Stephen Coate. "Workfare Meets Welfare: Arguments for Work Requirements in Poverty-Alleviation Programs." *American Economic Review* (March 1992).

Burtless, Gary. "When Work Doesn't Work." *Brookings Review* (Spring 1992).

Butler, Stuart M. "Power to the People: A Conservative Vision for Welfare." *Policy Review* (Spring 1987).

Congressional Digest. "Should the Family Welfare Reform Act of 1987 Be Passed?" (February 1988).

Davis, Angela. "Child Care or Workfare?" *New Perspectives Quarterly* (Winter 1990).

Edelman, Marian Wright. *Families in Peril: An Agenda for Social Change* (Cambridge, Mass.: Harvard University Press, 1987).

Ellwood, David. *Poor Support: Poverty in the American Family* (New York: Basic Books, 1988).

Glazer, Nathan. *The Limits of Social Policy* (Cambridge, Mass.: Harvard University Press, 1988).

Gueron, Judith M. "Work and Welfare: Lessons on Employment Programs." *Journal of Economic Perspectives* (Winter 1990).

Hopkins, Kevin R. "A New Deal for America's Poor: Abolish Welfare, Guarantee Jobs." *Policy Review* (Summer 1988).

Jencks, Christopher. "Can We Put a Time Limit on Welfare?" *The American Prospect* (Fall 1992).

Jencks, Christopher. *Rethinking Social Policy* (Cambridge, Mass.: Harvard University Press, 1992).

Jencks, Christopher, and Paul E. Peterson, eds. *The Urban Underclass* (Washington, D.C.: Brookings Institution, 1991).

Katz, Michael B. *In the Shadow of the Poorhouse* (New York: Basic Books, 1986).

Katz, Michael B. *The Undeserving Poor: From the War on Poverty to the War on Welfare* (New York: Pantheon Books, 1989).

Kelman, Steven. "A Case for In-Kind Transfers." *Economics and Philosophy* 2 (1986).

Lynn, Laurence E., Jr., and David deF. Whitman. *The President as Policymaker: Jimmy Carter & Welfare Reform* (Philadelphia: Temple University Press, 1981).

Marmor, Theodore R., Jerry L. Mashaw, and Philip L. Harvey. *America's Misunderstood Welfare State* (New York: Basic Books, 1990).

Mead, Lawrence M. "The New Welfare Debate." *Commentary* (March 1988).

Mead, Lawrence M. "The Hidden Jobs Debate." *The Public Interest* (Spring 1988).

Mead, Lawrence M. "Should Workfare Be Mandatory? What Research Says." *Journal of Policy Analysis and Management* (Summer 1990).

Murray, Charles. *Losing Ground: American Social Policy 1950–1980* (New York: Basic Books, 1984).

Piven, Frances Fox, and Richard A. Cloward. *Regulating the Poor: The Functions of Public Welfare* (New York: Vintage Books, 1971).

Sawhill, Isabel. "Poverty in the U.S.: Why Is It So Persistent?" *Journal of Economic Literature* (September 1988).

Schiller, Bradley R., and C. Nielson Brasher. "Workfare in the 1980s: Successes and Limits." *Policy Studies Review* (Summer 1990).

Udesky, Laurie. "How Workfare Hurts Kids: Welfare Reform and Its Victims." *The Nation* (September 24, 1990).

Wilson, William Julius. *The Truly Disadvantaged* (Chicago: University of Chicago Press, 1987).

Wiseman, Michael. "How Workfare Really Works." *The Public Interest* (Fall 1987).

3
PRIVATIZATION AND PUBLIC HOUSING POLICY
"Should Public Housing Be Sold to Tenants or Otherwise Privatized?"

Housing policy in the United States is a blend of public and private influences. While private markets are the primary means for allocating housing, substantial federal, state, and local government policies both directly and indirectly affect housing policy. Increasingly, because of budget cuts, direct expenditures are targeted chiefly to only the poorest individuals and families. Subsidized housing and public housing operating subsidies comprise the bulk of direct federal expenditures, and many states and localities have varying levels of commitment and expenditures in providing housing to the most needy. But by far the largest government role in housing is through "tax expenditures," or loopholes in the tax code that allow deductions for certain housing-related expenditures, most of which benefit upper-middle-class and wealthy individuals.* The largest housing tax expenditure is the ability of homeowners to deduct their mortgage interest payments from reported income. In 1990, the federal treasury lost over $35 billion from the mortgage interest deduction alone, another $12 billion on the deductibility of property taxes on owner-occupied homes, and a total of nearly $11 billion on other housing-related tax deductions.[1] Closing the mortgage interest deduction alone would more than pay for all expenditures of the United States Department of Housing and Urban Development. State and local tax expenditures on housing are considerable as well. Therefore, government efforts in housing tend to benefit the very poor and, to a much larger extent, wealthier Americans.[2]

The problems of crime, drug abuse, homelessness, welfare dependency, and lack of family cohesion are nowhere more concentrated than in urban public housing. In city after city, public housing projects have become a venue for gang warfare and rampant drug use, where children must be escorted to school for fear of violence and intimidation, and the elderly are afraid to ride in dark elevators. One writer reports, "some mothers even fear being robbed

---

* There are several reasons why most of the benefits from tax expenditures tend to benefit the wealthy. First, those who itemize their tax returns tend to be more prosperous because their expenditures are high enough to surpass the standard deduction. Second, when personal income tax rates are progressive, an equivalent tax deduction for wealthy individuals is larger than for lower-income persons, since their tax bracket is higher. For example, a $10,000 deduction for someone in a 33 percent tax bracket reduces the tax liability by $3,300, while someone in a 15 percent bracket saves just $1,500. Finally, since the wealthy tend to own more expensive homes, and therefore declare larger deductions, their savings are all the greater.

by their own drug-addicted children."[3] There are currently some 1.4 million units of housing in the public and Indian housing programs.[4] There were 1.2 million households and 3 million persons occupying public housing units in August of 1993, with an average household size of approximately 2.5 persons.[5] However, many of these units that would seem to be available are unoccupiable, some due to intolerable living conditions. Due to the limited number of public housing units, many who are legally eligible to receive public housing assistance cannot find an available unit. This has raised a problem of equity: Some are receiving significant government subsidies while others with similarly limited incomes are not. It has been argued that it is inherently unfair that some receive subsidized housing, better access to child care, training and recreation programs, etc., while others who are equally needy pay 70 to 80 percent of their income for housing, if they can afford housing at all.[6]

Many residents feel "trapped" in urban public housing projects, where the average length of occupancy is 91 months.[7] Many individuals living in the projects have little ability or incentive to make changes in the environment in which they live. With an average family income of $8,300 and an average of $1,830 in net family assets, most have no other housing opportunities given the expense of private real estate in the United States, particularly in large metropolitan areas. Many in public housing are also recipients of transfers from other welfare programs, such as Aid to Families with Dependent Children, food stamps, energy assistance, and other cash and in-kind benefits. In fact, for only 23 percent of public housing residents nationally do wages make up more than half of their income.[8] Furthermore, the ethnic mix of individuals living in public housing is anything but nationally representative. Fully 69 percent of public housing tenants are minorities, and in the largest cities public housing is more than 90 percent minority occupied. Eleven housing agencies manage complexes with more than 10,000 units, and three are massive with more than 30,000 units. For these very large complexes, the percentage of minority occupants jumps to 91 percent; indeed, as the size of units increases, the average percentage of minorities tends to rise as well.[9] Further, 36 percent of residents are elderly,[10] many if not most of whom live with fixed incomes based on Social Security or Supplemental Security Income. Over one-third of those living in public housing projects are single parents, and a full three-fourths of resident families are female-headed.[11] Therefore, changes in public housing policy affect some of the nation's least advantaged citizens.

Problems of crime, dilapidated buildings, drug abuse, and general social disorder have resulted in calls for fundamental reform of a public housing system that had its start more than one hundred years ago with a 1892 congressional study that investigated the slums of some large American cities.[12] This was followed by Theodore Roosevelt's 1902 Housing Commission, which made some of the first overt, if limited, policy recommendations to improve the supply of decent housing in the nation. The recommendations of this commission included the destruction of unsanitary housing, and the government purchase, renovation, and loan financing.[13] Despite these and other recommendations, it was not until the New Deal that the basis of modern housing policy was established. The Reconstruction Finance Corporation was authorized to make loans for low-income housing corporations, and the 1934 National Housing Act created the Federal Housing Administration and gave it the power to insure certain housing loans. While these developments provided the foundation, the Housing Act of 1937, which authorized loans to local Public Housing Authorities (PHAs), established the structure that still stands today.[14] For political reasons, however, much public housing was built in poor and minority areas of cities like New York and Chicago rather than wealthier and white neighborhoods. It is difficult to believe today that public housing at the time was seen to vastly improve on the dilapidated wooden tenements of the past.

The following years saw a large expansion in the number of housing services provided by the federal government, most being in the form of loans and loan guarantees. An important step for public housing was the 1969 Housing Act, which introduced the so-called Brooke Amendment limiting public housing rents to a maximum of one-fourth of tenant income.[15] Due to the cash flow restrictions that this imposed on many of those operating low-income housing, the federal government began to subsidize the operating costs of many public housing facilities.[16] The 1974 Housing Act created "Section 8" entitlements, which subsidized the rent of public housing tenants directly.[17] Public housing tenants now pay an average of $164 per month for their apartments. In 1992, Section 8 subsidies cost the Department of Housing and Urban Development (HUD) some $8 billion. HUD payments for non-Section 8 public housing totaled $2.9 billion.[18]

For many tenants of public housing projects, finding help in addressing the problems of public housing has been difficult. Security is in some cases nonexistent. One writer touring New York City public housing units observed: "Entrances almost always have broken locks, missing windowpanes, and vandalized intercoms. A key was necessary to come in by the main entrance in less than five percent of the buildings I visited, and I saw tenant patrols in only three percent. A young woman who was a caretaker in Brownsville reported, 'Every time we put a new lock in, they break it. Everybody just comes and goes, comes and goes. They don't even live in the building.' . . . Addicts sometimes steal the front doors of buildings to sell as scrap metal. . . . Many of the steps and landings were strewn with empty crack vials, used condoms, and excrement."[19] Tenants frequently find that the bureaucracies of many public housing authorities are unresponsive due to the fact that services are contracted with the housing authority and not directly with the tenants. Low-income residents of public housing are not a powerful political constituency and therefore have greater difficulty in obtaining assistance. Although most residents would like to live in better conditions, for many there is little incentive to seek work because rent levels in the projects are tied to a fixed level of income. Therefore, it pays to remain in public housing because of the unlikelihood of finding employment that would pay enough to allow them to move to better accommodations. These problems are exacerbated by the fact that the middle class has been driven out of many public housing units, leaving not a vibrant community as its creators had hoped but, as one writer put it, "increasingly . . . permanent residences for the indigent."[20] In New York City alone, it is estimated that more than 33,000 unauthorized families are sharing public housing units.[21] Eviction is hardly an attractive option when most of these persons would instead be homeless.

In response to the expense of public housing programs and the problems that have occurred, there have been movements to create Resident Management Councils to put management control of public housing units into the tenants' hands. Residents would contract services directly and schedule upkeep and maintenance themselves. By taking responsible control of the properties, a sense of community and self-worth would hopefully develop. However, many critics of public housing, while applauding the steps already taken toward resident empowerment, wish to take the process further. The Housing Act of 1987, which encouraged the establishment of Resident Management Council initiatives, also allowed for the full privatization of some public housing units. The units would be sold to the current low-income residents at a discounted price. Many believe that by giving home ownership to the residents, they would be encouraged to be more self-sufficient and would enter the job market more readily. Critics assert that most residents want to leave public housing, not own it, and efforts in this direction merely maintain overwhelmingly minority public housing ghettos.

In the first article below, Stuart Butler of the Heritage Foundation argues for public housing privatization, asserting that privatization is the surest method to increase the quality and availability of housing to the poor. He looks to the wave of privatization that swept Europe in the 1980s and is currently active in Eastern Europe as an opportunity to use privatization to revitalize housing in America's poorest areas. In the second article, John Atlas of a New Jersey legal services agency and Peter Dreier of the Boston Redevelopment Authority counter that public housing has not been a failure and that the majority of public housing units provide decent and affordable housing to the poor. They argue that privatization is not the key to success in improving public housing, but instead focus on the need for increased resources, better tenant screening, increased availability of public housing to the working poor, and the development of a social policy that stresses the creation of not-for-profit community developers. Their arguments follow.

Endnotes

1. U.S. Office of Management and Budget, *Budget of the United States Government, 1990, Special Analyses* (Washington, D.C.: U.S. Government Printing Office).
2. This was found to be true with California housing as well. See William S. Furry, *Housing Assistance in California: A Program Analysis* (Santa Monica: Rand Corporation, 1983).
3. Camilo Jose Vergara, "Hell in a Very Tall Place," *The Atlantic Monthly* (September 1989), p. 75.

4. Personal communication from H. Bruce Vincent, U.S. Department of Housing and Urban Development.

5. Ibid.

6. Paul A. Messenger, "Please Abolish My Job, Mr. Kemp: Confessions of a Public Housing Administrator," *Policy Review* (Winter 1990), pp. 47–48.

7. Personal communication with H. Bruce Vincent, U.S. Department of Housing and Urban Development; data from Report T18-5, Multifamily Tenant Characteristics System, received December 13, 1993.

8. Ibid.

9. Ibid.

10. Ibid.

11. Ibid.

12. George Sternlieb and David Listokin, "A Review of National Housing Policy," pp. 14–44 in Peter D. Salins, ed. *Housing America's Poor* (Chapel Hill: University of North Carolina Press, 1987).

13. Ibid.

14. Ibid.

15. Ibid.

16. Messenger, "Please Abolish My Job," p. 46.

17. Sternlieb and Listokin, "A Review of National Housing Policy."

18. U.S. Department of Commerce, Bureau of the Census, *Federal Expenditures by State for Fiscal Year 1992*, Table 2 (Washington, D.C.: U.S. Government Printing Office, 1993).

19. Vergara, "Hell in a Very Tall Place," pp. 74–75.

20. Ibid., p. 76.

21. Ibid.

YES

How Privatization Incentives Can Revive Inner-City Housing

Stuart M. Butler

Privatization attracted considerable interest around the world in the 1980s both as a device to inject new life into sagging, centrally planned economies and as a means of bolstering government finances through the sale of government assets or by cutting the cost of services by contracting with private suppliers. Today the new democratic countries of eastern Europe are counting on the privatization of inefficient state industries, among other measures, to jump-start their economies. Earlier in the decade several western European countries, most notably Britain, launched major privatization programs with similar objectives. Since 1980, Britain has privatized some $50 billion worth of assets, including the telephone system, the national airline, and over one million units of public housing.

Many American observers of the worldwide move to privatization, however, perhaps understandably have overlooked one element that has important implications for the United States. While the broad macroeconomic and financial benefits of privatization attract the headlines and the greatest interest, the *microeconomic* implications of a change in control or ownership can be even more significant. This is why a number of academics and public officials—among them Housing and Urban Development Secretary Jack Kemp—have grown increasingly interested in privatization as one potent tool to tackle America's blighted inner-city public housing.

The theory behind public housing is that by providing decent, affordable housing to the poor, families would be placed on the first rung of a ladder leading to economic and social independence. For some families that indeed is the reality. But for most low-income Americans, obtaining a public housing unit is the end of the road, a life sentence of dependency and crushing despair. Life in many projects consists of drug gangs running the neighborhood, inefficient or corrupt housing authorities that do little to maintain buildings, and an atmosphere of hopelessness that breaks the spirit of all but a few families. And the buildings decay along with the hopes of the people. Nearly 100,000 of the nation's 1.25 million public housing units are vacant or abandoned, most of them uninhabitable without huge expenditures on rehabilitation.

Yet among this general desolation there are small oases in which exciting changes can be seen. These illustrate the power of one form of privatization—allowing those receiving a government service to become their own providers.

The dramatic effects of a change in control or ownership have been seen in a number of privatization cases in Britain. Most notable has been the sale of public housing units to their tenants, at substantial discounts. When tenants become owners, they view their homes very differently. It is no exaggeration to say that it is possible to walk down a street in a British public housing project and pick out the units that have been sold to tenants. Ownership soon leads to fresh paint, spruced-up gardens, and little changes designed to place a stamp of individualism on the unit.

Large-scale tenant ownership of the kind enjoyed in Britain is still years away in the United States. But America's experience with tenant management of public housing—one step short of ownership—shows just how potent the incentives of private control can be.

Ironically, tenant management sprang up in the United States not as an enlightened experiment by progressive local housing authorities, but more often than not out of a desire of desperate governments to wash their hands of a "hopeless" project. The genesis of tenant management makes the results all the more remarkable. Take Cochran Gardens in St. Louis, a high-rise project only a stone's throw away from the infamous Pruitt-Igoe complex which became such an uncontrollable fiasco it was blown up in 1972. In the 1970s, Cochran was referred to as "Little 'Nam." Drug dealers and prostitution rings controlled entire floors, using the project much like an office block. Welfare and unemployment there had reached staggering levels.

By 1976 the tenants had had enough, and they petitioned the housing authority to allow them to manage the project themselves. The frustrated authority agreed to train the tenants in basic management techniques and to give the operating subsidy for the buildings to a tenant management corporation. It then handed over control to the residents.

Today Cochran is a model neighborhood. Emboldened with their new powers, tenants joined with the police to rid the project of drug dealers. And rather than continue maintenance contracts with firms that were cronies of the housing authority, the tenant team began to train residents to undertake maintenance work themselves, reducing costs while improving quality and creating jobs for unemployed residents. By 1985, over 350 jobs had been created by the new managers, most of them for project residents. These jobs were not just in maintenance positions. They were also in several project-based enterprises, such as a catering company, a roofing firm, and day care centers, each serving the surrounding area as well as Cochran itself.

Similar results have occurred in Boston, Washington D.C., and about a dozen other cities with tenant-managed projects. In each case despair drove residents to ask for the right to manage a rapidly deteriorating project, and in each case despair drove the housing authority to agree.

The key point to recognize about the tenant management experience is not so much that it is an example of the benefits of privatization, but that it shows the success of a particular *form* of privatization which incorporates unique incentives. In fact, privatization is nothing new in American public housing projects. Housing authorities have for decades contracted with private management and maintenance firms to serve public housing projects. The difference between tenant management and traditional private contracting is that the management firm consists of people who live in the project.

That turns out to be a very big difference. It is a difference summed up succinctly by Kimi Gray, a resident of the tenant-managed Kenilworth-Parkside project in Washington, D.C. "My engineer lives in the project," explains Gray, "so when the heat goes off he gets cold, too." When the city contracts with professional private managers and maintenance firms to run public projects, the result often is only a marginal improvement on cases where the city runs the project directly. Public housing tenants generally are not a powerful political constituency. So although tenants may grumble about dismal services due to inefficiency or corruption, most contractors and housing officials can safely ignore the complaints. City officials would never be so cavalier about services to politically active middle-class residents.

Tenant management changes these dynamics fundamentally. Now the people receiving the services pay the piper and thus call the tune. Instead of contractors needing only to satisfy an indifferent City Hall, or line the pockets of a few officials, they must now satisfy the tenants themselves—who have rather higher expectations. When tenants took control of Kenilworth-Parkside, Kimi Gray invited the heating firm representative that for years had given them dismal service to come to the project to discuss renewing the contract. She kept him waiting outside her office for two hours and then told him he had lost their business.

Tenant management allows the consumers of the services to shop around for service contractors, and thus it forces the contractors to compete on the basis of quality and price. In many instances, however, tenant managers choose to employ residents to perform basic maintenance, as in the case of Cochran. The new managers have powerful incentives to recruit employees from within the project. Not only does the use of local labor often reduce the costs, but by increasing the incomes of residents, it also means an increase in rental income for the project (in public housing rent is based on family income). Moreover, the managers have strong financial incentives to reduce vacancy levels and to improve rent collections. A detailed study of the Kenilworth project by the international accounting firm of Coopers & Lybrand found that between 1982 and 1985 rental income had jumped seventy-seven percent, thanks to a combination of improved collections, job creation, and a cut in the vacancy rate from eighteen percent (about the average for the city) to just six percent.

Tenant management and the use of resident labor also have been shown to contribute to sometimes-striking reductions in social problems within a project. In Kenilworth, for example, the crime rate has plummeted seventy-five percent and the rate of teenage pregnancy is down fifty percent. And thanks to the 130 jobs in the project created by the management team, once-absent fathers are returning home, helping to cut the welfare dependency rate by more than half.

The results achieved in tenant-managed projects are not due only to the financial incentives in this form of privatization. Just as important is the authority that comes with management by the residents themselves. One important feature of this authority is that tenants are willing to accept stringent rules from a resident corporation that they would never accept from City Hall. Resident managers are able to impose tough fines and other penalties against such things as graffiti, broken windows, and late payment of rent.

Thanks to the Housing Act of 1987, which explicitly encourages tenant management in public housing, and the enthusiastic support of it by HUD Secretary Kemp, projects controlled by tenants are likely to become increasingly common phenomena in America's inner cities. Many tenants are even thinking beyond resident management to resident ownership, arguing that they should have the same opportunities for home ownership as other Americans, and that they should be allowed, through ownership, to capture some of the improvements in property values resulting from their management successes.

The 1987 Act permits such full privatization at substantially discounted prices, and in 1988 Kenilworth became the first project to start along the road to ownership. Resident ownership of public housing is, admittedly, never likely to be common, but officials and politicians are far less skeptical about the idea than they were just five years ago, when ownership was first advanced seriously. The reason for this change of heart is twofold: first, the evident sophistication of tenant managers; and second, by reducing operating costs while boosting family incomes through job generation, tenant management has put the annual costs of ownership within reach of many more residents than had previously been assumed was possible.

Can this use of privatization in public housing projects really have a significant impact on America's inner cities? Yes, if policymakers understand why it works and extend the same principles to other policies governing inner-city neighborhoods. Tenant management works because people are much more willing to take tough action when they have real control over their lives, and because residents of public housing have every incentive to seek economical and quality services for the project. Mere tenant "involvement" in running projects does not work because it does not include real power and responsibility.

Thus tenant management needs to be combined with other steps that put the residents of the inner city in control of their own neighborhoods, so that they, as consumers, are able to call the shots rather than being forced to be the passive recipients of whatever is served up to them. In addition to contracting with tenants for public housing management, that means introducing another form of privatization—vouchers. Housing vouchers are needed to allow the poor to decide where *they* want to live, rather than being segregated into approved projects, so that the poor have an opportunity to move to neighborhoods with better job opportunities or schools. It also means vouchers in education, so that the poor would at last have a financial lever over the school system.

The great irony of these privatization approaches, which are often viewed as a conservative approach to inner-city revitalization, is that their message of "empowerment" is remarkably similar to the themes espoused by the architects of The Great Society. Yet whereas The Great Society focused more on political empowerment, intended to give the poor access to the resources of government, privatization takes the form of economic empowerment. The results of tenant management suggest this economic form of empowerment is more potent. By giving the poor the economic power and incentives to reshape their lives, through effective control or ownership of housing and other basic ingredients of a neighborhood, the tools of privatization thus may prove to be the crucial weapon needed to win the war on inner-city poverty.

NO

From "Projects" to Communities: How to Redeem Public Housing

John Atlas and Peter Dreier

After a quick visit to riot-torn Los Angeles in May this year, George Bush dusted off an old plan to privatize public housing and offered it as part of his face-saving plan to show he cares about America's cities. In fact, public housing represents less than 2 percent of the nation's housing supply, yet it looms large in public debate about national housing policy: Should we sell apartments to tenants? Demand better-behaved tenants? Evict drug dealers (and their families) from projects? Give tenants a stronger voice in management? Tear down developments? Replace them with housing vouchers?

In the midst of the broadest housing crisis since the Depression—declining home-ownership, scarce affordable rental housing, rising homelessness—why does public housing command so much attention?

In a conservative era, public housing seems to many Americans a metaphor for the failures of activist government. The conservative attack on public housing is part of a larger privatization agenda to reduce government and discredit public endeavors of economic uplift.

But unless defenders of activist government address public housing's real dilemmas, it will continue to serve as a decrepit symbol, mocking aspirations of public improvement. Restoring public housing's integrity will require not just programmatic reform but ideological and political revision as well.

The first thing to appreciate about public housing is that it has become the housing of last resort for the very poor—often those without jobs, skills, or hopes. Thus the dilemma is partly circular: public housing is likely to remain socially and politically unattractive until we alleviate poverty itself. To that end, one might imagine new public expenditure—on job-creating public works, human capital programs of training and education, as well as health care and child care. But such an agenda will not likely receive majority support unless the voters believe their tax dollars will be well spent. And there stands public housing, our most visible symbol of well-intentioned government gone awry.

Politically, public housing encompasses several voter backlashes—against crime, drugs, illegitimacy, violent youth, minorities, the "undeserving" poor, and government itself. Joining Ronald Reagan's welfare queen and George Bush's Willie Horton is the public housing drug dealer protected by the American Civil Liberties Union.

Where to break into the circle? There is today a broad consensus among social scientists, policy experts, and politicians that public funds by themselves will not cure the current epidemic of drugs, gangs, and violence in America's slums. Conservative Housing and Urban Development (HUD) Secretary Jack Kemp, liberal sociologist William Julius Wilson, and the Rev. Jesse Jackson all argue for self-help—that ghetto residents themselves must change the moral environment in which they live. But bootstrap lectures alone will not restore the physical, economic, and moral well-being of the ghettoes. Without public funds, self-help efforts are doomed to fail.

As we shall see, there are workable strategies to turn subsidized housing into livable communities. But they will require a revision of cherished beliefs across the political spectrum. Conservatives will have to abandon the idea that the marketplace, by itself, can provide affordable housing for the poor. And progressives will have to acknowledge that the rights of residents must be balanced with responsibilities to communities.

MYTH AND REALITY

The best-kept secret about public housing is that most of it actually provides decent, affordable housing to many people. Properly run, it remains one of the best options for housing the poor. There are 1.3 million public housing apartments and about 800,000 families on the waiting lists of the nation's 3,060 local housing authorities. Public housing developments often are no worse than privately owned, low-rent apartments; most, in fact, are better, which is why the waiting lists continue to swell. But because public housing involves tax dollars, it is more visible and open to public scrutiny.

Many projects, especially racially isolated high-rises in big cities, have indeed failed. These represent less than one-quarter of the nation's public housing, but they cast a giant shadow. The projects isolate and concentrate minorities dependent on welfare, suffering from high unemployment rates, teenage pregnancy, single parenthood, and a climate of serious crime. Some projects, like St. Louis's infamous Pruitt-Igoe homes, virtually ceased to function as viable communities. Pruitt-Igoe was eventually dynamited by the city not because of structural flaws but because it was an unlivable environment.

Today many public housing families face the daily fear of death from drugs, drug wars, or random shots that hit innocent victims. Children are afraid to walk to school, and elderly tenants, for whom hallways and elevators are as dangerous as streets, are afraid to leave their apartments. In these devastated neighborhoods, families are destroyed.

These projects have become the playgrounds for drug-dealing predators, as depicted in the 1991 movie *Straight Out of Brooklyn* by Matty Rich (who grew up in Brooklyn's Red Hook projects) and in Alex Kotlowitz's book chronicling life in the Chicago projects, *There Are No Children Here*. As they portray it, public housing has become more a trap than a ladder.

Were public housing's troubles inevitable? During the Depression, public housing began as an ad hoc public-works program to create jobs. From the program's formal legislative inception in 1937, it was aimed at providing housing for the "submerged middle class," those who could not find suitable housing in the private market but not the very poor with no means to pay rent. Senator Robert Wagner of New York, principal author of the Housing Act of 1937, declared, "There are some whom we cannot expect to serve . . . those who cannot pay the rent." Rents originally covered all operating expenses except debt service. The principal and interest on bonds floated by local housing authorities to construct the buildings were paid by the federal government.

For years, this arrangement worked. Vincent Lane, until recently the chairman of the Chicago Housing Authority (CHA), remembers when public housing was new. Four decades ago, Lane's family moved from the South to a cold-water flat opposite the CHA's Wentworth Gardens development. It boasted broad playgrounds, heat, hot water, and basketball courts. "I envied the kids in public housing," Lane recalls. "The best housing in the community was Wentworth Gardens."

By 1942, 175,000 public housing apartments—most in two-to-four-story buildings—were constructed in 290 communities. By 1946, another 195,000 units of "permanent" housing were built in areas where war industry or military bases had created new demand for housing. After the war, recognizing the pent-up demand for housing and fearing competition from public housing (which it claimed was an opening wedge for socialism), the real estate industry sabotaged the public housing program by pressuring Congress to limit it to the very poor. That new rule, embodied in the 1949 Housing Act, was the beginning of the decline of public housing.

From 1944 to 1951, minorities represented between 26 percent and 39 percent of all public housing tenants. By 1978, the figure reached over 60 percent. From 1950 to 1970, the median income of public housing residents fell from 64 percent to 37 percent of the national median. By 1988, the average income of public housing households was $6,539, one-fifth of the national average ($32,144). Today only about 40 percent of nonelderly households in public housing have a wage earner. Among big cities, the percentage of working poor is highest in New York City—about 60 percent—which perhaps explains why, with some exceptions, its public housing projects are among the best in the country.

The look of public housing, cheap and proud of it, contributed to the isolation of its residents. By constructing buildings often compared to warehouses, the program stigmatized "government housing," rendering it unattractive to even the lower middle class, who would rely instead on private builders for the American Dream.

High-rise designs, reflecting the need to minimize land costs, contributed to the rise in crime. One study found that in New York the difference between high-rise and low-rise projects was much more significant as an explanation for crime rates than was the ratio of welfare families. The study showed that the number of robberies in a housing project rose proportionately with its height.

Despite the popular stereotype, high-rises account for only 27 percent of public housing buildings (32 percent are garden apartments, 16 percent low-rise walk-ups, and 25 percent single-family homes or townhouses). But high-rise projects, most of them in the largest cities, account for many of the problems. Congress ended the construction of high-rises in the mid-1970s, except those built for the elderly.

Conservatives and the real estate industry also fought to ensure that participation by cities was voluntary and administration was local. Decisions about whether, or where, to build developments were left to local officials, often dominated by private real estate interests. Few units were built in affluent areas. As public housing became the home of blacks and other minorities, local control by white politicians contributed to patterns of racial segregation.

Since the 1960s, fast-rising operating expenses have far outpaced tenants' incomes. As a result, local authorities have lacked the income to provide day-to-day maintenance, deferring repairs and capital improvements. Rising energy costs in the early 1970s further strapped residents. Faced with a decaying stock of public housing, Congress appropriated additional subsidies so that tenants would pay not more than 25 percent (since Reagan, 30 percent) of their incomes on rent. But the additional funds were inadequate to meet operating expenses, so even the best-managed projects continued to deteriorate physically. Cutbacks during the Reagan era merely made a bad situation worse. A 1987 Abt Associates study estimated a $21.5 billion backlog in basic repairs and capital improvements for the nation's public housing stock.

SHARED MISTAKES

Looking back, it is fair to blame conservatives more than liberals for these policy mistakes. Conservative and real estate industry support was paid for with legislative compromises assuring that public housing, originally designed for the working poor and young families starting out, would instead be permanent housing for the very poor. As such, public housing became more unpopular politically, leading to a cycle of government neglect and underfunding which, in turn, led to poor construction design, inadequate maintenance, racial segregation, stigmatization, and further concentration of the very poor.

But liberals sometimes let public housing down, too. In the New Deal coalition, defenders of traditional public housing—mayors, building-trades unions, local civil servants—were often too tolerant of incompetent and paternalistic public housing management that increased tenant dependency and undermined community. Tenant management, as a remedy, entered the debate only in the late 1960s and never became the policy favored by HUD or by most local housing authorities.

At the same time, some of the most vocal advocates for the poor, including housing activists and poverty lawyers, became unwitting allies of conservatives. In a climate of declining resources, many antipoverty activists demanded that public housing give priority to the very poor and also turned mainly to the courts to protect tenant rights—often at the cost of further isolating the poor and undermining any management authority to bring order to public housing neighborhoods. Thanks to a new set of rights, disruptive residents were not disciplined. Tenants who could leave moved out; law-abiding tenants without other options became demoralized.

By the 1970s, many of these neighborhoods fell between two stools. Neither were they viable, self-governing communities, nor were they any longer governed by an externally imposed set of norms. This identity crisis played into the hands of private developers, who wanted a piece of the government-funded, low-income housing action. By the late 1960s, the housing industry convinced Congress to replace public housing with privately owned, subsidized housing (known by their statute numbers: Sections 236, 221d, and 8) that gave private developers tax breaks, low-cost mortgages, and rent subsidies to house the poor. These inefficient and costly programs led to widespread political abuses and eventually to the HUD scandals of the 1970s, which were repeated in the 1990s.

Tellingly, Jack Kemp has not focused on the troubles of privately owned, subsidized projects, despite the fact that there are more of these developments (1.9 million apartments) than there are public housing projects (1.3 million units). But while Kemp has usually spared private slumlords the antidrug and empowerment rhetoric that he directs at the public projects—a tactic that fits into neoconservatives' government-bashing agenda—the crime, drug, and social problems in these privately owned projects are as bad as, if not worse than, the problems plaguing government-owned projects. The tenants of privately owned, government-subsidized developments deserve the same attention and resources as their public housing companions.

Conservatives like Kemp address the need for self-help but not the need for resources, an approach that appeals to taxpayers who want solutions that cost no money. To reframe the conservative-dominated housing debate and to make public housing successful both for residents and in the eyes of the public, we must alter some basic assumptions.

First, we must turn developments into livable communities. That means insisting on better screening of applicants and tougher treatment of abusive tenants. It also means giving residents a stronger voice in management and, ultimately, ownership.

Second, social housing should not be for only the very poor. The homeless and the welfare poor deserve decent housing, but not at the expense of the working poor, who can help stabilize housing developments.

Third, public housing needs more money—for repairs, maintenance, and security, as well as social services, child care, and job-training programs that can help residents move into America's mainstream. But that money won't be forthcoming until America decides that public housing is worth saving.

Finally, traditional public housing needs to be one strand of a broader social housing strategy that relies more heavily on a new generation of competent and dedicated community nonprofit developers.

RIGHTS AND RESOURCES

Though today they stand as symbols of lawlessness, public housing projects until the 1960s were places of almost excessive law and order. Indeed, project managers nearly ruled with an iron hand, as Harry Spence, the court-appointed receiver of the troubled Boston Housing Authority from 1979 to 1984, described in a *Working Papers* interview ten years ago:

> Until the late 1960s, public housing . . . worked on a theory of despotism. The project manager was the despot. Longtime tenants will tell you there was a day when if my kid walked across the lawn, the manager came out and said you either stop that or you're out. That's now looked at almost nostalgically. And it depended almost entirely on the caliber of the manager. For much of the community, that unrestrained power was being used to enforce community norms. But often, it was abused, because there was a class gap between the manager and the tenants. It was a highly personalized and often vicious order.

The managerial despotism Spence recounts was finally overturned on grounds of both civil rights and civil liberties. Until the 1960s, public order in the projects was preserved partly through a system of fines for minor infractions such as littering, loitering, and petty vandalism. Tenants objected that fines were both a hardship for struggling families and—equally important—a source of sometimes arbitrary management.

In the late 1960s, as part of the civil rights movement, tenants protested to eliminate the system of fines and arbitrary evictions. The fight to challenge bad management and for tenant rights was aided by a new and formidable ally—the War on Poverty's legal services program and foundation-supported public interest law firms. The broader legal strategy was to persuade the courts to confer new rights, such as welfare and housing, upon the poor. In an era of judicial activism epitomized by *Brown* v. *Board of Education*, the underlying assumption was that an authoritative decision by the Supreme Court would alter patterns of behavior and that its affirmation of rights would make an important difference in the distribution of power and wealth.

It was as if a committee of concerned citizens raised $10 million of government and foundation money to help the poor with their housing problems and hired 150 lawyers but only a handful of organizers or other staff—and then was denied money to carry out the court-mandated remedies. This imbalance of resources skewed aid for the poor toward litigation. Early on there were significant victories in both welfare rights and housing. A spate of cases extended fair hearing rights to welfare recipients, debtors, employees, students, automobile drivers, prisoners, and, in 1967, public housing tenants. Subsequently, HUD adopted rules that guaranteed due process in eviction, admission, and other management practices.

But litigation neither redistributed wealth and power nor extended fundamental economic rights. Instead, the combination of the conservatives' penny-pinching and the liberal activists' focus on vindicating individual rights made daily life more insufferable for most residents. As housing and tenant activists became politically isolated—and the middle class became increasingly wary of programs to help the poor—no one seemed to care that many public housing agencies became rife with waste, patronage, and indifference. As Harry Spence observed:

In effect, the government responded by saying, "If we can't do it the old way, we're not going to do it at all. If we can't keep the unrestrained authority and the unrestrained segregation we had before, we won't do it at all. The courts have tied our hands. So screw this community. Wallow in your own misery."

Ask tenants who have lived through these changes what they would do to make the projects more habitable, and they typically urge tougher screening and eviction policies and reinstatement of fines—albeit with procedural safeguards. As one tenant leader put it, "The old way was sometimes arbitrary. But at least it helped parents keep their kids in line and keep out the criminals." The old rules also embodied a shared authority that has been lost. Tenants sense that removing the rules has boomeranged, that it was crucially connected with the loss of adult influence over the projects' teenagers.

The housing and antipoverty activists mistook community-supported restraints (such as applicant screenings) for racist repression because those procedures disproportionately affected blacks. Dan Wuenschel, head of the Cambridge Housing Authority in Massachusetts, put his finger on this dilemma in a speech to legal services attorneys:

> Public housing rises or falls on how well its developments function as communities in which parents can raise their children in an environment which is safe, which nurtures and permits growth toward successful adulthood. Elders must feel and be sufficiently secure to travel about their environment, to socialize, to shop without the fear of being mugged, or else they withdraw and wither and die much sooner than they should.
>
> I believe that in your zeal for your individual clients you are blinded to their collective effect on public housing communities. It often seems to us "public housers" that you view the newest law or regulation, listed by me as a burden, as a new challenge to be manipulated—to be "worked"—sort of like a new Nintendo game. . . . You don't see the fourteen-year-old Haitian girl who is beaten up by her drug dealing, neighbor pimp because she got pregnant. Our managers do—every day. If so, why would you appeal that individual's eviction if we got lucky and caught him or her on nonpayment of rent?

DRUG-RELATED EVICTIONS

Tougher eviction and screening requirements, while appealing to most tenants, raise some important concerns. For example, where will those families who have been denied admission to developments go? Will we throw due process out the window? Nowhere are these issues more salient than in the current debate on what to do about drugs in public housing.

Kemp has made "drug-free" public housing one of the Bush administration's high-profile domestic priorities. Kemp wants to bar anyone convicted of a drug offense—buying, selling, or using—from public housing. On the other side, many housing advocates, civil libertarians, poverty lawyers, and tenants believe that Kemp's emphasis on eviction to combat drug activity does little to solve the problem. They argue that tough antidrug tactics—such as evicting a person before he or she is convicted of a crime—violate constitutional rights to due process. Social service agencies complain that easy eviction policies merely shuffle problems from one government-run program to the next and create more homeless families and shattered lives. Stepped-up eviction practices, they say, have led to the eviction or harassment of innocent victims. For example:

- While his mother was at work, the adult son of a public housing tenant was arrested in her apartment on charges that he sold drugs to an undercover agent. Even though the son was not convicted and was fighting the charges, the housing authority tried to evict the mother, her daughter, and her three minor grandchildren.
- Another housing authority started eviction proceedings against a young working mother and her three small children. The mother separated from her husband because he became heavily involved with drugs and alcohol. The husband left the apartment and never lived there again, although he occasionally visited the project to see his children. He recently went to jail after pleading guilty to drug charges. Now the housing authority wants to put out the innocent spouse and her family.
- An eviction case was brought against a tenant who had lived in her apartment for seventeen years. The tenant's adult daughter, who lived with her, was arrested in front of the building. She was charged not with selling drugs but with possessing drug paraphernalia (a hypodermic needle). The mother, who worked full-time, had no idea her daughter had a drug problem. The daughter pleaded guilty, served her sentence, and is now trying to get into a rehabilitation program. The mother wanted to help her daughter stay off drugs. But the housing authority wanted to evict them both.

Lawyers for the National Housing Law Project (NHLP) criticize HUD officials for urging that public housing officials do not need to wait for a criminal conviction to seek to evict a family. According to HUD, a housing authority needs only to prove by a preponderance of the evidence in a civil court that the tenant being evicted engaged in illegal activity. To the NHLP and the ACLU, this looks like an overzealous federal government trampling on individual rights; evictions are civil proceedings that require a much lower burden of proof than criminal cases. "While drugs are a serious problem," says Connie Pascale, a legal aid lawyer in New Jersey, "evicting innocent family members or recovering addicts is not a real solution. Focusing mainly on evictions will only lead to more homeless families and upset, confused, and angry children."

Yet Kemp's drug-free public housing mission has struck a responsive chord, particularly among public housing residents who have seen their neighborhoods ravaged by drugs. Kemp's charge has also inspired some state legislatures to get tough on suspected drug dealers. A new amendment to New Jersey's landlord—tenant law provides that people can be evicted on drug allegations even if they have never been arrested. There need only be a "preponderance" of evidence that the person is using drugs. Hearings on these bills drew wide support from public housing tenants.

Recently, the Chicago Housing Authority and the Chicago Police Department jointly initiated "Operation Clean Sweep" to wipe out drugs in high-rise buildings. Under the program, the Chicago Police Department dispatches fifty to sixty officers to secure the perimeter and interior areas of a targeted building. There police officers gain control of all entrances to the buildings and all elevators and stairways. Maintenance personnel, protected by security guards, erect a fence around individual buildings and install doors and grates to maintain control. CHA teams enter the building to inspect each apartment and common areas to ensure that only tenants remain in the building. If drugs or other contraband are found, the police are called to make arrests. The building is then "secured" by fencing in the lobby, and residents are issued photo-identification cards. CHA typically institutes a visitation policy, restricting access to residents and guests. After the sweep, CHA repair crews remain at the building, making necessary repairs and readying vacant units for occupancy. CHA personnel also survey the social service needs of residents and then work to provide the needed services and referrals.

So far such sweeps in Chicago, Newark, and elsewhere have dramatically reduced drug activity and other crimes. They have also received praise from a variety of housing activists. The Philadelphia Housing Authority (PHA) stepped up attacks on drug offenders, but Virginia Wilks, president of the Tenants Council for the Richard Allen Homes, says the PHA was not vigilant enough: "If the evictions could be speeded up, then it would be a cure." Terry Clay, a PHA attorney, agrees: "Tenants have rights, but those rights had to be balanced against the rights of other tenants to live in a safe, drug-free environment."

As to the charge that innocent family members may be evicted, Judge Alan K. Silberstein of Philadelphia Municipal Court reflects widespread opinion. He told the *Philadelphia Inquirer*: "Tenants were responsible for what went on in the home. Many cases dealt with mothers who contended that they had no knowledge their teenage sons were selling drugs. If I'm judge, I say to them: 'If you can't stop him you'll be evicted.' Why should everyone else have to suffer because she can't control her son?"

Harry Spence, the former Boston housing receiver, summed up the case for a tough eviction program: "The issue is not whether some people are removed from the community by the BHA, or alternatively whether everybody gets to stay. The issue rather is: Who moves out, the perpetrator or the victim?"

While tough questions about rights remain unanswered, their burden should not fall on the backs of people who adhere to mainstream values. Society must extend some help to its most troubled citizens so they can function in our communities without endangering themselves or others. But the cost of that help must not be carried by decent public housing tenants, many of whom have already paid in lack of opportunity caused by an accident of geography, race, or class. It ought to be possible to screen prospective tenants and to expedite eviction of drug dealers while still retaining due process that can pass constitutional muster. By the same token, if the children of drug dealers are evicted, society needs to address their needs just as it addresses other neglected or abused children.

RESTORING COMMUNITY THROUGH SELF-GOVERNMENT

Well-meaning opposition to arbitrary authority must now be coupled with self-government by tenants—an effort to restore order and a sense of community. If public housing is to work, tenants must gain more control over their communities. That means giving tenants a stronger voice in management and resident selection, and, whenever possible, giving tenants individual or collective ownership of their own housing.

The past decade has witnessed a growing movement toward self-government and management in public housing. The first experiment in tenant self-management took place in St. Louis in the 1960s, in response to a rent strike and tenant protest. The idea expanded slightly in the 1970s but has become a serious topic of discussion since the mid-1980s. In 1984, President Reagan kicked off a three-year pilot program to encourage local housing authorities to sell units to tenants. The program made only 320 sales—a quarter of HUD's goal. The average income of households that purchased units was $16,673, more than double that of the typical public housing household.

In 1987, at the urging of Kemp (then a congressman), Congress passed a small program to fund Resident Management Corporations to run and eventually own public housing developments. Only about twenty resident management groups existed with any management experience; today there are more than 100 of them. Kemp, who was named HUD Secretary by President Bush in 1989, has made "tenant empowerment" the centerpiece of his agenda. The 1990 federal housing bill incorporated Kemp's vision by expanding federal funding for Resident Management Corporations and opportunities for tenants to purchase their complexes as resident-owned cooperatives. Kemp views resident management as a step toward "empowering" residents through home-ownership.

Kemp frequently travels with two charismatic tenant leaders—Kimi Gray and Bertha Gilkey—who have led efforts to turn around troubled public housing projects in Washington, D.C. (Kenilworth-Parkside) and St. Louis (Cochran Gardens), respectively. Kemp showcases these high-profile success stories to spread the gospel of tenant involvement. So far, however, Kemp has little to show for these efforts because of limited funding, the newness of the effort, and the resistance of most local housing authorities to relinquishing ownership or control.

In most resident-management efforts to date, tenants have only token influence. Local housing managers simply delegate responsibilities to tenant groups or co-opt compliant tenant leaders to deflect protest. Tenants get to sit on committees, perhaps hire management firms and personnel, and in some cases participate in setting some priorities for fund allocation. Only in a handful of cases—such as Boston's Bromley-Heath development—do tenants actually take over the management function. And given budget constraints, resident-managers often simply replace housing authorities as the target of tenant anger while forcing well-intentioned residents to administer austerity.

Kemp's efforts to sell public housing to residents, if successful, could dramatically reduce HUD's responsibility and financial commitment to low-income housing. Without subsidies, public housing tenants—who now pay 30 percent of their incomes for rent—are too poor to afford the monthly costs of home-ownership, even if the homes were sold for one dollar. Payments for the utilities and taxes alone, not to mention repair and maintenance needs, exceed their current rents. In the few success stories that Kemp promotes, HUD poured huge subsidies (for example, over $130,000 per unit at Kenil-worth-Parkside) to make these showcases work. HUD will only provide the buyers with subsidies for five years. After that, we could see a wave of foreclosures. Moreover, there are few safeguards to prevent the new homeowners from eventually selling their homes for a windfall profit, thereby reducing the housing stock available to the poor. Both initiatives, in effect, are decoys for Kemp's larger "privatization" agenda.

While there are many paths to tenant management and ownership, it works best where tenants take the initiative. The early success stories in tenant empowerment were triggered from the bottom up, by tenant protests. Local housing authorities, for example, conceded management prerogatives to settle rent strikes or other disruptive tactics. But there have also been successes where local housing authorities took the first steps. Thanks in part to Kemp's evangelical fervor, more local housing authority managers have now "seen the light" on tenant participation. They run the spectrum from resident advisory committees to tenant management to resident ownership.

Resident ownership should be the final stage of an organizing process that involves mobilizing tenants around day-to-day issues such as maintenance and crime, developing stable leaders, and winning stepping-stone victories, so that when tenants get to manage or own their projects, they have won something worth owning. Kemp often talks about tenant organizing. But so far, looking for quick results, he has been unwilling to fund that kind of genuine grass-roots empowerment.

Where tenant organizations gain a greater voice in running public housing, the conflict between individual prerogatives and community order is renegotiated. For example, at the Chicago Housing Authority, director Vince Lane encouraged residents to manage their own affairs. Tenants were offered rent rebates if they helped maintain graffiti-free walls. Others were trained to assist the newly formed CHA police force to bring community policing to the projects. Residents were asked to serve on management committees that screened new tenants. In some buildings, new Resident Management Corporations have taken on the responsibility for collecting rent checks. Some view

Lane's efforts as heavy-handed, paternalistic, even despotic; others see him as the CHA's savior after decades of mismanagement.

But what about the erosion of due process rights of those who are excluded? As noted, public housing is the last resort for most poor people. The number of eligible tenants far exceeds the number of apartments available, so most of the poor are "denied" admission. Screening does not exclude more tenants; it simply gives priority to certain tenants on criteria other than first come, first serve. Certainly excessive concern about criminal activity denies admission to some worthy people. But as Jim Sleeper has written:

> The Constitution has been suspended in many housing projects for years now by armed gangs who foreclose freedom of speech, freedom of assembly, freedom of association and property rights. . . . This is, in effect, a civil war, and we will have to choose sides even as we argue about causes and postbellum remedies, which must include massive social spending on education, health care, youth recreation, and more.

TAKING THE NEXT STEPS

Resident management and ownership are not panaceas for poverty. But where tenants are well-organized and exercise power, both physical and social conditions improve. Self-reliance replaces dependency. Residents stop being victims. What's more, experience suggests that ultimately, tenant-managed or -owned developments save funds because tenants have a greater stake in their homes and are less tolerant of destructive and costly behavior.

Kemp's 1990 initiative, the Homeownership Opportunities for People Everywhere (HOPE) program, is far too limited in scope and implementation. President Bush originally asked for $1 billion to fund HOPE, but when Congress finally approved the plan, funding had been reduced by 60 percent. Bush agreed to this lower figure because the legislative package that included HOPE also incorporated one of Bush's pet projects—the space station. However, in the aftermath of the Los Angeles riots, Bush is again requesting $1 billion in funding, and this time he may get it. He claims that this will allow 36,000 tenants to buy their apartments. But even for those tenants and tenant groups that win the HOPE competition, the grants are too small to be effective and too limited to sustain the kind of multiyear effort that is needed. Nor is there any guarantee that once tenants organize and are ready to buy, the funds for physical rehabilitation or ongoing operation of developments will be available.

The current approach may add a few more high-profile successes that Kemp can showcase, but it could lead to failure and demoralization for most tenants. HOPE will raise hopes but end in hopelessness because it does not provide the resources needed to fulfill its worthy goals. To work, HOPE must incorporate criteria that guarantee its residents a chance for real success:

- Congress must provide adequate funds so that tenants can organize—with the help of experienced organizers—to address day-to-day concerns (crime, for example, or maintenance) as a prelude to ownership.

- Tenants must be given the initial and ongoing training necessary to participate in management effectively, to create resident-run management corporations, and eventually to own their own developments.
- Congress must provide adequate subsidies so that the new owners can meet both the long-term and the day-to-day costs of homeownership. Better yet, working with tenant groups, HUD should repair the complexes before they are sold.
- The developments should be sold only as limited-equity cooperatives, not as single condos, to guarantee that this housing will continue to be available for low-income residents after the initial owners have left.
- Beyond bricks and mortar, HOPE should include funds to provide social programs—such as job training, child care, drug treatment, and community-based health care—and hire tenants for management and construction jobs.
- HOPE must ultimately become an entitlement program for all public and subsidized housing developments in the country, not a "demonstration project" for a lucky handful of people.

An expanded tenant-ownership program should not be a substitute for an ongoing federal commitment to expand the supply of affordable housing through a variety of approaches. One alternative is private, nonprofit housing sponsored by community organizations, churches, unions, and tenant groups. (See Peter Dreier and J. David Hulchanski, "Affordable Housing: Lessons from Canada," *TAP*, No. 2, Spring 1990.) With the support of many private foundations, local and state governments, and business groups, these nonprofit developers patch together resources to create low-income housing.

Such groups now have an enviable track record of constructing and rehabilitating housing for the poor. According to a recent survey sponsored by the National Congress for Community Economic Development, about 2,000 Community Development Corporations (CDCs) have produced 87,000 housing units in the past three years. Some housing experts view these CDCs as the next wave of housing reform; last year, Congress recognized this success by enacting the first federal initiative—the Community Housing Partnership program—to target funds for the nonprofit sector.

But these nonprofit groups and their housing projects face many of the same long-term problems that now confront public housing: securing adequate funding, stable and professional management, and a crime- and drug-free environment. Whether we rely on public housing, nonprofit organizations, or private landlords to house the poor, the same questions and issues remain.

Like every revolution, public housing has had its victims—in some cases the very people it was intended to help. In public housing projects, destroying arbitrary authority without replacing it with democratic authority left residents prey to overlords of the underclass, to criminals, and to drug abusers. In the new climate, where drug use was held to be a victimless crime and purity of procedure took precedence over community safety, residents of projects who had once been shackled by the inequality of law were now trapped by the absence of law.

Salvaging public housing will not, on its own, solve our housing crisis. Less than one in five low-income households receives any kind of federal housing assistance—the lowest level of any industrial nation. Just providing rent subsidies for all of them would cost over $25 billion a year. But Congress is unlikely to appropriate funds for rent subsidies, housing repair, or new construction by nonprofit community-based groups. As long as public housing remains a quagmire, providing the resources that will give the residents of these developments a greater voice in management and the skills to make their environment more livable will be a major step forward in helping the poor to help themselves. Admittedly, this will not substitute for a macroeconomic program to eradicate poverty. Admittedly, too, it will touch only a small percentage of America's 33 million poor, leaving the majority to fend for themselves in the private housing market. But if it works, it will help restore the public's confidence in activist government and in public and community enterprise.

DISCUSSION QUESTIONS

1. What role, if any, does the federal government play in providing housing? What about state and local governments? Why?
2. Should property that is public (belonging to the taxpayer) be turned over to private hands? How much of the real value should a potential owner pay for such a property?
3. Given America's well-known problems of homelessness, how do you think government could better respond to the problem of housing? Why?
4. In terms of qualifying for public housing (and other public assistance), should individuals be treated the same if their income level is the same or should other factors be taken into account?
5. How, if at all, does the nature of housing influence the sense of "community" in a neighborhood or block? How important is a sense of community in many of the problems described above? Why?
6. Is there any difference between spending money directly on housing programs and "spending money" through tax expenditures? Do you think they are treated different politically?
7. Is private enterprise better at providing some services than governments? Which ones? Why? Are governments better at providing some services? Why?
8. What do you think would be the impact of housing "vouchers" on housing segregation? What political influences might work for or against such a change? Why?

ADDITIONAL READINGS

Bratt, Rachel G. *Rebuilding a Low-income Housing Policy* (Philadelphia: Temple University Press, 1989).

Bratt, Rachel G., Chester Hartman, and Ann Meyerson, eds. *Critical Perspectives on Housing* (Philadelphia: Temple University Press, 1986).

Forrest, Ray, and Alan Murie. *Selling the Welfare State: The Privatisation of Public Housing* (London: Routledge, 1988).

Goering, John M., ed. *Housing Desegregation and Federal Policy* (Chapel Hill: University of North Carolina Press, 1986).

Harsman, Bjorn, and John M. Quigley, eds. *Housing Markets and Housing Institutions: An International Comparison* (Boston: Kluwer Academic Publishers, 1991).

Institute for Policy Studies. *The Right to Housing: A Blueprint for Housing the Nation* (Washington, D.C.: Institute for Policy Studies, 1989).

Kemp, Jack. "Houses to the People: An Open Letter to Boris Yeltsin." *Policy Review* (Winter 1992).

Kotlowitz, Alex. *There Are No Children Here* (New York: Doubleday, 1991).

Messenger, Paul H. "Public-Housing Perversity: A View from the Trenches." *The Public Interest* (Summer 1992).

Pynoos, Jon. *Breaking the Rules: Bureaucracy and Reform in Public Housing* (New York: Plenum Press, 1986).

Salins, Peter D., ed. *Housing America's Poor* (Chapel Hill: University of North Carolina Press, 1987).

Suchman, Diane R., with D. Scott Middleton and Susan L. Giles. *Public/private Housing Partnerships* (Washington, D.C.: Urban Land Institute, 1990).

U.S. Congressional Budget Office. *Current Housing Problems and Possible Federal Responses* (Washington, D.C.: Congressional Budget Office, 1988).

Vergara, Camilo Jose. "Hell in a Very Tall Place." *The Atlantic Monthly* (September 1989).

4

AIDS POLICY

"Does AIDS-Prevention Education Work?"

The pandemic of AIDS that has swept the world over the past two decades represents one of the most serious public health challenges that policymakers have ever faced. In 1990, the World Health Organization (WHO) estimated that between 8 and 10 million individuals had contracted the HIV virus globally and that some 283,000 had actually developed AIDS.[1] In July 1991 this figure rose to 10–12 million HIV-positive individuals.[2] Revised figures published in February 1992 put the number at 12 million.[3] WHO estimated in July 1994 that 17 million were infected and that 4 million people had full-blown AIDS, and predicted that by the year 2000, 30 to 40 million people will be infected by the virus, the greatest percentage of whom will be in Africa and Southeast Asia.[4]

Africa is a case of particular concern. Of the 17 million HIV-positive people, over 67 percent (over 11.4 million) are Africans.[5] Of the estimated 4.1 million women infected with the HIV virus globally in 1991, 81 percent live in Africa.[6] Uganda has the largest AIDS crisis of any African nation; it has been estimated that 25 percent of pregnant women in the capital city of Kampala were HIV positive in 1992. For those women in high-risk groups such as prostitutes, the rate of infection was estimated to be 75 percent.[7] In other African countries such as Burundi, Malawi, Tanzania, and Zambia, the infection rates for low-risk groups are estimated to be at least 25 percent.[8]

The federal Centers for Disease Control (CDC) reports that through September 1992, there were 242,146 cases of AIDS in the United States and its territories out of an estimated 1 to 2 million thought to be infected by the HIV virus.[9] As a cause of death, AIDS has been on the rise, from the fifteenth leading killer in 1988 to the eleventh just one year later;[10] it is estimated to be the eighth largest killer in 1993.[11] Of those who have developed AIDS, over 98 percent are adolescents or adults, with less than 2 percent under age thirteen.[12] The age group with the highest rate of AIDS for both sexes was 30–39 years, representing over 40 percent of all cases.[13] By September 1992, over 160,000 deaths in the United States since 1981 were attributable to AIDS.[14]

The term *AIDS*, the acronym for acquired immune deficiency syndrome, was first published in the *New England Journal of Medicine* in 1981; it was there that the evidence of a new immune deficiency disease was first made known.[15] (It should be noted that the onset of AIDS is when the visible symptoms of the HIV virus appear. Normally, this first occurs when an individual's T cell count falls below 300 and becomes increasingly severe as the T cell count continues its decline. Minor symptoms like rashes or intestinal problems are followed by more severe fatigue and general muscular and skeletal atrophy.) From this report, research progressed rapidly through CDC surveillance of the epidemiology of the disease. It was quickly realized that the disease had been in the United States for some time, perhaps a decade, but had avoided formal detection. It was also clear that the pattern of infection was in no way random: the disease was predominant in the large cities of both coasts and was concentrated in male homosexuals and intravenous drug users. For example, through 1992, 58 percent of AIDS cases were traced directly to men who had sex with other men;[16] another 23 percent of cases were attributed to IV drug usage.[17]

A virus was isolated from patients suffering from AIDS at the Institut Pasteur in France in 1983. This virus was found to attack the T4-type lymphocytes of the human immune system and was believed to be the cause of AIDS. The attack of the virus caused the breakdown of the immune system, which resulted in patient vulnerability to even common ailments. An illness that a healthy patient would easily recover from can be fatal to someone with AIDS. Over the next several years researchers continued to find viruses similar to the one discovered in France. The connection between the virus and AIDS became clear. In 1986 the International Committee for the Taxonomy of Viruses recommended that all viruses of this group be labeled together under the term "human immunodeficiency virus" or, as it has become better known, HIV.

As research on the nature of the virus continued, it became apparent that the virus was transmitted between individuals through bodily fluids, specifically blood and semen. This discovery made it clear why the disease was prevalent in homosexuals and intravenous drug users; both groups engaged in what was high-risk behavior for the transmission of the disease. However, despite the belief of many in the public, it was also apparent that this was not a disease that affected only these groups; there was clear evidence that heterosexual contact in certain instances could transmit the disease. Heterosexual contact was the mode of exposure in 6 percent of all AIDS cases in the population as a whole and in 36 percent of female AIDS cases.[18] Other forms of transmission included incidental exposure to tainted blood through transfusions, accidental clinical exposure, and fetal exposure. In 86 percent of pediatric cases of AIDS, the mode of exposure was through a mother at risk for HIV.[19]

Public ignorance of the disease to a large extent still exists. It was known quite early that there was no convincing evidence that HIV could be transmitted through casual contact and that animal or parasite transmission was not a source of infection. It was clear that risk of exposure to the disease could be lessened drastically by changes in personal behavior patterns or by taking precautionary measures. However, modifying individual behavior is anything but easy. As one anonymous person was quoted in the New York Times, "Getting a man to wear a condom isn't as simple as saying, 'You look better in a hat.'"

The disease remains incurable and is believed to be invariably fatal. Furthermore, there is no known vaccine; efforts to discover either a vaccine or cure have met with failure. The treatments that are known to extend the life and ease the suffering of those who contract the virus, such as AZT, impose enormous financial costs and also cause side effects in AIDS patients. The nature of the disease itself and its relationship to personal behavior patterns with regard to sexuality and drug use—and the public perceptions of those who contract the disease—make public policy decisions in this area particularly difficult in their combination of moral, economic, political, and civil rights dimensions.

The purity of the national blood supply was one of the first policy issues to be acted on at the federal level. With the rapid growth in knowledge about the HIV virus, it became possible to test for the presence of the virus in a patient or a blood sample by looking for the levels of the natural antibody that the immune system puts out in response to the virus. With the development of this test, the Reagan administration issued guidelines recommending the antibody test for the nation's blood supply in March 1985.[20] Further federal guidelines included recommending certain preventative measures be taken in workplaces where transmission was thought to be possible. This included health care workers, food handlers, and personal service workers. A statewide voter referendum put forth by Lyndon LaRouche in California in 1986 attempted to prohibit HIV-positive individuals from working in health care, food handling, and other industries where virus transmission was thought possible; it was extremely controversial and was ultimately defeated. To date, despite public fears, there have been only thirty-two documented cases of occupational transmission and only sixty-nine possible cases.[21] Also, most HIV-infected children were allowed to attend schools, although there were some incidents of children being excluded from educational institutions due to infection. One was the much-publicized case of Ryan White, a hemophiliac who contracted the HIV virus from a tainted blood transfusion and was banned from attending school in his hometown of Kokomo, Indiana. His case was one of the first to highlight the problems of AIDS discrimination in the United States. He died of AIDS in April 1990.[22]

Efforts to inform individuals and protect them from exposure from other sources have met with significant political and cultural resistance. The relationship of AIDS to sexual activity has illuminated divisions within American society. The epidemic has helped bring the issue of homosexuality to the forefront of American political debate, stirring controversy and raising questions of tolerance and understanding. Educating heterosexuals to the dangers of the disease has been a difficult issue politically as well and has been accomplished mostly through private organizations and through the efforts of schools and local governments. Promoting condom use, especially among the nation's youth, has proven divisive in many areas where the question of education conflicts with the beliefs of some parents in the virtues of abstinence. For the health policy official this creates the dilemma of balancing social concerns with the knowledge that proper use of a condom is the only device known to protect individuals from contraction when engaged in sexual activity.

The question of prevention among intravenous drug users has perhaps proven even more difficult. Fears of encouraging drug use through the distribution of clean needles to drug addicts have impeded many of the attempted programs. However, it is now known that the surest way to contract the virus is to share a needle with an infected individual and that IV drug use as a source of AIDS has been rising the most rapidly, from 11 percent of AIDS cases in 1981[23] to 23 percent through 1992.[24] Despite the dangers prevalent among this group, the 1992 Congress, in a major reorganization of the Alcohol, Drug Abuse, and Mental Health Administration, prohibited the use of federal funds for needle exchange programs.[25] This has meant that such programs have been attempted only at the state and local levels, such as New Haven's Needle Exchange Program.[26]

Federal funds allocated to combating the AIDS virus have increased each year, rising from a level of $8 million in 1983 to over $2.9 billion in 1990. The greatest share of these funds is allocated to basic research while the next largest share is paid out in direct medical costs, primarily through Medicaid.[27] Many AIDS activists feel the level of financial commitment to AIDS research is woefully inadequate in relation to the effects of the disease and attribute some of the federal government's ambivalence to publicize AIDS more forcefully to hostility toward gays. (A compelling account of the early years of political inattention and neglect of the AIDS problem is Randy Shilts's *And the Band Played On*.) Other activists argue that money is not enough and call for greater leadership by public officials, particularly the president, in forming a "sense of urgency."[28] Others raise the issue that on a per-victim basis, more money is spent on AIDS research than cancer research, although far more people die from cancer than AIDS. Consequently, some have called spending on AIDS research excessive relative to spending on other diseases (although not necessarily excessive in absolute dollars).

In the articles below, former U.S. Surgeon General C. Everett Koop argues that only through educating the young to be more sexually responsible than their "elders" can the threat of AIDS be controlled. He believes that teaching children about the threat of AIDS, if it is done in the right context, will not encourage promiscuity among youth. Representative William J. Dannemeyer of California and legislative counsel Michael G. Franc counter that the "education only" approach to AIDS control has been a failure due to its assumptions that people have strong will and self-control, which they believe is not the case. They claim that instead of relying on such measures to stem the spread of AIDS, it is better to take steps that "interrupt the chain of transmission" or ones that track and limit the activity of those who are infected. Their arguments follow.

Endnotes

1. Institute of Medicine, *The AIDS Research Program of the National Institutes of Health* (Washington, D.C.: National Academy Press, 1992), p. 24.

2. Dennis C. Weeks, "The AIDS Pandemic in Africa," *Current History* (May 1992), p. 208.
3. Ibid.
4. "Full-Blown AIDS Cases Estimated at 4 Million," *New York Times* (July 2, 1994), p. 8.
5. Weeks, "The AIDS Pandemic in Africa," p. 208.
6. Ibid.
7. Ibid.
8. Ibid, p. 209.
9. U.S. Centers for Disease Control, *HIV/AIDS Surveillance* (Washington, D.C.: U.S. Government Printing Office, October 1992), Table 1, p. 5.
10. U.S. Department of Health and Human Services, *Health United States 1991* (Washington, D.C.: U.S. Government Printing Office, 1992), Table 31.
11. "AIDS Is Top Killer among Young Men," *New York Times* (October 31, 1993), p. 13.
12. CDC, *HIV/AIDS Surveillance*, Table 2, p. 7.
13. Ibid., Table 7, p. 12.
14. Ibid., Table 8, p. 13.
15. M. S. Gottlieb, et al., "Pneumocystis Carinii and Mucosal Candidiasis in Previously Healthy Homosexual Men: Evidence of a New Acquired Cellular Immunodeficiency," *New England Journal of Medicine* 305 (December 10, 1981): 1425–1431.
16. CDC, *HIV/AIDS Surveillance*, Table 3, p. 8.
17. Ibid.
18. Ibid.
19. Ibid.
20. Philip R. Lee and Peter S. Arno, "AIDS and Health Policy," in John Griggs, ed. *AIDS: Public Policy Dimensions* (New York: United Hospital Fund Publications, 1987), p. 9.
21. CDC, *HIV/AIDS Surveillance*, Table 10, p. 14.
22. "The 'Miracle' of Ryan White," *Time* (April 23, 1990), p. 39.
23. Institute of Medicine, *The AIDS Research Program of the National Institutes of Health*, p. 24.
24. CDC, *HIV/AIDS Surveillance*, Table 3, p. 8.
25. "Drug, Mental Health Programs Revamped," *Congressional Quarterly Almanac, 1992*, p. 422.
26. U.S. General Accounting Office, *Needle Exchange Programs* (Washington, D.C.: GAO, March 1993).
27. U.S. Department of Health and Human Services, *Health United States, 92-1232* (Washington, D.C.: U.S. Government Printing Office, 1992), Table 128.
28. Jeffrey Schmalz, "Whatever Happened to AIDS?" *New York Times Magazine* (November 28, 1993), p. 81.

YES

Teaching Children about AIDS

C. Everett Koop

The AIDS epidemic officially began only six years ago, when the U.S. Public Health Service published the first five reports of persons struck down by *Pneumocystis carinii* pneumonia. These cases, involving "otherwise healthy homosexual males" living in Los Angeles, were considered "clinically unusual." Just *how* unusual is now a matter of history.

Today, the total number of AIDS cases on record in the United States is over 40,000. And the curve is rising dramatically. One or more cases have occurred in every state; in each of 17 major cities, the count has already topped 300. By 1991, according to estimates from the Centers for Disease Control (CDC), the number of AIDS cases may exceed 270,000.

This is a terrible disease, for which we do not yet have a cure. Nor do we have a vaccine, and one probably won't be generally available before the end of this century. Meanwhile, the mortality rate for AIDS is virtually 100 percent; over half the recorded victims of the disease are already dead, and the rest probably soon will be. The only thing we have that may work—and I repeat: "*may* work"—is education, education, and more education.

THE NEED TO CHANGE PRACTICES

The AIDS virus—also known as the "human immunodeficiency virus," or HIV—is transmitted from one person to another in blood or semen. In other body fluids, such as tears, saliva, sweat, and urine, the virus particle count is too low or is absent altogether. Hence, we have no substantiated cases of the AIDS virus being transmitted in water glasses, on toilet seats, by sneezes or coughs, and so on.

Certain sexual practices engaged in mainly by homosexual and bisexual men often produce semen *and* blood that are passed between partners. These men are the persons most at risk of catching AIDS, not because of their particular sexual orientation, but because of their sexual behavior *within* that orientation.

But practices can be changed. In fact, after several years of intensive AIDS education directed to homosexual and bisexual men, it appears that they have become more cautious and, as a result, the transmission of other diseases such as syphilis, gonorrhea, and hepatitis has, in fact, decreased. Because they each have a shorter incubation period than AIDS, we can track these diseases more easily for short-term data. We can only assume that the transmission of AIDS within this group has probably decreased as well.

The need to change practices is exactly the same issue for intravenous drug abusers, who constitute the second largest group of AIDS victims. The ones who use their own clean needles for each "fix" are killing themselves by abusing potent, addictive, illegal drugs. But they probably won't kill themselves through an AIDS-related disease.

Drug abusers tend *not* to be this fastidiously hygienic, however. About 90 percent of all heroin addicts borrow used and dirty needles, as well as other contaminated drug paraphernalia. These addicts are making absolutely sure that they die as early and as uncomfortably as possible. And when they engage in sex, they're shortening the lives of other people as well.

It's clear that if every homosexual and bisexual man used a condom during sex from this day forward, and if every IV drug abuser used only a clean needle for each fix, the epidemic of AIDS would slow down in those populations, gradually reach a steady state, and finally begin to recede as those who are already infected die off and no new victims take their places.

But that's only a theory. The reality is far more grim. Some homosexual and bisexual men have changed their sexual practices, but not all of them have. And we have no idea how many drug addicts may have heard our "clean-needle" message of AIDS prevention. Nor do we know how many have actually processed that information and, as a result, changed their behavior.

INNOCENT VICTIMS

So, the theory remains just that: a theory. The AIDS epidemic, in reality, is not going to level off and recede for many years to come. And the percentage of completely innocent victims of the disease could become increasingly significant. The overall number of AIDS cases will probably increase ninefold over the next five years, but the number of cases involving heterosexuals will increase about 20-fold.

At present, about 4 percent of all reported AIDS victims are heterosexuals—men and women who are neither homosexuals nor bisexuals nor IV drug abusers. Apparently, their only high-risk activity was to have had sexual relations with someone who was infected with the AIDS virus.

A common example could be that of a heterosexual man who has sex with an HIV-infected prostitute, then goes home and has sex with his unsuspecting wife or with other women, all of whom could receive the virus from him. Nothing very kinky about it, nothing very exotic, but all very tragic.

The tragedy is then compounded when one of these women becomes pregnant and passes the virus on to her newborn infant either in utero or in the birth canal during delivery.

It's true that the number of children born with AIDS is still quite small. They constitute just over 1 percent of the total number of all AIDS victims. A couple of years ago, however, *there weren't any*. Now, there are 470. In fact, some hospitals—in New York, New Jersey, and Washington, D.C., for example—have had to set aside isolation wards to take care of the rising number of infants infected with the AIDS virus (and who are frequently abandoned or orphaned).

Over half the babies born with AIDS are black. Another 25 percent of all babies born with AIDS are Hispanic. And just to increase our sense of horror at what is happening in the black and Hispanic communities, we suspect that these cases are vastly underreported.

What we're seeing with AIDS, therefore, is more tragic evidence of the demography of high-risk pregnancies and birth. In our society, such pregnancies are most likely to occur among black women under the age of 19 who are poor, not ready for work (usually without a high school diploma), and without ready access to sound health care.

This fact is in addition to what is emerging with more and more clarity regarding the incidence of AIDS among black adults. In the population generally, one of every eight Americans is black. But among Americans with AIDS, one of every four is black. Also, about a third of all black AIDS victims are IV drug abusers, which is also disproportionate.

This is catastrophic news for the black community, which already is under great economic and social stress. And it's also more evidence of the apparent inability of U.S. society in general to make much headway in helping young people control their own destinies.

TREATING OTHERS WITH RESPECT

In the absence of a vaccine or any miracle drug to stop AIDS, the best thing society can do to contain this epidemic is to present scientifically accurate and personally sensitive information about AIDS to our children. The objective is to make them a lot more responsible in their relationships than their elders have been. And before AIDS education even begins, a child should be given information relative to his or her own sexuality.

I've recommended that this be done in the context of a comprehensive school health curriculum, so that children may make the same kinds of intelligent, life-saving choices regarding their own sexuality as we hope they will in regard to their own dental health, their ability to handle anger and stress, their rejection of cigarettes and other drugs, and so on.

Instead of calling it "sex education," I'd like it called something like "studies in human development." Children should be learning all about themselves—about their unbelievable complexity, and especially about their own great value. If they are properly taught their own worth, we can expect them to treat themselves, and others, with great respect.

Human development instruction should keep pace with—and not anticipate—a child's own development and curiosity. It should begin in infancy, taught by parents through overt instruction and good role modeling, and by enlightened teachers armed with facts and useful materials.

Education in this country has traditionally been the responsibility of states and communities. That tradition should continue, but the federal role—getting factual, scientifically accurate information into the hands of local teachers—is also important. This year the Public Health Service is investing a million dollars in just such an activity. For example:

- Last December our CDC, the lead agency in our educational efforts, brought together an ad hoc group of advisors drawn from organizations such as the American Academy of Pediatrics, the National Congress of PTAs, the National Education Association, the School Board of the City of New York, and so on. This group produced a set of guidelines—which are responsive to, and consistent with, the needs of the community—for teaching about AIDS in the nation's schools.
- Under a grant from CDC, the Indiana Department of Health and Indiana University have jointly produced a manual on AIDS for students and teachers, copies of which are available from CDC in Atlanta.
- Cooperative agreements are being established with state education departments and local school districts to support their efforts in mounting programs to teach about AIDS. That program should be in place early this school year.

In these and related activities, there are some basic concepts in human development that ought to be conveyed. For example, I think children ought not to be afraid of sex. Still, I think it makes sense to suggest to them, as they approach pubescence, that abstinence at their time of life is by far the preferable option. Abstinence is in fact the only option that really prevents sexually transmitted disease.

But children grow up, and, as adults, not too many of them choose to be sexually abstinent all their lives. So what's next? I've advised that the next-best protection is a faithful, monogamous relationship; one in which they have only one continuing sexual partner who is equally faithful. Paraphrasing Lee Iacocca, I say: If you have a monogamous relationship, *keep* it; if you don't have one, *get* it.

But, again, not everyone is fortunate enough to achieve such a relationship. Many men and women who take marriage vows may practice monogamy, but not all of them do. So the next concept is: When in doubt, protect yourself. If you don't know what you're doing and with whom you're doing it, then don't do it. But if you go ahead anyway, then you must be absolutely certain that your partner is free of the AIDS virus. Otherwise, if you're a man, use a condom from start to finish; if you're a woman, make sure your partner uses a condom from start to finish. A condom is not perfect. But it's the best thing available for people who neither abstain nor are monogamous.

That's my basic message on sex and AIDS education for children. In my report of October 1986, I devoted fewer than 200 words to the subject. But for some people, those were 200 words too many! Because they believe that sex education in school will lead to promiscuity, they prefer that such instruction be given at home. I agree, but the fact is that most parents do not provide sex education to their children, so schools and churches must do it instead.

THE LARGER SOCIAL CONTEXT

I'm sure that some of the controversy about sex education and AIDS education reflects genuine concerns by parents and school officials regarding course content. But the discussion also reflects the continued ambivalence and confusion in our society about male–female relationships in general.

There is more to human relationships than just "good sex," and young people ought to be told that. We should encourage them to seek out relationships that are sensitive and affirmative—equitable relationships in which both adults are mutually loving, caring, respectful, and considerate.

We all want such relationships. But many people settle for much less. They tend to overemphasize sex because it's easier and can be accomplished with very little thought. This is the distorted message, delivered by so much of our popular media as well, that sex is most often a casual and even gratuitous act in which no one gets hurt, no one gets pregnant, and no one takes responsibility.

I suggest that we teach AIDS education at an appropriate moment within the context of a total sex education curriculum. But more fundamental is the *social* context that embraces sex education itself. And this is where we have to reach beyond the biology staff and secure the help of psychology and sociology staff as well.

The larger social context is the one in which men and women relate to each other generally in our society. And here, the evidence is not very inspiring.

Earlier this year, for example, I was briefed on a study—done for our National Institute of Mental Health by Dr. Mary Koss of Kent State University—that involved a representative sample of about 6,000 men and women who attend 32 colleges across the country.

Although these subjects were reasonably well-educated, middle-class individuals from workaday American families, 25 percent of the college men said they had committed some form of sexual aggression against a female companion one or more times. About 8 percent of the sample had tried to rape or *had* raped their companions. And half of them said that, given the chance, they'd do it again.

Twenty-five percent of this representative sample comes to 740 men. But 25 percent of the total male enrollment in U.S. higher education today is a *million and a half* men—a million and a half young men for whom male–female relationships are not caring, not respectful, certainly not loving, and hardly equitable.

Thus our job in the long run is to get through to these young men—and young women—and many millions more who are adolescent and preadolescent, and try to instill in them more positive and humane values. And our job right *now* is to advise them as follows: That they should be abstinent; if not abstinent, then monogamous; and if not monogamous, then at least supercautious.

We must tell young people the truth about AIDS and about the way it's spread. We must talk sense to them, and their parents, and their teachers. This is no rose garden. But we've got to make the effort. We have to educate and inform them, even though we do so in the midst of all the other complex aspects of sexual relations in America. Their lives are at stake, and so is the physical and spiritual life of this country.

NO

The Failure of AIDS-Prevention Education

William E. Dannemeyer and Michael G. Franc

For most of this century, public-health officials have relied on a few basic techniques to contain contagious diseases. They have assumed that serious infectious diseases can be controlled only by interrupting the chain of transmission. To do so they have attempted to locate carriers of the disease, to alert those who may have been exposed to it, to offer counseling to prevent further transmission, and to ensure that infected individuals desist from all activities that might spread the disease. Those who persist in knowingly spreading the disease have been subject to incarceration.

Almost every state requires public-health officials to follow these procedures with respect to diseases such as syphilis and gonorrhea. California, for example, requires physicians to report more than fifty infectious diseases to health authorities, including chancroid, infectious hepatitis, the plague, Rocky Mountain spotted fever, smallpox, syphilis, tuberculosis, and yellow fever.

Unfortunately, the AIDS epidemic has aroused political forces that have precluded the application of these traditional public-health measures to the human immunodeficiency virus (HIV). Only a handful of states have required that positive HIV test results be reported (confidentially) to patients, implemented a system to trace the contacts of people who test positive, or established procedures to deal with recalcitrant carriers. Even fewer have established programs that routinely offer voluntary HIV tests to people in high-risk areas when they come into contact with the public-health system—whether in hospitals or clinics, whether for sexually transmitted diseases or intravenous drug abuse.

Public-health officials instead have instituted anonymous testing for HIV. As University of Minnesota physician Dr. David Pence has explained, anonymous testing should not be confused with confidential testing. In an important 1987 address, Pence elaborated on this crucial distinction:

> Confidential testing means results are known only to the patient, his doctor, and public health officials. This is the standard practice throughout medicine. Anonymous testing means a person is tested without giving his name. This practice is unique to the HIV infection. *Con fidem* means "with faith or trust." A *nomos* means "without a name." In this juxtaposition of two Latin phrases we find the failure of our present policy.

Proponents of anonymous testing, Pence explains, have convinced the public-health establishment that neither the government nor the medical profession can be trusted. People at risk are given complete discretion over whether to request a test for HIV, and over whether to warn their sexual or needle-sharing contacts that they might be infected. Pence attributes the insistence upon anonymous testing to the Vietnam generation's suspicion of government's police power:

> At the heart of the debate [is] a discussion of the legitimate policing functions of local communities and their public health agencies. This is a difficult concept for the younger public health officials who have been raised in a cultural milieu hostile to police work. Most of the new generation officials are considerably more comfortable with their role as educators than their function as enforcers.

Those holding this view have great political power. In the waning days of the 100th Congress, for example, a unified public-health establishment helped defeat a proposal by Florida Representative Bill McCollum that would have required states to enact limited contact-tracing programs for spouses who may have been exposed to the AIDS virus. Many observers regarded the McCollum Amendment as a rather modest attempt to rein in the epidemic. Why should anyone object to warning the unsuspecting spouse of an intravenous drug user or a bisexual man that she may have been exposed to a fatal virus by someone without the moral courage to reveal his positive test results? Yet McCollum's proposal lost by the lopsided margin of 279 to 105.

THE EDUCATION-ONLY APPROACH

The response to the burgeoning AIDS epidemic to date has been confined to what we will call the education-only approach. This approach focuses exclusively on education to convince homosexuals and intravenous drug users to change their behavior in ways that will eliminate the risk of HIV transmission. Unfortunately, the education-only approach has failed miserably with respect to the urban underclass, the locus of the second wave of the AIDS epidemic. This second wave began in the inner cities' crack houses and shooting galleries and has now spread to the non-drug-using spouses, sexual partners, and offspring of intravenous drug users.

Those who accept the education-only approach assume that even the most desperate heroin or cocaine addicts can be taught the self-control required to use clean needles and engage only in "safe" sexual practices. They believe that these people will ascertain their HIV status, will inform their sexual partners of their high-risk behavior, and will never knowingly expose them to the AIDS virus. Education-only advocates think that heroin and cocaine addicts are able to control their actions so as to prevent HIV transmission.

This belief is naive. A study conducted by Dr. Mindy Thompson Fullilove, a San Francisco physician, focused on the sexual habits of two hundred black teenage crack users and found that 27 percent of them reported having had five or more sexual partners in the previous year, with 12 percent admitting to having had more than ten partners. Over one-third said that they never used condoms, and most of the rest said that they rarely used them—in spite of the fact that 80 percent understood their value in preventing the spread of HIV. The explanation for this behavior may lie in Fullilove's finding that almost half of those surveyed said that they had sex while high on drugs.

As Fullilove noted, "This is not an ignorant group." Their behavior instead results from the nature of intravenous crack use; users often exchange sex for drugs, which they then typically inject every five minutes to maintain their high. For such an incorrigible population, the only effective educational outreach would involve targeting unsuspecting heterosexual contacts.

In a recent sobering assessment of poverty trends in *Commentary*, Charles Murray agrees that the education-only strategy currently favored by most health professionals for fighting AIDS mostly fails to reach high-risk people in minority communities. Murray observes that since 1982 the number of AIDS cases reported to the Centers for Disease Control (CDC) has risen 3.8 times faster for blacks than for whites. Education alone, he notes, is ill-suited to reach members of the urban underclass. Murray contrasts such people with the homosexual men who accounted for the vast majority of the first victims of the AIDS epidemic:

> Homosexuals tend to be well-informed, and in many places well-organized, and have demonstrated their readiness to change behavior. Among blacks, by contrast, only 38 percent of AIDS cases involve homosexual, non-IV-drug-abusing males. Almost all of the rest are associated with drug abuse, heterosexual transmission, or transmission from mother to infant. Most of these cases occur in populations that are notoriously difficult to reach with educational programs: not only drug addicts, but the homeless, the chronically unemployed, those living in large inner cities.

The *Los Angeles Times* recently echoed Murray's observation in an editorial. It noted the growing incidence of HIV among blacks and Latinos in Los Angeles County and concluded: "There is no evidence that public health education efforts have succeeded in winning substantial behavior changes to safer sex practices in these groups and communities." Even the *Journal of the American Medical Association* (*JAMA*) editorialized recently that "behavior has not changed much and HIV-1 seroprevalence has continued to climb" in San Francisco, even though public-health authorities there have made "strenuous educational and intervention efforts" to reach intravenous drug users.

Physicians who treat drug-related cases of AIDS in the inner cities agree. One told the *Los Angeles Herald-Examiner* that interrupting the spread of the epidemic in these communities presents a unique challenge to health officials. "It's much harder for drug users," he said. Physicians must contend with "a bunch of poor people with chaotic, disordered lives," who cannot be expected to help themselves. "I don't think that that's a realistic expectation. We need to build a public health system for drug users."

AIDS IN THE INNER CITIES

In the absence of such a system, CDC data reveal that the AIDS epidemic is now spreading most rapidly among intravenous drug users. After several years in which the intravenous drug component of the epidemic accounted for about 17 percent of all cases reported to the CDC, in 1988 full-blown cases of AIDS among drug users suddenly jumped to 24 percent of all new cases, a rate that has continued in 1989. Should this trend persist, the epidemic will reach tens of thousands of inner-city residents, as the non-drug-using spouses, sexual partners, and offspring of intravenous drug users are infected.

The portents of disaster are apparent. Study after study of inner-city residents—both drug users and their sexual partners—indicates that the AIDS epidemic has reached the alarmingly high level that was common among homosexual males several years ago. The government's official estimates of the prevalence of AIDS have come under closer scrutiny, and many experts now conclude that the extent of the problem is much greater than was previously believed.

Dr. Rand L. Stoneburner of the New York City Department of Health reviewed the 7,884 deaths in New York City between 1978 and 1986 that had been listed as "narcotics-related" and found that many of them were also AIDS-related, even though AIDS was not officially listed as the cause of death. Stoneburner discerned "an increase in mortality among IV drug users in New York that is not captured by [the CDC's] surveillance definition [of] AIDS but is likely to be related to HIV infection." He estimates that the true number of HIV-related deaths in New York between 1982 and 1986 is at least 134 percent higher among drug users than was reported to the CDC. Dr. Stephen Joseph, the city's Health Commissioner, puts the figure at 150 percent.

An anonymous survey of HIV seroprevalence among newborns conducted by the New York State Department of Health confirms Stoneburner's fears that official figures understate the prevalence of AIDS. Through May 31, 1988, New York tested 133,781 newborn infants for HIV antibodies. A positive test result on a newborn clearly indicates that the mother is infected. These mothers, in turn, most likely contracted the virus from sharing needles or having sex with infected drug users or bisexual men. The results of the New York survey attest to the disturbing extent to which the epidemic has penetrated the general population, especially those who live in poor inner-city neighborhoods.

The statewide infection rate was 0.67 percent, about twice the infection rate found in the CDC sentinel hospital and college-campus surveys; it is cause for great concern. The pockets of infection in certain urban areas, however, tell the real story; in the five boroughs of New York City the infection rate was 1.29 percent. In the Bronx, which has one of the worst drug problems in America, the infection rate among pregnant women was 1.89 percent.

If nearly two of every hundred pregnant women in the Bronx are infected with the AIDS virus, one can only speculate what the infection rate in particular Bronx ghettos is, or what the rate is among the men who have sex with the women there or share their needles. The overall infection rate may exceed 10 percent in certain neighborhoods; the same New York State survey sampled 494 males who entered the Downstate Correctional Facility in New York City consecutively, and found an overall seroprevalence rate of 17.4 percent. The infection rate among those arrested in New York City exceeded 20 percent. Even in California, where the intravenous drug component of the epidemic had been thought negligible, between 2.5 and 3 percent of the state's prison population is seropositive.

A recent Citizens' Committee for Children survey, which covered twenty of the forty-eight hospitals with pediatric units in New York City, suggests that the epidemic is claiming many more victims than are listed in the CDC's official reports. The survey found that 828 children with CDC-defined AIDS or clinically apparent HIV infection received care in 1988. The city's Department of Health, however, reported only 14 CDC-defined AIDS cases in all forty-eight hospitals during this period. The underreporting in this instance missed HIV disabled children by at least a factor of six. Most ominously, the extent of pediatric infection may be worse; only eight of the hospitals surveyed stated that they report all such cases to the CDC.

In Baltimore, researchers screened over four thousand patients at several clinics specializing in sexually transmitted diseases; they found a seroprevalence rate of 5.2 percent, with the highest rates occurring among blacks and adult men. Almost 7 percent of men aged twenty-five to twenty-nine and 11.4 percent of those over thirty tested positive; yet only 7.1 percent of the men in the sample were homosexual or bisexual. The researchers concluded: "As many as 40 percent of seropositive men and 62 percent of seropositive women may have acquired HIV through heterosexual transmission. It can be expected that HIV infection rates will continue to increase among blacks of both sexes unless intervention programs for HIV infection that are aimed at minority groups are initiated immediately and prove to be successful."

INTRAVENOUS DRUG USERS AND THE FAILURE OF EDUCATION

We now know that we cannot expect an education-only approach to be successful. Greenwich House, a major substance-abuse treatment facility in New York City, recently completed a study funded by the American Foundation for AIDS Research (AmFAR) on the effectiveness of AIDS education for substance abusers. The researchers selected eighty-two clients, sixty-two of whom completed the study—that is, they returned for a follow-up evaluation three months after receiving the education.

The participants in the study were clearly the cream of the crop of intravenous drug users. As the researchers explained, the sample was biased in several important ways: "It was drawn from a clinic population, which is inherently self-selected; persons within that unique population further self-selected by deciding whether they would participate in the study; finally, erosion of the sample occurred due to dropouts." In addition, the participants were surprisingly well-educated for drug users. Fifty-four percent reported that they had attended college or even completed it; street users, who do not seek professional help, are much less educated. Since even this experiment's results were discouraging, similar efforts directed at the general intravenous-drug-using population are likely to fail dismally.

The participants in the Greenwich House study were ominously cavalier about their risk status. Only about one-third had been tested for HIV; one in five of this group did not even know the test results. Of those not tested, 46 percent said that they did not consider themselves at risk; 20 percent said that they simply did not want to know. Only 9 percent cited the fear that their confidentiality would be breached in explaining why they had not been tested—a strikingly low figure, given the importance that the education-only theorists attach to this fear.

Ironically, these drug users favor the very public-health measures that many health officials oppose. Seventy-six percent believe that infected individuals should be required by law to tell their sex partners; 63 percent favor mandatory HIV screening at all drug-treatment centers; 63 percent believe that those who knowingly transmit the AIDS virus should be incarcerated. In addition, 46 percent believe that giving out free needles will encourage drug use.

These drug users also doubt that people who are high on drugs will avoid risky activities. Three in four, for example, believe that drug users who need a fix will not worry about the condition of their needles; 86 percent assert that people who are high on drugs are less likely to use condoms. Four in five believe that people who want to have sex will do so, whether or not condoms are available. Two-thirds feel that men will not use condoms because they "make sex less pleasurable."

How effective was the educational program? The researchers concluded: "The overall knowledge gain among respondents indicated that the AIDS education seemed to have some effect. However, this did not seem to alter the sexual and drug practices of the sample in a substantial way."

Even this guardedly optimistic conclusion misses the main point. The results suggest that the participants actually knew less about safe sex and the dangers of needle sharing after the study than before it. In terms of "total" AIDS knowledge, 37 percent regressed and only 26 percent improved; with respect to "drug-related" AIDS knowledge, 23 percent lost ground and only 16 percent improved. Furthermore, more than twice as many regressed (21 percent) as advanced (10 percent) with respect to "sex-related" knowledge.

Three months after the study 41 percent of the participants knew the proper use of a condom. Unfortunately, when the study began, 49 percent answered the same question correctly. Participants in the study reported only slight decreases in vaginal, oral, and oral-anal sex. More than half the participants continued to engage in oral and vaginal sex three months after the completion of the study. There was virtually no change in the number of participants—about 10 percent—who engaged in anal sex.

Nor did the educational efforts deter drug use. More blacks and Hispanics injected drugs after the study (42 percent) than before it (33 percent), an increase that is perhaps reflected in the increase among those who injected cocaine (from 23 percent to 26 percent). The only progress occurred in the number of those who shared needles; the percentage dropped from seventeen to eight.

The most disturbing finding, however, was that 25 percent of the participants said that they would continue to have sex even if they learned that they were HIV positive.

THE HARLEM HOSPITAL CENTER STUDY

The Greenwich House researchers warned that their findings should not be generalized, due to the small number of participants in the study. But another study, conducted by a team at the Harlem Hospital Center in New York City and reported in the *Journal of the American Medical Association*, tested a much larger sample of drug users and reached many of the same conclusions.

The Harlem Hospital Center study surveyed 868 patients and forty-six staff members in the hospital's methadone-maintenance clinics with respect to their attitudes on AIDS. As in the Greenwich House study, the drug users were remarkably nonchalant about their risk. About half said they did not believe that they were at risk; only one in five had been tested; 15 percent of those who had been tested had not bothered to learn their test results.

Like their counterparts in the Greenwich House study, the patients strongly supported traditional public-health measures to control contagious diseases. Almost three quarters favored routine voluntary HIV testing at the clinic and more than half supported a *mandatory* testing program there. Again, large majorities supported partner-notification programs for sex partners (84.1 percent) and for those who share needles (80.2 percent). Majorities also favored less stringent confidentiality laws that would allow physicians, nurses, and counselors to learn of positive test results.

The staff also strongly preferred traditional public-health measures to control the epidemic—even though nearly all of the national health organizations based in Washington favor the education-only approach. Virtually all of the staff supported voluntary (97.8 percent) or mandatory (82.6 percent) testing at the clinics, and the reform of confidentiality laws to inform physicians, nurses, and counselors of positive test results. Large majorities also opposed the distribution of clean needles (73.9 percent) and bleach (65.2 percent) to intravenous drug users.

The survey also reinforced the conclusion that the education-only approach has done little to slow the spread of the epidemic. As in the Greenwich House study, the percentage of patients who reported sharing needles dropped from 20 percent in 1987 to 9 percent in 1988. Similarly, the percentage of patients reporting multiple sex partners dropped from almost 30 percent to 15 percent.

Although these results may seem encouraging, the researchers caution that they are unsatisfactory for such a high-risk group:

> Uninfected persons in intimate sexual or needle-sharing contact with a population group with a high prevalence of HIV infection must make *extreme* reductions in risk-taking behavior to prevent becoming infected. For example, if their associates are 50 percent infected, little protection would be gained by a reduction in the number of sex or needle-sharing partners from fifty to five, since they would still be heavily exposed to the virus.

In a high-risk group such as intravenous drug users, it is simply unacceptable for 15 percent to have sex with multiple partners and for 10 percent to share needles.

What is more, many intravenous drug users, especially men who share needles, have sex with nonusers. Debra L. Murphy of the Columbia University School of Public Health documented the sexual-behavior patterns of drug users and found that 40 percent of the women and 70 percent of the men have sex with people who do *not* use drugs. Fully 78 percent of male intravenous drug users who share needles report having sex with nonusers. Murphy undoubtedly understates the case when she concludes that intravenous drug users "may play a very important role" in exposing the general population to the AIDS virus.

THE AIDS OUTREACH INTERVENTION PROJECT

Armed with a $3.2 million grant from the National Institute on Drug Abuse (NIDA), the AIDS Outreach Intervention Project at the University of Illinois at Chicago is assessing HIV seroprevalence among a street population of intravenous drug abusers. Principle investigator Wayne Weibel and project director Herbert J. Horan employed former drug abusers to establish personal contact with Chicago drug users. By November 1988 the researchers had completed more than a thousand interviews with local users and conducted 956 HIV blood tests. The NIDA study, which will take three years to complete, represents the first systematic effort to establish the extent of the AIDS epidemic among intravenous drug users who have not sought counseling or otherwise attempted to end their habits—that is, habitual street users.

Preliminary results from the Chicago portion of the study confirm the hypothesis that drug users who seek professional help at clinics are much different from those who remain on the street. Tom Lampinen, a graduate student who worked on the project, reviewed demographic data from several Illinois testing sites and found "striking" differences between the users who are tested at these sites and the street users who participated in the study. Compared with those tested at the sites, the street users were less educated (2 percent had completed college compared to 26 percent), more likely to be unemployed (80 percent unemployed compared to 36 percent), and more likely to have injected heroin (92 percent compared to 54 percent). Demographically, those tested at the sites resemble the participants in the Greenwich House study.

Not surprisingly, the researchers found that state HIV test sites in Illinois may be overlooking substantial epidemics of HIV. The Outreach Project found a seroprevalence rate of 21 percent, with pockets of infection running as high as 30 percent on Chicago's west side. In contrast, the state test sites report infection rates of only 10 percent. Among those who were HIV-positive, the researchers found two distinct groups—those whose chronic drug use had diminished their sexual activity and those who exchanged sex for drugs. Over 34 percent of infected users reported having sex with eleven or more partners in recent months; only 10 percent of all those interviewed reported no sexual activity. Nine in ten admitted sharing needles; only 19 percent said that they sterilized them before injection.

PARTNERS OF INTRAVENOUS DRUG USERS

Recent data indicate that infected drug users are spreading the virus to their heterosexual partners. "Those who binge on cocaine and who trade sex for drugs," *JAMA* concluded in a recent editorial, "pose the risk of propagating HIV-1 beyond just the [intravenous drug abuser]. The impact on the heterosexual population is becoming evident in current statistics."

The editorial's author, Dr. Stanley Weiss of New Jersey Medical School in Newark, reported that the sexual partners of intravenous drug users now constitute the majority of AIDS cases attributed solely to heterosexual contact. Using CDC data, Weiss found that of 5,324 cases of AIDS among adults in New Jersey as of November 30, 1988, 54 percent were linked to heterosexual drug users and 8.4 percent to heterosexual contact alone. More alarmingly, of the first 1,112 cases diagnosed in 1988, 11.6 percent—almost three times the national average—were heterosexually acquired, with the majority coming from areas with spiraling drug-abuse problems. One team of researchers in the Bronx, in fact, interviewed and tested the drug-free partners of intravenous drug users and found a seropositivity rate of 48 percent, with seven of twelve male and forty-one of eighty-eight female partners testing positive.

Most of the heterosexual transmissions in these areas are from males to females. Women in these neighborhoods are the first victims of the education-only philosophy. As Dr. Janet Mitchell, Director of Perinatology at New York's Harlem Hospital Center, explained: "Women are often the last to know the habits of their partners."

Women are four times as likely as heterosexual men to acquire HIV through heterosexual intercourse, says Dr. Mary Guinan, an epidemiologist who works for the CDC in Atlanta. Guinan predicts that in five years heterosexual intercourse will overtake intravenous drug use—which currently accounts for 53 percent of all cases of full-blown AIDS among women—as the most common route of transmission among women.

Not all intravenous drug users, of course, hail from the worst urban ghettos. Dr. Jordan Glaser, Director of the Department of Infectious Diseases at Staten Island Hospital in New York, surveyed the heterosexual contacts of thirty-two HIV-positive middle-class intravenous drug users. The typical contact was a white, married woman in her thirties living in a household with an average income of $41,200. Most of the contacts were monogamous, had been married an average of six years, and reported only one lifetime partner. Needless to say, these contacts did not regard themselves as being at risk for HIV infection.

Thirty of the thirty-nine contacts agreed to be tested; seven were positive. Fewer than half of the contacts were even aware of their partner's drug habit at the start of the sexual relationship. Four learned of it upon being told of their positive test results. Reflecting on his findings, Dr. Glaser concluded that among intravenous drug users

> AIDS is a disease of monogamy, not promiscuity. . . . These cases are particularly disturbing to us as clinicians. This is because the women who became infected are for the most part innocent victims of their spouses' behavior. Some have only found out about their spouses' high risk behaviors upon being diagnosed HIV positive.

Dr. Guinan of the CDC believes that the extent of middle-class HIV infection is much greater than reported. "I know of many cases where the husband and wife are dead, they've left three children, and it's never been reported." Many women, especially, seek medical help from physicians who never think to look for HIV. Dr. Janet Mitchell of the Harlem Hospital Center believes *all* women admitted to hospitals in high-risk areas should be tested for HIV.

Support for Mitchell's observation comes from the most recent data from the military testing program. Since October 1985 there has been a statistically significant decrease in HIV infection among male recruit applicants, from 1.7 per 1,000 to 1.2 per 1,000. Among women, however, the seroprevalence rate has remained constant at between 0.7 and 0.8 per 1,000. This suggests that homosexual men and intravenous drug users, aware of their HIV status or suspecting that they are infected, have been removing themselves from the applicant pool while infected women continue to apply, unaware that they have been exposed to the fatal virus.

A POLICY RESPONSE

A coherent response to the AIDS epidemic in the inner cities requires: (1) confidential, identity-linked reporting of positive HIV test results to public-health authorities; (2) aggressive programs to alert unsuspecting sexual partners of those who test positive that they may be at risk; (3) elimination of barriers to testing, such as the requirement for written consent, now placed between physicians and their patients; (4) routine offering of voluntary HIV testing to those who come into contact with the public-health system in high-risk areas; and (5) criminal penalties for those who, knowing that they are infected, expose others to the virus.

Physicians should have complete discretion to test patients whom they believe to be at risk of infection. As David Pence has pointed out, testing a patient's blood is part of the implied consent that a patient grants his physician. This covenant between physician and patient allows the physician tremendous latitude in testing for infectious agents. "The AIDS virus," Pence concludes, "does not belong to a protected class. If it makes its way into a hospital, only a routine doctor's order is required to expose it." Obstacles to testing prevent high-risk individuals from receiving the best possible care.

The outlook for the measures advocated in this article has brightened considerably in recent months. On January 1 the most comprehensive public-health response to the epidemic went into effect in Rhode Island. After considerable political turmoil, State Health Commissioner H. Denman Scott persuaded the legislature to enact a sweeping measure that requires reporting; partner notification; and routine HIV testing of certain hospital patients, couples applying for marriage licenses, and members of several high-risk groups, including people treated for sexually transmitted diseases and intravenous drug use. The new law also requires testing for most of the state's prison population.

Perhaps the most significant assault on the education-only mentality occurred in a speech delivered in Montreal at the Fifth International Conference on AIDS by New York City Health Commissioner Joseph. Joseph told the conferees that "we are fast approaching a time when we will have no choice but to change some of our most basic HIV-related policies." He then announced his support for a system of confidential reporting of HIV infection, coupled with aggressive partner-notification programs to notify those at risk of infection. He predicted that these techniques "will become standard public-health applications for controlling HIV infection and illness."

Dr. Joseph's willingness to make this case publicly is extremely significant. New York City's AIDS caseload exceeds those of Los Angeles, Washington, Houston, and San Francisco combined, so the policy changes that New York City officials contemplate will be seriously considered by their counterparts elsewhere. As the extent of infection among intravenous drug users becomes more apparent, moreover, the policies advocated by Dr. Joseph may be adopted by other public-health officials looking for an alternative to the education-only approach.

A growing number of states, including Michigan, Oregon, Colorado, South Carolina, Utah, Ohio, and Arkansas, have adopted thoughtful measures to control the epidemic. Significantly, the state medical societies in New York, Pennsylvania, and Florida have all endorsed many of the public-health protections—notably, confidential reporting—advocated here. Unfortunately, the states that now require confidential reporting account for less than 10 percent of the cases of full-blown AIDS reported to date. Until the states with the largest pools of infection—notably California and New York—adopt these measures, HIV will continue to claim the lives of thousands of innocent residents in the inner cities. The time has come for public-health officials everywhere to reevaluate the education-only approach to the epidemic.

DISCUSSION QUESTIONS

1. Magic Johnson's dramatic public announcement that he tested HIV positive was subsequently followed by his retirement from the National Basketball Association. Part of his decision to retire resulted from comments that other NBA players had made who were fearful of contracting AIDS. Should people who are HIV positive be permitted to play professional contact sports? What about in high school or college? What impact do you think this would have on testing for HIV? What other implications would it have?
2. How should decision makers decide how much money to put into AIDS research compared to research on other deadly diseases, such as various forms of cancer? What factors should be considered?
3. Should persons who are HIV positive be permitted to immigrate into the United States? Why?
4. Should governments subsidize or otherwise encourage needle exchange programs? Why?
5. Should high schools distribute condoms free to students?
6. What efforts should the federal government make to address the growing AIDS problem?

ADDITIONAL READINGS

"A National Strategy on AIDS." *Issues in Science and Technology* (Spring 1989).

Anderson, Warwick. "The New York Needle Trial: The Politics of Public Health in the Age of AIDS." *American Journal of Public Health* (November 1991).

Bayer, Ronald. *Private Acts, Social Consequences: AIDS and the Politics of Public Health* (New Brunswick, N.J.: Rutgers University Press, 1991).

Camus, Albert. *The Plague* (New York: Knopf, 1957). Originally published 1948.

Falco, Mathea, and Warren I. Cikins, eds. *Toward a National Policy on Drug and AIDS Testing* (Washington, D.C.: Brookings Institution, 1989).

Humm, Andy, and Frances Kunreuther. "The Invisible Epidemic: Teenagers and AIDS." *Social Policy* (Spring 1991).

Jennings, Chris. *Understanding and Preventing AIDS* (Cambridge, Mass.: Health Alert Press, 1988).

Johnston, William B., and Kevin R. Hopkins. *The Catastrophe Ahead: AIDS and the Case for a New Public Policy* (New York: Praeger, 1990).

Kirp, David L. "Fighting AIDS in the Streets: Needle Exchange Comes of Age." *The Nation* (April 26, 1993).

Kirp, David L. "Innocent Victims: The Politics of Pediatric AIDS." *The Nation* (May 14, 1990).

Kirp, David L. "The AIDS Perplex." *The Public Interest* (Summer 1989).

Langone, John. *AIDS: The Facts* (Boston: Little, Brown, 1991).

McKenzie, Nancy F., ed. *The AIDS Reader: Social, Political, and Ethical Issues* (New York: Penguin Books, 1991).

Nelkin, Dorothy, David P. Willis, and Scott V. Parris, eds. *A Disease of Society: Cultural and Institutional Responses to AIDS* (Cambridge: Cambridge University Press, 1991).

O'Malley, Padraig, ed. *The AIDS Epidemic: Private Rights and the Public Interest* (Boston: Beacon Press, 1989).

Shilts, Randy. *And the Band Played On: Politics, People, and the AIDS Epidemic* (New York: St. Martin's Press, 1987).

U.S. National Commission on Acquired Immune Deficiency Syndrome. *America Living with AIDS: Transforming Anger, Fear, and Indifference into Action: Report of the National Commission on Acquired Immune Deficiency Syndrome* (Washington, D.C.: The Commission, 1991).

Weiss, Lowell. "HIV's Weak Link." *The New Republic* (October 7, 1991).

Zinbert, Norman E. "Social Policy: AIDS and Intravenous Drug Use." *Dædalus* (Spring 1989).

5

NATIONAL HEALTH INSURANCE

"Should the United States Adopt a Single-Payer System of National Health Insurance?"

Health care policy is perhaps the largest, most complex, and most politically volatile public issue facing the United States today. The fears of many Americans who had either lost health insurance or were afraid they would, coupled with Harris Wofford's upset victory in the 1991 Pennsylvania Senate campaign that was waged largely over the issue of health care, forced the issue to command national political attention. While health care reform has been on the public agenda for decades, it is now almost universally accepted that some type of reform is both necessary and inevitable. Groucho Marx once said that "a hospital bed is a parked taxi with the meter running," and many Americans are now finding that their ability to afford a hospital visit is increasingly threatened.

Health care is the fastest growing portion of the federal budget and, as a share of national income, has risen rapidly over the past several decades to encompass one-seventh of the U.S. economy. Between 1970 and 1991, national health care expenditures rose from $261 billion to over $750 billion, while per-capita national health care expenditures rose from $1,130 to over $2,700 (all in constant 1991 dollars). Total and per-capita health care costs are higher in the United States than in any other nation, and Americans have grown accustomed to access to the finest medical technology in the world. Nevertheless, despite massive expenditures, satisfaction with health care is frequently higher abroad, and the United States still trails many industrialized nations in important measures of health care quality, such as infant mortality rates.* The principal public policy problems are twofold: rapidly increasing costs and the lack of adequate health care coverage for tens of millions of Americans. Few argue that universal coverage can be achieved without substantial government involvement, but the means for addressing skyrocketing health care costs are hotly disputed.

The high cost of health care in the United States is attributable to several sources. While analysts disagree over which effects are most important, high

---

* Infant mortality rates in 1993 were approximately 8.4 per 1,000 live births in the United States, compared with 4.3 in Japan, 6.0 in France, 6.6 in Germany, and 7.0 in Canada. Some perspective is necessary here, however—infant mortality rates are 52 per 1,000 births in Turkey, 77 in Bolivia, 109 in Bangladesh, 159 in Afghanistan, and 162 in Somalia (*Statistical Abstract of the United States, 1993*).

on the list are rapid and increasingly costly technological advances, slow productivity growth in the health care industry, and a system in which nearly every incentive is to provide health care regardless of cost. (Since 1960, the share of out-of-pocket health care expenditures has fallen from over half to approximately one-quarter of all health care expenditures.) Other factors, such as an aging U.S. population, contribute to increasing costs as well. Some analysts, including Henry Aaron of the Brookings Institution, point to a number of factors that have been exaggerated as contributors to high health care costs, such as high administrative costs, medical malpractice insurance, and unhealthy lifestyles of American citizens. (Aaron argues that while lifestyle changes, such as quitting smoking, have important benefits, they will only minimally reduce health care costs, if at all, because beneficiaries will subsequently die from illnesses that are even more costly to treat.)[1]

Besides cost-containment measures, universal coverage is the other central element in health care reform proposals. Aside from the obvious personal anguish of not knowing whether one or one's family can receive proper medical attention, there are other social, economic, and distributive considerations of having so many individuals—estimates vary, but range to upwards of 37 million—without health insurance. Some cannot leave their jobs for fear of being denied health care insurance from a new employer due to "preexisting conditions" or ailments that a prospective insurer may regard as too expensive to cover, such as AIDS. Further, some argue that the lack of preventative care encouraged by some health insurance plans leads to medical emergencies that could have been avoided with proper initial care (health maintenance plans are generally an exception). As Senator Edward Kennedy said, "what we have today in the United States is not so much a health-care system as a disease-cure system." Many inner-city hospitals are deluged with patients needing emergency care, costs that the hospitals are forced to recover elsewhere, such as by increasing the costs to paying patients. Finally, it should be noted that the uninsured in the United States are not representative of the nation as a whole, but are disproportionately minorities and the poorly educated. According to a 28-month survey from February 1985 to May 1987, 5.9 percent of African Americans and 11.3 percent of Hispanics had no coverage for the entire period, compared with 4.0 percent of whites; 6.8 percent of those with less than twelve years of schooling had no coverage, compared with 3.7 percent with twelve to fifteen years of schooling and 1.5 percent with sixteen or more years of schooling.[2] Increasingly, however, health care reform has become a concern of middle America as well, with layoffs at all levels forcing those who never feared for coverage to do without. Moreover, even those currently insured fear losing health insurance should they transfer or lose their jobs.

Proponents of universal coverage argue also that access to basic medical care is a right that should be accorded all U.S. citizens regardless of their ability to pay. Universal coverage cannot be had without a massive redistribution in health care spending, however. Most of the redistribution would be progressive, depending on the financing mechanism, but also capricious.

For example, industries that currently provide health insurance, such as the automobile industry, would gain windfall benefits from a national system of health insurance, while industries that do not currently pay for health insurance would most likely experience losses. Therefore, the political obstacles to reform are as substantial as the political imperatives to do something. Any universal system will increase costs to the federal government, if only to cover the currently uninsured, and some schemes seek to replace private insurance with public financing.

One issue of health care reform that has drawn considerable media and scholarly attention is the applicability of the Canadian "single-payer" health care system to the United States. A smaller proportion of health care costs are financed publicly in the United States than in any other industrialized nation. In 1988, for example, 42 percent of health care expenditures in the United States were publicly financed, compared with 73 percent in Germany and Japan, 74 percent in France, and 86 percent in the United Kingdom. Indeed, no member of the Organization for European Cooperation and Development finances less than 60 percent of health expenditures publicly. (Aaron argues that the portion of a country's health care costs that are privately financed is positively related to health care costs; therefore, public financing could lower overall costs as well.) In the following articles, Theodore Marmor, professor of public policy and management at Yale University, argues that the Canadian health care system, while not perfect, can provide a workable model for health care reform in the United States. The similarity of Canada's political system to ours makes it an ideal country from which to learn. The three elements that make the Canadian system successful—universal coverage, centralized financial responsibility, and political accountability—could all be successfully transferred to the United States and would result in a vastly improved health care system. Taking the opposite stance, physician William Goodman questions the advisability of modeling health care reform after the Canadian system, emphasizing the negative aspects of that system, such as high and rapidly rising costs, difficulty in accessing special medical equipment, and the fact that demands on the system are open-ended while the funding is limited. While a similar system could be established in the United States, argues Goodman, its positive effects would be only temporary, and it would result in long-range catastrophe for both the economy and the health care system. Marmor and Goodman expand on these arguments below.

Endnotes

1. Henry J. Aaron, "Health Care Financing," in Henry J. Aaron and Charles L. Schultze, eds., *Setting Domestic Priorities: What Can Government Do?* (Washington, D.C.: Brookings Institution, 1992).
2. U.S. Department of Commerce, Bureau of the Census, *Statistical Abstract of the United States, 1991* (Washington, D.C.: U.S. Government Printing Office, 1991).

YES

Canada's Health-Care System: A Model for the United States?

Theodore R. Marmor

If there is any part of American life that is now regularly criticized as unaffordable, unfair, and uncontrollable, it is medical care. The claim that American medicine is "in crisis" is of course not new—both Senator Edward M. Kennedy (D-Mass.) and President Richard Nixon agreed on that in 1971. What is new is the extension of alarm to American business leaders, who are seriously worried about skyrocketing health-insurance premiums and whose complaints have transformed the media's coverage of American medicine.

One sign of this transformed discussion is the unexpected prominence of Canada's health-care system in American debates over what can and should be done about the medical care "crisis" in the United States. In the past two years especially, commissions and commentators have taken up the topic of serious reform in American medical care with vigor. The leaders of the Chrysler Corporation—particularly its flamboyant head, Lee Iacocca, but also its board member and the former United States secretary of health and human services, Joseph Califano—published widely cited pieces criticizing American medical practices and lauding Canada's national health insurance program. A new organization of American doctors—Physicians for a National Health Program—made Canada its model and published its recommendation of a "Canadian-style" plan in the *New England Journal of Medicine*.

Whatever the catalyst, the Canadian model gained popularity with media commentators, surprising Canadians so accustomed to American neglect. In the spring and summer of 1989, all three American television networks, National Public Radio, and the major newspapers offered stories on Canadian medical care and its financing. Congressional committees began to ask Canadian experts to testify, and political organizations sent parades of representatives to Canada on crash study tours. But the most striking evidence of the seriousness with which American commentators have taken the Canadian model were the attacks on it by the American Medical Association (AMA).

Under the seemingly innocently titled "Public Alert Program," the AMA committed $2.5 million in 1989 to "telling millions of Americans the facts about the Canadian health-care system." In a campaign reminiscent of its 1948 attack on President Harry Truman's proposed national health insurance scheme, the AMA began to place advertisements in the major media and to supply background materials for a blitz of editorials, opinion pieces, and reports about Canada.

Why should the AMA be so concerned about the Canadian example of national health insurance? Why, in turn, should the Health Insurance Association of America (HIAA) devote expensive staff energy to producing what amounts to a book asserting that no matter how appealing the Canadian model is, it would be neither politically acceptable nor practical to implement? The answer is not terribly complicated. Over the past five years, business, labor, and popular discontent with American medicine has crystallized. There is widespread political interest in substantial change, and the Canadian example has been used widely enough for criticism to warrant counterattack from those with the greatest stake in the status quo.

Contrary to the message of the AMA and the HIAA, the Canadian system not only works reasonably well—it pays for universal access to ordinary medical care, maintains a generally high level of quality, is administratively efficient, and restrains the growth of health-care costs far more effectively than any of the myriad cost-containment schemes tried in the United States—but is as adaptable to American circumstances as one could imagine a foreign model to be.

CAN THE U.S. LEARN FROM ABROAD?

Canada, France, and Germany provide their citizens with universal health insurance coverage at a cost of between 8 and 9.5 percent of gross national product (GNP). Britain, Japan, and Australia provide it for between 6 and 8 percent of GNP. The United States, as is so often noted, spends more than 12 percent of GNP on health care—more than any other country—and yet ranks below all the members of the Organization for European Cooperation and Development in terms of infant mortality and life expectancy. Yet for all the money spent, there are still some 35 million Americans without health insurance, and an undetermined number who have inadequate insurance. The United States is obviously doing something wrong.

When other countries achieve what the United States says it would like to attain, it makes good sense to look abroad. But for Americans there are particularly revealing difficulties in looking abroad for lessons—whether in government or commerce. The American public is somewhat skittish about America's uniqueness, educated to believe in a special mission and character of this "city on a hill." Crossnational comparisons can easily arouse xenophobia, with defenders of the status quo ever ready to invoke the claim that "America is just different."

Three dangers complicate the politics of American–Canadian health-care policy arguments. First is the widespread incidence of well-financed distortion, the myth-making exemplified by the AMA campaign. Second is the mistaken notion that if there is any way in which the two nations differ, they are not "comparable." (There are some hilarious examples of this fallacy of comparative difference in the recent media attention to Canada. One claim of Canada's irrelevance to the United States, written by a "surgeon from White Plains" for the opinion page of *The New York Times*, noted the fact that 90 percent of Canada's population lives within 100 miles of the American border.)

Less hilarious but more important working illustrations of the fallacy of comparative difference show up regularly in the comments of American health-care policy analysts. For instance, Alain Enthoven, a Stanford University economist who has closely examined American medical reform, frankly admits Canada's superior performance but challenges its relevance. In a debate in the summer of 1990 about what to do about America's medical "mess," Enthoven argued against wasting any more time talking about Canada. Canadian culture and politics are so different, he alleged, that a serious attempt to borrow from their undeniably good experience was "off the radar screen of American possibility."

The assertion that Canada's experience is not relevant is supported by sociologist Seymour Martin Lipset in his recently published work. According to Lipset, Canadians respect government far more than Americans do, a contention buttressed by the difference between the Canadian founding document and the American Declaration of Independence. According to their charter, Canadians are committed to "peace, order, and good government," while Americans look to the individualistic "pursuit of happiness."

Never has so much been claimed with so little evidence; serious comparative research on public opinion shows no fundamental difference between the North American publics—a somewhat wider range on the Canadian left to be sure, but a distribution that leads most comparativists to group the United States and Canada together as similar liberal democracies in their creeds.

Canada's path to and experience with national health insurance provides American policymakers with a perfect opportunity for crossnational learning. The United States shares with Canada a common language and political roots, a comparably diverse population with a similar distribution of living standards, increasingly integrated economies, and a tradition of fractious but constitutional federalism that makes political disputes similar though obviously not identical. Moreover, until Canada consolidated its national health insurance in 1971, the patterns and styles of medical care in both countries were nearly identical. (Indeed, Canadian regulators used the United States Joint Commission on Hospital Accreditation to judge their hospitals' acceptability until well after World War II.)

Three questions emerge in examining the Canadian health-care experience. The first is whether Canada's medical-care system is truly exemplary and worth importing. The second is whether a Canadian-style program is politically feasible in the United States. And third, even if desirable as a model and politically acceptable, can Canadian national health insurance be adapted to American circumstances?

CANADA'S EXEMPLARY PERFORMANCE

The basic outline of Canada's national health insurance is clear. The federal government conditionally promises each province that it will prepay roughly 40 percent of the costs of all necessary medical care. The federal grant is available so long as the province's health insurance program is universal (covering all citizens), comprehensive (covering all conventional hospital and medical care), accessible (no limits on services and no extra charges to patients), portable (each province recognizes the others' coverage), and publicly administered (under control of a public, nonprofit organization). All 10 provinces maintain health insurance plans satisfying these criteria. The provincial ministry of health is the only payer in each province. There are no complex eligibility tests or complicated definitions of insured services. Administrative costs, as a consequence, are negligible by American standards.

The practical dynamics of Canada's program are also simple, at least in outline. Annual negotiations between provincial governments and the providers of care determine the hospital budgets and the level of physicians' fees. As in the United States, most hospitals are nonprofit community institutions and physicians practice (under fee-for-service payment) in diverse individual and group settings. Patients choose their own doctors; doctors bill the province; and hospitals work from global budgets, not itemized billings. Disagreements over insurance claims, gaps in coverage, and bureaucratic incomprehensibility are, for practical purposes, nonexistent. Canadian patients and providers never have to file multiple claims to different insurers. (American Medicare beneficiaries might well have to file claims with three or more insurers, and a physician or hospital treating Medicaid patients might have to wait six months or more for payment.)

Most of the negative effects economic theory and Canadian doctors predicted—worrisome physician flight, rationing of lifesaving care, long queues, and technological obsolescence—have not emerged. There is, and has always been, some movement of highly trained, highly prized personnel from Canada to the United States. Physicians are no exception. But this trend was not greatly affected by Canadian national health insurance, and the numbers have always been small, not enough to offset a steady increase in the number of practicing physicians. As Table 5-1 shows, Canada's physician–population ratio has been, and remains, comparable to that of the United States.

TABLE 5-1
Physicians per 100,000 People, United States and Canada

Year	United States	Canada
1965	155	130
1970	159	146
1975	178	172
1980	201	184
1985	224	206
1987	234	216

Source: Organization for Economic Cooperation and Development, Health Care Systems in Transition: The Search for Efficiency (Paris, 1990), tables 27 and 61.

At the outset, the existing physician fee schedules of provincial medical associations were accepted by the provincial governments, although in most provinces payments were initially set somewhat below 100 percent to reflect the elimination of a doctor's risk of unpaid debts. Since that time, changes in the fee schedules have been negotiated by provincial medical associations and ministries of health. The typical process of setting fees is one of extended negotiation, not unilateral imposition. Physicians were the highest-paid professionals in Canada before the introduction of universal medical insurance; they still are.

RATIONING CARE

Canada does ration medical care. So does the United States and every other country in the world. What counts is not the presence of rationing (or allocation) but the basis for and the extent of restricted access to health care. The United States continues to ration by the ability to pay—a process largely determined by race, class, and employment circumstances. Access to care and the quality of care vary enormously, and many in the United States—particularly the poor or poorly insured—experience long waiting lists and substandard facilities, if they receive care at all. By contrast, Canada and most other developed countries try to provide a more uniform standard of care to the entire population. Medical care is allocated largely on the basis of relative medical need, which is determined by physician judgment, not by insurance status, bureaucratic rules, or arbitrary age limits.

At certain times and in some places, substantial waiting lists for selected surgical and diagnostic procedures occur. But the overall rates of hospital use per capita are considerably higher in Canada than in the United States. Most patients are cared for in a timely manner, and long waiting lists reflect managerial problems more than chronic shortages of facilities. Emergency care is available immediately to everyone.

There is no question that some expensive, high-technology items are not as available in Canada as they are in the United States. Canada has a full range of high-technology facilities, but in considerably less abundance and with little competition for market share. Expensive capital equipment is first approved only for highly specialized centers, and subsequent diffusion is closely controlled by provincial ministries of health. This control results in lower rates of use for some technologies in Canada—cardiac surgery, magnetic resonance imaging, lithotripsy, and so on (see Table 5-2). This is not necessarily a bad thing. Throughout North America, there is concern about the appropriate use of expensive new procedures. Inappropriate use is both financially costly and medically dangerous to patients.

The quality of a nation's health care is never simple to measure. Many critics view the slower diffusion and limited use of some new technologies in Canada as evidence of lower quality care. If quality is defined as more high-technology services regardless of relative effectiveness, then the United States

TABLE 5-2

Comparative Availability of Selected Medical Technologies, United States and Canada (units per million people)

Medical Technology	U.S.	Canada	Ratio: U.S./Canada
Open-heart surgery	3.26	1.23	2.7:1
Cardiac catheterization	5.06	1.50	3.4:1
Organ transplantation	1.31	1.08	1.2:1
Radiation therapy	3.97	0.54	7.4:1
Extracorporeal shock wave lithoscopy	0.94	0.16*	5.9:1
Magnetic-resonance imaging	3.69	0.46	8.0:1

Note: United States data are for 1987, Canada for 1989 except where indicated.
* 1988
Source: D. A. Rublee, "Medical Technology in Canada and the U.S.," *Health Affairs*, Fall 1989, p. 180.

certainly offers higher quality medical care. If, however, quality is defined by health results rather than by the use of high technology, then there is no evidence of a Canadian disadvantage. If life expectancy and infant mortality measure the quality of a health-care system, Canada has a definite advantage. And if consumer satisfaction is a critical component of quality, then both polls and political behavior put Canadian national health insurance well in the lead.

The generally high levels of Canadian satisfaction suggest the importance of the way health-care quality is distributed. When quality is defined as the best technologies and facilities available to the most privileged members of a population, rather than as the facilities available to the average individual, American medical care ranks among the best in the world. But major aspects of American medical care—the limited extent of immunization, the large number of pregnant women without regular medical attention, and the risk of bankruptcy from illness—would be considered intolerable in other comparably wealthy countries. Canada has fewer centers of technological excellence, but the average level of care is, by any definition, at least equal to that in the United States.

ADAPTING CANADA'S HEALTH-CARE SYSTEM

What would make the Canadian option not only more attractive to the American electorate, but also easier to implement in the American context? Part of the answer lies in distinguishing the necessary from the incidental elements of the Canadian success story in universal health insurance. The Canadian program combines three features that have made its cost, access, and quality acceptable over nearly 20 years of full-scale operation.

One of the features is universality of coverage. All Canadians are insured on the "same terms and conditions." This universality has made it politically impossible in Canada to deal with cost pressures by stealth or to permit end runs around the controls. Second, there is a clear center of financial responsibility in

Canada: a ministry of health or its equivalent in each province. Financing medical care under concentrated rather than fragmented auspices is crucial to the third component of Canada's system: clear political accountability for the cost and quality of and access to Canadian medical care. These three features—universal access, a responsible financing agency, and accountable political leaders to answer for the balance among cost, quality, and access—explain why Canada's performance has been superior to that of the United States.

But what do these features of the Canadian model mean for possible American adaptations? What sorts of changes could be made without losing what has been necessary for Canada's relatively successful experience with national health insurance?

Canada's universalism is strong in two ways. Every Canadian is literally on the same provincial health insurance plan as his or her neighbor—the equivalent of every Californian belonging to one Blue Cross/Blue Shield plan. What's more, Canadians have the same coverage under their provincial plan: "equal terms and conditions," not varied options. In the health sphere, Canada is probably more egalitarian than any other comparable industrial democracy. Private insurers are forbidden by law to sell supplementary coverage for publicly insured services. And to maintain the "equal terms" of access, Canadian doctors since 1984 have for all practical purposes been prevented from charging patients anything above the government's fee schedule.

Not all of these Canadian features are necessary for an acceptable form of universal health insurance. Canada did not start with such a firmly egalitarian version. The Hall Commission of 1964–1966, the royal commission that justified extending government hospital insurance to medical care, defined universal coverage as no less than 95 percent of the citizens in each province. While desirable on egalitarian grounds, literal universality has not been a necessary feature of Canada's success. American reformers need not insist on Canada's strong contemporary form of universal enrollment.

"Uniform" conditions would also be less compelling than in Canada. For Americans to be in the same boat does not necessarily require that the boat's cabins all be the same size or have the same view. What is essential is that the health insurance boat include most Americans on roughly comparable terms.

It is on the issue of the terms of benefits and the constraints on "supplementation" that the most acrimonious disputes are likely to break out. Could the United States (or a state) forego the Canadian ban on supplementary health insurance for services covered under a universal plan without losing financial control? Would it be unacceptable to permit physicians (or other medical professionals paid under fee-for-service arrangements) to charge their patients more than the agreed-on schedule of fees?

The answer here is ambiguous. On the first point, Canada has never experimented. But other nations with acceptable national health insurance programs have supplementary insurance that coexists with public coverage. As for charges that are above negotiated rates ("extra-billing" or "balance-billing" in the jargon of health economics), the answer is clearer. The ability to contain medical costs depends on establishing firm limits; extra-billing violates those limits and reintroduces barriers to access that universal health insurance is meant to lower. No successful national health insurance program has permitted this practice for long; Canada found over time that balance-billing became a serious problem in many communities, threatening both the uniformity of treatment and the access to treatment itself. Both supplementary insurance and extra-billing, when widespread, threaten equitable cost control.

FINANCING NATIONAL HEALTH CARE

Whether Canada's concentration of finance in provincial ministries of health has been crucial to its successful control of medical-care costs is the second issue to evaluate. Is the location of responsibility at the provincial as opposed to federal level vital? The other key question is whether Canada's public financing and direct governmental administration are required for political accountability: an identifiable budget accounts for a jurisdiction's overall health expenditure.

The crossnational evidence on the first question suggests that it is the concentration of financial responsibility, not its precise location, that is crucial to countervailing inflationary health-care cost pressures. Canada, by constitutional requirement, had no choice but to use provincial governments to administer health insurance. Great Britain, by contrast, concentrates financial responsibility in the national Ministry of Health, and Sweden does so in each of its county councils. The lesson for the United States is that there are options.

The second, more difficult question concerns the direct accountability of the processes by which health-care funds are raised and spent. Public financing makes Canadian outlays for health highly visible. At the same time, Canadian provinces could, and some did, use preexisting health insurance companies as political buffers between physicians and the government. In the mid-1960s, Ontario used these intermediaries to manage the flow of funds and the processing of claims. Such a buffer seemed important then as a concession to the deep hostility many Canadian doctors felt regarding government medical insurance. In fact, the Canadian provinces that used financial intermediaries at the outset abandoned them after a few years. They made administration complicated and more expensive and, once their role in moderating conflict was no longer necessary, they seemed useless (except to the insurance companies).

One can certainly imagine the use of such intermediaries in the United States. This, after all, has been the pattern with American Medicare since 1965—an arrangement that draws on private expertise and "economizes" on the number of public employees. Canadians found such indirect management cumbersome and more expensive to manage than direct administration. But contracting out financial tasks is certainly, on the Canadian evidence, compatible with political accountability.

In the United States of the 1990s, however, the crucial political problem facing national health insurance advocates is the public's hostility toward increased taxes. Can one imagine Canadian-style government health insurance working without direct public finance? In other words, what would be lost if, for example, state regulatory authorities set the terms of medical-care financing, negotiated with hospitals and physicians, and required that employers finance health insurance directly or pay into a state fund a fixed amount per employee? However the point is phrased, the question remains the same: Is it possible to have the right level of countervailing power without the fusion of taxing and negotiating responsibility?

The answer to that question is far from obvious. In some European countries—Germany in particular—national and state governments have played a powerful regulatory role without Canada's single-payer feature. The German government constrains the negotiations among physicians, hospitals, and the thousands of sickness funds without channeling social insurance financing through conventional public tax accounts. It sets the rules by which the parties operate and each of the sickness funds faces the full financial consequences of its members' medical care. There is both financial accountability and complicated administration in the German example. What the United States should notice is that it does not have the German history of lifelong involvement with one health insurance institution.

What this suggests is that the degree of responsibility for health financing—and the clarity about where that accountability lies—is not solely determined by the details of public finance. There are forms of mandated health insurance, which finances care on terms negotiated by public officials, that might closely resemble in practice the publicly financed, compulsory health insurance program found in Canada.

It is certainly possible to imagine mandated universal health insurance—with workable regulations drawn from German experience—working tolerably well in the United States. Such arrangements could address the problems of inflation, inadequate coverage, and political accountability, but less effectively than a system modeled after Canada's. The United States should be under no illusion here; there are choices available, with different tradeoffs among acceptability, effectiveness, and administrative complexity. What the United States has at the moment is a vicious circle of trouble; a system like Canada's is possible, but a less direct program would be an improvement.

This sort of reasoning led some policy analysts to suggest adapting the Canadian model along the lines suggested earlier. Their proposal treats the state health department as the negotiating agent of universal health insurance, insurance made universal by the accretion of mandated coverage for workers and their families, Medicare for those over 65 and the disabled, Medicaid for the poor, and a new insurance plan for those not in these categories. No one starting from a blank slate would seek this rather complicated version of universal coverage through aggregation, clear public responsibility for costs, and decentralized administration. But, as a third choice, it should be tolerable.

THE CASE FOR THE CANADIAN MODEL

In the early 1970s, American experts paid considerable attention to Canada's recently completed program of national health insurance. That scrutiny was part of the substantial interest in an American form of universal health insurance. When the realities of stagflation in the 1970s and early 1980s removed national health insurance from the American political agenda, the lessons of Canada's experience were put aside, hardly noticed except by specialists in health policy. The reawakening of American interest in Canada comes without anything like a widely shared American appreciation of how Canadian health insurance works in practice.

The result of that disparity between interest and knowledge is a very uneven discussion of what the United States can and cannot learn from its neighbor to the north, let alone what adaptations to American circumstances a conscious effort to borrow from Canada's example would entail. Instead, the discussion of Canadian health insurance resembles a shouting match, with enthusiasts pointing to evidence about citizen satisfaction and relatively low expenditures per capita and detractors arguing either that Canada is too different for the United States to take seriously as a model, or that the model itself is terrible because it creates long lines, causes doctors to emigrate, and disappoints patients.

If there is any country from which the United States can learn, it is Canada. Having had similar medical-care arrangements for most of the twentieth century, Canada and the United States have conducted over the past 20 years a fateful experiment in forms of medical finance. It is two decades and hundreds of billions of dollars too late to contend that the United States should have acted on Canadian lessons in the early 1970s. That option was simply not politically available in the economic aftermath of the first oil crisis in 1973. But that does not mean, in the 1990s and beyond, that Americans cannot learn from Canada's example.

The central lesson of the Canadian experiment is that the balance among cost, quality, and access is relatively easy to evaluate. What Canada illustrates clearly is that a sensibly organized national health insurance system can work in a political community like that in the United States, that universal coverage, coherent financial responsibility, and clear political accountability are the central ingredients of success, and that a population accustomed to the same standard of medical care as the United States can take pride in what in essence are 10 provincial Blue Cross/Blue Shield plans with comprehensive benefits to which everyone belongs as a matter of right. If that were understood clearly, the problems of adapting the Canadian model to America would seem less daunting.

NO

The Canadian Model: Could It Work Here?

William E. Goodman

With the increasing concern about deficiencies in health care delivery in the United States, and the Canadian experiment looming before you in the north, the question in the title of my talk was inevitable.

I was in private practice in Canada long before the advent of health insurance there and continued to practice for some 15 years after its introduction. From this experience, I can draw certain conclusions. However, to discuss the question that is before us, I must begin by asking some questions of my own.

CONSTITUTIONAL AND POLITICAL ISSUES

Because I acquired an honors degree in economics and political science before studying medicine, the first issue that came to my mind was whether it is constitutionally *possible* for the U.S. governments (state and/or federal) to institute (legally) a Canadian-style system.

Although you and I speak the same language, have much the same culture, are exposed to the same media influences, and spend a great deal of time in each other's countries, you must understand that the Canadian political structure, not to mention its national psyche, is very different from yours. Our parliamentary system, unlike your republican form, allows the man at the head of the party having a simple majority of seats in the House of Commons to do almost anything—and to get away with it. We have recently acquired a much-vaunted, so-called Charter of Rights. But unlike your Bill of Rights, it was so emasculated before being passed that it isn't worth the paper it's printed on. As for our psyches, the best way to compare them is to tell you that, while the key words in your Declaration of Independence are "life, liberty, and the pursuit of happiness," the key words in our constitution are "peace, order, and good government."

By and large, Canadians are middle-of-the-roaders who love security and hate to rock the boat. In contrast, Americans are a nation of protesters who tend to admire boat-rockers and self-made achievers. As Professor Russel Knight of the University of Western Ontario once said, "In the United States, everyone aspires to be an entrepreneur; in Canada, everyone wants to be a civil servant."

Notwithstanding these differences, both our governments learned long ago how to get around constitutional limitations and embarrassments. (Look at what's happened here since the passage of California's Proposition 13, and Washington's Gramm–Rudman Act.) In health care as in other matters, legislators have known since time immemorial that what could not be achieved by purely legislative measures could nonetheless be attained by fiscal arm-twisting—in other words, by bribery. *It's legal bribery, but still bribery, to make opponents an offer they can't refuse*. That's what happened in Canada. Under our constitution, the federal government has virtually no powers in health matters. Yet, by taxing *everyone* across the country indiscriminately, but offering billions of dollars in grants to *only* those provinces that introduced a national health insured system of the federal government's choice, it finally forced all of them to participate.

From what I know of your constitutional setup, I believe it would be much more difficult, in legal terms, for your government to impose its will on a reluctant State, reluctant public, or reluctant profession. Nonetheless, I expect that the outcome for the U.S. health care system will ultimately be determined by the power of the dollar, not by ringing Jeffersonian statements.

PUBLIC ACCEPTANCE

Even if a Canadian-style model is constitutionally possible here, a second question arises: Would your doctors, your hospitals, your diagnostic laboratories, your insurance companies, your employers, and, most of all, your patients be prepared to pay the enormous cost involved? A recent U.S. public opinion poll showed that, although a majority of Americans would love access to such a Canadian-patterned system, only a very small minority were prepared to pay even $50 more a year. (So much for the validity of polls.)

And the cost is not measured solely in dollars. Much more important costs are a lack of access to health care personnel, institutions, diagnostic and therapeutic facilities; waits for essential services and surgery that run into years; and what I regret to have to refer to as the "lowest-common-denominator" quality of medical care. More about the last later.

HEALTH CARE COSTS

It has been claimed that, according to the most recent statistics, Canadian medical care uses up about 8.6 percent of our gross national product, with full universal coverage, while U.S. health care consumes 12 percent of your GNP, even though some 35 million Americans reportedly have no health insurance at all. Without exploring possible reasons for the difference (e.g., leaving aside the fact that a lower percentage in Canada may actually mean a lower level of accessibility and quality), I find these figures highly suspect, based on previous experience with government statistics.

Our government's statisticians, like yours, are capable of enormous errors. Let me read you an Associated Press report from Washington, dated September 5, 1989:

Chagrined economists watched in horror as the government made revision after revision last month in data on past performance that they use in their prognostications. The net result was that the economy was not nearly as weak during the spring as originally thought. Consumers spent at least double the pace first reported, employment growth was much stronger, and the overall economy, rather than limping along at an anemic annual growth rate of 1.7 percent from April through June, actually grew at a healthy 2.7 percent rate. . . . The government's reports on factory orders and retail sales have been notoriously unreliable, and analysts have grown accustomed to looking at the figures with skepticism. . . . The Labor Department's monthly employment report—generally considered one of the most accurate economic measurements—veered far off the mark earlier this year. Almost half the actual job growth in April, May, and June was missed in the original report.

As you all know, politicians and their minions are past masters in the art of disguising, manipulating, and fudging figures to their advantage, in addition to making presumably honest but gigantic errors. You will remember, to quote Mark Twain, that there are three kinds of lies: lies, damn lies, and statistics.

However, even if we accept the estimate of the percentages of our respective GNPs devoted to health care costs, *the expense of health care in Canada is one of the major factors in a Canadian federal per capita debt and per capita annual deficit that is twice as bad as yours.* As to provincial budgets, over a third of the revenue is already committed to health care, and the proportion is rising inexorably.

Notwithstanding these huge expenditures, the obvious deficiencies of the system are such that everyone—the public, the hospitals, the media, the doctors and nurses, the health economists, the budgetary experts, and even the government's own representatives—speak incessantly about the crisis in our health care system. So what has gone wrong?

Apart from any political philosophy that you may espouse, be it free-enterprise or welfare-state, it's essential to realize that the basic and unalterable flaw in any system like the Canadian model is that, in economic terms, it is an open-ended scheme with closed-end funding. In other words, the potential demands are completely unrestricted, but the money to pay for them is not. It's like giving the public a no-dollar-limit, no-responsibility-for-payment medical credit card—an open invitation to unlimited abuse by both patients and doctors. Therein lies the politicians' dilemma: how to continue to buy votes with grandiose give-away schemes when it becomes evident that the money is running out. This is a generic problem, not confined to any one country or system of government. Its end result, no matter where practiced or how implemented, is always bankruptcy—unless major (and painful and politically very unpopular) changes are instituted in time, to the chagrin, disappointment, and detriment of the sick.

CANADIAN VIGNETTES: TRUE STORIES OF "UNIVERSAL ACCESS"

How does one define the "Canadian model"? Let me paint you a few scenarios—all taken from the pages of Canadian newspapers and magazines, or from our broadcast media.

1. *You're sick and need access to some special diagnostic or therapeutic equipment*, but because of the constraints of government global budgeting, your hospital (in this case the largest teaching hospital of the largest university faculty of medicine in Canada's largest city) can't afford it. Hospital administrators are having to go, hat in hand, begging for handouts from the general public or former patients, to buy the necessary machinery.

2. *You're sick and need to be admitted to your local community hospital but can't get in.* Notwithstanding the waiting list, many months long, of people with elective or urgent problems, the hospital has decided to close 12 percent of its beds—one in eight—taking them completely out of service because of the government's refusal to provide adequate funding. At the same time, the hospital is legally prohibited from accepting any additional private payments that might have permitted it to continue in full operation.

3. *You're sick and need cardiac bypass surgery*, but the list of patients waiting for similar and sometimes more urgent surgery is so long that your hospital admission is postponed 11 times in the year before you finally come to surgery. Or you die of cardiac disease before your turn comes up. This has happened to many patients.

4. *You need an elective procedure like a lens implant or hip transplant.* Since your hospital has used up the annual allotment that the government allows, you are willing to pay the cost of the prosthesis yourself, rather than waiting ten months or a year until the hospital receives a new allotment. The answer is no. *The government will not allow you to pay for your own procedure, and it is illegal for a doctor or hospital to participate in such a queue-jumping measure.* (Interestingly enough, if you're an American or other foreigner who has seen fit to come to Canada at your own expense for the surgery, it *is* permissible.)

As Professor Arnold Aberman put it:

> The monopoly on health care exercised by the government here is such that, if the government decides that *it* can't afford it, [Canadians] are not allowed [privately] to buy it.

The only way for Canadians to get around this idiotic rule is to leave the country to go to the U.S.A. for the diagnostic or therapeutic modality they require.

5. *Your wife, your mother, your sister, or your daughter is asymptomatic but wants the reassurance of mammography or a Pap smear to rule out early breast or cervical cancer.* She has great difficulty arranging this because the government has decreed to the profession that these procedures are justified only in certain age or other risk groups and are not required more often than at certain specified intervals. The criteria used for making such determinations are epidemiological and have nothing to do with the well-being of the individual patient. To use their own euphemistic words, the government asks: "Is it cost-effective? Can it withstand economic appraisal?"

6. *You've had a sudden myocardial infarction* and your family wants your doctor to administer the drug TPA or APSAC immediately. They have read that it is more effective than the streptokinase currently used in most Canadian

hospitals. The government or the hospital will not be willing to pay for the newer drug because it is much more expensive. And even if your family were willing to pay the extra cost themselves, permission for the doctor or hospital to use the drug might not be granted.

7. *You're a 37-year-old pregnant physician* in Vancouver and believe that you should have an amniocentesis to rule out genetic abnormalities in the fetus. By government edict, local doctors and hospitals cannot perform it, *even if you're willing to pay the total cost yourself,* unless you are over a certain age or have a specific history of genetic abnormalities. So you have to cross the border to Seattle if you wish to have the procedure, at considerable added expenditure of both time and money, *not* reimbursed by our government medical plan.

8. *You're a medical department head* in a university teaching hospital and need a certain complement of interns and residents for your department to function properly. But the government (which now pays the salaries of in-hospital personnel) says *no.* It thinks the country already has too many people in that specialty and besides, it can only afford half or two-thirds of the number you requested, so you'll have to make do with less. In most cases, the government even refuses to allow house officers to work without pay (as some are willing to do in order to acquire necessary practical experience and academic credit).

9. *You're head of housekeeping* in one of the largest university teaching hospitals in Montreal and need a minimum number of workers to keep the wards clean and tidy. "Sorry," says the hospital administrator. The halls may be littered with old cartons, soft drink cans, and other garbage, but with its limited government budget, the hospital has to cut corners somewhere. There is not even sufficient money to pay for the nurses who are desperately required—and nurses are far more important than floor cleaners.

10. *You're the mayor* in a small, remote northern Ontario community. Your community hospital desperately needs money to upgrade its facilities, the only ones available for a very large but sparsely populated region. In addition, you have great difficulty recruiting *any* doctors to settle and work in your rather less than desirable area. "That's your problem," say the provincial government authorities. They offer to give the hospital money only if, by refusing hospital privileges, you force any doctor working there to accept "capping," that is, maximum global annual payments.

11. *You're a family practitioner* and want to refer a patient with a particular problem to a particular specialist who has great expertise in that field. Unfortunately, he works in one of the hospitals in which doctors' incomes are capped annually, and he has already reached his maximum for the year. There being no incentive for him to work, since he would be earning absolutely nothing for the extra time and effort, he's off attending conferences, writing books, taking part in seminars, or even perhaps playing golf. Accordingly, your patient may have to wait eight to ten months for an appointment.

12. *You're a surgical specialist* doing cataract surgery or nasal surgery or arthroscopy. Tired of having a ten-month list of patients waiting for hospital facilities to become available, you decide to invest your own funds in your own first-class facility, thereby reducing your patients' wait to a couple of

weeks. "Uh, uh," says the government bureaucrat. First, you will have to have a special license. Second, the bureaucrats will decide if and where and by whom such facilities may be set up, what procedures they will be permitted to perform, and how much they will be allowed to charge. Furthermore, government control is such that they have the legal authority to walk in at any time without a search warrant to review your pattern of operations and your patient files and to seize any records they like.

13. *Your child has been born prematurely* and needs highly specialized neonatal care to survive. Too bad. Although you live close to a large city with teaching hospitals associated with a university medical faculty, many of the beds in the critical neonatal service lie empty, out of service because of lack of funding. No functioning bed is available for your child in the entire city, and he has to be flown hundreds of miles to another city, or perhaps across the border to Buffalo or Detroit, where such beds are much more readily found. It's true that under these circumstances the provincial government will pay for most of the hospital costs involved, but neither you nor your wife will be reimbursed for trips back and forth to that location, for the necessary hotel accommodations, for the long-distance telephone calls, or for lost wages. And there is no way to compensate a family for the emotional trauma of being hundreds of miles away from a loved one who is critically ill.

14. *You're a gourmet* who loves fatty French foods. You are approaching age 40 and have begun to worry about your cholesterol level. You ask your general practitioner or cardiologist to order the necessary laboratory tests. "Not necessary," says the health ministry—unless you're in a certain age group and demonstrate certain "identifying risk factors for coronary heart disease." Your GP isn't actually forbidden—yet—to order the tests, but he knows that if he does he'll be receiving telephone calls and letters from the ministry demanding that he justify his course of action. Net result: he probably won't order the test. As in most other areas of life, a threat, actual or implied, is sufficient for deterrence.

15. *You're an older physician* with a particular empathy for other old people and work 80-hour weeks visiting them at their homes or in nursing homes—calls that very few doctors are prepared to make nowadays and for which your patients are extremely grateful. But instead of receiving thanks from the health administrators, you are ordered to appear before a review committee. You've been "gouging the scheme," say the health police, costing the government thousands of dollars for "unnecessary visits"! You end up having to spend many hours of your precious time and many of your own dollars for a lawyer's services before you are completely exonerated by the quasi-judicial Medical Review Committee or the Health Disciplines Board.

16. *You're a specialist in private practice*, with a teaching appointment at a hospital affiliated with a medical school. Each year, the hospital, hit harder and harder by increasing costs due to technical advances and inflation, has been issuing more and more strident appeals to the medical staff for voluntary and sometimes not-so-voluntary donations to tide it over financial crises caused by government global budgets that often don't even cover the inflation rate.

Under our system, hospital appointments, especially those in university hospitals, are very limited; and your right to admit your patients to that hospital depends entirely on such an appointment. Your unwillingness to contribute annual "donations" on a scale deemed adequate by the hospital authorities may bring a veiled threat of freezing—or even termination—of your academic appointment. It's a form of hidden but nonetheless compulsory additional taxation, enforced by what is now essentially an arm of the government—the hospital. To quote the Dean of the Faculty of Health Sciences at one of our medical schools: "Governments across the country are in hot pursuit of cost containment. . . . The medical schools have become increasingly dependent on service income generated by practicing academic clinicians." So you have now become a de facto hospital employee, generating income for your employer not only by admitting your patients but also, willingly or unwillingly, sharing your own piece-work income with it.

17. *You're a radiologist* specializing in mammography, for which the government has heretofore paid a professional reading fee of $17.50. Now, because the incidence of breast cancer in women is about one in ten, the female public and particularly the militant feminist organizations have started clamoring for regular universal screening for adult women. To placate them, the government agrees to set up radiographic screening centers. However, because of the added cost, radiologists are informed that *since they should be able to read 40 such films per hour, the payment rate per patient will be reduced,* in Ontario to $10 and in British Columbia to $5.00. The radiologists' society, insisting that adequate readings cannot be done at a rate of more than eight per hour, is appalled, and predicts that such superficial mass-produced readings will result in missed cases of cancer. No matter: the health minister is interested in epidemiological, not individual outcomes.

18. *You have just been diagnosed as having cancer* and require immediate radiation therapy. You live in Canada's largest city, boasting the two largest cancer centers in the country, but you are told that both have such long waiting lists that they're not accepting new patients. You are instructed to report to a cancer center in a distant Canadian city, or more likely to an American center, at an enormous cost in time and inconvenience, as well as money, to you and your family.

19. *You are a doctor in a small community* in one of Canada's smaller provinces. Since these areas have trouble attracting doctors at the best of times, you're working to death trying to provide services to your patients. Along comes a politically appointed "Commission on Selected Health Care Programs," to tell you that:

a) The supply and activities of doctors will have to be controlled to stop spiralling health care costs; b) Doctors admit too many people to hospitals, run too many unnecessary tests, write too many prescriptions, and prescribe expensive brand-name drugs [instead of] generics; c) Doctors should be penalized if their patients are admitted to hospitals and not operated on within 48 hours or, if operated, are not released within their expected length of stay.

So much for professional independence.

20. *You're a long-suffering Canadian taxpayer* and have been comparing notes with American friends. If an American works full-time for a full year, your friends complain, the total burden of taxes is so heavy that it consumes his entire income from January 1 to May 3. In other words, he has to work four months of the year for the government. To your horror, you discover that the comparable figures for a citizen of Ontario are January 1 to July 7th! A Canadian has to work over *six* months solely to satisfy government's constantly increasing demand for taxes.

21. *You are a family doctor*, and a patient with a serious but not immediately life-threatening illness is furious when he's told that he'll have to wait three to six months for an appointment to see a particular specialist and six to 18 months for urgent hospitalization. What advice do you give him? The answer is obviously to buy a health insurance policy offered to Canadians by U.S. insurance companies for treatment in the U.S. Since 90 percent of Canadians live within 100 miles of the American border, it's no great problem for them to drive to Boston, Albany, Buffalo, Detroit, Cleveland, Seattle, or a dozen other border cities.

OTHER PROBLEMS

I'm sorry to overwhelm you with such a lengthy litany of horrors, but we see, hear, and read such repeated references in your media to the marvels of the Canadian model that I felt it essential you should know some of the warts on this much-touted scheme. I've restricted myself to the problems arising from the financial absurdity of the system. But there are many others, equally important: the total loss of medical confidentiality; the loss of morale and dedication among medical personnel; the loss of health care workers by emigration, change of vocation, or early retirement; the massive intrusion by the bureaucracy into the doctor–patient relationship; the civil servantization and inevitable unionization of the medical profession; and so on. It would take five more lectures of this length to describe in detail all the pernicious ramifications of socialized medicine, Canadian style.

WILL THE CANADIAN SYSTEM BE TRANSPLANTED?

Returning to the questions that I posed earlier: Could the U.S. government introduce a scheme like the Canadian one in this country, regardless of constitutional niceties? The answer is clearly yes. What the politicians can't do by purely legislative means, they will accomplish by financial coercion.

Will the U.S. accept it?

For the public, the answer, I'm sorry to say, is yes—overwhelmingly and gladly. They'd love it, because 95 percent of them won't understand its long-term effects on their lives, their liberties, their access to first-class medical care, or even on their pocketbooks. All they would know is that they had to pay nothing out of pocket at the time and place of actual medical service, at least initially. The vast majority of Canadians had and still have similar difficulties in associating "free" benefits on one hand with massive increases in taxes, public debt, and inflation on the other. Canadians still do not understand that their rapidly decreasing access to first-class medical care is an inevitable consequence of these "benefits."

As to industry, unionized facilities such as Lee Iacocca's Chrysler Corporation and many members of the National Association of Manufacturers have already indicated that they would welcome Canadian-style medicine with open arms. Why not? It would allow them to foist onto the general taxpayer most of the cost of their present employee health plans. In the long run, they'll rue the day, but industry tends to concentrate on the needs and stresses of the moment without much concern for the long-range perspective.

As to physicians, most would, sad to say, also approve of the Canadian scheme—whether because of inertia, as in older doctors; or out of a fatalistic resignation to what many consider inevitable; or because they realize, from the experience of the medical profession after introduction of national health insurance in other countries, that they will earn far *more* money than at present, at least for the first few years; or because they actually welcome increasing government intervention out of philosophical convictions, possibly due to having grown up in an increasingly welfare-state, do-gooder environment. Whatever the cause, I predict that over 80 percent of your doctors would raise no significant objection to national health insurance. Some will grumble and scream; some will threaten and issue bulletins; some may even withdraw services temporarily. But eventually, especially if significant financial or other penalties are involved, the rush to join the bandwagon will be overwhelming. This has been the experience in nations all over the world, and I see no reason to believe that U.S. response will be different. You have already seen a portent of this in the alacrity with which American doctors have joined HMOs or accepted Medicare assignment, even where it was not mandatory.

As to health-related industries, their acceptance will at first be grudging because of the perceived governmental regulation. However, I would remind you of American economics Nobel laureate George Stigler's famous pronouncement that regulation usually ends up benefiting those being regulated. Consider the billions of dollars earned by the defense industries under government regulation. Who minds a little supervision when the supervisors will approve a $650 toilet seat?

WOULD THE SYSTEM LEAD TO BANKRUPTCY?

The U.S. is still better off financially than Canada. But that situation will not long survive the introduction of a few of our open-ended social welfare schemes like national health insurance. Soon, the U.S., like Canada, would start lowering medical and institutional standards and reducing access to care. However, it takes a number of years for this to happen. In the meantime, the politician who fostered and promoted the system will be collecting votes, and the massively increased bureaucracy will have acquired a vested interest in maintaining and expanding the play. It took almost 20 years after the introduction of socialized medicine in Ontario for the politicians to grudgingly acknowledge, as our Minister of Health did last year, that "health care spending is on a collision course with economic realities." Yet any first-year economics student could have predicted, 20 years ago, exactly what would happen.

CONCLUSIONS

Let me give you the short answer to the question posed in the title of this address. If you define "could the Canadian model work here?" to mean "would it improve quality and accessibility of health care for a majority of Americans?" my answer is yes—but only temporarily. Your citizens, like ours, will experience only briefly the medical Utopia that they have been promised, and at an enormous and eventually unbearable cost. Given your government's already astronomical deficits, I would guess that the time before imminent financial collapse would be much shorter than in Canada—perhaps five years.

The crux of the problem in any national health insurance program like the Canadian one is the large and ever-increasing gap between politicians' extravagant promises, public expectations arising from those promises, and cruel financial reality. The reality, sad as it may seem, is that not even you, the richest country in the world, can afford everything for everybody for very long.

It's a pretty dismal picture, isn't it? Yet, if you think about it, this is a hopeful circumstance for AAPS [Association of American Physicians and Surgeons]. You and others who share your beliefs have a long and bitter struggle ahead, with many disappointments. But I'm convinced that in the long run, you'll prevail. You'll win, not only because you have the courage of your convictions and the will to continue fighting, but because the Canadian-style edifice that your opponents are in the process of constructing is built on sand.

DISCUSSION QUESTIONS

1. Should universal coverage be one of the primary goals of health care reform? Why or why not?
2. Arguments for health care reform generally rest on the premise that there are serious deficiencies in the present system of health care, though many disagree about what these deficiencies are. Are there deficiencies in the present system of health care? If so, what are these deficiencies? Would a single-payer system remedy these deficiencies?
3. Should health care reform come largely from the federal government, state governments, or both? Why?

4. Goodman compiles a list of grievances against the Canadian health care system, arguing that they are largely a result of the centralized, nonmarket nature of the Canadian system. Compile a similar list of grievances against the American system, and explain the cause of these problems in the American system.

5. Many have argued that adequate health care, like an adequate education, should be considered a right rather than a luxury and that governments must secure this right. Do you agree? Why or why not? Does your opinion on this question affect your opinion of the adequacy of the Canadian system?

6. Should businesses finance health care reform, or should financing be provided from public sources? What difference does it make, either politically or economically?

ADDITIONAL READINGS

Aaron, Henry J. "Health Care Financing," in Henry J. Aaron and Charles L. Schultze, eds. *Setting Domestic Priorities: What Can Government Do?* (Washington, D.C.: Brookings Institution, 1992).

Aaron, Henry J. "The Worst Health Care Reform Plan . . . Except for All the Others." *Challenge* (November/December 1991).

Arnould, Richard J., Robert F. Rich, and William D. White, eds. *Competitive Approaches to Health Care Reform* (Washington, D.C.: Urban Institute Press, 1993).

Bennett, Arnold, and Orvill Adams, eds. *Looking North for Health: What We Can Learn from Canada's Health Care System* (San Francisco: Jossey-Bass, 1993).

Enthoven, Alain C. *Theory and Practice of Managed Competition in Health Care* (New York: Elsevier, 1988).

Fein, Rashi. "Toward Adequate Health Care." *Dissent* (Winter 1988).

Fein, Rashi. "Health Care Reform." *Scientific American* (November 1992).

Haislmaier, Edmund F. "A Cure for the Health Care Crisis." *Issues in Science and Technology* (Spring 1990).

Kerrey, Robert. "Why America Will Adopt Comprehensive Health Care Reform." *The American Prospect* (Summer 1991).

Kopkind, Andrew. "Seizing the Historic Moment." *The Nation* (December 16, 1991).

Marmor, Theodore R., and Jerry L. Mashaw. "Canada's Health Insurance and Ours: The Real Lessons, the Big Choices." *The American Prospect* (Fall 1990).

Pauly, Mark, Patricia Danzon, John Hoff, and Paul Feldstein. "How Can We Get Responsible National Health Insurance?" *The American Enterprise* (July/August 1992).

Rivlin, Alice M., and Joshua M. Wiener. *Caring for the Disabled Elderly: Who Will Pay?* (Washington, D.C.: Brookings Institution, 1988).

Russell, Louise B. *Technology in Hospitals* (Washington, D.C.: Brookings Institution, 1979).

Seidman, Laurence S. "Reconsidering National Health Insurance." *The Public Interest* (Fall 1990).

Starr, Paul. "Health Compromise: Universal Coverage and Managed Competition under a Cap." *The American Prospect* (Winter 1993).

Starr, Paul. *The Social Transformation of American Medicine* (New York: Basic Books, 1982).

Taylor, Malcolm G. *Insuring National Health Care: The Canadian Experience* (Chapel Hill: University of North Carolina Press, 1990).

6

STATE HEALTH CARE POLICY

"Should Other States Follow the 'Oregon Plan' in Rationing Health Care under the Federal Medicaid Program?"

The Medicare and Medicaid programs were launched in 1965 as key components to ensure health care coverage for many Americans under President Johnson's Great Society program. Medicare, the health care insurance "entitlement" program for the elderly and some disabled, is a federally funded program for all who qualify for Social Security benefits. Medicaid, in contrast, is not an "entitlement," but is rather a joint federal and state means-tested program that provides health care coverage to low-income families (including the blind, elderly, and disabled covered by Supplemental Security Income). Medicaid costs are shared by the federal[1] and state governments, at a matching rate inversely related with a state's per-capita income,* but the program is operated strictly at the state level. The federal government sets broad guidelines, and states generally determine eligibility, coverage, and how the program will be administered. (Virtually all states have Medicaid programs.) As a result, who is eligible, which medical procedures are covered, levels of reimbursement for medical providers, and other fundamental program designs vary considerably from state to state. The federal government has in recent years expanded the list of required services for states to provide under Medicaid. Not surprisingly, states complain that federal requirements are not met with additional federal resources. Some states, like New York, also argue that the formula treats unfairly states with high per-capita income but many poor individuals. The federal government also penalizes states that provide procedures under Medicaid that are not politically acceptable; for example, the Hyde Amendment denied matching federal funds to states that provided abortion services to Medicaid recipients.

Medicaid recipients number more than 25 million nationwide, about 45 percent of whom are under age 16 and another 11 percent over age 65; 60 percent of recipients are white, 34 percent are African American, and 15 percent are Hispanic.† Although Medicaid is targeted to the poor (63 percent of Medicaid recipients are below the poverty level), a surprisingly small portion of Medicaid

---

* The minimum matching rate, for the richest states, is one federal dollar for every state Medicaid dollar spent, an amount that rises for poorer states.

† Note that the total exceeds 100 percent because under Census definitions, Hispanics can be of any race. All statistics quoted in this paragraph are from U.S. Census sources.

expenditures wind up in the hands of persons on AFDC (Aid to Families with Dependent Children) (68 percent of Medicaid recipients are on AFDC, but they receive only a quarter of expenditures). Instead, most expenditures are devoted to the permanently and totally disabled (38 percent) and the elderly (persons over age 65 receive 34 percent of Medicaid expenditures). Surely some or many of these individuals may be poor, but their basis of eligibility is not AFDC assistance, and the notion that Medicaid expenditures are largely a medical handout to able-bodied, working-age persons is unfounded. Indeed, it is not uncommon for elderly individuals who cannot afford costly long-term care to "spend down" their assets so as to qualify for Medicaid assistance; this of course has proven to be a costly drain on Medicaid resources as well.

Like other health care expenditures,[2] Medicare and Medicaid costs have increased dramatically. Real per-capita health and medical care costs have jumped from $365 in 1970 to nearly $1,000 twenty years later (the federal government pays 69 percent of total costs). There are about 35 percent more Medicare than Medicaid recipients, and total Medicare costs in 1990 were $109 billion (up 211 percent from 1980 costs) compared to $65 billion for Medicaid (up 136 percent from 1980 levels).[3] Medicaid is one of the most significant and fastest-growing programs targeted to the poor. Federal Medicaid spending comprises approximately 6 percent of total federal social welfare expenditures (including Social Security), but about 24 percent of all federal cash and noncash benefits for persons with limited income and 31 percent of total cash and noncash benefits for persons with limited income. Total (federal, state, and local) expenditures on Medicaid are three times that for AFDC, and there are more than twice as many Medicaid recipients as those receiving AFDC.

States have suffered from federal Medicaid coverage requirements, spiraling Medicaid costs, and growing numbers of eligible recipients; in response, states have either restricted eligibility or cut back on payments to doctors and hospitals. As a result, in many states doctors refuse to treat Medicaid patients, and the poor are sometimes shunted to public or university-run hospitals, many of which are forced to charge patients with private insurance higher rates in order to make up for low Medicaid reimbursements. Further, the inability of many poor Americans to find medical care leads many preventable medical problems to develop into more serious and expensive emergency treatments at hospitals.

Physician Arnold Relman has said that "health care is being converted from a social service to an economic commodity, sold in the marketplace and distributed on the basis of who can afford to pay for it." The result is that in the United States, health care is rationed: Some can afford private insurance or qualify for government assistance, and others cannot. The controversial "Oregon plan" for rationing Medicaid funds expands the eligibility for Medicaid at the expense of denying funding for certain medical procedures. The plan was conceived in the late 1980s when the Oregon state legislature faced a budget shortfall in Medicaid and considered further restricting program eligibility. The state considered instead a procedure whereby 709 medical procedures were ranked from highest to lowest on a benefit–cost scale, and the state would fund as many procedures as its Medicaid budget would allow. The ranking considered cost of care, the number of years over which the patient would benefit from care, and an assessment of the "quality of well-being" after the medical procedure. The first ranking, released in May 1990, was widely criticized because some life-threatening conditions were not covered while seemingly trivial concerns were. AIDS detection and prevention were relatively high on the list, while treatment for AIDS patients was low. The public outcry created the need to develop an alternative allocation scheme. The second ranking scheme did not consider cost, reduced the number of categories of care, and allowed officials to move treatments up on the list where obvious problems existed. The public's reaction was much more favorable to the second ranking, which formed the basis of Oregon's appeal to the federal government to grant it an exemption under Medicaid. That appeal was denied by the Bush administration, ostensibly because its application could violate requirements under the Americans with Disabilities Act, but was granted early in the Clinton administration.

The United States is a nation wealthy enough to continue spending prodigious sums on health care for all citizens, but at the cost of denying funds to other important public and private needs. If health care is to be rationed, two questions must be addressed. First, how much do Americans want to spend (both publicly and privately) on providing health care? Second, how should that amount of money be allocated? The Oregon plan addresses only a portion of the second question (how to allocate existing Medicaid funds), but the difficult moral question for rationing Medicaid (or any health care) funds is either which *procedures* will not be covered, or *who* will not be covered. In other words, how far down the list of procedures should Oregonians go in providing medical coverage for the indigent? Proponents of the Oregon plan, like John Kitzhaber, an Oregon state legislator and chief architect of the plan, argue that rationing is necessary, and by reallocating current expenditures, more people can be covered. Critics counter that the list is inappropriate and that Oregon spends too little money on Medicaid. More fundamentally, physician Robert Brook and Rand health policy analyst Kathleen Lohr argue that rationing health care is not necessary in light of the waste in current medical practices and that the effects of rationing will be disproportionately borne by the poor, elderly, and chronically ill. These opposing arguments are presented in the two articles below.

Endnotes

1. The principal federal agency overseeing and funding Medicaid is the Health Care Financing Administration (which controls Medicare as well) in the United States Department of Health and Human Services.
2. See the debate on national health insurance in Chapter 5.
3. U.S. Department of Commerce, Bureau of the Census, *Statistical Abstract of the United States, 1992* (Washington, D.C.: U.S. Government Printing Office, 1992).

YES

A Healthier Approach to Health Care

John Kitzhaber

Medicaid was created by Congress in 1965 to provide health care to poor people, with the federal and state governments sharing the costs. But the program is failing—it now serves a much smaller percentage of the poor than when originally enacted, and the states are buckling under the financial burden.

The economic crunch is due in part to the requirement that, in order to qualify for federal matching dollars, states must comply with a steady stream of federal Medicaid mandates to provide specific services or include certain populations. The resulting escalation of health care costs is forcing state legislatures across the country either to raise taxes or to limit investments in environmental protection, education, housing, law enforcement, economic development, and a host of other essential social programs.

This was the situation in Oregon in 1987 when the state legislature, faced with over $48 million in immediate social program needs and only $21 million available in the budget, voted to discontinue funding for most organ transplants for people on Medicaid. It was argued that these were high-cost procedures that would benefit only about 30 individuals during the next two years. The money was used instead to fund, among other things, basic preventive care for nearly 3,000 people with no health insurance coverage at all.

The legislature's decision received little attention at first. But in late 1987 a young boy with leukemia, unable to receive state funds to pay for a bone marrow transplant, died while his parents sought public contributions to finance the operation. The case prompted an effort in January 1988 to partially refund the transplant program for eight individuals in immediate need. This took the form of a motion before the Legislative Emergency Board, comprised of 17 legislators, which has the authority to appropriate money from an emergency fund when the legislature is not in session. After an emotional two-day debate, the motion was narrowly defeated.

The debate did not turn on the question of whether organ transplants have merit—clearly they often do. Nor was the question whether the state at that point had sufficient resources to make that particular appropriation. It did. Rather, the question was simply this: If the state was going to invest more money in its health care budget, where should the next dollar go? What was the policy that would lead us to fund transplants as opposed to further expanding the availability of prenatal care? What was the policy that would lead us to offer transplants to eight individuals as opposed to nine—or to 19? Where was the equity in giving sophisticated and costly services to a few Oregonians covered under Medicaid before providing basic health care services to other equally needy citizens, including many of the "working poor," who lacked any public or private coverage?

What became readily apparent was that Oregon had no health care policy. We were responding to a highly emotional issue and had no way whatsoever to evaluate whether funding transplants was the best place to invest state health care dollars. By appropriating the money, we in the legislature would know that another eight transplants could be performed. Yet we had no way of knowing—or being held accountable for—the consequences of not using that money to expand access to other individuals who were currently excluded from the system altogether.

This realization—that we were making decisions unguided by any specific policy and untempered by accountability—made the legislature step back and take a look at the national health care delivery system and the role states play in it. What we discovered was that there was no clear policy at the federal level either.

LEADERSHIP NEEDED

Faced with the lack of any clear federal leadership, we in Oregon came to realize that by default we had to assume responsibility for health care reform. This led us to develop the Oregon Basic Health Services Act, adopted in 1989 after an intensive legislative effort. The act was motivated by the desire to build a new system that recognizes the reality of fiscal limits, carefully defines the public policy objectives, and, most important, includes a mechanism to establish accountability for resource allocation decisions and for their consequences.

Let us consider each of these points in turn:

The reality of limits. Unlike the federal government, states are constitutionally required to operate within a balanced budget. Yet Congress has passed the buck to the states to raise substantial amounts of new revenue for Medicaid. In the Omnibus Budget Reconciliation Act of 1989, new mandates require states to provide Medicaid coverage for pregnant women and children up to the age of six who have family incomes below 133 percent of the federal poverty level. Furthermore, states must provide these clients nearly all "medically necessary" services—virtually everything our high-tech health care system has to offer—no matter the cost. Ironically, these new requirements were handed down just two months after the National Governors' Association, citing what it considered an imminent health care fiscal crisis, asked Congress for a two-year moratorium on Medicaid mandates. And in 1990, during the seemingly endless struggle to agree on its own budget, the federal government enacted a host of new mandates for the states, including the requirement that Medicaid cover all children born after 1983 until they turn 19.

The new mandates may seem laudable at first glance. But because they are not part of a comprehensive policy to deal with the problems of access for the poor, they have triggered unfortunate consequences. To support new mandates, states unwilling or unable to raise taxes or cut other social programs are often forced to change Medicaid eligibility standards for those individuals not specifically covered. This amounts to nothing more than "redefining the poor," throwing some people off the program to balance the budget.

To meet the 1989 mandates, nearly all states have restricted eligibility for women who are not pregnant and for children over the age of six. Alabama provides Medicaid coverage only to those families with incomes of less than 14 percent of the federal poverty level; California, which has the broadest coverage, includes those with incomes up to 79 percent of the poverty level. Yet, even in California, 5 million people are uninsured, and a measles epidemic rages among the more than 400,000 unimmunized children. Nationally, the average eligibility standard is under 50 percent of the poverty level, which means that a family of three with an annual income over $5,500 is regarded as too wealthy to qualify for Medicaid coverage in many parts of this nation.

Another action that states have sometimes taken to pay for new mandates is to cut provider reimbursement rates—that is, reduce the amount paid for medical services. But since some providers refuse to participate in the Medicaid program as rates drop, this can create yet another barrier to access. A recent Supreme Court ruling allowing hospitals to sue states for what they consider inadequate Medicaid reimbursement makes it less likely that states will take this approach and more likely that they will restrict eligibility further to control costs. The 1990 mandates exacerbate the cost squeeze by prohibiting reductions in reimbursement to pharmacists.

The current Medicaid program also runs afoul of fiscal reality in its assumption that all medical services and procedures are equally valuable and effective, an assumption directly contradicted by a growing body of information on medical outcomes. Although the latest federal Medicaid mandates require that all "medically necessary" services be provided, there is absolutely nothing in the system to measure which services are in fact necessary, or even effective. For example, Medicaid must pay for all services, including some of questionable or unproven benefit, for children 5 years of age and under, but it is not required to cover services of proven effectiveness for children 6 years and over.

The need for a clear policy. Unlike federal officials, Oregon's citizens and legislators believe that the policy objective is not simply to guarantee all state citizens access to health care, but rather to keep all of them healthy. The federal Medicaid program is based on the assumption that providing health care is the most important way to improve health. But we are convinced that health care is not necessarily synonymous with health. Indeed, it is clearly evident that the nation's enormous and increasing expenditure for health care has not actually made us healthier as a people. In 1988, for example, the United States led the world in health care spending with $1,926 per capita—far more than Canada (the second biggest spender at $1,370 per capita) and three times Great Britain's $711. Yet 19 countries have lower infant morality rates and 26 have better cardiovascular statistics. An American woman ranks seventh worldwide in life expectancy, and an American male stands tenth.

These statistics are often explained by noting that 35 million Americans, many of them the working poor, lack public or private health coverage. The reality is that the statistics reflect not so much a problem of access to health care as a failure to allocate sufficient resources to a variety of other social conditions that also affect health in important ways.

Women fail to get prenatal care, for example, not just because they lack health insurance, but also because of transportation problems, communication barriers, and the lack of day care. Infant mortality reflects more than just a lack of prenatal care; it also reflects poor housing, environmental pollution, teenage pregnancies, and the growing problem of substance abuse. We cannot improve the health of our state or nation if, for example, we continue to focus expenditures on the medical complications of substance abuse while ignoring the social conditions that lead to addiction. That means dealing with issues such as education, income maintenance, and economic opportunity. Yet when health care costs go up, these programs are jeopardized.

The need for accountability. If we accept the fact that the health care budget is ultimately finite, then it follows that an explicit decision to allocate money for one set of services means that an implicit decision has also been made not to spend money on other services. That, in essence, constitutes rationing of health care, and legislative bodies do it every budget cycle. But they do it implicitly, with no real accountability for the whole of their actions.

This issue is graphically illustrated by the national debate over costly high-technology medical interventions for a few individuals versus preventive care for large numbers of people. The struggle in Oregon over funding of transplants is a case in point, but examples abound across the country. In 1985, Illinois passed legislation guaranteeing up to $200,000 in state funds for any citizen needing an organ transplant and lacking health insurance. By making this huge fiscal commitment, the legislature engaged in implicit rationing by ignoring the fact that 60 percent of the state's black children were not even immunized against polio and that inner-city health clinics in Chicago were being closed because of a lack of revenue.

In Florida—a state that sets its Medicaid eligibility at a mere 35 percent of the federal poverty level—Governor Bob Martinez last year approved spending $100,000 in an attempt to save the life of a two-year-old boy who had nearly drowned after falling into a neighbor's swimming pool. Lung infection set in and coma followed. The child was transferred to a Minnesota hospital and put on a sophisticated lung bypass machine, even though medical experts admitted he would probably remain in a vegetative state or, at best, be severely impaired.

Policymakers in both states were able to take credit for highly visible operations that "save lives," but did not have to assume any accountability for the consequences of what they implicitly chose not to fund. "How are you supposed to put a price on saving one child?" said an aide to the Florida governor. "You can't look at it as all this money for one kid. The truth is, when you have a two-year-boy who is about to die, you don't have a hell of a lot of choice."

And it does seem, of course, that there isn't a choice, because the child is right in front of us. But each year in the United States, approximately 40,000 children die before their first birthday—with no national uproar because they are not in front of us. Many of these deaths—the result of implicit social and legislative decisions for which there is no accountability—are preventable.

The moral here is not that we should abandon high technology or cast away human compassion. Rather, we must recognize that today's system allows us to make crucial allocation decisions in a vacuum, to take the easy and popular way out and avoid having to weigh the overall social costs and benefits.

DETERMINING WHAT TO COVER

The Oregon Basic Health Services Act extends Medicaid eligibility to all persons with incomes below the federal poverty level, as the original legislation intended, thus establishing a definition of the poor based strictly on need—not on the complex and sometimes contradictory maze of federal "categories" and changing Medicaid mandates. It also requires comparable employment-based coverage for those with a family income above the federal poverty level, which brings the working poor into the system. By guaranteeing that virtually everyone in the state will have access to health care, the act fundamentally changes the issue from who is covered to what is covered.

In determining what services to cover, judgment should be made based on medical efficacy and cost-effectiveness of the services being purchased. The process we are using to accomplish this differs markedly from the current pattern of random federal mandates and piecemeal state insurance mandates, which are often based on the relative power of special interests. Rather, we are prioritizing health services according to the degree of benefit each service can be expected to have on the health of the entire population.

Responsibility for prioritizing health services is assigned to the Oregon Health Services Commission, an 11-member body appointed by the governor and confirmed by the State Senate after public hearings. To establish priorities, the commission developed a formula that considers the benefit likely to result from each procedure, the duration of that benefit, and the cost involved. Panels of physicians and an extensive review of medical literature were used to provide information on the appropriateness, efficiency, and outcomes of specific procedures. In addition to its evaluation of cost-effectiveness, the commission took into consideration social values such as quality of life, equity, and community compassion, which were ascertained through 47 public meetings held around the state.

In May 1990, the commission conducted an initial computer run to test the methodology. As expected, this revealed a number of problems. Unfortunately, the media and some critics of the act seized upon the results and widely represented them as the final Oregon "priority list," leaving the impression that the effort was fatally flawed. In fact, the computer run was but a necessary part of an orderly process to develop a credible ranking system, an effort that was never before attempted. It was hoped that the exercise would not only reveal problems, but also shed some light on how they might be rectified.

This proved to be the case. The problems identified included disagreement about how to define the "duration of benefit" for various types of diseases and treatments, the lack of standards on how to group similar diagnoses, and incomplete or inaccurate data on costs. These issues are now being addressed, and the final priority list is certain to be substantially different.

The final document will consist of a prioritized listing of condition/treatment pairs grouped into 26 categories including preventive care for children, health education, treatment of acute life-threatening conditions where treatment prevents death and leads to full recovery, treatment of fatal conditions with no improvement in life-span but with improvement in quality of life. These categories will then themselves be prioritized to reflect the social values developed from the community meetings process. Each budget cycle, the commission will review and update the list.

When the commission has completed its work, which is scheduled for late February 1991, the legislature will determine how many benefits on the priority list can be funded with existing revenue and how much additional revenue will be required to fund what the legislature considers an acceptable "basic" package. Because an estimated 77,000 citizens will be added to the Medicaid rolls, the legislature will almost certainly increase the total Medicaid appropriation.

We believe that the legislature will provide the extra funds for two reasons. First, legislators will know—for the first time—not only which services are being purchased with the new revenue, but also the effectiveness of the services and the value society places on them. Second, since preventive services are likely to be ranked highly, the investment will provide long-term cost savings by reducing the need for medical care later on.

TOWARD A BETTER SYSTEM

Certainly the Oregon Basic Health Services Act constitutes a major departure from traditional approaches to solving problems of access and cost, and therefore should be scrutinized closely. No policy reform of this magnitude can avoid opposition, and our proposal has met with three main criticisms.

The most frequent, and most emotional, is that the act discriminates against women and children. This charge arises from the fact that only about one-third of all Medicaid dollars spent in Oregon go for services to aid families with dependent children, whereas the rest go to purchase services for the aged, blind, and disabled—groups excluded from the prioritization process. Thus it is argued that only women and children will suffer any benefit reductions that might result.

The argument ignores a critical distinction. Virtually all medical services for the elderly, the blind, and the disabled are funded by the federally administered Medicare program, not Medicaid. Most of the services provided for these groups under Medicaid are not medical treatments but social services, such as assistance in eating, bathing, and mobility. These services do not lend themselves to the medical services prioritization model and can be provided outside an institutional setting. In fact, Oregon was the first state to be granted a federal waiver to use Medicaid funds for such services in home and community-based care, which we see as a less expensive and more humane alternative to institutionalization.

When these dollars are removed from the Medicaid pot, most of the remaining money is in fact spent on families with dependent children and, under the new act, on poor women and men without children. Also, the criticism confuses prioritization with resource allocation. Although social services were not prioritized, there is nothing in the legislation to prevent us from shifting some of these funds into the medical budget, if the public agrees that this is the best way to improve general well-being. Finally, this criticism ignores the thousands of women and children who are now ineligible for Medicaid but will be brought into the health care system by the act.

The second criticism is that before we resort to "rationing," we should eliminate waste from the current system. This assumes that we are not rationing health care now, which of course we are. And although the concern about eliminating waste is certainly valid, the Oregon proposal is one of the first to offer a systematic cost/benefit analysis by which such waste can be identified and attacked.

Third, some critics suggest that if we must ration health care, the rationing should apply to all members of society, not just the poor. We agree in principle but believe that progress toward that policy objective will have to occur in several steps. Moreover, the criticism is more applicable to the status quo than to the Oregon proposal. For one thing, Medicaid now covers fewer than half of the people living below the poverty level, whereas our act provides assistance to all needy people.

In addition, the federal system offers public health care subsidies to virtually everyone in the United States except those who have no private insurance coverage and who are not eligible for either Medicaid or Medicare. In 1990 the government will spend about $45 billion on Medicaid (states will contribute another $33 billion) and $105 billion on Medicare; and because employer contributions to health insurance premiums are not taxable, the government will provide a subsidy of well over $50 billion to the middle class.

Neither the Medicare subsidy nor that offered through the tax exclusion considers financial need—you get the subsidy regardless of your personal wealth. The irony—indeed, the hypocrisy—is that there are about 16 million working but uninsured Americans (plus their dependents) whose taxes help underwrite Medicaid, Medicare, and the tax exclusion but who are not eligible for any public subsidy themselves and cannot afford to pay private premiums.

Congress should correct the inequities in the current federal system of health benefits. In the meantime, we believe that Oregon is doing what a state can do to address today's implicit rationing of health care.

FEDERAL PERMISSION NEEDED

Oregon's proposal, passed by large bipartisan majorities in both houses of the state legislature and enjoying widespread public support, deserves the chance to move forward. What is needed is to have the federal government grant Oregon a waiver allowing the state to redesign the current package of mandated benefits. The waiver can be granted administratively by the Health Care Financing Administration (HCFA)—the agency that manages Medicaid—or granted statutorily by Congress. Because of the importance of this effort, and since HCFA has never awarded a waiver of this scope before, we are pursuing both routes.

Although the administrative waiver has not yet been formally submitted, HCFA officials have reviewed our draft proposal and offered technical recommendations that will be incorporated into the final request. Agency administrator Gail Wilensky, who generally favors allowing states to set up demonstration projects, has indicated that she will recommend approval of the waiver if it meets the agency's technical review.

HCFA has asked that the formal waiver request not be submitted until the Oregon Health Services Commission has completed its priority list and the legislature has established funding levels. If the commission meets its proposed deadline of late February 1991, the legislature should be able to make its appropriation in April or May.

Once the waiver is submitted, HCFA will convene a panel of health care experts to pass judgment. The agency expects the review process to take about six months, which means Oregon would be able to implement the new program early in 1992. If the agency can shorten its review to two or three months, as we have requested, the program could be operating as early as July, the start of Oregon's next fiscal year.

At roughly the same time our request is sent to HCFA, we will formally ask Congress to grant approval for the Secretary of Health and Human Services to issue the necessary waiver. It is important to note that our suggested waiver language asks for a waiver only if the secretary "determines that the standard of health benefits meets the basic health needs of the eligible population." We are also requesting a public comment period prior to any action by the secretary to allow our critics to examine the proposed benefit package before a waiver is granted.

Although the entire Oregon congressional delegation is supporting the waiver, two individuals are particularly well placed for the upcoming debate. Senator Bob Packwood is the ranking Republican on the Senate Finance Committee, which has jurisdiction over the Medicaid program in the Senate, and Congressman Ron Wyden, a Democrat, sits on the House Subcommittee on Health and the Environment, which oversees Medicaid in the House. In addition, support has been expressed by Senator Bob Kerry (D-Nebr.), Congressman Jim McDermott (D-Wash.), and Congressman Roy Rowland (R-Ga.).

Other states will be watching how Oregon's proposal fares at HCFA and in Congress. Colorado, Michigan, Iowa, Nebraska, Arizona, Massachusetts,

Oklahoma, Alaska, and California have expressed considerable interest in our approach. Two states, Colorado and Michigan, have actually drafted similar legislation. In Colorado the legislation was introduced in early 1990; although the bill ultimately failed in committee, it precipitated valuable debate on the question of resource allocation. Most of the other states are waiting to see if Oregon is granted a waiver before beginning the difficult work of developing their own plans.

We believe it is clearly in the national interest to let Oregon put its plan into operation. Whether we are right or our critics are right cannot be known unless the plan is tried. At a minimum the experience will provide information that will be invaluable in addressing the health care crisis in America. If the plan succeeds, it can serve as a pattern for other states and, we hope, lead eventually to the kind of realistic and comprehensive federal action that the nation so sorely needs.

NO

Will We Need to Ration Effective Health Care?

Robert H. Brook and Kathleen N. Lohr

The central health policy issue for the remainder of the decade, if not the century, is whether the nation will accept and act on the premise that it must ration effective medical services. Rationing can be simply defined as any set of activities that determines who gets needed medical care when resources are insufficient to provide for all. Put another way, it is the provision of some service to one patient at the risk of denying it to an equally deserving patient. At the most basic level, it is the problem clinicians face in deciding who to treat when not all can be treated.

The rhetoric of the times conveys the impression that only the rationing of care—either by direct means (for example, by denying the patient access to a certain procedure) or by some general economic mechanism (such as increasing deductibles in health insurance policies or reducing income eligibility levels for Medicaid)—will halt the persistent escalation in health care costs and expenditures, which now constitute more than 10 percent of the nation's gross national product.

Most of the health policy debate today focuses on how best to implement rationing and which mechanisms to use, not on whether rationing is necessary. We believe that the correct question is whether deliberate rationing of services by nonmedical or nonclinical means is needed. The answer, we contend, is "no."

The nation has little experience with direct rationing except, perhaps, with scarce, costly, high-technology services such as intensive or neonatal care or, in more distant times, kidney dialysis. The nation is gaining experience, however, with certain economic approaches to rationing such as higher patient cost sharing. At the same time evidence is mounting that these approaches proportionately lower the use of both effective services (those services that provide demonstrable health benefits that outweigh risks and side effects) and ineffective services. (We include in this definition of effective some services that others might exclude, namely, services for which the marginal benefit to health is positive but does not exceed the marginal cost. That is, our view of effective services would incorporate situations in which the patient benefits from the service but not to the extent that it is worth the cost to society.)

The rationing issue is not an idle or merely intellectual one, because the social costs of rationing can be high. If the country decides to ration effective services, no matter how well it does so, it will have a greater impact on the elderly, the poor, and the chronically ill than on the rich, the middle class, or the healthy. With explicit, stringent rationing, people with resources will find ways to obtain needed medical services; those lacking such resources will do without, at least temporarily. Three studies come to mind, two from the United States and one from Great Britain.

Along with numerous colleagues we have just completed a major social experiment on the effects of differing levels of cost sharing on health. About 2,000 families in six sites in the United States were given health insurance that differed only in the amount of money the family members were required to pay out of pocket. All of the insurance plans were generous and covered most medical services. The people in the plans were representative of the U.S. population, except the elderly were excluded. They chose their own physicians and paid on a fee-for-service basis. Expenditures were 40 percent higher on the plan in which services were free than on the plans that required patient cost sharing.

These large differences in expenditures had negligible, if any, effects on the health of the average adult or child. However, at the end of the experiment, low-income children with anemia may have been worse off with cost sharing. And low-income adults who were sick, especially with hypertension, were also worse off on the cost-sharing plans. Because of their resulting higher blood pressure, these adults on the cost-sharing plan had an estimated 15 percent greater chance of dying within five years than those on the free-care plan. These outcomes can be attributed to the lower physician contact resulting from cost sharing.

In a recent cost-cutting effort, California eliminated its Medicaid (Medi-Cal) program for 270,000 medically indigent adults. (Medically indigent adults are Medicaid recipients between the ages of 21 and 65 who receive state Medicaid benefits because they are poor and medically needy but who are not eligible for federal assistance programs such as those that serve the aged, blind, disabled, and families with dependent children.) A common problem among the medically indigent is high blood pressure, and most such patients had their blood pressure under control until the program was terminated. When they lost their health insurance coverage, many of these individuals developed un-controlled hypertension. Within the first six months after loss of insurance, the relative risk of dying in this population increased by 40 percent. The morbidity and mortality problems persisted during the ensuing year, although eventual restoration of coverage to some helped reverse the adverse effects of losing coverage.

Great Britain provides another example. That country rations health care by spending per capita about one-fourth of what is spent by the United States. Under the British National Health Service, the queues for certain types of services such as elective, but needed, surgery are long. Correspondingly, the use of private means to obtain such services, among those who have the means, is substantial. For instance, about one-fourth of all elective total hip replacements in England and Wales are paid for privately. The extent of private payment is all the more telling because the British National Health Service enjoys wide and enthusiastic public support, and the people of Great Britain have relatively low incomes (at least in comparison to incomes in the United States) and presumably less discretionary income with which to cover private fees. Even so, many people are willing to pay to obtain medical care promptly; those without adequate financial resources, on the other hand, wait in queues.

Evidence that rationing effective services in the United States may be unnecessary comes from three areas: the wide variation in per-person rates of use of all forms of medical care, the unproven effectiveness of many procedures used to diagnose and treat illness, and the unquestioned assumption among both medical practitioners and the public that doing more or at least doing something is preferable to doing nothing.

First, the per-person rates of use of certain services vary widely in this country among people who appear to be similar in all the characteristics that usually predict use. These characteristics include basic health status, age, sex, and other demographic, social, and economic factors.

Examples are numerous and telling:

- Per-person medical expenditures for elderly residents of Miami, Florida, are more than twice as high as those for seniors in Rochester, New York.
- Hospital use is 60 percent higher in the North Central regions of the country than in the West.
- The rates of use of computerized tomography (CAT) scans to diagnose problems affecting the brain per patient discharged from acute care hospitals were seven times higher in the West North Central states (Iowa, Kansas, Minnesota, Missouri, Nebraska, North Dakota, and South Dakota) than in the Mountain states (Arizona, Colorado, Idaho, Montana, Nevada, New Mexico, Utah, and Wyoming).
- The use of procedures such as coronary angiography, a common diagnostic procedure for detecting blockages of the arteries serving the heart, varies by as much as threefold across major geographic areas of the country.
- In 1981 the percentage of women in Detroit whose babies were delivered by cesarean section was about 10 percent; in Washington, D.C., the figure was 24 percent.
- In areas of the country with an average population of about 300,000, the rate of total knee replacements among the elderly varied sixfold in the early 1980s.
- In the United States, Canada, and England and Wales, the rates of prostatectomy in men varied by a factor of two and a half; the rates of hysterectomy in women varied by a factor of three; and the rates of removal of the gall bladder in women varied by a factor of five.

If the figures at the lower end of these ranges represent appropriate and adequate care, then 30 percent to 50 percent of the nation's health bill might be said to consist of expenditures on care that produces little or no demonstrable health benefit. If these ineffective services were selectively eliminated, the pressure to ration effective services would be markedly relieved. However, if the figures at the upper end of these ranges represent adequate care, then expenditures on health care do not appear so out of line. The question is, what is appropriate?

Unfortunately, the medical or clinical data with which to determine whether procedures are generally overused or underused are sparse. Some information, however, can be marshaled. Consider, for instance, the appropriateness of hospital use. A hospital day, which is an expensive commodity, is termed appropriate if the services provided can be done only while the patient is hospitalized and if these services are medically effective; that is, they will do more good than harm. Recent studies indicate that about 25 percent of all hospital days are inappropriate because the services performed did not require hospitalization. For example, the only care the patient received may have been oral medication, which could just as easily have been taken at home.

Having an unnecessary operation or diagnostic test also represents inappropriate care. If such services are provided in the hospital setting, and if they are the only reason for that hospitalization, then the percentage of hospital days that are inappropriate rises dramatically. Preliminary work in a few hospitals suggests that one-third or more of coronary angiographies and coronary artery bypass surgeries may be medically inappropriate; that is, the risk to the patient is, on average, as great as the procedure's benefit. Similar results have been found for carotid endarterectomies (a procedure to remove clots in arteries leading to the brain) performed in selected Veterans Administration hospitals. If these results, which have not been obtained from hospitals selected for poor performance or questionable practices, are representative of all hospitals, then the 30 percent to 50 percent figures cited earlier may not appear farfetched. They may even be an underestimate.

Some of the nation's health care dollars go to services and technologies whose efficacy (performance under ideal circumstances, for example by the best physicians and in the best hospitals) and effectiveness (performance under ordinary circumstances such as in the common private practice setting) have never been satisfactorily examined. Even when the efficacy of a surgical procedure or new drug has been demonstrated, it is not clear that results achieved under these ideal conditions will also be achieved by the average practitioner. More studies are needed that describe the risks and benefits of procedures when performed by the average practitioner. Carotid endarterectomy, for example, may be an appropriate procedure for some patients, but only when the surgeon's postoperative complication rate is very low. If the average surgeon who performs the procedure has a higher complication rate, then the risk to the patient may outweigh the benefit.

Further, many medical practices in use today gained wide acceptance well before the nation became alarmed about the spiraling costs of medical care and before concerns with benefits and risks came under the scrutiny of policymakers and researchers. Today, ethical considerations and various technical problems often preclude scientific examination of the efficacy and effectiveness of these "accepted" practices. The scarcity of information about which technologies or practices are efficacious or appropriate in which clinical circumstances obviously complicates the task of trying to avoid rationing effective services.

Another problem relates to the "do something" mentality. One manifestation of this problem is that physicians have not been taught how to put an accurate value on additional diagnostic information. The urge to obtain yet more (relatively uninformative) data pervades the diagnostic process, and the consequences of this attitude are subtle, costly, and sometimes harmful. It may, for instance, obscure the diagnosis of something as simple as appendicitis in patients coming to an emergency room with belly pain.

An example from a recent book by David Sackett and his colleagues is illustrative. A 35-year-old man goes to a physician with nonexertional chest pain that occurs after a heavy meal. No other cardiovascular risk factor is present. After taking a personal history and doing a physical examination, the physician concludes that the patient has about a 5 percent chance of having coronary artery disease. The question, then, is whether he should order an exercise stress test to determine more conclusively whether the patient has heart disease, even though the odds are about 19 to 1 that the patient does not.

Many physicians would automatically order the stress test. If the test were positive, a dye study of the circulation of the heart (coronary angiography) would be ordered. If a blockage of the left main coronary artery were eventually found (an unlikely event in this example), then coronary artery bypass surgery would be performed. If no untoward events occurred during the test or operation, the diagnostic and therapeutic process would be declared a success.

If, however, 1,000 such patients were put through this process, more harm than good would probably be done, and at great cost. The stress test is not totally accurate in ruling illness in or out (respectively, "sensitive" or "specific" in technical terms). Thus, some patients will suffer from being falsely labeled as ill or having heart disease; others who truly have heart disease may be incorrectly reassured about their state of health. An occasional patient, who may or may not have heart disease, could suffer a serious complication of the test or even die. Because all these problems can and do occur with this test, the net gain (in either accurate information or improved health status) from administering it to 1,000 men, each of whom has only a 5 percent chance of having coronary disease in the first place, is less than its associated risks.

The point can be generalized. Deciding to use a diagnostic technology, even a relatively inexpensive one, can be both harmful and costly. Greater knowledge about the sensitivity and specificity of diagnostic tests, better appreciation of the strengths and limitations of such tests in specific clinical situations, and wider application of formal decision analysis skills (skills that physicians typically do not learn or apply in daily practice) would go far to rationalize medical practice and reduce costs. Moreover, patients appear willing to give up the "more is better" philosophy for tests or procedures when their physicians explain why the test or procedure is not needed.

From these bits of evidence, we can speculate that perhaps one-third of the financial resources devoted to health care today are being spent on ineffective or unproductive care. If these expenditures could be identified and reduced, explicit rationing or stringent economic measures would not be necessary. Even if the above calculations are slightly off and the nation's total health bill increased slightly as a proportion of gross national product, these changes would nonetheless help produce a health care system that is based on demonstrably effective services and is more responsive to the needs of all citizens.

Eliminating inefficiency in the medical system, however, will not be easy. It will require changes in federal policies, funding decisions, and medical education, and it will necessitate an extensive research effort to assess the quality of care. In addition, some of the necessary steps will challenge traditional practices and ingrained habits of both the medical profession and the public. Because such changes are difficult and time-consuming to implement, it is important to begin the discussion now. Three topics deserve special attention: competing interests of the public and the medical community, competing needs for privacy and information, and threats to the hospital industry.

Perhaps the greatest challenge will be to resolve the competing interests of the public and the medical community and encourage physicians to become more efficient providers of care. Some experts argue that in an effort to remold physician practice and curtail costs, remuneration for doctors should be drastically cut, for example, by subjecting them to a rigid fee schedule or by bringing them under the umbrella of an organized, salaried system. Understandably, the medical profession objects to these attacks on its livelihood and autonomy. We maintain that these changes are not necessary if physicians are willing to become more accountable to the public.

Greater accountability will entail two substantial changes in the way the medical profession performs its work. First, doctors must make publicly available adequate information about their performance. Second, they must use that information to become more effective providers.

In the first area, physicians must support—in principle, practice, and funding—rigorous, performance-based review. Such a review program would aim to ensure that physicians provide adequate quality of care as efficiently as possible. It would probably require national criteria and standards and a nationwide data bank. Information on inpatient care, for instance, might be gathered through surveillance activities like those now performed by the Centers for Disease Control in Atlanta to gather data on deaths from infectious diseases. In this case the surveillance would be focused on, say, excess or avoidable hospital deaths or rates of unnecessary use of specific procedures. Population-based studies and the tools of clinical epidemiology and decision analysis should become central features of the review program.

Further, this set of activities implies appreciable change for medical education and professional peer review. Physicians must be trained to think in epidemiological terms. In addition, a comprehensive, performance-based review program requires a strong commitment by knowledgeable physicians to take the lead in designing and fostering new approaches to quality assurance. For example, practicing physicians should be subjected to a review of the actual care they provide to their patients, a step that would go significantly beyond the current system for certification and recertification, which is largely based on taking courses and passing written exams.

If physicians are to become more effective providers, state and federal policies must be modified to provide incentives for doctors to improve their performance. For instance, the reciprocal rights and obligations of physicians to participate in publicly funded programs, such as Medicare or Medicaid, should be redefined. Eligibility to participate might be curtailed or denied to those practitioners who are shown, through performance-based review, to be inefficient or poor providers. At a minimum, physicians who provide inferior care should be required to bring their practices up to standard; physicians who provide good care inefficiently should not receive full reimbursement from the public treasury. Thus, two physicians may obtain the same good outcome; that one does it twice as expensively as the other does not necessarily warrant any higher reimbursement. Such a policy might go a long way in motivating physicians to learn how to use resources more appropriately.

In short, physicians might maintain their present forms of practice and levels of payment by accepting more responsibility for delivering effective medical care as efficiently as possible. Physicians should seriously consider this trade-off between autonomy and public accountability.

To ensure access to effective care, the public will have to make a similar trade-off. Determining what is effective medical care requires obtaining from patients or their medical records information about complaints, symptoms, signs, and illnesses and linking that information to the care rendered and the outcome achieved. The difficulty and expense of acquiring such information to date can be attributed in part to concerns about privacy and confidentiality. For example, because of strict interpretations of how best to protect confidentiality, researchers are sometimes required to obtain separate releases from patients, physicians, and hospitals to interview patients or to gain access to information in medical records, even when such information would never be released on an individual patient basis.

The lay public, as well as physicians, will need to temper concerns about privacy of medical records if the rationing of effective care is to be avoided. Giving prior authorization to researchers to use medical records to evaluate and improve the health care delivery system will be one important step in this direction. (Such data collection must, of course, be conducted with strict attention to confidentiality, but this has always been a hallmark of rigorous scientific investigation in medicine.)

Innovative procedures for data collection will also be necessary. As already mentioned, one possibility might involve a nationwide data bank for outpatient care, perhaps using personal computers within doctors' offices to obtain information directly from patients about this treatment. (Such information would be collected confidentially—the nurse or physician would not have access to it—and would be aggregated across patients.)

As do physicians, the public faces a trade-off. In exchange for easing the process of obtaining information vitally needed to evaluate medical care, the public is entitled to assurance from the federal government that, in the long run, access to effective medical care will be maintained, if not strengthened.

Efforts to eliminate ineffective care will likely have one immediate major impact: contraction of the hospital industry, perhaps by as much as one-fourth to one-half of all acute hospital beds. Such contraction will be painful and hard to manage equitably, and it is not clear who should take the lead among government officials, hospital owners, and boards of trustees. The guiding principle should be to retain those hospitals that deliver high-quality care; where needed, assistance in becoming more efficient users of resources should be provided. Evaluating which hospitals provide high-quality care will require data on patient outcomes. For hospital evaluation, the need for performance-based review and for better access to medical record information is the same as for physician-care evaluation. For instance, systems to categorize hospital mortality and to identify facilities with greater-than-expected mortality rates have been developed. Before they are routinely applied, however, a good deal of investigation into their reliability and validity is needed. In addition, the process of determining which hospitals should close should be public, with the active participation of elected community representatives.

Development of an equitable and responsive health system need not entail rationing effective services. Reaching this goal requires, among other things, greater public accountability by physicians for their performance and greater cooperation by the public in making available the information needed to support performance-based review. The medical profession may cooperate for altruistic reasons, financial reasons, or both. Motivation is not on trial here. The public may support such a step if it believes full-scale rationing can thereby be avoided. Everyone may lose a little in making this system a reality, but the nation may gain a health system that effectively and efficiently meets the needs of all Americans.

DISCUSSION QUESTIONS

1. Do you think health care currently is rationed in the United States? If so, how? Does health care need to be rationed? If so, how should health care be rationed?
2. Is health care a right to all Americans, regardless of ability to pay?
3. Should every citizen be entitled to free health care of any type (face-lifts, heart surgery, psychological help, dental care, eyeglasses, mammograms, etc.)? If not, what criteria should be used to determine which medical care is included in a national medical plan and which is not?
4. Some argue that health care does not need to be rationed because massive waste can be eliminated instead. What is "waste" in health care? Is it likely that people will agree which medical treatments are wasteful?
5. Besides the issue of rationing health care, the Oregon Medicaid plan brings up questions of federalism. Should states be allowed to allocate Medicaid funds as they please, or should the federal government exert substantial control? Why?
6. What constraints, if any, do states face in allocating medical care compared with the federal government?
7. Is the Oregon plan "playing God"? Is this avoidable?
8. Should Medicaid be an exclusively federally funded program, like Medicare, or should states retain significant authority?

ADDITIONAL READINGS

Aaron, Henry J., and William B. Schwartz. *The Painful Prescription: Rationing Hospital Care* (Washington, D.C.: Brookings Institution, 1984).

Blank, Robert H. *Rationing Medicine* (New York: Columbia University Press, 1988).

Bovbjerg, Randall R., and John Holahan. *Medicaid in the Reagan Era: Federal Policy and State Choices* (Washington, D.C.: Urban Institute, 1982).

Churchill, Larry R. *Rationing Health Care in America: Perceptions and Principles of Justice* (Notre Dame, Ind.: University of Notre Dame Press, 1987).

Greenberg, Warren. *Competition, Regulation, and Rationing in Health Care* (Ann Arbor, Mich.: Health Administration Press, 1991).

Haynes, Pamela L. *Evaluating State Medicaid Reforms* (Washington, D.C.: American Enterprise Institute, 1985).

Lohr, Kathleen N., and M. Susan Marquis. *Medicare and Medicaid: Past, Present, and Future* (Santa Monica, Calif.: Rand, 1984).

Menzel, Paul T. *Strong Medicine: The Ethical Rationing of Health Care* (New York: Oxford University Press, 1990).

Strosberg, Martin A., et al., eds. *Rationing America's Medical Care: The Oregon Plan and Beyond* (Washington, D.C.: Brookings Institution, 1992).

U.S. Congress, Office of Technology Assessment. *Evaluation of the Oregon Medicaid Proposal* (Washington, D.C.: Office of Technology Assessment, 1992).

Vladeck, Bruce C. "Unhealthy Rations." *The American Prospect* (Summer 1991).

Wiener, Joshua M. "Oregon's Plan for Health Care Rationing." *The Brookings Review* (Winter 1992).

Wiener, Joshua M., and Raymond J. Hanley. "Winners and Losers: Primary and High-Tech Care under Health Care Rationing." *The Brookings Review* (Fall 1992).

PART II
ECONOMIC POLICY

7
INDUSTRIAL POLICY

"Should the Federal Government Play a Greater Role in Promoting Specific Industries or Technologies?"

Industrial policy is the catchphrase for any form of government direction of industrial efforts, including tax incentives, direct subsidies, relaxation of anti-trust controls, international trade tariffs, and political suasion to open foreign markets. The public policy debate typically proceeds by assuming that the United States does not currently have an industrial policy, and therefore the debate is over whether it should. In fact, the United States already has a form of an industrial policy in place today, albeit an uncoordinated one. There are numerous tax subsidies to particular industries (oil and natural gas, home builders, health care providers), direct subsidies to other industries (loggers, farmers), tariffs on imported products to favor domestic industries (sugar, textiles), government-owned or -controlled enterprises (federal laboratories, a chip-making consortium called Sematech), and federally funded research and development that benefits many industries and universities. Few observers, outside of the industries that benefit directly from such government help, support the current patchwork of federal control of domestic industry. Therefore, the question is more appropriately whether these government policies should be abolished entirely or whether a more systematic direction of capital should replace the current haphazard industrial policy.

On one side, free-market advocates believe that government intervention in business investment can only lead to either inept policy or, more insidiously, manipulation of government funds by well-organized industry interests. Capital, they believe, is most appropriately allocated by free markets that will channel resources where they are most valuable. Opponents of industrial policy argue that government funds will be directed to the most politically powerful interests. Therefore, a free-market allocation is always preferred to a political allocation, and industrial policy opponents prefer to frame the issue as: Should government be in the business of picking winners and losers? Their answer is a resounding no.

On the other side, industrial policy supporters prefer that the question be rephrased in this way: Should government promote emerging industries and technologies that will, over the long run, stimulate domestic employment and wages? Interventionists point to successes in government–industry cooperation, such as the Defense Advanced Research Project Agency's (DARPA) successes in fostering emerging technologies and promoting commercial successes. This group argues that government and industry are inextricably—and appropriately—intertwined in a modern economy and that the federal government should invest in technologies and industries that will provide high-skill and high-wage jobs for Americans. Industrial policy supporters point also to the fact that the fastest-growing economies in the world (many of them Asian, including China) are characterized by substantial government involvement in allocating capital and human resources.

Underlying the debate is the simmering comparison of the role of the U.S. federal government in promoting industries with that of the Japanese government, whose vaunted Ministry of International Trade and Industry (MITI) has been heralded by some as leading Japan out of post–World War II ruin. James Fallows, Washington editor of *The Atlantic Monthly* who has written extensively on competitiveness and Asian economies, holds that government involvement can substantially increase a nation's long-term economic viability. He maintains that American economic rules are insufficient to explain economic competitiveness, using the once-thriving U.S. semiconductor industry as an example. Karl Zinsmeister of the American Enterprise Institute takes issue, arguing that government involvement in the economy is inefficient. He cites Japan's MITI as an example of the failure of governmental industrial policy, such as its attempt to force Japanese automobile companies into one, its failure to recognize the potential of Sony and transistors manufacturing, and its failed meddling in oil markets. According to Zinsmeister, many of Japan's most successful industries are those that were *not* targeted by MITI, and the success of these industries can be credited to the educational system, the high savings rate, and the strong sense of family unity of the Japanese people. The most effective policy for developing a vibrant economy, argues Zinsmeister, is to reduce, not increase, governmental involvement in the economy. Their positions are amplified below.

YES

Looking at the Sun

James Fallows

This is not supposed to be an ideological age, but the ideas we use to explain events are very powerful. The idea that Communist control of Vietnam would lead to Communist control of all of Asia required the United States to fight there. Standing up to the Viet Cong and the North Vietnamese represented a chance to correct the mistake made when no one stood up to Hitler—or so it seemed while the domino theory prevailed. In economics the idea that there can't ever be too much competition, or that the government will gum up whatever it touches, requires us to assume that whatever the market decides is for the best.

During last year's presidential campaign the columnist George Will off-handedly reminded his readers that the "lesson of the late 20th century" was government's inability to hit whatever economic target it set for itself. Therefore it was folly for the Democrats under Bill Clinton even to talk about devising a "national economic plan." The significance was that Will could say this offhandedly, and he could safely assume that most educated Americans would agree.

> Aspiring planners of national economies were thick on the ground, here and especially in Europe, as recently as the 1940s and 1950s. But recent history has been chastening, at least to people paying attention. . . . Planners say, with breezy confidence: Why wait for billions of private decisions in free markets to reveal possibilities and preferences? Government in the hands of clever people like us can know what is possible and preferable.

Suppose this paragraph, and the idea behind it, had been a little different. Suppose it had said,

> Aspiring planners of national economies were thick on the ground in America as recently as the 1950s. Even now they dominate the governments of Europe, except for England, and those of East Asia, except for Hong Kong.
>
> Perhaps it's just a coincidence, but each of these "except for" countries is the industrial sick man of its region. The European planners have succeeded in some ways but failed in many others. In East Asia, government in the hands of clever people has generally achieved what it set out to do.
>
> This history might be chastening to people paying attention to what it really means—but that's hard for us, because we like people to talk to us in English, and the Anglophone world tells us not to question what we already think.

This, of course, would represent a different idea, which would fit reality into different patterns, leading to different results. With another mental map of the world, people might feel differently about the nature of economic change. The prevailing American idea requires us to view industrial rises and falls as if they were the weather. We can complain all we want, but in the long run there's nothing much we can do, except put on a sweater when it's cold. Or the American idea makes economic change seem like an earthquake: some people are better prepared for it than others, but no one can constrain the fundamental force. A different idea—that industrial decline is less like a drought than like a disease, which might be treated—would lead to different behavior.

In the early 1960s American strategists "knew" certain things about military power. They knew that the most dangerous potential conflict was between the two superpowers. If the United States and the Soviet Union were not fighting each other, then either of them would beat whichever lesser power it faced. It was hard to make those ideas fit the facts of Vietnam and Afghanistan. American economists "know" certain things about business competition now. It is very hard to make those ideas fit the facts of the semiconductor industry, America's great success story of the early 1980s.

The story matters more than others, because of the importance of semiconductor chips to high-tech industrial growth. But even if the products themselves were insignificant, the gap between how Americans think about industry and what happened to this particular industry would be provocative. Americans have learned to explain away industrial failure with reasons that seem to make sense when applied to TV makers, or the Big Three of Detroit, or traditional heavy industry. These reasons—shortsighted management, obstinate unions, neglect of education and investment—do not fit the semiconductor case. A better understanding requires a look at ideas that are in very limited circulation among people educated and trained in English-speaking countries—ideas in direct conflict with all that we "know."

THE AGE OF INNOCENCE

California is blessed with a sense of newness, and in 1980 that sense was especially vivid. The Santa Clara Valley had just been baptized Silicon Valley and was the center of the semiconductor industry for the entire world. The new buildings to house that industry looked fresh and almost flimsy without seeming cheap. They were like mushrooms that spring up after a rain, fragile but in their own way perfect. In the downtown of Cupertino, one of the newest and freshest-looking of Silicon Valley's cities, stood a public library with a large sculpture shaped like a conquistador's helmet. Against it the sun emitted a coppery glow. Such structures were this new economy's answer to the concert halls and art museums that had gone up in Detroit and Chicago in the previous century: people were making money, and they were spreading it around.

Just a few blocks from the library was one of the main sources of the money, Apple Computer, which was then growing so rapidly that its offices were scattered among half a dozen rented sites. If Cupertino had had a sky-scraper, from its top you would have been able to see the other great successes of the valley. They included Intel, with headquarters in Santa Clara; Hewlett-Packard, in Palo Alto; the upstart Zilog, in Cupertino, which had been founded by exiles from Intel; and a host of others.

Within a few years it would become difficult to remember the sense of amazement and all-embracing promise that had emanated from Silicon Valley. But in the years before 1980 the industry did things never done before, creating things no one had ever seen. As Detroit had at the turn of the century, when new car companies were springing up practically overnight, Silicon Valley conveyed the sense that its industries were remaking the world around them—and, as in Detroit earlier, some of the people who had made the original discoveries were still in charge.

The manufacturers of the valley could be divided into three main catego-ries. At the top of the industrial food chain were the computer makers—compa-nies like Apple and Hewlett-Packard, whose brand names the public knew and whose products sat on desks in offices and homes. Below the computer makers were the semiconductor makers—Intel, Motorola, Texas Instruments, Zilog, National Semiconductor, and many others. As the industry grew through the 1980s, the public came to know their names as well, but until very late in the decade, when computer users around the country began buying extra RAM or faster processors for their home computers, the semiconductor makers sold their products to the computer industry and other industrial consumers. At the base were the semiconductor-equipment companies—Varian, Eaton, and Perkin-Elmer, among others. They were virtually invisible to the public, but without them Intel and Motorola could not have made chips, and without chips Apple and HP could not have made computers.

The varied branches of this industry were working together in California just the way American economic theory said they should. Few companies in this industry were big and integrated. Most were small, specialized, and agile. The giants of those days, IBM and Xerox, were present in the valley but served largely as brooder houses from which ambitious engineers and breakthroughs in basic research would emerge. (AT&T's Bell Labs had played the same role in the industry's early days.) Every branch of the industry seemed unchallengeably strong—as U.S. car makers had seemed in the 1950s, as U.S. software houses believe themselves to be today.

Japanese manufacturers, who had already created problems for other, less advanced-seeming American industries, were barely on the map. At the urging of the Japanese government a number of big Japanese firms—Toshiba, Hitachi, Fujitsu, NEC—were by the mid-1970s building both chips and computers. But they still relied overwhelmingly on American suppliers for chip-making equipment; they had no way to match it on their own.

Because of everything that was going right in Silicon Valley, its workers—and most of the American public—saw a kind of commonsense economic *and moral* logic to its rise. These industries were forward-looking and flexible. They used advanced technology and they created good jobs. They invested for the long run; they thought of labor and management as a team; they weren't crying for government protection, as so many of America's "sunset" industries were. Opinion polls in the 1980s still showed great American confidence in the country's technical prowess. Koreans might move from textiles to steel, Japanese from steel to cars, but Americans would move from cars to computer chips, and who could tell what would come next?

THE SUDDEN COLLAPSE

Less than ten years later everything about this industry had changed. The very companies that had supposed they demonstrated the moral superiority of the American way of doing business seemed by the late 1980s to be making the opposite point.

Through the late 1970s American companies dominated chip making and the manufacture of semiconductor equipment—the machines used to produce chips. Of all the machines in the world used to make semiconductors in the middle and late 1970s, about 85 percent came from America; about 80 percent of those used in Japan were American.

By 1982 Japanese semiconductor companies were making more "dynamic random access memory" chips, or DRAMS (pronounced "dee-rams"), than American firms. These DRAM products are what most computer users think of as "memory chips." Three years later Japan's production of semiconductor products as a whole exceeded America's. As Japanese companies increased their output of chips, they also turned to Japanese suppliers for chip-making equipment. By 1985 American equipment makers had barely 25 percent of the market in Japan, already the world's largest and fastest-growing market.

The best-publicized American success was in the area of microprocessors—the chips that interpret the instructions in computer programs and control the operations of the computer as a whole. The two American powerhouses in microprocessor making were Intel and Motorola. Intel had started out as a memory-chip company—indeed, it had invented the DRAM chip in 1969—but, like many others, had been forced out of that business as Japanese producers came in. Unlike the others, however, it had found a new and amazingly lucrative niche in producing microprocessors. Motorola, which had been actively fighting trade wars in Japan, and whose processor chips were used in the Macintosh and in a variety of industrial applications, also prospered.

Each of the two companies had worked to have its chips designed into major computer operating systems. Intel's chips dominated the IBM-compatible world of computers running DOS, Microsoft Windows, and OS/2; Motorola's ran the Macintosh and other Apple products. These relationships provided a steady cash flow that buoyed Intel and Motorola when the rest of the American semiconductor industry was foundering.

In 1978 the two largest merchant semiconductor firms in the world were Texas Instruments and Motorola. (IBM was ranked as the world's largest producer, but it used chips for its own products, unlike the merchant firms that sold the chips they made.) By 1983 Japanese semiconductor companies were spending more on new facilities than American ones. By 1985 they were spending more on research and development. By 1986 the top three merchant firms were NEC, Hitachi, and Toshiba, and there were six Japanese firms among the ten world leaders. At that time, according to one report, "most non-Japanese producers of DRAMs had been eliminated from the world market or marginalized; Japanese firms controlled 90 percent of world production of 256K DRAMs." Even AT&T was leaving the DRAM business by the end of the decade. Early in 1991 I met a minister of the Korean government who had come to Washington to try to put together alliances of Korean and American technology firms. If they tried to make it on their own, he said, they were both certain to be eclipsed by Japanese firms.

The chips were raw material for other advanced products: they went into computers, VCRs, and increasingly into cars. NEC, Hitachi, and Toshiba were best known not for the chips they sold but for their computers, VCRs, machine tools, and similar finished goods that incorporated chips. The United States has twice as many people as Japan, an economy that through the 1980s was more than twice as large as Japan's, and a computer-and-semiconductor industry that was regarded as leading the entire world. Yet in 1988 Japan's *consumption* of semiconductors—its use of them as components for cars, computers, and countless other high-value products—was greater than America's.

In addition to providing the supplies for computer makers and other "downstream" industries, the chip makers were themselves major customers. They bought from the "upstream" equipment makers that made the complex and expensive capital goods necessary to produce chips. As the American semiconductor industry dwindled, so did the related American industries that bought from and sold to it. In theory this need not have happened—American etcher makers could sell equipment to Hitachi rather than to Advanced Micro Devices; American computer makers could get all the DRAM chips they needed from NEC rather than from sources nearby in Silicon Valley. But it didn't work that way.

As the semiconductor industry grew in Japan, it evolved in such a way as to promote linkages with other Japanese firms—and prevent them with non-Japanese firms. In the mid-1970s Japan's Ministry of International Trade and Industry launched its VLSI projects, the most visible of numerous efforts to coordinate the growth of Japan's computer-related industries. The acronym stood for "very-large-scale integration," and the projects involved preferential access to capital, government-sponsored research, strategies for licensing technology from foreign (mainly American) suppliers, and other means to help Japanese producers overcome the foreign lead in high-tech production.

By the logic of American-style economic theory, such government-sponsored efforts were both unnecessary and self-defeating. They were unnecessary because if customers in Japan wanted chips, chip-making machines, or computers, they could always just buy them from suppliers in other countries. There was no need to create new industries from scratch. And the efforts were self-defeating because government interference would raise the price that

Japanese industrial customers had to pay, handicapping the firms that used the chips.

Japanese commentators, when writing in English, often claim that precisely this logic prevailed in Japan. "We Japanese, like people everywhere, import when other countries can provide competitively attractive goods and services," one famous Japanese spokesman asserted this year. Yet this nationality-blind, purely price-minded mentality cannot explain the way the Japanese semiconductor industry grew. The strategy of developing high-tech manufacturing abilities within Japan rather than buying high-tech goods from outside Japan succeeded.

With each passing year Japanese firms had a larger share in every part of the industry: machinery, chips, and computers. By the end of the 1980s American equipment makers—the companies that produced the specialized, ultra-precision equipment for each of the twenty-five-plus steps necessary to make a semiconductor—still outsold Japanese suppliers in every part of the world except Japan. But the market inside Japan had become so large, and was so thoroughly dominated by Japanese suppliers, that Japanese equipment makers outsold American ones worldwide.

In Japan the companies that made chips were tightly connected to the companies that bought chips—and connected by something beyond the prospect of business advantage which momentarily binds buyers to sellers in the American marketplace. The closest analogy from American life is the military. Just as the U.S. Air Force, with its allies in industry and Congress, competes bitterly against the Army and the Navy (and their respective allies) for budget dollars and prestige, so do Toshiba, NEC, and Fujitsu, with their allies, compete bitterly against one another for primacy and market share. Yet each kind of competitor recognizes limits to its rivalry. Fundamentally it is on the same team as its rivals, and at certain points all must suppress their immediate interests for the common good. According to Western economic theory there is virtually no "shared interest" among business competitors. Members of the American military system, and of the Japanese business system, need no theory to articulate why they are on the same side.

THE UNEXPECTED CHIP SHORTAGE

In 1985, just as the last non-Japanese producers of DRAM chips were about to drop out of the business because of sustained low-priced exports from Japan, a strange thing happened. For at least two decades the price of chips had steadily gone down. Factories became bigger and more efficient. Producers learned how to eliminate defects, which meant they had fewer flawed chips to throw away, which in turn reduced the overall cost per finished chip. Yet starting that year 256-kilobyte DRAM chips started to become expensive and scarce. Prices went up, and stayed up, as they never had before.

One of the industry's chronic headaches had been the "learning curve," a rapid fall in the price of a new chip six or eight months after it was introduced.

Financial experts at Intel in 1980 explained to me that the retail price of a chip began to plummet once competitors figured out how to make it. Previously exotic products like 64K chips and 80286 processors became mere commodities, and forces of supply and demand drove the price through the floor. This was a blessing for consumers, but it meant that companies had to be quick to develop new products, so that they could earn their profits in those first six or eight months of premium pricing. In the past, high prices had always led to increased supply—the more the money that was coming in, the more of it the companies reinvested in factory space. But as the price of 256K chips mysteriously rose, Japanese companies did not invest in any more 256K production space.

The exact causes of the DRAM shortage are still hotly debated in Japan and the United States. In brief, most discussion in America assumed that the United States itself had caused this price rise, through its complaints about Japanese "dumping" of chips in the previous three years. Reports published in Japan suggested that the Japanese industry itself engineered the rise, taking advantage of the OPEC-like control it had finally attained over chip supplies. Either way, the results were unmistakable. An American high-tech industry that had fed on chips, using more and more memory to produce bigger and faster machines, was suddenly cut off from its supply. Chip prices were going up, defying the industry's collective experience—and no matter what the price, some chips seemed impossible to find.

Officials of the Ministry of International Trade and Industry (MITI) began regulating the flow of precious DRAM chips out of the country, much as oil ministers had regulated output during OPEC's heyday. MITI had long maintained a list of goods subject to government approval before they could be sold to customers in China. An official of Hitachi, one of Japan's major DRAM producers, said that during the shortage "it was easier to get approval from MITI to sell [goods subject to government control] into China than it was to get approval to sell DRAMS into the United States." Japanese producers that were strong in DRAMS but relatively weak in other semiconductor products, such as "application-specific integrated circuits," or ASICS, began offering package deals to American customers on a take-it-or-leave-it basis: We'll let you have DRAMS if you'll buy our ASICS. American computer makers bought expansion boards from Japanese suppliers simply to strip off and use the DRAM chips.

The shortage was intense through most of 1988. Its most enduring effect was to aggravate a division between two branches of the American high-tech industry, chip makers and computer makers. In Japan these industries generally saw themselves as allies—and in many cases were actually part of the same firm. In America the chip and computer makers were often at odds. For the chip makers, of course, higher chip prices meant higher revenues. For the computer makers, higher chip prices meant higher costs. So although the American computer makers might theoretically agree that it was wrong for Japanese chip makers to dump chips, at least in the short term the dumping was a boon. More important, although the evil of dumping was theoretical, the hardship caused by the chip shortage was immediate for the U.S. computer makers. Most of them retained a "never again" mentality after the 1988 short-age. They realized the dangers of exposing themselves to another DRAM shortage by antagonizing suppliers in Japan.

These disagreements came to a famous climax early in 1990. IBM had spent much of the previous year pushing for a new U.S. chip-making consortium. The idea behind the project was that America's biggest chip-using and chip-making companies would band together to help strengthen the domestic semiconductor industry. Computer companies such as Digital Equipment and Hewlett-Packard—which, like IBM, used tremendous numbers of chips—would join semiconductor companies such as Intel and LSI Logic in building a large, advanced chip-making facility to be called U.S. Memories. The computer companies would then commit themselves to buying a certain share of the plant's future output, even if in the short term they could obtain chips more cheaply from Japanese or Korean suppliers. The project's backers argued that in the long term the computer companies and the whole domestic high-tech industry would be stronger if American-owned chip companies survived.

U.S. Memories had been proposed in 1988, during the great chip shortage. As it held its first organizational meetings, in 1989, chip prices began drifting down. By the summer of 1989 another chip glut seemed to be in the making. Japanese manufacturers had expanded their output, and U.S. computer makers could get all the chips they wanted at good prices. In September of 1989, amid falling chip prices, Apple Computer announced that it wouldn't support U.S. Memories. Apple spokesmen said there was no need for the project, now that DRAM chips were cheap and plentiful again. By November, Compaq, Sun Microsystems, Unisys, and Tandy had all rejected U.S. Memories as well.

At a showdown meeting in Dallas on January 10, 1990, Sanford Kane, the president of U.S. Memories, asked the remaining partners to state explicitly how much money they would put up and how many U.S. Memories chips they would buy. IBM and Digital were the only two computer companies to make significant commitments. Hewlett-Packard, one of the original supporters of the plan, backed off. By the end of the meeting it was clear that U.S. Memories was dead.

"These guys have a tactical view of the world; they don't think strategically," Sanford Kane told Stephen Kreider Yoder, of *The Wall Street Journal*, shortly after the meeting. They were able "to so quickly forget that a year ago they were screaming for this"—that is, for some alternative to Japanese suppliers. "For them, it's 'Don't worry, be happy.' Just close your eyes and blindly go on." Kenneth Flamm, then a semiconductor expert at the Brookings Institution and now a Pentagon official in the Clinton Administration, said in the same article that the U.S. Memories failure "goes to prove Akio Morita's contention that U.S. business has a ten-minute time horizon."

With a longer perspective, those who argued for a U.S. consortium said, computer companies would realize how deeply they were threatened by reliance on foreign suppliers. If, for instance, Compaq was selling laptop computers in competition with Toshiba, but both of them relied on Toshiba chips and screens from Sharp, then in the long run Compaq would lose.

At about the time U.S. Memories failed, Ingolf Ruge, a German technology expert, said,

> The goal of the Japanese . . . is a world monopoly on chips. They have even announced this publicly, and they are acting with this in mind. About a year ago, all Japanese manufacturers suddenly cut back on production, shooting prices way up. This monopolistic policy is currently costing companies like Nixdorf [a major German computer maker] tens of millions of Deutschmarks.

DEBILITATING DEPENDENCE

Through the early 1990s American politicians would often threaten to deny the American market to foreign manufacturers as a way of getting what the United States wanted. Since America was by far the world's biggest importer, this was sometimes a plausible threat. In 1992 Japan, for instance, sent 28 percent of all its exports to the United States, its largest customer, and only six percent to its second largest customer, Hong Kong. But the threat was less plausible than many Americans believed, because in many areas Japanese companies were the only known suppliers. The American market for fax machines was large, but there were no domestic manufacturers. In 1991 the U.S. Office of Technology Assessment issued a report on international competition in high-tech manufacturing. It concluded that for a number of steps in the semiconductor-making process Japanese companies were the only suppliers. No American companies had the machinery or technical know-how to compete.

Also in 1991 one Japanese electronics maker irritated the U.S. government by selling equipment to Iran. Some federal agencies proposed punishing the company by refusing to buy its products. The main resistance came from the Pentagon: the American military realized that it could not develop several projects it had under way if the company were barred from selling in the United States. During the brief war against Iraq the U.S. military grumbled about the difficulty of getting supplies and crucial parts from Japanese industries; the Japanese government, after all, was much less enthusiastic about the war than the American government was. The most celebrated American weapons used during that war, including the Patriot missiles that intercepted some of the Iraqi SCUDs, all relied for their operation on a kind of ceramic chip packaging that no American company produced in significant quantities.

Several years earlier the National Security Agency, which is in charge of intercepting, processing, encoding, and decoding millions of messages a year, took the extraordinary step of setting out to build its own semiconductor-manufacturing facility. It went to this extreme to avoid having to buy foreign-manufactured semiconductors, which could conceivably be tainted with virtually undetectable yet potentially catastrophic viruslike hostile programming. Despite its determination to avoid relying on foreign sources the NSA found that it could not. For certain kinds of semiconductor-manufacturing equipment it had no alternative but to buy from suppliers in Japan.

The NSA was asked what it would do when its foreign-made machines needed servicing, as they inevitably would. Would it allow service representatives from the parent company to come to its supersecret premises and work on the machines? A government official involved in buying the machines smiled ruefully, according to another U.S. government official who witnessed the exchange, and replied, "Oh, we'd never risk having a foreign citizen enter the facility. If we can't fix it ourselves, we'll just throw that piece of equipment out and purchase a new one, even if it means several million dollars for replacement instead of several hundred dollars for repair."

Just before the Gulf War the Defense Intelligence Agency circulated a highly classified and controversial draft report about the American military's growing dependence on Japanese high-tech equipment. The report warned that the Japanese government was explicitly considering how it could exploit the military's dependence to gain additional leverage over the United States.

In 1990 Andrew Grove, one of the founders of Intel, gave a speech contrasting the Japanese and American semiconductor industries. Among the most striking differences, he said, was how much denser and deeper the Japanese network of suppliers was. One Japanese company had decided to get into the DRAM business and was up and operating within about a year. For immediate service it could call on suppliers of machinery and components located in Japan. "At one point," Grove said, "there were twelve hundred vendor employees"—that is, representatives of companies making the components and machinery—"swarming all over the location where this company's first factory was being built." He added, "We couldn't do this in the United States for love or money. There are no twelve hundred vendor employees and there are no dozens of relevant suppliers."

By the early 1990s American semiconductor and computer companies were routinely complaining to the government, but their complaints had taken on a strange new fatalistic tone. In many cases they were not even asking for a better opportunity to sell to Japanese customers, or to sell in competition with Japanese firms in other markets around the world. Rather, they were complaining because they were having trouble *buying* the best chip-making equipment from Japanese suppliers. In the fall of 1991 a report from the General Accounting Office said that a third of the American companies it surveyed had had problems buying up-to-date components from Japanese suppliers, even though the components were already for sale within Japan. Among the crucial components were flat display screens for laptop computers and the most modern versions of "steppers" for producing semiconductors. One company said that the delays had cost it $1.4 billion in sales, and another said the problems in getting display screens had put it "essentially out of business." William Spencer, the president of an American chip-making consortium called Sematech, was asked early last year which kind of silicon wafers U.S. manufacturers would be using in the long run. "That's easy to answer," he said. "It depends on what Japan, and to a degree Germany, will sell us. We no longer have sufficient silicon sources of our own, so what we can make depends on what they will sell us."

At about the same time, several American newspapers carried the news that Intel, clearly the giant of Silicon Valley, had nearly perfected a technology called "flash memory," which could revolutionize the electronics business yet again. Because normal computer chips do not store information when the power is off, computers require bulky storage devices, especially hard-disk drives. Flash memory retains its contents when the machine is turned off, so it could eventually eliminate disk drives. Perhaps more important, it could add enormous amounts of memory to small devices not normally thought of as computers, from toys to compact-disc players to organizers like the popular Sharp Wizard series.

This looked like a comeback for the American industry—and it was so reported in a euphoric story in *The Washington Post*, in February of last year. But on the same day the *Post* story appeared, Jacob Schlesinger, of *The Wall Street Journal*, presented the same news in a very different light. Intel had come up with the technology—based, for once, on an invention that originated in Japan. But Intel could not *make* the chips. Even Intel—touted throughout the American press last year as the classic high-tech success—lacked both the money and the manufacturing capacity. It would rely on Sharp to do the actual production work. "The Intel–Sharp pact shows growing American dependence on Japan, even when the U.S. has the technological edge," the *Journal* story concluded.

From Intel's point of view the alliance with Sharp would help avoid another peril. The most valuable customers for flash-memory chips would be consumer-electronics companies—the ones that made TVs, VCRs, computer games. Those companies were mainly based in Japan. Everything in Intel's experience indicated that if it did not form a partnership with a Japanese company it would eventually be frozen out of this new market.

Just before the war against Iraq began, in December of 1990, the Nomura Research Institute, which is connected to one of the world's largest stock-brokerage houses, Nomura Securities, of Tokyo, released its survey of the semiconductor and computer industries. Anyone who has tried to talk delicately around an unpleasant truth ("Well, I'm sure Johnny is trying his best in math") could recognize the tone of this document. For instance, "The widely held view is that the declining market share indicates loss of American competitiveness, but we believe this is not necessarily the case."

The report sympathetically but firmly stated that American firms simply could not compete in the future.

> As the memory capacity of DRAMs increased, management of the manufacturing process and the capability to make massive capital investments became the major determinants of competitiveness, and since Japanese companies were stronger than U.S. companies in both respects, their share of the world market expanded rapidly. . . . A second trend is that the U.S. will fade as a growth market.

And so on. It is difficult for Americans to compete with Japan's "oligopolistic dominance," which came from "weeding out of weaker companies unable to keep up with heavy capital expenditure," the report said. "In the technology-intensive computer and semiconductor industries, the basic trend since the start of the 1980s—market share gains by Japanese companies, market share losses by American companies—will likely continue in the 1990s." Whenever American firms started to show weakness, the report said, they usually went on to collapse. "The U.S. market is hard on losers. Companies that have reached the limits of growth rarely have a chance to come back." Large Japanese firms, in contrast, simply did not go bankrupt, and were able to buffer losses in one division with earnings from another.

The Nomura report—which was intended for domestic Japanese consumption rather than for inspection by Americans—included a nightmare version of a Horatio Alger story. It concerned a young, talented, and ambitious American software engineer known as Mr. A. He starts with a big high-tech company, as would his counterpart in Japan. Then this company is acquired in a hostile takeover and Mr. A is laid off—a fate that would not befall his counterpart in Japan. He moves to a fast-growing company but is laid off again when business slows down. He joins yet another company but, hardened by his experience, resolves to "keep the knowledge and skills he was acquiring to himself as a means of ensuring his job security." After five years with this firm Mr. A considers jumping ship and starting his own firm, with the help of venture capitalists. The Nomura report drew these lessons:

> Mr. A's experiences in the status- and class-conscious culture of the American company suggest why the United States is so imbued with an entrepreneurial spirit, yet why American industry is so sloppy when it comes to factory productivity and quality control.

"CULTURAL" EXPLANATIONS

How can we explain what happened to the American semiconductor industry? The familiar reasons for industrial failure—greedy bosses, pigheaded unions, rampant short-termism, overregulation by the meddlesome state—don't seem to apply.

The Japanese explanation is simpler. During the 1980s most Japanese high-tech industries thrived. Japanese commentators and politicians are quick to see the "unique" traits of the Japanese people as the explanation for almost any phenomenon in Japan. Therefore Japanese discussions of the semiconductor industry have stressed "harmonious" working patterns, attention to detail, and related Japanese characteristics that supposedly make it natural for Japanese companies to excel.

At a Hitachi semiconductor factory on the island of Kyushu, in 1986, I walked through fabrication areas that looked very much like their counterparts in Texas and California. The hardware and the procedures seemed so similar. Why were Hitachi and other Japanese manufacturers doing so much better?

"The starting level of production is not so different here from in America," the manager who was escorting me said—in English, since he had studied for a while in the United States. He paused, and indicated thoughtfulness with the distinctive Japanese gesture of "teeth-sucking." (This involves opening the mouth, putting the bottom teeth against the upper lip, and inhaling, with a sucking, slurping sound. Its body-language message is "Whew! I need to think about this for a minute.") When he recovered, he said, "The starting level is similar—but ours improves much more rapidly than in America. There is a difference of culture. It is often said that we Japanese are united as a single people, or even race. In the U.S. there are so many people with different backgrounds and religions and races, it is harder to work together in harmony—unless you are all Swedes in Wisconsin."

Americans themselves have, in their time, fallen back on ethnic theories to explain success or failure. But ethnicity and race are no longer part of any respectable discussion of business trends. Instead the emphasis is on the ultimate justice of the market. We all assume that the efficient companies will survive and the inefficient will fail. Governments can try to tamper with this law of nature, by offering subsidies or shielding producers from foreign competition. But in the short run these attempts will harm a nation's consumers, by raising prices, and in the long run they will weaken the nation's producers, by delaying the moment when old industries are cleared away so that new ones can rise.

In the late 1980s this view was summed up in a grim comment made by a Republican official during a meeting about American semiconductor makers. Sometimes the words have been attributed to Richard Darman, the director of the Office of Management and Budget, and sometimes to Michael Boskin, the chair of the Council of Economic Advisers. Sometimes they have been attributed to someone else. Each of the supposed speakers denies uttering the sentence, but the underlying argument, if not the specific wording, accurately reflects a position all of them have held for years: "If our guys can't hack it, then let 'em go."

This vision of "creative destruction," in the famous words of Joseph Schumpeter, is indispensable as a guide to most economic activity. But it can't quite explain the semiconductor case. All the familiar variants of the "If they can't hack it" argument apply to certain parts of the American economy, but they don't tell us what went on in Silicon Valley.

Consider several elements of the standard analysis. The first and most familiar part is that American management has simply forgotten why it is in business. Too many companies are run by financiers, not engineers or production experts. The executives have feathered their own nests, ignored and mistreated their workers, been too lazy to learn what it takes to please German or Japanese customers, and in general failed to do their best.

A second, related explanation is that American products have become shoddy and backward—and a nation that still excels in basic science has forgotten how to put its inventions to commercial use. The most popular Japanese products of the 1980s were typically hatched in American labs. The United States is following the unwholesome trail blazed by the English, who by the 1930s were famed for having brilliant tinkerer-inventors but an increasingly feeble manufacturing base. Before and during the Second World War, British scientists came up with most of the crucial breakthroughs in radar technology. Yet the high-volume production was done in America, where the huge wartime investment in radar provided a foundation for the postwar American electronics industry.

The third standard belief is that American managers have been ruinously focused on the short term. Given a choice between spending $10 million for new equipment that will pay off in five years and using the money to boost earnings next quarter, they have too often pumped up the earnings, because their own pay is tied to results *right now*.

All these failings are serious, and one or more of them may seem to explain what has gone wrong when we examine American businesses that are failing. But they weren't failings of the semiconductor industry in 1980, when it was on the verge of its precipitous decline.

By the rules that American politicians and journalists use to explain success or failure, there was no obvious reason why the industry should have been eclipsed so fast—indeed, relatively much faster than any of the "bad" old industries like steel and cars. The semiconductor industry was in trouble less than two decades after its basic product was invented and barely one decade after its most rapid growth. It is as if other industries in which the United States now considers itself dominant—movies and music, pharmaceuticals, university education, software—were on the skids by the end of the nineties. A Saturn plant for GM, a mini-mill for steel makers, a radical new program of teaching Japanese or German in the schools—all these might be necessary for ginning up the economy. But on the evidence of what happened to Silicon Valley, perhaps those things would not be sufficient. Maybe our understanding of competition is not sufficient either.

DIFFERENT GOVERNMENTS, DIFFERENT SYSTEMS

Peter Drucker, the business strategist, in his 1989 book *The New Realities* gave one view of how Japan had changed the competitive landscape.

> The emergence of new non-Western trading countries—foremost the Japanese—creates what I would call *adversarial* trade. . . . Competitive trade aims at creating a customer. Adversarial trade aims at dominating an industry. . . . Adversarial trade, however, is unlikely to be beneficial to both sides. . . . The aim in adversarial trade . . . is to drive the competitor out of the market altogether rather than to let it survive.

Most American commentators have offered narrower explanations for competitive shifts. For example, Michael Porter, of the Harvard Business School, claims several times in his lengthy 1990 book *The Competitive Advantage of Nations* that Japanese chip makers succeeded mainly because they were quicker-moving than their American competitors. They made the crucial switch from one form of chip technology to another (from "bipolar" to "metal oxide") faster than the Americans—and this switch, Porter says, "catapulted the Japanese to industry leadership."

But this explanation only raises further questions. Why, exactly, would American businesses have been slower to switch from one kind of chip to another, especially when in the preceding decade they had seen more clearly than anyone else the importance of moving fast? Was it simply that they were complacent and satisfied, like the barons of Detroit or Pittsburgh in their dominant days? That doesn't seem likely—the rhetoric that poured out of Silicon Valley in those days was full of exhortations to stay alert, to adapt or die, to keep moving ahead. Had they forgotten that there were competitors overseas? Did they dismiss them, the way auto makers had dismissed the tinny, laughable cars from Japan? Hardly. Even in 1980 Silicon Valley rang with analyses of the "Asian challenge."

Individual firms in America may have made strategic errors, and individual firms in Japan may have been persistent and skillful and shrewd. But something else was going on that shaped the actions of these firms, and its effects sometimes dwarfed what any one firm could do. Something was going on that did not often show up in the speeches and the editorials about quality control and foreign-language training and good morale on the factory floor. That something involved factors left out of standard discussions of "improving competitiveness."

One of these missing factors was government. On its way up and on its way down, the semiconductor industry was driven not just by private companies—although they made every crucial operating decision and came up with every new design—but by a network of government–business interactions. The role of the government is often considered an embarrassing afterthought in American or British discussions of how economies should work. Yet in America, as in every other country that spawned a semiconductor industry, government incentives and pressures shaped the way the industry grew. All around the world the design, production, and marketing of chips were carried out by private firms. It was these firms—America's Intel and Japan's Toshiba, Korea's Samsung and France's Thomson—that journalists and politicians mainly discussed. But each firm took the shape it did largely because of policies imposed by its government.

Last year the Semiconductor Industry Association published a history of the industry, which says that the industry's growth since the 1950s can be divided into five stages. The first four are these:

1) The pioneering American efforts in the 1950s and 1960s to develop transistors and integrated circuits, and to learn to make them efficiently and in large quantities.

2) The Japanese entry into the field in the 1960s and subsequent rapid catch-up with American producers in the 1970s and 1980s.

3) The effort of European manufacturers, principally Philips, of Holland, and Siemens, of Germany, to survive in the business in the 1980s, despite the American technical lead and the Japanese competitive surge.

4) The emergence of other East Asian producers, especially those in Korea, to challenge the Japanese in the late 1980s.

Every one of these steps, the history says, depended fundamentally on government policies. Using the emphasis of italics the authors wrote,

> *Government policies have shaped the course of international competition in microelectronics virtually from the inception of the industry, producing outcomes completely different than would have occurred through the operation of the market alone.*

The SIA authors are not, of course, purely detached historians; their organization has lobbied for the U.S. government to respond more aggressively to Japan's industrial policy for semiconductors. And the SIA can offer evidence to substantiate its view of events. Let's consider the various stages again.

U.S. genesis. American companies led the world in semiconductor technology thanks to their own efforts, expenditures, and ingenuity—but also thanks to U.S. government support. The government did not directly finance the crucial research that led to integrated circuits, but the companies making these investments understood that if the products were successful, the Department of Defense and NASA would be standing in line as customers.

For instance, in 1962 NASA announced that it would use integrated circuits—the first simple chips, produced by Texas Instruments, Fairchild Semiconductor, and other suppliers—in the computer systems that would guide Apollo spacecraft to the moon, and the Air Force decided to buy ICs to guide its Minuteman missiles. Every history of the semiconductor business regards these contracts as a turning point; they guaranteed a big and relatively long-term market, which no private purchaser could have offered at the time.

The early government purchases let manufacturers increase their volume of production. As volume went up, price went down, and commercial customers began buying more and more chips. This was not an explicit "industrial policy," but it had the same effect: it gave the companies a reason to invest in new products and new factories.

The Defense Department played another crucial role. Government contracts had paid for some of the research that led to patents. In those cases the Defense Department required the companies, in effect, to share the patents with the American industry as a whole. Sharing with foreign producers was at this time moot, since there were virtually none; moreover, the Defense Department could use national security as a justification for excluding foreign-owned companies. By normal market logic, a company would have no incentive to share its discoveries for nothing. But the government insisted that such discoveries be treated as a public good. This naturally made it easier for small companies, which became the hallmark of Silicon Valley, to find niches and go to work.

The U.S. government did not run a single semiconductor factory, and no doubt would have failed if it had tried. But it provided conditions that *could not otherwise have existed*, especially the reliable markets in the crucial early years, and thereby got the industry off the ground. The government has never directly operated farms either—and if it had, it would have been less efficient than the sturdy, self-disciplined folk who settled the American heartland. Yet many of the farmers received their land through government land grants; the territory was originally mapped by government (often Army) cartographers; new seeds were continually developed by the government's agricultural experiment stations. The government did not directly make airplanes, even during the Second World War, and if it had, they would not have been as good as those made by Boeing or Lockheed or what was then known as Douglas Aircraft (and is now McDonnell Douglas). But, even more than with semiconductors, the government provided the initial market—directly, through the War Department, and indirectly, through air-mail contracts that got fledgling airlines going. Americans still talk about "government interference" and "industrial policy" as if they faced a choice between grim, Soviet-style central planning and entrepreneurs completely on their own. In reality, even as lively and entrepreneurial an American industry as semiconductors reflects a mixture of visible and invisible hands.

Japanese ascendancy. The role of government in the rise of the Japanese industry is more familiar and is taken for granted. Without heavy government involvement, Japan's semiconductor industry would not exist. In the beginning, during the decade or two or three after the Second World War, non-Japanese firms had difficulty exporting to Japan, were virtually forbidden to invest in Japan, and were forced to license their advanced technology to Japanese producers at fees set by the Japanese government if they hoped to do business in Japan at all.

These aspects of Japanese policy had long-lasting consequences—in the 1960s and 1970s foreign suppliers could not build up the relationships with customers in Japan which, they now know, are essential for doing business there—and the rules established by the Japanese government had nothing to do with enhancing free-market competition as an end in itself. Market forces were *tools*: Sony and Matsushita and NEC and Toshiba competed against one another as hard as they could. But the goal—building an industry in Japan run by Japanese people—was decided on and carried out by the government.

Why does this matter? Because it is so much at odds with the prevailing American idea about why industries rise and fall. Michael Porter says that Japanese semiconductor makers succeeded because of the fierce "internal competition" in Japan. This is a favorite theme in analyses of Japanese success: because Japanese companies had to try so hard to stay alive at home, they were naturally better prepared for competition overseas. Yes, competition inside Japan is intense. But is that what made IBM and Texas Instruments decide to license Japanese patents?

A leading trade economist, Gary Saxonhouse, says that the postwar Japanese emphasis on high-value manufacturing is a "natural" part of Japan's high literacy rate and "factor endowment." With a lot of people and with not much space, the Japanese naturally tend to produce sophisticated, valuable products. In isolation this may sound logical enough. But it doesn't fully explain how Japan went from having virtually no semiconductor industry in 1970, when it was already crowded and the people were already well educated, to holding the lead in 1990—or why the foreign share of its market remained constant through the eighties, no matter what ups and downs were occurring in technology and market position and corporate strength elsewhere in the world.

"If our guys can't hack it"—this is a natural reflection of everything we have been taught about industrial development. But a more realistic view is the conclusion of one authoritative history of the industry, *Competing for Control*, by Michael Borrus. "State policy would not have succeeded without the efforts, investments, and strategies of Japanese industry," it says. "But the industry would almost certainly have failed without the state."

Phases three and four of the industry's growth, according to the SIA account, were *European survival* and the appearance of the *new East Asian entrants*. In each case, as with the U.S. and Japanese examples, government policy made a decisive difference. European governments unashamedly promoted national champions in technology. The French government, in an effort to promote a domestic high-tech industry, subsidized the installation of Minitels, computer terminals for looking up phone numbers and other simple functions, in most homes. The Korean case is less familiar to the Western public but even more overt. Chun Doo Hwan, who took power after the previous strongman was kicked out in a coup, believed in state-run industrialization. In the mid-1980s his advisers persuaded him, in the words of a magazine report, that "the only way to crack the world semiconductor market would be to orchestrate a massive development project involving every important Korean company in the business." By the end of the decade analysts from the World Bank—which is committed to the proposition that state guidance usually fails—concluded about Korea that "there is no doubt that the government has sought explicitly to encourage the development of high-tech industries like computers and semiconductors by designating them 'strategic industries' entitled to certain preferential treatment."

That is, the growth and survival of semiconductor industries has not been just a matter of "hacking it," or fostering competition, or having good schools—although each of these ingredients has played a part. In fact the evidence seems to run exactly the other way. Every country that has waited for the industry to develop "naturally," through the flux and play of market forces, is waiting still. Canada is as populous and as committed to education as some countries that now make semiconductors. It had as much natural advantage for the semiconductor industry in 1980 as Korea did—indeed, much more, since it was richer, better educated, and closer to major markets and research centers in the United States. Hong Kong ten years ago had as much natural inclination for making semiconductors as Singapore—it was just as crowded, just as much influenced by Confucian culture. The governments of Korea and Singapore deliberately cultivated the industry; the governments of Canada and Hong Kong did not. Korea and Singapore now have a semiconductor industry; Canada and Hong Kong do not. Governments may not be able to pick winners, but they seem to be able to make winners.

WHEN GOVERNMENT INTERFERES

And there was a fifth stage in the modern semiconductor industry. The authors of the industry study called it *"U.S. revival."* "Recovery" or "respite" might be a more appropriate term. Starting in the late 1980s some parts of the U.S.-based industry flickered back to life. The graph lines showing worldwide market share for American-made chips dropped steadily through the late 1970s and the early 1980s—and then, around 1988, ticked slightly up again. Graphs for each specific kind of chip—processors, memory chips, ASICs—all showed similar changes at about the same time.

What happened? Was the main factor the fall in the dollar's value, which made American chips cheaper for buyers around the world? Probably not—there had been very little correlation between currency changes and worldwide market share before 1988. (That is, when the dollar went up, American market share went down. When the dollar went down, American market share also went down.) Was it owing to a dramatic improvement in American education? Hah. Was it because the companies themselves tried harder in the late eighties than they had in the golden age of the early eighties? Perhaps. The kings of the American industry, Intel and Motorola, kept racing each other with new designs and improved manufacturing processes. The industry in general, like the American auto makers it had once scorned, put new emphasis on quality and service.

But something else happened at about this time: the U.S. government intervened—"interfered," if you prefer—in the workings of the market to protect American manufacturers. In 1986 the United States and Japan signed the Semiconductor Trade Arrangement, which was renewed and modified in 1991. The results of these negotiations differed from most trade agreements in that they did not attempt to remove barriers or create a level playing field in the Japanese market. The agreement was, in effect, a quota bill, paying less attention to the rules of competition in Japan than to the result. In 1986 the two governments expressed their "expectation" that by the end of 1991 U.S. companies would supply 20 percent of the semiconductors bought in Japan. At the time this agreement was signed, U.S. companies accounted for less than 10 percent of the Japanese market—and about 65 percent of the market in the rest of the world. (The deadline for reaching 20 percent was later extended to 1992.)

The Japanese government hotly denied that this "expectation" was any kind of enforceable promise. When talking to American politicians and reporters Japanese government officials often claimed, doing their best to keep a straight face, that setting a market-share target would mean government interference with private enterprise. Surely the Americans didn't want that! Yet Japanese press reports made clear that the government was behaving internally as if it believed it had to meet the target of 20 percent. MITI was twisting the arms of big Japanese industries, encouraging them to design in foreign chips when they planned new products.

In 1987 the U.S. government also decided to support Sematech, the chip-making consortium. Its purpose was to encourage American semiconductor companies to cooperate in research areas too risky or expensive for any of them to undertake independently. The government offered research contracts and subsidies to defray research costs. The cost to the federal government was $100 million a year, which was matched by contributions from the industry. And in the wake of all this government "interference" the fortunes of the American semiconductor industry finally improved. The American share of the Japanese market had remained flat, at about 10 percent, through the years when it was supposedly determined by pure market forces. It began rising, into the teens, in the late 1980s, and it neared 20 percent late in 1992, just as the Semiconductor Trade Arrangement had specified.

CAPITALISM AND PLAIN CAPITAL

What happened in Silicon Valley says something about exactly where our standard economic theories may mislead us. Beneath all the ups and downs of high-tech competition, one difference between the Japanese and American industries matters more than anything else. The Japanese companies *had more money*. They could build newer and bigger factories, because they had more capital to invest. They could prevail in price wars, because they had bigger war chests with which to cover losses. They could retain their work forces, because in recessions they did not have to lay employees off. They could invest in ten potentially promising technologies at once (and fail at nine of them), because their R&D budgets allowed more room to experiment.

According to the deepest assumptions of capitalism, governments can never outguess the market about where money should go. All that governments can—and should—do is make sure the necessary signals flow. Signals come in the form of prices; therefore the paramount goal is to "get prices right." After that everything should work on its own.

This vision of capitalism is like the American vision of democracy. The government has no right to define what a good society may be. All it can do is set the rules by which people express their views, exercise their rights, and cast their votes. According to American theory, if the system is fair, the results by definition must be good. So it is with the business system: if competition is on a level playing field, if new competitors can enter the game, if customers can choose freely and fairly among the offerings, then whatever happens will be for the best. The right amount of money will be available for investment and the right number of new ideas will pop up for putting the money to use.

By this logic the semiconductor industry in 1980 was structured about as well as any industry could be. It was fluidity and frictionlessness exemplified. The chip-making merchant firms of the valley acted as much like the "economic men" of academic theory as real human beings ever will. In the textbooks, economic man goes through life calculating the costs and benefits of different decisions—and is not swayed by irrational or sentimental concepts, including "Buy American" (or, for that matter, "Buy Japanese" or "Buy French"). The economic men who ran companies in Silicon Valley had every reason to sell equipment to whoever came up with money—even when they knew that many of the buyers might in the long run become their competitors.

In the early 1980s Silicon Valley companies raced one another to get more customers, to remove cost and waste from their operations, to increase their production runs. Every one of these steps drove prices down, down, down. The more intense the competition, the lower the prices—and the lower the prices, the thinner the profit margin. In the search for higher profits firms were forced to innovate once again.

If the American approach boiled down to getting prices right, the Japanese approach boiled down to getting enough money—not worrying about theoretical efficiency, not being concerned about the best rules for competition, but focusing only on getting the nation's money into the hands of its big manufacturing firms. If companies could get more money than their competitors, they would eventually prevail, no matter how "fair" the competition might be. This was a view of capitalism that depended on capital. It did not concentrate on rules but focused instead on one goal: to build industry as quickly as possible. It was a means of catching up, and it worked.

What was most mysterious about this approach, from the Western perspective, was that it seemed to be divorced from normal calculations of profitability. American semiconductor officials, when preparing a dumping complaint against their Japanese rivals, found in 1985 a portion of a Hitachi sales presentation that emphasized the "win at any cost" spirit. It said,

> Quote 10% Below Competition
> If they requote . . .
> Bid 10% under again
> The bidding stops when Hitachi wins . . .
> Win with the 10% rule . . .
> Find AMD and Intel sockets . . .
> Quote 10% below their price . . .
> If they requote,
> Go 10% *again*
> Don't quit until you *win*!

ANOTHER WORLD

When the American industry was doing everything right according to American economic theory, it began to collapse. When European, Japanese, and Korean producers broke all the rules of American "market rationality," they started to pull ahead. The very existence of the American industry could not be explained by natural market forces—nor could its implosion, nor could its partial recovery in the late 1980s. Every one of these trends reflected not just market forces, not just the dead hand of the state, but some interaction between the two that is usually missing from the public debate.

You don't have to care about semiconductors, or really even about economics, to be intrigued by this tension. A well-established set of theories, which undergirds our national policy and runs through nearly every speech and editorial about America's economic health, cannot explain what has happened in a major industry in the real world. Academic economists have offered nuances and refinements of the theories which more closely fit the facts of the semiconductor case. For example, they emphasize that the "externalities" of a high-tech industry can make it sensible for governments to subsidize the industry's growth. Strong semiconductor and aircraft industries generate high-wage jobs and make it easier to attract other high-value industries in the future; therefore governments may be sensible in offering subsidies, even though the simplest version of economic theory says that the choice should be left strictly to the invisible hand. But very few of these refinements make their way into the public debate, where we're usually presented with the stark choice between free markets and state control.

We can resolve this tension by disregarding the evidence—as most of us do when concentrating on consumer products like cars and TVs rather than semiconductor chips as the symbol of trade problems. We can invent exceptions and special clauses to account for the variation—much as the Ptolemaic astronomers did when they tried to fit the motion of the planets into their theory that the sun revolved around the earth. Or—we can look again at our basic ideas.

NO

MITI Mouse: Japan's Industrial Policy Doesn't Work

Karl Zinsmeister

Over the past two decades, sharp increases in international business competition and the pace of commercial innovation have sent a series of tremors rippling through the U.S. economy. Highly visible industries—such as steel and automobiles—contracted and restructured. Venerable airlines, banks, and retailers failed. Even in thriving industries like computers, some high-flying pioneers ignominiously bit the dust. When the early 1990s brought recession followed by the doldrums of sluggish economic growth, many Americans seemed to panic. Looking for ways to soup up American output, they gave the White House keys to Bill Clinton, who promised "economic change."

Candidate Clinton made it clear that the way he would pursue long-term change was through increased governmental steering of the economy. "Mr. Clinton wants to pull the American economy in the direction of the managed capitalism found in Japan and Western Europe, where governments play a larger role than Washington in shaping industries and markets," summarized the *New York Times* in 1992.

CLINTON'S MANAGED CAPITALISM

In the first months of the new administration we have begun to see exactly how President Clinton intends to use the federal apparatus to try to shape American industry. In late February, he unveiled an expansive new industrial policy with $17 billion of funding. The president proposes to remake the Commerce Department's National Institute of Standards and Technology into an aggressive, new technology-targeting agency. He says he will use U.S. national laboratories to do more research for private companies. He wants a national network of government-run "manufacturing extension" centers, a joint government–corporate program to develop "clean" cars, and a major government push to build a grid of so-called information superhighways across the country. The president says he will transfer billions of dollars from defense research into new programs that are supposed to produce civilian products instead. He has announced that the Pentagon's Defense Advanced Research Projects Agency will be renamed simply the Advanced Research Projects Agency, to reflect a wider set of responsibilities.

More efforts along these lines surely are coming. Last year Mr. Clinton campaigned on his "Rebuild America Fund," to which he proposed to allot $80 billion of fresh spending over a four-year period so that a government network of railways and roads, communications lines, and environmentalist public-works projects could be built. He endorsed a plan by Democratic senators to create a Civilian Technology Corporation that would coordinate private research and channel public funds to specific industries and companies.

Upon taking office, President Clinton set up a new National Economic Council in the White House to monitor trade patterns and protect "vital" domestic companies and sectors. Mr. Clinton originally conceived this panel as an "Economic Security Council," out of the notion that government's national security responsibilities extend directly into the realm of business and industry oversight.

He appointed as his chief economic adviser Laura D'Andrea Tyson, an unorthodox economist who argues that selective protectionism, subsidies to damaged and/or critical industries, and managed trade—meaning government negotiations to divide up the global business pie—will improve the well-being of American consumers. Ms. Tyson welcomes the idea of the federal government picking winners among technologies, and writes that it would be "criminal" to waste the peace dividend by failing to spend it subsidizing commercial technology.

The new administration also has hinted at a taste for trade protection and business subsidies. At his Little Rock economic summit last December, the president-elect listened sympathetically as corporate executives bemoaned foreign competition, and commiserated with them over the plight of the ailing old-line enterprises. Protectionist pressure has since been building fast, with big companies and unions from the airline, auto, steel, oil, semiconductor, agriculture, textile, apparel, and movie industries already in line by Inauguration Day. At the end of January, Commerce Secretary Ron Brown levied steep tariffs on steel imports, and the Treasury Department began a review that could increase duties on minivans and sport-utility vehicles from 2.5 percent to 25 percent. In late February, Mr. Brown testified that the administration might formally charge Japanese automakers with "dumping"—selling their cars too cheaply in the United States.

MEDDLERS IN MARKETS

Some of the president's closest advisers have been calling for measures along these lines for many years. Longtime Clinton pal Ira Magaziner, who has been appointed senior White House adviser, urges an energetic industrial policy that would use public funds to subsidize or even create companies to compete with foreign firms. He calls for "American companies to get the kind of help from the U.S. government that virtually every other nation gives its business."

Clinton confidant Derek Shearer, who is on record endorsing nationalized government investment in critical businesses, promises the president will have a special "Japan policy." Financier Felix Rohatyn, a major Clinton campaign donor and one of his informal economic advisers, has proposed in the past, in tandem with Jesse Jackson, that politicians should use the accumulated pension funds of public employees for major industrial and public works projects around the country in order to provide state stimulus to the economy. In his book *Putting People First*, Mr. Clinton suggests that both private and public pension funds could be tapped as a source of funding for government infrastructure projects.

Robert Reich, economic director on the transition team and now the U.S. secretary of labor, has a long history of support for government industrial planning. In March 1992, he proclaimed to the *Washington Post* that "industrial policy is back, far more respectable than it was before. These ideas were anathema in the 1980s. But the world has changed since then. The Japanese leviathan is that much larger, the European Community looks more menacing, the erosion of the U.S. industrial base is that much more apparent."

The Clinton economic agenda is still taking form, but we know enough about the views of the president and certain critical advisers to expect that lots of experiments in government industrial management lie ahead. Whether the talk is of "infrastructure spending" or "trade realignment" or "technology targeting," the consistent new emphasis in the White House will be on increased planning, spending, and intervention by Washington overseers.

COPYING THE JAPANESE?

Referring to other nations where government does more steering of the economy, Mr. Clinton argued during his campaign that we ought to "copy our competitors." The economic manipulations of France and some other European countries sometimes have been cited by Clintonites as examples. But today's favorite model for advocates of greater political orchestration of business activity is Japan. White House economic adviser Tyson argues that the "[Japanese] example may well provide the prescription . . . for our own economic revival."

"Now that the competition between centrally planned socialism and market capitalism is over, interest in Japan's alternative way of organizing a market economy should be greater than ever before," argues Alan Blinder, President Clinton's second appointment to the Council of Economic Advisers. As part of a longer paean to Japanese industrial management written in 1992, Mr. Blinder rudely dismissed the conclusion of many economists that "government intervention is a mere detail, and probably harmful" to the Japanese economy. Actually, he asserted, in Japan "the government not only tells businesses what they ought to do, but the companies frequently listen . . . the system undeniably works." Mr. Blinder concludes: "Perhaps Americans should spend less time cajoling the Japanese to be more like us and more time considering whether we might do better by being more like them."

It isn't only the Clintonites who want us to copy the Japanese. Democratic presidential candidate Paul Tsongas built his whole primary campaign around the idea that "industrial policy is what Japan has. . . . It is what we must have as well. . . . American companies need the U.S. government as a full partner if they are to have any hope of competing internationally." Indeed, every one of the Democratic candidates for president in 1992 came out in favor of a national "industrial policy" during the primaries, as did scores of congressmen in the House and Senate. "The success nations such as Japan have had by adopting industrial policies is one of the reasons laissez faire has given way to savoir faire among the Democrats," argued the *Boston Globe* during the presidential primary season.

IF YOU CAN'T BEAT 'EM . . .

The most visible advocate of the Japanese model, of course, is Ross Perot. "You've get to target the industries of the future. If you study MITI [the Ministry of International Trade and Industry] in Japan, it works," he asserts loudly.

Even a few businessmen—who traditionally have been very skeptical of government picking winners and losers in commerce—have lately adopted an "if-you-can't beat-'em, join-'em" attitude. "The government of Japan has acted. . . . The United States, too, must act. . . . The United States must have an industrial policy," argues Jerry Sanders, the outspoken CEO of electronic chipmaker Advanced Micro Devices. One informal survey of several hundred U.S. executives doing business in Japan recently found that two-thirds of all respondents answered "yes" to the question, "Do you feel that the United States should develop an industrial policy similar to Japan's?" A 1991 poll by the *Harvard Business Review* found that 74 percent of American business managers now think the government should "actively help" corporations doing business overseas. *Business Week* magazine carried a splashy 1992 feature story trumpeting "Industrial Policy" on its cover in huge letters. "Should the United States have an industrial policy?" asked the editors. "The answer is 'Yes.'"

Unfortunately, most of today's boosters of Japanese-style industrial policy for the United States don't understand either the true strengths of the Japanese economy or its unreported weaknesses. They seem to believe, along with many other Americans, that the Japanese have triumphed in nearly all their economic endeavors, and that benevolent guidance by the Japanese government is the real source of these successes. They are wrong on both counts.

MITI'S CHECKERED HISTORY

In popular fable, the grand intelligence behind Japan's spectacular economic rise has been the Ministry of International Trade and Industry, or MITI. Beginning after World War II, MITI bureaucrats used their broad powers to distribute Japan's limited commercial resources and assign tasks for the rebuilding of the shattered economy. In those early years, when markets were in shambles, companies were destroyed, and private economic management had nearly collapsed, the Japanese may have had little choice. But from the beginning, MITI's attempts to manage the economy led to serious foul-ups and misdirections.

In the 1950s, for instance, MITI worked vigorously to force the Japanese automobile industry into a single company—because planners were certain multiple competitors would only weaken each other. To their very good fortune, ministry officials were unable to strong-arm the private manufacturers into accepting their vision of one, two, or (by 1961) "at most" three Japanese auto firms. Today Japan has nine vibrantly rivalrous auto builders, and experts agree that it is the fierce competition among them that has driven the industry to its current levels of excellence.

At just about the same time MITI was trying to shrink the Japanese auto sector, it was pressuring other companies to avoid what is viewed as a dead-end in electronics. In 1953, a small company named Sony went to MITI to ask permission to buy transistor-manufacturing rights from Western Electric. MITI was not impressed with the technology, or with Sony, and didn't want to squander scarce foreign currency on either. Permission to make the purchase was refused, and a great enterprise was nearly suffocated in its crib. Fortunately, company founder Akio Morita was persistent, and he eventually badgered the bureaucrats into giving Sony the go-ahead.

Meanwhile, MITI was pushing other sectors of the Japanese economy down paths that would lead to disappointment and wasted resources. The steel industry is a good example. In this country, Japanese steel is commonly thought of as a MITI triumph, but actually it has been a drag on the nation.

After a giant, force-fed buildup during the 1960s and 1970s, many of Japan's blast furnaces fell idle through the 1980s. Over the last five years, more than 50,000 steelworkers have had to be laid off, and costly but underutilized plants have been scrapped. Massachusetts Institute of Technology economist Paul Krugman describes Japanese steel as "the success that never was," and says MITI's buildup of the industry probably "reduced Japanese national income." MITI's expensive attempts to build up the aluminum and non-ferrous metal industries in Japan were even worse debacles.

MITI's efforts to "target" the "industries of the future" have failed in many other sectors too. Indeed, the ministry has misfired far more than it has succeeded. Intensive and repeated MITI efforts to build up Japan's aircraft and aerospace industries, for instance, have produced only inferior products at absurd prices, and little or no world demand. Decades-long attempts to jump-start a biotechnology industry have been equally disappointing.

COMPUTER CRASH

Another grandly fruitless MITI venture was the Sunshine Project, initiated in 1974 with the intent of achieving quick breakthroughs in alternative sources of energy. "All that was produced for sure were jobs for superannuated bureaucrats," one observer has commented. Shades of the U.S. government's "synfuels," "shale oil," and Clinch River reactor debacles.

MITI also made an enormous mess of Japan's oil industry. The ministry set prices, allocated production quotas, forbade foreign competitors, and otherwise dabbled and interfered. The result was huge financial costs to both government and industry, consumers saddled with a serious misallocation of filling stations, wholesale gas prices nearly double the world market levels, and a very weak set of energy companies. MITI floundered in similar ways in the petroleum-based chemical manufacturing industry, another vital sector in any economy today.

MITI's aggressive efforts in oil "failed to produce true international competitors," states Harvard professor Michael Porter. In the late 1980s a deregulation plan was put together to pull government out of this sector.

Another example of MITI's pump-priming disappointments is the computer industry. Although the sector was first targeted nearly three decades ago, most Japanese computer products continue to lag behind their competitors, in little demand outside their sheltered domestic markets. Nimbler American companies set almost all industry standards, and even have used technological leapfrogging, superior manufacturing, and speedier product cycles to take back submarkets once believed to be slated for Japanese dominance. (Printers, hard drives, and notebook and palmtop computers are examples of this.) "In the mid-1980s, people like me were fearing that Japanese companies would take over the U.S. personal computer market in no time. Today, I find them a surprisingly ineffective force," states Andrew Grove, CEO of Intel Corporation, which has led U.S. manufacturers to dominance in today's microchip industry. Software has been the subject of a separate MITI push—to even less effect. According to Japanese scholar Koji Shinjo, the "government promotion policies" that have supported the Japanese computer industry "conceal serious problems."

One of MITI's most ambitious programs of all, the so-called Fifth Generation Computer Project, inspired much fear in other countries when it commenced in 1983. The well-funded 10-year effort coordinated the work of eight companies in a newly built government laboratory. Its widely trumpeted goal was to produce the world's first thinking, "artificially intelligent" computers. The project has fallen far short of its aims, however, having produced no fundamental technical advances or marketable products, and the program now is being phased out.

WHITE ELEPHANTS

MITI is not the only meddler. Japan's other government industries have engineered many costly failures in industrial policy. Some of the biggest follies have been portrayed in the Western press as smashing successes. Take shipbuilding: starting in the 1950s, the Ministry of Transport went on a shipbuilding binge, instituting a tariff to keep out British and West German competitors and encouraging the buildup of the world's largest yards and highest-volume industry. By the late 1970s, however, worldwide overbuilding and changing cargo patterns turned Japan's yards into white elephants.

Because they were following government incentives instead of market signals, Japanese shipbuilders monumentally miscalculated the demand for and profitability of their product. Even at its peak, the industry never netted a penny. The set-up costs had been high, and excess capacity plus competition from Korea, Northern Ireland, and other builders kept margins unhealthily slim. When the downturn came, losses were huge. The government had to step in again, this time to shrink the industry to a quarter of its former capacity. Where just a few years before they had been injecting growth hormones, the bureaucrats now were dispensing "adjustment aid."

Another boondoggle engineered by the Ministry of Transport is the Japanese national railway. The railway is known to most Americans primarily for its impressive high-speed "bullet trains," the *shinkansen*. What is less well appreciated is the fact that until it was finally privatized in 1987 in the face of financial crisis, the agency had hundreds of thousands of featherbedded employees, continual strikes, poor service, serious overcrowding on some lines with gross overservice on others, and losses that averaged more than $20 million a day. This was despite heavy government subsidies and very high fares—in the 13 years before privatization, ticket prices were increased 11 times.

"Everybody thinks the Japanese national railway is a success but it is the worst failure imaginable. It loses five times as much per passenger mile as any other railroad," pointed out Peter Drucker shortly before the privatization. Like many other government-dependent businesses around the globe, the railway's biggest problem was special-interest pressure to build and operate unprofitable but politically popular lines. A breathtaking $279 billion in debt accumulated by the agency ended up on the public books, a burden to be carried by Japanese taxpayers for decades. There is a warning in this for Bill Clinton, who has spoken often of his plans to have the government build "high-speed rail lines" in the United States.

STIFLED TELECOM

Railways are not the only sector where the Japanese government's transportation policy has gone off the tracks. Government coddling also has made the Japanese airline industry extremely inefficient. Until 1986, government-run Japan Airlines (JAL) held a monopoly on overseas flights, and All Nippon airways (ANA) had a virtual monopoly on domestic flights. Tickets were so costly that relatively few Japanese could afford to fly.

When JAL was finally privatized, its managers found that the cozy regulatory cocoon they enjoyed for so many years left them ill-prepared for the fierce global competition that is now the norm in air transport. JAL currently is one of the highest-cost carriers in the world, and its share of travel to and from Japan recently has fallen by one-sixth. American carriers, which honed their operations after being released from government regulation a decade earlier, are far more competitive on the major trans-Pacific routes.

Telecommunications is another important economic sector that has been stifled by governmental embrace in Japan. The national telecommunications monopoly NTT is being privatized at last, but is still two-thirds state-owned and it is not lean or mean. Domestic phone calls cost 50 percent more in Japan than in the United States, and calling abroad from within Japan is far more expensive than calling in. Service is much less innovative in Japan. Cellular phones, for instance, only recently have caught on, due to clumsy regulation by the Ministry of Posts and Telecommunications.

Meanwhile, equipment makers also lag behind their competitors. "Japanese companies are at a disadvantage because they don't have enough competition in their home markets," says consultant Francis McInerney. Both consumers and companies have paid the price for Japan's industrial policy in telecommunications.

FINANCIAL FEUDALISM

Bureaucratic manipulation has gravely wounded Japan's financial sector, which these days often is described as "feudal." Ministry of Finance doting has kept Japan's banks, life-insurance companies, and stockbrokering firms in an inefficient backwater state, and in the past several years many institutions have careened toward serious solvency troubles. Government policies also are directly responsible for the recent collapse of Japan's stock market, and for the disastrous speculation in land and real estate markets that has made home-owning impossible for most young Japanese workers—homes are up to 10 times more expensive than in America.

The farm policies of the Ministry of Agriculture can only be characterized as a fiasco. Their penalties are multiple: Japanese consumers must pay exaggerated prices for food—twice as much as Americans, as a share of family income. In a time of damaging labor shortages in Japan, fully 9 percent of the workforce is tied up in farming, versus 3 percent in the United States. And large amounts of prime urban land are locked away in inefficient crop production instead of being used for desperately needed housing or commercial buildings.

Westerners have the idea that the crowding and poor physical amenities endured by the Japanese people are the unavoidable result of their island topography. Actually, there is much more land within an hour's travel of Tokyo than there is in New York, and a lot more of it is open—Tokyo's population density within a six-mile radius of the city center is 39,000 persons per square mile, versus around 65,000 in Paris and Manhattan. Tokyo feels so overstrained because only half the land in the metropolitan area has been developed. There are still 125,000 farmers within the city, working tiny plots that average less than 6,500 square feet each. McKinsey and Co. consultant Kenichi Ohmae reports that the land available for housing and offices within 30 miles of Tokyo could quadruple if the government would change its policy of protecting farming "in the national interest."

Thanks to heavy state strictures on store operations, Japan's goods distribution and retailing network is also very inefficient. It normally takes five to 10 years to get government permission to open a new store in Japan. Goods must pass through twice as many sticky fingers on their way from factory to buyer as in America or Britain. "Our distribution system is really an unofficial jobs program subsidized in full by the consumer," observes opposition politician Wakako Hironaka. These measures elevate consumer prices a punishing 60 to 100 percent.

The list of industrial policy failures in Japan goes on and on. Japanese pharmaceutical firms are second-rate internationally, in large measure due to protectionism and meddling by the Ministry of Health. Government attempts to aid and protect the Japanese mining industry have been boondoggles.

FAILING THE SCREEN TEST

A major disappointment currently in the making concerns high-definition television (HDTV). Twenty-five years ago the Japanese government began to set targets for a new HDTV broadcasting standard. More than a billion dollars later (in 1991), the state-owned NHK television network pushed the world's first working system into operation. Industrial policy advocates in the United States, who had been agitating unsuccessfully for a similar $1.5-billion effort by the U.S. government, moaned that we had once again been outfoxed on a hugely valuable technology.

Actually, it was the Japanese bureaucrats who outfoxed themselves. In their office-bound wisdom, the targeters picked the wrong—and now seriously obsolete—technology. American companies, following consumer and market signals, have developed a far more advanced digital HDTV standard, and are now poised to dominate video transmission and reception in the coming decades. Federal Communications Commission chairman Alfred Sikes, the U.S. official in charge of broadcasting oversight, concluded from the episode that "bureaucrats determined to freeze the frame on fast-moving industries lock their companies and citizens into second-class products."

BEHIND IN PRODUCTIVITY

If industrial policy in Japan has had so many failures, then how did Japan become such a juggernaut today? The answer comes in two parts.

Part one: Japan is not a juggernaut. The Japanese economy is one of the splendid successes of our lifetime, having grown about twice as fast since World War II as most of its industrial counterparts. Despite the hoopla, however, media and academic reports often ignore the fact that Japan, like every nation, continues to have plenty of weak and potholed sectors in its economy.

An inventory of the consumer goods in American houses and garages is not a good way to gauge Japan's overall productive strength. After all, manufacturing represents only about one-fifth to one-third of the economy in any industrial nation today, and Japan's manufacturing successes are further concentrated in a relatively narrow—albeit highly visible—band of consumer goods, such as electronics and cars.

A broader-spectrum comparison of economic output in Japan and the United States done in 1989 by professors at Harvard University and Tokyo's Keio University found that Japanese efficiency was lower than U.S. levels in 16 of 29 major industries, including communications, transport, construction, retailing and services. Japan's Labor Ministry reported in 1992 that overall, U.S. workers are 1.6 times as productive as Japanese workers. A more selective and detailed study done in 1992 by McKinsey Global Institute—with assistance from several economists, including Nobel laureate Robert Solow—also found that most U.S. enterprises were more productive than Japanese counterparts, particularly in the service sector—which includes banking, airlines, and phone companies, not just fast-food restaurants. While the Japanese have many superb companies and industries, their economy also has lots of weak spots.

TWO JAPANESE ECONOMIES

Most of the weakest areas in Japan are those that have been subsidized or otherwise shielded by the government. That's part two of the explanation of how the Japanese arrived where they are today even though targeting and so forth did not work: The fact is, they succeeded for reasons unrelated to industrial policy. Indeed, it may be most accurate to say the Japanese succeeded in spite of industrial policy. In his recent book *The Competitive Advantage of Nations*, Harvard professor Porter does not credit Japanese planners at all. "Government policy in a range of industries," he writes, "has had the effect of undermining competition and sheltering inefficient competitors, lowering the overall productivity of the Japanese economy."

Many of Japan's strongest businesses—like consumer electronics, cameras, robotics, precision equipment, pianos, bicycles, watches and calculators, numerically controlled machine tools, and ceramics—developed mostly on their own, without much help from MITI or other agencies. And where government mandarins have intervened most actively—like shipbuilding, agriculture, petrochemicals, and aerospace—they often have done little more than provide costly life support to fossils and failures.

There are actually two Japanese economies—one vibrantly competitive, one bloated and inefficient and kept afloat by bureaucratic fiat. As Masaru Yoshitomi, director-general at the government's Economic Planning Agency, concedes, Japan's less efficient industries amount to "a welfare system within the private sector."

Ministry planning is not the source of Japan's economic vigor. The real credit lies elsewhere: with her strong, serious primary education system; with the extraordinarily high savings rates of her people and all the government policies that encourage that; with her low inflation and low tax policies; and with her powerfully cohesive families that allow youngsters to grow into productive citizens and workers (only 5 percent of all Japanese children currently live in broken homes, compared with 28 percent in this country). The Japanese are a fantastically disciplined people who probably would make any economic structure look good.

Maybe the most important factor driving the nation's success is the fierce market competition that reigns wherever it is allowed in Japan—remember those nine different Japanese car companies. Japanese economist Ryutaro Komiya argues that "vigorous competition . . . in spite of . . . the strong inclination of the government ministry responsible for an industry to suppress competition" has been a key to the vitality of the Japanese economy. Professor Porter of Harvard describes hot competition as "perhaps the most essential underpinning" of Japanese achievement.

THE JAPANESE TURN AWAY

Certainly government steering is not the secret. "The idea that central planning is responsible for Japan's success is a myth," says former White House economist David Henderson. "Japan's is an economy driven by firms, not government," says Professor Porter. While MITI and other government agencies "have preserved unproductive firms in dozens of industries," Professor Porter concludes from his massive research, "only a handful of the more than 60 industries involved have subsequently achieved significant international success." Japanese industrial policy, in other words, has failed far more often than it has succeeded.

Bailouts, more than start-ups, have been the main work of Japan's finaglers. Behind all the talk of targeting "infant industries of the future," most ministry resources have been funneled to elderly, even senile, industries of the past. Decliners rather than ascenders have absorbed the bulk of the money. Even when targeters have managed to hit the right industry, their success at hitting the right firm at the right time in the right way, without doing more harm than good, has been minimal.

For these reasons, the Japanese now are discarding industrial policy and government management of their economy—a widely underreported fact in the West. The privatizations of the national railway, the national airline, the telephone monopoly, and the deregulation efforts affecting the oil industry have already been discussed. Deregulation and sharp reductions in ministry guidance are also underway in banking and financial services. The once tightly controlled retail and distribution sector is seeing some relaxation. Numerous government tariffs are being removed or lowered.

Meanwhile, many of MITI's formal powers have been allowed to lapse. Of course, bureaucracies never surrender authority easily, and some of Japan's agencies are still clawing to retain their powers of economic direction. But the movement away from the planned and targeted economy is unmistakable.

Japan's fling with industrial policy was closely linked with its predicament of transforming itself from a poor, war-devastated nation into a developed one, and most of the overt governmental prodding took place in the 1950s and 1960s. As their economy became richer and more elaborate, the Japanese discovered that state force-feeding interferes with growth more than it helps. "In my time, our job was simple," says Naohiro Amaya, a central MITI official during Japan's postwar rebuilding. But now, he continues, the economy has become too complicated for government ministers to manipulate effectively. His successors are "trying to solve many complex equations simultaneously." Most Japanese leaders came to this same conclusion some years ago. As the *Wall Street Journal* summarizes, "there is an emerging consensus among the public and the business community that an economy guided by the government . . . is ill-suited to the needs of modern Japan."

The irony is that just as the Japanese are fleeing national business management, some Americans (and even more the Europeans) are edging toward it. Today's "severe danger," economics writer and Japan expert Bill Emmott warns, is that America, panicked by the reality of stiffened global competition, "will learn from the wrong Japanese example, will emulate something that Japan has in fact abandoned."

ON TRACK THE AMERICAN WAY

Americans have high economic expectations. Sometimes this leads us to exaggerate our problems and overlook successes. From mid-1982 to mid-1990, after all, the U.S. economy grew an impressive 31 percent after inflation. That meant 18 million brand-new jobs, per-capita disposable income rising by one-fifth after inflation, and added production equivalent to the entire output of the West German economy—all in less than a decade.

While we often hear claims these days that the United States can't compete as an exporter anymore, the truth is that American exports have more than doubled in real dollar value since the mid-1980s. The United States now sells more than $400 billion worth of goods to other countries annually. By comparison, Japanese exports total around $300 billion, and theirs recently have been rising at a much slower 3-percent annual rate.

It is true the United States has economic problems that need fixing. And it is true that some proud American companies lately have been outperformed by foreign competition. But our economy still contains a multitude of internationally unsurpassed sectors, and hundreds of American firms recently have made impressive comebacks. In 1992, for example, U.S. computer chip manufacturers stunned pundits by retaking the world market share lead from the Japanese. In most emerging branches of the business, U.S. companies—written off just a few years ago—once again are setting the pace. Meanwhile,

European attempts to compete in semiconductors by using tariffs and huge government subsidies made their position worse.

Private restructurings are also boosting many other American industries back into world leadership. U.S. steelmakers are again the lowest-cost producers. Machine tool makers have pulled back to the front of their pack. It is becoming increasingly clear that over the next decade American firms even will regain a strong position in home electronics—a niche filled almost exclusively by imports in recent years.

Or take even that sorest of sore spots, the auto industry. In 1992 Japanese automakers actually lost a point and a half of market share in the United States, and they will lose more this year. Detroit completely dominates today's two fastest growing sales niches: sport/utility vehicles—like Jeeps—and minivans. Minivans and utility vehicles now account for a fifth of the total U.S. vehicle market, and that share is rising fast. Domestic makers sell 90 percent of them.

Every one of the Japanese car companies except Honda (which is cutting production sharply this year) has recently been losing money in the United States—to the collective tune of $4 billion a year. They are all reducing new investment, canceling products, and leaving models on the market longer between overhauls. Meanwhile, Ford and Chrysler are now on solid footing, and GM is building good cars while finally undertaking the financial restructuring it long has needed.

IMPROVING WHAT WE DO BEST

Many Japanese competitors recently have discovered that what goes up also can come down. Total Japanese industrial production was nearly 9 percent lower in 1992 than in the year previous. Corporate profits have declined for three consecutive years—the first time that has happened since World War II. The Japanese stock market has lost half its value since 1990. Land prices are down by one-third. Several major banks are at risk of failing. Even marquee industries like consumer electronics are suffering. Sony will show a 70-percent decline in earnings in the fiscal year just now ending. The Japanese certainly will continue to have one of the world's most competitive economies for the foreseeable future, but they are not invincible. Over the next decade, weak spots in their system will become increasingly apparent.

If the United States is to prosper in the years ahead, it will do so not by aping the Japan of the 1960s, but by solving its own problems and refining what it does best. Instead of dabbling in industrial decision-making and subsidies that would amount to corporate welfare, our government should concentrate on refashioning our miserable public education system, on mending our families so children can grow up responsibly, on reducing our national expenditures and deficit, on freeing our entrepreneurs from suffocating controls, and on making our tax code friendlier to investment and savings and less protective of consumption.

The great global economic lesson of the last generation is that earnest centralized management—even in as mild a form as existed in post-war Japan—always will bring less prosperity than open market competition. It will be a tragedy if the new American administration, in the name of aiding American "competitiveness," ignores that vital lesson here at home.

DISCUSSION QUESTIONS

1. What is industrial policy? Can you give some examples of private industry that are substantially unaffected by government policy?
2. Arguments for and against an industrial policy seem to share the goal of creating a "strong" economy. What is meant by a strong economy, and why is it important?
3. In what way does the debate over industrial policy intersect with the debate over free trade or protectionism? In what ways do the debates vary?
4. Fallows and Zinsmeister each choose one of several ways to make an argument for and against an industrial policy. What are some other arguments for and against industrial policy? Are there more convincing arguments?
5. States often develop policies to benefit particular industries or businesses that are valued by citizens of that state (e.g., dairy price-support programs to benefit farmers and preserve open space). Do the arguments for and against an industrial policy apply to specific state programs?
6. In many ways, arguments between those who favor and those who oppose an industrial policy reveal the dichotomy between those who believe that government can play a constructive role in the economy and those who think it cannot. Which approach do you favor, and how do you apply this approach to other policy areas? When should governments intervene? When should private industry be left alone?
7. What role do governments have in establishing the conditions under which "free markets" can operate?

ADDITIONAL READINGS

Amsden, Alice H. "East Asia's Challenge—to Standard Economics." *The American Prospect* (Summer 1990).

Breyer, Stephen. *Regulation and Its Reform* (Cambridge, Mass.: Harvard University Press, 1982).

Dertouzos, Michael L., Richard K. Lester, and Robert M. Solow. *Made in America: Regaining the Productive Edge* (Cambridge, Mass.: MIT Press, 1989).

Etzioni, Amitai. "Caution: Industrial Policy Is Coming." *Challenge* (September/October 1992).

Fallows, James. *More Like Us: Making America Great Again* (Boston: Houghton Mifflin, 1989).

Fallows, James. "How the World Works." *The Atlantic Monthly* (December 1993).

Florida, Richard, and Donald F. Smith Jr. "Keep the Government Out of Venture Capital." *Issues in Science and Technology* (Summer 1993).

Industry Week. "Do We Need a National Industrial Policy?" (March 18, 1991).

Lindblom, Charles E. *Politics and Markets* (New York: Basic Books, 1977).

Reich, Robert B. "An Outward-Looking Economic Nationalism." *The American Prospect* (Spring 1990).

Reich, Robert B. "Who Do We Think They Are?" *The American Prospect* (Winter 1991).

Tolchin, Susan J. "Halting the Erosion of America's Critical Assets." *Issues in Science and Technology* (Spring 1993).

Tyson, Laura D'Andrea. "They Are Not Like Us: Why American Ownership Still Matters." *The American Prospect* (Winter 1991).

Vernon, Raymond. "A Strategy for International Trade." *Issues in Science and Technology* (Winter 1988–89).

Vogel, David. *Fluctuating Fortunes: The Political Power of Business in America* (New York: Basic Books, 1989).

Weaver, R. Kent, and Bert A. Rockman, eds. *Do Institutions Matter?* (Washington, D.C.: Brookings Institution, 1993).

8
ENERGY POLICY
"Should the United States Have a National Energy Policy?"

One of the principal factors driving modern industrial economies is a supply of usable energy. Indeed, it is difficult to imagine a modern economy without prodigious sources of energy. The United States is an extreme case, however. Excluding the oil-dominated countries of the Middle East, per-capita energy consumption in the United States is nearly the highest in the world (only Canada's is slightly higher), more than twice as high as Britain, France, Italy, Japan, and Germany.[1] Part of the reason why U.S. consumption is so high is that energy prices are so low. For example, as of January 1, 1991, one gallon of premium fuel sold for an average of $1.43 in the United States, compared with $2.44 in Panama, $2.55 in Britain, $3.61 in Belgium, $2.92 in Morocco, $3.90 in Japan, $3.86 in France, and $5.10 in Italy.* Another reason is that per-capita GNP is higher in the United States than in most other nations, much of it dependent on energy. Despite these factors, many believe that Americans are simply wasteful energy consumers. The profligacy of U.S. energy consumption is typified (if exaggerated) by socialite Betsy Blooming-dale's comment in 1982 that she saved energy "by asking my servants not to turn on the self-cleaning oven after seven in the morning."

But while total U.S. energy consumption rose from 66.4 quadrillion British thermal units (or quads) in 1970 to 81.4 quads in 1990, per-capita energy consumption remained unchanged (at 327 million Btus), and energy consumption per dollar of GNP fell from 27,500 Btus in 1970 to 19,600 twenty years later.[2] Oil and other petroleum products have long been the most important fuel for the U.S. economy. The versatility of oil, from heating to electrical generation to automotive fuel, made it the perfect source of energy for a heavily industrialized economy. By 1973, a critical year for energy, oil usage made up 47 percent of all energy consumed (measured in Btus), up from a level of 39 percent in 1949.[3] In addition to increasing U.S. energy consumption, since 1970 there have been significant changes in the types of energy used. Petroleum products represented 44 percent of total energy use in 1970, falling slightly to 41 percent by 1990; natural gas also fell from 33 percent of total energy use in 1970 to 24 percent by 1990. Coal and nuclear power increased as a percentage of energy use over the same

---

* Several countries' prices were below that of the United States, including Mexico ($0.87), Saudi Arabia ($0.54), and Venezuela ($0.27), all large petroleum-producing nations (*Statistical Abstract of the United States, 1993*, p. 866).

twenty-year period: Coal rose from 18 percent of energy use in 1970 to 23 percent in 1990; nuclear power jumped from 0.3 percent in 1970 to 7.6 percent by 1990.[4] Nevertheless, petroleum remains the dominant source of energy in the U.S. economy and is the one source with which it is least endowed. The result has been a sharp increase in imported oil, from 7.5 quads in 1970 to approximately 17 quads today.

The world faced a major disruption in its supply of energy for the first time in 1973 when the oil cartel of the Organization of Petroleum Exporting Countries (OPEC), a group of nations whose primary export commodity was petroleum, began its first embargo of the United States and other countries that were seen as supporters of Israel during the Yom Kippur War.[5] The cartel (a group of producers that controls a large-enough share of a product market to be able to influence its price) restricted the supply of oil products available to the global market, causing shortages and drastically increasing the price for fuel. In the span of one year, the real per-barrel price of crude oil jumped 59 percent, from $12.31 in 1973 to $19.58 in 1974 (both in constant 1992 dollars).[6]

In 1970, U.S. net imports represented just 23.5 percent of its total petroleum consumption, jumping to 34.8 percent by 1973.[7] Of all oil imported into the United States in 1973, half was imported from OPEC nations, with 15 percent of total imports coming from Arab OPEC nations.[8] The average real price of leaded gasoline jumped 24 percent, from $1.23 per gallon in 1973 to $1.52 in 1974 (both in constant 1992 dollars).[9] Home heating oil prices rose with the price of gasoline, taking a large bite out of households' disposable income, particularly those in the northeast where oil heating is most prevalent. The average real price for heating oil increased from $0.72 per gallon in 1973 to $1.03 per gallon in 1974, a rise of 43 percent in just one year (in constant 1992 dollars).[10] Industrial and commercial transportation fuel was likewise more expensive. This translated into higher prices in virtually all products as firms had to incorporate increased energy costs into the price of their goods and services, fueling inflation. Besides increases in prices there were long gasoline lines—and short tempers—as retailers were restricted in the amount of gasoline they could sell to individual customers, a memorable experience for drivers who lived through "gasless Sundays," odd and even gasoline distribution based on license plate numbers, and other forms of rationing.

The resulting increase in the cost of energy from the OPEC oil squeeze had a dramatic impact on the economy of the United States, as well as other Western industrialized democracies and countries in the Third World. The United States was forced into a major recession; indeed many economists attribute the simultaneously high levels of unemployment and inflation, known as stagflation, of the 1970s to the OPEC embargo. While other structural factors are clearly at work, 1973 remains a defining year in terms of flagging U.S. economic growth (and indeed for much of the industrialized world). Median per-capita family income rose only slightly, from $34,774 in 1973 to $35,939 by 1991 (both in constant 1991 dollars), far below the rates of income growth since World War II.[11]

Calls for energy conservation and independence quickly followed the 1973 crisis. The Nixon administration saw the passage of the Emergency Petroleum Allocation Act of 1973, which gave the government the right to allocate petroleum resources by mandate in times of shortages. It also extended oil price controls that had been established by the White House in 1971. The Nixon administration also implemented a national 55-mile-per-hour speed limit on the nation's highways in early 1974 and authorized construction of the trans-Alaska oil pipeline. The federal government became highly concerned that the defense of the nation was seriously threatened by U.S. vulnerability to supply shocks of any kind. The political instability of the Middle East, which held over 62 percent of the world's proven reserves of oil,[12] as well as the proximity of the USSR to that region, was a source of major concern to government officials. The Strategic Petroleum Reserve was created in 1974 to maintain an emergency supply of oil should the nation need it.

With the Carter administration, energy policy continued to move toward conservation and increasing energy supplies. The first part of the National Energy Act of 1978 deregulated natural gas prices over a three-year period. Petroleum price controls also began to be phased out. At the same time, coal, with which the United States is endowed in abundance, was encouraged as a major source of energy. The act further changed utility rate structures so that the true cost of supplying energy would be represented and also set a schedule of taxes and tax breaks that sought to increase energy conservation and development of new resources, such as new discoveries of petroleum and the development of alternative forms of energy. Funding for programs to develop alternative sources of energy from solar, wind, geothermal, and water power was initiated or increased significantly, as were projects that sought to extract energy from new sources such as so-called synfuels, produced by squeezing oil from coal and shale. Government began to subsidize many domestic producers of oil who could not have competed on the world market as well as oil company efforts at oil exploration. Despite these efforts at conservation and reduced dependence, U.S. reliance on imported oil grew steadily throughout the rest of the 1970s. By 1979, when the second oil crisis due to the revolution in Iran struck the United States, dependence on foreign oil had grown from 34.8 percent in 1973 to 43.1 percent, with 70.5 percent of that coming from OPEC sources and 38.2 percent of the total from Arab OPEC nations.[13]

The election of President Reagan in 1980 marked a change in energy policy, with little government involvement in energy markets. Part of this was due to the philosophical orientation of the Reagan administration to involve government as little as possible in directing resources, and part of it was due to falling oil prices. The Reagan administration removed the remaining price controls on gasoline. By 1985, dependence on foreign oil had fallen to 27.3 percent, with 42.5 percent from OPEC sources.[14] However, lessened dependency on foreign oil was to be short-lived. With the reestablishment of a secure oil market and the weakening of OPEC's position, per-barrel crude oil prices fell significantly during the 1980s. Between 1981 and 1986, oil prices fell 67.9 percent in real terms and fluctuated only mildly through 1990.[15] The result has been a steady increase in foreign imports relative to domestic energy consumption. By 1991, foreign oil dependency had climbed again to 39.5 percent, 61.3 percent of which originated in OPEC nations.[16]

With Iraq's invasion of Kuwait in August 1990 and the subsequent U.S. military confrontation with Iraq in early 1991, energy security once again became a more central concern of both government and the American people. The war in the Persian Gulf was a major oil shock. It was estimated that gasoline prices rose from an average of $1.08 per gallon for regular unleaded on August 1, 1990, to $1.25 per gallon by August 10. In the first week of the invasion, the spot price for a barrel of West Texas intermediate crude increased by more than a third. By the end of September, the price per barrel had reached nearly $40.[17] World oil prices subsequently fell as Iraq was forced out of Kuwait.

As former Secretary of Energy James Schlesinger said regarding U.S. energy policy, "The only thing we learn from history is we learn nothing from history."[18] The United States continues to rely on worldwide oil markets, with little government intervention, to dictate oil prices. A senior vice president of Texaco noted that "our energy policy is to take the cheapest oil in the world, regardless of source, and take our chances that it will continue to be cheap and available."[19] On one hand, supporters of this strategy argue that this is how many goods and services are allocated in the world economy, and energy is just one of them. Further, they denounce critics' assertions that we are running out of fossil fuels. While true on its face, they argue that we will never completely run out of petroleum because if it still has value in use, shortages will simply drive up the price, causing a (perhaps frantic) search for substitute forms of energy, including more oil exploration. And, they might tell skeptics, if you are so sure that oil will soon become scarce, in which case oil prices should rise dramatically, go out and become rich by purchasing (presumably cheap) oil futures on the commodities market (and reselling them later when oil is expensive). The fact that most people do not is evidence, they argue, of the fact that oil is sufficiently plentiful and that current prices reflect copious supplies. Finally, they argue that predicting the future of energy markets is folly, pointing to a comment made in 1955 that "nuclear powered vacuum cleaners will probably be a reality within 10 years" and Henry Luce's suggestion in 1956 that "by 1980, all 'power' (electric, atomic, solar) is likely to be virtually costless."

Those advocating a larger government role in energy policy do so motivated by several factors. R. Buckminster Fuller noted that "society cannot continue to live on oil and gas. Those fossil fuels represent nature's savings accounts which took billions of year to form." Others have urged conservation measures, noting that "there isn't a gasoline shortage. There's a driving surplus." Further concern over energy issues in the late 1980s and the early 1990s centered around questions of environmental degradation. The threat of global warming became a major concern; some argue that only by implementing a national strategy designed to reduce carbon emissions (by reducing fossil-fuel dependence), such as by the use of solar and geothermal energy, can global warming be slowed (the nuclear power industry sees this as perhaps its last hope for continued life in the United States). Other environmental concerns center around oil spills, offshore drilling, and oil exploration in sensitive ecosystems such as the proposed drilling in Alaska's Arctic National Wildlife Refuge. Further arguments for a national strategy to conserve energy relate to issues of economic competitiveness. Some economists and government policymakers feel that by reducing U.S. energy usage, firms could reduce energy costs, thereby allowing them to sell their products abroad at a more competitive price. They argue that abatement would furthermore free up enormous amounts of now-wasted capital that could be reinvested in the economy. Advocates point to several strategies for implementing a national energy policy, including supply-side measures such as subsidizing alternative energy sources and demand-side measures such as various forms of energy taxes and corporate average fuel economy (CAFE) standards for automobiles.

In the articles that follow, Christopher Flavin of the Worldwatch Institute argues that reducing oil dependence is critical and that the time is now to aggressively change course toward a policy of encouraging the use of renewable energy sources. Irwin Stelzer of the American Enterprise Institute counters that the history of past government intervention, from the American experience in the 1970s to the planning and controls of Communist and former Communist nations, argues strongly against strategies for energy usage. He contends that reliance on the free market, even if it is imperfect, is a better solution than that proposed by Flavin. Their articles follow.

Endnotes

1. U.S. Department of Commerce, Bureau of the Census, *Statistical Abstract of the United States, 1991* (Washington, D.C.: U.S. Government Printing Office, 1991), p. 854.
2. U.S. Department of Commerce, Bureau of the Census, *Statistical Abstract of the United States, 1993* (Washington, D.C.: U.S. Government Printing Office, 1993), p. 563.
3. U.S. Department of Energy, Energy Information Administration, *Annual Energy Review 1991* (Washington, D.C.: U.S. Government Printing Office, 1992), Table 3.
4. *Statistical Abstract of the United States, 1993*, p. 563.
5. Alfred A. Marcus, *Controversial Issues in Energy Policy* (Newbury Park, Calif.: Sage Publications, 1992), pp. 57–63.
6. In nominal dollars, this was a jump from $3.89 in 1973 to $6.87 per barrel in 1974 (*Annual Energy Review 1991*, Table 68).
7. *Statistical Abstract of the United States, 1991*, p. 563; *Annual Energy Review 1991*, Table 58.
8. *Annual Energy Review 1991*, Table 58.
9. This is 38.8 cents per gallon in 1973 and 53.2 cents in 1974 (*Annual Energy Review 1991*, Table 73).
10. This is 22.8 cents per gallon in 1973 and 36.0 cents in 1974 (*Annual Energy Review 1991*, Table 73).

11. *Economic Report of the President, 1993* (Washington, D.C.: U.S. Government Printing Office, 1993), p. 380.
12. *Annual Energy Review 1991*, Table 117.
13. Ibid., Table 58.
14. Ibid.
15. Ibid., Table 68.
16. Ibid., Table 58.
17. U.S. Department of Energy, Energy Information Administration, *Energy Facts 1990* (Washington, D.C.: U.S. Government Printing Office, 1990), pp. 2–3.
18. Quoted in Matthew L. Wald, "After 20 Years, America's Foot Is Still on the Gas," *New York Times* (October 17, 1993), p. E4.
19. William K. Tell, senior vice president of Texaco, quoted in Wald, "After 20 Years."

YES

Beyond the Gulf Crisis: An Energy Strategy for the '90s

Christopher Flavin

President Bush has demonstrated that the U.S. commitment to protect Persian Gulf oil is more than rhetorical. He has not yet done the same regarding our domestic energy policy, which continues to founder in a sea of rhetoric nearly devoid of clear goals or programs. While the United States has spent more than a decade preparing its troops to fight a desert war in the Persian Gulf, it has allowed its oil imports to rise so high that U.S. vulnerability to events in this politically unstable region has been greatly increased.

Deputy Secretary of Energy W. Henson Moore explained the administration's perspective in early 1990 when he wrote, "We anticipate a decade of relative stability" in world oil markets. He attempted to sum up the Bush energy policy but did not even mention the problem of rising U.S. oil imports. The Energy Department was apparently no better prepared than the rest of the administration, which was providing Saddam Hussein with high-tech weapons only weeks before his tanks overran Kuwait.

THE UNITED STATES AND THE PERSIAN GULF

Even without Saddam Hussein, the world oil situation has been deteriorating steadily in recent years. The Middle East's share of the world oil market is rising at more than one million barrels per day each year; the world is again as dependent on the Persian Gulf as it was in 1980. Indeed, since 1980, the Middle East's share of world oil reserves has risen from 59 percent to 68 percent. Meanwhile, production in the United States and the Soviet Union, the two largest producers, is falling. Contrary to Secretary Moore's conclusions, steep oil price hikes during the '90s are a virtual certainty, even without Saddam Hussein's assistance.

OPEC is not only back in the driver's seat, but is increasingly dominated by the major Persian Gulf producers, such as Saudi Arabia and Iraq. One-fifth of global reserves are now under Iraq's direct control, and over one-half are in the immediate area of the Persian Gulf. Before this crisis, the major Middle Eastern producers still had three million barrels per day worth of spare capacity, most of which is now being used to help weather the embargo of Iraq and Kuwait. But current trends would eliminate all that reserve by the mid-'90s, leaving almost no reserve margins in case of future political upheavals.

The United States bears considerable responsibility for the deterioration in the world oil picture. Throughout the '80s, the Reagan Administration sought to eliminate virtually every government program aimed at reducing oil dependence. It has now been over a decade since the Congress passed significant legislation to reduce U.S. oil consumption. The Bush Administration has eased back on the rhetoric, but is in most respects carrying on with a Reagan-like energy policy. The short-run response to the Persian Gulf crisis is similarly weak. Drivers are exhorted to pump up their tires, and local officials are encouraged to scrap environmental limits in order to save a few thousand barrels of oil.

President Bush has failed to project a vision of the country's energy future or to make the tough political choices that are needed. As a former oil company executive, he waxes enthusiastic about oil drilling in several of the country's valuable protected areas. But the oil in question is by all accounts minimal; pursuit of that oil is a feeble attempt to resurrect a policy that has failed on its own terms. This policy can be redirected when the Department of Energy delivers its National Energy Strategy to the President in December. Unfortunately, it is not yet even clear whether the administration has embraced the obvious goal of reducing U.S. oil imports. To carry through on that goal, the United States would need to develop a convincing way to improve the energy efficiency of the U.S. economy—particularly of the motor vehicles that now account for nearly two-thirds of U.S. oil consumption. Improved efficiency is far and away the quickest and most cost-effective means of reducing oil dependence. It would also boost the nation's economic competitiveness and strengthen its environmental health.

THE U.S. OIL OUTLOOK

From the mid-'70s until 1986, the U.S. energy situation improved considerably, under the dual influence of high oil prices and an array of policies designed to do everything from weatherizing buildings to commercializing alcohol fuels. As a result, the U.S. economy has grown by 50 percent since 1973, while energy use has increased by less than 7 percent. The U.S. economy is nearly 30 percent more energy-efficient than it was in 1973, which has made it possible to cut the national fuel bill by $150 billion annually. U.S. oil imports fell from a high of nearly nine million barrels per day in 1978 to just five million barrels per day in 1985.

During the past five years, U.S. oil consumption has risen rapidly, and import dependence has again grown to nearly nine million barrels per day. The American Petroleum Institute, the National Petroleum Council, and the U.S. Department of Energy have all released major studies that point with alarm to these trends and argue that U.S. economic health and national security will be threatened by the forces now at work.

The decline in domestic U.S. oil production is a major factor in this deterioration. As the world's pioneering oil producer, the United States has already heavily exploited its oil reserves and has a reserves-to-production ratio of just nine years, far lower than the 100-plus years available to most Persian

Gulf producers (see Table 8-1). The heavy investments that went into U.S. oil exploration a decade ago delayed the decline in production that began in 1971. However, even when prices were at their zenith, U.S. oil production in the lower forty-eight states was still 20 percent below its peak level. Today, it is 35 percent below its peak. Meanwhile, oil from Alaska's North Slope, which temporarily compensated for declines elsewhere, peaked at about two million barrels per day in 1988 and has declined by over 12 percent since then.

Far from being a victim of world oil market fluctuations, the U.S. oil industry benefited from the OPEC-led price increases of the '70s. These high prices temporarily misled U.S. oil producers into thinking they could still compete with low-cost Middle Eastern oil. To the contrary, U.S. oil production will inevitably decline. Interior Department figures show that of the country's thirteen largest oil fields, seven are at least 80 percent depleted.

As finding oil in the United States has become more difficult, the amount of oil discovered per foot of exploratory well has fallen to less than half the rate that prevailed in the early '70s. The average U.S. oil well yields just fourteen barrels of oil, compared to 2,500 barrels in Saudi Arabia. As oil becomes more difficult to find and extract, average U.S. oil extraction costs have reached at least five times those in the Middle East. The U.S. industry can no longer compete at the world price. The 1.6 million barrel per day decline in U.S. oil production since 1985 is among the steepest ever recorded, but it is only the beginning of a downward trend. The Department of Energy's *Annual Energy Outlook* projects that crude oil production in the lower forty-eight states will fall from 6.12 million barrels per day in 1988 to 4.9 million barrels per day in 2000 at crude oil prices of $28 per barrel.

While domestic production was falling, consumption was up 10 percent between 1985 and 1989. By 1989, imports made up 42 percent of consumption. In three of the first seven months of 1990, the United States imported more oil than it produced. The cumulative decline in oil and natural gas liquids

TABLE 8-1
World Oil Reserves and Production by Region

	1980 Oil Reserves (billion barrels)	1989 Oil Reserves (billion barrels)	Years of Reserves Remaining at 1989 Production Rates
Middle East	362.0	660.3	110
Latin America	69.5	125.2	51
USSR & E. Europe	65.8	59.9	13
Africa	55.1	58.8	28
North America	39.2	42.4	10
Western Europe	23.2	18.4	13
Asia & Australasia	40.1	46.8	20
Total	654.9	1011.8	245

Source: British Petroleum, *Statistical Review of World Energy*.

production in the continental United States and Alaska could increase U.S. dependence on oil imports to 75 percent by the year 2000.

In short, the United States no longer has an abundant, low-cost energy resource that can substitute for other economic weaknesses. Indeed, in the future the U.S. energy picture is likely to grow closer to that of Europe and Japan, which lack cheap domestic energy sources and yet have been able to develop economies that function well in a high energy cost environment. The United States uses around twice as much oil per unit of GNP and per person as do the European nations.

OIL SUPPLY OPTIONS

Still, the inclination of the oil industry and the Bush Administration is to deal with the country's energy problems by pursuing the increasingly difficult goal of expanding the country's oil output. Given the declining U.S. oil resource base, this is an uphill battle. The agenda of the oil companies centers on opening up pristine areas in Alaska and off the coast of California for drilling. While these projects would undoubtedly boost oil company profits, they would hardly alter the country's dangerous level of oil dependence. The Arctic Refuge is an example. Damage to the ecology of the Refuge is virtually guaranteed. At the same time, the Interior Department's official figures show that the chances are against finding enough oil to be extracted. In the recent past, oil companies have estimated much higher success rates for Alaska and offshore oil projects, invested hundreds of millions of dollars in their development, and come up completely dry.

The Interior Department's 1987 report, *Arctic National Wildlife Refuge, Alaska, Coastal Plain Resource Assessment*, calls attention to the belief that, "the 1002 area is currently the unexplored area in the United States with the greatest potential to contain giant and supergiant fields"—a statement that reflects not the oil riches of the Refuge but the meager oil exploration prospects now remaining in the United States. The Interior Department's mid-range estimate of the Arctic Refuge resource is only 3.2 billion barrels. That is about as much oil as the United States consumes every six months, or far less than one percent of worldwide ultimately recoverable oil resources. This is an important figure because it is the overall world supply/demand balance that determines oil prices. Even when global supplies are tight, price will not be appreciably affected by the small amounts of Arctic National Wildlife Refuge oil.

The Department of the Interior also focuses at some length on the presumed economic benefits of 3.2 billion barrels of oil, estimated at $79.4 billion (undiscounted). This figure looks impressive, but the United States currently has an *annual* energy bill of over $400 billion; these revenues spread over a thirty-year period would be less than one percent of the annual national energy bill. Moreover, this oil would still have to be paid for by consumers; the benefits to the economy and job creation would be limited. If 3.2 billion barrels of oil are extracted from the Arctic Refuge over thirty years, as estimated by the Interior Department, then production will average 290,000 barrels per day. This would restore only a fraction of the oil production the United States is projected to lose by the turn of the century—the earliest that this new oil could be made available. Oil thought to be available in offshore California fields is even smaller in magnitude.

Since 1985, U.S. oil imports have risen by over three million barrels per day, or ten times the projected yields of Arctic Refuge oil. Further increases in U.S. oil imports are, as the Department of Energy points out, almost guaranteed in the years ahead. Trying to stem this tide with Arctic Refuge oil is like trying to stop a major fire with a teacup.

Even in the unlikely event that oil is extracted from the Arctic Refuge, this "success" would have an almost imperceptible impact on the U.S. energy situation. U.S. oil import dependence would at best be lowered by a few percentage points for a limited period of time, delaying by less than a year the major energy adjustments the United States must make. Indeed, there is something pathetic about the world's first major oil producer desperately sucking oil out of a national treasure to maintain wasteful practices that our industrial competitors are abandoning.

Even if continuing to expand fossil fuel consumption could achieve the economic goals claimed, it would undermine our environmental future. Fossil fuels are the main source of air pollution now choking rural areas and cities alike. In addition, rising levels of carbon dioxide and other gases are irrevocably altering the world's climate, and according to scientists could make the world warmer fifty years from now than at any time in human history.

The main cause of this phenomenon is fossil fuel combustion, which adds six billion tons of carbon to the atmosphere each year, more than one ton for each person on the planet. Although there is now evidence that global temperatures have already begun to rise, the implications of such a warming are not fully understood. They could well include serious disruptions in agriculture and the flooding of densely populated coastal areas. In response, several governments have begun to develop energy policies aimed at reducing emissions of greenhouse gases. As the Netherlands, Denmark, and Japan all recognize, improved energy efficiency will have to play the largest role in reducing carbon dioxide output over the next two decades, and this can only occur with active government intervention. Fortuitously, these policies will also help to reduce oil consumption.

A FAILED ENERGY POLICY

From the mid-'70s until the mid-'80s, the United States was well on the road to easing its oil dependence. Oil imports had fallen to just one-third of consumption as energy efficiency improved throughout the economy. These gains were in part a result of higher energy prices, but they were also induced by a series of successful energy policies. While synthetic fuels projects collapsed and nuclear research programs led nowhere, other policies led to notable gains.

These include energy price deregulation, energy conservation and renewable energy tax credits, minimum efficiency standards for cars and appliances, home weatherization programs, federal and state utility reforms, and federal funding of research and development on energy-efficient and renewable energy technologies.

The improved energy efficiency of the U.S. economy since 1973 has saved the equivalent of 5 billion barrels of oil in 1989, or 14.5 million barrels per day. This is fifty times the potential contribution from the Arctic Refuge, and studies indicate that energy efficiency's contribution could be doubled to the equivalent of more than 20 million barrels of oil per day by 2000. President Reagan entered office determined to eviscerate most of these programs, claiming that energy was a matter for the private sector, not for public policy. Initially, he sought to abolish the Department of Energy and then appointed a dentist to be his first Secretary of Energy. Even the solar collectors atop the White House were torn down. Congress saved the Department and resisted many of his policies, but President Reagan eventually got most of what he wanted. By the late '80s, most of the tax credits for energy conservation and renewable energy sources had expired. And federal budgets for key areas of energy research and development had been cut by 80 percent.

The $194 million being spent on all energy efficiency research and development in 1990 is equivalent to about four days' worth of spending on the U.S. military forces now in the Persian Gulf. Nearly 70 percent of the Department of Energy's budget goes to nuclear weapons production and cleanup. The remaining federal energy budget continues to be dominated by spending on fossil fuels and a host of nuclear technologies that have virtually no chance of making a contribution during the next few decades.

The Reagan Administration and Congress also permitted automobile fuel economy standards to lapse at the level achieved in 1986. For several years, the administration even provided the auto industry with exemptions to the standards already in place. As a consequence, new cars rolling off Detroit's assembly lines in 1989 were actually less efficient than those of the previous year. This is a costly reversal. Automobiles are at the root of U.S. oil dependence. Some 43 percent of the country's oil is now used in automobiles. Another 20 percent is used in other forms of transportation such as air travel and trucking. If average fuel economy were just seven miles per gallon higher, we would be importing two million fewer barrels of oil each day, and be in a much better position to withstand the effects of the embargo on Iraq.

REDUCING OIL DEPENDENCE

While President Bush used the words "energy conservation" as U.S. troops were on their way to the Persian Gulf, in a year and a half in office he has not proposed any significant policies to reduce dependence on imported oil. The steady rise in U.S. oil imports during the Reagan Administration has continued during the Bush presidency.

Means are available to reverse this trend. We can make our cars, buildings, and industries far more fuel-efficient than they are today. And we can gradually develop clean renewable fuels to run our vehicles. The record of the recent past demonstrates the enormous potential of energy efficiency. Keeping up with out Japanese and European competitors requires continued efforts to improve efficiency and cut national energy bills.

The first step in this direction would be for the United States to develop a "least cost energy plan" that would fairly weigh all new sources of energy supply and conservation, and consider various energy policies on the basis of their ability to achieve national goals. Recent experience and numerous analytical studies show that improved energy efficiency is the fastest and least expensive means of reducing dependence on foreign oil. Simply raising new car fuel economy from the current average of 27 miles per gallon to 40 miles per gallon would reduce U.S. oil consumption by 2.8 million barrels per day by the year 2005. This is nearly ten times the rate of extraction that the Department of Interior thinks is possible from the Arctic National Wildlife Refuge.

The automotive technologies to accomplish these goals are at hand. Prototype vehicles than run over 70 miles per gallon have been developed, though they have not yet reached the marketplace. These include improved engines, more efficient transmissions, and greater use of lightweight synthetic materials. The projected additional cost for a 40-mile-per-gallon car is $500, according to Marc Ledbetter of the American Council for an Energy-Efficient Economy. This sum would be more than offset by gasoline savings of over $2,000 during the life of a typical car. Overall, such technologies can save gasoline at a cost of about 43 cents per gallon or one-third the current retail price.

Strong programs are also needed to continue the energy efficiency revolution that began to sweep U.S. buildings in the '70s and '80s. These programs can greatly reduce the use of natural gas, freeing up gas to replace oil in other sectors. However, in recent years, the federal government has provided little support for those who are considering reducing their household or office energy consumption. This year the Bush Administration recommended an 85 percent cut in federal grants in this area. Energy efficiency improvements that have occurred so far only scratch at the potential to develop new energy-efficient technologies. Refrigerators, air conditioners, lights, and buildings can all be powered at a fraction of their current energy requirements.

The past decade's efficiency improvements were driven largely by high energy prices which have since fallen. Moreover, the government has yet to address seriously the market imperfections that cause underinvestment in energy efficiency. Without energy policy reforms, the efficiency potential will not be realized, and oil imports will remain high. One strategy that has been effectively employed in New England is to encourage utilities to invest hundreds of millions of dollars in improved energy efficiency by rewarding them with high rates of return on those investments.

BEYOND OIL

Ultimately, freeing the world of oil dependence will mean harnessing the world's abundant reserves of renewable energy resources such as solar, wind, and biomass energy. None of these offers an immediate large-scale alternative to liquid petroleum, but over the coming decades they can begin to form the basis of a non-fossil-fuel transportation system.

While steady progress has occurred in many of the technologies to harness these resources, it has been slowed by low oil prices and declining federal budgets. The U.S. government spends a pittance on all of these technologies combined—$138 million annually or one-fifth the estimated cost of a B-2 bomber. Nonetheless, a host of renewable energy technologies have made it to the commercial market, producing power from wind turbines, solar power plants, and geothermal facilities at competitive prices. California, which is the hotbed of this activity, has 17,000 wind turbines in place and gets over 40 percent of its electricity from renewable energy sources. Renewable energy has greatly reduced California's consumption of oil and natural gas. These results stem not just from California's abundant resources but from a concerted state effort to encourage renewable energy development.

Renewable energy technologies deserve at least as much support as they received a decade ago—$1 billion annually in 1990 dollars. With such a commitment, private investment would itself increase rapidly, and renewable energy sources would begin to make a significant additional contribution to U.S. energy supplies before the '90s were out.

Using renewable energy for transportation will require substantial investments in delivery, storage, and combustion systems. Electric vehicles, for example, can run on electricity coming from any source. General Motors, Fiat, and other companies already have such vehicles under development. Even more promising is the prospect of nonpolluting hydrogen cars. Hydrogen can be produced directly from water, using solar or other renewable energy sources. The hydrogen can then be moved around the country by pipeline and stored in large tanks.

It will take time to develop a hydrogen-based transportation system, but Germany already has an integrated national program to develop all aspects of a hydrogen-powered transport system—to be centered around massive solar installations in southern Europe and northern Africa. Involved in the program are research institutes, pipeline companies, engineering firms, and the automobile industry. Mercedes Benz and BMW already have prototype hydrogen-powered cars.

TOWARD A NATIONAL ENERGY STRATEGY

The concerted German effort highlights a major weakness of U.S. energy policy. It has no clear goals, resources are scattered over miscellaneous technologies, and funding is guided by today's shortsighted industrial interests rather than by a strategic view of the country's energy future. If we continue in this direction, we will not only sacrifice our national security and environment, but the economy as well. The Germans and Japanese, for example, are now outspending us on key solar technologies that are likely to become major competitive industries in the future.

The coming months will be a window of opportunity for U.S. energy policymaking, which is often driven by crisis. Not only is there the chance to consider important new legislation, but President Bush is scheduled to unveil a National Energy Strategy that has been underway for more than a year. With the dangerous implications of our lack of an energy policy now clearly demonstrated, the National Strategy provides an opportunity to implement a plan to reduce oil dependence and improve energy efficiency. Steps to improve automobile fuel economy, to boost energy efficiency research and development budgets, and to reinstate programs encouraging home weatherization are among the policy steps that would help curb our dependence on the Persian Gulf.

Unfortunately, Secretary of Energy James Watkins now appears to be retreating from the notion he voiced a year ago of a strong, comprehensive energy strategy. Rather, the Secretary has spoken recently of lists of options to be delivered to the President in December, at which point they may well be eviscerated by White House political advisors and lobbyists from the energy and auto industries. Meanwhile, just this September, the Bush Administration successfully defeated the most effective short-run policy—legislation before the U.S. Senate that would have raised U.S. new car fuel economy to 40 miles per gallon by the year 2000.

The United States can no longer afford to lurch from one oil crisis to another. The stakes will only grow as the Middle East's share of the world oil market continues to increase in the years ahead. The technology is available to end this explosive cycle. With American lives now on the line and with tens of billions of dollars likely to be spent in the Gulf in the next year alone, it is high time we got serious about "energy security."

NO

National Energy Planning Redux

Irwin Stelzer

Romanians do without electricity for large parts of the day. Poles and East Germans choke in the pollution from inefficient electric generating plants. The British public pays a 20-percent surcharge on its electric bills to pay for past nuclear sins of its then-nationalized power system. Russian oil production, suffering from years of government mismanagement, is in decline. China is unable to harness its vast resources of natural gas. Americans, meanwhile, have enjoyed ample supplies of relatively inexpensive oil and natural gas, and—so far—haven't had to worry too much about whether their lights will go on when they flip a switch.

The lesson seems obvious: market economies, even those with some regulated sectors, deliver adequate supplies of energy, when and where it is needed, at reasonable prices and with tolerable social costs; centrally directed, planned economies don't. Unfortunately, James Buchanan's observation that "the accumulation of empirical evidence must ultimately dispel romance" is not applicable to bureaucrats, even Republican bureaucrats, who inhabit the well-lit, air-conditioned offices of the White House and the Department of Energy.

So, last year President Bush directed the DOE (an agency Ronald Reagan and his vice president promised to abolish) "to lead an inter-agency effort to develop a National Energy Strategy . . . [to] serve as a blueprint for energy policy and program decisions." Pursuant to that directive, Secretary of Energy James Watkins "opened a dialogue with the American people," holding fifteen public hearings, receiving more than a thousand written submissions, and compiling a hearing record of some 12,000 pages. This resulted in a 230-page "Interim Report," which will form the basis for still more public comment, en route to a year-end "first edition of the National Energy Strategy." In the words of a triumphant DOE press release, "the report will provide a baseline for development and analysis of energy options."

The bipartisan applause for this effort is deafening. The General Accounting Office, not notable for its support of Republican initiatives, has only good things to say about this one: "We support the initiative to develop a national energy strategy and believe that such a strategy is sorely needed and long overdue." Rather than trust consumers and the marketplace, the GAO is eager for government to "propose initiatives for guiding future energy choices. . . ."

THE COSTS OF GOVERNMENT INTERVENTION

The cause of those who argue for government intervention in energy markets received a fillip over this summer when Iraq appropriated for itself Kuwait's oil reserves. This put a total of 7 percent of the world's oil production, and 20 percent of its reserves, into the hands of an expansionist despot who, among other things, wants to keep oil prices at levels that the so-called "price doves" among his fellow cartelists have so far avoided. Surely, the planners' skills are needed to offset the machinations of Saddam Hussein.

Grizzled observers of past efforts to forge a national energy policy are taking tight hold of their wallets. If history teaches anything, it is that government interventions in energy markets create shortages (natural gas, gasoline), gluts (natural gas), raise costs (electricity), and lead to enormous inefficiencies.

This country has suffered through President Nixon's "Project Independence," launched in 1973 to enable us, in his words, "to meet our own energy needs without depending on any foreign sources." Since then, imported oil has risen from 35 percent to almost 50 percent of our supply. Nixon also treated us to a gasoline-allocation scheme that led to long lines at all pumps except those on Capitol Hill that were reserved for congressmen. President Carter repeated that error by promulgating federal controls on thermostat settings, substituting sweaters for oil and gas heat and sweating for air conditioning. This he called the Moral Equivalent of War, a macho analogy to real war that was somewhat reduced in force by its unfortunate acronym—MEOW.

Presidents have not acted alone in this silliness. In 1978 Congress chipped in with the National Energy Conservation Policy Act. Section 682 of the act contains this "finding": "The Congress recognizes that bicycles are the most efficient means of transportation." The image of Tip O'Neill and Ted Kennedy pedaling up Capitol Hill to support this measure is amusing.

All of these efforts to manipulate the energy economy would be more amusing if they had not been so costly. After the first OPEC price shock, attempts to control oil prices cut billions off our GNP and contributed to the inflation that plagued the 1970s. Attempts to prevent the use of natural gas in utility boilers increased both electricity prices and pollution levels—all to conserve a fuel now in excess supply. Legislation to force electric companies to buy power from independent firms jacked up supply costs and contributed to an inefficient increase in generating capacity.

That President Bush should consider reinserting the government into the energy business should, on reflection, come as no surprise. As vice president he responded to a collapse in oil prices with a widely publicized appeal, made during a visit to Saudi Arabia, for stable (most observers took this to mean higher) oil prices. Fortunately, President Reagan shot down his lieutenant's effort to transfer large amounts of income from the vice president's oil-consuming Maine neighbors to his oil-producing Texas neighbors.

But President Bush's ardor for some sort of national energy strategy, rather than fluctuating, market-determined prices, remains uncooled. Like his predecessors—indeed, like most politicians here and abroad—he finds it difficult to leave energy pricing, and demand and supply decisions, to consumers and producers interacting in a free market.

The most obvious reason for continued government attention to the energy economy is that powerful pressure groups are affected by what goes on in those markets. Tales of oil barons and their more modern corporate counterparts lobbying for government favors dot American history books. From the days of Teapot Dome, and earlier, the oil industry has had an intense interest in the leasing of oil lands. It also has had a huge stake in import policy, at times winning quotas or tariff protection that would turn Lee Iacocca green with envy.

In short, government action (or inaction) in energy markets means money. Higher oil or natural-gas prices send a huge flow of dollars from New England and the Midwest southward, just as surely as will the taxpayer bailout of the savings-and-loan depositors. Lower or controlled prices reverse the regional flow, conferring windfalls on northern consumers, and devastating the economy of Texas—the home state at various times of presidents, Senate and House leaders, and key cabinet officers. The *Economist* estimates that every one-dollar fall in the price of oil costs Texas 25,000 jobs. The stakes are simply too high for politicians to adopt a consistent hands-off attitude toward energy markets.

SOCIAL CONTROL AND ENERGY POLICY

These financial motives are so transparent, and so easily understood, that actions taken in pursuit of them only occasionally cause problems. When oil companies bribe federal officials (Teapot Dome) or attempt to buy senators (natural-gas decontrol), or when oil-industry opponents raise a cry about "obscene profits," the issues are on the table for all to see.

This is not the case with those who use energy policy as an instrument for implementing their broad social agenda. In the late 1970s we were treated to the Club of Rome and similar groups' fears that the world was running out of resources and that stringent efforts to curb consumption were essential. This view had its roots in the sumptuary mentality of the Middle Ages, derived in turn from ancient Greek and Roman statutes limiting expenditures on funerals, per-capita entertainment, and dress. Malthus resurrected this nervousness about over-consumption in a mixture of economics and moral judgments that found its way into President Carter's piety: "[T]oo many of us now tend to worship self-indulgence and consumption. . . . [P]iling up material goods cannot fill the emptiness of lives which have no confidence or purpose." In short, small is beautiful, less is more. It was a short jump from that view to establishing a national energy policy that was "the moral equivalent of war," to be won by establishing "a new conservation ethic." For if one believes that Americans are overly self-indulgent consumers of material goods, energy policy is the perfect tool to exorcise that devil. Car pools instead of stereophonic privacy when driving to work; the equality of mass transit, enforced by restrictions on gasoline and vehicle use; summer thermostats at 78°, winter settings at 65°, frosty refrigerators and manually cleaned ovens, substituting manpower for electric power: all have been ingredients of various national energy plans. All, if effectively implemented (often an impossibility), save energy and satisfy the yearnings of the Malthuses, Carters, and their ilk for a return to a simpler, more austere, and therefore more virtuous life.

Such a change, whatever one thinks of it, in what we have come to call "life style" is only tangentially related to energy policy, which is merely the lever used to pry Americans from their attachment to material things. It should come as no surprise that groups that worry about Americans' attachment to material goods oppose nuclear power as too dangerous, coal as too dirty, and oil as environmentally unacceptable because of the effect of offshore drilling and, lately, oil spills. Their preference is conservation—reduced demand rather than increased supply.

OIL AND OUR NATIONAL SECURITY

Not all proponents of a national energy policy share this minimalist view of the good life, of course. Others worry about national security, which they believe is threatened by an excessive reliance on imported oil. With America now dependent on such supplies for almost 50 percent of its oil needs, those concerns are not irrational. After all, the oil embargo and the oil price "shocks" of the 1970s did contribute to the stagflation of the late 1970s, costing us dearly in income and jobs. And the more recent Middle East crisis may well produce more of the same. This can be avoided, interventionists argue, by subsidizing domestic production, setting import quotas, or mandating reductions in gasoline consumption.

There are two responses to this argument for a national energy policy. The first is that the 1990s are not the 1970s. We have learned, for one thing, that price controls are not an efficient response to supply interruptions or price spikes. The imposition of price controls in the 1970s encouraged excessive consumption in response to the artificially lower prices and discouraged the development of domestic supplies.

We have also learned the modern value of Joseph's Biblical advice to the Pharaoh about lean years following fat ones. Our strategic reserve of oil now totals 600 million barrels. the equivalent of eighty-one days' supply. In addition, we have diversified our sources of crude-oil supplies: 70 percent of our imports come from Venezuela, Mexico, Canada, and other nations outside of Arab OPEC.

The second response to those who see a national energy policy as necessary to national security is more complicated, since it cuts across several of the energy industries. It stresses the need to adopt a program that makes markets work better, rather than one that substitutes the heavy hand of government for the invisible hand of Adam Smith.

TARIFFS AND THE "TRUE" COSTS OF OIL CONSUMPTION

Economists have long recognized that markets efficiently allocate resources only so long as the prices attached to the products in question correctly reflect the costs of producing those products. Those costs include the labor and capital employed in the production process, and the cost of what on the surface appear to be free goods, clean air and water being the most notable. It is now widely accepted that many production processes, especially those involving the burning of fossil fuels, consume environmental resources. To the extent that the cost of those resources is not reflected in the prices of those fuels, consumers receive an erroneously low price signal, causing them to overconsume. That much seems clear to all parties to the dispute over energy policy, from Governor Sununu to the greenest environmentalist. Their squabble is over how much these environmental resources cost, and how best to force producers to reflect those costs in prices.

Not so obvious, except when some crisis bursts upon us, is the fact that the importation of oil also imposes costs that are not reflected in the price of crude oil. For one thing, the impact of imports on our rate of inflation, balance of payments, and national defense, combined with the effect of our incremental consumption on world oil prices, means that current oil prices do not reflect all the externalities associated with our level of oil imports: even the cartel price is below the true marginal cost of that oil to us. This means that America consumes more imported oil than is economically optimal.

To achieve an optimal level of consumption, the price of imported oil must be raised high enough to reflect its true marginal cost to society. This can most efficiently be accomplished by a tariff of about $10 per barrel, according to an estimate by Harvard's William Hogan. Such a device would, of course, adversely affect domestic oil consumers. But it would do so only because those consumers are not now paying the full cost that their oil consumption imposes on society. In short, a properly conceived tariff would end their subsidy. And it would sop up economic rents otherwise available to the OPEC cartel and its fellow travellers, while at the same time providing a more efficient incentive to the development of new technologies than would the subsidization of the "promising" technologies so beloved of environmentalists (solar, wind), construction engineers (synthetic fuels), and farmers (grain-based motor fuel).

Note that imposition of such a tariff is entirely consistent with leaving the energy business to the market. It merely gets the price signals right, and then lets consumers decide how much imported oil to use, and domestic energy producers how much oil (or alternative fuels) to produce. The alternative of doing nothing encourages overconsumption of deceptively low-priced imported oil. And the alternative of quotas involves the government in deciding just who gets how much of the bargain-basement petroleum.

The failure of past allocation systems, many devised in response to previous Middle East eruptions, is proof enough that the most recent (Iraqi) threat is no basis for an interventionist national energy policy. Saddam may get prices up, largely because we failed to do so first with a tariff. But higher prices produce far fewer dislocations than a government rationing scheme—it is one thing to pay more for gasoline, another not to be able to get any because some bureaucrat allocated too much to the wrong place. And a policy of getting prices right, by internalizing the environmental costs of fossil-fuel use and reflecting the economic and security costs of imported oil in its price, would have other salutary effects. It would increase the relative attractiveness of conservation techniques—with energy prices at higher, economically efficient levels, it would pay for more people to insulate their homes, drive more slowly, and turn off the lights when leaving home—without a web of government rules limiting energy consumption. And it would encourage the reappraisal of nuclear power now being whispered in policy-making circles, by changing the relative costs of fossil fuels and nuclear-generated power.

A NUCLEAR REVIVAL?

The American nuclear program is now moribund. Although some 112 licensed and operating nuclear reactors now provide about 20 percent of the nation's electricity, no new plants have been ordered since 1978, and several have been cancelled. The reasons for this state of affairs include inept management of, and huge cost overruns on, nuclear projects; changing federal safety regulations; state rate regulations that levy *ex post facto* penalties on companies investing in plants that hindsight proved not to be needed, just yet; an inability to devise a politically acceptable means of disposing of nuclear waste; media that consider Jane Fonda an authoritative source of scientific information; politicians who pander to local hysteria by closing down plants that are completed and ready to produce needed energy; and, until recently, a slowdown in the growth of demand for electrical energy.

Whether or not the nuclear program in American will recover—with newly designed, smaller, and safer plants having a role in the next century—is difficult to determine. Experience has taught that it is foolish to rely on the optimistically low cost estimates of committed technologists, or on the counter-claims of conservationists who specialize in very high cost estimates. Both proponents and opponents of nuclear power regularly fail to concede the obvious: predicting the costs of nuclear power and comparing them with those of oil, gas, and coal plants is extraordinarily difficult. What Oxford's George Yarrow calls "the balance of advantage between the alternatives" depends on the course of coal, oil, and gas prices well into the next century, the long-term level of interest rates, and the course of environmental and safety regulation—variables that no responsible economist can forecast with an easy conscience.

Fortunately, there is no need for policy makers to adjudicate these disputes over cost projections: that's what the market is for. For the past decade the market has been saying that it will not commit capital to the construction of nuclear plants, given the prospects for demand growth, the costs of constructing the plants, and the regulatory environment in which the electric-utility industry operates. Ordinarily, those who support the market-determined solutions to energy problems would applaud the decisions to cancel plants, and the refusal of the industry to start new ones. But the world of nuclear power is no ordinary one.

For the current sorry state of our nuclear industry is due only in part to the low demand and high cost projections that entrepreneurs have faced. It is due equally to the asymmetry of risk created by state regulators. If a nuclear plant is built on time and within the projected cost, the utility is permitted to earn a modest, so-called "reasonable" return on that investment. If the power produced proves to be cheaper than that from fossil-fuel plants, the benefits are passed on to consumers in the form of lower electric rates. But if the plant significantly overruns its costs projections, or is late, or proves to add to excess capacity for some time (these plants take a decade to build, and often are not "needed" at the moment of completion), the investor is likely to face a regulator who will deny him a return on, and possibly a return of, the billions of dollars of capital committed to the plant. Unless this asymmetry is eliminated, markets cannot perform their function of determining whether it is appropriate for investors to risk their capital on the construction of nuclear plants to meet future power needs. If we are even to find out who is right—those who think that nuclear power has a cost-effective role to play in our energy future, or those who argue that it is wildly expensive, and that small gas-fired plants and conservation are more efficient—this asymmetry must be eliminated. We don't need nuclear subsidies; we do need a system of regulation that permits markets to work—that is, to reward entrepreneurs who guess right and to penalize those who guess wrong.

FORECASTING ENERGY DEMAND

Until recently, resolution of this issue was more important to the private investors who had committed billions to nuclear plants than it was to the broader national interest. With substantial excess generating capacity available in most parts of the country, few large power plants of any sort were needed. But that circumstance may well be changing. Economists at the Federal Reserve Bank of Boston have reported what New Englanders know: utilities in the region have had to invoke "emergency operating procedures in order to cope with the region's peak demands for electricity." New York utilities may, but will not certainly, be able to meet projected demands later in this decade. Wisconsin utilities and regulators are reported in the trade press to be scrambling to figure out how to supply the power their customers will need in a few years. Florida utilities resorted to rolling blackouts when severe cold weather hit the state last winter. "We . . . will need to build a lot of generating capacity over the next ten years," concludes Federal Energy Regulatory Commission Chairman Martin Allday. Now seems to be the time when the market should be freed to appraise the nuclear option.

This conclusion seems unassailable even if we recognize that forecasts of energy demand are notorious for their unreliability; the joke in the trade is that energy forecasters were invented to make economic forecasters look good. The reasons for past failures to forecast the demand for energy with any accuracy are partly technical and partly institutional. On the technical side, such forecasts rely on elaborate econometric models, which depend heavily not only on data relating to the energy industry (prices, quantities demanded, etc.), but also on forecasts of GNP, one of the driving forces behind energy demand. As a consequence, any error in forecasting the general level of economic activity—and current debates over whether we are headed into a recession or are to be blessed with a renewed spate of growth suggest how difficult economic forecasting is—has a magnified effect on energy-demand forecasts.

Equally important is the fact that energy forecasting, as it has been practiced, is a mixture of analysis and self-serving numbers manipulation. Since the financial community now tends to frown upon utilities with large construction programs—the fear being that regulators will not permit an adequate return on newly invested capital—the pressure on all utilities is to forecast zero or low growth, so that analysts will be persuaded that the company will not be raising and investing new capital in the industry. On the other hand, a new generation of would-be energy czars prefers a high-growth scenario, since it desperately needs an impending shortage in order to support its arguments for government intervention in one form or another. After all, a crash program to build subsidized nuclear plants, or to require people to use less energy, or to require more fuel-efficient cars, makes no sense unless there is a projected shortage of energy.

LET MARKETS DO THE WORK

The good news is that whereas central planners need consensus forecasts, market economies don't. Market-driven economies are ecumenical enough to include those who predict oversupply, and those who see an opportunity for profit in building new plants. The latter risk their capital, in the hope of profit if they guess right, in the certainty of losses if they guess wrong.

Unfortunately, that description of a functioning capitalist response to consumer needs doesn't quite fit the existent energy market. And both the private and public sectors are to blame.

On the private side, large elements of monopoly power operate to prevent supply from efficiently meeting demand. In the electric-power industry some companies can use their control of transmission capacity to prevent competitors from getting cheaper power to market, and railroads use their control of rights-of-way to prevent coal-slurry pipelines from competing effectively with rail carriers.

On the public side we have statutes that require utilities to buy power from inefficient suppliers, regulations that have been used to confiscate shareholders' investments in power plants, and subsidies for various forms of energy that appeal to one or another set of legislators.

Given this leaky fountain pen, the federal energy bureaucracy is preparing to don a pair of rubber gloves—the National Energy Strategy. It is true, of course, that the White House and the DOE have been careful to emphasize their desire to rely on market forces. But their understanding of that term has so far been broad enough to include proposals to subsidize domestic oil and gas production, and solar research. In this post-Reagan era the willingness to let markets provide answers seems to be waning. Most politicians, after all, are rivals of markets; the more we rely on the latter, the less power we confer on the former.

The alternative to the development of a new grand strategy is to use existing tools to make markets work better. Prices should be made to reflect the economic cost of each energy source, and regulators should be required to allow investors a reasonable chance to earn profits commensurate with the risks that they take. Also, monopoly positions should be challenged, so that competitive suppliers of energy—oil, nuclear, coal, and conservation technologies—can have equal access to markets. Subsidies, be they for Senator Dole's corn farmers or the greens' solar advocates, should be eliminated.

This freeing up of markets is not a national energy policy, as that term is generally understood. It is a program to permit private entrepreneurs to go about the business of satisfying consumer needs, confining regulation to those areas in which effective competition is not feasible. (Just as economic deregulation of airlines coexists comfortably with stringent safety regulation, so reliance on market forces can coexist with safety and other rules for nuclear plants, coal mining, and the use of oil tankers.) A program to make markets work better is, in short, a means of making a centrally constructed energy plan, or strategy, unnecessary.

Such a market-improving series of steps is intrinsically superior to any government-instituted energy plan. This is so not because government officials are less able than their private-sector counterparts, but rather because the mistakes that the government makes are carved in stone: it takes time, sometimes years or even decades, before Congress or a government agency even recognizes that it has made a mistake, let alone remedies it. Private-sector errors, on the other hand, are less enduring. We do not have to wait for the businessman to discover his own errors, because his competitors will discover his errors for him. If an oil-company executive sends inadequate supplies to a particular region, that will merely create an opportunity for his competitors; they will try to capitalize on it by increasing their supplies to the very region that the first executive undersupplied. If private-sector investors back a technology that does not work, they go bust; if the government backs one, more taxpayer money can always be conscripted to continue the program.

Recent history supports this view. Even the imperfectly competitive and partly regulated markets that constitute our energy economy have provided effective cures for many of the problems that began with OPEC's unsheathing of "the oil weapon" in the early 1970s. The grip of OPEC has been loosened because the extortionate prices set by the cartel induced consumers to use less oil, and producers to develop alternative supply sources. The oversupply in the electric-power business is being whittled away by demand growth and by asset write-downs, the latter resulting in demand-stimulating lower prices. The natural-gas glut is being worked off, ever so slowly, and contractual problems hanging over from the days of price regulation are being resolved. The environmental costs of fossil-fuel consumption (and, some say, more) will be reflected in prices when the new Clean Air Act comes into effect. And plans are slowly being drawn up by utilities and independents to build plants to meet future electricity needs. As a sailor, President Bush should know that, in such circumstances, steady as she goes is a much wiser course than a lurch to port.

DISCUSSION QUESTIONS

1. What do you think is the impact of price controls on gasoline? Who stands to benefit and to lose from such a policy? Is it equitable or fair?
2. What impact does increasing CAFE standards have? How does the price of gasoline affect the political will to raise CAFE standards?
3. Why, if at all, should the government be actively involved with allocating energy (and not, for example, toasters, houses, and other consumer items)?
4. How is the U.S. government involved with energy policy? Is it really a "hands-off" policy?
5. What are some advantages and disadvantages of substantially raising the gasoline tax? Who would benefit? Who would lose? What political actors are especially powerful?
6. What is the relationship between energy use and environmental quality?
7. Do you support nuclear power as a means of reducing fossil-fuel consumption (and thereby reducing the threat of global warming)?
8. How much importance should the United States place on developing supply-side responses to energy in relation to curtailing or changing energy demand? Why?

ADDITIONAL READINGS

Chubb, John E. "U.S. Energy Policy: A Problem of Delegation," in John E. Chubb and Paul Peterson, eds. *Can the Government Govern?* (Washington, D.C.: Brookings Institution, 1989).

Cullingworth, J. Barry, ed. *Energy, Land, and Public Policy* (New Brunswick, N.J.: Transaction Publishers, 1990).

Davis, David. *Energy Politics*, 4th ed. (New York: St. Martin's Press, 1993).

Gilbert, Richard J., ed. *Regulatory Choices: A Perspective on Developments in Energy Policy* (Berkeley: University of California Press, 1991).

Hartnett, James. "National Energy Policy: Its History and the Need for an Increased Gasoline Tax." *California Western Law Review* (1991–92).

Maclean, Douglas, and Peter G. Brown, eds. *Energy and the Future* (Totowa, N.J.: Rowman and Littlefield, 1983).

Marcus, Alfred Allen. *Controversial Issues in Energy Policy* (Newbury Park, Calif.: Sage Publications, 1992).

McKee, David L., ed. *Energy, the Environment, and Public Policy: Issues for the 1990s* (New York: Praeger, 1991).

Mead, Walter J. *Energy and the Environment: Conflict in Public Policy* (Washington, D.C.: American Enterprise Institute, 1978).

Nemetz, Peter N., and Marilyn Hankey. *Economic Incentives for Energy Conservation* (New York: Wiley, 1984).

Nivola, Pietro S. *The Politics of Energy Conservation* (Washington, D.C.: Brookings Institution, 1986).

Rogers, James E., Jr. "The Need for a National Energy Policy." *Vital Speeches* (May 15, 1991).

Rosenbaum, Walter A. *Energy, Politics, and Public Policy*, 2d ed. (Washington, D.C.: Congressional Quarterly Press, 1987).

Sawhill, John C., ed. *Energy Conservation and Public Policy* (Englewood Cliffs, N.J.: Prentice-Hall, 1979).

Sawhill, John C., and Richard Cotton, eds. *Energy Conservation: Successes and Failures* (Washington, D.C.: Brookings Institution, 1986).

Yergin, Daniel. *The Prize: The Epic Quest for Oil, Money, and Power* (New York: Simon & Schuster, 1992).

9
BUDGETARY POLICY

"Should Balancing the Budget Be a Major Federal Priority?"

Since the late 1970s, the federal budget deficit has attracted prominent national attention commensurate with its dramatic escalation. Real federal budget deficits have mushroomed since the 1970s, from $10.2 billion in 1970 to $127 billion in 1980 to over $300 billion by 1993 (all in 1993 dollars). In nominal dollars, prior to 1982 no budget deficits exceeded $100 billion (even during World War II), while from 1982 to the present, no deficits have been less than $100 billion. Federal budget *deficits*—the difference between annual federal revenues and expenditures—should not be confused with the federal *debt*, however. The gross federal debt—which in 1993 exceeded $4 trillion—is the total amount of money owed by the federal government to creditors, mostly the public. (Since the public holds about three-fourths of the debt, the U.S. federal government owes U.S. citizens over $3 trillion; U.S. securities holders therefore find themselves paying taxes in order to pay themselves principal and interest on Treasury bill holdings.) Annual interest payments on the federal debt alone now total more than $200 billion, or about 15 percent of federal expenditures, although lower interest rates have recently saved the federal government billions of dollars in debt financing.

At one level, the severity of the budget deficit depends on how the information is presented. In dollar terms, the dramatic increases in budget deficits are outlined above. However, as a percentage of U.S. Gross Domestic Product (GDP), which rose from $2.6 trillion in 1980 to over $6 trillion by 1993, deficit increases are less pronounced. The deficit as a percentage of GDP was 2.8 percent in 1980, compared with 5 percent in 1992. Further, annual deficits in relation to annual revenues are today nowhere near historic levels. During the early 1940s deficits ran as high as $54.6 billion, compared with just $24 billion in federal receipts (and therefore $78.6 billion in expenditures). Although the wartime situation is unique, current deficits are far below federal receipts. Even the magnitude of the public debt is not historically unprecedented, viewed as a percentage of GDP: In 1946, the debt represented 127.5 percent of GDP, compared with just over 70 percent of GDP in 1993. However, federal debt as a percentage of GDP had been decreasing steadily since World War II, to just 34 percent of GDP in 1980, and only began to increase in 1982. In 1941, B. C. Forbes wrote: "Washington's spending is giving me the jitters. The Administration tosses out billions and billions as if they were pennies. . . . A federal debt of $100 billion—one hundred thousand millions—looms." Today, an annual *deficit* target of $100 billion appears unreachable.

There are several reasons why the mounting federal debt and budget deficits have raised concern, including economic, political, and moral anxieties. Economists worry that because budget deficits mean that the government is borrowing heavily just to maintain current expenditures, it crowds out private borrowing and therefore private investment. The concern is not for the deficit itself, but for its impact on investment and therefore future economic productivity. National saving rates of 6 to 10 percent from the 1950s to the 1970s were common, but fell precipitously in the 1980s to below 4 percent of the Gross National Product. During the same period, other industrialized countries were saving over 10 percent of their GNP, and Japan was saving 15 to 20 percent. While no one knows for sure why savings rates dropped sharply in the 1980s, some economists attributed much of the decline to heavy federal government borrowing, which, they argue, crowded out private investment (and therefore replaced private investment with public spending). A related economic problem is that government borrowing increases the demand for investment funds, driving up interest rates worldwide and reducing investment opportunities. Finally, economists have warned that much of the federal deficit spending in the 1980s was financed by foreign governments (which purchased government securities or IOUs, like Treasury bills). Should the availability of foreign capital evaporate, the U.S. economy could see long-term stagnation or even decline; should foreign capital continue to finance U.S. debt, then increasingly the United States is "owned" by other nations.[1] Either way, they point out, the United States is worse off.

Politically, budget deficits have been criticized for what they indicate about the ability of political institutions (particularly Congress and the president) to make difficult spending and revenue decisions. The now quite public congressional votes to increase the debt ceiling and near constant political wrangling over the annual budget have eroded the public's faith in elected representatives to handle the problem. This is exacerbated by the growth in "entitlement" programs (particularly in health care and income security) that far surpasses the growth of revenues. The final and perhaps most intuitive reason for the public's concern for budget deficits is a moral one: It represents the inability of our society to live within its means, instead saddling future generations with the burden of paying for current expenditures. The more than $4 trillion debt will have to be paid for eventually (if only the interest payments to finance it), and every year the budget deficit adds to the total that future generations will owe. As former Colorado governor Richard Lamm put it, "Christmas is a time when kids tell Santa what they want and adults pay for it. Deficits are when adults tell the government what they want—and their kids pay for it."

Many members of the public underestimate the difficulty of balancing the budget, however, particularly with the strong antitax sentiment dominating budget politics. A brief look at the composition of federal budget expenditures shows why it is all but impossible for spending cuts to eliminate the budget deficit. Social insurance programs (Social Security, Medicare, Medicaid, and the like), national defense, and interest payments on the debt comprise more than three-fourths of all federal spending. Therefore, remaining budget cuts must come from grants to state and local government, child nutrition programs, law enforcement, environmental protection and cleanup, education, highway programs, research, and other federal programs with wide support. Indeed, David Stockman, former director of the Office of Management and Budget, once presented President Reagan with a list of federal programs from which Reagan could either take a "nick" or a "whack" in order to reduce expenditures. After Stockman tallied the cuts chosen by the president, he realized that Reagan had made only trivial cuts.[2] If a conservative president like Ronald Reagan could not bring himself to cut spending anywhere near the amount necessary to eliminate the deficit, many wondered who could. As a result, many liberals saw the mounting budget deficits in the 1980s as an attempt by conservatives to curtail any new spending initiatives, particularly on social programs. While this arguably succeeded, increasingly conservatives fear that deficits coupled with the political unwillingness to cut popular spending programs will lead to increased taxes and therefore an expanded role for government. Proposals for addressing the problems caused by budget deficits have ranged from constitutional controls (such as a balanced budget amendment), to Gramm–Rudman legislative requirements to reduce deficits, to a recent proposal by economists William Gale and Robert Litan to require individuals to save more.[3]

In contrast, others believe either that budget deficits are not harmful or that compared with the political and economic costs of eliminating deficits, we are better off tolerating them. For example, some economists on the political left believe that budget deficits should take a backseat to more important economic priorities and advocate additional deficit spending on jobs, infrastructure, and other investment programs to further stimulate the economy. They contend that a portion of government spending should be considered investment. After all, governments build and repair roads, subsidize basic and applied research, and pursue other investment decisions. They argue that government spending does not necessarily crowd out private investment; it simply changes the type of investment. Some economists on the political right argue that reducing deficits should be a priority in the hopes that balanced budgets will be achieved by cutting federal spending, not by raising taxes. But the main source of disagreement is not ideological but one of degree: Are the costs imposed by budget deficits greater than the costs of eliminating them? Different economists predict conflicting (and plausible) scenarios as a result of continuing budget deficits. The policy question therefore centers not around whether budget deficits are good or bad—other things being equal, few economists, even ardent Keynesians, advocate long-term deficits of the magnitude faced in the 1980s and early 1990s. The question instead is whether reducing the budget deficit should be a major federal priority that overshadows other budgetary issues. Economists Charles Schultze of the Brookings Institution and Robert Eisner of Northwestern University take up two opposing positions of this multifaceted issue below.

Endnotes

1. See, for example, Martin and Susan Tolchin, *Buying into America: How Foreign Money Is Changing the Face of Our Nation* (New York: Times Books, 1988).
2. David Stockman, *The Triumph of Politics* (New York: Harper and Row, 1986).
3. William G. Gale and Robert E. Litan, "Saving Our Way Out of the Deficit Dilemma," *Brookings Review* (Fall 1993). This proposal does not reduce the deficit, but does address the central concern of many economists: the low rate of national savings.

YES

Of Wolves, Termites, and Pussycats or, Why We Should Worry about the Budget Deficit

Charles L. Schultze

For more than six years now the nation has been unable to muster the political consensus needed to deal decisively with the immense federal budget deficit. One of the reasons is that the public and the Congress are faced with three quite different and conflicting views about the economic consequences of persistent large deficits.

One view often heard on Wall Street, in international financial circles, and among some economists is that continued failure to reduce the U.S. budget deficit threatens to cause an economic crisis, characterized by a plummeting overseas value of the dollar, soaring interest rates, and a severe recession exacerbated by financial disturbances.

In marked contrast, several prominent economists and public opinion makers have recently been arguing that the problem of the budget deficit has been vastly overstated and that excessive concern about it is getting in the way of addressing more serious economic and social problems. Here the left of center finds common ground with the supply-siders of the far right. Robert Eisner, Robert Heilbroner, and the left wing of the Democratic party join Jack Kemp, Arthur Laffer, and other supply-siders. Although they come from different analytic and ideologic backgrounds, they all arrive at a common set of conclusions deemphasizing the importance of the deficit.

Still a third viewpoint, shared by the majority of economists who have addressed the problem, and among whom I find myself, holds that the consequences of perpetuating large budget deficits will be neither explosive nor harmless. Rather, by reducing sharply the nation's already low rates of saving and investment, the deficits will slowly and almost imperceptibly but inexorably depress the potential growth of American living standards.

In an economic bestiary, the conventional Wall Street view of the deficit might be characterized as the wolf at the door; the second view as the domesticated pussycat; and the third as the termites in the basement.

IS A CRISIS COMING?

It is not at all inevitable that the maintenance of today's large budget deficits will bring on some kind of cyclical crisis. There *are* risks ahead that could be reduced if the deficits were smaller. Nevertheless, with competent management

231

by the Federal Reserve, the United States can very probably continue to muddle through, maintaining economic stability despite high budget deficits, as it has done for the past six years. Those who worry about a crisis, however, see one coming in the form of a "dollar strike." In this scenario, foreigners, observing that budget and current account deficits remain high, suddenly lose confidence in the U.S. economy and desert the dollar in droves. The dollar's exchange value plummets, import prices soar, and the U.S. price level rises sharply. To prevent this one-shot rise in the price level from pushing up wages and turning into a persistent and possibly accelerating wage–price spiral, the Fed has no option but to tighten monetary policy severely, raise interest rates sharply, and put the economy through the wringer of a recession.

This chain of events, while not impossible, is also not very likely. In the years ahead downward pressure on the dollar may well continue, but a precipitous dollar collapse is not at all probable. A failure by the United States to reduce its budget deficit would set off a dollar flight only if international investors began to think that the Federal Reserve might become unwilling to stomach the higher interest rates needed to neutralize any inflationary, excess demand effects of the budget deficit.

But the Fed for the past six years has had both the will and the political freedom to do the unpleasant things needed to deal with budget deficits much larger than those now in prospect. Moreover, at an unprecedentedly early stage of the recovery from the 1982 recession, it showed its willingness to push real interest rates far above their historical norms to keep the pace of expansion within bounds. And with U.S. interest rates already well above those in West Germany and Japan, a sudden plunge in the dollar would likely be self-limiting as dollar assets began to look more and more like a good buy.

All in all, the wolf-at-the-door thesis is not likely to prove out so long as the Fed continues to pursue a credible set of noninflationary policies—a quite reasonable assumption given recent history.

THE COLLAPSE OF NATIONAL SAVING

That we may be able to muddle through, sustaining large budget deficits without a cyclical crisis, does not mean that the deficits do no harm and that we can ignore them. In addition to providing a stable prosperity today, a successful economy must also make provision for tomorrow. It ought to save a reasonable fraction of its income to invest in increasing the stock of productive capital in the hands of the nation's citizens. This accumulation of wealth will in turn contribute to the growth of national living standards.

Yet the national rate of saving and wealth has fallen substantially in recent years. And it is in this important aspect of economic performance that the high level of the federal budget deficit continues to damage the American economy.

National saving consists of two major components—private saving and government saving. A government deficit represents *dis*saving, since an equivalent amount of private saving is absorbed in financing the deficit, leaving that much less available for national investment. The U.S. *net* national saving rate has fallen dramatically, from an average of 8 percent of national income during the first three decades of the postwar period to an average of 2.6 percent in the last two years. Both elements of saving declined. The private saving rate dropped by about three percentage points, to 6.4 percent in 1987–88. And dissaving from the government budget deficit rose to more than 5 percent in 1986 before falling back to just under 4 percent. That means that the United States has been on a spending spree throughout the 1980s, sharply raising the proportion of its income devoted to the combination of consumption and government spending and correspondingly decreasing the fraction of income it saves for the future.

Had the United States been forced to rely only on its own saving, domestic investment would have fallen as sharply as saving did. But because the country was able to finance a major part of its spending spree by borrowing heavily from abroad, rather than by having to scale back investment here at home, net domestic investment in housing construction and business plant and equipment fell by less than two percentage points, compared with the 5½ point drop in the national saving rate. As a result more than half of America's net domestic investment is now financed, directly and indirectly, from other countries.

Had the country adjusted to its lower private and public saving rates by radically cutting domestic investment in productive assets, the nation's productivity growth, which has already slowed, would have slowed even more, further depressing the growth of American living standards. But because we adjusted to the lower saving rate principally by borrowing from abroad, our living standards will suffer for a different reason—out of our future national income we will have to pay a continuing portion to foreign investors in the form of interest payments on the massive overseas debts we have been accumulating.

If we continue to consume this unprecedentedly large fraction of our national income—a fraction that is excessive in comparison either with our own history or with other industrial countries—the future can develop in two possible ways, neither of which is attractive. First, at today's high U.S. interest rates, foreigners might continue to find the United States an attractive place to invest some of their funds. The dollar would not fall, and the U.S. balance of payments deficit, after declining a bit more, would stabilize at a high level. The United States would continue indefinitely to borrow large sums from abroad, steadily increasing the future diversion of national income to overseas interest payments, and further depressing the future path of American living standards.

The second alternative is that foreign investors, despite high U.S. interest rates, might reduce their demand for dollar investments as they perceive a growing risk to the exchange value of their dollar holdings. In that case, the flow of foreign funds into the United States would decline. And then in corresponding amount, we would have to cut back domestic investment here at home to match our own shrunken national saving. The growth of U.S. living standards would suffer, not by further diversion of national income to overseas interest payments, but by a further slowing of the growth in national investment, productivity, and real wages. Either way, so long as the country overspends by running a large budget deficit in conjunction with low private saving, the future growth of the net incomes available to American citizens and their children will be gradually, but surely, eroded.

MAKING MOLEHILLS OUT OF MOUNTAINS

Let me turn to the arguments which suggest that the federal budget deficit is not a serious national problem. To start with, a number of people quarrel with the way the budget deficit *or* private saving is defined. With a proper definition, so the argument goes, the national saving and budget deficit problems would be seen to be minimal.

One set of these views, generally associated with Robert Eisner of Northwestern University, comes from the left. There are four strings to Eisner's bow. First, he would adjust the budget deficit for the effect of inflation on the public debt. Because inflation reduces the real value of that debt, some part of the interest payments received by government bondholders—equal to the inflation rate times the public debt—has to be considered not as income to be consumed, but as an asset transfer needed to restore the real value of wealth and consequently to be saved. Under this view, the part of the deficit that is represented by the inflation adjustment is not income, does not increase demand for consumer goods, and does not lower the national saving rate. It should be subtracted from the deficit. If it were, the current deficit would equal 2½ percent of national income, not the 3½ percent commonly cited. By the mid-1990s the inflation-adjusted deficit would fall to about 1 percent of national income.

It may make sense to subtract the inflation adjustment when estimating the "true" size of the budget deficit, as Eisner suggests. But the whole question is irrelevant to the issue at hand. Making the inflation adjustment does not change the estimate of *national* saving one iota. If the inflation adjustment is subtracted from the deficit because it is not truly income to bondholders, then current statistics overstate not only the budget deficit but also the income and the saving of those same bondholders. The Eisner adjustment simply reallocates national saving among its components: less private saving, less government dissaving, with no net effect on national saving itself. Moreover, the inflation adjustment as a share of national income has recently been the same as it was on average between 1955 and 1980; the *increase* in the budget deficit since that base period, and its share of the responsibility for the decline in national saving, is just about the same whether the inflation adjustment is made or not.

Second, Eisner argues that some of the federal deficit finances the accumulation of public capital, which adds to the nation's productive wealth. On this account too the true deficit, excluding government capital formation, would be smaller than shown by the current unified budget deficit. To construct such a budget, one must not only subtract gross capital outlays from total government expenditures, but also add depreciation to other operating outlays. Excluding military weapons from the definition of productive capital, which I think is only reasonable, the federal government's net capital accumulation now runs at $7 billion a year—hardly enough to affect the measured size of the deficit. Net investment by state and local governments is larger—$22 billion in 1987. But that investment as a share of national income has fallen substantially since the pre-1980 period. Including such investment in the definition of national saving would magnify the size of the recent saving decline.

Third, Eisner and others say that because state and local governments are running a large surplus, the budget deficit for total government is much smaller than the deficit for the federal government alone. In fact, state and local governments are now running a small deficit in their operating budgets. As defined in the national income accounts, their budgets include the pension funds of state and local employees, which are large surpluses. Were these same employees in the private sector, however, those surpluses would be considered as part of personal saving; it is only a freak of the national income accounting system that treats them as part of the government budget. . . . In any event, no matter whether these pension fund accumulations are classified as private or as public saving, it does not change in one whit the measure of national saving and the fact of its collapse in recent years.

A final point Eisner and others make is that a substantial reduction in the budget deficit would lead to recession, lower national income, and lower, not higher, saving. According to this view, it is unlikely that the policy mix could be shifted sufficiently toward monetary ease to offset the demand-depressing effect of fiscal restraint. That is reminiscent of Keynesian arguments from 30 to 40 years ago: "You can't push on a string with monetary policy." Whatever its validity in explaining events of the 1930s or the first postwar decade when the U.S. economy was flooded with cash, the argument is sheer nonsense in the current economic environment. If the economy were in a recession, if monetary policy were already quite relaxed, and if interest rates were at very low levels, then further monetary ease might be unable to offset the effect of a fiscal tightening. But the economy is at or close to full employment, and real interest rates are far above historical norms, conditions under which the old Keynesian fears of the inefficacy of monetary policy to stimulate demand are groundless.

There is indeed a practical limit to the speed at which monetary policy can effectively offset a shift in fiscal policy. The budget deficit ought to be eliminated not all at once but over a number of years. But I lose little sleep worrying that Congress and the president will suddenly agree on an excessively rapid reduction in the budget deficit—it is, to borrow a phrase from Senator Daniel Patrick Moynihan, forty-fifth on my list of fears, following right after my fear of being eaten alive by piranhas.

THE BRADFORD THESIS

In a recent paper David Bradford of Princeton raises another major objection to the analysis underlying the standard observation that the national saving rate has fallen sharply. According to the usual definition, saving is that part of the national output (or income—the two are the same) that is *not* consumed by individuals and government. It is what is available each year to invest in additions to the nation's stock of productive assets—principally residential housing, business plant and equipment, and investment abroad. Bradford argues that this definition is wrong. National saving, he believes, should be defined as the change in the inflation-adjusted market value of the nation's assets. It should therefore count not only annual additions to the stock of assets but also changes in their value, including realized and unrealized capital gains.

His definition paints a very different picture of the recent behavior of the national saving rate. Measured as the change in the real market value of the nation's assets, net national saving averaged 11 percent of national income in the three decades from 1951 through 1980. It also averaged 11 percent in 1985–87. (As might be expected however, annual fluctuations in the saving rate, so defined, were huge; the average annual change in the saving rate was 15 percent of national income, and in several years the saving rate rose or fell by 30 percentage points!)

After all, says Bradford, it is the present value of the stream of future income from wealth that counts. If, for any reason, the market puts an increased value on a given set of assets, that real capital gain represents a legitimate increase in national wealth just as much as an increase in the physical volume of assets does—it presumably represents an increase in the current value of the future stream of national income expected to flow from those assets. The existing cost-based measure of national saving and wealth is therefore inappropriate, either for use in investigating private saving behavior or as a measure of national saving performance.

For purposes of understanding the consumption and saving behavior of individuals, changes in the market value of their wealth, including capital gains, may be quite relevant. But the aggregate change in the market value of individuals' wealth is not at all a relevant measure of national saving performance.

We are interested in the volume of national saving, and the investment in productive assets that it makes possible, because additions to those assets contribute to future national income and production. But future national income can also change for reasons that have nothing to do with the volume of saving—for example, the future pace of scientific and technological advance may speed up or slow down, or the overseas price of oil may surge or collapse. To some extent expectations about such future developments can affect the current price of corporate stocks, increase or decrease the market value of corporate assets, and so affect the measure of national saving as defined by Bradford. But such developments, however much they affect future national income, have nothing to do with the contribution of current saving and investment to future national income, and hence the capital gains or losses on existing assets these developments generate do not belong in the measure used to evaluate the nation's saving and investment performance.

An even more important objection to the Bradford measure of saving is that the sum of changes in the market value of business enterprises and real estate may have little to do with changes in national productive wealth. Several examples help make this point clear. Legal limits on the supply of taxicabs in New York City, through restrictions on the number of cab medallions, have increased the financial value of those medallions tremendously and thus the wealth of the individuals or businesses who own them. If entry into the taxi business were made free, the financial value of the medallions would collapse, but national wealth would not have fallen; indeed, the future national income would rise. Or, assume a sudden and well-forecasted halt to all new innovations in the United States. The future obsolescence of the existing stock of tangible capital assets would fall to zero, and stock prices of firms owning those assets would soar, but future national production would decline.

To take another case, imagine a sudden large increase in population. Urban land values would skyrocket, even as the disamenities of urban living would increase sharply. This change in market value surely would not mean that the nation had added to its saving, its investment, and its productive wealth. As a final example, suppose that a law were passed prohibiting new entry into any existing line of business. The market value of existing firms would sharply increase, but clearly national wealth would not.

In short, changes in the aggregate of the market value of existing firms and residential real estate often tell little about changes in national wealth. Rather, the proper measure for assessing the nation's saving performance is the definition of national saving used in the Commerce Department's national income accounts—namely, the difference between national income and consumption (by government and bondholders), which, in turn, is equal to the increase in the physical volume of productive assets.

THE BARRO HYPOTHESIS

Let me turn to a quite different set of arguments that suggest the budget deficit is not a big problem, even from the standpoint of national saving and investment. Represented here are a wide variety of subcategories of different schools of thought. First is the argument put forward by Robert Barro of Harvard, which has some adherents among academic economists. According to this view, infinitely farsighted, ultrarational, and highly beneficent consumers and taxpayers save to achieve long-term, generation-spanning wealth objectives for themselves and their children. Any increases in their immediate disposable income, from a deficit-creating tax cut or transfer payment, are perceived to imply equally large tax increases (plus interest on accumulated debt) to be paid in the future either by themselves or their heirs. They will, therefore, save all of the current increase in income, putting it aside to pay for the future tax increases, to preserve their long-term wealth objectives.

By this reasoning, changes in the budget deficit do not affect national saving, but instead set in motion exactly offsetting movements in private saving.

Thus, according to Barro, the recent fall in national saving was not caused by the large growth in the budget deficit, and a reduction in the deficit would not raise national saving.

On the surface, this view is grossly contradicted by the events of the last five years. The increase in the federal budget deficit was accompanied by a decrease, not an increase, in private saving. But the proponents of the Barro hypothesis have argued that in the absence of the growing federal deficit, private saving would have fallen even further than it actually did. The large rise in stock prices, they say, provided stockholders with large unanticipated increases in their wealth, sharply reducing their incentive to continue saving; thus, had the budget deficit not risen, the personal saving rate would today be even lower than it is.

Douglas Bernheim of Stanford University, in a recent paper for the National Bureau of Economic Research, summarized the theoretical underpinnings and empirical evidence for the Barro hypothesis and concluded, convincingly to me, that it does not stand up. Some additional evidence also contradicts the Barro hypothesis. But let me leave this particular point for the moment and turn to another set of views which holds that the budget deficit is not an important problem.

Some people note that the budget deficit has already fallen from 5½ to 3½ percent of national income and even with no further cuts will drop to 2 or 2½ percent of national income by the mid-1990s. Moreover, they argue, favorable demographic trends will soon reverse the recent decline in private saving. For a long time the country has experienced a falling proportion of adults in the high-saving group (age 35 to 60). But that group will soon grow much larger as the baby boom ages, and personal saving will return to earlier levels. With the budget deficit declining, and personal saving likely to increase, national saving will not remain at its current low level—certainly it will not remain low enough to warrant incurring the economic costs of the tax increase that would be required to eliminate the budget deficit.

To deal with these arguments three questions must be considered. First, is the personal saving rate only temporarily low; can it be expected to rise again? Second, would a cut in the budget deficit increase national saving, or, as Barro maintains, would it simply result in smaller private saving? Third, what sort of a national saving rate should this country be aiming for, anyway?

The personal saving rate has been falling since the mid-1970s. (Personal saving constitutes about two-thirds of private saving, the remainder being contributed by retained business earnings.) To determine what factors may have been responsible for the decline in personal saving, I fit an econometric equation relating the personal saving rate to other economic developments, including those most often cited as being important saving determinants. I first fit the equation to data for the years 1956 through 1980, and then used the relationships shown there to "forecast" forward the course of personal saving over the next seven years, 1981–87. The relationships developed for the earlier period closely tracked the path of the saving rate since 1980, suggesting that the equation is a good representation of the factors determining saving and permitting me to draw the following conclusions.

- An increase in the budget deficit does raise personal saving and vice versa, but only temporarily. It takes time for taxpayers to adjust their consumption when tax cuts or increased transfer payments raise their income. Very soon, though, personal saving returns to its old level. Contrary to Barro's hypothesis, only an insignificant fraction of a permanent increase in the budget deficit is offset by an increase in personal saving.
- A rise in the value of stock prices (adjusted for inflation) does reduce the personal saving rate. About 1 percentage point of the 3¼ percentage point drop in the personal saving rate since 1982 can be attributed to the rise in stock prices since then.
- Changes in the proportion of the population in different age groups do not appear to have been significant factors in changing the personal saving rate. The proportion of high-saving age groups in the population declined steadily from the mid-1960s to 1981, while the personal saving rate rose slightly and then fell. The proportion of high savers stabilized after 1981 and then began to edge up while the saving rate continued to fall sharply. (Not surprisingly, the statistic representing the population share of high savers did not explain any of the fall in personal saving.)

The stock market, the short-run effects of changes in the budget deficits, and other factors incorporated in my equation do not fully account for the drift downward in the personal saving rate after 1975. On the basis of admittedly scanty evidence, this downtrend appears to have halted around 1985. The annual rate of decline was just about the same from 1975 to 1980 as from 1980 to 1985. There are several economic theories about saving motivations which imply that a slowdown in the long-term rate of growth of per capita income will lead to a fall in the saving rate. And after 1973 the growth of per capita income in the United States did slow down. But it is impossible to determine from the data whether or not this decline in income growth is responsible for the downtrend in the personal saving rate.

SAVING TARGETS

In the short run the saving rate fluctuates substantially, and that fact together with uncertainty about the causes of the 1975–85 downtrend make it difficult to predict the future course of private saving. Nevertheless, at a minimum, there is no warrant to believe either that favorable demographic trends will raise the saving rate or that a large part of today's low rate is a temporary aberration that will soon disappear. Until events demonstrate otherwise, the prudent course is to assume that the personal saving rate will continue somewhere near its present level.

If both the personal and business saving rates stay at roughly their recent level, total private saving will run at about 7 percent of national income, compared with a 9¼ percent average in the 30 years before 1980. What does this projection mean, then, for setting targets for the balance in the federal budget in the 1990s?

Let me start by setting a very conservative, minimal target for national saving, namely the rate of saving that—on its own without further reliance on overseas borrowing—would be needed to support enough investment to maintain the annual rate of productivity growth at its current level of 1 percent. The rate of growth in output per worker is determined by the pace of technological advance, the increase in workers' skills, and other similar factors, plus the amount of investment in capital goods. We have no evidence to believe that the pace of advance in technology, workers' skills, and other such factors will speed up. Given a continuation of the current rate of advance, we can calculate the specific amount of investment, and therefore the specific amount of saving, that will be needed to maintain the current rate of productivity growth.

The saving rate required in the next decade or so to support the investment necessary to achieve this "business-as-usual" objective will not be as high as the saving rate for the decades before 1980. That is so for three reasons. First, the projected growth of the labor force is lower, so the increase in the capital stock necessary to equip the new workers is less.

Second, the pace of technological advance has apparently slowed since the earlier years, so the opportunities to invest profitably in additions to the stock of capital per worker are less. Third, according to the statisticians at the Department of Commerce, the quality-adjusted prices of computers and related equipment, which now constitute a large fraction of business investment, are falling rapidly, as the speed and capability of computers steadily increase. Each average dollar of saving now buys more capital equipment than it used to, producing more investment bang per saving buck.

To maintain the rate of productivity advance at its current pace, then, net investment needs to run somewhere between 5 and 5½ percent of national income. And if the country is no longer going to rely on an inflow of foreign saving, it will have to save 5–5½ percent of its national income to finance that investment. That investment rate is much lower than the 7.6 percent of national income devoted to domestic investment during the 1956–79 period. But it is much larger than the current national saving rate of 3 percent.

Even so, the business-as-usual saving objective is not ambitious enough by a long shot, because it does not take into account the demographic crunch that will come early in the next century when the baby boomers begin to retire and the ratio of retirees to active workers rises steeply. To avoid putting a major burden on the next generation of workers, the nation's saving, investment, and income growth should be increased over and above business as usual.

The magnitude of the additional saving needed is reasonably well represented by the growing annual surplus in the nation's Social Security and other retirement trust funds. The decision, taken in 1978 and 1983, to have this generation of workers pay for a larger portion of its own Social Security retirement benefits can be translated into economic reality only if the annual surpluses in the Social Security trust funds are used to increase national saving, the stock of national wealth, and the future level of national income above what would otherwise have occurred. In practical terms, that means national saving ought to be increased above the business-as-usual level by the amount of the annual surplus in the Social Security and federal retirement trust funds.

Allowing for some increase in payroll taxes to support hospital insurance under Medicare, which is not now fully funded, those surpluses should amount to about 2½ percent of national income by the mid-1990s, which when added to the business-as-usual requirement of 5–5½ percent, gives a target national saving rate of about 8 percent. This more ambitious objective is approximately equal to the pre-1980 average.

If the private saving rate is in the neighborhood of 7 percent, as I expect, then achieving an 8 percent national saving rate would require a government *surplus* of about 1 percent of national income, where the budget is defined to include Social Security. Without further action to raise taxes or cut government spending, however, a budget *deficit* of 2 percent of national income is likely out into the 1990s. Therefore, tax increases and government spending cuts amounting to some 3 percent of national income will be needed to achieve this conservatively defined set of national saving targets. And by the mid-1990s that will require almost $200 billion of budgetary actions.

You might ask why not try to encourage private saving with various tax concessions and incentives. But that is a loser's game. The payoff to such schemes is small, by the estimates of all but enthusiasts, and the revenue losses involved will end up raising the budget deficit by far more than they stimulate private saving, leaving behind a net decrease in national saving.

We have no really powerful tools to raise the national saving rate to a reasonable level other than through eliminating the budget deficit and transforming it into a modest surplus. In turn, I am absolutely certain that goal cannot be accomplished without a relatively substantial tax increase. Unfortunately, neither the American people nor their political leaders yet seem willing to accept one.

NO

Our Real Deficits

Robert Eisner

Budget deficits of $300 billion! A federal debt over $3 trillion! Repeated trade deficits that have made the United States "The World's Greatest Debtor Nation!" A savings and loan bailout to "cost the taxpayer" $500 billion! What are we to make of these astronomical numbers and apocalyptic proclamations? They are dear to politicians, press, and assorted pundits, but what is their substance? Is the overweening attention they attract obscuring the real issues facing our nation and its economy? And is it preventing vital policy planning and decisions?

This is not going to be an article of gloom and doom. As I write, we have apparently slipped into a recession that cost more than 200,000 jobs in one month, and promises to get worse—no one can honestly say how much worse—before it gets better. Justified concern has been expressed both about where we are now and whether we are providing properly for our future. We also slipped into a brief but fairly expensive war, with initial "off-budget" funding requests running over $60 billion and uncounted billions more anticipated to replenish military stockpiles and compensate for at least some of the war's destruction and political consequences. Paradoxically, war expenditures serve generally to combat recessions, but they also drain resources from investment in the future.

Still the United States remains the globe's greatest economic power. We are the nation with the greatest total wealth and the highest average standard of living—whatever that means—with the exception of any surviving oil sheikdoms and possibly Sweden and Switzerland. We are the envy of much of the world. We are the (probably misunderstood) model for many of our former antagonists in the old communist empire, as their efforts at a transition from Stalinist command socialism to a market (and capitalist?) economy make matters worse before, it is hoped, they get better.

Our economy, though, is far from perfect. There is trouble now, and there is trouble ahead. To find a cure for our troubles we shall have to disabuse ourselves of some very widespread myths and face up to some ignored realities.

FAULTY CONCEPTS AND FAULTY MEASURES

It is hard to know where to start on the myths of deficits and debt. Many people talk about them: few know, literally, what they are talking about. First, the numbers and statements in our opening paragraph, however closely they reflect widespread assertions, are false on their face. Even without basic revisions to give them real economic content, the official deficit should be put not at $300 billion but at $162 billion. The relevant measure of the federal debt is not the total gross public debt of $3.2 trillion but the debt held by the public, a more modest $2.5 trillion, from which might well be subtracted some $235 billion of Treasury securities held by the Federal Reserve.

The figures purporting to make the United States the world's greatest debtor nation have little to do with debt. They are calculated as the difference between the value of foreign investments in the United States and investment by Americans in the rest of the world. These values have been so inappropriately and inconsistently calculated that the source of the figures, the Bureau of Economic Analysis of the U.S. Department of Commerce, has ceased publishing their totals pending a review and revision of the underlying methodology. The savings and loan bailout figure of $500 billion is put forth on the basis of double-counting—the original capital amount plus accruing interest. By that measure the federal debt, if it is not paid off, is infinite, because interest payments will keep accumulating forever.

THE DEFICIT AND THE REAL CHANGE IN DEBT

Many observers, including countless TV newspeople and newspaper headline writers, do not even seem able to distinguish between the federal deficit and the national debt. The deficit, of course, is in principle the change in debt. If an individual starts with a debt of $100,000 and spends $40,000 when his income is $30,000, he must borrow $10,000 to finance the shortfall (or sell off assets) and his (net) debt goes to $110,000.

So it is too, or would be if we measured right, for the federal government. With a current debt held by the public, that is, outside of the government itself, of close to $2,500 billion and a deficit of, say, $200 billion over the year, the debt at the end of fiscal 1991 would go to $2,700 billion. And here we stumble on one of the critical failures of official measures of the deficit; they do not adjust the value of the debt for inflation.

To understand the necessity and nature of the needed inflation correction, we have to recognize first that the central significance of the federal government's net debt is not to the government itself but to the holders of that debt, essentially the American people and their businesses, banks, insurance companies, and pension funds; contrary once more to popular mythology, the proportion of that debt held by foreigners remains little more than 15 percent, less than it was a decade ago. The greater the federal debt, therefore, the wealthier, in holdings of Treasury securities, are the American people.

A federal deficit of $200 billion in effect showers the United States with close to $200 billion more in *assets* in the form of Treasury bills, notes, and bonds or, if the securities end up owned by Federal Reserve banks, the money that they back. The effect of this increase in perceived wealth (except for the unlikely incidence of worry that taxes will be higher in the future as a consequence of the increase in debt) is to make us less inclined to save and more inclined to spend. It is in this way that deficits generally prove stimulative to the economy. By giving us greater wealth in the form of Treasury securities they increase our purchases and keep business humming.

Thus, deficits frequently, in fact much more often than not, prove good for us. Properly measured deficits over the past four decades have been positively correlated with subsequent increases in GNP and *decreases* in unemployment. The one way deficits can be bad is if they are *too* large. But for them to be too large they must be bringing about a demand to purchase more than can be produced. The consequence then is rising prices and inflation. Measures to combat the inflation, such as tight money and higher real interest rates, may then "crowd out" desirable investment.

If deficits are to be seen as significant because they increase debt, it must be the real debt that increases, that is, that debt after adjustment for inflation. Clearly the person who had $100,000 at the beginning of the year and $101,000 at the end of the year will not long see herself as richer if she has to reckon that prices have risen 4 percent. In real terms her $100,000 is now worth only about $97,000 compared to a year ago. That person will spend less, not more.

And what is true for the individual will be true for the economy as a whole. A deficit will increase spending to the extent that public holdings of Treasury securities have risen more than inflation. To gauge how much those holdings have gone up in real terms, and hence how large the *real* deficit is, we must adjust for inflation. With inflation running at about 4 percent and the debt held by the public at about $2,500 billion, this is an adjustment of some $100 billion, more or less than half, depending on how it is measured, of the anticipated deficit over this year.

PECULIAR ACCOUNTING

There are further corrections to be made to official measures. For one thing, private business and state and local governments keep separate capital budgets. The business income or profit-and-loss statement includes only "current" expenses, not the outlays for new machinery or the building of factories; it counts only the depreciation on those assets as a current cost. If the federal accounts were to be kept in similar fashion and we were to substitute depreciation for current outlays labeled by the Office of Management and Budget as "investment," we would knock another $70 billion or so off our measure of the deficit.

And if we were to note that some $130 billion of federal outlays are grants-in-aid to state and local governments, we might see it as all the more appropriate to balance federal deficits by at least the $40 billion or so of state and local government surpluses. Adding in this correction would finally move our total government budget to surplus.

Another way of looking at this is to note the ratio of debt to income. For individuals, businesses, or government, since debt is increasing (if only because of inflation but also along with general growth), an appropriate question is whether it is increasing faster than income. For the nation, the relevant income is national income, or gross national product. To keep the ratio of debt to GNP constant, debt must grow at the same rate as GNP. For our recent 7-percent growth of GNP, the deficit that, again, is the increase in debt, would come to $175 billion currently, pretty close to the deficit we are actually running and, since the debt–GNP ratio is now three-sevenths, 3 percent of a growing GNP in the future.

There is plenty of room for the debt–income ratio to rise if we see any reason for that. True, it was considerably less—about 25 percent before the large deficits of the 1980s—but it was well over 100 percent at the end of World War II, which ushered in a period of substantial prosperity and growth. In spite of all the hullabaloo to the contrary, the deficit now is not too large. And reducing it now, as the economy plunges into recession, can only further reduce purchases of the nation's output and aggravate that recession.

PHONY NEW GRAMM–RUDMAN NUMBERS

The pressure to reduce the deficit is fueled in part by other strange games of accounting. Indeed, the new budget deal, the "Budget Enforcement Act of 1990," compounds existing peculiarities so that, in the face of a "unified budget" deficit of $220 billion for fiscal year 1990, it can raise the old Gramm–Rudman 1991 target from $64 billion to $327 billion and claim a $35-billion deficit reduction.

A major reason for the jump in the Gramm–Rudman numbers is the new edict requiring that these numbers not reflect the unified budget total, but rather be measured exclusive of the net inflow of tax revenues into the social security trust funds. The combined trust fund surplus came to $58 billion in 1990 and is projected in the new budget at $60 billion in 1991. Removing these positive components from the total makes the "deficit," restricted arbitrarily to the rest of the budget, that much higher. Political rhetoric about protecting the sanctity of social security aside, this requirement does not make economic sense, any more than would excluding defense expenditures of $300 billion from a unified budget reportedly in deficit by $220 billion and then asserting that the budget is truly in surplus by $80 billion. The deficit's impact on the economy relates to the difference between total expenditures and total tax revenues, regardless of where the Congress or the administration chose to deposit them. Hence it relates to the increase in the debt held by the public, not to the accounting entries of debt "held" in trust funds.

Another reason for the spurt in the deficit numbers is the improper inclusion of the "costs" of the S&L bailout. Those came to $58 billion in fiscal 1990 and have been projected at $112 billion for 1991. These amounts, however, are merely financial transactions signifying no new government expenditures or commands on the nation's economic resources. They entail putting on different kinds of paper a debt that the government already has to S&L depositors as a consequence of insurance of those deposits. They do not add to the net wealth of the public, although by preventing S&L depositors from losing their money they do preserve that wealth. They are not properly part of the budget deficit and, despite all the contrary rhetoric, they have nothing to do with "the taxpayer." They are no proper excuse for raising taxes or demanding cuts in government expenditures.

Including social security and excluding the S&L bailout, as is recommended by the Congressional Budget Office, puts both the 1990 deficit and the pre-recession-projected 1991 deficit at $162 billion. Under the criterion of preventing an increase in the debt–GNP ratio, these figures are within the bounds. The war against Iraq, of course, brought a significant increase in the deficit but, unless it leads to more subsequent military spending, that impact may be viewed as a temporary aberration. Stability of the debt–GNP ratio is further disturbed by the recession, which has driven the growth of GNP well below its recent 7-percent per year, and has already contributed to the larger 1991 figure of $207 billion projected by the administration in its 1992 budget document. A severe recession, though, is just the time when we should allow the debt–GNP ratio, along with the deficit, to grow.

In a fundamental, long-run sense, then, the total budget is now in balance; there is no real deficit. Projections for the years ahead, if legislated expenditure ceilings are observed, in fact indicate a real surplus. And that, as we shall explain, is a matter more for concern than for cheers.

REAL DEFICITS

In a still more fundamental sense, our economy—and our society—are not in balance. The real issues are not mismeasured financial magnitudes. They are rather the distribution of income and product and well-being among our current population. They are the composition of our output as between public and private goods and among public goods. They are the decisions that we make now that will affect life well into the next century.

On the level of the budget, the critical problem is not the amount of spending or how it is financed. It is its composition. Some two-thirds of federal expenditures for goods and services go for "national defense." The great bulk of those expenditures, aside from their function in preserving "the offensive option" for crises in the Persian Gulf or elsewhere, are shown more than ever, with the inability to curtail them sharply with the end of the cold war, to be related at least as much to preserving jobs and profits as national security.

In the past decade, the inequality of distribution of the national income has increased sharply. The rich have gotten richer, the poor poorer, and those in the middle have been squeezed. Tax changes in the first half of the decade, with huge cuts for upper income groups and investment "incentives" that increased capital gains while the rate at which they were taxed was cut, aggravated the inequality, as did the lowering of "safety nets" and the starving of uplift programs. The tax reform of 1986 improved horizontal equity, reducing some of the glaring loopholes, but did little if anything on balance to level the playing field as between traditional winners and losers.

THE FALSE ISSUES OF NATIONAL SAVING AND INVESTMENT

The budget deficits of the eighties did actually contribute significantly to bringing the economy out of its deep recession of 1982–83. Unemployment, which had reached a post–World-War-II high of 10.7 percent, was cut in half before beginning to inch up again in 1990. A widespread lament, however, was that these deficits were bringing on a consumption binge and "crowding out" private domestic investment. To the argument that in fact gross private domestic investment as a percent of GNP remained at or close to its previous highs (16 and 17 percent), the retort was that it was being financed by foreigners. Our net foreign investment had turned negative and, further, depreciation or capital consumption had increased so that national saving, the sum of net private domestic investment and net foreign investment, had declined. We were hence not providing enough for future productivity, and a considerable part of the fruits of that productivity would be going to foreign owners of American stocks, bonds, and real assets.

This argument too, though, is out of focus. As long as we maintain a prosperous, growing economy, without restrictive fiscal or monetary policy, private investment in a reasonably free market economy can and should be expected to take care of itself. Business can be expected to invest in what is productive and therefore profitable. And if foreigners choose to invest here they can do so to a greater extent than we invest abroad only so far as we import more than we export. That jointly determined outcome may, unfortunately, stem from restrictive monetary policy that raises real interest rates and hence the value, and cost, of the dollar, thus making U.S. goods unduly expensive to foreigners and foreign goods unduly cheap for Americans. But if that is not the cause, there is nothing to fear here either.

In contradiction to the statements about our "debtor" status, receipts on U.S. assets abroad in the third quarter of 1990 still exceeded payments on foreign assets in the United States, by 8 percent—$33.08 billion to $30.63 billion, or about a $10-billion surplus at annual rates. Even if the current account deficit—negative net foreign investment—continued at its swollen Gulf-crisis rate of $100 billion a year for five years it would bring only a trivial move to net payments of capital income to foreigners. At a 4-percent real rate of return, the cumulated net acquisition of $500 billion of U.S. assets would entail new net payments to foreigners of only $20 billion per year, which would be well under three-tenths of one percent of our GNP. Given the surplus we are still enjoying, we would then have a net deficit on capital income of not much more than one-tenth of 1 percent of GNP, a level that would hardly justify any of the alarm so often expressed. And indeed, with the dollar allowed to fall, our trade balance would improve and the value of our foreign-currency denominated assets as well as the income from them would grow in relevant, dollar terms, so that even this minimal swing to deficit in our capital income accounts might not eventuate—particularly if we could learn to cut our military expenditures abroad.

THE REAL ISSUES

Having put in their proper place, cut down to size, or dismissed most of the deficits that receive so much misguided attention, I must point now to the real and important deficits, perhaps better known to some of the readers of this journal. Private tangible investment in a free market economy, once government has played its part with nonrestrictive and sufficiently stimulative fiscal and monetary policy, can safely and properly be left to find its own level. The real rub is in intangible investment, including investment in human capital, and in public investment—everything that is not automatically pulled along by the actuality or the lure of private profits.

We can begin to see the wastage and failure to develop human capital in the figures for unemployment. In January 1991, it was counted at over 7,715,000, or 6.1 percent of the total labor force. Unemployment was little over 3 percent during the height of the Vietnam War and close to 1 percent during World War II. We should not require wars to reach minimum unemployment levels.

Yet those contrasting numbers present only a small part of the problem. The widely cited unemployment numbers include only those people not working at all who are either looking for work or not looking because they are awaiting recall by their employers. Workers reduced to part-time employment "for economic reasons," even to an afternoon a week in a car-wash, constitute 5,510,000 more, not included in the total. Also excluded are "discouraged workers," 941,000 of them in the fourth quarter of 1990, who have despaired of finding another job and hence have stopped looking. And most important, uncounted millions in inner cities as well as outlying ghettos remain outside the labor force, outside the mainstream of the economy, poorly educated if at all, a deadweight loss to society as well as to themselves.

Elimination of this human waste requires public policy and public investment. A private firm cannot take into account social costs when it lays off workers. If a tight government budget or tight money deprive a firm's customers of the purchasing power necessary to buy its products, the firm cuts production and employment. Efforts to reduce the budget deficit as an economy slips into recession, whether by cutting government payments or expenditures or by increasing taxes, only aggravate the deficit in purchases, deepen the recession, and add to unemployment.

Further, since we do not have a slave economy, private employers lack adequate incentive to offer basic educational skills to workers. If they do take a chance on an underprivileged youth, and the investment in his employment is successful, they retain only part of the fruits of that investment. Some of it is retained by the worker and much of the rest goes to his next employer.

There is a similar problem with investment in basic research that will over the long run keep us at an advancing, technological frontier. By its nature, and all the more so in a free society, basic research involves the free and open interchange of ideas. Since the people who undertake it are thus unable to keep its benefits to themselves, it is likely to prove inadequate without public support.

In the way of public investment, the needs are more and more evident in our decaying highway system, in crumbling bridges, in skies crowded with planes waiting to land at overcrowded airports, in staggering problems of waste disposal, in the lack of resources devoted to protecting and improving our environment of land, water, and air. One set of estimates suggests the need to double, from $13 billion to $26 billion annually, the expenditures to attain and maintain minimum standards on existing highways. These estimates also suggest $50 billion needed to repair or replace 240,000 bridges, $1 billion a year more just to maintain existing flying conditions, $11 billion to clean up nuclear and non-nuclear military waste, $3 billion for non-military hazardous waste, and $2.4 billion to comply with the Clean Water Act.

And then there are $2 billion in unmet needs for Head Start and early education, $5 billion for education for "at-risk" youth, $7 billion to support long-term health insurance, $4 billion to repair existing public housing. One estimate has set at least $130 billion annually as the shortfall in the nation's investments to tackle some of these most grievous problems.

The United States, the only developed country without a comprehensive system of health insurance, ranks with the worst in infant mortality. In standardized tests in math and science for 13-year-olds, given in a number of advanced countries in Asia, Europe, and North America, Untied States students came out dead last. Where will that stand us in international economic competition in the twenty-first century? George Bush declared that he intended to be the "education president." But new resources to put into education are declared not available or, in perhaps a convenient rationalization, unnecessary.

Our so painfully arranged and much ballyhooed Budget Enforcement Act of 1990, pretty much a successor to Gramm–Rudman–Hollings, promised to reduce what it denotes as budget deficits by an average of close to $100 billion annually over five years. It would accomplish this very considerably by sharply limiting increases in the aggregate of real "discretionary" domestic expenditures. Any of the hoped-for "peace dividend" that might remain after the Gulf War and its aftermath can be used only to reduce the deficit. The nonmilitary, domestic expenditures would not even grow with the population or total product, let alone meet any of the needs just indicated. One may doubt whether, with a slowing economy, this law will even reduce the "deficits" to which it refers. It can only stand in the way of reduction of the real deficits faced by our nation and its economy.

DISCUSSION QUESTIONS

1. Do you think the federal budget deficit is an important problem? Why? What tax increases and/or expenditure cuts would you advocate in order to reduce or eliminate the deficit?
2. Is there a difference between personal debt (which totaled nearly $800 billion in 1991) and the debt of the federal government? Why?
3. Would a balanced budget amendment to the Constitution address the problem?
4. Why do you think the Gramm–Rudman deficit reduction law fails to curb deficits?
5. Why is the level of national savings important?
6. William Gale and Robert Litan argue that a mandatory savings plan would increase savings and would be more easily accomplished politically than trying to balance the budget. Do you agree?
7. How, if at all, is the federal budget deficit related to the trade deficit? What implications do you think eliminating the trade deficit would have on the budget deficit? Why?
8. There are clearly some costs in eliminating the budget deficit. What are the most important costs? What are the benefits of reducing or eliminating the deficit? Do the benefits justify the costs?
9. Who is most likely to be affected by cuts in the budget deficit? Does this depend on how the deficit is curtailed? How?

ADDITIONAL READINGS

Anderson, Arne. *A Progressive Answer to the Fiscal Deficit* (Washington, D.C.: Economic Policy Institute, 1989).

Baker, Dean, and Todd Schafer. "The Clinton Budget Package: Putting Deficit Reduction First?" *Challenge* (May–June 1993).

Blinder, Alan S. *Hard Heads, Soft Hearts* (Reading, Mass.: Addison-Wesley, 1987).

Chubb, John E., and Paul E. Peterson, eds. *Can the Government Govern?* (Washington, D.C.: Brookings Institution, 1989).

Eisner, Robert. "Clinton, Deficits, and the U.S. Economy." *Challenge* (May–June 1993).

Eisner, Robert. "Debunking the Conventional Wisdom in Economic Policy." *Challenge* (May–June 1990).

Eisner, Robert. "Budget Deficits: Rhetoric and Reality." *Journal of Economic Perspectives* (Spring 1989).

Gale, William G., and Robert E. Litan. "Saving Our Way Out of the Deficit Dilemma." *Brookings Review* (Fall 1993).

Greider, William. *The Education of David Stockman and Other Americans* (New York: E.P. Dutton, 1981).

Heilbroner, Robert, and Peter Bernstein. *The Debt and the Deficit: False Alarms/Real Possibilities* (New York: W.W. Norton, 1989).

Krugman, Paul. *The Age of Diminished Expectations: U.S. Economic Policy in the 1990s* (Cambridge, Mass.: MIT Press, 1990).

Penner, Rudolph G. "What Worries Me Now About Federal Deficits." *Across the Board* (July/August 1989).

Roberts, Paul Craig. "Reaganomics and the Crash: The Fallacious Attack on the Twin Towers of Debt." *Policy Review* (Winter 1988).

Schick, Allen. *The Capacity to Budget* (Washington, D.C.: Urban Institute Press, 1990).

Schultze, Charles L. *Memos to the President* (Washington, D.C.: Brookings Institution, 1992).

Stockman, David. *The Triumph of Politics* (New York: Harper and Row, 1986).

Weaver, R. Kent. *Automatic Government* (Washington, D.C.: Brookings Institution, 1988).

White, Joseph, and Aaron Wildavsky. "How to Fix the Deficit—Really." *The Public Interest* (Winter 1989).

Wildavsky, Aaron. *The New Politics of the Budgetary Process*, 2d ed. (New York: HarperCollins, 1992).

10
URBAN POLICY
"Are Enterprise Zones Effective Tools in Developing Inner Cities?"

The chaos of the 1992 riots that gripped Los Angeles in the wake of the verdict in the Rodney King beating case left many Americans stunned; not since the riots in the Watts neighborhood of Los Angeles and then in Newark, Detroit, and other major cities in the mid-1960s had Americans witnessed a domestic uprising of such ferocity and magnitude. It was clear that the verdict in the King case was merely a catalyst to a reaction whose source was much deeper. Inner cities have suffered from chronic levels of crime, poverty, lack of educational opportunity, and unemployment, all compounded by the flight of financially successful former city residents to more affluent and suburban areas. The unemployment rate for young African-American and Hispanic males (42 percent and 28.2 percent, respectively) far exceeds the rate for young whites (18.4 percent).[1] In some urban areas the minority youth unemployment rate exceeds 50 percent. Nearly a third of African-American families are living below the poverty level, compared to 8 percent of white families.[2] A particularly alarming statistic is that there are more young African-American males entering prisons than colleges and universities. The issue of urban America has not been high on the public agenda since the late 1960s and early 1970s. However, fear of further uprisings in the wake of the Los Angeles riot and a realization of the conditions that inner-city residents face each day have recently brought the plight of these groups back to the forefront of policy debates (albeit episodically).

The reasons for the apparent decline of America's inner cities that began in the 1960s and accelerated in the 1970s and 1980s are highly complex and controversial. Discriminatory housing policies, public housing segregation, rising tax rates, the "deindustrialization of America" and the rise of the service economy, the extension of welfare programs in Lyndon Johnson's Great Society, cuts in federal funding, stagnating real incomes, large increases in immigrants (who concentrate in large cities), and white flight to suburban areas are only some of the reasons that have been cited. For whatever reasons, many cities across the nation face a situation of little hope, with mounting social problems and a declining tax base.

Policy concerning economic development of the inner cities and other depressed areas has more recently focused on the concept of enterprise zones and other market-based alternatives. The idea of enterprise zones was first implemented in England during the 1970s. Enterprise zones are areas that are designated, or more popularly "green-lined," as economically depressed and in need of assistance in attracting economically viable establishments. The assumption behind enterprise zones is that businesses will not ordinarily locate to economically depressed areas due to the costs involved. In the inner cities, businesses must pay extra costs in the form of security, higher insurance rates, and renovation of the relatively depreciated capital in the area. In economically depressed rural areas, firms face high transportation costs and often must pay large sums for needed infrastructure development. Firms in both cases find it difficult to hire employees with sufficient educational training to successfully meet job requirements. Rather than direct government invest-ment, enterprise zones seek to attract private-sector employment into areas that the private sector has neglected. This is accomplished by offering financial incentives to potential employers that will locate their businesses within the green-lined areas. Examples of incentives include business tax reductions, capital gains tax reductions, investment tax credits, or other tax breaks tied to employing enterprise zone residents. Further benefits might include regulatory relief, funds for worker training, and infrastructure investments such as roads, streetlighting, and sewers, all of which would entice an incoming business. The trick for successful enterprise zones is to identify firms that, with a small additional subsidy, would find it profitable to locate within the zones. Doing so, however, is anything but straightforward.

Thirty-five states had enterprise zone legislation as of 1993, and over 1,500 areas had been designated as enterprise zones. Although federal enterprise zone legislation was passed in 1987 providing authority to designate 100 federal enterprise zones, there were no appropriations attached to the package to create incentives in the zones; then-Secretary of Housing and Urban Development Jack Kemp, one of the earliest proponents of enterprise zones, did not act on the bill because he felt that to enact a package without substance was "flawed" in that it failed to give any tax breaks to businesses entering a zone.[3]

The goal of enterprise zones is to offer enough benefits to a firm to outweigh the costs of doing business in the zone. The benefits to the city and state governments in which the zone is located accrue in the form of increased tax revenue from the economic activity in the area and reduced direct costs from welfare, unemployment transfers, and activities such as policing and incarceration of individuals in the criminal justice system. Ideally, expenditure savings offset the losses in tax revenue and the expenditures involved.[4] Federal tax and regulatory relief are much greater incentives than what most states can offer. Some have argued that the depth of the incentives necessary to attract business is so great that it can best be accomplished with federal assistance.[5] However, in a sense, states already use a form of enterprise zones to lure firms into their borders by offering tax breaks and other financial inducements. Enterprise zones are supposed to target areas where market forces would otherwise not direct capital.

Critics of enterprise zones contend that they do not create new jobs but are likely to take jobs from other areas in a "zero-sum" game. It is argued that the businesses that would benefit most from moving to an enterprise zone are already located in areas that are nearly as depressed as the green-lined zones but do not qualify for green-lining. The result, it is claimed, is that helping one area might very well come at the expense of others. Another argument against the zones is that firms may use the benefits of zones to reap profits from locational decisions that they would have made anyway. It is possible that companies might attempt to "extort" benefits from state and local governments in order to move to or stay within an enterprise zone. There is evidence of this already. When Chrysler threatened to shut down one of its plants in Illinois, the plant was declared an "enterprise zone" by the governor, entitling Chrysler to a $15 million subsidy.[6] Illinois later set up a $100 million package in order to benefit a Chrysler-Mitsubishi plant in Bloomington.[7] There has been some evidence that the success of enterprise zones enacted at the state level has been tied more to infrastructure and community development and also the marketing of the zones than to tax and regulatory relief, but the evidence is as yet unclear.[8] Finally, there are political reasons to doubt that enterprise zone expenditures will be distributed purely on merit. To the extent that Congress becomes involved with allocating expenditures, the result could be distributing funds widely (at the extreme, one enterprise zone per congressional district) in order to ensure a winning political coalition.

In the first article below, former HUD secretary Jack Kemp argues that the problems of poverty and economic development in areas where poverty is the greatest can be solved only by unleashing the powers of "entrepreneurial capitalism." He contends that this can be accomplished only by providing incentives to engage in market transactions, such as deregulation, privatization, and a decrease in business taxes. Kemp believes that the enterprise zone is the right tool to bring these incentives to the poorest areas. Sar Levitan and Elizabeth Miller of the George Washington University Center for Social Policy Studies counter that the way enterprise zones are currently constructed, they are merely a zero-sum game, transferring jobs and investment, not creating them. Instead they argue for an increased presence of the federal government in the poorest areas and believe that the government must provide large expenditures on human and physical capital if these areas are to escape the grips of poverty. Their arguments follow.

Endnotes

1. U.S. Department of Commerce, Bureau of the Census, *Statistical Abstract of the United States, 1993* (Washington, D.C.: U.S. Government Printing Office, 1993), Table 635.
2. *Statistical Abstract of the United States, 1992,* p. 39. The percentage for African-American families is 29.3 percent and for individuals 31.9 percent.
3. Jeffrey L. Katz, "Enterprise Zones Struggle to Make Their Mark," *Congressional Quarterly Weekly* (July 17, 1993), p. 1880.
4. Even if they did not fully offset the losses, it is hoped that they would cost less than the previous programs.
5. Katz, "Enterprise Zones," p. 1880.
6. Robert Guskind, "Enterprise Zones: Do They Work?" *Journal of Housing* (January/February 1991), p. 49.
7. Ibid.
8. Katz, "Enterprise Zones," p. 1880.

YES

Tackling Poverty: Market-Based Policies to Empower the Poor

Jack Kemp

When President Bush asked me to serve as his Secretary of Housing and Urban Development, I was thrilled to have the opportunity to make HUD and its programs into models of "progressive conservatism" in action. Because free-market economics is the only real solution to relieve and eliminate poverty, I was excited by the prospect that the free enterprise approach would finally become the basis of federal policies to combat poverty and despair.

My long-standing conservative views have only been strengthened under the impact of my new practical experiences at HUD. I have visited pockets of poverty in ghettos and barrios all over America. I have seen and spoken with people living in the depths of poverty, despair, and, in some cases, hopelessness. I have met families torn apart by drugs, and have talked to elderly women living in public housing, who are prisoners in their own homes for fear of drug-pushing gangs. From East Los Angeles, to Harlem and the South Bronx, to Miami's Overtown, to Motown and Chicago, the grinding poverty and crippling despair many Americans live with highlight the unkept promises of the Great Society.

Conservatives who believe in change, reform, and progress must become the vanguard of a crusade to end the scourge of poverty as a way of life, a crusade to be regarded as a great cause: putting economic opportunity, free enterprise, jobs, homeownership, and hope within the reach of every American man, woman, and child. To do anything less than we can to give every person the opportunity to achieve his or her capacity is to deny all of society the enrichment of each person's unique talents and potential.

The agenda set by President Bush for my stewardship at HUD reaffirms our commitment to the Lincolnian roots of the Republican Party and to the self-evident truths of all mankind—a commitment to the idea that all our nation's people should have the opportunity to share in the blessings of freedom, democracy, and equality of opportunity.

It is no accident that the root word for "civilization" is "the city": urban life has generally been the fountainhead of movements for political as well as cultural development. Not only are our cities home to millions of Americans, especially minorities and recently arrived immigrants, usually very poor; the cities traditionally have been centers of educational opportunity and cultural diversity, helping those seeking social and economic opportunity to move into the mainstream of prosperity and become fully integrated into American society.

ABOLISH POVERTY, NOT HUD

The postwar era's erosion of the urban economic base weakened the cities' ability to provide these essential services to citizens most in need of them. Clearly the restoration of the economic base of our great urban centers must be a priority. The key to extending the historic national prosperity of the Reagan years into the nation's distressed inner cities lies in unlocking the greatest catalyst of economic growth and job creation—entrepreneurial capitalism. Without jobs and an equity share in the system, poor people can hardly be expected to afford decent housing. Without a steady source of income they cannot become economically self-sufficient and independent. Employment is the necessary first step out of the poverty trap and into the social and economic mainstream. All too often, unfortunately, the federal government has acted not as a stimulus to job creation but as a barrier separating would-be small business men and women from entrepreneurship and creativity.

The response by some on the left and the right to the mistaken federal barriers to enterprise as well as to the recently exposed scandals involving political favoritism at HUD (by both Democratic and Republican administrations) has been to abolish HUD. I do not agree. Poverty, not HUD, is what needs to be eliminated. To further that goal, I have proposed more than 50 sweeping recommendations to eliminate political discretion, strengthen management and financial controls, and better target programs to the poor. In addition, President Bush has announced a major new initiative called HOPE, which stands for Homeownership and Opportunity for People Everywhere. HOPE includes at least 10 policy initiatives that together are designed to move the American dream of homeownership and economic opportunity closer to realization for those Americans who have yet to participate fully in the blessings of freedom.

KNOCKING DOWN BARRIERS TO ENTERPRISE

For more than 10 years I have pushed for the creation of enterprise zones in the inner cities, which would provide sizable tax incentives to unleash the entrepreneurial spirit and energies now stifled by oppressive tax rates and burdensome government regulation. We must knock down government-erected barriers between risk and reward for inner-city entrepreneurs. To start with, we need to reduce the capital gains tax nationwide and eliminate it entirely within enterprise zone boundaries, as President Bush has proposed. This tax-cut strategy will create powerful incentives for risk takers to put their energy and ideas into new ventures in distressed areas. This bold act would also unlock the precious seed capital needed to start new businesses. Those who paint the capital gains tax cut as a tax break for the wealthy—rather than what it really is, an incentive for the poor who want to work and become wealthy—are simply engaging in a reactionary political game of class envy.

We must reward rather than punish people for moving from the welfare roll to the payroll. Consider today's perverse incentives facing poor people struggling to get on the first rung of the ladder of opportunity. They face an effective marginal tax rate of over 100 percent. We populist conservatives believe human nature responds rationally to economic incentives and rewards, so we can hardly be surprised when unemployed Americans facing such disincentives to work do not snap up entry-level jobs. We should eliminate income taxes on workers' wages up to 160 to 170 percent of the poverty level.

I have no doubt that inner-city entrepreneurs would respond to opportunities that offer real financial rewards. There could be an explosion of real economic activity, and the entrepreneurial, managerial, and creative talents of urban residents now boxed into mediocrity could be unleashed and could flourish. While Congress has been gridlocked for years over enterprise zones, enterprise zone-style programs in 37 states and the District of Columbia have saved or created an estimated 180,000 jobs and spurred about $9 billion in private investment in poor areas. These state zones have worked quite well despite their lack of federal tax incentives.

New Jersey's urban enterprise zone program, for example, is stimulating private investment and job creation. According to a recent study, enterprise zones in Camden, Newark, Trenton, Jersey City, Elizabeth, Orange, and other depressed communities have created 9,193 jobs through mid-1988, $243 million in payroll, $1.8 billion in output, and $803 million in private investment in 1987 and 1988 alone. In fact, New Jersey's enterprise zone program has created so much new economic activity in the zones that the program has raised an estimated $1.90 to $5.20 of new tax revenue for every dollar of tax incentives they provided—fresh proof of the supply-side revenue gains from marginal rate reductions.

Some states, unfortunately, have preferred complex, capital-based tax incentives that appeal only to large corporations. Development of a strong, local business community is also important in revitalizing depressed neighborhoods. Small business owners have a direct stake in their community and strengthen the social fabric. And, small businesses are often the most innovative and responsive, producing the products and services most in demand by the community. Because most small businesses have little or no tax liability in the initial years of operation, enterprise zone incentives for small businesses should be designed to attract seed capital, improve cash flow, and enhance entrepreneurial activity.

Skeptics should remember that similar broad-based incentives helped create over 20 million new jobs in the 1980s, two-thirds of which were produced by small businesses with 20 or fewer employees. Giving people, including inner city and rural poor people, the opportunity to succeed and make the most of their God-given talents is what the American dream is all about, and that is what enterprise zones are designed to achieve.

OWNERSHIP FOR ALL

Enterprise zones are but one powerful tool for eliminating barriers to entrepreneurship, job creation, and economic growth in the inner cities. As Stuart

Butler of The Heritage Foundation points out, enterprise zones should be viewed as an economic tactic within an emerging overall strategy of stimulating creativity and empowering poor Americans. Nowhere is this strategy more evident than in the resident management and ownership movement that is sweeping public housing communities across the country.

Many liberals, it seems, believe that people who live in public housing are not capable of keeping a decent, safe home or even of caring for themselves. My plan for privatization recognizes that empowering poor people can be part of the solution. Scores of men and women living in public housing—true entrepreneurs filled with concern for their families, like Kimi Gray at Washington's Kenilworth-Parkside—began to articulate a different view from the liberals', calling for the residents, not the government, to make the decisions about managing their neighborhoods. Led by heroic women like Mildred Haley at Bromley Heath in Boston, Bertha Gilkey at Cochran Gardens in St. Louis, Chicago's Irene Johnson at LeClaire Courts, and Alicia Rodriguez of Estrada Court in East Los Angeles, public housing tenants today are retaking their housing from the drug pushers, criminals, and bullies. Growing numbers of urban homesteading families are being inspired by the possibility of managing their communities and the dream of one day owning their own homes.

Private homeownership is essential to the movement. One of the oldest lessons in history is that private property ownership is the strongest incentive to advancing people's skills and talents. It is the key as well to both maintaining property in good condition and increasing prosperity for more to share. One of the most effective means of learning entrepreneurial skills is through participating in the management of the family's own home. In fact, the word "economics" comes from a Greek word for "household management."

Anyone who doubts whether empowering the poor can turn around a public housing project should visit one. Since the start of resident management at Chicago's notorious Cabrini-Green project, a major portion of the community has been recovered from the gangs and drug dealers. And since D.C.'s Kenilworth-Parkside's resident management program began, drug abuse and teen-age pregnancies have declined, rent collections and college enrollments have risen, and over 130 former welfare recipients are now gainfully employed. Fiscal conservatives worried about the cost to the taxpayer should know that the Coopers & Lybrand accounting firm estimates that moving Kenilworth-Parkside alone to resident management will save the government $4.5 million over 10 years. Multiply that by the thousands of similar projects around the nation, and the economic benefit alone will richly repay our modest investment in resident management and ownership.

THE HIGH COST OF RED TAPE

It is especially satisfying to me to help the poor realize their dream of home-ownership. But, the affordable housing problem covers a broad spectrum of the market. The average new home price in September 1989 had jumped to $162,000, and in some areas the cost of new homes has risen so steeply that middle-income families are losing hope of buying their first house anytime in the near future. The affordability problem is aggravated by large down payment requirements and high mortgage interest rates. The high prices and tightening supply of new homes in turn is pushing up rents, especially in large urban centers. While all tenants suffer, many of the unemployed at the bottom of the economic ladder simply cannot afford to house their families at such rents, and become homeless.

When a market is unable to increase supply and production at reasonable cost, we should look first at the legal barriers to production and commerce. Local impact (development) fees, application processing costs, building codes, zoning and land use restrictions, and no-growth policies are greatly increasing construction costs, while rent control laws are restricting the expansion and maintenance of rental housing.

In one of the more extreme cases, Orange County, California, a Golden State Project report says that regulations, delays, and fees may almost double the price of a standard-size home. In New Jersey, recent studies suggest that one-third of new home prices is attributable to regulatory restraints imposed by four or five layers of government simultaneously, resulting in expensive legal costs, skyrocketing land prices, and delays that may add years to the time it takes to complete construction.

Some estimate that every $1,000 rise in the price of housing disqualifies 300,000 middle-income families, forcing them to remain in the rental market. Since the additional cost of red tape on a new home is relatively constant, builders tend to construct more luxurious and expensive homes that appeal to wealthy buyers who can tolerate the bureaucratic add-on expenses. This results in a market gap in the middle-income range, thus increasing the demand for more rental housing.

As President Bush has said, all levels of government must reexamine some well-intended housing policies that in fact decrease our housing supply, particularly excessive regulations that unnecessarily add tends of thousands of dollars to the cost of housing or create perverse incentives that allow existing housing to deteriorate. To carry out that reexamination I will convene a Blue Ribbon Commission on Affordable Housing that will recommend ways of removing these barriers. I agree with President Bush's own recommendation that HOPE funding not be made available to any locality or state until it has identified barriers to affordable housing within its jurisdiction and taken steps to remove them.

Unfortunately, the bulk of the restraints on new home construction originate at the lower levels and cannot be reached by federal agencies directly. President Bush's HOPE initiative, however, contains a major new proposal to get at the roots of the housing affordability problem by creating 50 Housing Opportunity zones throughout the country, within enterprise zones. Housing Opportunity zones are intended to pump money into poor urban and rural areas where the housing stock is deteriorating, yet local regulatory and tax barriers are stopping rehabilitation and new construction. Cities competing to be designated a Housing Opportunity zone will be required to offer a plan to eliminate barriers to home construction and improvement. I am convinced that improvements in housing quality and affordability will result from the freer markets in the Housing Opportunity zones.

Also, HUD is attempting to ease the personal financial problems of buying a home by improving conditions in mortgage financing markets for low- and moderate-income and first-time buyers. We are looking at the tax code for ways to provide more tax incentives for homeownership, such as using IRAs to fund first-time buyers' down payments. With respect to low-income renters, I have strongly supported expansion of housing vouchers to give the poor added market power and more flexibility and choice in meeting their housing needs.

GOOD-SHEPHERD CONSERVATISM

There are many issues outside the portfolio of programs that I manage as Secretary of HUD that need to be addressed in order to realize our goal of steady reduction of poverty.

Most important is to keep the U.S. economy growing rapidly without inflation. The Federal Reserve's priority should be to stabilize the dollar and keep interest rates as low as possible without reigniting inflation. And because I believe that guaranteeing money that is honest and stable in value is an important progressive and populist step, I support the monetary policy mandated by the Founding Fathers in the Constitution, which says that the dollar should be as good as gold.

Moreover, we now live in an age in which the world's economies have been so integrated that economic borders are meaningless. Policies that pretend to "protect" businesses and jobs by isolating trade within national borders threaten employment, prosperity, price stability, and technological innovation; they also raise the specter of Depression-era international trade wars. Open international commerce allows American consumers to share in a global market of goods and services while maximizing the demand abroad for the best products working Americans can produce. To be sure, this does not excuse us as a compassionate society from putting in place programs such as workers compensation benefits and new skills training to ease the problems of workers dislocated by global economic shifts.

Lincoln once said that he never had a moral sentiment that did not spring from the Declaration of Independence, by which he meant the statement that all human beings are created equal in their dignity and rights. I can think of no other idea so clearly consistent with progressive conservatism as the extension of equal human and civil rights to all Americans. From the Voting Rights Act of 1965, guaranteeing the franchise for black and other minority Americans, to the struggle for the right to life, to the effort to relieve the tax burden on the American family, we all must be engaged in bringing the ideal of the equal rights of the individual ever closer to real achievement.

We conservatives must demonstrate by both our words and our actions that at the center of our political and social philosophy is the idea of the good shepherd—that we want the whole globe someday to be free, prosperous, and democratic.

The body of evidence grows daily that people everywhere have pinned their hopes for their own and their families' futures on the possibility of creating free economic and political markets in their countries. The ideas of democratic capitalism have triumphed the world over, but the struggle to turn those ideas into political reality everywhere has not yet been completed. As President Bush has said, the decade of the '90s must be the decade of global democracy.

NO

Enterprise Zones Are No Solution for Our Blighted Areas

Sar A. Levitan and Elizabeth I. Miller

Even in the best of times, poverty and high unemployment remain the rule for blighted areas. To help these areas, the Bush administration has advocated the designation of distressed neighborhoods as enterprise zones. Once designated as an enterprise zone, they would be entitled to special tax reductions and relief from regulation. The underlying rationale for enterprise zones is that a reduction of taxes, regulation, and other "government imposed barriers" will result in an infusion of capital into depressed neighborhoods. This, in turn, will lead to more business operations and an overall net gain in investment and jobs. Empirical evidence is lacking, however, that reducing federal taxes and relaxing regulations will alleviate the problems of inner cities.

Taxes play at best a secondary role in business investment decisions. Other factors—including the availability of a skilled labor force, proximity to transportation and markets, local amenities, and the physical security of the sites—play a far more important role when businesses consider expansion, relocation, or starting a new venture. High unemployment, poverty, and crime weigh against investing in blighted areas, as do dilapidated infrastructures and inferior services and amenities. Modest tax incentives and deregulation alone do not provide adequate inducements to offset the deterrents of locating in a blighted area.

Many believe an infusion of small businesses is needed to vitalize blighted areas. The Bush administration argues that a reduction in government financial and regulatory barriers, as proposed in enterprise zones, will encourage small businesses and entrepreneurs to start new businesses in zones. Tax incentives and deregulation, however, would have at best a nominal impact in increasing the number of startup businesses. Entrepreneurs do not decide to start businesses because of marginal tax relief. In addition, most small firms would be unable to utilize the tax credits offered in proposed enterprise zone legislation, because few businesses in their early years have the tax liabilities needed to take advantage of tax breaks.

Two policy options for administering aid to designated areas are tax expenditures and direct subsidies. Advocates of unfettered free markets argue that policies based on direct assistance have failed because their reliance on subsidies fosters a dependence on government handouts. This, they assert, stifles free enterprise and interferes with market forces. They contend that tax breaks, in contrast, encourage free enterprise and business growth. The distinction free-market advocates draw between direct subsidies and tax exemptions is not persuasive; both policies distort free-market operations. Enterprise zones are subsections of larger economic markets, yet tax breaks and deregulation apply only to the zones. Enterprise zone theory is premised on government intervention in the market to favor a designated area. It follows that the subsidies accompanying designation may diminish the competitive capabilities of firms outside the boundaries of the zone, which may be equally depressed. Due to government intervention, these firms will have a distinct disadvantage compared to their zone competitors.

Compared with direct subsidies, revenue foregone through the tax code is normally an ineffective mechanism for revitalizing blighted areas. Tax expenditures proposed in enterprise zone legislation have few strings attached to their use. There is no guarantee that the income produced by the tax expenditures will benefit the zone or its residents. A company can choose to pocket profits generated by the tax credits rather than reinvest in the zone or hire zone residents. Direct government grants or subsidized loans usually provide safeguards, requiring subsidies be used for their intended purposes.

PENDING LEGISLATION

In March 1992, Congress passed enterprise zone legislation—it was included in the Democratic tax package, but President Bush vetoed the bill. The two major bills presently before the Congress, sponsored by the Bush administration and the chairman of the House Ways and Means Committee, Dan Rostenkowski, offer only tax cuts. Although the bills differ in their choice of allowable tax expenditures, the main recipients of tax subsidies in both bills are investors, not residents or local proprietors (see Table 10-1). Rostenkowski's bill rewards employers for hiring zone residents while the administration's bill offers a nominal subsidy to employees. The remaining assistance goes to investors.

The major difference between the two bills is the cap Rostenkowski places on the amount of tax incentives available to businesses and investors in a given

TABLE 10-1
Comparison of the Administration and Rostenkowski Bills

Provisions	Administration (HR23)	Rostenkowski (HR11)
Job credit for employer	None	10 percent of wages and health insurance paid to zone residents
Refundable tax credit to employees	5 percent of qualified wages; annual maximum of $525 per worker	None
Stock deduction	Stock deductions for ordinary losses	Deductions of worthless stock
Capital gains	Permanent exclusion	Deferral of capital gains
Financing of child care facilities	None	60-month amortization and rehabilitation credits

year. The provision is intended to preclude the escalation of program costs. Without the cap, the unforeseen costs that arose from tax-free industrial development bonds may be repeated. Before they were restricted, tax-free industrial development bonds accounted for significant revenue loss to the federal government without commensurate returns. Also, in the absence of a cap on capital gains, investors may develop the area, displacing the old residents with new buildings.

The administration opposes placing a cap on the dollars spent for the program because a cap would require the government to allocate tax subsidies to businesses. According to the administration, this would entail the appointment of a local "zone czar" charged with earmarking subsidies for individual businesses. The administration conveniently ignores the fact that by selecting a limited number of areas to receive federal assistance, the administrator charged with designating zones implicitly becomes a zone czar.

Many assumptions, some arbitrary, have to be made in order to estimate the costs of the proposed legislation. Given the size and caps of the Rostenkowski bill, a ball park estimate by the Congressional Joint Taxation Committee has placed its costs over four years at $2 billion:

- $200 million, 1st year;
- $400 million, 2nd year;
- $600 million, 3rd year;
- $800 million, the 4th year.

Because the administration's bill allows fifty zones, twice the number authorized in Rostenkowski's bill, its cost would be at least doubled. The administration, however, imposes no caps on the generous incentives it offers. It costs will remain uncertain, but could initially deplete the Treasury by significantly larger amounts than that estimated for the Rostenkowski bill. Depending on the zones that are designated, the level and type of investment in the zones, and the number of employees hired, just to name a few variables, the administration's bill could cost ten times the projected amount of the Rostenkowski bill. It is unlikely, however, that an enterprise zone program will be limited to fifty zones, further increasing its costs.

Aside from the magnitude and type of incentives a viable enterprise zone initiative would offer, the designation process of the zones is likely to preclude a successful program. Placing limits on the number of areas receiving federal aid creates political problems. Every member of Congress will insist that his or her district or state receive a fair share of the federal funds appropriated for enterprise zones. Past federal programs that were geographically targeted, including the Area Redevelopment Act (ARA) and Model Cities, were expanded to include a much larger number of areas than originally intended. The designer of ARA envisioned it would help a few dozen areas. By the time the bill was signed into law, one of every five counties qualified, and a year later over 1000 counties were included in the ARA program. Originally designed for three cities, the model cities program ballooned to encompass over 120 cities.

Expansion of the ARA and model cities programs was a political necessity to secure congressional passage, but it diminished the ability of these programs to achieve their goals by spreading their resources too thinly.

Enterprise zone legislation may face the same fate. Besides the administration bill that authorizes fifty zones, two other bills have been introduced in the current Congress: one authorizes 100 zones in rural areas, and the other calls for twelve zones on Indian reservations. Although the needs of impoverished rural areas and Indian reservations are not in question, these bills indicate the likelihood that an enterprise zone program, if enacted, would repeat the experience of earlier federal legislation addressed to aid depressed areas. The original rationale for an enterprise zone initiative was to target assistance to truly blighted areas, but history shows that in a political arena, achieving this goal is difficult if not impossible.

If Congress succeeds in limiting the number of areas eligible for designation, federal officials will have to choose among qualified areas because pending legislation does not establish rigorous criteria for designation. The selection of zones will offer difficult decisions for officials. If they choose areas with potential for redevelopment, then the most needy and poorest areas will be bypassed by the program because they are the least likely to succeed. If they decide to assist the most blighted areas, they would need to limit sharply the number of eligible zones since these communities require relatively large investments. Focusing on the needs of the most blighted areas would diminish potential support for the program because success would be hard to demonstrate and more viable areas would resent spending a disproportionate share of the program's resources on the poorest areas. In either case, areas in extreme distress would be hard put to take advantage of the proposed enterprise zone benefits, casting doubt on the viability of the program.

In line with the 1990 deficit reduction legislation, an enterprise zone initiative would entail either an equal cut in other discretionary domestic programs or a tax increase. Although neither alternative is palatable to the administration or Congress, proponents of the legislation have failed to face up to this conundrum. Scarce funds from established and proven social programs should not be used to experiment with an initiative grounded in supply-side economics. Given other domestic priorities, the pending enterprise zone proposals should not be placed at the top of the administration or congressional wish list.

STATE EXPERIENCE

While Congress has debated enterprise zone legislation during the last decade, thirty-seven states and the District of Columbia have enacted enterprise zone programs designed to combat the blight of inner city and rural areas. Pending federal legislation relies on tax breaks, but state governments have taken a multifaceted approach to enterprise zone programs. The diversity of economic development tools utilized by state enterprise zones has resulted in more varied assistance packages, but the total resources allocated for state programs are meager. Despite state differences, tentative results fail to demonstrate enterprise zones' ability to revitalize blighted areas.

The experience of state enterprise zone programs reinforces the view that politics creates obstacles to limiting the number of zones. Illinois state legislators were unable or unwilling to deny zone benefits to most areas that applied for designation. Beginning with a generous forty-eight zones, the state has since qualified twice that number. Kentucky and New Jersey used other "innovative" means to expand eligibility. They enlarged their zones' physical boundaries to include relatively affluent areas. This, of course, detracts from the original purpose of helping depressed communities.

In designating enterprise zones, several states used a zone's potential for growth as a controlling factor for designation. Indiana and New Jersey favored areas with a strong potential for becoming economically viable. Their policies promised a high probability of "success" because they excluded the most needy areas. In contrast, Michigan selected an extremely depressed area, and tax incentives alone failed.

State experiences indicate that few small businesses are able to take advantage of most tax concessions. Only sale tax exemptions were found to be useful to small businesses. Because small businesses normally receive their initial capital from friends and family, tax concessions on nonexistent stock and capital gains were inconsequential to them. In addition, most small businesses could not use tax credits unless they were refundable. This presents strong doubts whether small businesses have been able to take advantage of state programs. Because small businesses may not be able to partake in the incentives, they may be placed at a competitive disadvantage with the larger, established firms able to obtain the subsidies.

The employment and training of zone residents, particularly the disadvantaged, were not a prime consideration when states designed and implemented enterprise zone policies. For example, 40 percent of businesses operating in New Jersey's zones and unable to qualify for zone benefits claimed that to operate profitably they could not meet the state's requirement of hiring 25 percent of their work force from zone residents. The surveyed firms indicated that a better trained work force would improve business conditions in zones. In the absence of educational and basic skills training programs, state zone policies have been of little help to the long-term unemployed and unskilled, who should be prime targets for assistance. Enterprise zone policies created few net jobs or businesses. The majority of the new businesses that moved into state enterprise zones were either relocating firms or businesses that would have started without government incentives. The jobs they created would have existed without the subsidies but might have been situated outside the zone. Zones' gains were other areas' losses.

The limited tax resources of the states were a serious impediment to successful enterprise zone programs. Excluding unemployment insurance payroll taxes, state taxes account at most for five percent of total business expenses, which sharply limits the tax credits states can offer. Whatever the value of states as laboratories for social experimentation, their zone policies and programs strongly indicate that states are ill equipped to revitalize blighted areas.

EMPOWERMENT: A VISION BASED ON FAITH

Conceptually, enterprise zone legislation is an attractive policy. The proposed programs appear to offer an innovative and targeted strategy for revitalizing depressed areas. The administration has described enterprise zones as offering "empowerment," a buzzword currently in vogue with fiscal conservatives wishing to help the poor. Using a free-market approach, advocates claim their goal is to bestow power on the poor and enable them to forge their destinies. The rhetoric surrounding enterprise zones distorts reality and tends to obfuscate the needs of blighted area residents along with the real costs of their rehabilitation. Empowerment cannot be achieved on the cheap and is not a substitute for direct help.

The overall effectiveness of a federal enterprise zone program is problematic. Pending bills do not address the principal cause of distress—the idleness or waste of blighted area residents. "Empowering" zone residents requires that they become economically self-sufficient. For this to happen, residents need to be able to compete effectively in the labor market. Tax expenditures will not accomplish this, nor will they provide the mechanisms needed to "empower" zone residents. Many residents lack the basic skills needed for most jobs. Only when residents are empowered with a good education and salable skills will residents be able to raise themselves out of poverty. Educating and training people require direct expenditures. None of the bills addresses this issue. For these reasons, the proposed assistance is not likely to succeed in combating urban or rural economic depression.

The initial advocates of enterprise zones argued (and some still do) that the program will be costless; the resulting investments will more than compensate the government for lost tax revenue. The same people, however, also promised that the 1981 tax cuts would raise federal revenue and reduce the national deficit. Because business start-ups and employment have not significantly increased in state zones and are unlikely to do so in federal zones, there is little reason to believe federal enterprise zones will increase net federal revenue.

The most a federal enterprise zone program can hope for is a zero-sum game as investments are transferred from nonzone areas to zones. Redistribution of investment could have a detrimental effect on neighboring areas, except when a business leaves a full employment area, which is a rarity these days. Most blighted areas are surrounded by neighborhoods whose economies may be only marginally better or even worse than that of the zones. Directing investment away from contiguous areas may further destabilize their economies.

In the real world, an effective enterprise zone program will require direct expenditures. Stuart M. Butler of the Heritage Foundation, a staunch advocate of enterprise zones, has argued that an attractive tax and regulatory climate is only one precondition for economic development. Testifying before a House Ways and Means subcommittee he stated, "Other ingredients are required if economic development is to occur. Action needs to be taken . . . to tackle the staggering increase in drug use and crime within the inner cities. . . . " These "other ingredients" will not come free and without them, tax incentives alone will fall far short of inducing business to expand or relocate in enterprise zones. State experiences have shown that improvements in physical appearance, service, and infrastructure are extremely important to revive an area.

Reliance on the private sector to correct the ills of blighted areas is based on a wish lacking empirical support. It is not the responsibility of the private sector to improve the physical and human infrastructures of decayed areas. In fact, the private sector abandoned these areas for more attractive and safer environments in the suburbs or outside the United States, which exacerbated the deterioration of inner cities and impoverished rural areas. Tax reductions and relaxed regulations in and of themselves will not bring businesses back to depressed communities. And tax expenditures are not without their costs. Cuts in taxes will lead to lost government revenue on top of unprecedented deficits. The shortfall will be met either by a reduction in services provided by the government or by raising revenues. In either case, the community pays for the tax cuts.

Past attempts to aid depressed areas at both the state and federal levels have demonstrated the complexity of the problems blighted areas face. If the federal government were serious about combating blight, it would need to address economic deprivation wherever it exists as well as its causes. The deep-seated problems of inner cities and impoverished rural areas cannot be easily alleviated, although it can be argued that every little bit helps. As currently proposed, however, the alleviation of deprivation in one area is likely to come at the expense of contiguous areas. Robbing Peter to pay Paul has been tried before, but it is hardly a model for a new initiative.

Should Congress decide to spare a few billion dollars to aid residents of depressed communities, it should consider investing the funds in rehabilitating depressed communities with direct investments in human and physical infrastructures. Existing antipoverty programs are examples of human resource programs able to help people in blighted areas. A judicious expansion of these efforts and the creation of jobs for the poor wherever chronic high unemployment persists are likely to prove a more effective approach to attacking the deep-seated problem of inner city and rural poverty than experimenting with unproven and doubtful programs.

Assisting the residents entails improving their education and skill levels. Once the residents are able to compete effectively for employment, it will not be necessary to bring job opportunities to their back yards. Equipped with the necessary skills, they will be able to travel outside the zone to earn a living. Improvements in amenities and infrastructure should address, at a minimum, transportation facilities, police protection, and the educational and training system. This is the most effective strategy to empower the residents of blighted communities.

DISCUSSION QUESTIONS

1. What do you think are the principal reasons why firms do not locate into certain depressed areas? Will financial inducements change those decisions? Why?
2. Who are the chief beneficiaries of enterprise zones?
3. Should enterprise zones be the responsibility of the federal government or conducted mostly by states and localities? Why?
4. Are there other ways to revitalize depressed urban and rural areas besides enterprise zones? What are they? How do their advantages and disadvantages compare with those of enterprise zones?
5. Some have criticized enterprise zones because they target funds to firms rather than directly to the individuals who live in depressed economic conditions. Is this an appropriate criticism? Why?

ADDITIONAL READINGS

Byron, Christopher. "Zone Offense." *New York* (May 25, 1992).

Goldsmith, William W. "Enterprise Zones: If They Work, We're in Trouble." *International Journal of Urban and Regional Research* (September 1982).

Guskind, Robert. "Enterprise Zones: Do They Work?" *Journal of Housing* (January/February 1990).

Hall, Peter. "Enterprise Zones: A Justification." *International Journal of Urban and Regional Research* (September 1982).

Harrison, Bennett. "The Politics and Economics of the Urban Enterprise Zone Proposal: A Critique." *International Journal of Urban and Regional Research* (September 1982).

Jacobs, Jane. *Cities and the Wealth of Nations: Principles of Economic Life* (New York: Random House, 1984).

Mounts, Richard. "The 'Urban Enterprise Zone' Hustle." *Commonweal* (March 13, 1981).

Rubin, Marilyn. "Urban Enterprise Zones: Do They Work? Evidence from New Jersey." *Public Budgeting and Finance* (Winter 1990).

Wolf, Michael Allan. "Whatever Happened to Enterprise Zones?" *Urban Land* (February 1991).

PART III
INTERNATIONAL POLICY

11

INTERNATIONAL TRADE POLICY

"Should the Federal Government Vigorously Pursue International Free-Trade Policies?"

The turnaround in the U.S. position in world economic trade has been remarkable. From 1946 to 1981, the United States generally enjoyed a trade surplus by exporting more goods and services than it imported. Beginning in 1982, however, the United States has imported vastly more in value than it exports, a difference peaking at $163 billion in 1987, even in the face of declining oil prices.[1] But does the trade deficit matter? How does it affect U.S. living standards and public policy? What are the advantages of free trade? Does protectionism help or hurt the U.S. economy? Is it true, as Eugene Debs said, that "every war of trade becomes a war of blood"?

First, it is important to clarify the difference between the trade deficit and its counterpart, the budget deficit. Although the two are economically related,* their meanings are distinct. The budget deficit applies only to federal government expenditures, while the trade account is the value of goods and services exported from the United States minus those imported (if the number is positive, it is a trade surplus; if it is negative, it is a trade deficit). The trade deficit—and some of its impacts—can be viewed from the perspective of an individual who buys more goods and services from others than she sells (typically, in the form of labor in return for wages). Purchases that exceed one's income can only be financed (short of theft) by selling assets or writing lots of IOUs. Essentially, this is not so different from what happened in the United States in the 1980s. Just as individuals need to deplete their savings or assets in order to purchase more than their income currently allows, the huge U.S. trade deficits of the 1980s were largely financed by selling assets, including corporations, real estate, and stocks.†

---

* While the linkage between budget and trade deficits is disputed, a simple theoretical connection exists. Growing budget deficits (as experienced in the United States in the 1980s) reduce national savings, the argument runs, because they gobble up resources that would instead have gone to private investments. In the absence of world capital markets, domestic interest rates would have skyrocketed due to the enormous government demand for investment. Instead, however, government deficits were largely financed from foreign capital, and if the United States is selling more assets to foreigners than it purchases from abroad, then its current account balance must show a trade deficit.

† It should be noted that not all foreign investment in the United States has been successful, particularly large real estate purchases made prior to plummeting land values in the late 1980s.

If the federal government wanted to, it could easily reduce or eliminate the trade deficit, either by devaluing the dollar (which tends to make foreign-made goods more expensive for U.S. citizens to buy and U.S. goods relatively cheaper for foreigners) or erecting additional trade barriers (like tariffs, other import restraints, or export subsidies). This, however, entails some costs; for example, foreign products like automobiles would be more expensive to U.S. consumers, and therefore U.S. living standards would likely decline. This begs the question: How important is it to eliminate or reduce the trade deficit? Oddly enough, for all the attention the trade deficit receives, many economists believe that its economic impacts are minor in relation to national wealth. Nevertheless, just as continued budget deficits mean that the federal government owes people money in the future, a growing trade deficit means that the U.S. economy owes foreigners future payments as well (although they are now small in relation to the entire economy). Perhaps more problematic is the political issue that increasingly national sovereignty is endangered by foreign ownership of U.S. assets.[2] Others, however, take a more benign view of foreign investment in the United States, pointing out that it signals world-wide belief in a productive American future.

Before we investigate arguments for protectionism—some of which spring from a reaction against mounting trade deficits—it is important to understand why an overwhelming majority of economists favor free trade. Basically, the advantages of free trade were first explicated by the economist David Ricardo, who described the (somewhat counterintuitive) benefits to all countries of "comparative advantage." Suppose, for example, that there exist just two countries, and one can produce every commodity more cheaply than the other. Ricardo argued that even in this extreme case, it made sense for the productive country to specialize in producing what it made most efficiently, while the unproductive country produces those goods that it makes efficiently relative to its other productive capacity and that of the other nation.* In short, although one country may enjoy an absolute advantage in producing goods, the relevant consideration is the comparative advantage relative to other nations' capabilities. Why? Because total output will be greater if both nations specialize rather than if one country produces both goods.† As a commonly used example illustrates, Woodrow Wilson was a faster typist than his secretary, but it still made sense for him to lead the nation and leave the typing to his secretary. In other words, the total output of Wilson and his secretary would drop if Wilson performed both tasks, even though he was better at both. Economists therefore argue that tariffs or other restraints of trade—in this example, reducing or prohibiting the "trade" between Wilson and his secretary—reduce total output and therefore the wealth of both nations. Argu-

---

* Ricardo's argument was based on his labor theory, which has since been replaced by relative price ratios; if the ratio in prices between any two goods in any two countries is different, then gains from trade are possible.

† This assumes constant returns to scale, or a fixed ratio of inputs to output (e.g., that doubling output will require exactly doubling inputs).

ments for free trade are therefore mostly about efficiency in production, or getting the most out of productive inputs like workers and capital. There is little sense in growing bananas in the United States and apples in Panama, economists argue, when each country is better off specializing in production and then trading. Even where free-traders acknowledge that protectionism saves U.S. jobs, they contend that it does so at great cost. For example, a study by Gary Hufbauer and Kim Elliott of the Institute for International Economics found that protectionism in twenty-one of the most protected U.S. industries results in saving 191,000 jobs but at an annual cost of $170,000 apiece (compared to the average hourly pay in those industries of $7.76). Most economists therefore argue that everyone would be better off if protectionist tariffs were eliminated—thereby lowering prices to consumers—and workers who lost jobs compensated accordingly. (At $170,000 per job, there is plenty of room for mutual benefit to consumers and workers.)

Advocates of some form of protectionism—an increasingly vague term meant to designate any form of government intervention to advance domestic economic interests at the expense of foreign economic interests—argue (as with the argument over industrial policy) that there is no such thing as free trade because government intervention is found everywhere, from building roads to subsidizing research to erecting trade barriers to subsidizing farm exports. Proponents of protectionism range from those hoping to protect personal economic interests to those concerned more broadly with the long-term interests of the nation's economy. An example of the former motivation is the ability of domestic textile concerns to maintain import quotas on clothing, which raises the price of imported clothing relative to domestically produced clothing, thereby conferring a competitive advantage to domestic producers. How can a small industry induce democratically elected representatives (e.g., Congress) to deliver it substantial benefits at the expense of higher clothing prices for millions of citizens? One argument maintains that because benefits are concentrated and costs widely diffused, there is an incentive for textile manufacturers to lobby heavily to protect their privileged position, while there is little corresponding incentive for individual consumers to lobby for what amounts to only a modest reduction in clothing costs for them (although cumulatively, the amounts are substantial).* Therefore, these types of protectionist measures that benefit a small minority can be sustained even when a vast majority of citizens are made worse off as a result.

Another political motivation for protectionist measures is attributable to the fact that removing import barriers will cost jobs that are readily visible, and therefore will be strongly contested politically, while the political support for new jobs that will be created is minimal. Economist Charles Schultze called this political response the principle of "do no direct harm."[3] He argues that for political reasons governments cannot directly harm constituents' inter-

---

* This is known as the "free-rider" problem, whereby some individuals will free-ride on the effort expended by others.

ests; because government policies necessarily create winners and losers, costs can only be imposed if they are disguised, such as through the higher prices of Japanese automobiles due to "voluntary" export restraints negotiated by the United States. Not surprisingly, recessions and poor or stagnant economic times increase calls for protectionism because of fears for job losses in certain fields and the difficulty in finding new jobs.

A more sophisticated and publicly interested defense of some forms of protectionism relies on the findings of the "new international economics," sometimes referred to as economic geography.[4] Economic geographers point out that where firms locate depends both on historical accident and where other firms and customers already are located, such as the emergence of the manufacturing belt in the Northeast and the Great Lakes region, computer technology in Silicon Valley in California, and so on.[5] Therefore, the argument runs, if nations can create advantages that encourage the development of an industry within their borders, and if there are economies of scale that preclude multiple centers of production in different countries,* then nations can control entire industries by providing "seed money" to launch their efforts. Jet aircraft represents one example. As a leading proponent puts it, "If you want to explain why the U.S. exports aircraft, you should not look for underlying aspects of the U.S. economy [as economists traditionally have done]; you should study the historical circumstances that gave the United States a head start in the industry."[6] Therefore, by protecting infant industries that promise to develop goods, particularly ones that provide spillover benefits to other industries or benefits to national security as well (such as semiconductors), proponents argue that protectionism will not reduce the long-term standard of living (as free-trade backers argue), but instead will advance those high-skill, high-wage jobs that every nation covets.

The debate over free trade mixes both political and economic arguments, and increasingly those related to environmental and labor standards concerns as well. For example, environmental protectionists argue that free trade will lead to multinational corporations moving high-polluting industries to developing nations with lax environmental standards, thereby polluting other lands and moving jobs out of industrialized nations. Some economists counter that wealthier nations are better able to afford strong environmental protection, and that free trade advances global wealth and therefore the ability of developing nations to preserve or enhance their environmental quality.[7] Environmental, labor, and other distributive implications of trade complicate the economics and politics of free trade. In the articles below, economist Robert Litan of the Brookings Institution and attorney Peter Suchman argue for promoting free trade, followed by Robert Kuttner's support for managing trade in order to protect economic sovereignty.

---

* Economies of scale refer to the cost advantages of large producers over small producers, the result being that a handful of large producers will drive small producers out of the market through competition, in the extreme case resulting in a natural monopoly of one large firm.

Endnotes

1. These figures, compiled by the U.S. Department of Commerce, are based on the balance on current account, which includes merchandise, services, investment income, and unilateral transfers.
2. Martin and Susan Tolchin, *Buying into America: How Foreign Money Is Changing the Face of Our Nation* (New York: Times Books, 1988).
3. Charles L. Schultze, *The Public Use of Private Interest* (Washington, D.C.: Brookings Institution, 1977).
4. See, for example, Paul Krugman, *Geography and Trade* (Cambridge, Mass.: MIT Press, 1991).
5. A relatively nontechnical discussion can be found in Krugman, *Geography and Trade.*
6. Paul Krugman, *The Age of Diminished Expectations* (Cambridge, Mass.: MIT Press, 1990), p. 109.
7. See Herman E. Daly, "The Perils of Free Trade," *Scientific American* (November 1993); Jagdish N. Bhagwati, "The Case for Free Trade," *Scientific American* (November 1993).

YES

U.S. Trade Policy at a Crossroad

Robert E. Litan and Peter O. Suchman

Since the end of World War II the United States has been perhaps the leading advocate among industrialized nations of liberalized international trade. It was the motivating force behind the General Agreement on Tariffs and Trade (GATT), the seven major trade negotiations pursued under its auspices, and the significant reductions in tariffs that these negotiations have produced.

Tariff liberalization, quite predictably, has promoted both trade and interdependence. The ratio of world exports to gross national product (GNP) has climbed throughout the postwar era, especially in the last two decades. This is a healthy development. It implies that nations increasingly have found it cheaper to buy their goods abroad than to produce them at home, affording consumers around the world a wider choice of goods at less cost than if nations had continued to hide behind the high tariffs that they introduced in the 1930s.

Two principles underlie this success. First, the widespread reductions in tariff barriers were made possible only through multilateral bargaining. The industrialized countries formed GATT largely because of the economies in negotiation that could be purchased if a large number of countries reduced their trade barriers simultaneously rather than successively on a bilateral basis over a long period of time.[1] Second, the GATT members agreed on the rules that should govern trade rather than on the results—import and export levels and balances of trade—that individual countries might find desirable or appropriate. In addition, the GATT parties agreed on a framework for resolving bilateral disputes over particular rules.

In the last few years, however, many in the U.S. academic, business, and policy-making communities have raised significant questions about each of these principles. The critics argue that the GATT multilateral framework is no longer viable: it is unsuited for reducing nontariff barriers, it lacks an effective enforcement mechanism, and the members themselves have lost interest in continued negotiations. One prominent economist, Lester Thurow, has even pronounced the GATT to be dead.[2] The preferred alternative is bilateral or regional trade negotiations or even "free trade arrangements" (FTAs), such as those the United States recently completed with Israel and Canada.

Thurow and other critics go one step further. In their view, the new less-than-multilateral negotiations should specify outcomes. Unlike tariffs, which are easily observable and readily monitored, many nontariff barriers can be invisible and inherently difficult, if not impossible, to negotiate away. Results rather than rules should therefore become the centerpiece of trade negotiations.

There are many indications that support within the United States for the rules-oriented, multilateral approach to freer trade is rapidly eroding and that U.S. trade is indeed at a critical crossroad. In this article, we discuss the reasons for this trend, distinguishing along the way fact from myth. We then outline the major shifts in trade policy that critics of the old regime have advanced. We conclude that the critics are wrong. It is in the interest of the United States to vigorously renew its commitment to reducing trade barriers on a multilateral basis without specifying trade outcomes. But this country is unlikely to be successful unless it also undertakes certain measures at home to attack the major sources of current trade tensions.

SOURCES OF DISSATISFACTION

Four key factors have been undermining the commitment of U.S. policy-makers and business leaders to the GATT framework.

The trade deficit. The dominant influence, unrelated to the operation of the GATT, is the dramatic deterioration in U.S. trade performance. From a positive $7 billion balance in 1981, the U.S. current account (which includes trade in both goods and services) fell to a deficit of $154 billion only 6 years later, before improving modestly in 1988 to $144 billion.

As important as the U.S. deterioration is the dramatic improvement in the trade positions of the world's other two industrial leaders, the Federal Republic of Germany (FRG) and Japan. Until 1982 the ratio of the current account to total output in these three countries generally hovered within one percentage point of balance. There has been a sea change since. The U.S. current account has fallen deeply into deficit (more than 3% of GNP); the mirror image is true for Japan and the FRG.

It is no coincidence that in 1985, around the time these trade imbalances became substantial, the U.S. Congress began debating the original version of what eventually became the 1988 Trade Act.[3] Although complex and technical in nature, that proposal essentially was designed to dramatically weaken the U.S. commitment to multilateralism in trade policy. Instead, the bill proposed a unilateral tightening of U.S. laws against unfairly traded imports—those that are dumped, unlawfully subsidized, or in violation of our intellectual property laws. Perhaps most controversial was the amendment to the original proposal offered by Richard Gephardt (D-MO), now House majority leader, that would have rejected the "rules-oriented" principle of trade law as well.[4] It would have required certain of our major trading partners, notably, the FRG, Japan, and Brazil, to reduce their trade surpluses with us over a 10-year period, or otherwise be subject to U.S. import tariffs and quotas to achieve that objective.

Fearing that a congressional trade initiative would turn strongly protectionist and thus risk a round-robin of retaliatory measures by our trading partners, the Reagan Administration followed a two-part strategy to weaken support for the legislation. First, it displayed a new "get tough" policy on unfair trade by launching complaints against South Korea and Brazil under the prevailing version of Section 301 of the U.S. trade law,[5] authorizing retaliation against countries that unreasonably discriminate against the importation of U.S. products. Second, abandoning the previous free-market attitude toward exchange rates, newly installed Secretary of the Treasury James Baker negotiated in September 1985 a coordinated depreciation of the dollar against major European and Japanese currencies. The Plaza Accord, as it was called, was designed to reduce the overall U.S. trade deficit by cheapening U.S. exports in terms of foreign currency while raising the dollar price of U.S. imports. In fact, during the following 18 months, until the dollar was stabilized in the Louvre Agreement, the dollar fell by roughly 35% in real terms (adjusted for differences between countries in the rate of inflation) against an average of ten major currencies.[6]

The Administration's initiatives bought valuable time and helped ease the political pressure for a protectionist trade bill. In particular, the depreciation of the dollar eventually halted the monthly rise in the trade deficit figures. The monthly deficit hit its peak in the fourth quarter of 1987 at $14 billion, but by mid-1988 was down to roughly $10 billion. Still, with so much political time and energy invested in trade legislation, Congress was not to be deterred from taking some action, which it did in the summer of 1988.

Significantly, the final bill signed by President Reagan contained a modified version of the original Gephardt amendment that continued to reflect a new unilateral direction in U.S. trade policy. Quickly dubbed "Super 301," this provision requires the U.S. government (not the GATT) to identify the countries that we (not the GATT) believe most burden our exports through their "unreasonable" policies (whether or not they violate GATT or any other international agreement) and then authorizes the President to retaliate against them if they do not agree within a short period to change those policies. Super 301 gets its name from the preexisting Section 301 of the trade law, which contains similar authorization without requiring the President to so publicly identify specific countries as priority "unfair traders."

Exchange rate pessimism. The pressure for the United States unilaterally to take even more aggressive actions against trading practices of other countries nevertheless remains and is likely to intensify. The principal reason stems from a phenomenon labeled by some as "exchange rate pessimism," a powerful second force for weakening the long-standing U.S. commitment to a multilateral rules-oriented trade policy.

Simply put, the pessimists submit that movements in exchange rates do not have a significant effect on trade patterns and thus trade rules must be changed to guarantee an improvement in the U.S. trade balance.[7] For example, it is thought in some quarters that the substantial decline of the dollar since 1985 did not "work" because the U.S. trade deficit continued to deteriorate through 1987. Frequently noted is the anti-import bias in Japan relative to other industrialized countries. In 1986, for example, Japan imported only 4.4% of its manufactured goods, compared to 13.8% for the United States and 37.2% for the FRG.[8] This apparent discrimination against imports, it is said, accounts for the fact that despite the near doubling of the value of the yen against the dollar between 1985 and 1988, the U.S. trade deficit with Japan has actually remained stuck at roughly $50 billion.[9]

In fact, economists have repeatedly shown through statistical tests that the pessimists are wrong: trade flows are clearly responsive to changes in prices of both imports and exports.[10] Roughly speaking, these studies demonstrate that for every one percentage point change in prices, the volumes of both exports and imports also change by at least one percentage point. To be sure, not all movements in exchange rates are reflected in prices of traded goods. Foreign exporters to the United States, in particular, have not passed on in the form of higher dollar prices to U.S. consumers a substantial fraction of the dollar depreciation since 1985.[11] Nevertheless, several well-known econometric models have tracked U.S. trade performance remarkably well through the 1980s by using the standard statistical relation between trade flows and exchange rates.

For example, Helkie and Hooper, whose statistical estimates of U.S. trade behavior are used at the Federal Reserve Board, projected in 1984 the U.S. current account 2 years ahead.[12] Their projections for 1985 and 1986 erred by only 1.1%. More recently, Bryant averaged the current account forecasts of five well-known trade models made both in January 1987 and December 1987, correcting for changes since the earlier projection in dollar exchange rates, oil prices, and GNP.[13] The projections are highly accurate for 1988 (Table 11-1). The revised current account projections for 1989 appear somewhat optimistic, but the dollar rose in value after those projections were made, which helps account for the slower rate of current account improvement likely to be recorded in 1989.

Why then has the U.S. trade picture brightened so modestly in the face of the substantial dollar depreciation since 1985? The principal answer lies in the mathematics of the trade deficit and the sheer momentum for continuing deficits that the numbers build in. In 1984, before the dollar began to fall, the dollar volume of U.S. imports exceeded U.S. exports by nearly 60%—$346 billion to $224 billion. Thus, even if both exports and imports continued to grow at the same rate thereafter, the trade deficit would have widened simply

TABLE 11-1
Average Projections of the U.S. Current Account Deficit of Five Econometric Models

	Billions of Dollars		
Projections	*1987*	*1988*	*1989*
January 1987 projections	141	133	146
Adjusted projection for December 1987 exchange rates, oil prices, and GNP growth	142	125	108
Actual	144	127	121*

* Annualized figure based on extrapolation of first two quarters.

because imports have been able to advance from a larger base. Indeed, without the dollar's decline since 1985, it has been estimated that the U.S. current account would have fallen into deficit by roughly $200 billion in 1988, instead of the $127 billion that was actually recorded.[14] Similar reasoning explains why the U.S. bilateral trade deficit with Japan has barely moved since 1985.[15]

This is not to deny the real nontariff trade barriers maintained in Japan. Lawrence has calculated that based on its state of economic development, Japan's imports of manufactures are approximately 40% below international standards. But despite these barriers, movements in the yen–dollar exchange rate have clearly affected trade between the two countries. Between 1980 and 1985 when the dollar rose in nominal terms against the yen by 5%, Japanese purchases of U.S. goods increased by just 6% (from $20.8 billion to $22.1 billion). But from 1985 to 1988, a period when the dollar fell by 53% against the yen, U.S. exports jumped by 70% (from $22.1 billion to $37.4 billion).[16]

Still, although the pessimists may severely understate the effects of exchange rate movements, if the level of the dollar remains roughly where it has been through most of 1989, pressures almost certainly will intensify for the United States to move away from its traditional multilateral, rules-oriented trade policy even further. Given the arithmetic momentum behind continued trade deficits, exports must grow at a substantially faster pace than imports in the future simply for the U.S. trade deficit to remain where it is. But that is not likely to occur unless U.S. exports get significantly cheaper in terms of foreign currency, that is, unless the dollar continues to fall. For example, four well-known trade models project that improvement in the overall U.S. current account will bottom out in 1990 and resume its upward climb thereafter (Table 11-2), given various levels of the dollar exchange rate from December 1987 through November 1988, when the value of the dollar was lower than at this writing and thus even more hospitable to trade improvement.

A multipolar world. Perhaps no event in the 1980s has been more unexpected than the significant easing of East–West tensions. At the same time, U.S. economic hegemony has disappeared. The United States is now a net debtor nation, owing increasing sums to Japan, the FRG, Taiwan, and other

TABLE 11-2
Alternative Projections of the U.S. Current Account Balance[29]

Study	Date	Real Exchange Rate Basis	Projections (billions of current dollars)			
			1989	1990	1991	1992
OECD	December 1988	2 November 1988	−116	−108		
DRI-Gault	December 1987	July 1988	−134	−154	−177	−201
Bryant	January 1988	December 1987	−108	−113	−127	
Cline	November 1988	4th quarter 1987	−119	−130	−143	−153

Sources: OECD, Organization for Economic Cooperation and Development; DRI, Data Resources Institute.

nations with large trade surpluses. In short, in both economic and political spheres the bipolar world that we lived in before 1980 has been replaced by a world increasingly governed by multiple centers of economic and political strength.

Paradoxically, the emergence of a multipolar world may be weakening commitments to the system of multilateral trade rules and negotiations. The GATT was formed in 1948 very much as the free world economic counterpart to the formal and informal political–military alliances formed between the United States and many other countries after World War II. In particular, at least in its early stages, the GATT was dominated by the United States and was seen in a bipolar context. The Soviet Union was not a founding member and still does not belong today, although recently it has expressed interest in joining.

The thawing of the Cold War and the splintering of economic and political influence around the world weaken the relative importance of the United States and thus subtly undermine continued commitments by other nations to the multilateral trade process. In addition, whereas in the United States freer trade was perceived to be in the interest of many industries because they were more productive than their foreign counterparts and thus wanted access to their markets, now many U.S. industries have lost their competitive edge.[17] In such an environment, freer trade can mean severe disruption, loss of jobs, and lower profits—outcomes that make it politically difficult at home for the United States to continue its leadership of the trade liberalization movement.

Weaknesses in the GATT. Finally, the GATT itself has weaknesses. These have existed since the GATT was formed, but they have been seen as more irritating as tariff barriers have been reduced and as other trade tensions have surfaced.

First, the GATT lacks an effective enforcement mechanism. Ironically, it was the U.S. Congress that was primarily responsible for this defect when it rejected the formation of a multilateral enforcement arm for GATT, the International Trade Organization. Second, the GATT fails to cover large areas of trade: agricultural products, services, and textiles (governed by a multi-country system of quotas arranged under the Multi-Fiber Arrangement).[18]

Third, and perhaps most important, an increasing share of trade within the industrialized countries is being burdened by nontariff trade barriers, especially so-called "voluntary restraint agreements" (VRAs) designed to circumvent the letter of the GATT.[19] VRAs are technically legal because they are negotiated "voluntarily" between importing countries, such as the United States (one of the worst offenders in the 1980s, with restrictions on imports of steel and automobiles), and their exporting trading partners. But the "voluntariness" of VRAs is clearly a fiction, and it is widely understood that they run afoul of the spirit of the GATT.

To many, the weaknesses in the GATT highlight the futility of the organization and the multilateral process of negotiation that it represents and encourages. To others, the missing links in the GATT, much like the nuclear weapons stockpiles of the major military powers, represent challenges for future negotiators to overcome. The GATT members are now addressing this challenge as part of the current Uruguay Round of trade negotiations, scheduled for completion by the end of 1990.[20]

OPTIONS FOR U.S. TRADE POLICY

The factors weakening the U.S. commitment to the postwar multilateral, rules-oriented trade regime have prompted a vigorous debate within the political and academic communities in this country about what principles should govern U.S. trade policy in the future. Three schools of thought, somewhat overlapping, have emerged.

The first, and least revolutionary of the alternatives, advocates that the United States itself fill the enforcement void in the GATT by playing the role of "super-cop." The United States has already embarked down this path, not only in adopting the new Super 301 provisions of the 1988 Trade Act, but in President Bush's decision in May 1989 under those provisions to single out Japan, Brazil, and India as countries engaged in discriminatory practices and thus "priority" targets for our retaliation if those practices are not soon ended.[21]

The second alternative also focuses on rules, but it advocates bilateral FTAs with other like-minded countries—Mexico, South Korea, Taiwan, and even Japan—modeled on the recent FTAs the United States negotiated with Canada and Israel, as well as the more ambitious integration effort now under way in Europe. The FTA policy model, which urges the bilateral negotiation of new rules on many subjects not covered or imperfectly covered by GATT (including investment, services, and agriculture), is thus more forward looking than the "super-cop" approach, which seeks unilateral enforcement of existing rules (that the United States sets) on a case-by-case basis.

Frustration with the slow pace of GATT negotiations has been a principal rationale advanced for the United States to seek more FTAs. The Tokyo Round, for example, took 6 years to complete (from 1973 to 1979). The current Uruguay Round was launched in the early 1980s and may not even be completed on schedule in 1990. Thus, the Reagan and Bush Administrations have pushed FTAs precisely in order to prod the GATT to move faster. Three well-known economists have recently offered a different justification: The world trading system is going "bilateral" in any event, so we might as well accept that fact and ensure that that process moves in a constructive rather than destructive direction.[22]

The third trade policy alternative would jettison not only the emphasis on multilateral action but on rules as well. Instead, it would "manage trade" by having the United States set bilateral trade targets with our trading partners. The targets could cover only our exports to them or our overall trade balance (as the Gephardt amendment advocated). Similarly, the targets could be set for individual products or industry sectors or could cover all trade.[23]

A CRITIQUE OF THE CRITICS

Each of the suggested alternatives to the traditional multilateral, rules-based trade policy followed by the United States has its appeal. But each also holds dangers that we think outweigh any benefits they may achieve.

The least risky, but also least promising, alternative is the United States as super-cop. As President Bush's decision under the Super 301 provision demonstrated, there will always be competing foreign policy objectives that any chief executive must take into account in deciding whether to single out individual countries as "unfair traders." It is widely assumed, for example, that the Administration exempted the European Community nations from the priority list primarily in order to avoid exacerbating then-worrisome tensions within the North Atlantic Treaty Organization over an appropriate response to the Soviet Union's nuclear arms reduction proposals.

But even President Bush's minimalist 301 effort has its risks. Several of the practices targeted by the President, notably India's trade-related investment measures and its insurance practices, are not covered by the GATT. If, therefore, we retaliate against these measures, our actions would violate the GATT and entitle the targeted countries lawfully to retaliate against us. Critics also have been too quick to dismiss the efficacy of the GATT enforcement mechanism. Of the 75 disputes brought before the GATT through September 1985, 88% were settled or dropped by the complaining country.[24] By circumventing the GATT dispute resolution mechanism, we weaken the commitment of other nations to lawful settlement of trade disputes.

Bilateral or regional FTAs do not offer a much better solution, and conceivably, could produce a worse one. The premise underpinning the case for more FTAs—that GATT negotiations take too long—is questionable. In fact, once the parties in the Tokyo Round got down to hard bargaining, agreement was reached in only 18 months, about the same time that was consumed in the United States–Canada talks.[25] Similarly, the tough negotiating in the current Uruguay Round did not really begin until President Bush assumed office, and even if completed late, in 1991 for example, would take less than 3 years—a major accomplishment given the round's ambitious objectives.

Moreover, as pioneering as they were, the FTAs with Canada and Israel were relatively limited in scope. Neither dealt with the highly controversial issues that are now being discussed in the Uruguay Round, including agricultural subsidies, protection of intellectual property rights, and restrictions on services and investment, or the subjects that inevitably would be on the table in future FTA discussions with other countries. Indeed, if the advocates are right that many restrictions against imports are extralegal and thus not amenable to international agreement—such as the complex Japanese distribution system, for example—then FTAs could disadvantage the United States; we would further open our market without meaningful reciprocal concessions.

More FTAs could actually harm world trade. In purely economic terms, such arrangements have two offsetting effects: although they may promote more efficient location of production within the areas covered by the agreements and thus enhance trade and consumer welfare, they may also divert trade from other countries outside the agreement to those inside. Although the net effect of these two tendencies will differ in different cases, it is noteworthy that three of the recent advocates of more bilateral arrangements have also estimated that the 1992 integration effort with the European Community will divert more trade than it creates.[26]

More fundamentally, however, further movement by the United States—the leader of multilateral trade liberalization efforts since the end of World War II—toward bilateral or regional pacts runs a serious risk of undermining, if not unraveling, the GATT. Indeed, given the current inward-looking focus of the Europeans and Canada's new-found partnership with the United States, who would be left to lead the liberalizing process in the GATT if we, too, abandon our commitment to multilateralism? The answer is no one.

Instead, nations would quickly enter a free-for-all to obtain from each other the best deal each could. The world trading system would thus degenerate into a complicated maze of discriminatory bilateral and regional arrangements. Frictions would dramatically increase over "rules of origin" because it would then become all-important to know from which country imports and exports had "originated." In a world of multinational enterprises that often manufacture products in multiple locations, disputes about rules of origin could lead to serious trade rifts and would lead to substantially more red tape and uncertainty for all those involved in international trade.

Finally, the managed trade alternative rests on equally shaky premises and holds perhaps the greatest dangers of all. The principal argument for managed trade—that product-specific bilateral negotiations, especially those with Japan, are worthless—is simply not correct. As Lawrence has shown, the Advisory Committee for Trade Policy and Negotiations has unwittingly provided data in its report recommending managed trade that, in fact, demonstrate the success of previous negotiations with Japan.[27] Between 1985 and 1987, U.S. exports to Japan of medical drugs and equipment, electronics, forest products, and telecommunications—sectors targeted by the U.S. trade negotiators—collectively increased by 47%, or twice the growth of all U.S. exports to Japan during this period.

In any event, the setting of trade targets would be counterproductive. If the targets were bilateral trade balances, it is more than likely that foreign countries would be happy to comply by restricting their exports to the United States rather than liberalizing imports. Like the VRAs that have limited the exports of Japanese cars and steel, these new restrictions would simply raise the price of goods exported to the United States and increase the profits of the foreign producers. Meanwhile, forcing foreign consumers to buy U.S. products they have not voluntarily chosen to purchase can hardly enhance the attractiveness of American goods overseas.

PREFERRED TRADE POLICY

If none of the alternative trade policy regimes offer significant advantages, what then should be done about America's obvious trade problems—reflected in its $100 billion-plus trade deficit?

The answer most economists have given has been frequently heard, routinely ignored, but still remains correct. In a world of flexible exchange rates, a nation's trade balance—or more accurately, its current account balance—is fundamentally determined not by its trade policies but rather by its spending patterns.

By definition, the current account balance measures the difference between a nation's saving and investment. High-saving countries like Japan that do not invest all of their savings at home export the surplus and invest the proceeds abroad. Low-saving countries like the United States that invest more than they save must import the difference and borrow from abroad to finance their current account deficits. Exchange rates are the primary medium through which shifts in spending patterns influence the trade balance. As a nation increases its saving relative to its investment, its interest rates fall and so does its exchange rate, as investors seek assets denominated in currencies where yields are higher. Conversely, as a nation decreases its saving relative to its investment, its interest rates rise and so does its exchange rate.

Until the 1980s, the United States invested what it saved and thus ran a current account balance near zero. In this decade, however, U.S. savings rates as a share of net national output, both public and private, have fallen dramatically relative to our investment rates, which have also fallen (Table 11-3). The shortfall in domestic saving required for investment has required us to import the difference, both in capital and goods, from abroad.[28]

In short, the cure for our trade imbalance lies in either substantially raising the fraction of national income that is saved or lowering the fraction that is invested. Clearly, the first of these choices is more palatable, if more painful, than the second.

It is not widely appreciated, however, that the removal of foreign trade barriers will have little effect on our trade position. In the short run, lower barriers would permit an increase in our exports and thus reduce the overall deficit. But a declining deficit shrinks the available supply of dollars on the market and thus drives up the dollar exchange rate. A higher dollar, in turn,

TABLE 11-3
U.S. Investment–Saving Balance, Expressed as Percentage Shares of Net National Product[30]

Savings and Investment	1951–1980	1984–1986	1987–1988
Saving			
Private	9.2	8.1	6.3
Government deficit	−1.2	−5.0	−4.0
(state and federal)			
Total national saving*	8.0	3.1	2.4
Domestic investment	7.6	6.2	5.9
Net U.S. investment abroad*	0.4	−3.2	−3.5
(current account balance)			

* Totals may not add due to rounding.

discourages exports and encourages imports. Over the long run, therefore, lower trade barriers have no effect on the trade balance.

By the same reasoning, it is a mistake to blame the deterioration in our trade accounts on unfair trade. Between 1981 and 1988, the U.S. trade position declined with every major trading area around the world, except the nations of the Organization of Petroleum Exporting Countries (OPEC) (where the United States benefited greatly from the drop in oil prices) (Table 11-4). This pattern makes it difficult to believe that a worldwide conspiracy to discriminate against U.S. imports could have suddenly developed only in this decade.

It is, nevertheless, in our interest to remove unfair impediments to our exports; doing so will raise the dollar exchange rate at which the United States can achieve balanced trade. A higher value of the dollar, other things being equal, permits American citizens to buy more imports for a given dollar expenditure and thus to enjoy a higher standard of living. The critical trade policy question, therefore, centers on what strategy can best be used to achieve a significant reduction in foreign trade barriers.

In our view, the best approach lies not in abandoning the rules-oriented, multilateral strategy that the United States has pioneered since World War II, but instead in reaffirming the commitment to that strategy and enlisting the vigorous participation of our trading partners. At a purely political level, we think that other countries that maintain trade barriers are more likely to lower them in response to international pressure, lawfully applied through the GATT, than solely in response to U.S. complaints. Indeed, our "lone ranger" attitude toward other nations' trade barriers runs a severe risk of tarnishing our broader political influence. For example, U.S. relations with both Japan and South Korea have already been severely strained as a result of our constant pressure on particular trade issues. Resentment builds, meanwhile, as the United States continues to demonstrate an inability to significantly reduce its national overspending, which other countries think, quite correctly, is the overwhelming reason for their trade surpluses with us.

The United States even runs broader geopolitical risks if it abandons its mantle of leadership on multilateral trade liberalization. It is fitting to recall the history of the period between the two major world wars of this century,

TABLE 11-4
U.S. Trade Balance by Region

	Billions of Dollars	
Country	1980	1988*
Canada	−0.5	−12.1
Japan	−8.6	−49.2
Western Europe	12.4	−15.1
OPEC	−30.5	−9.8
All other countries in the world	−0.1	−38.9

* First three quarters at annual rate.

when the rise of rival trading blocs contributed significantly to the tensions that led to World War II. Similar tensions led to repeated conflicts in the 17th and 18th centuries. Only when Great Britain, espousing the free trade principles of Adam Smith and David Ricardo, emerged as the dominant world power in the 19th century did these conflicts abate. The United States assumed this mantle of leadership toward free trade after World War II and until now has promoted increased liberalization, more trade, and improvements in living standards around the world.

It would be a severe mistake for the United States to abandon its leadership role simply because of its inability to address the root causes of trade difficulties abroad and its economic weaknesses at home. In the long run, we should realize that trade is still a positive sum game, not the zero sum game some have now contended. We should not be distracted by current tensions into wrecking the multilateral trade system that has helped bring all of the nations that participate in it to unprecedented levels of economic well-being.

ENDNOTES

1. In 1948, the GATT originally had 23 signatory countries; membership has since expanded to more than 90 countries.
2. L. C. Thurow, "GATT is dead," address before the World Economic Forum, Davos, Switzerland, January 1988.
3. *Omnibus Trade and Competitiveness Act of 1988.*
4. W. Schneider, "Democrats handed a big trade issue," *Natl. J.* (14 May 1988), p. 1322.
5. *Trade Act of 1974*, Sect. 301.
6. An account of the events leading up to these two agreements is given by Y. Funabashi [*Managing the Dollar: From The Plaza To The Louvre* (Institute for International Economics, Washington, DC, 1988)]. Some economists assert, however, that the Plaza Accord played very little role in the dollar's depreciation, arguing that the dollar was substantially overvalued at the beginning of 1985 and would have come down of its own accord in the absence of this agreement.
7. For example, see C. Prestowitz, Jr. [*Trading Places* (Basic Books, New York, 1988)].
8. *Analysis of the U.S.–Japan Trade Problem*, Report of the Advisory Committee for Trade Policy and Negotiations to the United States Trade Representative (Washington, DC, February 1989), p. 56.
9. J. Fallows, *Atl. Mon.* **263**, 40 (May 1989).
10. A sample of the recent literature includes reports by P. R. Krugman and R. Baldwin [*Brookings Pap. Econ. Activity (BPEA)*, pp. 1–56 (1987:1)] and R. Z. Lawrence [in *American Living Standards: Threats and Challenges*, R. E. Litan et al., Eds. (Brookings Institution, Washington, DC, 1988), pp. 23–65].
11. C. Mann, *Fed. Res. Bull.* **72**, 366 (June 1986).
12. W. L. Helkie and P. Hooper, in *External Deficits and the Dollar*, R. C. Bryant et al., Eds. (Brookings Institution, Washington, DC, 1988), pp. 10–56.
13. R. C. Bryant, "The U.S. External Deficit: An Update," Brookings Discussion Papers in International Economics (Brookings Institution, Washington, DC, January 1988). The models include Data Resources, Lexington, MA; Japanese Economic Planning Agency Model; Federal Reserve Board Staff Multi-Country

Model; the Global Economic Model of the National Institute for Economic and Social Research, London; and the Multicountry Model of John Taylor of the President's Council of Economic Advisers.

14. C. F. Bergsten, *America in the World Economy* (Institute for International Economics, Washington, DC, 1989), p. 85.

15. R. Z. Lawrence, *Brookings Pap. Econ. Act.* **2,** 517 (1987).

16. Data are from the *Economic Report of the President, 1989* (Government Printing Office, Washington, DC, 1989), pp. 427–431.

17. M. L. Dertouzous, R. K. Lester, R. M. Solow, and the MIT Commission on Industrial Productivity, *Made in America* (MIT Press, Cambridge, MA, 1989).

18. W. R. Cline, *The Future of World Trade in Textiles and Apparel* (Institute for International Economics, Washington, DC, 1987); L. H. Clark, "How 'managed trade' would really work," *The Wall Street Journal,* 9 November 1989, p. 16.

19. C. C. Coughlin and G. E. Wood, *Fed. Res. Bank St. Louis Rev.* (January–February 1989), p. 35.

20. A guide to the negotiations is presented by J. M. Finger and A. Olechowski [*The Uruguay Round: A Handbook on the Multilateral Trade Negotiations* (The World Bank, Washington, DC, 1987)].

21. Japan was criticized for unreasonably protecting its satellite and lumber industries, Brazil for protecting its computer software industry, and India for its discriminatory investment licensing system. B. Stokes, "Off and running," *Nat. J.* (17 June 1989), p. 1562.

22. R. Dornbusch, P. R. Krugman, Y. C. Park, *Meeting World Challenges: U.S. Manufacturing in the 1990s* (Eastman Kodak Company, Rochester, NY, 1989).

23. Managed trade has a number of advocates, including Prestowitz (*7*), the Advisory Committee for Trade Policy and Negotiations (*8*), and H. Kissinger and C. Vance [*For. Aff.* **66,** 899 (summer 1988)].

24. U.S. International Trade Commission, *Review of the Effectiveness of Trade Dispute Settlement Under the GATT and Tokyo Round Agreements* (Publication 1793, U.S. International Trade Commission, Washington, DC, 1985).

25. J. J. Schott, *More Free Trade Areas?* (Institute for International Economics, Washington, DC, 1989), p. 22.

26. This view is discussed in (*22*), p. 21.

27. R. Z. Lawrence, "The yen for results," *Financial Times,* 7 June 1989, p. 25.

28. For a more thorough discussion, see W. D. Nordhaus [*Challenge* (July–August 1989), p. 22].

29. W. R. Cline, *American Trade Adjustment: The Global Impact* (Institute for International Economics, Washington, DC, 1989), p. 15.

30. T. E. Mann and C. L. Schultze, *Brookings Rev.* **7,** 3 (winter 1988/89).

NO

Managed Trade and Economic Sovereignty

Robert Kuttner

The contemporary problem of the global political economy is that nations are losing sovereignty to private economic actors, yet the very turmoil of an unregulated market intensifies the pressure of nations to secure acceptable outcomes for their citizens. Despite the impetus toward an integrated global private economy, the nation-state remains the instrument of political mediation. The state, not private corporations or banks, remains accountable to its citizens for their economic welfare, and it bears the ultimate fiscal responsibility. Moreover, the polity remains the arena in which social contracts are negotiated. Yet the growing imbalance between an integrated, unregulated global economy and a weakened set of national and supranational instruments for its governance deprives individual nations of the machinery to deal constructively with those dislocations. The Keynesian nation-state has lost most of its economic rudder—not to supranational public authority but to internationalized private capital.

The confusion about the appropriate role for the state and the market is at its most muddled in the thinking about the desirable norms for the trading system that governs cross-border commerce, where the reach of the state is weakest and that of private capital strongest. The confusion is perhaps most severe in the United States, because the United States, as guarantor of the global system and purveyor of the ideal of liberal trade, is increasingly unsure how to reconcile those twin goals with its own national interest as an economy. For the most part, official opinion seems to think that the remedy for the dislocations of laissez-faire is more laissez-faire.

The United States, as the hegemon and as the nation most ideologically committed to economic liberalism, experiences these dilemmas most acutely because it is the least conscious of them. By the lights of orthodox economics and the ideology of the Reagan and Bush administrations, the remedy for the range of international economic problems is the perfection of free trade. But other trading nations, lacking the effortless commercial dominance that post-war America once enjoyed, feel far less guilty about using the economic instruments of the state. Long accustomed to higher levels of both exports and imports as a share of gross national product (GNP) and lacking the American sense of special responsibility for the system as a whole, they developed survival skills and institutions of economic adjustment and development that the United States lacks.[1]

In some countries, such as Japan, South Korea, France, and Brazil, these strategies have been overtly mercantilist. These nations have been willing to use the economic power of the state to promote industrial development, to shelter home markets, and to seek trade surpluses. Other successful small trading nations, such as Sweden and Austria, while supporting a generally open trading system, have devised their own mechanisms of adaptation and indirect subsidy that violate the norms of liberal trade in more subtle ways. Still other nations, in the Pacific Basin, most of them small, have achieved rapid growth by combining entrepreneurial dynamism with very low wages and state support, turning themselves into export powerhouses by letting their domestic consumption lag their production for world markets. Though this is ostensibly a subsidy, it is better understood as a different form of free riding on the trading system, since it depresses demand nationally and hence globally and creates lopsided trade surpluses that are the reciprocal of other nations' trade deficits.

In general, the United States has been the advocate of the purest version of free trade. Most other nations have loyally given lip service to these United States-inspired norms while devising pragmatic measures necessary for their survival in a global economy. At the same time, the United States has been far from the paragon of economic liberalism that it often professed itself to be. Yet because of its fierce ideological commitment to laissez-faire, United States departures from it have typically been poorly thought out, lacking in long-term industrial goals, and generally not helpful either to the trading system or to America's own economic self-interest.

There is thus a grave dilemma, both for the global trading system and for the United States as its chief architect and sponsor. Many other nations have demonstrated, by their actions if not their words, that they are not interested in a system of pure free trade. By some calculations, more than half the cross-border trade that takes place today operates by some other standard than the norms of classical free trade.[2] Yet, curiously enough, the volume of trade continues to increase substantially faster than the growth of total world GNP. The sins against liberal trade vary from economic-development initiatives undertaken by poor countries that might be justified as variations on the traditional "infant industry" loophole, to de facto industrial policies cloaked in national defense, to covert market-closing measures undertaken by the world's richest and most successful trade-surplus nations.

A different order of problem is the institutional disjuncture between trade negotiations, debt negotiations, and the other policy-making machinery that establishes rules for the global economy. One set of diplomats, at the General Agreement on Tariffs and Trade (GATT) in Geneva, is hectoring Third World nations to open their markets to United States, European, and Japanese manufactured goods. A different set of bureaucrats, associated with the World Bank, the International Monetary Fund (IMF), and the private creditor banks, is pressing debtor nations to reduce their imports and increase export earnings. Finally, the most pressing, overarching trade questions, such as the problem of chronic Japanese and West German surpluses and United States deficits in manufactured goods, are widely acknowledged, but these issues are not part of the GATT portfolio; they seem to be on the diplomatic agenda everywhere *but* at the trade talks. Once again, the assumption of liberal economics is that if "barriers" are removed then the "correct" pattern of trade will naturally ensue. The question of Japan's chronic surplus, or of balance in the trading system, are not issues per se, except to the extent that illegitimate trading practices can be demonstrated. Desperation remedies, such as the Gephardt amendment, are then branded as illegitimate because they flout the stated norms of the trading system that the United States champions.

The GATT system, of which more shortly, has only limited criteria for differentiating "good" violations of laissez-fair from bad ones. Aside from giving nations the right to countervail and being somewhat indulgent of statist policies in developing countries, the GATT does not effectively parse out departures from free trade; it has no mechanism for ensuring rough balance in the total calculus of mercantilism. The basic GATT norm is nondiscrimination and the basic GATT goal ever-freer universal market access. All "trade distorting" subsidies are presumed to be bad. All departures from the principle of multilateral nondiscrimination are deemed regrettable. Economic-development schemes, viewed through the GATT lens, are generally damned as merely protectionist, and it is never conceded that they might have positive-sum benefits in the form of technological gains or redistributions of production.

Advocates of liberal trade tend to see themselves as possessors of special virtue, maintaining the dikes against tides of self-serving protectionism. It is presumed that more laissez-faire is invariably better than less, even though economic theory says this is not necessarily true in an imperfect world. There is no taxonomy for sorting out a world of necessary second bests in practice and little recognition of the necessity of economic management, except through the reluctant toleration of escape-clause relief and other "safeguards," in GATT jargon, which are supposed to be temporary and used sparingly.

If this is a problem for the GATT system, it is a special problem for the United States, which tends to see its own self-interest as identical to the liberalism of the trading system as a whole. The United States seems to think that its special mission is to bring laissez-faire to the world, rather than to hammer out with its trading partners a sustainable mixed system that tolerates some state involvement in the economy while maintaining a rough overall balance and providing the United States an equitable share of benefits and costs.

The prevailing United States ideology of economic liberalism eschews industrial goals for the United States. In principle, it is none of the government's business where steel or automobiles or semiconductors or videocassette recorders or civilian aircraft are produced. If production migrates, this must be the market speaking. If the invisible hand operates through the guiding hand of foreign industrial policies, this is deemed to make no significant difference. Classical trade theory holds that if other nations are stupid enough to subsidize their export industries, American consumers ought to welcome the gift. These presumptions have four consequences, all of them negative for the United States national self-interest and confusing to the trading system.

First, the lack of a set of United States industrial goals means that it is impossible to have any trade goals for United States policy, except exhorting other nations to practice laissez-faire in the American image. In practice, this makes America's industrial fate partly the captive of other nations' industrial policies. Second, because the United States continues to view itself as the political leader of the Western world, it is reluctant to play tactical hardball on trade issues, lest it alienate key geopolitical allies. Third, when exhortation fails to achieve equitable results or to open markets, the United States is reluctant to resort to explicit market-sharing remedies, because this, of course, would be a version of the managed trade it claims to disdain and would violate the very ideology it is promoting. Finally, and perhaps most seriously, its devotion to the ideal of laissez-faire means that those United States departures from liberal trade that do intermittently occur are undertaken guiltily and without strategic purpose and are seen by United States officials as unfortunate concessions to domestic politics rather than as economic-development initiatives.

The cases are legion. For example, the United States disingenuously imposed a quota regime on automobiles, disguised as voluntary export restraints (VERs). This allowed Japan to determine just what was exported to the United States and to capture the quota rents; it also exposed Americans as perfect hypocrites. The United States backed into an "industrial policy"—for motorcycles (!)—via a trade-relief case but disdained one for the far more consequential machine-tool industry. It has long had a highly protectionist regime for agriculture, which it does not know how to dismantle, except by having everyone else forswear all price regulation for farm products, which other nations regard as unrealistic and probably cynical. It has had an extensive and unacknowledged industrial policy for aircraft via the Pentagon. And because national defense is the one available loophole in the otherwise seamless ideology of laissez-faire, the Pentagon has sponsored an industrial (and trade) policy for semiconductors, high-definition television, and even an advisory body to the secretary of defense, drawing the seemingly logical conclusion that the Pentagon should widen that sole loophole and simply take over the task of modernizing all of American industry.[3]

An even more stunning example of the self-defeating cost of political hegemony married to laissez-faire economics is American export control. The United States takes a far harder line than its allies in restricting the export of advanced technologies to Soviet bloc nations. This policy not only requires extensive export controls on East–West trade but also limits the ability of United States high-tech producers to export to friendly nations (lest sensitive products be transshipped to the East). As a consequence, United States producers lose billions of dollars' worth of export business—a 1988 report by the National Academy of Science conservatively estimated the 1985 annual export loss at $9.3 billion—while other nations understandably view the United States stance of promoting free commerce with one hand while tightly regulating it with the other as confusing, if not idiotic.

In the prevailing ideology, perfect laissez-faire is presumed to be not only the first best but the only defensible goal. As even most orthodox economists will admit when pressed hard enough, it is neither. But without any criteria or taxonomy for sorting out second bests in a necessarily mixed world economy that can never attain pure free trade, this self-defeating pattern keeps recurring. It is the purpose of this essay to explain and evaluate the available second bests. Contrary to the standard assumptions of free traders, the case for managed trade is not simply a set of special pleadings in behalf of retrograde industries but reflects a dissenting analysis of political economy, of the dynamics of trade, and of the interconnections between trade and geopolitics.

THE NEW VIEW

American policy has embraced an increasingly pure devotion to free-trade principles at the precise time that some orthodox economists are having serious second thoughts about whether the traditional theory of comparative advantage is reliable, either as a description of how trade really works or as a norm for optimal policy. The New View has emerged in the work of Paul Krugman, an eminently respectable neoclassical economist at the Massachusetts Institute of Technology and once the staff trade specialist on the Reagan Council of Economic Advisers, and in related work by Avinash Dixit, James Brander, Barbara J. Spender, and numerous others.

In order to understand the significance of the New View, it is important to recall some of the implications of the Old View, as set forth by David Ricardo in 1817.[4] According to the Old View, countries have *inherent* comparative advantages in particular products because of some intrinsic national characteristics. Ricardo himself simply assumed that international differences in resources and technology would give each country a comparative advantage in certain good that it could produce with relatively lower labor costs. Later, the Swedish economists Eli Heckscher and Bertil Ohlin argued that comparative advantages were due to differences in "factor proportions": the relative abundance of land, labor, and capital in each country, compared with the relative intensities with which these factors are used in producing various commodities.[5] As formalized by Paul Samuelson, this theory required the assumptions of identical technology in all countries as well as perfect competition in all markets.[6] Under these and other, more technical, conditions, each country will export those goods that incorporate relatively more of its relatively abundant factors.

Whether in the traditional Ricardian or more modern Heckscher-Ohlin-Samuelson (HOS) variant, the Old View had the powerful implication that *there is a naturally ordained pattern of trade*. The location of industries is not arbitrary: with free trade, industries will automatically be located where they can be most efficiently operated. There are some subtle differences between the two variants. The Ricardian emphasis on different technological capabilities of nations implicitly admits that social institutions and public policies can potentially affect a nation's "inherent" comparative advantages. The HOS view, on the other hand, implies a more extreme bias against intervention, since this theory holds technology constant and assumes that only natural and immutable "endowments" of productive factors matter to trade. But both theories imply that there is a unique allocation of industries among countries that is economi-cally efficient at any point in time and that this allocation can be achieved only through free trade.

The New View rejects this conclusion of the Old View. The New View asserts that the location of manufacturing production in the world is not a reflection of any inherent comparative advantages in the traditionally understood sense but is essentially the result of historical accidents. The indeterminacy of industrial loca-tion reflects several characteristics of the advanced global economy. These include increasing returns to scale and the ability of firms to "slide down the learning curve." In essence, innovators compete on the basis of entrepreneurial and techno-logical prowess rather than factor endowments. Technological leadership can sometimes flow from such arguably "natural" endowments as a skilled labor force (which itself reflects the policy influence of education and training interventions), but it can also be the deliberate result or fortuitous by-product of more explicit national policy to promote technology.

The significance of the New View is borne out by, among other indicators, the large amount of intraindustry trade, in which trading partners both export and import similar products—a phenomenon that is not predicted by the standard theory of specialization based on comparative advantage. As Klaus Stegemann has observed in studying intraindustry specialization in the context of European integration: "Which country makes which products within any manufacturing industry . . . cannot be explained exclusively on the basis of differences in natural ability or factor proportions. Variables such as entrepre-neurial initiative, investment in human capital, research and development, product design, economies of scale, and learning by doing were recognized to be crucial for the expansion of intra-industry trade."[7] These, in turn, are subject to policy intervention. Such intervention, if it leads to technological breakthroughs, may even produce positive-sum benefits.

A somewhat narrower strand of the New View holds that much interna-tional trade can be understood as a form of imperfect competition, in which some producers enjoy supernormal profits, or "rents." Contrary to standard theory, such rents are not instantly competed away but persist as innovators enjoy an array of niche positions. Since these rents are widespread, a nation that captures them gains an advantage over its competitors, both in the form of profits and in the continuation of technological dominance. Particular trade policies (tariffs, subsidies, export taxes, and so on) can, under certain circum-stances, be shown to raise national income by extracting more of these rents at the expense of foreigners. The deliberate use of such instruments is referred to as "strategic trade policy." These insights embellish an older literature on imperfect competition in international trade, dating back to the early 1900s. However, it is not necessary to demonstrate the presence of oligopolistic rents to show that the capture of leading industries can produce beneficial externalities or that the location of industries may be historically contingent. These points are logically separate.

James A. Brander and Barbara J. Spencer at the University of British Columbia term the process of capturing such rents "profit shifting."[8] Work by Lawrence Katz and Lawrence Summers adds the idea that since most of industry's costs are ultimately labor costs, capturing industries that enjoy supernormal profits also benefits that nation's work force (i.e., its citizens). Workers can capture a share of the profit in the form of wage premiums, or "labor rents," and over time may earn these "rents" by becoming more knowledgeable and hence more productive.[9]

If the location of production, especially in advanced industries, is fundamentally arbitrary, it is arguably subject to manipulation by national-policy interventions, whether microeconomic ones aimed at capturing positions in emerging industries, human capital policies aimed at improving the quality of the work force, or macroeconomic ones intended to influence savings rates, capital costs, and so on. However, the more orthodox version of the New View, while it has blown a big hole in the traditional theory of comparative advantage, has stopped well short of advocating industrial policies for two reasons, one ideological and the other technical.

Ideologically, most orthodox economists remain sufficiently steadfast neo-classicists to harbor grave doubts about the competence of collective action, particularly on the part of politicians responsive to interest groups, to undertake economically optimal policies that could improve on decisions of the market. This enterprise is deemed particularly perilous for the United States, whose political system is said to be uniquely vulnerable to special-interest groups. ("The trouble with picking winners," Senator William Roth recently declared, "is that each Congressman would want one for his District."[10]) Moreover, the technical economics demonstrating the possibility of welfare-enhancing strategic trade policy are dependent on the assumptions of the particular model. Changing an assumption can change whether a particular policy instrument (e.g., tariff, subsidy) ought to be used. Since there are potentially grave informational difficulties in knowing which model can be applied to any given industry, it may be safer to do nothing than to risk using the wrong instrument.

The typical New View paper, especially by economists wishing to keep their neoclassical union cards, takes care to include the disclaimer that even if profit shifting or interventions aimed at generating positive externalities are possible in theory, they are implausible in practice. According to Krugman, most economists who subscribe to the New View are uneasy about giving aid and comfort to mercantilists. Krugman concluded a rueful essay titled "Is Free Trade Passé?" by threading his way between contradictory positions: "To abandon the free trade principle in pursuit of the gains from sophisticated intervention could . . . open the door to adverse political consequences that would outweigh the potential gains. It is possible, then, both to believe that comparative advantage is an incomplete model of trade and to believe that free trade is the right policy."[11]

Nonetheless, the New View radically alters the context of debate, for it removes the premise that nations like Japan that practice strategic trade could not, by definition, be improving their welfare. It means that orthodox economists now concede that advocates of industrial policy are not, by definition, economic illiterates. And it invites a far more subtle policy debate on the instruments and the purposes of departures from Ricardian trade, which is no longer optimal by definition, after all.

FREE TRADE VERSUS FREER TRADE

If economic theory now admits that economic possibility is not directed by the invisible hand and that the textbook characterization of free trade as "first best" does not describe reality, then it becomes advisable to consider the possible second bests—not textbook free trade but *freer* trade. The vain attempt to pursue pure laissez-faire not only disadvantages United States industry but also leaves the world trading system with a dishonest and inefficient blend of subsidy, suboptimal investment, and subterfuge.

In practice, managed-trade modes can improve on the free-trade model, not as it exists in the textbooks but as it actually operates in a world of nation-states. Pure free trade is improbable, and different nations are likely to operate their domestic economics according to fundamentally different rules and structures. Yet it should nonetheless be possible to design a trade regime and a set of operating principles for United States policy that permit dissimilar nations to trade with one another without producing lopsided outcomes. The actual experience of three industries in which the organization of United States trade has consciously departed from the principles of laissez-faire will reveal both good and bad design elements of second-best trade regimes.

In the case of textiles and apparel, the Multifiber Arrangement (MFA) provides a good illustration of a reasonably successful managed-trade regime. The MFA seeks to manage the rate of import growth, thus allowing time for domestic producers to phase out of some production and to automate in other areas where advanced capital can compete with cheap labor. The limitation on a ruinous free-for-all has helped limit worldwide excess capacity and has given new exporting nations the ability to predict and plan for their probable share in a steadily expanding market. Far from retarding innovation, the predictability has facilitated new capital investment in both the industrial and developing nations.

The steel industry offers a good example of what happens when other nations' mercantilism coexists with the United States pretense that free trade reigns. In the 1970s, newly industrializing nations invested heavily in steel capacity. That new capacity came on line just in time for the global economic slowdown following the two oil shocks. The result was a worldwide squeeze on steel earnings and pressure to dump subsidized steel on the world's only large open market: the United States. Because of an unwillingness to admit forthrightly what was occurring, the United States government let serious damage occur before finally negotiating a *fourth*-best solution in the form of "voluntary" export restraints. This is an industry that cries out for a regime that reconciles the desire of major nations to retain some domestic steel production with a common interest in reciprocal reduction of worldwide subsidy costs and global excess capacity.

The semiconductor industry illustrates the reality that different nations simply play by different rules. The Japanese semiconductor industry is part of a conglomeration of horizontally integrated electronics firms. It epitomizes the Japanese habit of pursuing technological prowess and market share, notwithstanding what in America would be unacceptable short-term losses. There is no GATT-wide conception of antitrust, and conventional antidumping remedies are not adequate to handle the complexities of semiconductor trade. Moreover, it is clear that the three major trading areas—the United States, Japan, and the European Community (EC)—consider semiconductors so important that they are determined to retain domestic production capacity. Here, even the United States put aside its principles and negotiated a quasi-cartel with Japan, although it has failed to produce the United States market share in Japan that was promised. As in steel, the national and global interest would be served by a regime that acknowledges the reality of managed trade yet promotes competition, innovation, and freer trade.

This brief review of three industries suggests that if nations wish to retain domestic production capacity and not cede their entire market to foreign suppliers, it is possible to design relatively liberal and balanced managed-trade regimes: not free trade but freer trade. However, several caveats are in order.

First, no single template fits all industries. In textiles and apparel, the "threat" to established producers is from low-wage countries; the problem of emerging worldwide excess capacity is tempered by the fact that "capacity" is rather less expensive and long lived than in steel. Moreover, there is plenty of competition among advanced nations to keep competitive pressure on one another and no reason to cartelize that portion of the industry. A regime based on limiting the total rate of increase of imports has been moderately successful—though it produces far more imports in excess of the stipulated quotas than the domestic industry wants.

In steel, on the other hand, the problem is worldwide subsidy and overcapacity, coupled with a near universal desire among nations to retain steelmaking facilities. The present nonregime is a series of purely tactical expedients. The necessary remedy may be a more explicit managed regime based on market shares. In semiconductors, though a reciprocal import-share regime would solve the problem in the home economies of producer nations, it would require an entirely new set of negotiated common principles to establish norms of behavior in third-country markets.

Second, the suitability of managed-trade regimes in some products—steel, textiles, semiconductors, and some farm products, among others—does not mean that a generic system of managed trade is wanted or needed. Ideally, the norm should be roughly that of the GATT—relatively liberal trade, based on the familiar principles of multilateral most-favored-nation (MFN) nondiscrimination, national treatment, with limited tolerance for market-distorting subsidies, quotas, and market-closing devices. A GATT-like system should be the residual because that is relatively simpler and cleaner (though, as the long complex history of dumping disputes attests, it is not nearly so simple and clean as its defenders claim).

Even if a liberal trade regime is the residual, however, it is clear that some important nations do not really wish such a regime in some key products. A departure from liberal norms in those product areas need not result in net losses of allocative efficiency. Indeed, such a departure may bring net benefits, if the problems of overcapacity and glut can be frankly addressed, negotiated, and resolved (as they apparently have been in textiles).

The most logical candidates for a managed-trade regime are products for which nations are currently restraining trade and for one reason or another wish to retain or develop technological and production capacity. In that case, if there is widespread reluctance to observe the norms of liberal trade, a frankly acknowledged managed-trade regime, with a balance-of-benefits as the core principle, is vastly preferable to the current patchwork of subterfuges and imbalanced concessions. If, at some point, the members of the GATT wish to shift their managed-trade regime, say in wheat, toward freer and freer trade, that is of course their prerogative.

If managed trade in key industries is legitimate, the United States becomes much freer to press its trading partners—not simply to practice laissez-faire in their own economies (the traditional United States diplomatic goal) but to bring a balance of obligations and benefits to the trading system. The United States is also freed to define industrial goals for its own domestic economy and strategies for carrying them out. Such strategies might or might not require targeted industrial policies in any given sector. Under a managed-trade regime for semiconductors, the United States might choose to subsidize semiconductor research and development via a Sematech consortium. In the case of steel, the United States might decide that holding foreign subsidized steel to a 25 percent market share is sufficient to allow a renaissance in American steel through free-market principles, with only a reinvestment quid pro quo and some retraining aid as minimalist industrial policies.

A balance-of-benefits approach is also a better way of reconciling the reality of widespread domestic economic interventions with equity and comity in the trading system as a whole. Simply countervailing against other nations' subsidies or market-closing policies is no solution. In an emerging industry, such as high-definition television, where each major region wishes to develop production capacity, a balance-of-benefits approach could attempt to calculate and negotiate limits on the total amount of subsidy. Nations that wanted their products to be freely traded would have to abide by those limits. Alternatively, a portion of each nation's domestic market could be reserved for domestic suppliers, and the rest could be available for imports, perhaps with auctioned quotas. If trading nations eventually grew weary of ruinous subsidy wars as the industry matured, reciprocal reductions in subsidies could be negotiated.

The recent United States position on farm trade is a splendid illustration of the best being the enemy of the good when it comes to reciprocal reduction of subsidy and oversupply. In the recent Montreal midterm review of the GATT round, the EC urged the United States to pursue a medium-term program of reciprocal reduction of subsidies, with some tolerance for supply and price management and a mutual respect for historical regional export markets. The United States took the position that it would agree to this interim approach only if Europe joined the United States in a grandiose commitment to absolutely free trade in agriculture by the year 2000. The Europeans rightly saw that as a cynical maneuver that the United States delegation contrived in order to seem absolutely devoted to the freest possible trade while winking to assure domestic farm interests that no capitulation was genuinely contemplated. The predictable diplomatic result was impasse. Even the nations that are the lowest-cost producers and the most committed to liberal trade in agriculture, such as Canada and Australia, shared the EC view that partially managed trade in farm products was the only conceivable route toward freer trade.

The point that free traders need to comprehend is that a regime of partially managed trade can be the route to relatively freer and more sustainable trade, as well as to a more balanced and sustainable role for the United States in the system. They should also note that this approach would inject a greater degree of multilateralism into the trading system. At present, in the mind of free traders, the ideal of "multilateralism" is irrevocably yoked to the ideal of "liberal," for both historical and ideological reasons. But these two ideals are logically separable. It is possible to have a trading regime that is slightly less liberal in that it tolerates some explicitly managed trade but is also more genuinely multilateral than the present system in which various subterfuges invariably involve bilateral side deals that do real harm both to the multilateral norms and to the flow of commerce.

There is also the question of overall balance in the trading system. Here, major nations with chronic trade surpluses need to be regarded as free riders. When a nation runs a chronic surplus, it produces more goods than it consumes. That allows the surplus nation to enjoy the benefits of a rather tight fiscal and monetary policy—low rates of interest and inflation—without suffering from a high unemployment rate, because that unemployment is exported. It means, in turn, that the surplus nation's domestic industry has lower capital costs than its competitors, which is likely to lead to a higher rate of productivity growth and hence to exacerbate the imbalance. Surplus nations are a source of exported austerity; they force other nations to depress demand to reduce their current-account imbalances.

Keynes had the right answer. Incentives should be structured into the international monetary and trading systems to encourage surplus nations to expand both their economies and their markets for imports. One approach would be to "tax" nations with chronic surpluses and to have the tax capitalize Third World development and refinancing funds. The Super-301 approach is another remedy. But skeptics are right to be somewhat wary of this remedy, because it makes the United States the aggrieved party, when in fact the aggrieved party ought to be the trading system as a whole.

Here again, if the United States can let go of the twin ideas that the trading system is its special responsibility and that the only defensible set of rules for that system are Ricardian ones, then the United States will paradoxically be in a better position to bargain for systemwide reciprocity, based on the principles of roughly balanced benefits and roughly balanced trading accounts. The European Community proposed something like this standard for the Uruguay Round, but the United States rejected it as smacking too much of managed trade.

With a balance-of-benefits approach, there are several tests of whether a particular nation is playing fair. Over time, it must have overall rough balance in its trade accounts. If it is a party to one of the specific managed-trade arrangements outlined above, it must honor them. And its overall pattern of departures from free trade—such as market closings, subsidies, and cartels— must not exceed some negotiated norm. The scheme for holding nations accountable must be elevated to systemwide accountability rather than nation-by-nation retaliation; that would be a real gain for multilateralism. If, for example, Japan is party to a steel arrangement that requires it to open 25 percent of its markets to steel imports and it fails to comply, there should be some automatic consequence imposed by the GATT and not by the United States government (which is worried about military bases). A logical consequence would be that other nations close their 25 percent import markets to Japanese steel.

This essay necessarily treats the subject partly from a systemic perspective—how a managed-trade system could work while still providing the benefits of relatively open commerce and competition. It is also worth dwelling on the United States national interest in such a system. Because of its devotion to the GATT, the United States typically regards all departures from liberal trade as short-term tactical expedients, to be unilaterally given up as soon as possible. By recognizing that managed trade is sometimes the best available option, the United States will be better prepared to differentiate short-term tactical maneuvers from long-term strategic economic goals.

Some Americans willing to embrace a modest dose of planning but skeptical of mercantilism have posed the choice as "protectionism" versus "adjustment."[12] Supposedly, protection means keeping other people's products out, and adjustment means temporary restraints while labor and capital are redirected to "higher value added" sectors, using the policy tools of reskilling workers and perhaps discreetly allocating some capital or subsidizing research. The trouble with this high-sounding middle ground is twofold. First, it does not indicate what to do when other nations' mercantilism pushes the United States out of industries where it would like to maintain some self-sufficiency (steel happens to be a very high value-added industry) and where United States industry is actually or potentially very competitive. Second, while professing to reject laissez-faire purism, it in fact embraces most of the Ricardian shibboleths about trade.

TOWARD A MIXED SYSTEM

Trade theory now holds that the location of production in manufactures is not necessarily dictated by inherent comparative advantages. In an imperfect world, national policies can and do capture or create advantages. Substantial

trade in which cheap labor, climate, or the presence of natural resources significantly affect relative production costs still proceeds along Ricardian lines. But
semiconductors, for example, will be produced most efficiently wherever the
best technology has been developed and applied. This is not only true for high-
tech products; German firms have successfully applied advanced production
technology to the textile industry and remain competitive in global markets
on the basis of efficient capital rather than cheap labor.

Politically, the United States has pursued free trade, not because it is
necessarily economically optimal either for the United States or for the world
economy (though it has convinced itself that it is), but because liberal trade
is a logical imperative if one cares to play the role of hegemon. This made
sense in the early postwar period, when as the leading nation the United States
gained from free trade because its industry was dominant and its products
were superior. But America's system goals as hegemon and its national goals
as an economy are no longer identical. In order to maintain its hegemonic
role, the United States has tolerated asymmetries in the trading system and
contorted its domestic responses to the pressures of trade in a fashion that has
done serious harm to the United States domestic economy, as well as to the
sustainability of the global trading system.

Laissez-faire fails, either as an empirical description of what is or as a
normative ideal for what should be, on several grounds. Contrary to classical
economics, economies are not self-regulating. History shows that purely private economic forces, left to their own devices, wreak social havoc, distributive
injustice, and economic instability, which in turn produce political consequences that are far worse than a preventive dose of economic management.
It is not even clear that free markets optimize outcomes in the narrow sense
of allocative efficiency.

However, to acknowledge that laissez-faire is a false lodestar and that the
costs of a hegemonic role have become economically unsustainable for the
United States is not to know precisely what a mixed system ought to look
like. It is tricky enough to design a mixed system within national borders,
where sovereignty is a settled question. A mixed system is far more difficult
to fashion across national frontiers, in a realm where political sovereignty is
widely dispersed. Clearly, a mixed system is far messier than a system of
perfectly free trade—though the fairer comparison is with the existing system,
which is also highly messy. And even if one could design an ideal system
to regulate a global mixed economy, there remains the political problem of
negotiating one's way from here to there.

In the United States trade debate, there has been a remarkable confusion
of ends with means and of goals with tactics. Incredibly, advocates of tactical
hardball aimed at opening closed markets overseas find themselves accused of
sabotaging "free trade"—as if enforcing fair play among all trading partners
were a betrayal of the principle. Thus, in discussing managed alternatives to
free trade, one needs to clarify when these are merely tactical responses to
other nations' refusal to honor free-trade norms, as the "Super-301" provision
of the 1988 Trade Act is held to be, versus economic-development initiatives

that make sense in their own terms. Because of the widespread support among American conservatives for laissez-faire, domestically as well as globally, departures from Ricardian trade are usually defended only in tactical terms and seldom as necessary measures of domestic industrial development.

This essay assumes that departures from Ricardian trade in most countries are seldom merely tactical. Moreover, there are sectors in which managed trade makes sense to achieve stabilization, to enhance productive innovation, and to get nations to operate according to rules that are at least universal and reciprocal, if not Ricardian. The United States should not manage trade in, say, semiconductors merely as a lever to win concessions that move the entire system toward freer semiconductor trade. For the moment, retaining and restoring United States capacity in that crucial sector take priority over liberalization of markets as a trade-system goal, especially if America's major trading partners insist that they wish to develop and maintain their own semiconductor capacity. It is not helpful to disguise that goal as a tactic aimed to make Japan "play fair" and open its market to products that the United States may no longer make, thanks to earlier Japanese mercantilism.

On the other hand, there may be industries and moments when nations conclude that the sum total of interventionist subsidies and other market manipulations are imposing total costs that exceed benefits and may wish to negotiate reciprocal limits on such subsidies and greater mutual market access. Agriculture—in which trade does take place more nearly according to comparative advantages—is a case in point. One must also be clear about whether allowing room for industrial policy and complementary managed trade is to be understood as a unilateral attempt to capture advantage at the expense of other nations or whether managed trade can have positive-sum benefits for the system as a whole in the form of technological innovation, stabilization, and diffusion of productive wealth. To the extent that the United States wishes to remain an influential and well-behaved citizen of the trading system (though perhaps not its hegemon), it does not wish to revert to Japan-like unilateralism.

TRADE POLICY IN THE NATIONAL INTEREST

Much of the debate about free trade, managed trade, industrial policy, and so forth is confused by implied conceptions of the "national interest." From the perspective of traditional economic liberalism, questions of national interest are limited to narrow military and geopolitical security. There is also a supposed abstract and generalized consumer interest in free trade, which is treated in isolation from the influence of trade on domestic productive employment. To the extent that an open trading system wins friends for the United States, liberal trade complements traditional national-security goals. In this conception, there is no room for an economic national interest defined in terms of industrial objectives, nor are there geopolitical economic goals beyond those that supposedly flow naturally from free markets. By definition, the freest possible market yields results that are "natural" and hence optimal. Even if other trading nations violate those norms, the United States still allegedly gains both economic and geopolitical advantage by practicing liberal trade. The possibility of a national interest colliding with Ricardian trading norms is thus neatly excluded by definition.

This perspective, however, begs several questions. In practice, one can identify several concrete goals for the United States economy, which do not necessarily result from a conventional free-trade environment—particularly when that environment is lopsided. These goals include full employment at decent wages, rapid productivity growth, rising levels of real income distributed equitably, retention of technological leadership in a broad spectrum of major industries, maintenance of a skilled work force, and so on.

It is conventional to argue that "we" must do this or that for the economy to thrive, but it is not always clear to whom "we" refers. For example, the interests of American-based banks and multinational corporations, which are key advocates of liberal trade, are not always identical to the goals of high and rising living standards for the American people and the maintenance of technological leadership within the United States. The relative merits of different approaches to trade policy need to be weighed against true national objectives (rather than narrow corporate ones), and in the context of other United States foreign-policy objectives, with which trade objectives sometimes compete.

We now have come full circle to the aspirations of the early postwar regime: the ceding of some national economic sovereignty to supranational public authority, the better to permit individual nations to operate mixed economies at home. In the late 1940s, this vision stalled because the real supranational authority was the hegemonic supremacy of the United States. But in the 1970s and 1980s, as national sovereignty has been ceded to global private capital and the hegemonic position of the United States has weakened, the American protectorate became no longer entirely viable. The fact that the two emerging rival centers of economic power—the EC and Japan—are both more comfortable with a mix of mercantilism and liberalism makes it that much more likely that a mixed trading system is the only durable alternative and that the rules should acknowledge the reality. This essay has suggested that, by adjusting its hegemonic ambitions to its economic capacity and by modifying its concomitant devotion to laissez-faire as a standard for itself and others, the United States will be in a better position both to work toward a sustainable, multilateral trading regime and to define and advance its own national interests. But, obviously, ceasing to play the hegemonic role will involve not only a change of habits; it will involve a loss of perquisites.

Readers should not mistake this observation for the wish that the United States play a less influential global role. There was a time when the United States loomed so large that it could play the role of hegemon and serve its national economic interests as well as its goals for the trading system and for the Western alliance. And for the most part, the United States threw its economic weight around in a remarkably enlightened fashion. The issue is not whether it would be nice to maintain that role; the relative shrinkage of the

United States economy makes such a role unsustainable. The issue is how best to adjust to the new realities.

Playing a different role will require a drastic revision of some foreign-policy fundamentals. If the United States ceases to function as hegemon, it will no longer be able to confer economic benefit in exchange for geopolitical foreign-policy goals. It will be more subject to the discipline of membership in a global system. It may have to defer more to European and Japanese wishes with regard to East–West issues, Third World debt, arms control, the environment, and other policy areas where the United States has generally expected that if its views do not always carry the day at least they frame the agenda. It may have to defer more to Third World interests, too. All of this might even be salutary. Fortuitously, these shifts are also happening just as the Soviet Union is becoming more respectful of pluralism.

The scholars who investigate the logic of hegemony and global economic stability are divided on the question of whether a stable global order is possible on the absence of a hegemonic nation. The interwar period is a chilling precedent. But clinging to the illusion of American hegemony in a laissez-faire world will only weaken the United States economy and the global economic order. The United States is no longer preeminent, and most other nations favor a mixed form of capitalism rather than laissez-faire. The United States had better work toward the goal of a stable, pluralist system because all the economic indicators suggest that a pluralist world now exists.

ENDNOTES

1. Peter Katzenstein, *Small States in World Markets* (Ithaca, N.Y.: Cornell University Press, 1985), chapters 1 and 2; and Peter Gourevitch, *Politics in Hard Times* (Ithaca, N.Y.: Cornell University Press, 1986), chapters 5 and 6.
2. Pat Choate and Juyne Linger, "Taylored Trade: Dealing with the World as It Is," *Harvard Business Review* (January–February 1988), 91.
3. Defense Science Board Report to the Secretary of Defense (Fuhrman Report), Washington, D.C., October 1988.
4. See David Ricardo, *Principles of Political Economy and Taxation*, 3d ed. (1821; Cambridge: Cambridge University Press, 1951).
5. See Eli Heckscher, "The Effect of Foreign Trade on the Distribution of Income" (1919), in *Readings in the Theory of International Trade*, ed. Howard S. Ellis and Lloyd A. Metzler (Philadelphia: Blackiston, 1950); and Bertil Ohlin, *Interregional and International Trade* (Cambridge, Mass.: Harvard University Press, 1933).
6. See Paul A. Samuelson, "International Factor-Price Equalisation Once Again" (1949), in *International Trade: Selected Readings*, 2d ed., ed. Jagdish Bhagwati (Cambridge, Mass.: MIT Press, 1987).
7. See Klaus Stegemann, "Policy Rivalry among Industrial States: What Can We Learn from Models of Strategic Trade Policy?," *International Organization* 43 (Winter 1989): 75–76.
8. See James A. Brander, "Rationales for Strategic Trade and Industrial Policy," in *Strategic Trade Policy and the New International Economics*, ed. Paul Krugman (Cambridge, Mass.: MIT Press, 1986), 23–46; Barbara J. Spencer, "What Should Trade Policy Target?," in ibid., 69–90; and Stegemann, 75.

9. See Lawrence Katz and Lawrence R. Summers, "Can Inter-Industry Wage Differentials Justify Strategic Trade Policy?" (Cambridge, Mass.: National Bureau of Economic Research, September 1988).
10. William Roth (Speech to Chicago Council on Foreign Relations, 11 April 1989).
11. Paul Krugman, "Is Free Trade Passé?," *Journal of Economic Perspectives* 1 (Fall 1987): 143.
12. Robert B. Reich, "Beyond Free Trade," *Foreign Affairs* 61 (Spring 1983): 733–804; and Gary Clyde Hufbauer and Howard F. Rosen, *Trade Policies for Troubled Industries* (Washington, D.C.: Institute for International Economics, 1986).

DISCUSSION QUESTIONS

1. What is "free trade"? Can you give an example? Can you think of some examples where the concept of "free trade" is ambiguous?
2. What is the intention of various "protectionist" measures? How well do you think they accomplish their stated purposes?
3. Some critics of free trade believe that protectionist measures conceal a political agenda. How important is domestic politics in controlling multinational trade agreements? Is this appropriate?
4. Should the United States enter in multilateral free-trade zones in, say, the Americas? Should the United States pursue bilateral agreements with other industrialized nations, such as Germany and Japan? Why or why not?
5. What is the relationship between trade policy and industrial policy? How do the two relate? How do they differ?
6. Do you think free trade will improve or diminish environmental quality in developing nations over the long run? Why? What will be the likely impact on the environmental quality of developed nations?
7. Economists tend to focus on the overall impacts of free trade. Who do you think is helped by free trade? What individuals are harmed?

ADDITIONAL READINGS

Bhagwati, Jagdish N. *Protectionism* (Cambridge, Mass.: MIT Press, 1988).
Bhagwati, Jagdish N. *The World Trading System at Risk* (Princeton, N.J.: Princeton University Press, 1991).
Bhagwati, Jagdish N. "The Case for Free Trade." *Scientific American* (November 1993).
Daly, Herman E. "The Perils of Free Trade." *Scientific American* (November 1993).
Gaster, Robin. "Protectionism with Purpose: Guiding Foreign Investment." *Foreign Policy* (Fall 1992).
Koechlin, Timothy, and Mehrene Larudee. "The High Cost of NAFTA." *Challenge* (September–October 1992).
Krugman, Paul. *The Age of Diminished Expectations* (Cambridge, Mass.: MIT Press, 1990).
Krugman, Paul. *Geography and Trade* (Cambridge, Mass.: MIT Press, 1991).
Krugman, Paul. "The Narrow and Broad Arguments for Free Trade." *American Economic Review* (May 1993).

Kuttner, Robert. *The End of Laissez-Faire: National Purpose and the Global Economy After the Cold War* (New York: Knopf, 1991).

McKenzie, Richard B. "American Competitiveness—Do We Really Need to Worry?" *The Public Interest* (Winter 1988).

Morris, Robert. "An Open Trade Alternative for the Next President." *The Brookings Review* (Summer 1988).

Mussa, Michael. "Making the Practical Case for Freer Trade." *American Economic Review* (May 1993).

Nau, Henry R. *The Myth of America's Decline* (New York: Oxford University Press, 1988).

Nivola, Pietro S. "More Like Them? The Political Feasibility of Strategic Trade Policy." *The Brookings Review* (Spring 1991).

Prestowitz, Clyde. "More Trade Is Better Than Free Trade." *Technology Review* (April 1991).

Reich, Robert B. "We Need a Strategic Trade Policy." *Challenge* (July—August 1990).

Reich, Robert B. *The Work of Nations: Preparing Ourselves for 21st-Century Capitalism* (New York: Knopf, 1991).

Stelzer, Irwin M. "The New Protectionism." *National Review* (March 16, 1992).

Tyler, Gus. "The Myth of Free Trade: Is It Part of the 'Moral Law'?" *Dissent* (Spring 1988).

Wendt, Timothy. "Strategic Trade: Protecting American Economic and Political Interests." *APS: Proceedings of the Academy of Political Science* (1990).

12
IMMIGRATION POLICY
"Should the United States Allow Substantial Increases in Immigration?"

Although Ambrose Bierce's *Devil's Dictionary* defines an immigrant as "an unenlightened person who thinks one country better than another," immigration has been seen as a vehicle for advancement by many. Immigration policy around the world is a contentious debate that mixes issues of race, class, economic security, culture, and xenophobia. Turkish immigrants in Germany, Korean immigrants in Japan, Mexican and Haitian immigrants in the United States, Sudanese immigrants in Egypt (not to mention Kurds, Palestinians, gypsies, and others without homelands) have all suffered from their status as "outsiders." But alongside the social unrest and violence that sometimes accompany immigrants' experiences are great success stories, perhaps nowhere more evident than the social, economic, and cultural vibrancy that immigrants have provided in the United States. But while many citizens reflect approvingly on the hard work ethic embodied by immigrants in the past, there is increasing skepticism and concern that immigration no longer provides benefits to the United States that it once did. Indeed, a recent public opinion poll conducted in New York State found that fewer than half of the respondents believed that the welcoming inscription of the Statue of Liberty—"Bring me your tired, your poor, your huddled masses yearning to breathe free"—was still relevant today. Perhaps more surprising, this applied equally to the immigrants surveyed as well.

The number and composition of immigrants to the United States have changed dramatically over the past century. Both in absolute numbers and percentage of the U.S. population, immigration was at its peak between 1901 and 1910, when 8.8 million immigrants entered the United States, more than one for every 100 natives. Immigration rates dropped precipitously during the Great Depression decade of 1931 to 1940 and rose only slowly during the next decade; in both decades, fewer than one immigrant per thousand natives entered the country.[1] Rising in number by more than one million per decade thereafter, immigration exceeded 6 million in the 1980s, yet still represented fewer than three immigrants per thousand natives.

Because of changes in immigration policy as well as changes in the political and economic conditions of other countries, the origins of immigrants to the United States have changed markedly as well. In 1907, when the single largest influx of immigrants (1.285 million) was admitted, over 93 percent (1.200 million) came from Europe (including eastern Europe); nearly half of all immigrants were from Italy and central Europe, and only about 42,000 came from the Americas. By 1989, of the nearly 1.1 million immigrants, not one European country was in the top ten countries of origin of U.S. immigrants. Instead, immigrants hailed from, in descending order, Mexico, El Salvador, the Philippines, Vietnam, Korea, China, India, the Dominican Republic, Jamaica, and Iran. European immigrants comprised less than 8 percent of the total, compared with slightly more than 8 percent from the Caribbean and over 9 percent from Central America.

The focus of most public and media attention has been on illegal immigration. Immigrants generally enter illegally in one of two ways: crossing the border illegally or overstaying temporary work, student, or tourist visas. Most Americans think of the "immigrant problem" as stemming from illegals from Mexico and Central America crossing surreptitiously into California or Texas or of Haitians and Cubans in dangerously crowded boats pouring into southern Florida. Some commentators, however, suggest that more significant issues relating to the welfare of the United States stem from legal immigration. More than 6 million immigrants were admitted legally in the 1980s alone, compared with an estimated 3–4 million illegal immigrants living in the United States (estimates vary widely, however). (Of course, individuals emigrate from the United States as well, at a rate of approximately 160,000 per year; indeed, nearly a third of immigrants at some point emigrate.) Annually, approximately 750,000 immigrants enter legally, compared with an estimated 100,000 to 300,000 illegal entries. Despite the emphasis on immigration policy in the past decade, the percentage of the population that is foreign-born has declined from 13 percent in 1920 to 7 percent today. Some suggest that excessive attention has focused on illegal immigration and too little on the far more numerous legal immigrants, particularly their job skills.

U.S. immigration policy has undergone significant changes, and these changes have propelled many of the shifts in immigrant composition outlined above. Early responses to immigration in the late nineteenth century reflect xenophobic impulses and attempts to exclude certain classes of individuals, such as prostitutes, convicts, those with communicable diseases like tuberculosis, political radicals, and for the most part Asians. Some states even imposed head taxes on immigrants before the Supreme Court struck down their constitutionality.[2] A national-origins quota system began in the 1920s, where the national composition of immigrants was based on the composition of the U.S. population; for example, if 5 percent of U.S. citizens were of Polish origin, then 5 percent of immigrants could be admitted from Poland. The 1965 amendments to the Immigration and Nationality Act finally dropped the national-origins quota system, which effectively gave preference to European immigrants, and instead substituted a policy where 80 percent of numerically limited visas were dedicated to close relatives of U.S. citizens; the other 20 percent were to be allocated based on labor skills. (Further, an unlimited number of people could enter the United States if they were spouses, parents, or minor children of U.S. citizens.) This led to dramatic increases in the number of Asian and Latin American immigrants. In addition, as economist George Borjas points out, "only 4 percent of legal immigrants admitted in 1987 actually entered the United States because of their skills."[3] (This is not to say, of course, that 96 percent of immigrants were unskilled, only that their basis of admission was a criterion other than skill.) The Immigration Reform and Control Act of 1986 was directed toward the problem of illegal immigration. It granted amnesty to aliens in the United States since 1982 and to agricultural workers and made hiring illegal aliens unlawful. The Immigration Act of 1990 expanded the number of immigrants who could enter the United States by approximately 40 percent and focused more attention on attracting those with greater skills, particularly by permitting more employer-sponsored entrants.

The issue of immigration leads to numerous policy disputes—such as whether English should be the official language in schools—but perhaps the most contentious part of the debate centers around the degree to which immigrants displace native workers, causing unemployment and declining wages. Because immigrants are not distributed uniformly across the country— more than three-fourths live in California, Florida, Illinois, New Jersey, New York, and Texas, with an even higher percentage when illegals are added—political debates occur most often in large immigrant cities or in the states listed. Immigration opponents argue that with a fixed job base, new workers, particularly immigrants willing to work for lower wages, will push natives out of jobs or at a minimum will force natives to reduce wage demands in order to keep their jobs. Besides the wage–job drain, immigration opponents complain of the high costs of social support programs, such as public schools and health care, that exhaust the resources of native taxpayers, particularly in the large cities and border states where immigrants congregate. This not only serves to raise the cost to taxpayers, but dilutes the political willingness of taxpayers to finance increasingly expensive social welfare programs intended to benefit the native poor.

Immigration supporters counter that far from reducing jobs, immigrants create them. Supporters point to studies showing that not only are immigrants more likely than natives to start new businesses, and therefore to hire additional workers directly, but that immigrants also create jobs through spending on goods and services. More immigrants mean greater needs for basics such as shoes, food, and housing, which translate into additional native jobs to provide for immigrants' demands. As it turns out, most studies show that immigration has little net impact either on the wages of native workers or the unemployment rate. Even in the case of the Mariel boatlift from Cuba, when 125,000 largely unskilled Cuban exiles descended on the Miami labor market virtually overnight, researchers found that there was no discernible impact on the wages or the unemployment rate of even unskilled workers, either white or nonwhite. Further, supporters of increased immigration concede that immigrants may drain local resources in providing education and health care services, but that overall immigrants pay more in taxes than they receive in public services. The problem is that federal taxes comprise the bulk of tax receipts from immigrants, forcing localities to bear the economic burden of providing for immigrants' needs with little federal support.

Views on immigration do not always fall neatly along an ideological spectrum. Prominent conservatives variously support and oppose greater immigration, and the same can be said of liberals. A third view focuses not on the absolute numbers of immigrants, but on their job skills and educational background. This group holds that by allowing immigrants to enter the United States based only on familial relations (and not, for example, based on job skills or educational achievement), the United States is losing out in the worldwide competition for skilled labor to foreign economic competitors like Australia and Canada, which award immigration on a merit-based point system. The focus of reform, these adherents argue, should be on improving the job-skill composition of immigrants rather than on the number of immigrants per se. Supporters of current policy counter that immigration based on family connections provides immigrants with important social and economic connections that can speed their entrance into the labor market and social milieu. Economists Julian Simon of the University of Maryland and Vernon Briggs of Cornell University take up the debate below.

Endnotes

1. U.S. Department of Commerce, Bureau of the Census, *Historical Statistics of the United States: Colonial Times to 1970* (Washington, D.C.: U.S. Government Printing Office, 1975); U.S. Department of Commerce, Bureau of the Census, *Statistical Abstract of the United States, 1993* (Washington, D.C.: U.S. Government Printing Office, 1993).
2. George J. Borjas, *Friends or Strangers* (New York: Basic Books, 1990).
3. Ibid., p. 32. This section draws heavily on Borjas's work and that of Peter Schuck, "The Great Immigration Debate," *The American Prospect* (Fall 1990), pp. 100–118.

YES

The Case for Greatly Increased Immigration

Julian L. Simon

By increasing somewhat the flow of immigrants—from about 600,000 to about 750,000 admissions per year—the immigration legislation passed by Congress late in 1990 will improve the standard of living of native-born Americans. The bill represents a sea change in public attitude toward immigration; it demonstrates that substantially increasing immigration is politically possible now. That's all good news, and we should celebrate it.

The bad news is that the legislation does not *greatly* increase immigration. The new rate is still quite low by historical standards. A much larger increase in numbers—even to, say, only half the rate relative to population size that the United States accepted around the turn of the century—would surely increase our standard of living even more.

The political problem for advocates of immigration is to avoid the letdown to be expected after the passage of this first major legal-immigration bill in a quarter-century. And since the new law seems to contemplate additional legislation (by providing for a commission to collect information on immigration), it is important to educate the public about how immigration benefits the nation as well as the immigrants.

Increased immigration presents the United States with an opportunity to realize many national goals with a single stroke. It is a safe and sure path—open to no other nation—to achieve all of these benefits: 1) a sharply increased rate of technological advance, spurred by the addition of top scientific talent from all over the world; 2) satisfaction of business's demand for the labor that the baby-bust generation makes scarce; 3) reduction of the burden that retirees impose upon the ever-shrinking cohort of citizens of labor-force age, who must support the Social Security System; 4) rising tax revenues—resulting from the increase in the proportion of workers to retirees—that will provide the only painless way of shrinking and perhaps even eliminating the federal deficit; 5) improvement in our competitive position vis-á-vis Japan, Europe, and the rest of the world; 6) a boost to our image abroad, stemming from immigrants' connections with their relatives back home, and from the remittances that they send back to them; and 7) not least, the opportunity given to additional people to enjoy the blessings of life in the United States.

All the U.S. need do to achieve these benefits is further to relax its barriers against skilled immigrants. Talented and energetic people want to come here. Yet we do not greatly avail ourselves of this golden opportunity, barring the door to many of the most economically productive workers in the world.

If immigration is such an across-the-board winner, why aren't we welcoming skilled and hardworking foreigners with open arms? These are some of the reasons: 1) The public is ignorant of the facts to be presented here; it therefore charges immigrants with increasing unemployment, abusing welfare programs, and lowering the quality of our work force. 2) Various groups fear that immigrants would harm their particular interests; the groups are less concerned with the welfare of the country as a whole. 3) Well-organized lobbies oppose immigration, which receives little organized support. 4) Nativism, which may or may not be the same as racism in any particular case, continues to exert an appeal.

THE DIMENSIONS OF PRESENT-DAY IMMIGRATION

The most important issue is the total number of immigrants allowed into the United States. It is important to keep our eyes fixed on this issue, because it tends to get obscured in emotional discussions of the desirability of reuniting families, the plight of refugees, the geographic origin and racial composition of our immigrant population, the needs of particular industries, the illegality of some immigration, and so on.

The Federation for American Immigration Reform (FAIR)—whose rhetoric I shall use as illustration—says that "[i]mmigration to the United States is at record levels." This claim is simply false: Figure 12.1 shows the absolute numbers of legal immigrants over the decades. The recent inflow clearly is far below the inflow around the turn of the century—even though it includes the huge number of immigrants who took advantage of the 1986 amnesty; they are classified as having entered in 1989, although most of them actually arrived before 1980. Even the inclusion of illegal immigrants does not alter the fact that there is less immigration now than in the past.

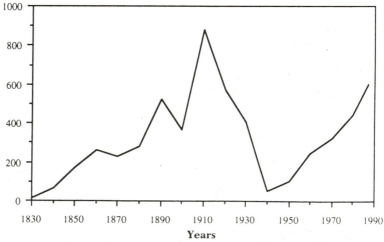

FIGURE 12.1. **Annual Number of U.S. Immigrants (in 1,000s)**

Economically speaking, more relevant than these absolute numbers is the volume of immigration as a proportion of the native population, as shown in Figure 12.2. Between 1901 and 1910 immigrants arrived at the yearly rate of 10.4 per thousand U.S. population, whereas between 1981 and 1987 the rate was only 2.5 percent of the population. So the recent flow is less than a fourth as heavy as it was in that earlier period. Australia and Canada admit three times that many immigrants as a proportion of their populations.

Another way to think about the matter: in 1910, 14.6 percent of the population was born abroad, but in 1980 less than 6 percent of us were. Not only is the present stock of immigrants much smaller proportionally than it was earlier, but it also is a small proportion considered by itself. We tend to think of ourselves as a "nation of immigrants," but less than one out of fifteen people now in the U.S. was born abroad, including those who arrived many years ago. Who would guess that the U.S. has a smaller share of foreign-born residents than many countries that we tend to think have closed homogeneous populations—including Great Britain, Switzerland, France, and Germany? We are a nation not of immigrants, but rather of the descendants of immigrants.

Furthermore, the absorption of immigrants is much easier now than it was in earlier times. One has only to read the history of the Pilgrims in Plymouth Colony to realize the enormity of the immediate burden that each new load of immigrants represented. But it is the essence of an advanced society that it can more easily handle material problems than can technically primitive societies. With every year it becomes easier for us to make the material adjustments that an increase in population requires. That is, immigrant assimilation becomes ever less of an economic problem—all the more reason that the proportion of immigrants now seems relatively small, compared with what it was in the past.

Unfortunately, despite recent changes favoring skilled immigrants, our present admissions policy remains largely nepotistic. Most visas are granted

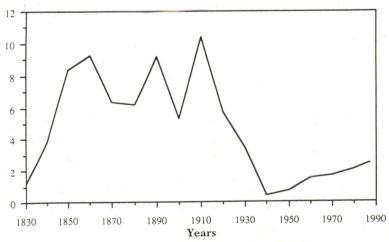

FIGURE 12.2. **Immigrants to the U.S. per 1,000 Inhabitants**

to foreigners who have family connections here. Even with the 1990 legislation, the U.S. will admit only about 110,000 people—perhaps 20 percent of all immigrants—on the basis of their job skills. Compare our policy with Australia's, which admits almost 50 percent of its immigrants according to "economic" criteria, and only 30 percent as relatives of citizens. Many of those whom we admit via family preferences also are skilled, of course, but it would be beneficial to us as well as fair to deserving foreigners to admit more people on the basis of merit alone. Indeed, George Borjas of the University of California at Santa Barbara has presented evidence that the economic "quality" of immigrants with given levels of education has declined in recent decades—though the magnitude of the decline remains controversial; the likeliest explanation for the decline is an increase in the proportion of immigrants who are admitted as relatives rather than on their merits alone. On the other hand, Harriet Duleep of the U.S. Civil Rights Commission has recently shown that despite the different admissions policies of the U.S. and Canada (which uses a point system), immigration affects the economies of the two countries similarly—probably because families carefully evaluate the economic potential of relatives before deciding to bring them in.

For years, phony inflated estimates of the stocks and flows of illegal immigrants were bandied about by opponents of immigration in order to muddy the waters. Since the 1986 Simpson-Mazzoli law's amnesty we know that the numbers are actually quite modest, much lower than even the "mainstream" estimates cited in the press. So that scarce no longer serves as an effective red herring for opponents of immigration.

MALTHUSIAN AND OTHER OBJECTIONS

Now let us consider the costs and benefits of immigration—even though economic issues may not be the real heart of the matter, often serving only as a smoke screen to conceal the true motives for opposition. Only thus can one explain why the benefits of immigration do not produce more open policies. Because opponents of immigration wield economic argument to justify their positions, however, we must consider their assertions.

Malthusian objections to immigration begin with "capital dilution." The supposed "law of diminishing returns"—which every economics text explains should not be thought of as a law—causes output per worker to fall. The "law" is so marvelously simple, direct, and commonsensical that it easily seduces thought—especially among academics, for whom such abstractions are bread and butter. Its simplicity also makes the Malthusian notion excellent fare for the family newspaper. In contrast, the arguments that demonstrate the inapplicability of Malthusian capital dilution in the context of immigration are relatively complex and indirect. As a consequence, simple—though incorrect— Malthusianism easily attracts adherents.

Nowadays, however, the most important capital is human capital—education and skills, which people own themselves and carry with them—rather than capitalist-supplied physical capital. The bugaboo of production capital has been laid to rest by the experience of the years since World War II, which taught economists that, aside from the shortest-run considerations, physical capital does not pose a major constraint to economic growth. It is human capital that is far more important in a country's development. And immigrants supply their own human capital.

The main real cost that immigration imposes on natives is the extra capital needed for additional schools and hospitals. But this cost turns out to be small relative to benefits, in considerable part because we finance such construction with bond issues, so that we operate largely on a pay-as-you-go basis. Immigrants therefore pay much of their share.

The supposed cost that most captures the public's imagination, of course, is welfare payments. According to popular belief, no sooner do immigrants arrive than they become public charges, draining welfare money from the American taxpayers, and paying no taxes.

Solid evidence gives the lie to this charge. In an analysis of Census Bureau data I found that, aside from Social Security and Medicare, about as much money is spent on welfare services and schooling for immigrant families as for citizens. When programs for the elderly are included, immigrant families receive far *less* in public services than natives. During the first five years in the U.S., the average immigrant family receives $1,400 in welfare and schooling (in 1975 dollars), compared with the $2,300 received by the average native family. The receipts gradually become equal over several decades. Arthur Akhbari of St. Mary's College in Canada has shown that recent Canadian data produce almost identical results. And Duleep's finding that the economic results of Canadian and U.S. immigration are quite similar, despite the different admissions systems, adds weight to the conclusion that U.S. immigrants pay much more in taxes than they receive in benefits.

Of course there must be some systematic abuses of the welfare system by immigrants. But our legislative system is capable of devising adequate remedies. Even now there are provisions in the Immigration and Naturalization Act that deny visas to aliens who are "likely to become public charges" and provide for the deportation of immigrants who have within five years after entry become public charges "from causes not affirmatively shown to have risen after entry."

As to illegal immigrants and welfare, FAIR typically says that "[t]axpayers are hurt by having to pay more for social services." Ironically, several surveys—for example, one by Sidney Weintraub and Gilberto Cardenas of the University of Texas—show that illegals are even heavier net contributors to the public coffers than legal immigrants; many illegals are in the U.S. only temporarily and are therefore without families, and they are often afraid to apply for services for fear of being apprehended. Illegals do, however, pay taxes.

Some cities and states with disproportionately high immigration do incur significant costs and complications when immigrants first arrive. They deserve sympathy and perhaps federal assistance, though officials should note that immigrants' federal taxes will later effectively pay for such temporary assistance.

THE NON-THREAT OF DISPLACED NATIVE WORKERS

The most dramatic argument against immigration—the bogeyman in the mind of organized labor, which has been its most powerful political opponents since the nineteenth century—has been that foreigners take jobs held by natives and thereby increase native unemployment. The logic is simple: if the number of jobs is fixed, and immigrants occupy some jobs, there must be fewer available jobs for natives.

In the shortest run, the demand for any particular sort of worker is indeed inflexible. Therefore, additional immigrants in a given occupation must to some degree lower wages and/or increase unemployment in that occupation. For example, the large recent influx of foreign physicians increases the competition that U.S. physicians face, lowering their earnings. But because immigrants come with a variety of skills, workers in most occupations feel little impact. And in the longer run, workers in most occupations are not injured at all.

A good-sized body of competent recent research shows that immigration does not exacerbate unemployment, even among directly competing groups; in California, for instance, immigrants have not increased unemployment among blacks and women. And the research, done by several independent scholars from a variety of angles, uses several kinds of data. For example, Stephen Moore and I systematically studied immigration's effects upon overall unemployment, by looking at the changes in unemployment in various U.S. cities that have experienced different levels of unemployment. We found that if there is displacement, it is too little to be observable.

The explanation is that immigrants not only take jobs, but also create them. Their purchases increase the demand for labor, leading to new hires roughly equal in number to the immigrant workers. Immigrants also create jobs directly by opening new businesses. A Canadian government survey of immigrants, which should also describe U.S. experience, found that almost 5 percent—ninety-one of the 1,746 males and 291 single females in its panel sample—had started businesses within their first three years in Canada. Not only did they employ themselves, but they also employed others, creating a total of 606 jobs. Thus the total of 2,037 immigrants personally created roughly 30 percent as many jobs as they collectively held. Furthermore, these numbers surely rose rapidly after the three-year study period; after one year seventy-one self-employed immigrants had created 264 jobs, compared with the ninety-one immigrant entrepreneurs and 606 jobs observed after three years.

We can interpret this result as follows: even if one native Canadian was pushed out of a preexisting job by every five immigrants—an improbably high number—this effect would be more than made up for by the new jobs, occupied by natives, created by the immigrants' businesses.

The businesses that immigrants start are at first small, of course. But surprisingly, small businesses are the most important source of new jobs. And immigrant entrepreneurs tend to succeed in a dynamic economy, because they are innovative and mobile.

Furthermore, potential immigrants are well aware of labor–market conditions in the U.S. and they tend not to come if there is little demand for their skills. Natives tend not to be harmed even in the few industries—like the restaurant and hotel businesses—in which immigrants concentrate, because natives do not want jobs in these industries. Evidence for this comes from experiments conducted by the Immigration and Naturalization Service and San Diego County. In one case, 2,154 illegal aliens were removed from jobs, but the California State Human Resources Agency had almost no success in filling the jobs with U.S. citizens.

Wages are admittedly pushed downward somewhat in industries and localities in which immigrants are concentrated. Barton Smith and Robert Newman of the University of Houston found that adjusted wages are 8 percent lower in the Texas border cities in which the proportion of Mexicans is relatively high. Much of the apparent difference is accounted for by a lower cost of living in the border cities, however. And because immigrants tend to be heterogeneous in their skills, their presence does not disproportionately affect any particular industry; and of course salaries rise in the occupations that few immigrants enter. (Indeed, if immigrants were spread evenly throughout all occupations, wages would not fall in any occupation.) At the same time, immigrants, who consume a wide variety of goods and services, increase the demand for labor across the range of occupations.

TAX PAYMENTS

If immigrants paid relatively little in taxes they might still burden natives, despite using fewer welfare services. But data on family earnings, which allow us to estimate tax payments, show that this is not at all the case.

Immigrants pay more than their share of taxes. Within three to five years, immigrant-family earnings reach and pass those of the average American family. The tax and welfare data together indicate that, on balance, an immigrant family enriches natives by contributing an average of $1,300 or more per year (in 1975 dollars) to the public coffers during its stay in the U.S. Evaluating the future stream of these contributions as one would a dam or harbor, the present value of an immigrant family—discounted at the risk-free interest rate of 3 percent—adds up to almost two years' earnings for a native family head. This means that the economic activities of an average immigrant family reduce the taxes of a native head of household enough to advance his or her possible date of retirement by two years.

Curiously, contemporary welfare-state policies render immigration more beneficial to natives than it was in earlier times when welfare was mainly voluntary. There are two main reasons why today's immigrants make net contributions to the public coffers. First, far from being tired, huddled masses, immigrants tend to come when they are young, strong, and vibrant, at the start of their work lives. For example, perhaps 46 percent of immigrants are in the prime labor-force ages of twenty to thirty-nine, compared with perhaps 26 percent of natives. And only 4 percent of immigrants are aged sixty or over, compared with about 15 percent of natives. Second, many immigrants are well educated and have well-paying skills that produce hefty tax contributions.

Because immigrants arrive in the early prime of their work lives, they ward off a major looming threat to U.S. economic well-being. This threat is the graying of the population, which means that each working native has an increasing burden of retired dependents to support. In 1900, there were five and one-half people aged twenty-five to fifty-four for each person aged sixty and above, whereas the Census Bureau projects that in the year 2000 the ratio will shrink to two and one-half to one—resulting in a burden that will be more than twice as heavy on workers.

Being predominantly youthful adults, immigrants mitigate this looming problem of more retired natives being supported by fewer workers. Indeed, immigration is the only practical way to alleviate the burden of increasing dependency that native workers would otherwise feel.

In the public sphere this means that immigrants immediately lessen the Social Security burden upon native workers. (The same holds for the defense burden, of course.) And if there is a single factor currently complicating the government's economic policies, it is the size of Social Security payments and other assistance to the aged. Immigration—and the resulting increase in tax payments by immigrants—provides the only way to reduce the federal budget deficit without making painful cuts in valued services.

BOOSTING PRODUCTIVITY

Most important in the long run is the boost that immigrants give to productivity. Though hard to pin down statistically, the beneficial impact of immigration upon productivity is likely to dwarf all other effects after these additional workers and consumers have been in the country a few years. Some of the productivity increase comes from immigrants working in industries and laboratories that are at the forefront of world technology. We benefit along with others from the contribution to world productivity in, say, genetic engineering that immigrants could not make in their home countries. More immigrants mean more workers, who will think up productivity-enhancing ideas. As Soichiro Honda (of motorcycle and auto fame) said: "Where 100 people think, there are 100 powers; if 1,000 people think, there are 1,000 powers."

It is well to remember that the development of the atomic bomb hinged on the participation of such immigrants as Enrico Fermi, John von Neumann, and Stan Ulam, among many others. Contemporary newspaper stories continue this historical saga, noting the disproportionate numbers of Vietnamese and other Asian immigrant youths who achieve distinction in competitions such as the Westinghouse Science Talent Search. Ben Wattenberg and Karl Zinsmeister of the American Enterprise Institute write that among the forty 1988 finalists, "22 were foreign-born or children of foreign-born parents: from Taiwan, China, Korea, India, Guyana, Poland, Trinidad, Canada, Peru, Iran, Vietnam, and Honduras." They also note that one-fourth of recent valedictorians and salutatorians in San Diego have been Vietnamese, and that thirteen of the seventeen public high school valedictorians in Boston in 1989 were foreign born. Sometimes it seems as if such names as Wang Computers and Steven Chen dominate our most vigorous industry.

THE BOTTOM LINE

An economist always owes the reader a cost–benefit assessment for policy analysis. So I combined the most important elements pertaining to legal immigrants with a simple macroeconomic model, making reasonable assumptions where necessary. The net effect is slightly negative for the early years, but four or five years later the net effect turns positive and large. And when we tote up future costs and benefits, the rate of "investment" return from immigrants to the citizen public is about 20 percent per annum—a good return for any portfolio.

Does all this seem to be a far-out minority view? In 1990 the American Immigration Institute surveyed prominent economists—all the ex-presidents of the American Economic Association, and then-members of the Council of Economic Advisers—about immigration. Economists ought to understand the economic effects of immigration better than others, so their views are of special interest. More than four-fifths of the respondents said that immigration has a very favorable impact on economic growth; none said that its impact is unfavorable. Almost three-fourths said that illegals have a positive economic impact. And almost all agree that recent immigrants have had the same kind of impact as immigrants in the past.

THE REAL REASONS FOR OPPOSITION

I began by citing various reasons for our failure to take in more immigrants, despite the clear-cut benefits of doing so. The first is ignorance of the benefits described above. Second is the opposition by special interests, such as organized labor (which wants to restrict competition for jobs) and ethnic groups (whose members often fear that immigration will cause their proportion of the population to decrease). The third reason is well-organized opposition to immigration and a total lack of organized support for it.

FAIR, for example, has a large budget—it amassed $2,000,000 in revenues in 1989—and a large staff. It supports letter-writing campaigns to newspapers and legislators, gets its representatives onto television and radio, and is in the rolodex of every journalist who writes on the subject. Several other organizations play a similar role. On the other side, until recently no organization advocated more immigration generally. Now at least there is the fledgling American Immigration Institute; and the de Tocqueville Institute did excellent work on immigration in 1989 and 1990, before taking on other issues.

The fourth check to immigration is nativism or racism, a motive that often lies beneath the surface of the opposition's arguments.

Rita Simon of American University, who has studied the history of public opinion toward immigrants, has found that the arguments against immigration have remained eerily identical. In the first half of the nineteenth century, Irish immigrants in New York and Boston were seen as the unassimilable possessors of all bad qualities. One newspaper wrote: "American has become the sewer into which the pollutions of European jails are emptied." Another asked: "Have we not a right to protect ourselves against the ravenous dregs of anarchy and crime, the tainted swarms of pauperism and vice Europe shakes on our shores from her diseased robes?"

The 1884 platform of the Democratic party stated its opposition to the "importation of foreign labor or the admission of servile races unfitted by habit, training, religion or kindred for absorption into the great body of our people or for the citizenship which our laws confer."

Francis Walker, Commissioner General of the Immigration Service, wrote in 1896:

> The question today is . . . protecting the American rate of wages, the American standard of living, and the quality of American citizenship from degradation through the tumultuous access of vast throngs of ignorant and brutalized peasantry from the countries of Eastern and Southern Europe.

In the 1920s the *Saturday Evening Post* also directed fear and hatred at the "new immigrants" from Southern and Eastern Europe: "More than a third of them cannot read and write; generally speaking they have been very difficult to assimilate. . . . They have been hot beds of dissent, unrest, sedition and anarchy."

Although statements like these are no longer acceptable in public, many people still privately sympathize with such views. One can see the traces in nativist codewords that accuse immigrants of "disturbing national homogeneity" and "changing our national culture."

IMPROVING OUR POLICIES

In addition to admitting more immigrants into the United States, we should also consider instituting other desirable changes in policy. Specifically, we must go further to increase the benefits that accrue to the United States from the inflow of highly educated people with high productive potential—especially people with technical skills. To its credit, the 1990 legislation will increase the flow of talented people by increasing the proportion of immigrants who are admitted because of their economic characteristics rather than their familial ties to U.S. citizens. This was worth doing to reduce nepotistic "family connections" admissions, and to treat meritorious applicants without such connections more fairly.

The new system does not greatly increase the flow of highly skilled people, however. An additional 100,000 or so immigrants will be admitted under the new provisions for economic selection; only 40,000 will be skilled people, the other 60,000 being their dependents. The overall increase in numbers admitted will yield perhaps another 30,000 highly skilled people. This is still only a small—though a most valuable—increment to our economy.

The 1990 legislation also contains a beneficial provision allowing entry to people who will invest a million dollars and create employment for ten Americans. Although this provision will not be as profitable for natives as an outright sale of the opportunity to immigrate, as permitted by some other countries, it does move in the right direction. But the new law does not go far enough; it permits entry to a maximum of only 10,000 persons per year under this provision—a piddling number by any standard.

Another policy that the U.S. might employ is simply to give permanent-resident visas to foreigners studying in the U.S. Many foreign students already find ways to remain under the present rules—about half of them students of engineering and science. And even more foreign graduates would remain if they could, which would push up our rate of progress even more.

Furthermore, if young foreigners knew that they could remain in the United States after completing their education here, more would choose to study here. This would provide multiple benefits to the United States. Given assurance that they could remain, these students could pay more realistic tuition rates than are now charged, which would benefit U.S. universities. And these increased rates would enable universities to expand their programs to serve both foreign and native students better. Best of all would be the increased number of highly competent scientific and managerial workers who would be part of the American work force.

In addition, a large number of students requires a larger number of professors. And a larger number of openings for professors, especially in such fields as engineering and science, would attract more of the world's best scientists from abroad. This would enhance the process that has brought so many foreigners who subsequently won Nobel prizes to the U.S.—to the advantage as well as the honor of this country.

POLITICAL ADVANTAGES

Political power and economic well-being are intimately related; a nation's international standing is heavily influenced by its economic situation. And today the future of any country—especially of a major country that is in the vanguard with respect to production and living standards—depends entirely on its progress in knowledge, skill, and productivity. This is more true now than in the past, because technology changes more rapidly than in earlier times. Even a single invention can speedily alter a country's economic or military future—consider, for example, the atom bomb or the computer—as no invention could in the past, even the invention of the gun. That's why immigration safely, cheaply, and surely provides the U.S. with perhaps the greatest opportunity that a country has ever had to surpass its political rivals.

And the best way for the U.S. to boost its rate of technological advance, and to raise its standard of living, is simply to take in more immigrants. To that end, I would suggest that the number of visas be increased by half a million per year for three years. If no major problems arise with that total (and there is no reason to expect a problem, since even another one or two million immigrants a year would still give us an admissions rate lower than we successfully coped with in earlier times, when assimilation was more difficult), then we should boost the number by another half-million, and so on, until unexpected problems arise.

Immigration policy presents the U.S. with an opportunity like the one that faced the Brooklyn Dodgers in 1947, before blacks played baseball on any major-league team. Signing Jackie Robinson and then Roy Campanella, at the price of antagonizing some players and club owners, put the Dodgers way ahead of the pack. In the case of immigration, unlike baseball, no other "team" can duplicate our feat, because immigrants mainly want to come here. All we need is the vision, guts, and ambition of Dodger general manager Branch Rickey. (A bit of his religious zeal mixed in would do no harm.)

Can we see our national interest clearly enough to reject unfounded beliefs that some groups will lose jobs to immigrants, and to surmount the racism that remains in our society? Or will we pay a heavy price in slower growth and lessened efficiency for maintaining our prejudices and pandering to the supposed interests of groups—organized labor, environmentalists, and others—whose misguided wishes will not benefit even them in the long run?

NO

Immigration Policy: Political or Economic?

Vernon M. Briggs Jr.

As the United States enters the last decade of the twentieth century, its labor market is in transformation. New forces that are restructuring the nation's employment patterns are altering the demand for labor. At the same time, the labor supply is in a period of rapid growth in size and unprecedented changes in composition. Assessing the evolving situation, then Secretary of Labor Elizabeth Dole proclaimed in late 1989 that the nation's labor force was "woefully inadequate to meet the changes that lie ahead." Many other knowledgeable observers have expressed similar concerns. The nature of the workforce is emerging as the number one economic issue confronting the nation. The implications extend not only to the competitiveness of the economy and to the preparedness of the labor force but, given the multiracial and multicultural makeup of the population, to the prospects for maintaining domestic tranquility.

The forces altering the nature of labor demand in the United States are the same confronting all industrialized nations. They are associated with the pace of technological change, the expansion of international trade and shifts in consumer spending preferences. Conceivably, the effects of reduced military spending may soon be added to the list. The consequences of these influences are reshaping the nation's occupational, industrial, and geographic employment patterns. Employment in most goods-producing industries and in many blue-collar occupations is declining, while it is increasing in most service industries and many white-collar occupations. Regional employment trends are extremely unbalanced, with growth generally more pronounced in urban than in rural areas and particularly strong in the Southwest and weak in the Midwest and Prairie regions.

The concurrent forces being exerted on the supply of labor, however, constitute a uniquely American experience. Over the twelve-year period ending in 1988, the U.S. labor force increased by about one-third more than the combined growth of the other nine major industrial nations of the free world (see Table 12-1). Moreover, much of the labor force growth in the other industrialized nations was in the form of increases in unemployment rather than in employment. In all cases, the growth in employment in these nations, compared with the United States, ranged from minimal to modest.

Even more significant than the rapid growth of the U.S. labor force are the differential growth rates of its component groups, depicted in Table 12-2. Women have accounted for two-thirds of the increase in workers since the mid-1970s and are projected to do the same during the 1990s. Minorities

TABLE 12-1
Changes in Labor Force, Employment, and Unemployment in 10 Industrialized Nations between 1976 and 1988 (thousands)

	Labor Force			Employment			Unemployment		
	1988	*1976*	*Change*	*1988*	*1976*	*Change*	*1988*	*1976*	*Change*
United States	121,669	96,158	25,511	114,968	88,752	26,216	6,701	7,406	−705
Canada	13,275	10,203	3,072	12,245	9,477	2,768	1,031	726	305
Australia	7,974	6,244	1,730	7,398	5,946	1,452	576	298	278
Japan	60,860	53,100	7,760	59,310	52,020	7,290	1,550	1,080	470
France	23,590	22,010	1,580	21,180	21,020	160	2,410	990	1,420
Germany	28,580	25,900	2,680	26,770	25,010	1,760	1,810	890	920
Italy	22,660	20,300	1,850	20,870	19,600	1,270	1,790	700	1,090
Netherlands	6,560	4,890	1,670	5,940	4,630	1,310	620	260	360
Sweden	4,540	4,149	391	4,467	4,083	384	73	66	7
United Kingdom	28,150	25,290	2,860	25,740	23,810	1,930	2,410	1,480	930

Note: All data for foreign nations are adjusted to approximate U.S. definitions.
Source: U.S. Department of Labor.

TABLE 12-2
Civilian Labor Force and Participation Rates by Sex, Race, and Hispanic Origin,* 1976 and 1988, and Moderate Growth Projections to 2000

Group	Participation Rate (%)			Level (in thousands)			Change (in thousands)		Percent Change		Growth Rate (%)	
	1976	1988	2000	1976	1988	2000	1976–1988	1988–2000	1976–1988	1988–2000	1976–1988	1988–2000
Total, 16 and over	61.6	65.9	69.0	96,158	121,669	141,134	25,511	19,465	26.5	16.0	2.0	1.2
Men, 16 and over	77.5	76.2	75.9	57,174	66,927	74,324	9,753	7,397	17.1	11.1	1.3	0.9
Women, 16 and over	47.3	56.6	62.6	38,983	54,742	66,810	15,759	12,068	40.4	22.0	2.9	1.7
Whites, 16 and over	61.8	66.2	69.5	84,767	104,756	118,981	19,989	14,225	23.6	13.6	1.8	1.1
Men	78.4	76.9	76.6	51,033	58,317	63,288	7,284	4,971	14.3	8.5	1.1	0.7
Women	46.9	56.4	62.9	33,735	46,439	55,693	12,704	9,254	37.7	19.9	2.7	1.5
Blacks, 16 and over	58.9	63.8	66.5	9,565	13,205	16,465	3,640	3,260	38.1	24.7	2.7	1.9
Men	69.7	71.0	71.4	5,105	6,596	8,007	1,491	1,411	29.2	21.4	2.2	1.6
Women	50.0	58.0	62.5	4,460	6,609	8,458	2,149	1,849	48.2	28.0	3.3	2.1
Asian and Other, 16 and over	62.8	65.0	65.5	1,826	3,709	5,688	1,883	1,979	103.1	53.4	6.1	3.6
Men	74.9	74.4	74.6	1,036	2,015	3,029	979	1,014	94.5	50.3	5.7	3.5
Women	51.6	56.5	57.5	790	1,694	2,659	904	965	114.4	57.0	6.6	3.8
Hispanics, 16 and over	60.7	67.4	69.9	4,279	8,982	14,321	4,703	5,339	109.9	59.4	6.4	4.0
Men	79.6	81.9	80.3	2,625	5,409	8,284	2,784	2,875	106.1	53.2	6.2	3.6
Women	44.1	53.2	59.4	1,654	3,573	6,037	1,919	2,464	116.0	69.0	6.6	4.5

* Persons of Hispanic origin may be of any race.
Source: U.S. Department of Labor.

327

(blacks, Hispanics, and Asians) are sustaining growth rates that greatly exceed those of whites, which means that their respective proportions of the labor force are increasing while the proportion of whites is shrinking. And black males continue to experience the greatest employment difficulty: black males have the lowest labor force participation rates. Blacks are the only racial or ethnic group in which the absolute number of female workers exceeds that of male workers—a pattern that, as Table 12-2 shows, is projected to worsen.

Women in general and minorities in particular (with the possible exception of Asian Americans) have had fewer opportunities to be trained, educated, or prepared for the occupations that are forecasted to increase most in the coming decade. They are disproportionately concentrated in occupations and industries already in decline or most vulnerable to decline in the near future. None of the nation's major international competitors are faced with comparable pressures to accommodate so many new job seekers or to adjust to such rapid changes in the gender and racial compositions of their respective labor forces.

HISTORIC ROLE OF IMMIGRATION POLICY

For present purposes, however, concern is about the one element that impinges on the size and diversity of the U.S. labor force and that is virtually unknown in other nations: the role of immigration. Since the mid-1960s, mass immigration has again surfaced as a distinguishing feature of life in the United States. Indeed, a recent study of contemporary American society stated that the single feature that continues to distinguish the United States from other industrialized nations is that "immigration continues to flow at a rate unknown elsewhere in the world."

With immigration currently accounting for 30–35 percent (depending on what estimate of illegal immigration is applied) of the annual growth of the U.S. labor force, it is essential to know how immigrants—regardless of their mode of entry—fit into the labor market transformation process. After all, our immigration policy is a purely discretionary act of the federal government. The flow of immigrants is one aspect of labor force size and character that public policy should be able to control and shape to serve the national interest.

In general, immigration policy prior to World War I was consistent with economic development trends and labor force requirements of the United States. Throughout its first century, the country had neither ceilings nor screening restrictions on the number and type of people permitted to enter for permanent settlement. In this preindustrial stage, the economy was dominated by agricultural production. Most jobs required little training or educational preparation. Policymakers did not need to concern themselves with human resource preparation issues. Because a vast amount of land was largely unpopulated, an unregulated immigration policy was consistent with the nation's basic labor market needs.

When the industrialization process began in earnest during the later decades of the nineteenth century, the newly introduced technology of mechanization required mainly unskilled workers to fill manufacturing jobs in the nation's expanding urban labor markets. The same can be said of the other employment growth sectors of mining, construction, and transportation. Pools of citizen workers existed who could have been incorporated to meet those needs—most notably the recently freed blacks of the former slave economies of the rural South. But mass immigration from Asia and Europe became the chosen alternative. Before long, however, immigration from China and Japan was banned in response to negative social reactions, so various ethnic groups from eastern and southern Europe became the primary source of new workers during this era.

From purely an efficiency standpoint, the mass immigration of the late nineteenth century and the first two decades of the twentieth century was also consistent with the labor market needs of the nation. Jobs created during this expansive era typically required little in the way of skill, education, literacy, or fluency in English from the workforce. The enormous supply of immigrants who came during this time generally lacked these human capital attributes but nonetheless reasonably matched the prevailing demand for labor. The technology of that period asked little in the way of human resource preparation. Available jobs required mainly blood, sweat, and tears, and most immigrants as well as most native-born workers amply provided all three.

Beginning with the outbreak of World War I, however, the nation experienced a sharp contraction in immigration. After the war, the United States imposed its first quantitative screening on the number of immigrants to be admitted. Moreover, the pervasive negative social reactions to many of the new ethnic groups also led to the adoption of overtly discriminatory qualitative restrictions. These restrictive actions were embodied in the Immigration Act of 1924 (often called the National Origins Act). Qualitative screening standards were enacted that favored immigrants from western and northern Europe, disfavored all other Europeans, banned virtually all Asians, and ignored most Africans. Immigration from the Western Hemisphere, however, was not included in the ceiling or the national origin quotas. It has only been since 1968 that Western Hemisphere immigration has been subject to prevailing immigration ceilings and their admission provisions.

In the 1920s, the expanding domestic economy was characterized by the widespread introduction of the assembly line method of production. The adoption of capital-intensive mass production techniques no longer required unlimited numbers of workers. Assembly line technology, however, still required largely unskilled workers. To meet these needs, employers had to turn to domestic labor surpluses. They found these pools of underutilized workers in the nation's massive rural economy. During the 1920s, the rural population declined for the first time. Among the new supply of workers to respond to these urban job opportunities were the native-born blacks of the rural South who finally began their exodus to the large cities of the North, the South, and the West Coast.

The depression decade of the 1930s, with its general surplus of unemployed job seekers, was followed by the war years of the 1940s, when tight labor markets caused previously existing artificial barriers to the employment of women and minority groups to weaken, providing access to a wide array of jobs that were hitherto unavailable to these domestic sources of labor. These inclusive developments occurred when even the low entry quotas of prevailing immigration laws were not being met.

The pent-up demand for products and the forced saving of the World War II era led to economic prosperity in the 1950s. During this period of general affluence, the United States was finally forced to confront the legacy of racial inequality that had plagued it since its inception. The Civil Rights movement was launched in earnest and soon spread throughout the South and elsewhere, culminating in passage of the Civil Rights Act of 1964. This legislation sustained the principle that overt racism would no longer be tolerated. It was only logical that the next step would be to purge racist practices from the nation's relations with the external world.

NONECONOMIC FOCUS OF NEW POLICY

Enactment of the Immigration Act of 1965 ended the era of using immigration for racial and ethnic discrimination. It also ushered in the era of mass immigration that has continued to this day. Virtually dormant for more than forty years, this sleeping giant from America's past was aroused. Instead of seizing the opportunity to craft a new immigration policy to meet some positive definition of the public interest, however, Congress created a policy aimed primarily at fulfilling the private interests of its legal residents. It sharply increased immigration levels and adopted a politically popular new admission system based on the concept of family reunification; 80 percent of total visas available each year were reserved for various categories of adult relatives and extended family members of American citizens. In addition, immediate family members (spouses, minor children and parents) of each adult visa holder were made exempt from all quotas and were usually admitted automatically. In other words, noneconomic considerations held sway as the guiding principle for designing the nation's revised immigration policy.

In response to mounting humanitarian pressures and difficulties in accommodating refugees under the legal immigration system, Congress passed the Refugee Act of 1980. This bill separated refugee admissions from the legal immigration system and, in the process, created a new entry route with no annual ceiling. The number of refugees admitted each year varies depending on the amount of political pressure exerted by special interest groups on the president, who has the authority to set the number of refugees to be admitted each year after a largely *pro forma* consultation with Congress. Subsequent annual figures have ranged from a low of 67,000 refugees in 1986 to a high of 217,000 refugees in 1981. The admission figure for 1991 was 131,000. Obviously, no labor market test is applied to refugee admissions. The preponderance of refugees since 1980 has been from Third World nations in Asia, the Caribbean area, and Central America. Most have been deficient in their levels of skill, education, and English language proficiency. Many have clustered together in a handful of urban enclaves.

The complex admission systems for both legal immigrants and refugees have proved easy to circumvent, however. Illegal immigration has flourished, and because of its nature, the exact number of illegal immigrants can never be known. Official estimates are that in the 1980s the flow was about 200,000 a year, but this figure is suspected of being far too low. Apprehensions—admittedly a poor indicator—have soared from 110,000 in 1965 to a high of 1.7 million in 1986. The figure for 1990 was 1,087,786. Despite four generous amnesty programs in 1986 in which a combined total of more than 3.2 million illegal immigrants were allowed to legalize their status, it is believed that there are still close to 4 million illegal immigrants in the United States and that their ranks mount by the day. Of course, illegal immigrants enter without regard to their preparation for available jobs or to the effect they might have on citizen workers with comparable skills or education. Likewise, no labor qualifications were imposed on the amnesty recipients whose entry into the labor force has now been legitimized. As with refugees, most illegal immigrants and amnesty recipients have been from less economically developed nations, and suffer deficiencies in their skills, training, education, and ability to speak English. They, too, have tended to cluster in enclaves—mainly in urban areas but also in some rural communities where labor-intensive agricultural methods prevail.

Finally, the immigration system permits certain foreign workers to be employed in the United States under specified labor market circumstances. Known as nonimmigrant workers, their numbers have been growing steadily and are now in excess of 300,000 a year. There are no annual ceilings on the total number of nonimmigrant workers who can be admitted. They are employed in a variety of occupations, ranging from agricultural workers to nurses, engineers, professors, and scientists. Most nonimmigrant workers can be admitted only if qualified citizen workers cannot be found. But typically, merely perfunctory checks are made to test for citizen availability. Supposedly the nonimmigrant workers are admitted only for temporary periods, but their visas can be extended in some cases for up to five years. The increasing dependence of U.S. employers on nonimmigrant workers is a symptom that something is seriously wrong with the current system. It implies that the legal immigration system lacks the direction and the flexibility to respond to legitimate shortages of qualified workers to fill real job vacancies.

POLICY CONTRARY TO NATIONAL WELFARE

In altering admission standards and enlarging the scale of immigration flows since 1965, no one foresaw that the U.S. economy was entering a new phase of fundamental change. Even after the new employment trends became evident, the congressional committees responsible for designing immigration policy essentially ignored them. Therefore, it can be said unequivocally that, for the first time in the nation's history, immigration policy not only is inconsistent with labor force needs but also may be counterproductive to the country's welfare.

By definition, immigration policy can influence the quantitative size of the labor force as well as the qualitative characteristics of those it admits. Currently, there is little synchronization of immigrant flows with demonstrated needs of the labor market. With widespread uncertainty as to the number of illegal immigrants, refugees and nonimmigrant workers who will enter in any given year, it is impossible to know in advance of their actual entry how many foreign-born people will annually join the U.S. labor force. Moreover, whatever skills, education, linguistic abilities, talents, or locational settlement preferences most immigrants and refugees possess are largely incidental to why they are admitted or enter.

The labor market effects of the politically driven immigration system are twofold. Some immigrant and nonimmigrant workers have human resource endowments that are quite congruent with labor market conditions currently dictated by the economy's needs, and some are desperately needed because of the appalling lack of attention paid by policymakers to the adequate preparation of citizens for that labor market. But many do not. The majority must seek employment in declining sectors of goods-producing industries (such as agriculture and light manufacturing) or low-wage sectors of the expanding service sector (like restaurants, lodgings, and retail enterprises). Such immigrants—especially those who have entered illegally—are a major reason for the revival of "sweat shop" enterprises and the upsurge in the child labor violations reported in the nation's urban centers. The revival of such Third World working conditions in many cities is nothing for America to be proud of, regardless of whether these immigrants actually displace citizen workers in exploitive work situations.

Unfortunately, many citizen workers who are among the urban working poor or underclass are also to be found in many of the same declining occupations and industries. A disproportionately high number of these citizens are minorities—especially young people and women. As these citizen groups grow in both absolute and percentage terms, the logic of fair play would say that they should have the first claim on available jobs and opportunities for employment preparation. The last thing these citizen groups need is more competition from immigrants for the declining number of low-skill jobs that provide a livable income or for the limited opportunities for training and education that are available to low-income workers.

A LEGISLATED RETREAT FROM REALITY

On the last day of its legislative session, the 101st Congress passed the Immigration Act of 1990. President Bush signed it into law on November 19, 1990. Although its terms indicate more awareness of potential labor market effects than does extant immigration law, its primary focus is on increasing the quantity of immigrants. When the new law takes effect on October 1, 1991, legal immigration will increase by more than 35 percent over present levels to 700,000 people a year. Like the law it replaces, the new law gives short shrift to the specific human capital endowments of those to be admitted or to the general labor market conditions of the U.S. economy that may prevail at any given time. Thus, the new legislation largely perpetuates the notion that immigration policy—despite its magnitude—has little responsibility for its economic consequences.

While the new law does increase the number of immigrants admitted without regard to family ties to 140,000 visas a year, the actual percentage of work-related visas to the total number of visas remains the same, 20 percent, as under the present law. Hence, there is no real change in policy focus.

Actually, the use of the 140,000 figure to indicate the number of work-related immigrants to be admitted each year is a gross overstatement of what the law actually provides. This is because the work-related slots include not only the eligible workers themselves but also their "accompanying family members." As a result, the number of actual needed workers specifically admitted under the work-related provisions will be far fewer—perhaps only one-third or less of the total annual figure of 140,000 admissions. It is likely, therefore, that the majority of those admitted under the work-related provisions will actually be admitted only because they too are family members. Moreover, any work-related slots that are not used in any given year are to be added to those slots available solely for family-related admissions.

In addition, the law introduces questionable new entry routes, especially for "investor immigrants" who can now "buy their way in." It also resurrects one of the most reprehensible features of U.S. immigration history: "diversity immigrants"—the use of national origin criteria for admission. Many Americans, for instance, will be shocked to learn that 40 percent of the 40,000 diversity visas for each of the next three years are specifically reserved for immigrants from one country—Ireland.

By any fair reading the new immigration law can only be seen as a retreat from any quest to tailor immigration policy to labor market needs.

The U.S. labor market does not face a shortage of labor *per se*. The labor force is conservatively projected to grow by an annual average of 1.6 million workers to the year 2000—or by 19.5 million workers over the decade, as shown in Table 12-2. Moreover, this "official" projection grossly understated immigration flows at the time it was made and has become obsolete by subsequent legislative developments. The Department of Labor projection estimated that 100,000 illegal immigrants a year would enter the country when the figure is now known to exceed this by several multiples; it made no allowance for the more than 3 million former illegal immigrants who received approval of their amnesty petitions since 1988 or for the subsequent family reunification implications associated with their admission; it used an estimate of annual legal immigration of 400,000 a year when the figure has been closer to 500,000 immigrants and will rise to 700,000 when the Immigration Act of 1990 takes effect in late 1991; and it totally omitted any allowance for annual admission of refugees. In fact, in 1989 the total number of immigrants from all sources admitted for permanent residence was 1,090,924—the highest figure for any single year since 1914. And this figure did not include any estimate of the additional illegal immigrant flow, or of the growing number of nonimmigrants permitted to work in the United States on a temporary basis during that year, or of refugees who must wait one year before they can adjust their status to become resident aliens.

In the context of a continuation of significant labor force growth, and with persistent unemployment rates already in the high 6 percent range, it is inconceivable that the United States will have a shortage of potential workers in the 1990s. What the nation faces is a shortage of qualified labor. In this case, the appropriate remedy is to address the evolving problem of a mismatch between the skills of the citizen workforce and the emerging skill and education requirements of the workplace. In other words, the real need is for an expanded national human resource development policy for citizen workers, not for a continuing increase in immigrants who are admitted mainly without regard to their human capital attributes.

No technologically advanced industrial nation that has 27 million illiterate and another 20–40 million marginally literate adults need fear a shortage of unskilled workers in its foreseeable future. Indeed, immigration—especially that of illegal immigrants, recent amnesty recipients and refugees—is a major contributor to the growth of adult illiteracy in the United States. To this degree, immigration, by adding to the surplus of illiterate adult job seekers, is serving to diminish the limited opportunities for poorly prepared citizens to find jobs or to improve their employability by on-the-job training. It is not surprising, therefore, that the underground economy is thriving in many urban centers. Moreover, the nature of the overall immigration and refugee flow is also contributing to the need for localities to expand funding for remedial education and training and language programs in many urban communities. Too often these funding choices cause scarce public funds to be diverted from being used to upgrade the human resource capabilities of the citizen labor force.

On the labor supply side, the incidence of unemployment, poverty, and adult illiteracy is much higher and the educational attainment levels significantly lower for blacks and Hispanics than for non-Hispanic whites and Asians. In addition, blacks and Hispanics are disproportionately employed in industries and occupations already in sharpest decline—the goods-producing industries and blue-collar occupations. Thus, the most rapidly increasing groups in the labor force are precisely those most adversely at risk from the changing employment requirements. Unless public policy measures are targeted to their human resource development needs, many members of both groups, as well as other vulnerable segments of the general population, will have dim employment and income prospects in the emerging postindustrial economy.

If the policy of mass and unguided immigration continues, it is unlikely there there will be sufficient pressure to enact the long-term human resource development policies needed to prepare and to incorporate these citizen groups into the mainstream economy. Instead, by providing both competition and alternatives, the large and unplanned influx of immigrant labor will serve to maintain the social marginalization of many citizen blacks and citizen Hispanics. If so, the rare chance afforded by the employment trends of the 1990s to reduce significantly the economically disadvantaged population and the underclass will be lost for another generation. It will also mean that job opportunities will be reduced for the growing numbers of older workers who may wish to prolong their working lives and for the vast pool of disabled citizens who were only recently extended employment protection by the Americans with Disabilities Act of 1990.

In other words, a substantial human reserve of potential citizen workers already exists. If their human resource development needs were addressed comprehensively, they could provide an ample supply of workers for the labor force needs of the 1990s and beyond. If the prevailing character of the nation's immigration policy is not changed, the immigration system will almost guarantee that many citizens from these groups will remain potential or marginal workforce participants. As matters stand, immigration policy represents a major obstacle to the achievement of a politically stable, fully employed and truly equitable society.

APPROPRIATE FEDERAL POLICY

Napoleon said that "policy is destiny." As the United States enters the 1990s, evolving employment patterns overwhelmingly reveal a preference for skilled and educated workers as well as a diminished parallel demand for job seekers who lack these human capital endowments. The nation is facing the worst possible situation: a shortage of qualified workers coexisting with a surplus of unqualified job seekers, with clear racial dimensions as to who is in which grouping.

In this context, the appropriate role of immigration policy is clear. Immigration policy must be made strictly accountable for its economic consequences. It should be a targeted and flexible policy designed to admit only persons who can fill job vacancies that require significant skill preparation and educational investment. The number annually admitted should be far fewer than the number needed. Immigration should never be allowed to dampen two types of market pressures: (1) those needed to encourage citizen workers to invest in preparing for vocations that are expanding; and (2) those needed to ensure that government bodies provide the requisite human resource development to prepare citizens for the new types of jobs that are emerging.

Because it takes time for would-be workers to acquire skills and education, immigration policy can be used on a short-run basis to target for permanent settlement experienced workers who possess these abilities. But the preparedness, or lack thereof, of the domestic labor force is the fundamental economic issue confronting the United States. Over the long haul, citizen workers must be prepared to qualify for jobs that have the greatest growth potential.

Legal entry should be restricted to skilled and educated immigrants because America has an abundance of unskilled and poorly prepared would-be workers. With job prospects for unskilled and semiskilled workers becoming dimmer by the day, long-term human resource strategy must be predicated on ways to enhance the employability of workers facing reduced demand for their services and to prevent future would-be workers from facing such dismal prospects. That too many of those lacking sufficient skills and education are from the nation's growing minority populations only adds urgency to this domestic challenge. The United States cannot allow the labor force to continue to polarize along racial and class lines if it hopes to prosper and persevere.

Obviously, refugees will continue to be admitted without regard to labor market criteria. Nonetheless, it behooves the federal government to provide all financial assistance necessary to prepare refugees to meet employment requirements of the local communities in which they are settled.

Refugees are admitted as the result of federal government policy decisions, and the government alone should bear the full financial costs associated with their job preparation. It is also imperative to strengthen federal policy in order to reduce illegal immigration. To accomplish this, it will be necessary to tighten restrictions on the use of fraudulent documents, to devote more funds and human resources to enforcement of employer sanctions, and to introduce penalties on apprehended illegal immigrants found to be employed.

The national goal of all elements of the U.S. human resource development policy must be to build a high-wage, high-productivity labor force along the lines being pursued by Japan and West Germany. In the process, shortages of qualified labor offer America a rare chance to reduce its persistently high levels of unemployment, to improve the lot of its working poor, and to rid itself of a large underclass. These shortages can force public human resource development policy and private sector employment practices to focus on the need to incorporate into the mainstream economy many citizens who have been left out in the past.

In this precise context, William Aramondy, president of the United Way, recently said, "We have the biggest single opportunity in our history to address two hundred years of unfairness to blacks. If we don't, God condemn us for blowing the chance." The major threat to the opportunity he correctly identified is perpetuation of the nation's politically dominated immigration policy. Immigration policy must cease being a cause of U.S. economic problems and instead be redirected to become a source of solutions.

DISCUSSION QUESTIONS

1. What impact do you think emigration has on countries like Mexico, China, Greece, and others?
2. Should the United States emphasize job skills in deciding who is allowed to enter the country legally?
3. What impact, if any, does increasing global trade have on immigration? What are the implications?

4. Should U.S. cities receive additional federal assistance because most immigrants live in cities?
5. What benefits do you think immigrants provide to the United States? What are the costs?
6. Are there differences in the challenges faced by today's immigrants compared with immigrants in the early twentieth century? If so, what are these differences? How should this affect public policy, if at all?
7. One option for dealing with illegal immigrants has been to increase border patrols. Another is to impose sanctions on employers hiring illegal immigrants. How should the United States deal with the problem of illegal immigrants? What other policy options are available?

ADDITIONAL READINGS

Abrams, Elliott, and Franklin S. Abrams, "Immigration Policy—Who Gets In and Why?" *The Public Interest* (Winter 1975).

Borjas, George J. *Friends or Strangers: The Impact of Immigrants on the U.S. Economy* (New York: Basic Books, 1990).

Chiswick, Barry R. *The Employment of Immigrants in the United States* (Washington, D.C.: American Enterprise Institute, 1983).

Congressional Digest (October 1989) (on the Immigration Act of 1990).

Conner, Roger L. "Answering the Demo-Doomsayers." *Brookings Review* (Fall 1989).

Fix, Michael, and Paul Hill. *Enforcing Employer Sanctions: Challenges and Strategies* (RAND-Urban Institute, May 1990).

Glazer, Nathan. *Ethnic Dilemmas, 1964–1982* (Cambridge, Mass.: Harvard University Press, 1983).

Harrison, Lawrence E. "America and Its Immigrants." *The National Interest* (Summer 1992).

Holden, Constance. "Debate Warming Up on Legal Migration Policy." *Science* (July 15, 1988).

Hutchinson, E. P. *Legislative History of American Immigration Policy, 1798–1965* (Philadelphia: University of Pennsylvania Press, 1981).

Morris, Milton D. *Immigration—The Beleaguered Bureaucracy* (Washington, D.C.: Brookings Institution, 1985).

Schuck, Peter H. "The Great Immigration Debate." *The American Prospect* (Fall 1990).

Simon, Julian L. "Why Control the Borders?" *National Review* (February 1, 1993).

Wattenberg, Ben J., and Karl Zinsmeister. "The Case for More Immigration." *Commentary* (April 1990).

13

INTERNATIONAL ENVIRONMENTAL POLICY

"Should the United States Take Immediate Action to Address the Threat from Global Warming?"

The effects of environmental pollutants, it is increasingly believed, can have global consequences with profound ecological, economic, and political ramifications. During the hot summer of 1988, Dr. James Hansen of NASA testified before Congress that the earth was becoming warmer and that human activity was responsible for some of this warming, known as the "greenhouse effect." Although this was not the first time the warning had been sounded, many public officials responded with alarm. Senator Al Gore, for example, called it "an ecological crisis without precedent in historic times." Many in the environmental community consider global warming to be one of the most important environmental risks facing the planet, and they caution that ignoring important signals of impending climate change may pose irreversible and dire consequences for life on earth. The most important international manifestation of this concern was the 1992 United Nations Conference on Environment and Development (UNCED) in Brazil, where signatory nations agreed to reduce greenhouse gas emissions (like methane, CFCs, nitrous oxides, ozone, and other trace gases) to 1990 levels. President Clinton on Earth Day of 1993 reversed the prior administration's opposition to the agreement and has committed the United States to the reduction.* Freezing greenhouse gas emissions at current or 1990 levels will not halt the increase in atmospheric *concentrations*, however. Therefore, even taking the steps outlined in UNCED will not prevent the likely increase in global temperatures expected over the next 100 or so years.†

Hansen's claims of global warming have been vigorously disputed by various members of the scientific community, however, and substantial scientific uncertainty remains over both the nature and causes of climate change. There is no dispute that a greenhouse effect exists; indeed, without this phenomenon the earth would be cold and lifeless due to its inability to trap heat radiating from the sun. (It is seldom recognized that the major contributor to

---

* Environmentalists have criticized President Clinton because of his reliance on voluntary reductions of greenhouse gases rather than a fuel tax or some form of energy or carbon tax.

† Some estimates suggest that in order to maintain existing concentrations of greenhouse gases, cuts of up to 80 percent of carbon emissions would be required (U.S. Office of Technology Assessment, *Preparing for an Uncertain Climate*, p. 2).

the greenhouse effect is not a man-made pollutant but rather water vapor.) Scientists for the most part agree that carbon emissions and airborne concentrations have been rising, that global temperatures probably increased over the past 150 years, and that there is a natural greenhouse effect. What remains inconclusive is how much future temperatures will rise, whether human activity is to blame for the increase in temperatures, and what the impacts will be.

Complicating the ability to determine whether the earth's temperature is increasing or not is the fact that there is no single measure of the earth's temperature. Not only does the earth's temperature vary significantly from one region to the next, but it varies widely due to differences in the time of day, cloud cover, volcanic activity, and other natural changes as well. Indeed, two reputable scientific sources disagree over whether the oceans warmed or cooled during the 1980s.[1] Recent temperature readings from satellite data generally have shown an absence of global warming trends, but they have been recorded only since 1979 and measure temperatures within four miles of the earth's atmosphere (and therefore not temperature changes that most affect life on the earth's surface).[2] Thermometer readings on the earth's surface have indicated some warming trends, although some contend that these modest increases (less than half a degree) are only part of a long cycle of temperature fluctuations that mark earth's natural history. The most alarming reports of global warming are not the product of recorded data, however, but are based on projections by sophisticated climate models that simulate changes in earth temperatures as a result of the expected increased concentrations of greenhouse gases. Some projections show that global temperatures will rise by six degrees Celsius or more within a century. Even if this were to occur, scientists have yet to determine whether the ice sheets of Greenland or Antarctica would melt (causing a large rise in sea level), what the ecological effects would be (e.g., plants grow more vigorously, but there may be reduced soil moisture), whether cloud cover would increase (which could mitigate the greenhouse effect), and whether other feedback mechanisms in the earth's climate would worsen or dampen the predicted warming. Clearly, industrialized nations whose economies are relatively unaffected by climate change (agriculture, which is most affected, plays a relatively minor role in the economy) will suffer less than developing nations where a large portion of economic output is driven by agriculture. Furthermore, coastal areas will presumably be hardest hit by predicted rising sea levels (due to melting ice), but the impacts have yet to be carefully assessed.[3]

One public policy problem is that individual nations are reluctant to act unilaterally to reduce greenhouse gas emissions because of the "free-rider" problem. If one nation reduces carbon emissions, it bears the full cost of doing so yet reaps only a portion of the worldwide benefits in the form of reduced global warming. Therefore, for each individual nation, the costs of reducing carbon emissions most likely outweigh the benefits that accrue to its citizens. Because of the spillover benefits of reducing greenhouse gas emissions, it is in the interest of all nations to cooperate to jointly attack the problem. It is because of this "prisoner's dilemma" that international agreements to address global problems are necessary. However, international cooperation is complicated by the fact that many large carbon emitters are not wealthy, industrialized nations that can afford emissions reductions. The United States is the largest contributor of greenhouse gases, both on an absolute and per-capita basis, largely due to its heavy reliance on burning coal for electricity. Interestingly, the top *per-capita* carbon emitters are industrialized nations (such as the United States, Australia, Canada, Germany, Britain, Italy, France, and Spain), while the largest *total* emitters of carbon include many developing countries (such as China, Brazil, India, and Indonesia). Therefore, substantially reducing total emissions will require sacrifices from developing nations, necessitating technology transfers and perhaps direct compensation from industrialized countries.

At the heart of the global warming controversy is how societies should make public policy decisions in the face of substantial scientific uncertainty. A recent report by the Office of Technology Assessment concludes that "most policy decisions made in the near future about how to respond to the specter of climate change will be made in light of great uncertainty about the nature and magnitude of potential effects."[4] Advocates of reducing greenhouse gas emissions have argued that because of the underlying uncertainty, prudence dictates that governments act now to avoid irreversible and possibly catastrophic future consequences. In other words, they argue it is better to be safe than sorry. Others urge waiting until more data are available with which to make more sound policy decisions. They argue that spending resources now may be unnecessarily expensive or may attack the wrong problems, and they urge additional study of the problems and the ways humans can cope with future climate changes. Basically, proponents of both sides of the issue argue that society must avoid what are called Type I and Type II errors. In this case, a Type I error is one that ignores the problem when it actually exists; if nations do not act, there is the chance that global warming will have catastrophic consequences for life on earth. A Type II error is where society acts to avoid a problem that does not really exist; if nations do act and global warming is later found to have been a false concern, then resources would have been wasted. Therefore, neither option is truly "playing it safe" because there are costs to being wrong in either direction. The issue is whether sufficient information is available and if the consequences (both of acting and not acting) warrant immediate action to address possible global warming.

In the first article below, Representative Claudine Schneider correctly points out that "As scientists debate the validity of these climate models, policymakers must decide what to do." ("What to do" can, of course, mean doing nothing.) She argues that relying on adaptation to climate change is "foolhardy," likening this strategy to "Let's wait until the ship hits the sand, then figure out what to do." Instead, she argues that reducing greenhouse gas emissions should be done in concert with other beneficial changes, such as enhancing U.S. competitiveness through improving energy efficiency, reducing reliance on fossil fuels, improving research and development, and halting deforestation. Schneider concludes that her proposals require "no sacrifice" because of the advantages that can be had from greenhouse gas reductions. Jeffrey Salmon of the George C. Marshall Institute takes the view that very little science is driving a great deal of fear over climate change, which he terms an "eco-scare." He asserts that man-made impacts on climate change are marginal and criticizes the models that predict impending disaster. Instead, he argues that a strategy of waiting for better information is the only prudent course of action. Their articles follow.

Endnotes

1. They are the U.S. National Oceanographic and Atmospheric Administration's Comprehensive Ocean Atmosphere Data Set and the U.K. Meteorological Office's Global Ocean Surface Temperature Atlas (Boyce Rensberger, "Blowing Hot and Cold on Global Warming," *Washington Post National Weekly Edition* [August 2–8, 1993], p. 38).
2. Rensberger, "Blowing Hot and Cold."
3. See William D. Nordhaus, "Reflections on the Economics of Climate Change," *Journal of Economic Perspectives* (Fall 1993).
4. U.S. Office of Technology Assessment, *Preparing for an Uncertain Climate* (Washington, D.C.: Office of Technology Assessment, 1993), p. 2.

YES

Preventing Climate Change

Claudine Schneider

Last summer, American farms suffered multibillion dollar crop losses from a devastating drought. Thousands of square miles of dry forests went up in smoke as fires raged uncontrollably. Entire communities were left homeless and destitute in the wake of hurricanes Gilbert and Helene. And smog blanketed many cities as a mass of hot air hovered over the country. "It must be the greenhouse effect," was the comment made over and over again by members of Congress. Media coverage had sensitized most Americans to the peril posed by the unchecked growth of greenhouse gas emissions, and the unpleasant weather seemed to be a preview of what we can expect if global climate models are accurate in their predictions.

As scientists debate the validity of these climate models, policymakers must decide what to do. Two opposing schools of thought are emerging: One school promotes adaptation, the other prevention.

Advocates of the adaptation approach argue that we should wait until more scientific evidence is in, which will allow us to take more targeted actions. They worry that premature efforts to cut greenhouse gases may needlessly disrupt the world economy. But by the time we are sure that the greenhouse effect is with us, it will be too late to reverse it; the only recourse will be adaptation. To my mind, this approach is too much like the crisis management tactic of "Let's wait until the ship hits the sand, then figure out what to do" so prevalent in public policymaking today.

Luckily, many conclude that inaction with respect to global warming is foolhardy. When symptoms of an illness appear, they say, a remedy should be sought. Thus there is growing support for a preventive strategy, which means reducing the emissions of greenhouse gases—primarily carbon dioxide (CO_2), but also chlorofluorocarbons (CFCs) and methane. For example, the recommendations of the 1988 Toronto Conference on the Changing Atmosphere include a call for at least a 20 percent reduction in global CO_2 emissions below the 1987 level by the year 2005, and a 50 percent reduction by the year 2015. This goal has been endorsed by the Prime Ministers of Canada and Norway. The Global Warming Prevention Act (H.R. 1078), which I recently introduced, and Senator Tim Wirth's National Energy Policy Act (S. 324) seek a 20 percent reduction by the end of the century.

Noting that society is at risk from the threat of global warming, the National Academy of Sciences recently called on President Bush to take a leadership role in gaining international consensus on this difficult issue and urged the president to adopt "prudent" policies to slow the pace of global climate change. Prudence dictates reducing our dependency on fossil fuels, which are the primary source of CO_2; phasing out most ozone-depleting chlorofluorocarbons and other halocarbons, which are also destroying the ozone layer; halting deforestation and promoting reforestation (trees remove CO_2 from the air whereas burning them releases it); and adopting agricultural and livestock practices that minimize forest conversion and reduce methane emissions. Slowing population growth will also have a profound impact.

Securing these changes will not be easy. Altering the ways of 240 million Americans, let alone 5 billion human beings worldwide, poses a formidable challenge. Confronting the vested economic interests adamantly opposed to change is an equally daunting task for political leaders. Moreover, the greenhouse peril must compete with other serious, and more immediate, environmental problems such as acid rain, urban ozone, indoor air pollution, the cleanup of contaminated nuclear weapons production facilities, and the disposal of toxic wastes.

The slow pace of climate change breeds complacency, but we must remember that the climate will also be slow to respond to after-the-fact solutions. We must begin now to adopt the good stewardship practices that will reduce the likelihood of human-induced climate disruption. Fortunately, congressional testimony received over the past several years indicates a wide range of actions to reduce greenhouse gases that are already cost-effective and many others that could be given sufficient research and development. Rapid progress has already begun on reducing CFC emissions, and many of the suggestions for minimizing other threats to the climate have been incorporated into legislative proposals.

The path to pursue is one that not only reduces emissions of greenhouse gases but that makes economic sense as well. Each choice we make should spur multiple benefits. Stephen Schneider, a climate expert at the National Center for Atmospheric Research, calls this the "tie-in" strategy: Take those actions that reduce the trade deficit, free up capital, save consumers money, and enhance the competitiveness of U.S. industry, as well as reduce greenhouse gases.

In this spirit, the Global Warming Prevention Act builds upon existing federal programs and newly proposed legislation that can help slow climate change as well as achieve these multiple purposes. By linking these disparate efforts in a coordinated program and adding a few initiatives focused primarily on climate change, we can increase the likelihood that Congress will approve a plan sufficiently comprehensive to alter the conditions that threaten to disrupt the climate. In spite of the global nature of the problem, the emphasis is on domestic policy because the United States is the major producer of greenhouse gases—contributing approximately 20 percent of the total—and the place where we as Americans have the ability to take immediate action. In addition, we cannot expect other countries to listen to our advice until we lead by example.

MORE BANG FOR THE BTU

The most impressive tie-in advantages result from improving energy efficiency. We have already witnessed the power of this approach in responding to the energy crisis of the 1970s. Seeking to reduce oil imports and energy costs, scientists and engineers spawned a veritable revolution in product design and manufacturing techniques. The result was the emergence of an enormous new energy "resource." One can now "produce" energy by using light bulbs that are four times as efficient as conventional models or by living in a superinsulated home that requires only one-tenth as much energy for heating as a typical home.

Such innovations still await widespread adoption. But so far, even the modest improvements that have been made in America's stock of buildings, vehicles, factories, and appliances have secured dramatic results. Since 1973, energy efficiency gains have displaced the equivalent of 14 million barrels of oil per day, saving Americans more than $150 billion per year. In addition, CO_2 emissions are 50 percent lower than they otherwise would have been. Foreign oil imports are less than half of what they would have been, lowering the annual trade deficit by more than $50 billion. Efficiency gains worldwide have been instrumental in spawning a global oil glut, collapsing world oil prices, curtailing OPEC's power, and reducing inflation rates fanned by high energy costs.

How much efficiency is possible? A staggering amount, according to a study by the Global End-Use Oriented Energy Project based in part at Princeton University's Center for Energy and the Environment. For example, the international research team's 50-year energy scenario, based on extensive (but fare from exhaustive) use of efficiency improvements, projects that it would be technologically feasible and economically compelling to hold energy use constant and reduce CO_2 emissions over the next half century even as world population doubled and gross world product quadrupled.

Converting the potential of energy efficiency to reality will not be easy. Formidable institutional barriers, market imperfections, and outdated public policies prevent most of these savings from being realized. But the federal government can take several steps to improve things.

Electric utilities, which produce one-third of U.S. CO_2 emissions, are an opportune place to begin. The administration can provide leadership by using the National Energy Policy Plan, which it must submit biannually to Congress, to establish cost-effective energy efficiency as a national goal. By ranking the full range of energy supply- and demand-side efficiency options in order of their cost-effectiveness, the plan would let all utilities know what they should be doing to reduce energy use and CO_2 emissions. The administration can tap the expertise of the National Academy of Sciences' Energy Engineering Board, which has convened an expert committee to study implementation of least-cost planning.

But as many regulatory commissioners and utility executives are beginning to learn, identifying low-cost efficiency options is only the first step. The current regulatory structure perversely penalizes a utility for pursuing a cost-effective energy efficiency strategy. Saving kilowatts can dramatically reduce a utility's earnings. Some states, such as Maine and California, are introducing far-reaching regulatory changes that will make it possible for a utility to increase profits while reducing total sales through energy saving improvements. (See

David Moskovitz, "Cutting the Nation's Electric Bill," *Issues*, Spring 1989.) Other state utility commissions should follow their lead.

The federal government can facilitate the least-cost planning process in several ways. First, the Department of Energy can expand its existing Least-Cost Utility Planning (LCUP) program. This technology transfer initiative, begun in 1986, links the government's national laboratories with the research arms of the gas and electric utility industries and the state public utility commissions. The LCUP collects and disseminates information on the mechanics of least-cost planning, the cost-effectiveness and reliability of supply- and demand-side technologies, and utility experience in using them.

The potential for energy savings is reflected in the success of the federally mandated Northwest Electric Power and Conservation Plan. Begun in 1980 when it became clear that the region had exhausted the supply of cheap federally produced hydropower, the plan established a rigorous least-cost planning process for Washington, Oregon, Idaho, and Montana. By focusing on low-cost energy efficiency measures, these states were able to indefinitely defer the need for all 16 planned generating plants, preventing the expenditure of billions of dollars in construction costs and keeping electric rates low.

In addition to sharing technical information, LCUP should conduct case studies of states that experimented with efficiency-minded regulatory reform. Because conditions vary significantly among states, detailed studies that explain why a particular action was necessary and how it works will be essential to other states that want to craft their own regulatory strategies. My legislation calls for increasing LCUP funding from $1 million to $15 million, a pittance compared to the $200 billion the United States spends on electricity each year and the projected $75 billion a year that will be required to build new generating plants in the 1990s unless we succeed in reducing electricity demand.

Another step is to amend the Public Utilities Regulatory Policy Act of 1978 to require all states to implement least-cost planning procedures. A dozen states have already begun this process, and another dozen are considering it, but there is no reason for any state not to do it. In addition, the Federal Energy Regulatory Commission, which now regulates more than one-fourth of wholesale electricity sales, should be required to adopt a least-cost planning process. Until now, FERC has entirely ignored the role of energy efficiency in meeting demand.

Finally, the federal government should incorporate least-cost planning into U.S. bilateral and multilateral assistance programs. The Agency for International Development, the World Bank, and the other international development banks are allocating only one percent of all energy project funds to energy efficiency. The developing countries desperately need electricity and lack the capital to build new power plants. Efficiency improvements can spur economic activity without draining off scarce investment capital. In Brazil, for example, José Goldemberg, rector of the University of São Paulo and the former president of São Paulo's electric and gas utilities, found that the use of high-efficiency lights, motors, and appliances could eliminate the need for two-thirds of planned utility plant construction between now and the year 2000, saving $30 billion.

PRODUCTIVE R&D

Transportation, particularly automobiles and light trucks, is responsible for almost one-third of U.S. carbon emissions, as well as a large fraction of tropospheric ozone and acid rain pollutants. Market forces are not sufficient to spur optimal efficiency because the cost of gasoline comprises only about 20 percent of the total cost of operating a car. Even doubling the price of gasoline, as many countries have done, would not give consumers enough incentive to demand cars that get more than 35 miles per gallon (mpg).

Several policies to reduce fuel use in transportation are already in effect. Since 1975, the Corporate Average Fuel Economy (CAFE) standards have required U.S. manufacturers to achieve a minimum average efficiency among all new cars sold. The fuel economy of new U.S. cars doubled between 1974 and 1985 as the standard rose gradually to 27.5 mpg. Under pressure from manufacturers, the standard was relaxed to 26 mpg in 1986, 1987, and 1988. President Bush recently announced that the standard will be raised to 27.5 mpg in 1990. We should continue gradually increasing the standard over the next decade to 45 mpg for cars and 35 mpg for light trucks, thereby eliminating the need for 15 billion barrels of oil.

Some manufacturers argue that more demanding standards will make it impossible to produce the big cars consumers want and to provide adequate safety for drivers. But Department of Transportation studies indicate that the use of technologies such as continuously variable transmissions, multivalve engines, and advanced lightweight materials will make it possible to achieve 48 mpg in large cars. A few four- and five-passenger prototypes have done much better. As for safety, design is more important than weight. Chevrolet's 4,100-pound 1985 Astro minivan, for example, was one of the worst performers in crash tests; the high-mileage 2,600-pound Chevy Nova had the best crash test rating of any of the new cars tested that year.

Volvo's prototype mid-sized passenger sedan, the LCP 2000, indicates what is technologically feasible. Road tested at a combined city/highway mileage of 75 mpg, the car exceeds EPA's stringent safety standards, accelerates to 60 mph in 11 seconds, and is expected to cost no more than current models.

One drawback of the CAFE standards is that a manufacturer cannot force consumers to choose its more efficient models and therefore cannot guarantee that it will meet the specified average for all cars sold. Congress, therefore, should reinforce the efficiency mandate by strengthening the existing gas guzzler tax, which is levied on any car that gets less than 22 mpg and rises as the mileage falls. I propose increasing the amount of the tax, gradually increasing the kick-in mileage to 32 mpg by 2004, and extending it to light trucks, which are currently exempt. In addition, I propose a "gas-sippers" rebate of up to $2,000 on the purchase of the most fuel-efficient vehicles.

Industry should not have to bear the entire research burden for developing more efficient cars. The Department of Energy (DOE) spends a piddling $50 million per year on all transportation R&D, while the nation is spending $100 billion a year on gasoline. DOE needs to increase its research on auto efficiency, particularly in areas that will have near-term commercial application. To ensure that the money is spent wisely, Congress should ask the National Academy of Sciences to do a thorough review of fuel economy R&D opportunities and recommend priorities for the DOE program.

Underpinning all of these efforts must be a stable federal research and development effort, working jointly with private industry. A 50 percent cut since 1980 in the federal energy efficiency R&D budget has meant that there have been no new research projects begun this decade. These budget cuts seem particularly shortsighted in light of the spectacular success of federal energy efficiency R&D. According to a 1987 analysis by the American Council for an Energy Efficient Economy, the $16 million that DOE spent on cooperative projects with industry to develop heat pumps, more efficient refrigera, new ballasts to improve the efficiency of fluorescent lights, and glass coatings that control heat loss and gain through windows will help save the country billions of dollars through energy savings.

Federal R&D can be especially productive in the areas of building design and industrial processes. The annual utility bill for the nation's buildings is $160 billion, but the fragmented building industry spends almost nothing on energy efficiency R&D. The federal government can coordinate research with the 28,000 homebuilders and 150,000 special trade contractors to tap energy savings in virtually every part of the building, from the foundation to the roof and from the heating and cooling system to the windows.

Similar savings can be found in industry. Generic research in industrial process efficiency can lead to significant savings across many industries, but no individual company will reap sufficient benefit to justify funding the research itself. The Global Warming Prevention Act therefore calls for the creation of a number of industrial research centers to conduct joint projects with industry to improve the efficiency of manufacturing processes. This effort will not only reduce greenhouse gases and other pollutants but will enhance industrial competitiveness by cutting production costs.

REPLACING FOSSIL FUELS

Efficiency improvements alone will not be enough, but they will buy us time to develop renewable energy sources that do not produce greenhouse gases. The world's renewable resource base is enormous. According to a 1985 report by the Department of Energy (DOE), a 25-year research and development effort could make it possible to economically extract 85 quads of renewable energy in the United States. Combined with efficiency improvements, this amount could conceivably meet virtually the entire U.S. energy demand in 2010. But the necessary work is not being done. The federal R&D budget for renewable energy has fallen from more than $800 million in 1979 to a proposed $130 million in 1990—less than one percent of DOE's total budget.

With such a vast potential available and opinion polls reporting a high public regard for solar energy, why has there been so little progress? There are several reasons. In part, the outstanding success of energy efficiency has eclipsed the promise of sun power. In the wake of an oil glut and collapsed energy prices, the market for renewable energy technology virtually disappeared. Moreover, ill-conceived public policies did little to advance the infant solar industry toward maturity. R&D efforts were misplaced, emphasizing giant centralized projects, rather than capitalizing on the inherently dispersed and diffuse nature of solar energy flows. Tax incentives, while well-intentioned, were in some ways counterproductive. Pegged to system cost rather than energy production, the solar tax credits favored expensive "gold-plated" systems over low-cost options such as passive solar design.

Although some solar technologies will require more R&D before they are economically competitive, many untapped opportunities are now available. For example, large-scale use of solar-generated electricity may still be a decade away, but the use of daylight in buildings is feasible now—and lighting accounts for 25 percent of all U.S. electricity use. DOE's Solar Energy Research Institute estimates that designing buildings to take advantage of daylight could provide one-fourth of lighting requirements. Daylighting should therefore be an integral part of all least-cost utility planning programs.

Several other renewable energy technologies are also in widespread practice or ready for use. Passive solar space heating has become an essential part of energy efficient building practice in northern climates, and solar water heating is being used in hundreds of thousands of buildings throughout the country. Although very cost-effective, these technologies are not being used to their full potential because many consumers lack information about their value, because renters have no incentive to invest in their homes, and because builders compete on home price rather than on operating costs. Least-cost planning programs need to include financial incentives or building standards that promote use of these established renewable energy technologies.

Photovoltaic cells and high-temperature solar thermal systems offer economically attractive ways of meeting utility peak power demands during summer, and wind power offers the same potential during cold weather. Biomass-derived ethanol is already in use in blends with gasoline, and biogas from waste could be used to fuel new, highly efficient aircraft-derived gas turbines. In fact, Sweden plans to use biogas-fired turbines as one of the replacements for nuclear power, which it is phasing out over the coming decade.

Renewable energy sources, primarily hydropower and biomass, supply close to 10 percent of total U.S. energy needs. To tap the full potential of renewable energy, the federal government must reverse the decline in R&D funding. Government spending still reflects pre-greenhouse thinking. DOE will spend $1 billion on fossil fuel research this year, seven times what it will spend on all renewable energy technologies combined. At a time when we should be exploring every opportunity for replacing fossil fuels, this simply makes no sense.

In addition, the government itself can make a concerted effort to use renewable energy. Federal buildings, military bases, and public housing continue to ignore cost-effective investments in solar technology and energy-saving measures. Federal procurement guidelines should be made more stringent in requiring this use.

Likewise, national and multinational assistance to developing countries should include more attention to renewable energy technologies. For example, the World Bank, which currently underwrites the cost of diesel water pumps should also subsidize solar-powered pumps, which are just as cost-effective, more reliable, and also useful for operating filters to remove waterborne parasites. Stimulating use of photovoltaic cells would also enable the industry to reduce prices by scaling up production processes.

FOREST RELIEF

Between 10 and 20 percent of greenhouse gas emissions are due to the deforestation of some 11 million hectares annually. One "Yellowstone Park" is disappearing every month; a forested area the size of Pennsylvania is ravaged every year. Reforesting efforts are pathetically weak, with just one tree replanted for every 10 cut down. At the current rate of deforestation nearly half the world's remaining forests will be lost within the next several generations.

Most of the world's forests—and those forests that are disappearing most rapidly—are found in developing countries, particularly Brazil and other countries with Amazonian forest, Central America, the Philippines, Indonesia, Ivory Coast, Madagascar, and Ghana. These governments believe, quite rightly, that fossil fuel use in the industrialized world is the major cause of CO_2 build-up and that the wealthy countries should bear the economic burden of reducing CO_2 emissions. President José Sarney of Brazil recently made it clear that he has no intention of letting the developed countries dictate Brazilian forest policy. Immediate economic needs and political realities in Brazil, not the long-term fears of the industrialized world, will guide Brazil's decisions.

Nevertheless, we cannot forget that preserving the tropical forests, which contain more than three-fourths of the world's biological diversity, has obvious tie-in appeal. The world relies heavily on the forests for a wide variety of products, including many important medicines. But as the forests disappear, plant and animal species are becoming extinct at a rate not witnessed since the demise of the dinosaurs 65 million years ago. We are in danger of losing an irreplaceable natural resource just as advances in molecular biology and genetic engineering are enhancing our ability to use it.

The importance of the tropical forests makes it incumbent on the United States to find a way to encourage their preservation. Self-righteous—and self-serving—homilies will not do. But through policy analysis, technological assistance, and financial aid, the United States can show Brazil and others how current practices are unsound and how alternatives can benefit them economically as well as environmentally.

An important first step is to identify policies that promote deforestation without providing economic benefits. Brazil's policies to encourage Amazonian cattle ranching are a case in point. For decades cattle ranchers received tax credits, low-interest loans, generous depreciation schedules, and other benefits as a reward for converting forests to ranches. By 1980, ranches accounted for three-fourths of cumulative forest conversion. John Browder of Tulane University has pointed out that although ranchers have profited enormously because of government subsidies, with returns on equity of more than 200 percent, for the typical 20,000-hectare cattle ranch the present value of the investment without subsidies is a loss equal to 55 percent of the total investment costs. These supposed economic development policies cost the Brazilian economy billions of dollars as well as the loss of mullions of hectares of irreplaceable natural resources. Many other developing countries, often with the help of national and multinational aid agencies, have made the same mistakes.

The developing countries will act to preserve the forests when they are convinced that it is in their interest to do so. The rural poor in developing countries need to grow food to survive, and the countries need to produce products for export. Cleared tropical forest land can be farmed (though only for a few years), and timber is a valuable export product. To reduce the incentive to destroy the forests, it is necessary to improve the productivity of agriculture on already cleared land and to find a way to generate wealth from the forests without destroying them.

The United States should expand on the pioneering work by the Agency for International Development (AID) to develop agroforestry, the nondestructive use of forest land to produce food and other products. For example, since 1965, AID forester Michael Benge has been demonstrating the advantages of leucaena, a fast-growing, nitrogen-fixing species that enriches the soil while serving as live fencing and producing forage for livestock and fuel wood. The National Academy of Sciences has published a series of handbooks on multiuse species for agroforestry in developing countries, and these could readily serve as the foundation for an expanded effort by AID and other development organizations.

Finally, we cannot forget that a rapidly growing population increases the pressure to burn fossil fuels and to use forests to produce energy and provide new land for farms and ranches. The United States pioneered family planning efforts to stabilize population growth several decades ago, long before most developing countries with high birth rates saw any need. Ironically, now that these same developing countries have reversed their positions and recognized the need to step up such efforts, the United States is steadily reducing its funding commitment to international family planning assistance.

Efforts to reduce CO_2 emissions through improving energy efficiency and tapping renewable energy sources can be overwhelmed by the increased energy needs that will accompany a growing world population. Every three years the world is adding a population the size of the United States, 95 percent of it in developing countries. Improving the standard of living in developing countries without increasing energy use is difficult enough without having to deal with the increased needs of a growing population. As a first step, the United States needs to double its international family planning funds. Developing countries need the means to control population growth—for their economic well-being and for the health of the planet.

The prevention approach to global climate change clearly entails an ambitious public policy agenda. Can we justify such a program with a few computer models? No, but we don't have to. Government initiatives to use energy more efficiently, to develop safe renewable alternatives to fossil fuels, to preserve tropical forests, and to slow population growth make economic and environmental sense even if climate disruption was not a danger.

If further research increases the certainty that we face rapid global warming, we will have to consider more dramatic measures. What I have proposed requires no sacrifice, and by setting in motion efforts that will steadily reduce CO_2 emissions, it will reduce the severity of measures needed if we find that the climate is changing more quickly than predicted.

NO

Greenhouse Anxiety

Jeffrey Salmon

Of all the environmental calamities that might be visited on the earth, none has attracted more attention or aroused more fear than global warming. Countless newspaper and television reports have warned us that mankind is altering the earth's delicate thermostat by spewing tons of carbon dioxide (CO_2) into the atmosphere, mainly by burning coal and oil. According to the global-warming theory, CO_2—along with other man-made gases such as methane—will enhance the earth's natural "greenhouse effect" to the point of an uncontrollable temperature rise, leaving civilization reeling under the double punishment of farmland drought and catastrophic flooding caused by melting polar ice caps.

On the face of it, the greenhouse effect would seem to be an unlikely candidate for the apocalypse. After all, most predictions suggest the earth's temperature might increase by only a few tenths of a degree per decade, and everyone knows forecasting the weather more than a day ahead is a hit-or-miss proposition. Why then should we take seriously weather predictions years into the future? Nonetheless, the warnings sounded by those who believe that global warming is upon us outmatch even the grimmest rhetoric of the cold war.

Congressman Henry Waxman thinks global warming "may be the greatest single threat to life on this planet." Vice President Al Gore has said that greenhouse warming is an "ecological crisis without precedent in historic times," and that any dispute of this judgment is not "worthy of recognition." While not going quite so far, the former head of the Environmental Protection Agency (EPA), William Reilly, has called this the most serious environmental problem facing our nation.

Energized by greenhouse anxiety, and by the determined advocacy of Vice President Gore, the entire environmental agenda has become a central part of President Bill Clinton's long-term legislative program. Early on, the administration signaled its eagerness to work with the green lobbyists by coordinating its energy-tax plan with the Sierra Club, the Environmental Defense Fund, and other established environmental groups in Washington. And just before Earth Day, President Clinton, reversing Bush-administration policy, announced he would commit the U.S. to the specific goals of the climate treaty signed at the Earth Summit last June in Rio de Janeiro. "Unless we act now," Clinton said, "we face a future in which the sun may scorch us, not warm us."

Naturally, the environmental lobby was delighted with the President's performance. But the lobby has an even more serious agenda in mind. Dramatically increased automobile fuel efficiency, and indeed the eventual phasing-out of the internal-combustion engine; carbon taxes; the ultimate elimination of coal- and oil-fired energy production; binding international agreements to reduce carbon-dioxide emissions—these are just a few of the items on the menu of proposed policies. Going even further, the UN Intergovernmental Panel on Climate Change (IPCC)—the major force behind last year's Rio summit—contends that *immediate* reductions of *over 60 percent* in "greenhouse emissions from human activities" are needed just to stabilize CO_2 concentrations at today's levels. Other observers put the figure at closer to 80 percent.

The impact of such numbers is difficult to fathom. According to the Department of Energy, for the U.S. alone, even a 20-percent reduction in CO_2 emissions by the year 2000—the goal President Clinton has committed us to achieving—would require a carbon tax forcing the price of electricity to double, oil prices to triple, and the cost of coal to quintuple. Since the U.S. emits only 30 percent of the earth's greenhouse gases, stabilizing CO_2 emissions worldwide would require much more draconian measures still: it would require a fundamental restructuring of the global economy.

Is any of this necessary? Do we face a looming catastrophe? In fact the answer is No. Whatever role might be played by global warming in domestic and international politics, there is *no* solid scientific evidence to support the theory that the earth is warming because of man-made greenhouse gases.

To the contrary, the weight of science indicates that carbon emissions from power plants, cars, and the like have only a marginal impact on the climate. As Robert White, president of the National Academy of Engineering, put it correctly in 1989: "We are confronted with an inverted pyramid of knowledge: a huge and growing mass of proposals for political action is balanced upon a handful of real facts."

How did this happen?

II

To understand the political history of global warming it is necessary to begin where the greenhouse argument itself begins, with the science.

The actual greenhouse effect is a natural phenomenon, existing for eons before humans even appeared on the scene. It comes largely from water vapor in the atmosphere which warms the earth by trapping some of the heat from the sun and keeping it in the lower atmosphere. Carbon dioxide, methane, and other gases also trap heat, but most greenhouse heating comes from water vapor. The warming effect of all these gases combined maintains average global temperatures at a comfortable 65°F. Without the greenhouse effect, the average temperature would be about 10° below zero, and the earth would resemble the planet Mars.

To today's ruckus over the greenhouse effect has very little to do with the actual greenhouse effect, which everyone agrees we cannot live without. Instead, the issue concerns the changes that human activities, particularly the burning of fossil fuels, have produced and will produce on the earth's natural climate-control system.

There are many unknowns about that system, but also some generally acknowledged facts. Scientists agree that people have added a great deal of CO_2 to the air over the last 100 years, mostly by driving cars and burning coal and oil for energy. Sometime in the middle of the next century we may double the amount of CO_2 in the atmosphere.

Alone, this substantial addition of greenhouse gases might have gone unnoticed by everyone but a handful of experts. Indeed, from the 1940's through the 1970's, while greenhouse gases were pouring into the atmosphere, global temperatures actually fell, and there was much talk in scientific circles about the possibility that we were headed into a new ice age. But this 30-year cooling period interrupted 100 years of generally warmer weather, during which the earth's temperature rose by about 1°F. The global-warming scare rests largely on the coincidence of the global increase in atmospheric CO_2 and this one-degree rise in temperature. (When it comes to global temperature averages, a little can make a great difference—in growing seasons, rainfall, and general weather patterns. But that is a different story.)

The increase in CO_2 in the atmosphere over the last 100 years, the one-degree temperature rise since 1880, the economic impact of climate change— these, too, are not matters of much debate within the scientific community. What scientists wonder about is not whether man-made greenhouse gases influence temperature, but by how much.

They have been trying to figure this out for some time. Early estimates, based on a projected doubling of CO_2 in the atmosphere, ranged from as little as 2°F to as much as 10°F. They were regarded as useful experiments, but of limited forecasting value. By the 1960's, though, advances in computer technology gave meteorologists the opportunity to build more sophisticated models using the enormously complex physics which controls weather patterns.

Today's so-called consensus view on global warming, as expressed by the IPCC, suggests that at the current rate of growth in greenhouse gases, average temperatures should already be increasing by approximately half-a-degree Fahrenheit each decade, and should reach 4°F by the middle of the next century. These estimates, which have been used to great effect by environmentalists, are based on computer simulations of future climate change, or, as they are called in the trade, General Circulation Models. In fact, *every* greenhouse forecast—every dire prediction of dangerous heat waves, droughts, flooding, radically shifting weather patterns, and the like—is the result of computers attempting to model the myriad factors that influence climate change.

As the IPCC report notes in its summary, "We have substantial confidence that models can predict at least the broad-scale features of climate change." Actually, however, the body of the report, which was written and reviewed by climate scientists, raises all kinds of doubts about the models' reliability. Climate modeling is a difficult and expensive proposition, and modelers themselves are the last to claim that their computers give them much predictive power.

And for good reason. The General Circulation Models attempt to mimic our climate system by using a mathematical simulation of the earth and its oceans and atmosphere. Unfortunately, the mechanisms of our climate are extremely complicated. Take cloud cover, one of the most obvious factors in climate change. Clouds create a problem for the greenhouse models because their influence far outweighs any possible effect of man-made emissions. It is nearly impossible to predict what kinds of clouds will form, or even whether they will serve to enhance or diminish global warming. Depending on your assumptions, you can have the model arrive at pretty much whatever answer you want.

To gain an idea of how reliable models are, consider how poorly they predict climate changes we have *already* experienced. And if they are incapable of accounting for the past, how will they be able to predict the future?

Over the last 100 years, greenhouse gases in the atmosphere increased by the equivalent of a 50-percent rise in CO_2. Given this increase, the models used by the IPCC would predict a warming of about two degrees over the same 100-year period. But as we have seen, temperatures have increased by only about half that amount—meaning the models have already exaggerated the greenhouse effect by a factor of two.

Even more striking, most of the one-degree warming observed over the last century took place before 1940, while most man-made greenhouse emissions entered the atmosphere *after* 1940. How are greenhouse gases to account for a temperature rise that occurred before they existed?

It gets worse. According to IPCC estimates, the increasing amount of greenhouse gases in the atmosphere should have driven global temperatures up by half a degree in the 1980's alone. Yet satellite measurements of global temperatures, which are the most accurate known, show no significant warming in the 1980's. Where the IPCC's models predicted half a degree, the satellites tell us there was an increase of less than one-tenth of a degree—meaning the models exaggerated by at least a factor of five.

There are other problems with the General Circulation Models. In addition to forecasting a general warming of the earth, the computer simulations predict the specific types of warming that should occur. For example, the Northern Hemisphere should warm more than the Southern, higher latitudes more than lower, and arctic regions most of all. These distinctive characteristics make up the so-called "greenhouse signal." If these changes had actually occurred, it would be a sign that the warming observed over the last 100 years had indeed been caused by man-made carbon emissions.

But no greenhouse signal has been found. There has been no significant difference in temperature trends between the two hemispheres, or between the high and low latitudes, and no significant warming in the arctic.

III

In a recent review of the debate over global warming, Richard Lindzen, Sloan Professor of Meteorology at MIT, noted that up until the 1980's, predictions based on computer models "were considered interesting, but largely academic, exercises—even by the scientists involved." What changed in the 1980's was that climate became a political issue. One of the first indications was a 1983 EPA press release claiming that dangerous global warming would occur sometime within the decade, causing sea levels to rise and several coastal cities to go under water. Environmental groups picked up the theme and added it to their already robust list of impending ecological disasters.

Something else changed as well. It is highly unlikely that the scare talk of environmentalists would have made the headway it did among politicians and the general public without the support of leading scientists. By the late 80's, that support was forthcoming.

It was in the stifling summer of 1988 that the greenhouse effect was, as the *Washington Post* put it, "propelled from the scientific journals to the nightly news." On June 23, with the thermometer hitting 98° in Washington, D.C., James Hansen, chief of NASA's Goddard Institute, and a well-known climate expert, announced before a Senate committee that "the greenhouse effect has been detected and it is changing our climate now. . . ." Even more significantly, Hansen said he was "99-percent confident" that current temperatures represent a "real warming trend" rather than natural climate variability.

Hansen's testimony had the effect he must have intended. "We have only one planet," declared the Senate committee chairman, J. Bennett Johnston. "If we screw it up, we have no place to go. The greenhouse effect has ripened beyond theory." Senator Dale Bumpers, sounding a populist note—"What you have is all the economic interests pitted against our very survival"— thought that Hansen's testimony "ought to be a cause for headlines in every newspaper of the country." And so it was. As Stephen Schneider, a climatologist and a major advocate of policies to halt global warming, summed up the reaction to Hansen's report: "Journalists lived it. Environmentalists were ecstatic."

Hansen's testimony, spectacular as it was, constituted only one of a series of endorsements offered by members of the scientific elite to the global-warming scenario. Perhaps the most dramatic was a January 1991 statement sponsored by the Union of Concerned Scientists (UCS) and signed by 700 members of the National Academy of Sciences and over 50 Nobel laureates. There, the UCS warned that burning fossil fuels could cause global temperatures to rise by some 9°F [*sic*] over the next 100 years. "This process," said the scientists, "could have catastrophic consequences for climate, agriculture, plant and animal species, and coastlines worldwide." Global warming, the statement concluded, was "the most serious environmental threat of the 21st century."

In the face of statements like this, it is no wonder that politicians should take it as established fact that "the greenhouse effect is here" (to quote Hansen again), or should conclude, as then-Senator Timothy Wirth did in 1990, that there were no credible scientists who questioned global warming. But that was most assuredly not the case. In response to Senator Wirth's statement, the late columnist Warren Brookes compiled and published a list of 50 peer-reviewed articles, well-known in the scientific community, which contradicted various parts of the global-warming theory. Moreover, as Richard Lindzen has noted, only a few of those who signed the UCS statement were climate specialists, and after the appeal was released, the president of the National Academy of Sciences warned his colleagues against speaking on subjects about which they could claim no special knowledge.

Environmentalists, of course, have hardly been deterred by this. Backed, as they assert, by the scientific establishment, they have tended to show open irritation at any attempt to question the threat they have proclaimed. Vice President Gore simply dismisses disagreement as bickering that gets in the way of what needs to be done. Others may admit there are doubts, but say we need to act anyway, as an insurance policy. "Uncertainty is no excuse for complacency," argues the UCS.

Here too, as it happens, they are mistaken. According to Michael Schlesinger of the University of Illinois, even if the worst global-warming scenarios were true—which they emphatically are not—delaying a response for five years to wait for more research would cost only one-tenth of a degree of additional warming, so negligible as to be lost in the natural fluctuations of global climate.

To greenhouse advocates, however, global warming is clearly more than just another eco-scare. It is "a powerful symbol," in Gore's words, "of the larger crisis" allegedly brought on by the whole thrust of modern industrial society. Concern for the environment, writes the Vice President, must therefore now become the "central organizing principle of world civilization." Resistance to this notion threatens "a kind of global civil war between those who refuse to consider the consequences of civilization's relentless advance and those who refuse to be silent partners in the destruction."

In this view, the scientists who have lent their authority to the idea that we are on the edge of such a "destruction," who have promoted the apocalyptic vision of an earth on fire, are men of courage. But there are other ways to interpret their behavior. Scientists willing to go public with greenhouse anxiety, however wildly exaggerated, have found themselves honored by environmentalists and touted by a panic-mongering press: as *Popular Science* noted, Stephen Schneider was "near-canonized by the media" for "sounding the tocsin" on global warming. And now that President Clinton has endorsed the specific goals of the Rio treaty, the scientists would seem to have won ratification in the highest political circles of the land.

At the same time, it would be wrong to suggest that their skewed version of reality has completely carried the day. Even some mainstream journalists have lately begun to question whether all the fuss about the greenhouse effect makes any sense, and whether the immense costs of reducing CO_2 emissions are really justified. Thus, the *New York Times*, in a recent series of hard-hitting articles on trendy environmental scares, pointed in particular to exaggerated fears of global warming. Even the thoroughly green magazine *Garbage* published a tough-minded cover story in its February/March issue that totally undercut the basic premises of dangerous global warming. In April, a two-part CBS miniseries, *The Fire Next Time*—an eco-version of the 1983 nuclear-war epic, *The Day After*— was panned by a number of critics, in part for its ludicrous hyping of the greenhouse effect.

While these examples are hardly definitive proof of a greater sobriety about environmental issues in general, they do signal a potentially healthy turn. One hopes, however, that skepticism will be applied not only to the environmental lobby, but also to the scientists who have collaborated in its gross distortions. These scientists, who have promoted the idea of an earth on fire, should have their own feet held closely to the flames they have helped to ignite. In the end, one of the saddest revelations of the whole global-warming scare has been how easy it is to exploit the ambitions of some members of the scientific elite. Undoing the harm this has done to the credibility of the scientific community may be the work of generations.

DISCUSSION QUESTIONS

1. Can greenhouse gas emissions be reduced without cost to the economy? If so, why have individuals and firms not already done so?
2. How should social decisions be made in the face of scientific uncertainty?
3. Are there any benefits from global warming?
4. Global warming will not affect all nations and all regions equally. Who do you suppose is most affected? Who is least affected? How does this affect the domestic and international politics of climate change agreements?
5. Should compensation be paid to developing nations to reduce carbon emissions? If so, what form should that compensation take (cash, technology transfers, etc.)?
6. What industries would be most harmed by a carbon tax (a tax based on the carbon content of the fuel)? What political interests in the United States do you think would support or oppose a carbon tax? Why?
7. Do you think there is greater uncertainty over the course of action with respect to global warming than with other major policy decisions (addressing crime, trade, AIDS, etc.)?
8. How can the United States and other nations prepare for the effects of global warming? How do you think it will affect *you*?
9. Psychologists have found that most individuals have a far greater fear of events with large negative consequences even when the probability of occurrence is low (e.g., nuclear power plant meltdown) and much less fear of large everyday risks (e.g., driving). Why do you think that is the case? How, if at all, should this finding affect the debate over global warming? Should it affect public policy decisions generally?
10. Some have suggested that U.S. companies be allowed to meet greenhouse gas reduction goals through investment abroad (e.g., by preserving forests, modernizing or even closing aging industrial facilities, etc.). What are the implications of this? Is it a good idea? Or should U.S. firms be forced to make their reductions in the United States only?

ADDITIONAL READINGS

Abrahamson, Dean Edwin, ed. *The Challenge of Global Warming* (Washington, D.C.: Island Press, 1989).

Chichilnisky, Graciela, and Geoffrey Heal. "Global Environmental Risks." *Journal of Economic Perspectives* (Fall 1993).

Cline, William R. *The Economics of Global Warming* (Washington, D.C.: Institute for International Economics, 1992).

Gore, Al. *Earth in the Balance* (Boston: Houghton Mifflin, 1992).

Haas, Peter M., Robert O. Keohane, and Marc A. Levy, eds. *Institutions for the Earth* (Cambridge, Mass.: MIT Press, 1993).

Intergovernmental Panel on Climate Change. *Climate Change 1992* (Cambridge: Cambridge University Press, 1992).

McKibben, Bill. *The End of Nature* (New York: Anchor Books, 1989).

Michaels, Patrick J. *Sound and Fury: The Science and Politics of Global Warming* (Washington, D.C.: Cato Institute, 1992).

National Academy of Sciences. *Policy Implications of Greenhouse Warming* (Washington, D.C.: National Academy Press, 1991).

Nordhaus, William D. "Reflections on the Economics of Climate Change." *Journal of Economic Perspectives* (Fall 1993).

Organization for Economic Cooperation and Development. *Climate Change Policy Initiatives* (Paris: OECD, 1992).

Organization for Economic Cooperation and Development. *The Costs of Cutting Carbon Emissions: Results from Global Models* (Paris: OECD, 1993).

Scheraga, Joel D. "Combating Global Warming." *Challenge* (July/August 1990).

Speth, James Gustave. *Environmental Pollution: A Long-term Perspective* (Washington, D.C.: World Resources Institute, 1989).

U.S. Office of Technology Assessment. *Changing by Degrees: Steps to Reduce Greenhouse Gases* (Washington, D.C.: Office of Technology Assessment, 1991).

U.S. Office of Technology Assessment. *Preparing for an Uncertain Climate* (Washington, D.C.: Office of Technology Assessment, 1993).

United Nations. *Combating Global Warming: Study on a Global System of Tradeable Carbon Emission Entitlements* (New York: United Nations, 1992).

Weyant, John P. "Costs of Reducing Global Carbon Emissions." *Journal of Economic Perspectives* (Fall 1993).

Wittwer, Sylvan H. "Flower Power: Rising Carbon Dioxide Is Great for Plants." *Policy Review* (Fall 1992).

World Climate Conference (edited by J. Jager and H. L. Ferguson). *Climate Change: Science, Impacts and Policy* (Cambridge: Cambridge University Press, 1991).

PART IV
RIGHTS AND
REGULATIONS

14

AFFIRMATIVE ACTION/EQUAL OPPORTUNITY

"Is Affirmative Action an Effective Means to Advance the Interests of Minorities?"

Affirmative action programs designed to promote the economic and social standing of African Americans and other minorities have become one of the most bitterly divisive social issues in the United States. Part of this has to do with differing views on what affirmative action means; in short, what action is being affirmed? An earlier view held that because of past discrimination and subjugation, current hiring practices, housing policies, and other private and public endeavors were unfair to minorities. Therefore, it was argued, legislative action should ensure *equal opportunity* before the law. The Civil Rights Act of 1964 and the Voting Rights Act of 1965 were efforts in this direction and continue to enjoy widespread support today. But the question remains: What level of action is necessary to ensure an "equal playing field" for all individuals? Dick Gregory contrasted civil rights with human rights: "*Civil rights*: What black folks are given in the U.S. on the installment plan, as in civil-rights bills. Not to be confused with *human rights*, which are the dignity, stature, humanity, respect, and freedom belonging to all people by right of their birth." Is equal opportunity before the law in employment, housing, and education enough? Or are more active policies required?

Sammy Davis Jr. said in 1965, "Being a star has made it possible for me to get insulted in places where the average Negro could never *hope* to go and get insulted." Proponents of affirmative action programs claim that racial preference in hiring is justified on the grounds of past discrimination against African Americans, given this country's long history of slavery and racial segregation. As Malcolm X stated in 1964, "I don't see an American dream; . . . I see an American nightmare. . . . Three hundred and ten years we worked in this country without a dime in return." Furthermore, recent evidence of discriminatory lending practices on mortgages by some banks suggests that legislation prohibiting such behavior does not preclude de facto discrimination. However, while most Americans continue to profess the need to promote racial equality and to fight practices of racial discrimination, a majority of white Americans feel that affirmative action programs have gone too far and have become a source of reverse discrimination. Some believe that while the fight for juridical equality is a just goal, affirmative action programs have the effect in many cases of discriminating against more highly skilled white workers in order to favor otherwise less qualified minority applicants. This view is especially pronounced in areas where jobs are scarce and economic times difficult.

While a majority of both African Americans and white Americans polled in 1991 favored equal opportunity programs in general, 82 percent and 55 percent, respectively,[1] when asked if African Americans and minorities should receive hiring preference in order to make up for past discrimination, only 10 percent of whites believed this to be a justified course of action; 64 percent of African Americans, however, thought that this was an appropriate measure.[2] When the question turned to one of minorities receiving preferred admission to colleges, 16 percent of whites favored such a policy compared with 58 percent of African Americans.[3] In a 1990 poll over a third of African Americans thought that race relations had gotten worse in the past five years, compared with 26 percent who thought that conditions had improved.[4]

Politicians have played on these opinions in the electorate with much effectiveness, sometimes subtly and sometimes overtly, particularly for rallying the white blue-collar vote. Republican Senator Jesse Helms of North Carolina, when facing a strong challenge from an African-American opponent, became infamous for a campaign commercial that played off of whites' fears of losing job opportunities to minorities only on the basis of race. The infamous Willie Horton advertisement by the Bush campaign in 1988, which recounted an incident where a convicted African-American felon on furlough from a Massachusetts prison brutalized a white Maryland family, further fed racial fears. In Louisiana the political success of David Duke, a former Grand Wizard of the Ku Klux Klan, was perhaps the most obvious manifestation of the political salience of race in electoral politics in the late 1980s and early 1990s. Of a more subtle nature, President Bush tried in 1990 to cast the Civil Rights Act, which forced businesses to set aside a certain number of positions for minority candidates, as a "quota bill," knowing that most Americans opposed hiring quotas. The importance of race in American politics can scarcely be overstated. Thomas and Mary Edsall write that "Race is no longer a straightforward, morally unambiguous force in American politics; instead, considerations of race are now deeply imbedded in the strategy and tactics of politics, in competing concepts of the function and responsibility of government, and in each voter's conceptual structure of moral and partisan identity."[5]

Affirmative action programs got their first test in 1941 when President Roosevelt created the Fair Employment Practice Committee, which ordered defense contractors to cease discriminatory practices in hiring. However, the Roosevelt order was not accompanied by any form of sanction for companies that did not comply, and the committee was dissolved in 1946. Twenty years later the Kennedy administration, in response to growing concerns over racial segregation, particularly in the South, extended that rule to all federal contractors and gave it teeth. The administration authorized the creation of a commission to collect employment statistics, investigate contractor practices, and impose sanctions against those not in compliance.[6] However, it was not until the Civil Rights Act of 1964, passed a year after the "March on Washington" in support of equal rights, that discrimination was outlawed in hiring practices, in places of public accommodation, and in programs receiving federal assistance; the act also created the Equal Employment Opportunity Commission

(EEOC). The Voting Rights Act of 1965 and other related civil rights legislation of the time further sought to prevent racial discrimination. In 1965, President Lyndon Johnson took this a step further by ordering companies doing business within the federal government to put into writing affirmative action plans that would hire minorities in order to make up for past discrimination and injustices.[7] It was hoped that such actions would have the effect of eventually eliminating barriers to African Americans and other minorities and would promote full equality in employment. A 1972 amendment to the Civil Rights Act strengthened the authority of the EEOC by including state and local governments and labor organizations within its purview.[8]

Several Supreme Court rulings extended the power of affirmative action programs throughout the 1960s and 1970s. In the 1971 case *Griggs* v. *Duke Power* the Court ruled against the use of employment criteria such as high school diploma requirements or literacy tests, frequently used as barriers to the hiring of minorities.[9] In the 1978 landmark case *Regents of the University of California* v. *Allan Bakke*, the Supreme Court ruled that admissions policies of public educational institutions were permitted to take race into account (although the Court ordered that Bakke must be admitted to the medical school, from which he later graduated). In *United Steelworkers of America* v. *Weber*, the Court in 1979 approved preferential treatment for African Americans in private institutions (in this case, for training programs). Both the *Bakke* and *Weber* cases were decided by 5 to 4 votes, however.

A retrenchment in affirmative action enforcement ensued during the Reagan administration. Attorney General Edwin Meese argued against the minority hiring practices of affirmative action before the Supreme Court in 1985, and during the late 1980s a more conservative Court handed down several decisions that made it more difficult to prove discrimination in hiring practices, thus making enforcement of affirmative action programs all the more difficult. For example, the 1989 *City of Richmond* v. *J.A. Croson Company* decision invalidated a provision requiring Richmond's contractors to set aside 30 percent of their business for minority-owned companies. It is with the newer definition of affirmative action that political and constitutional problems arise.

Those opposing affirmative action maintain that by establishing quotas or otherwise giving advantage to minority applicants over whites, unjust discrimination against whites results. Furthermore, some economists argue that a freely competitive market in labor is the most efficient method of meeting employer needs and that free markets punish discrimination because employers would pay an economic cost by hiring inferior white applicants over better-qualified minorities, putting them at a competitive disadvantage. Some civil rights advocates and liberals also question the effectiveness of such programs, believing that they might be increasing racial tensions overall by creating the perception that minorities are poorly qualified for employment and need compensatory discrimination to be hired. They further argue that the benefits of affirmative action have gone mainly to middle-class African Americans and have done little to advance the interests of poorer ones.[10] In the second article below, Professor Shelby Steele of San Jose State University argues that this stigmatizes successful minorities and women, both in education and employment, who are viewed by some as being in their position solely due to their "unequal status." It is not so much that some liberals oppose affirmative action per se, but rather they believe that affirmative action has accomplished little for those most in need and that their political capital is best expended elsewhere to advance the interest of minorities. As one put it, "Democrats are now all too conscious of the price they have paid for *appearing* to be the party of quotas."[11]

A minority of Americans support an aggressive brand of affirmative action, however.[12] Among members of the preeminent civil rights groups, the NAACP and Urban League, for example, support for the program remains strong. These groups feel that affirmative action has translated into advances for African Americans that would not have occurred otherwise. While expecting affirmative action to eliminate poverty is unrealistic, they argue, large gains have been made in minority representation in public and private institutions as a result of affirmative action programs. Many members of the Democratic Party also continue to have a strong interest in preserving affirmative action for electoral as well as personal reasons.

In the first article below, Professor Stanley Fish of Duke University argues that critics' assertions that affirmative action represents "reverse racism" are strongly misleading because the two types of "racism" are not equivalent. The racism felt by minorities derives from oppressors who have sought to deny voting rights, education, and economic parity to another group. "Racism" against whites (in the form of affirmative action) is a result of past actions, not an attempt to subjugate one group based only on its race. He argues that affirmative action must be viewed in the historical context of more than two hundred years of oppression. Calls for an "even playing field" (ostensibly by eliminating affirmative action) are designed, Fish argues, to keep an already tilted playing field in favor of whites. The article in support of affirmative action by Fish is next, followed by Steele's article in opposition.

Endnotes

1. "Public Opinion and Demographic Report," *The American Enterprise* (September/October 1991), pp. 82–83.
2. Ibid.
3. Ibid.
4. Ibid.
5. Thomas Byrne Edsall with Mary D. Edsall, "Race," *The Atlantic Monthly* (May 1991), p. 53.
6. Paula Dwyer, Howard Gleckman, Troy Segal, Tim Smart, and Joseph Weber, "Race in the Workplace: Is Affirmative Action Working?" *Business Week* (July 8, 1991), p. 50.
7. Bron Raymond Taylor, *Affirmative Action At Work* (Pittsburgh: University of Pittsburgh Press, 1991), p. 21.
8. In 1989, the EEOC received 55,952 charges of discrimination, resolved 66,209 charges (some of these were from previous years), and enforced affirmative action

laws by court actions 598 times. The actions of the EEOC resulted in $127 million in monetary benefits for victims of discrimination. In 1989, appropriations allocated to the EEOC for its operation were $181 million (U.S. Equal Employment Opportunity Commission, *Fiscal Year 1989 Annual Report* [Washington, D.C., 1989]).

9. Taylor, *Affirmative Action At Work*, pp. 22–23.
10. See W. J. Wilson, "Race-Neutral Programs and the Democratic Coalition," *The American Prospect* (Spring 1990).
11. Paul Starr, "Civil Reconstruction: What to Do without Affirmative Action," *The American Prospect* (Winter 1992), p. 9.
12. This is true even when the question is framed as action intended to redress past wrongs. See Starr, "Civil Reconstruction."

YES

Reverse Racism or How the Pot Got to Call the Kettle Black

Stanley Fish

I take my text from George Bush, who, in an address to the United Nations on September 23, 1991, said this of the UN resolution equating Zionism with racism: "Zionism . . . is the idea that led to the creation of a home for the Jewish people. . . . And to equate Zionism with the intolerable sin of racism is to twist history and forget the terrible plight of Jews in World War II and indeed throughout history." What happened in the Second World War was that six million Jews were exterminated by people who regarded them as racially inferior and a danger to Aryan purity. What happened after the Second World War was that the survivors of that Holocaust established a Jewish state—that is, a state centered on Jewish history, Jewish values, and Jewish traditions: in short, a Jewocentric state. What President Bush objected to was the logical sleight of hand by which these two actions were declared equivalent because they were both expressions of racial exclusiveness. Ignored, as Bush said, was the *historical* difference between them—the difference between a program of genocide and the determination of those who escaped it to establish a community in which they would be the makers, not the victims, of the laws.

Only if racism is thought of as something that occurs principally in the mind, a falling-away from proper notions of universal equality, can the desire of a victimized and terrorized people to band together be declared morally identical to the actions of their would-be executioners. Only when the actions of the two groups are detached from the historical conditions of their emergence and given a purely abstract description can they be made interchangeable. Bush was saying to the United Nations, "Look, the Nazis' conviction of racial superiority generated a policy of systematic genocide; the Jews' experience of centuries of persecution in almost every country on earth generated a desire for a homeland of their own. If you manage somehow to convince yourself that these are the same, it is you, not the Zionists, who are morally confused, and the reason you are morally confused is that you have forgotten history."

A KEY DISTINCTION

What I want to say, following Bush's reasoning, is that a similar forgetting of history has in recent years allowed some people to argue, and argue persuasively, that affirmative action is reverse racism. The very phrase "reverse racism" contains the argument in exactly the form to which Bush objected: In this country whites once set themselves apart from blacks and claimed privileges

368

for themselves while denying them to others. Now, on the basis of race, blacks are claiming special status and reserving for themselves privileges they deny to others. Isn't one as bad as the other? The answer is no. One can see why by imagining that it is not 1993 but 1955, and that we are in a town in the South with two more or less distinct communities, one white and one black. No doubt each community would have a ready store of dismissive epithets, ridiculing stories, self-serving folk myths, and expressions of plain hatred, all directed at the other community, and all based in racial hostility. Yet to regard their respective racisms—if that is the word—as equivalent would be bizarre, for the hostility of one group stems not from any wrong done to it but from its wish to protect its ability to deprive citizens of their voting rights, to limit access to educational institutions, to prevent entry into the economy except at the lowest and most menial levels, and to force members of the stigmatized group to ride in the back of the bus. The hostility of the other group is the result of these actions, and whereas hostility and racial anger are unhappy facts wherever they are found, a distinction must surely be made between the ideological hostility of the oppressors and the experience-based hostility of those who have been oppressed.

Not to make that distinction is, adapting George Bush's words, to twist history and forget the terrible plight of African-Americans in the more than 200 years of this country's existence. Moreover, to equate the efforts to remedy that plight with the actions that produced it is to twist history even further. Those efforts, designed to redress the imbalances caused by long-standing discrimination, are called affirmative action; to argue that affirmative action, which gives preferential treatment to disadvantaged minorities as part of a plan to achieve social equality, is not different from the policies that created the disadvantages in the first place is a travesty of reasoning. "Reverse racism" is a cogent description of affirmative action only if one considers the cancer of racism to be morally and medically indistinguishable from the therapy we apply to it. A cancer is an invasion of the body's equilibrium, and so is chemotherapy; but we do not decline to fight the disease because the medicine we employ is also disruptive of normal functioning. Strong illness, strong remedy: the formula is as appropriate to the health of the body politic as it is to that of the body proper.

At this point someone will always say, "But two wrongs don't make a right; if it was wrong to treat blacks unfairly, it is wrong to give blacks preference and thereby treat whites unfairly." This objection is just another version of the forgetting and rewriting of history. The work is done by the adverb "unfairly," which suggests two more or less equal parties, one of whom has been unjustly penalized by an incompetent umpire. But blacks have not simply been treated unfairly; they have been subjected first to decades of slavery, and then to decades of second-class citizenship, widespread legalized discrimination, economic persecution, educational deprivation, and cultural stigmatization. They have been bought, sold, killed, beaten, raped, excluded, exploited, shamed, and scorned for a very long time. The word "unfair" is hardly an adequate description of their experience, and the belated gift of "fairness" in the form of a resolution no longer to discriminate against them legally is hardly an adequate remedy for the deep disadvantages that the prior discrimination has produced. When the deck is stacked against you in more ways than you can even count, it is small consolation to hear that you are now free to enter the game and take your chances.

A TILTED FIELD

The same insincerity and hollowness of promise infect another formula that is popular with the anti-affirmative-action crowd: the formula of 'ie level playing field. Here the argument usually takes the form of saying "It is undemocratic to give one class of citizens advantages at the expense of other citizens; the truly democratic way is to have a level playing field to which everyone has access and where everyone has a fair and equal chance to succeed on the basis of his or her merit." Fine words—but they conceal the facts of the situation as it has been given to us by history: the playing field is already tilted in favor of those by whom and for whom it was constructed in the first place. If mastery of the requirements for entry depends upon immersion in the cultural experiences of the mainstream majority, if the skills that make for success are nurtured by institutions and cultural practices from which the disadvantaged minority has been systematically excluded, if the language and ways of comporting oneself that identify a player as "one of us" are alien to the lives minorities are forced to live, then words like "fair" and "equal" are cruel jokes, for what they promote and celebrate is an institutionalized unfairness and a perpetuated inequality. The playing field is already tilted, and the resistance to altering it by the mechanisms of affirmative action is in fact a determination to make sure that the present imbalances persist as long as possible.

One way of tilting the field is the Scholastic Aptitude Test. This test figures prominently in Dinesh D'Souza's book *Illiberal Education* (1991), in which one finds many examples of white or Asian students denied admission to colleges and universities even though their SAT scores were higher than the scores of some others—often African-Americans—who were admitted to the same institution. This, D'Souza says, is evidence that as a result of affirmative-action policies colleges and universities tend "to depreciate the importance of merit criteria in admissions." D'Souza's assumption—and it is one that many would share—is that the test does in fact measure *merit*, with merit understood as a quality objectively determined in the same way that body temperature can be objectively determined.

In fact, however, the test is nothing of the kind. Statistical studies have suggested that test scores reflect income and socioeconomic status. It has been demonstrated again and again that scores vary in relation to cultural background; the test's questions assume a certain uniformity in educational experience and lifestyle and penalize those who, for whatever reason, have had a different experience and lived different kinds of lives. In short, what is being measured by the SAT is not absolutes like native ability and merit but accidents like birth, social position, access to libraries, and the opportunity to take vacations or to take SAT prep courses.

Furthermore, as David Owen notes in *None of the Above: Behind the Myth of Scholastic Aptitude* (1985), the "correlation between SAT scores and college grades . . . is lower than the correlation between weight and height; in other words you would have a better chance of predicting a person's height by looking at his weight than you would of predicting his freshman grades by looking only at his SAT scores." Everywhere you look in the SAT story, the claims of fairness, objectivity, and neutrality fall away, to be replaced by suspicions of specialized measures and unfair advantages.

Against this background a point that in isolation might have a questionable force takes on a special and even explanatory resonance: the principal deviser of the test was an out-and-out racist. In 1923 Carl Campbell Brigham published a book called *A Study of American Intelligence*, in which, as Owen notes, he declared, among other things, that we faced in America "a possibility of racial admixture . . . infinitely worse than that faced by any European country today, for we are incorporating the Negro into our racial stock, while all of Europe is comparatively free of this taint." Brigham had earlier analyzed the Army Mental Tests using classifications drawn from another racist text, Madison Grant's *The Passing of the Great Race*, which divided American society into four distinct racial strains, with Nordic, blue-eyed, blond people at the pinnacle and the American Negro at the bottom. Nevertheless, in 1925 Brigham became a director of testing for the College Board, and developed the SAT. So here is the great SAT test, devised by a racist in order to confirm racist assumptions, measuring not native ability but cultural advantage, an uncertain indicator of performance, an indicator of very little except what money and social privilege can buy. And it is in the name of this mechanism that we are asked to reject affirmative action and reaffirm "the importance of merit criteria in admissions."

THE REALITY OF DISCRIMINATION

Nevertheless, there is at least one more card to play against affirmative action, and it is a strong one. Granted that the playing field is not level and that access to it is reserved for an already advantaged elite, the disadvantages suffered by others are less racial—at least in 1993—than socioeconomic. Therefore shouldn't, as D'Souza urges, "universities . . . retain their policies of preferential treatment, but alter their criteria of application from race to socioeconomic disadvantage," and thus avoid the unfairness of current policies that reward middle-class or affluent blacks at the expense of poor whites? One answer to this question is given by D'Souza himself when he acknowledges that the overlap between minority groups and the poor is very large—a point underscored by the former Secretary of Education Lamar Alexander, who said, in response to a question about funds targeted for black students, "Ninety-eight percent of race-specific scholarships do not involve constitutional problems."

He meant, I take it, that 98 percent of race-specific scholarships were also scholarships to the economically disadvantaged.

Still, the other two percent—nonpoor, middle-class, economically favored blacks—are receiving special attention on the basis of disadvantages they do not experience. What about them? The force of the question depends on the assumption that in this day and age race could not possibly be a serious disadvantage to those who are otherwise well positioned in the society. But the lie was given dramatically to this assumption in a 1991 broadcast of the ABC program *PrimeTime Live*. In a stunning fifteen-minute segment reporters and a camera crew followed two young men of equal education, cultural sophistication, level of apparent affluence, and so forth around St. Louis, a city where neither was known. The two differed in only a single respect: one was white, the other black. But that small difference turned out to mean everything. In a series of encounters with shoe salesmen, record-store employees, rental agents, landlords, employment agencies, taxicab drivers, and ordinary citizens, the black member of the pair was either ignored or given a special and suspicious attention. He was asked to pay more for the same goods or come up with a larger down payment for the same car, was turned away as a prospective tenant, was rejected as a prospective taxicab fare, was treated with contempt and irritation by clerks and bureaucrats, and in every way possible was made to feel inferior and unwanted.

The inescapable conclusion was that alike though they may have been in almost all respects, one of these young men, because he was black, would lead a significantly lesser life than his white counterpart: he would be housed less well and at greater expense; he would pay more for services and products when and if he was given the opportunity to buy them; he would have difficulty establishing credit; the first emotions he would inspire on the part of many people he met would be distrust and fear; his abilities would be discounted even before he had a chance to display them; and, above all, the treatment he received from minute to minute would chip away at his self-esteem and self-confidence with consequences that most of us could not even imagine. As the young man in question said at the conclusion of the broadcast, "You walk down the street with a suit and tie and it doesn't matter. Someone will make determinations about you, determinations that affect the quality of your life."

Of course, the same determinations are being made quite early on by kindergarten teachers, grade school principals, high school guidance counselors, and the like, with results that cut across socioeconomic lines and place young black men and women in the ranks of the disadvantaged no matter what the bank accounts of their parents happen to show. Racism is a cultural fact, and although its effects may to some extent be diminished by socioeconomic variables, those effects will still be sufficiently great to warrant the nation's attention and thus the continuation of affirmative-action policies. This is true even of the field thought to be dominated by blacks and often cited as evidence of the equal opportunities society now affords them. I refer, of course, to professional athletics. But national self-congratulation on this score might pause in the face of a few facts: A minuscule number of African-Americans ever receive a paycheck from a professional team. Even though nearly 1,600 daily newspapers report on the exploits of black athletes, they employ only seven full-time black sports columnists. Despite repeated pledges and resolutions, major-league teams have managed to put only a handful of blacks and Hispanics in executive positions.

WHY ME?

When all is said and done, however, one objection to affirmative action is unanswerable on its own terms, and that is the objection of the individual who says, "Why me? Sure, discrimination has persisted for many years, and I acknowledge that the damage done has not been removed by changes in the law. But why me? I didn't own slaves; I didn't vote to keep people on the back of the bus; I didn't turn water hoses on civil-rights marchers. Why, then, should I be the one who doesn't get the job or who doesn't get the scholarship or who gets bumped back to the waiting list?"

I sympathize with this feeling, if only because in a small way I have had the experience that produces it. I was recently nominated for an administrative post at a large university. Early signs were encouraging, but after an interval I received official notice that I would not be included at the next level of consideration, and subsequently I was told unofficially that at some point a decision had been made to look only in the direction of women and minorities. Although I was disappointed, I did not conclude that the situation was "unfair," because the policy was obviously not directed at me—at no point in the proceedings did someone say, "Let's find a way to rule out Stanley Fish." Nor was it directed even at persons of my race and sex—the policy was not intended to disenfranchise white males. Rather, the policy was driven by other considerations, and it was only as a by-product of those considerations—not as the main goal—that white males like me were rejected. Given that the institution in question has a high percentage of minority students, a very low percentage of minority faculty, and an even lower percentage of minority administrators, it made perfect sense to focus on women and minority candidates, and within that sense, not as the result of prejudice, my whiteness and maleness became disqualifications.

I can hear the objection in advance: "What's the difference? Unfair is unfair: you didn't get the job; you didn't even get on the short list." The difference is not in the outcome but in the ways of thinking that led up to the outcome. It is the difference between an unfairness that befalls one as the unintended effect of a policy rationally conceived and an unfairness that is pursued as an end in itself. It is the difference between the awful unfairness of Nazi extermination camps and the unfairness to Palestinian Arabs that arose from, but was not the chief purpose of, the founding of a Jewish state.

THE NEW BIGOTRY

The point is not a difficult one, but it is difficult to see when the unfairness scenarios are presented as simple contrasts between two decontextualized persons who emerge from nowhere to contend for a job or a place in a freshman class. Here is student A; he has a board score of 1,300. And here is student B; her board score is only 1,200, yet she is admitted and A is rejected. Is that fair? Given the minimal information provided, the answer is of course no. But if we expand our horizons and consider fairness in relation to the cultural and institutional histories that have brought the two students to this point, histories that weigh on them even if they are not the histories' authors, then both the question and the answer suddenly grow more complicated.

The sleight-of-hand logic that first abstracts events from history and then assesses them from behind a veil of willed ignorance gains some of its plausibility from another key word in the anti-affirmative-action lexicon. That word is "individual," as in "The American way is to focus on the rights of individuals rather than groups." Now, "individual" and "individualism" have been honorable words in the American political vocabulary, and they have often been well employed in the fight against various tyrannies. But like any other word or concept, individualism can be perverted to serve ends the opposite of those it originally served, and this is what has happened when in the name of individual rights, millions of individuals are enjoined from redressing historically documented wrongs. How is this managed? Largely in the same way that the invocation of fairness is used to legitimize an institutionalized inequality. First one says, in the most solemn of tones, that the protection of individual rights is the chief obligation of society. Then one defines individuals as souls sent into the world with equal entitlements as guaranteed either by their Creator or by the Constitution. Then one pretends that nothing has happened to them since they stepped onto the world's stage. And then one says of these carefully denatured souls that they will all be treated in the same way, irrespective of any of the differences that history has produced. Bizarre as it may seem, individualism in this argument turns out to mean that everyone is or should be the *same*. This dismissal of individual difference in the name of the individual would be funny were its consequences not so serious: it is the mechanism by which imbalances and inequities suffered by millions of people through no fault of their own can be sanitized and even celebrated as the natural workings of unfettered democracy.

"Individualism," "fairness," "merit"—these three words are continually misappropriated by bigots who have learned that they need not put on a white hood or bar access to the ballot box in order to secure their ends. Rather, they need only clothe themselves in a vocabulary plucked from its historical context and made into the justification for attitudes and policies they would not acknowledge if frankly named.

NO

A Negative Vote on Affirmative Action

Shelby Steele

In a few short years, when my two children will be applying to college, the affirmative-action policies by which most universities offer black students some form of preferential treatment will present me with a dilemma. I am a middle-class black, a college professor, far from wealthy, but also well removed from the kind of deprivation that would qualify my children for the label "disadvantaged." Both of them have endured racial insensitivity from whites. They have been called names, have suffered slights and have experienced first hand the peculiar malevolence that racism brings out of people. Yet they have never experienced racial discrimination, have never been stopped by their race on any path they have chosen to follow. Still, their society now tells them that if they will only designate themselves as black on their college applications, they will probably do better in the college lottery than if they conceal this fact. I think there is something of a Faustian bargain in this.

Of course many blacks and a considerable number of whites would say that I was sanctimoniously making affirmative action into a test of character. They would say that this small preference is the meagerest recompense for centuries of unrelieved oppression. And to these arguments other very obvious facts must be added. In America, many marginally competent or flatly incompetent whites are hired everyday—some because their white skin suits the conscious or unconscious racial preference of their employers. The white children of alumni are often grandfathered into elite universities in what can only be seen as a residual benefit of historic white privilege. Worse, white incompetence is always an individual matter, but for blacks it is often confirmation of ugly stereotypes. Given that unfairness cuts both ways, doesn't it only balance the scales of history, doesn't this repay, in a small way, the systematic denial under which my children's grandfather lived out his days?

In theory, affirmative action certainly has all the moral symmetry that fairness requires. It is reformist and corrective, even repentent and redemptive. And I would never sneer at these good intentions. Born in the late 1940's in Chicago, I started my education (a charitable term, in this case) in a segregated school, and suffered all the indignities that come to blacks in a segregated society. My father, born in the South, made it only to the third grade before the white man's fields took permanent priority over his formal education. And though he educated himself into an advanced reader with an almost professorial authority, he could only drive a truck for a living, and never earned more than $90 a week in his entire life. So yes, it is crucial to my sense of citizenship, to my ability to identify with the spirit and the interests of America, to know that this country, however imperfectly, recognizes its past sins and wishes to correct them.

Yet good intentions can blind us to the effects they generate when implemented. In our society affirmative action is, among other things, a testament to white good will and to black power, and in the midst of these heavy investments its effects can be hard to see. But after 20 years of implementation I think that affirmative action has shown itself to be more bad than good and that blacks—whom I will focus on in this essay—now stand to lose more from it than they gain.

In talking with affirmative-action administrators and with blacks and whites in general, I found that supporters of affirmative action focus on its good intentions and detractors emphasize its negative effects. It was virtually impossible to find people outside either camp. The closest I came was a white male manager at a large computer company who said, "I think it amounts to reverse discrimination, but I'll put up with a little of that for a little more diversity." But this only makes him a half-hearted supporter of affirmative action. I think many people who don't really like affirmative action support it to one degree or another anyway.

I believe they do this because of what happened to white and black Americans in the crucible of the 1960's, when whites were confronted with their racial guilt and blacks tasted their first real power. In that stormy time white absolution and black power coalesced into virtual mandates for society. Affirmative action became a meeting ground for those mandates in the law. At first, this meant insuring equal opportunity. The 1964 civil-rights bill was passed on the understanding that equal opportunity would not mean racial preference. But in the late 60's and early 70's, affirmative action underwent a remarkable escalation of its mission from simple anti-discrimination enforcement to social engineering by means of quotas, goals, timetables, set-asides and other forms of preferential treatment.

Legally, this was achieved through a series of executive orders and Equal Employment Opportunity Commission guidelines that allowed racial imbalances in the workplace to stand as proof of racial discrimination. Once it could be assumed that discrimination explained racial imbalances, it became easy to justify group remedies to presumed discrimination rather than the normal case-by-case redress.

Even though blacks had made great advances during the 60's without quotas, the white mandate to achieve a new racial innocence and the black mandate to gain power, which came to a head in the very late 60's, could no longer be satisfied by anything less than racial preferences. I don't think these mandates, in themselves, were wrong, because whites clearly needed to do better by blacks and blacks needed more real power in society. But as they came together in affirmative action, their effect was to distort our understanding of racial discrimination. By making black the color of preference, these mandates have reburdened society with the very marriage of color and preference (in reverse) that we set out to eradicate.

When affirmative action grew into social engineering, diversity became a golden word. Diversity is a term that applies democratic principles to races and cultures rather than to citizens, despite the fact that there is nothing to indicate that real diversity is the same thing as proportionate representation. Too often the result of this, on campuses for example, has been a democracy of colors rather than of people, an artificial diversity that gives the appearance of an educational parity between black and white students that has not yet been achieved in reality. Here again, racial preferences allow society to leapfrog over the difficult problem of developing blacks to parity with whites and into a cosmetic diversity that covers the blemish of disparity—a full six years after admission, only 26 to 28 percent of blacks graduate from college.

Racial representation is not the same thing as racial development. Representation can be manufactured; development is always hard earned. But it is the music of innocence and power that we hear in affirmative action that causes us to cling to it and to its distracting emphasis on representation. The fact is that after 20 years of racial preferences, the gap between median incomes of black and white families is greater than it was in the 1970's. None of this is to say that blacks don't need policies that insure our right to equal opportunity, but what we need more of is the development that will let us take advantage of society's efforts to include us.

I think one of the most troubling effects of racial preferences for blacks is a kind of demoralization. Under affirmative action, the quality that earns us preferential treatment is an implied inferiority. However this inferiority is explained—and it is easily enough explained by the myriad deprivations that grew out of our oppression—it is still inferiority. There are explanations and then there is the fact. And the fact must be borne by the individual as a condition apart from the explanation, apart even from the fact that others like himself also bear this condition. In integrated situations in which blacks must compete with whites who may be better prepared, these explanations may quickly wear thin and expose the individual to racial as well as personal self-doubt. (Of course whites also feel doubt, but only personally, not racially.)

What this means in practical terms is that when blacks deliver themselves into integrated situations they encounter a nasty little reflex in whites, a mindless, atavistic reflex that responds to the color black with negative stereotypes, such as intellectual ineptness. I think this reflex embarrasses most whites today and thus it is usually quickly repressed. On an equally atavistic level, the black will be aware of the reflex his color triggers and will feel a stab of horror at seeing himself reflected in this way. He, too, will do a quick repression, but a lifetime of such stabbings is what constitutes his inner realm of racial doubt. Even when the black sees no implication of inferiority in racial preferences, he knows that whites do, so that—consciously or unconsciously—the result is virtually the same. The effect of preferential treatment—the lowering of normal standards to increase black representation—puts blacks at war with an expanded realm of debilitating doubt, so that the doubt itself becomes an unrecognized preoccupation that undermines their ability to perform, especially in integrated situations.

I believe another liability of affirmative action comes from the fact that it indirectly encourages blacks to exploit their own past victimization. Like implied inferiority, victimization is what justifies preference, so that to receive the benefits of preferential treatment one must, to some extent, become invested in the view of one's self as a victim. In this way, affirmative action nurtures a victim-focused identity in blacks and sends us the message that there is more power in our past suffering than in our present achievements.

When power itself grows out of suffering, blacks are encouraged to expand the boundaries of what qualifies as racial oppression, a situation that can lead us to paint our victimization in vivid colors even as we receive the benefits of preference. The same corporations and institutions that give us preference are also seen as our oppressors. At Stanford University, minority-group students—who receive at least the same financial aid as whites with the same need—recently took over the president's office demanding, among other things, more financial aid.

But I think one of the worst prices that blacks pay for preference has to do with an illusion. I saw this illusion at work recently in the mother of a middle-class black student who was going off to his first semester of college: "They owe us this, so don't think for a minute that you don't belong there." This is the logic by which many blacks, and some whites, justify affirmative action—it is something "owed," a form of reparation. But this logic overlooks a much harder and less digestible reality, that it is impossible to repay blacks living today for the historic suffering of the race. If all blacks were given a million dollars tomorrow it would not amount to a dime on the dollar for three centuries of oppression, nor would it dissolve the residues of that oppression that we still carry today. The concept of historic reparation grows out of man's need to impose on the world a degree of justice that simply does not exist. Suffering can be endured and overcome, it cannot be repaid. To think otherwise is to prolong the suffering.

Several blacks I spoke with said they were still in favor of affirmative action because of the "subtle" discrimination blacks were subject to once they were on the job. One photojournalist said, "They have ways of ignoring you." A black female television producer said: "You can't file a lawsuit when your boss doesn't invite you to the insider meetings without ruining your career. So we still need affirmative action." Others mentioned the infamous "glass ceiling" through which blacks can see the top positions of authority but never reach them. But I don't think racial preferences are a protection against this subtle discrimination; I think they contribute to it.

In any workplace, racial preferences will always create two-tiered populations composed of preferreds and unpreferreds. In the case of blacks and whites, for instance, racial preferences imply that whites are superior just as they imply that blacks are inferior. They not only reinforce America's oldest racial myth but, for blacks, they have the effect of stigmatizing the already stigmatized.

I think that much of the "subtle" discrimination that blacks talk about is often (not always) discrimination against the stigma of questionable competence that affirmative action marks blacks with. In this sense, preferences make scapegoats of the very people they seek to help. And it may be that at a certain level employers impose a glass ceiling, but this may not be against the race so much as against the race's reputation for having advanced by color as much as by competence. This ceiling is the point at which corporations shift the emphasis from color to competency and stop playing the affirmative-action game. Here preference backfires for blacks and becomes a taint that holds them back. Of course one could argue that this taint, which is after all in the minds of whites, becomes nothing more than an excuse to discriminate against blacks. And certainly the result is the same in either case—blacks don't get past the glass ceiling. But this argument does not get around the fact that racial preferences now taint this color with a new theme of suspicion that makes blacks even more vulnerable to discrimination. In this crucial yet gray area of perceived competence, preferences make whites look better than they are and blacks worse, while doing nothing whatever to stop the very real discrimination that blacks may encounter. I don't wish to justify the glass ceiling here, but only suggest the very subtle ways that affirmative action revives rather than extinguishes the old rationalizations for racial discrimination.

I believe affirmative action is problematic in our society because we have demanded that it create parity between the races rather than insure equal opportunity. Preferential treatment does not teach skills, or educate, or instill motivation. It only passes out entitlement by color, a situation that in my profession has created an unrealistically high demand for black professors. The social engineer's assumption is that this high demand will inspire more blacks to earn Ph.D's and join the profession. In fact, the number of blacks earning Ph.D's has declined in recent years. Ph.D's must be developed from preschool on. They require family and community support. They must acquire an entire system of values that enables them to work hard while delaying gratification.

It now seems clear that the Supreme Court, in a series of recent decisions, is moving away from racial preferences. It has disallowed preferences except in instances of "identified discrimination," eroded the precedent that statistical racial imbalances are prima facie evidence of discrimination, and, in effect, granted white males the right to challenge consent degrees that use preference to achieve racial balances in the workplace. Referring to this and other Supreme Court decisions, one civil-rights leader said, "Night has fallen . . . as far as civil rights are concerned." But I am not so sure. The effect of these decisions is to protect the constitutional rights of everyone, rather than to take rights away from blacks. Night has fallen on racial preferences, not on the fundamental rights of black Americans. The reason for this shift, I believe, is that the white mandate for absolution from past racial sins has weakened considerably in the 1980's. Whites are now less willing to endure unfairness to themselves in order to grant special entitlements to blacks, even when those entitlements are justified in the name of past suffering. Yet the black mandate for more power in society has remained unchanged. And I think part of the anxiety many blacks feel over these decisions has to do with the loss of black power that they may signal.

But the power we've lost by these decisions is really only the power that grows out of our victimization. This is not a very substantial or reliable power, and it is important that we know this so we can focus more exclusively on the kind of development that will bring enduring power. There is talk now that

Congress may pass new legislation to compensate for these new limits on affirmative action. If this happens, I hope the focus will be on development and anti-discrimination, rather than entitlement, on achieving racial parity rather than jerry-building racial diversity.

But if not preferences, what? The impulse to discriminate is subtle and cannot be ferreted out unless its many guises are made clear to people. I think we need social policies that are committed to two goals: the educational and economic development of disadvantaged people regardless of race and the eradication from our society—through close monitoring and severe sanctions—of racial, ethnic or gender discrimination. Preferences will not get us to either of these goals, because they tend to benefit those who are not disadvantaged—middle-class white women and middle-class blacks—and attack one form of discrimination with another. Preferences are inexpensive and carry the glamour of good intentions—change the numbers and the good deed is done. To be against them is to be unkind. But I think the unkindest cut is to bestow on children like my own an undeserved advantage while neglecting the development of those disadvantaged children in the poorer sections of my city who will most likely never be in a position to benefit from a preference. Give my children fairness; give disadvantaged children a better shot at development—better elementary and secondary schools, job training, safer neighborhoods, better financial assistance for college and so on. A smaller percentage of black high school graduates go to college today than 15 years ago; more black males are in prison, jail or in some other way under the control of the criminal-justice system than in college. This despite racial preferences.

The mandates of black power and white absolution out of which preferences emerged were not wrong in themselves. What was wrong was that both races focused more on the goals of those mandates than on the means to the goals. Blacks can have no real power without taking responsibility for their own educational and economic development. Whites can have no racial innocence without earning it by eradicating discrimination and helping the disadvantaged to develop. Because we ignored the means, the goals have not been reached and the real work remains to be done.

DISCUSSION QUESTIONS

1. What does "affirmative action" mean to you? Is your definition different from "equal opportunity"?
2. What do you think the appropriate goal for affirmative action should be?
3. What groups, if any, should qualify for special consideration under affirmative action plans? Armenian Americans? Jews? Italians? What criteria are necessary or sufficient for inclusion?
4. Do you believe that the "playing field" is now even with respect to race, or are one or more groups relatively advantaged? If it is not level, what action(s) would improve racial parity in education and employment?

5. Is affirmative action "reverse racism"? In what ways are the two concepts similar? In what ways are they different?
6. How do you feel about affirmative action being used as a "divisive" issue in political campaigns? Do such campaigns add to racial tension, or is it "just politics"? How do you think that such campaigns influence people's attitudes toward "racial justice"?

ADDITIONAL READINGS

Altschiller, Donald, ed. *Affirmative Action* (New York: H.W. Wilson, 1991).

Boxill, Bernard R. *Blacks and Social Justice* (Lanham, Md.: Rowman & Littlefield, 1992).

Carter, Stephen L. *Reflections of an Affirmative Action Baby* (New York: Basic Books, 1991).

Clayton, Susan D., and Faye J. Crosby. *Justice, Gender, and Affirmative Action* (Ann Arbor: University of Michigan Press, 1992).

D'Souza, Dinesh. *Illiberal Education* (New York: The Free Press, 1991).

Eastland, Terry, and William J. Bennett. *Counting by Race: Equality from the Founding Fathers to Bakke* (New York: Basic Books, 1979).

Edsall, Thomas Byrne, with Mary D. Edsall. *Chain Reaction: The Impact of Race, Rights, and Taxes on American Politics* (New York: Norton, 1991).

Graham, Hugh Davis. *The Civil Rights Era: Origins and Development of National Policy, 1960–1972* (New York: Oxford University Press, 1990).

Kluger, Richard. *Simple Justice: The History of Brown v. Board of Education and Black America's Struggle for Equality* (New York: Knopf, 1976).

LaNoue, George R. "Social Science and Minority 'Set-Asides.'" *The Public Interest* (Winter 1993).

Reynolds, William Bradford. "Affirmative Action and Its Negative Repercussions." *The Annals of the American Academy of Political and Social Science* (September 1992).

Rosenfeld, Michel. *Affirmative Action and Justice: A Philosophical and Constitutional Inquiry* (New Haven, Conn.: Yale University Press, 1991).

Sowell, Thomas. "Affirmative Action: A Worldwide Disaster." *Commentary* (December 1989).

Sowell, Thomas. *Preferential Policies: An International Perspective* (New York: W. Morrow, 1990).

Steele, Shelby. *The Content of Our Character: A New Vision of Race in America* (New York: St. Martin's Press, 1990).

Sunstein, Cass R. *After the Rights Revolution* (Cambridge, Mass.: Harvard University Press, 1990).

Taylor, Bron Raymond. *Affirmative Action at Work: Law, Politics, and Ethics* (Pittsburgh: University of Pittsburgh Press, 1991).

Taylor, William L., and Susan M. Liss. "Affirmative Action in the 1990s: Staying the Course." *The Annals of the American Academy of Political and Social Science* (September 1992).

Tollett, Kenneth S. "Racism and Race-Conscious Remedies." *The American Prospect* (Spring 1991).

Tummala, Krishna K., ed. *Equity in Public Employment Across Nations* (Lanham, Md.: University Press of America, 1989).

Wilson, William J. "Race-Neutral Programs and the Democratic Coalition." *The American Prospect* (Spring 1990).

Wyzan, Michael L., ed. *The Political Economy of Ethnic Discrimination and Affirmative Action: A Comparative Perspective* (New York: Praeger, 1990).

15
DRUG POLICY
"Should Drugs Be Legalized?"

Lenny Bruce said in 1967 that "Pot will probably be legal in ten years. Why? Because in this audience probably every other one of you knows a law student who smokes pot, who will become a senator, who will legalize it to protect himself. But then no one will smoke it anymore. You'll see." The only element of Bruce's prediction that turned out to be true is that current senators have admitted to smoking marijuana in their college days. Nevertheless, drug legalization or decriminalization is beginning to loom large in modern policy debates. The current surgeon general, Joycelyn Elders, has recommended that the government study the idea of legalizing drugs (after backing off from a personal comment that she supports such an idea),[1] joining a growing list of politicians—many of them big-city mayors—who have publicly supported such a move.

The rising tide of urban violence has frequently been tied to the enormous profits that can be had from the sale of illegal drugs. It is estimated that 6.2 percent of the 21,505 homicides committed in 1991 were drug-related.[2] Furthermore, 13.3 percent of all prison inmates in 1989 committed their offenses in order to obtain money for the purchase of drugs; this includes 32 percent of robberies, 31 percent of burglaries, 23 percent of frauds, and 3 percent of homicides.[3] State and local authorities made over one million arrests for drug violations in 1991, three-fourths of them for possession offenses (compared with sale and manufacturing violations).[4] These events have driven a public outcry to take action to stem the flow of narcotics and especially their availability to children.*

Perhaps more than any other policy debate in this volume, the issue of drug legalization defies simple ideological characterization. Proponents range from libertarian academics to big-city mayors to those on the far political left, while opponents of legalization include conservatives and liberals alike. Therefore, unusual political coalitions can be found on either side of the debate. The political reaction to the "drug problem" has been based on two different strategies. Those who feel that the best approach to dealing with the problem of drugs is to emphasize expanding drug treatment programs, drug awareness programs, and strict sentencing for users compose the "demand side." Others believe that efforts should focus on utilizing law enforcement to interdict the shipment of drugs and to crack down heavily on the sale and

---

* The level of public concern has varied greatly, however, from a peak of 54 percent of respondents stating that drugs were the most important problem in 1990, compared with just 4 percent in early 1992 (*New York Times* [July 28, 1992]).

use of drugs, or "supply side" responses. Governmental policy has reflected both trends.

The success of the latest "war on drugs" that was initiated during the 1980s has been a subject of much controversy. Congress has passed the 1986 Antidrug Abuse Act, the 1988 Antidrug Abuse Act, the International Narcotics Control Act (INCA) of 1989, and the INCA of 1992. Expenditures on combating illegal drugs have risen more than 750 percent since 1981 to nearly $13 billion today. The stepped-up effort to fight the manufacture, distribution, and consumption of drugs during this period included the Partnership for a Drug Free America, Nancy Reagan's "Just Say No" campaign, increased community awareness programs, the creation of the Office of National Drug Control Policy (the so-called "drug czar"), and significantly increased funding of law enforcement units for drug interdiction efforts. Funding at the federal level for drug control policies was $12.2 billion in fiscal year 1993, with well over half of that figure (65 percent) going to supply-side efforts such as law enforcement and related military agencies.[5] Approximately $5.6 billion in supply-side spending was devoted to domestic law enforcement and the remaining $2.3 billion to international efforts, including interdiction. The majority of the remaining $4.3 billion (or 35 percent) for demand-side expenditures went to fund health-related agencies and other demand-reduction efforts.[6] The allocations for the demand component at the federal level were divided between prevention efforts, which received $1.7 billion, and treatment programs, which received $2.6 billion.[7] In 1991, individual states spent nearly $3.25 billion on alcohol and drug abuse services such as treatment and prevention. Of this money, treatment programs received nearly five times as much as prevention efforts.[8]

This additional effort had mixed results for interdiction efforts. For example, in 1985 the Drug Enforcement Administration (DEA) seized 338 clandestine drug laboratories, 18,000 kilograms (kg) of cocaine, 745,000 kg of marijuana, and 447 kg of heroin. Between 1985 and 1989, seizures of cocaine rose dramatically, reaching a peak in 1989 of 82,000 kg, then falling slightly to 77,000 in 1992. Seizures of marijuana declined steadily through 1991 to 108,000 kg but then nearly doubled to 201,000 kg in 1992. Heroin seizures showed no definite trend but reached a peak level of 1,100 kg in 1991. Total seizures of property by DEA officials amounted to some $857 million in 1992,[9] and the roughly estimated street value of cocaine, marijuana, and heroin seized in 1992 was some $27 billion.[10] Assessing whether this trend means success or failure of drug policy is difficult, however. On one hand, more drugs seized may indicate that DEA is doing a better job. On the other, more drugs seized may mean that more drugs are available, and the DEA is merely confiscating its normal share of a larger pool of drugs. Therefore, success or failure should not hinge solely on interdiction statistics. Despite the efforts of the U.S. and foreign governments, criminal organizations are estimated to generate over $300 billion from the illegal sale of drugs.

Furthermore, the national "drug czar" has been criticized as nothing more than a symbolic coordinator of numerous and disparate federal agencies with little power to shape policy. Supporters maintain that a more coherent national policy has resulted from the office's efforts. The Clinton administration slashed funding for the office early in its tenure while simultaneously elevating the director's position to the cabinet level.

A number of other important substantive issues over drug policy continue to be debated. One is whether funds directed toward interdiction, which many consider to have failed miserably, would be better spent on prevention and treatment instead. Supporters argue that while treatment does not always work, it is far more cost effective than imprisonment. Moreover, drug cases have clogged the federal court system, and judges are forced to push civil cases aside in order to handle the vast number of drug-related cases (despite large funding increases).

Recent trends show a tendency toward decreasing drug usage in all population groups. The annual use for some selected drugs* has fallen significantly for youth (ages twelve to seventeen) and young adults (ages eighteen to twenty-five). In 1974, 19 percent of those aged twelve to seventeen admitted to having used marijuana "during the past year"; this figure rose to a high of 24 percent in 1979, but receded to 10 percent by 1991. (There was a significant downward acceleration in this trend beginning in 1985.) A similar overall trend existed for cocaine: in 1974, 2.7 percent admitted to having used cocaine during the previous year, 4.2 percent in 1979, and 1.5 percent in 1991. Data on heroin usage in this age group have been limited but showed a significant drop in usage levels from 0.6 percent to 0.2 percent from 1990 to 1991.[11] While larger percentages of the eighteen to twenty-five age group are using drugs, the trends over time are similar to those of youth. For marijuana, 34 percent admitted use in 1974, 47 percent in 1979, and 24 percent in 1991. For cocaine, 8 percent admitted use in 1974, 20 percent in 1979, and under 8 percent by 1991. The same data indicated that heroin use declined from 0.8 percent in 1974 to 0.3 percent in 1991.[12] Among adults aged twenty-six and older the percentages were significantly lower. For this group marijuana usage went from 3.8 percent in 1974, reached a high of 10.6 percent in 1982, and then declined to 6.6 percent in 1991.[13] Cocaine saw a rise from a negligible amount in 1974 to a high of 4.2 percent in 1985, dropping to 2.3 percent in 1990.[14] Available data for heroin usage show that between 0.1 and 0.2 percent of adults in this age group admitted use since 1988.

Perceptions of drug usage have also shifted in recent years. In many school circles, drug use is no longer an approved or encouraged activity. The percentage of high school seniors who fear "great risk" to themselves from occasional use of cocaine increased from 54 percent to 75 percent from 1985 to 1991. There was a similar increase (from 24 percent in 1985 to 40 percent in 1991) in fear regarding marijuana.[15] A similar trend has been found in young adults aged nineteen to thirty.[16] These changing perceptions, as well

---

* Drug categories include marijuana and hashish, inhalants, hallucinogens, cocaine, heroin, nonmedical use of stimulants, sedatives, tranquilizers, analgesics, and alcohol.

as the increased interdiction efforts of law enforcement, have not affected high school seniors' perceptions of the availability of illicit drugs, however. In 1985, it was reported that 86 percent of high school seniors felt that it was "fairly" or "very" easy to obtain marijuana, 49 percent felt the same way about cocaine, and 21 percent for heroin. In 1992, slightly fewer (83 percent) believed marijuana was fairly or very easy to obtain, but more believed cocaine (53 percent) and heroin (35 percent) were more readily available than seven years earlier.[17]

Attitudes toward drug legalization have changed throughout the 1980s. In 1980, 26 percent of high school seniors felt that marijuana should be completely legalized; by 1986 that figure had shrunk to 15 percent but by 1992 had risen to 19 percent. Twenty-six percent of high school seniors felt in 1980 that marijuana use should always be a crime, rising to 48 percent by 1992.[18] College freshman have shown a similar shift in attitude, although one more pronounced than members of the population at large. A national survey in 1980 reported that 25 percent of the U.S. population thought that marijuana should be made legal, declining to 18 percent in 1991. The trends reported indicate that the preference for drug legalization increases for males, for those with higher incomes, and for those with greater education.

Proponents of drug legalization argue that current high street prices for illegal drugs encourage criminal activity. Legalization would drastically reduce the price of drugs and thereby all but eliminate crimes committed to obtain drugs, to protect distribution networks, etc. Further, drug purity could be regulated and the distribution supervised, thereby reducing poisoning and abuse. Legalization proponents sometimes encourage a concomitant tax on drugs to fund treatment and education programs. (Of course, if the drug tax is set too high, the advantages of legalization evaporate as drug prices are once again driven upward.) Ethan Nadelmann of Princeton University is one of the leading proponents of this position. He writes below that current and past efforts at drug control have been failures, and the costs that those efforts impose on society far outweigh any benefit gained. He responds to critics by acknowledging the potential for abuse, but argues that the dangers of drug use have been vastly overstated.

Opponents of drug legalization point out that if the price of drugs falls enough to have the positive effects that supporters argue, it will encourage greater use (and therefore addiction) to narcotics. Just because the "war on drugs" has not been an obvious success does not mean that eliminating the crime eliminates the problem, any more than legalizing assault would reduce violence, they maintain. Political scientist James Q. Wilson of UCLA argues that the high price of drugs due to their illegality has had a strong effect on reducing the number of new addicts. He claims that legalizing drugs would be extremely costly to society and that the difficulties involved in treating addictions—and the moral and ethical dilemmas presented by legalization—argue strongly against it.

Endnotes

1. Indeed, the White House press secretary said of the proposal, "Basically, it's not going to happen" (Stephen Labaton, "Surgeon General Suggests Study of Legalizing Drugs," *New York Times* [December 8, 1993], p. A23).
2. U.S. Department of Justice, Bureau of Justice Statistics, *Drugs and Crime Facts, 1992* (Washington, D.C.), pp. 8–9.
3. Ibid.
4. Ibid.
5. Personal correspondence from John Carnevale at the Office of National Drug Control Policy, received December 1, 1993.
6. Ibid.
7. Ibid.
8. U.S. Department of Justice, Bureau of Justice Statistics, *Sourcebook of Criminal Justice Statistics 1992* (Washington, D.C.: U.S. Government Printing Office, 1993), Table 1.12.
9. U.S. Department of Commerce, Bureau of the Census, *Statistical Abstract of the United States, 1993* (Washington, D.C.: U.S. Government Printing Office, 1993), Table 317.
10. U.S. Drug Enforcement Administration, *Illegal Drug Price/Purity Report* (July 1993).
11. *Sourcebook of Criminal Justice Statistics 1992*, Table 3.96.
12. Ibid., Table 3.97.
13. Ibid.
14. Ibid.
15. Ibid., Table 2.74.
16. Ibid., Table 2.75.
17. Ibid., Table 2.76.
18. Ibid., Table 2.79.

YES

The Case for Legalization

Ethan A. Nadelmann

What can be done about the "drug problem"? Despite frequent proclamations of war and dramatic increases in government funding and resources in recent years, there are many indications that the problem is not going away and may even be growing worse. During the past year alone, more than thirty million Americans violated the drug laws on literally billions of occasions. Drug-treatment programs in many cities are turning people away for lack of space and funding. In Washington, D.C., drug-related killings, largely of one drug dealer by another, are held responsible for a doubling in the homicide rate over the past year. In New York and elsewhere, courts and prisons are clogged with a virtually limitless supply of drug-law violators. In large cities and small towns alike, corruption of policemen and other criminal-justice officials by drug traffickers is rampant.

President Reagan and the First Lady are not alone in supporting increasingly repressive and expensive anti-drug measures, and in believing that the war against drugs can be won. Indeed, no "war" proclaimed by an American leader during the past forty years has garnered such sweeping bipartisan support; on this issue, liberals and conservatives are often indistinguishable. The fiercest disputes are not over objectives or even broad strategies, but over turf and tactics. Democratic politicians push for the appointment of a "drug czar" to oversee all drug policy, and blame the Administration for not applying sufficient pressure and sanctions against the foreign drug-producing countries. Republicans try to gain the upper hand by daring Democrats to support more widespread drug testing, increasingly powerful law-enforcement measures, and the death penalty for various drug-related offenses. But on the more fundamental issues of what this war is about, and what strategies are most likely to prove successful in the long run, no real debate—much less vocal dissent—can be heard.

If there were a serious public debate on this issue, far more attention would be given to one policy option that has just begun to be seriously considered, but which may well prove more successful than anything currently being implemented or proposed: legalization. Politicians and public officials remain hesitant even to mention the word, except to dismiss it contemptuously as a capitulation to the drug traffickers. Most Americans perceive drug legalization as an invitation to drug-infested anarchy. Even the civil-liberties groups shy away from this issue, limiting their input primarily to the drug-testing debate. The minority communities in the ghetto, for whom repealing the drug laws would promise the greatest benefits, fail to recognize the costs of our drug-prohibition policies. And the typical middle-class American, who hopes only that his children will not succumb to drug abuse, tends to favor any measures that he believes will make illegal drugs less accessible to them. Yet when one seriously compares the advantages and disadvantages of the legalization strategy with those of current and planned policies, abundant evidence suggests that legalization may well be the optimal strategy for tackling the drug problem.

Interestingly, public support for repealing the drug-prohibition laws has traditionally come primarily from the conservative end of the political spectrum: Milton Friedman, Ernest van den Haag, William F. Buckley, and the editors of the *Economist* have all supported it. Less vocal support comes from many liberals, politicians not among them, who are disturbed by the infringements on individual liberty posed by the drug laws. There is also a significant silent constituency in favor of repeal, found especially among criminal-justice officials, intelligence analysts, military interdictors, and criminal-justice scholars who have spent a considerable amount of time thinking about the problem. More often than not, however, job-security considerations, combined with an awareness that they can do little to change official policies, ensure that their views remain discreet and off the record.

During the spring of 1988, however, legalization suddenly began to be seriously considered as a policy option; the pros and cons of legalization were discussed on the front pages of leading newspapers and news magazines, and were debated on national television programs. Although the argument for legalization was not new, two factors seem to have been primarily responsible for the blitz of media coverage: an intellectual rationale for legalization—the first provided in decades—appeared in my article in the Spring issue of *Foreign Policy* magazine; more importantly, political legitimacy was subsequently bestowed upon the legalization option when Baltimore Mayor Kurt Schmoke, speaking to the National Conference of Mayors, noted the potential benefits of drug legalization and asked that the merits of legalization be debated in congressional hearings.

The idea of legalizing drugs was quickly denounced by most politicians across the political spectrum; nevertheless, the case for legalization appealed to many Americans. The prominent media coverage lent an aura of respectability to arguments that just a month earlier had seemed to be beyond the political pale. Despite the tendency of many journalists to caricature the legalization argument, at long last the issue had been joined. Various politicians, law-enforcement officials, health experts, and scholars came out in favor of drug legalization—or at least wanted to debate the matter seriously. On Capitol Hill, three or four congressmen seconded the call for a debate. According to some congressional staffers, two dozen additional legislators would have wanted to debate the issue, had the question arisen after rather than before the upcoming elections. Unable to oppose a mere hearing on the issue, Congressman Charles Rangel, chairman of the House Select Committee on Narcotics, declared his willingness to convene his committee in Baltimore to consider the legalization option.

There is, of course, no single legalization strategy. At one extreme is the libertarian vision of virtually no government restraints on the production and sale of drugs or any psychoactive substances, except perhaps around the fringes, such as prohibiting sales to children. At the other extreme is total government control over the production and sale of these goods. In between lies a strategy that may prove more successful than anything yet tried in stemming the problems of drug abuse and drug-related violence, corruption, sickness, and suffering. It is one in which government makes most of the substances that are now banned legally available to competent adults, exercises strong regulatory powers over all large-scale production and sale of drugs, makes drug-treatment programs available to all who need them, and offers honest drug-education programs to children. This strategy, it is worth noting, would also result in a net benefit to public treasuries of at least ten billion dollars a year, and perhaps much more.

There are three reasons why it is important to think about legalization scenarios, even though most Americans remain hostile to the idea. First, current drug-control policies have failed, are failing, and will continue to fail, in good part because they are fundamentally flawed. Second, many drug-control efforts are not only failing, but also proving highly costly and counter-productive; indeed, many of the drug-related evils that Americans identify as part and parcel of the "drug problem" are in fact caused by our drug-prohibition policies. Third, there is good reason to believe that repealing many of the drug laws would not lead, as many people fear, to a dramatic rise in drug abuse. In this essay I expand on each of these reasons for considering the legalization option. Government efforts to deal with the drug problem will succeed only if the rhetoric and crusading mentality that now dominate drug policy are replaced by reasoned and logical analysis.

WHY CURRENT DRUG POLICIES FAIL

Most proposals for dealing with the drug problem today reflect a desire to point the finger at those most removed from one's home and area of expertise. New York Mayor Ed Koch, Florida Congressman Larry Smith, and Harlem Congressman Charles Rangel, who recognize government's inability to deal with the drug problem in the cities, are among the most vocal supporters of punishing foreign drug-producing countries and stepping up interdiction efforts. Foreign leaders and U.S. State Department and drug-enforcement officials stationed abroad, on the other hand, who understand all too well why it is impossible to crack down successfully on illicit drug production outside the United States, are the most vigorous advocates of domestic enforcement and demand-reduction efforts within the United States. In between, those agencies charged with drug interdiction, from the Coast Guard and U.S. Customs Services to the U.S. military, know that they will never succeed in capturing more than a small percentage of the illicit drugs being smuggled into the United States. Nor surprisingly, they point their fingers in both directions. The solution, they promise, lies in greater source-control efforts abroad and greater demand-reduction efforts at home.

Trying to pass the buck is always understandable. But in each of these cases, the officials are half right and half wrong—half right in recognizing that they can do little to affect their end of the drug problem, given the suppositions and constraints of current drug-control strategies; half wrong (if we assume that their finger-pointing is sincere) in expecting that the solution lies elsewhere. It would be wrong, however, to assume that the public posturing of many officials reflects their real views. Many of them privately acknowledge the futility of all current drug-control strategies, and wonder whether radically different options, such as legalization, might not prove more successful in dealing with the drug problem. The political climate pervading this issue is such, however, that merely to ask that alternatives to current policies be considered is to incur a great political risk.

By most accounts, the dramatic increase in drug-enforcement efforts over the past few years has had little effect on the illicit drug market in the United States. The mere existence of drug-prohibition laws, combined with a minimal level of law-enforcement resources, is sufficient to maintain the price of illicit drugs at a level significantly higher than it would be if there were no such laws. Drug laws and enforcement also reduce the availability of illicit drugs, most notably in parts of the United States where demand is relatively limited to begin with. Theoretically, increases in drug-enforcement efforts should result in reduced availability, higher prices, and lower purity of illegal drugs. That is, in fact, what has happened to the domestic marijuana market (in at least the first two respects). But in general the illegal drug market has not responded as intended to the substantial increases in federal, state, and local drug-enforcement efforts.

Cocaine has sold for about a hundred dollars a gram at the retail level since the beginning of the 1980s. The average purity of that gram, however, has increased from 12 to 60 percent. Moreover, a growing number of users are turning to "crack," a potent derivative of cocaine that can be smoked; it is widely sold in ghetto neighborhoods now for five to ten dollars per vial. Needless to say, both crack and the 60 percent pure cocaine pose much greater threats to users than did the relatively benign powder available eight years ago. Similarly, the retail price of heroin has remained relatively constant even as the average purity has risen from 3.9 percent in 1983 to 6.1 percent in 1986. Throughout the southwestern part of the United States, a particularly potent form of heroin known as "black tar" has become increasingly prevalent. And in many cities, a powerful synthetic opiate, Dilaudid, is beginning to compete with heroin as the preferred opiate. The growing number of heroin-related hospital emergencies and deaths is directly related to these developments.

All of these trends suggest that drug-enforcement efforts are not succeeding and may even be backfiring. There are numerous indications, for instance, that a growing number of marijuana dealers in both the producer countries and the United States are switching to cocaine dealing, motivated both by the promise of greater profits and by government drug-enforcement efforts that place a premium on minimizing the bulk of the illicit product (in order to avoid detection). It is possible, of course, that some of these trends would be even more severe in the absence of drug laws and enforcement. At the same time, it is worth observing that the increases in the potency of illegal drugs have coincided with decreases in the potency of legal substances. Motivated in good part by health concerns, cigarette smokers are turning increasingly to lower-tar and -nicotine tobacco products, alcohol drinkers from hard liquor to wine and beer, and even coffee drinkers from regular to decaffeinated coffee. This trend may well have less to do with the nature of the substances than with their legal status. It is quite possible, for instance, that the subculture of illicit-drug use creates a bias or incentive in favor of riskier behavior and more powerful psychoactive effects. If this is the case, legalization might well succeed in reversing today's trend toward more potent drugs and more dangerous methods of consumption.

The most "successful" drug-enforcement operations are those that succeed in identifying and destroying an entire drug-trafficking organization. Such operations can send dozens of people to jail and earn the government millions of dollars in asset forfeitures. Yet these operations have virtually no effect on the availability or price of illegal drugs throughout much of the United States. During the past few years, some urban police departments have devoted significant manpower and financial resources to intensive crackdowns on street-level drug dealing in particular neighborhoods. Code-named Operation Pressure Point, Operation Clean Sweep, and so on, these massive police efforts have led to hundreds, even thousands, of arrests of low-level dealers and drug users, and have helped improve the quality of life in the targeted neighborhoods. In most cases, however, drug dealers have adapted relatively easily by moving their operations to nearby neighborhoods. In the final analysis, the principal accomplishment of most domestic drug-enforcement efforts is not to reduce the supply or availability of illegal drugs, or even to raise their price; it is to punish the drug dealers who are apprehended, and cause minor disruptions in established drug markets.

THE FAILURE OF INTERNATIONAL DRUG CONTROL

Many drug-enforcement officials and urban leaders recognize the futility of domestic drug-enforcement efforts and place their hopes in international control efforts. Yet these too are doomed to fail—for numerous reasons. First, marijuana and opium can be grown almost anywhere, and the coca plant, from which cocaine is derived, is increasingly being cultivated successfully in areas that were once considered inhospitable environments. Wherever drug-eradication efforts succeed, other regions and countries are quick to fill the void; for example, Colombian marijuana growers rapidly expanded production following successful eradication efforts in Mexico during the mid-1970s. Today, Mexican growers are rapidly taking advantage of recent Colombian government successes in eradicating marijuana in the Guajira peninsula. Meanwhile, Jamaicans and Central Americans from Panama to Belize, as well as a growing assortment of Asians and Africans, do what they can to sell their own marijuana in American markets. And within the United States, domestic marijuana production is believed to be a multi-billion-dollar industry, supplying between 15 and 50 percent of the American market.

This push-down/pop-up factor also characterizes the international heroin market. At various points during the past two decades, Turkey, Mexico, Southeast Asia (Burma, Thailand, and Laos), and Southwest Asia (Pakistan, Afghanistan, and Iran) have each served as the principal source of heroin imported into the United States. During the early 1970s, Mexican producers rapidly filled the void created by the Turkish government's successful opium-control measures. Although a successful eradication program during the latter part of the 1970s reduced Mexico's share of the U.S. market from a peak of 87 percent in 1975, it has since retained at least a one-third share in each year. Southwest Asian producers, who had played no role in supplying the American market as late as 1976, were able to supply over half the American market four years later. Today, increasing evidence indicates that drug traffickers are bringing unprecedented quantities of Southeast Asian heroin into the United States.

So far, the push-down/pop-up factor has played little role in the international cocaine market, for the simple reason that no government has yet pushed down in a significant way. Unlike marijuana- and opium-eradication efforts, in which aerial spraying of herbicides plays a prominent role, coca-eradication efforts are still conducted manually. The long anticipated development and approval of an environmentally safe herbicide to destroy coca plants may introduce an unprecedented push-down factor into the market. But even in the absence of such government pressures, coca growing has expanded rapidly during the past decade within Bolivia and Peru, and has expanded outward into Colombia, Brazil, Ecuador, Venezuela, and elsewhere. Moreover, once eradication efforts do begin, coca growers can be expected to adopt many of the same "guerrilla farming" methods adopted by marijuana and opium growers to camouflage and protect their crops from eradication efforts.

Beyond the push-down/pop-up factor, international source-control efforts face a variety of other obstacles. In many countries, governments with limited resources lack the ability to crack down on drug production in the hinterlands and other poorly policed regions. In some countries, ranging from Colombia and Peru to Burma and Thailand, leftist insurgencies are involved in drug production for either financial or political profit, and may play an important role in hampering government drug-control efforts. With respect to all three of the illicit crops, poor peasants with no comparable opportunities to earn as much money growing legitimate produce are prominently involved in the illicit business. In some cases, the illicit crop is part of a traditional, indigenous culture. Even where it is not, peasants typically perceive little or nothing immoral about taking advantage of the opportunity to grow the illicit crops. Indeed, from their perspective their moral obligation is not to protect the foolish American consumer of their produce but to provide for their families' welfare. And even among those who do perceive participation in the illicit drug market as somewhat unethical, the temptations held out by the drug traffickers often prove overwhelming.

No illicit drug is an difficult to keep out of the United States as heroin. The absence of geographical limitations on where it can be cultivated is just one minor obstacle. American heroin users consume an estimated six tons of heroin each year. The sixty tons of opium required to produce that heroin represent just 2–3 percent of the estimated 2–3,000 tons of illicit opium produced during each of the past few years. Even if eradication efforts combined with what often proves to be the opium growers' principal nemesis—bad weather—were to eliminate three-fourths of that production in one year, the U.S. market would still require just 10 percent of the remaining crop. Since U.S. consumers are able and willing to pay more than any others, the chances are good that they would still obtain their heroin. In any event, the prospects for such a radical reduction in illicit opium production are scanty indeed.

. . . Interdiction, like source control, is largely unable to keep illicit drugs out of the United States. Moreover, the past twenty years' experience has demonstrated that even dramatic increases in interdiction and source-control efforts have little or no effect on the price and purity of drugs. The few small successes, such as the destruction of the Turkish-opium "French Connection" in the early 1970s, and the crack-down on Mexican marijuana and heroin in the late 1970s, were exceptions to the rule. The elusive goal of international drug control since then has been to replicate those unusual successes. It is a strategy that is destined to fail, however, as long as millions of Americans continue to demand the illicit substances that foreigners are willing and able to supply.

THE COSTS OF PROHIBITION

The fact that drug-prohibition laws and policies cannot eradicate or even significantly reduce drug abuse is not necessarily a reason to repeal them. They do, after all, succeed in deterring many people from trying drugs, and they clearly reduce the availability and significantly increase the price of illegal drugs. These accomplishments alone might warrant retaining the drug laws, were it not for the fact that these same laws are also responsible for much of what Americans identify as the "drug problem." Here the analogies to alcohol and tobacco are worth noting. There is little question that we could reduce the health costs associated with use and abuse of alcohol and tobacco if we were to criminalize their production, sale, and possession. But no one believes that we could eliminate their use and abuse, that we could create an "alcohol-free" or "tobacco-free" country. Nor do most Americans believe that criminalizing the alcohol and tobacco markets would be a good idea. Their opposition stems largely from two beliefs: that adult Americans have the right to choose what substances they will consume and what risks they will take; and that the costs of trying to coerce so many Americans to abstain from those substances would be enormous. It was the strength of these two beliefs that ultimately led to the repeal of Prohibition, and it is partly due to memories of that experience that criminalizing either alcohol or tobacco has little support today.

Consider the potential consequences of criminalizing the production, sale, and possession of all tobacco products. On the positive side, the number of people smoking tobacco would almost certainly decline, as would the health costs associated with tobacco consumption. Although the "forbidden fruit" syndrome would attract some people to cigarette smoking who would not otherwise have smoked, many more would likely be deterred by the criminal sanction, the moral standing of the law, the higher cost and unreliable quality of the illicit tobacco, and the difficulties involved in acquiring it. Nonsmokers would rarely if ever be bothered by the irritating habits of their fellow citizens. The anti-tobacco laws would discourage some people from ever starting to smoke, and would induce others to quit.

On the negative side, however, millions of Americans, including both tobacco addicts and recreational users, would no doubt defy the law, generating a massive underground market and billions in profits for organized criminals. Although some tobacco farmers would find other work, thousands more would become outlaws and continue to produce their crops covertly. Throughout Latin America, farmers and gangsters would rejoice at the opportunity to earn untold sums of gringo greenbacks, even as U.S. diplomats pressured foreign governments to cooperate with U.S. laws. Within the United States, government helicopters would spray herbicides on illicit tobacco fields; people would be rewarded by the government for informing on their tobacco-growing, -selling, and -smoking neighbors; urine tests would be employed to identify violators of the anti-tobacco laws; and a Tobacco Enforcement Administration (the T.E.A.) would employ undercover agents, informants, and wiretaps to uncover tobacco-law violators. Municipal, state, and federal judicial systems would be clogged with tobacco traffickers and "abusers." "Tobacco-related murders" would increase dramatically as criminal organizations competed with one another for turf and markets. Smoking would become an act of youthful rebellion, and no doubt some users would begin to experiment with more concentrated, potent, and dangerous forms of tobacco. Tobacco-related corruption would infect all levels of government, and respect for the law would decline noticeably. Government expenditures on tobacco-law enforcement would climb rapidly into the billions of dollars, even as budget balancers longingly recalled the almost ten billion dollars per year in tobacco taxes earned by the federal and state governments prior to prohibition. Finally, the State of North Carolina might even secede again from the Union.

This seemingly far-fetched tobacco-prohibition scenario is little more than an extrapolation based on the current situation with respect to marijuana, cocaine, and heroin. In many ways, our predicament resembles what actually happened during Prohibition. Prior to Prohibition, most Americans hoped that alcohol could be effectively banned by passing laws against its production and supply. During the early years of Prohibition, when drinking declined but millions of Americans nonetheless continued to drink, Prohibition's supporters placed their faith in tougher laws and more police and jails. After a few more years, however, increasing numbers of Americans began to realize that laws and policemen were unable to eliminate the smugglers, bootleggers, and illicit producers, as long as tens of millions of Americans continued to want to buy alcohol. At the same time, they saw that more laws and policemen seemed to generate more violence and corruption, more crowded courts and jails, wider disrespect for government and the law, and more power and profits for the gangsters. Repeal of Prohibition came to be seen not as a capitulation to Al Capone and his ilk, but as a means of both putting the bootleggers out of business and eliminating most of the costs associated with the prohibition laws.

Today, Americans are faced with a dilemma similar to that confronted by our forebears sixty years ago. Demand for illicit drugs shows some signs of abating, but no signs of declining significantly. Moreover, there are substantial reasons to doubt that tougher laws and policing have played an important role in reducing consumption. Supply, meanwhile, has not abated at all. Availability of illicit drugs, except for marijuana in some locales, remains high. Prices are dropping, even as potency increases. And the number of drug producers, smugglers, and dealers remains sizable, even as jails and prisons fill to overflowing. As was the case during Prohibition, the principal beneficiaries of current drug policies are the new and old organized-crime gangs. The principal victims, on the other hand, are not the drug dealers, but the tens of millions of Americans who are worse off in one way or another as a consequence of the existence and failure of the drug-prohibition laws.

All public policies create beneficiaries and victims, both intended and unintended. When a public policy results in a disproportionate magnitude of unintended victims, there is good reason to reevaluate the assumptions and design of the policy. In the case of drug-prohibition policies, the intended beneficiaries are those individuals who would become drug abusers but for the existence and enforcement of the drug laws. The intended victims are those who traffic in illicit drugs and suffer the legal consequences. The unintended beneficiaries, conversely, are the drug producers and traffickers who profit handsomely from the illegality of the market, while avoiding arrest by the authorities and the violence perpetrated by other criminals. The unintended victims of drug-prohibition policies are rarely recognized as such, however. Viewed narrowly, they are the 30 million Americans who use illegal drugs, thereby risking loss of their jobs, imprisonment, and the damage done to health by ingesting illegally produced drugs; viewed broadly, they are all Americans, who pay the substantial costs of our present ill-considered policies, both as taxpayers and as the potential victims of crime. These unintended victims are generally thought to be victimized by the unintended beneficiaries (i.e., the drug dealers), when in fact it is the drug-prohibition policies themselves that are primarily responsible for their plight.

If law-enforcement efforts could succeed in significantly reducing either the supply of illicit drugs or the demand for them, we would probably have little need to seek alternative drug-control policies. But since those efforts have repeatedly failed to make much of a difference and show little indication of working better in the future, at this point we must focus greater attention on their costs. Unlike the demand and supply of illicit drugs, which have remained relatively indifferent to legislative initiatives, the costs of drug-enforcement measures can be affected—quite dramatically—by legislative measures. What tougher criminal sanctions and more police have failed to accomplish, in terms of reducing drug-related violence, corruption, death, and social decay, may well be better accomplished by legislative repeal of the drug laws, and adoption of less punitive but more effective measures to prevent and treat substance abuse.

COSTS TO THE TAXPAYER

Since 1981, federal expenditures on drug enforcement have more than tripled—from less than one billion dollars a year to about three billion. According to the National Drug Enforcement Policy Board, the annual budgets of the Drug Enforcement Administration (DEA) and the Coast Guard have each risen during the past seven years from about $220 million to roughly $500 million. During the same period, FBI resources devoted to drug enforcement have increased from $8 million a year to over $100 million; U.S. Marshals resources from $26 million to about $80 million; U.S. Attorney resources from $20 million to about $100 million; State Department resources from $35 million to $100 million; U.S. Customs resources from $180 million to over $400 million; and Bureau of Prison resources from $77 million to about $300 million. Expenditures on drug control by the military and the intelligence agencies are more difficult to calculate, although by all accounts they have increased by at least the same magnitude, and now total hundreds of millions of dollars per year. Even greater are the expenditures at lower levels of government. In a 1987 study for the U.S. Customs Service by Wharton Econometrics, state and local police were estimated to have devoted 18 percent of their total investigative resources, or close to five billion dollars, to drug-enforcement activities in 1986. This represented a 19 percent increase over the previous year's expenditures. All told, 1987 expenditures on all aspects of drug enforcement, from drug eradication in foreign countries to imprisonment of drug users and dealers in the United States, totaled at least ten billion dollars.

Of course, even ten billion dollars a year pales in comparison with expenditures on military defense. Of greater concern than the actual expenditures, however, has been the diversion of limited resources—including the time and energy of judges, prosecutors, and law-enforcement agents, as well as scarce prison space—from the prosecution and punishment of criminal activities that harm far more innocent victims than do violations of the drug laws. Drug-law violators account for approximately 10 percent of the roughly 800,000 inmates in state prisons and local jails, and more than one-third of the 44,000 federal prison inmates. These proportions are expected to increase in coming years, even as total prison populations continue to rise dramatically.[1] Among the 40,000 inmates in New York State prisons, drug-law violations surpassed first-degree robbery in 1987 as the number one cause of incarceration, accounting for 20 percent of the total prison population. The U.S. Sentencing Commission has estimated that, largely as a consequence of the Anti-Drug Abuse Act passed by Congress in 1986, the proportion of federal inmates incarcerated for drug violations will rise from one-third of the 44,000 prisoners sentenced to federal-prison terms today to one-half of the 100,000 to 150,000 federal prisoners anticipated in fifteen years. The direct costs of building and maintaining enough prisons to house this growing population are rising at an astronomical rate. The opportunity costs, in terms of alternative social expenditures foregone and other types of criminals not imprisoned, are perhaps even greater.[2]

During each of the last few years, police made about 750,000 arrests for violations of the drug laws. Slightly more than three-quarters of these have not been for manufacturing or dealing drugs, but solely for possession of an illicit drug, typically marijuana. (Those arrested, it is worth noting, represent little more than 2 percent of the thirty million Americans estimated to have used an illegal drug during the past year.) On the one hand, this has clogged many urban criminal-justice systems: in New York City, drug-law violations last year accounted for more than 40 percent of all felony indictments—up from 25 percent in 1985; in Washington, D.C., the figure was more than 50 percent. On the other hand, it has distracted criminal-justice officials from concentrating greater resources on violent offenses and property crimes. In many cities, law enforcement has become virtually synonymous with drug enforcement.

Drug laws typically have two effects on the market in illicit drugs. The first is to restrict the general availability and accessibility of illicit drugs, especially in locales where underground drug markets are small and isolated from the community. The second is to increase, often significantly, the price of illicit drugs to consumers. Since the costs of producing most illicit drugs are not much different from the costs of alcohol, tobacco, and coffee, most of the price paid for illicit substances is in effect a value-added tax created by their criminalization, which is enforced and supplemented by the law-enforcement establishment, but collected by the drug traffickers. A report by Wharton Econometrics for the President's Commission on Organized Crime identified the sale of illicit drugs as the source of more than half of all organized-crime revenues in 1986, with the marijuana and heroin business each providing over seven billion dollars, and the cocaine business over thirteen billion. By contrast, revenues from cigarette bootlegging, which persists principally because of differences among states in their cigarette-tax rates, were estimated at 290 million dollars. If the marijuana, cocaine, and heroin markets were legal, state and federal governments would collect billions of dollars annually in tax revenues. Instead, they expend billions on what amounts to a subsidy of organized crime and unorganized criminals.

DRUGS AND CRIME

The drug/crime connection is one that continues to resist coherent analysis, both because cause and effect are so difficult to distinguish and because the role of the drug-prohibition laws in causing and labeling "drug-related crime" is so often ignored. There are four possible connections between drugs and crime, at least three of which would be much diminished if the drug-prohibition laws were repealed. First, producing, selling, buying, and consuming strictly controlled and banned substances is itself a crime that occurs billions of times each year in the United States alone. In the absence of drug-prohibition laws, these activities would obviously cease to be crimes. Selling drugs to children would, of course, continue to be criminal, and other evasions of government regulation of a legal market would continue to be prosecuted; but by and large the drug/crime connection that now accounts for all of the criminal-justice costs noted above would be severed.

Second, many illicit-drug users commit crimes such as robbery and burglary, as well as drug dealing, prostitution, and numbers running, to earn enough money to purchase the relatively high-priced illicit drugs. Unlike the millions of alcoholics who can support their habits for relatively modest amounts, many cocaine and heroin addicts spend hundreds and even thousands of dollars a week. If the drugs to which they are addicted were significantly cheaper—which would be the case if they were legalized—the number of crimes committed by drug addicts to pay for their habits would, in all likelihood, decline dramatically. Even if a legal-drug policy included the imposition of relatively high consumption taxes in order to discourage consumption, drug prices would probably still be lower than they are today.

The third drug/crime connection is the commission of crimes—violent crimes in particular—by people under the influence of illicit drugs. This connection seems to have the greatest impact upon the popular imagination. Clearly, some drugs do "cause" some people to commit crimes by reducing normal inhibitions, unleashing aggressive and other antisocial tendencies, and lessening the sense of responsibility. Cocaine, particularly in the form of crack, has gained such a reputation in recent years, just as heroin did in the 1960s and 1970s, and marijuana did in the years before that. Crack's reputation for inspiring violent behavior may or may not be more deserved than those of marijuana and heroin; reliable evidence is not yet available. No illicit drug, however, is as widely associated with violent behavior as alcohol. According to Justice Department statistics, 34 percent of all jail inmates convicted of violent crimes in 1983 reported having used alcohol just prior to committing their offense. The impact of drug legalization on this drug/crime connection is the most difficult to predict. Much would depend on overall rates of drug abuse and changes in the nature of consumption, both of which are impossible to predict. It is worth noting, however, that a shift in consumption from alcohol to marijuana would almost certainly contribute to a decline in violent behavior.

The fourth drug/crime link is the violent, intimidating, and corrupting behavior of the drug traffickers. Illegal markets tend to breed violence—not only because they attract criminally-minded individuals, but also because participants in the market have no resort to legal institutions to resolve their disputes. During Prohibition, violent struggles between bootlegging gangs and hijackings of booze-laden trucks and sea vessels were frequent and notorious

occurrences. Today's equivalents are the booby traps that surround some marijuana fields, the pirates of the Caribbean looking to rip off drug-laden vessels
en route to the shores of the United States, and the machine-gun battles and
executions carried out by drug lords—all of which occasionally kill innocent
people. Most law-enforcement officials agree that the dramatic increases in
urban murder rates during the past few years can be explained almost entirely
by the rise in drug-dealer killings.

Perhaps the most unfortunate victims of the drug-prohibition policies have
been the law-abiding residents of America's ghettos. These policies have largely
proven futile in deterring large numbers of ghetto dwellers from becoming
drug abusers, but they do account for much of what ghetto residents identify
as the drug problem. In many neighborhoods, it often seems to be the aggressive gun-toting drug dealers who upset law-abiding residents far more than
the addicts nodding out in doorways. Other residents, however, perceive the
drug dealers as heroes and successful role models. In impoverished neighborhoods, they often stand out as symbols of success to children who see no other
options. At the same time, the increasingly harsh criminal penalties imposed
on adult drug dealers have led to the widespread recruitment of juveniles by
drug traffickers. Formerly, children started dealing drugs only after they had
been using them for a while; today the sequence is often reversed: many
children start using illegal drugs now only after working for older drug dealers.
And the juvenile-justice system offers no realistic options for dealing with this
growing problem.

The conspicuous failure of law-enforcement agencies to deal with this
drug/crime connection is probably most responsible for the demoralization of
neighborhoods and police departments alike. Intensive police crackdowns in
urban neighborhoods do little more than chase the menace a short distance
away to infect new areas. By contrast, legalization of the drug market would
drive the drug-dealing business off the streets and out of the apartment buildings, and into legal, government-regulated, tax-paying stores. It would also
force many of the gun-toting dealers out of business, and would convert others
into legitimate businessmen. Some, of course, would turn to other types of
criminal activities, just as some of the bootleggers did following Prohibition's
repeal. Gone, however, would be the unparalleled financial temptations that
lure so many people from all sectors of society into the drug-dealing business.

THE COSTS OF CORRUPTION

All vice-control efforts are particularly susceptible to corruption, but none so
much as drug enforcement. When police accept bribes from drug dealers, no
victim exists to complain to the authorities. Even when police extort money
and drugs from traffickers and dealers, the latter are in no position to report
the corrupt officers. What makes drug enforcement especially vulnerable to
corruption are the tremendous amounts of money involved in the business.
Today, many law-enforcement officials believe that police corruption is more

pervasive than at any time since Prohibition. In Miami, dozens of law-enforcement officials have been charged with accepting bribes, stealing from drug dealers, and even dealing drugs themselves. Throughout many small towns and rural communities in Georgia, where drug smugglers en route from Mexico, the Caribbean, and Latin America drop their loads of cocaine and marijuana, dozens of sheriffs have been implicated in drug-related corruption. In New York, drug-related corruption in one Brooklyn police precinct has generated the city's most far-reaching police-corruption scandal since the 1960s. More than a hundred cases of drug-related corruption are now prosecuted each year in state and federal courts. Every one of the federal law-enforcement agencies charged with drug-enforcement responsibilities has seen an agent implicated in drug-related corruption.

It is not difficult to explain the growing pervasiveness of drug-related corruption. The financial temptations are enormous relative to other opportunities, legitimate or illegitimate. Little effort is required. Many police officers are demoralized by the scope of the drug traffic, their sense that many citizens are indifferent, and the fact that many sectors of society do not even appreciate their efforts—as well as the fact that many of the drug dealers who are arrested do not remain in prison. Some police also recognize that enforcing the drug laws does not protect victims from predators so much as it regulates an illicit market that cannot be suppressed, but can be kept underground. In every respect, the analogy to Prohibition is apt. Repealing the drug-prohibition laws would dramatically reduce police corruption. By contrast, the measures currently being proposed to deal with the growing problem, including better funded and more aggressive internal investigations, offer relatively little promise.

Among the most difficult costs to evaluate are those that relate to the widespread defiance of the drug-prohibition laws: the effects of labeling as criminals the tens of millions of people who use drugs illicitly, subjecting them to the risks of criminal sanction, and obligating many of these same people to enter into relationships with drug dealers (who may be criminals in many more senses of the word) in order to purchase their drugs; the cynicism that such laws generate toward other laws and the law in general; and the sense of hostility and suspicion that many otherwise law-abiding individuals feel toward law-enforcement officials. It was costs such as these that strongly influenced many of Prohibition's more conservative opponents.

PHYSICAL AND MORAL COSTS

Perhaps the most paradoxical consequence of the drug laws is the tremendous harm they cause to the millions of drug users who have not been deterred from using illicit drugs in the first place. Nothing resembling an underground Food and Drug Administration has arisen to impose quality control on the illegal-drug market and provide users with accurate information on the drugs they consume. Imagine that Americans could not tell whether a bottle of wine contained 6 percent, 30 percent, or 90 percent alcohol, or whether an aspirin tablet contained 5 or 500 grams of aspirin. Imagine, too, that no controls existed to prevent winemakers from diluting their product with methanol and other dangerous impurities, and that vineyards and tobacco fields were fertilized with harmful substances by ignorant growers and sprayed with poisonous herbicides by government agents. Fewer people would use such substances, but more of those who did would get sick. Some would die.

The above scenario describes, of course, the current state of the illicit drug market. Many marijuana smokers are worse off for having smoked cannabis that was grown with dangerous fertilizers, sprayed with the herbicide paraquat, or mixed with more dangerous substances. Consumers of heroin and the various synthetic substances sold on the street face even severer consequences, including fatal overdoses and poisonings from unexpectedly potent or impure drug supplies. More often than not, the quality of a drug addict's life depends greatly upon his or her access to reliable supplies. Drug-enforcement operations that succeed in temporarily disrupting supply networks are thus a double-edged sword: they encourage some addicts to seek admission into drug-treatment programs, but they oblige others to seek out new and hence less reliable suppliers; the result is that more, not fewer, drug-related emergencies and deaths occur.

Today, over 50 percent of all people with AIDS in New York City, New Jersey, and many other parts of the country, as well as the vast majority of AIDS-infected heterosexuals throughout the country, have contracted the disease directly or indirectly through illegal intravenous drug use. Reports have emerged of drug dealers beginning to provide clean syringes together with their illegal drugs. But even as other governments around the world actively attempt to limit the spread of AIDS by and among drug users by instituting free syringe-exchange programs, state and municipal governments in the United States resist following suit, arguing that to do so would "encourage" or "condone" the use of illegal drugs. Only in January 1988 did New York City approve such a program on a very limited and experimental basis. At the same time, drug-treatment programs remain notoriously underfunded, turning away tens of thousands of addicts seeking help, even as billions of dollars more are spent to arrest, prosecute, and imprison illegal drug sellers and users. In what may represent a sign of shifting priorities, the President's Commission on AIDS, in its March 1988 report, emphasized the importance of making drug-treatment programs available to all in need of them. In all likelihood, however, the criminal-justice agencies will continue to receive the greatest share of drug-control funds.

Most Americans perceive the drug problem as a moral issue and draw a moral distinction between use of the illicit drugs and use of alcohol and tobacco. Yet when one subjects this distinction to reasoned analysis, it quickly disintegrates. The most consistent moral perspective of those who favor drug laws is that of the Mormons and the Puritans, who regard as immoral any intake of substances to alter one's state of consciousness or otherwise cause pleasure: they forbid not only the illicit drugs and alcohol, but also tobacco, caffeine, and even chocolate. The vast majority of Americans are hardly so

consistent with respect to the propriety of their pleasures. Yet once one acknowledges that there is nothing immoral about drinking alcohol or smoking
tobacco for non-medicinal purposes, it becomes difficult to condemn the consumption of marijuana, cocaine, and other substances on moral grounds. The
"moral" condemnation of some substances and not others proves to be little
more than a prejudice in favor of some drugs and against others.

The same false distinction is drawn with respect to those who provide the
psychoactive substances to users and abusers alike. If degrees of immorality
were measured by the levels of harm caused by one's products, the "traffickers"
in tobacco and alcohol would be vilified as the most evil of all substance
purveyors. That they are perceived instead as respected members of our community, while providers of the no more dangerous illicit substances are pun-
ished with long prison sentences, says much about the prejudices of most
Americans with respect to psychoactive substances, but little about the morality
or immorality of their activities.

Much the same is true of gun salesmen. Most of the consumers of their
products use them safely; a minority, however, end up shooting either themselves or someone else. Can we hold the gun salesman morally culpable for
the harm that probably would not have occurred but for his existence? Most
people say no, except perhaps where the salesman clearly knew that his product
would be used to commit a crime. Yet in the case of those who sell illicit
substances to willing customers, the providers are deemed not only legally
guilty, but also morally reprehensible. The law does not require any demonstration that the dealer knew of a specific harm to follow; indeed, it does not
require any evidence at all of harm having resulted from the sale. Rather, the
law is predicated on the assumption that harm will inevitably follow. Despite
the patent falsity of that assumption, it persists as the underlying justification
for the drug laws.

Although a valid moral distinction cannot be drawn between the licit and
the illicit psychoactive substances, one can point to a different kind of moral
justification for the drug laws: they arguably reflect a paternalistic obligation
to protect those in danger of succumbing to their own weaknesses. If drugs
were legally available, most people would either abstain from using them or
would use them responsibly and in moderation. A minority without self-
restraint, however, would end up harming themselves if the substances were
more readily available. Therefore, the majority has a moral obligation to deny
itself legal access to certain substances because of the plight of the minority.
This obligation is presumably greatest when children are included among
the minority.

At least in principle, this argument seems to provide the strongest moral
justification for the drug laws. But ultimately the moral quality of laws must
be judged not by how those laws are intended to work in principle, but by
how they function in practice. When laws intended to serve a moral end inflict
great damage on innocent parties, we must rethink our moral position.

Because drug-law violations do not create victims with an interest in notify-
ing the police, drug-enforcement agents rely heavily on undercover operations,

electronic surveillance, and information provided by informants. These techniques are indispensable to effective law enforcement, but they are also among the least palatable investigative methods employed by the police. The same is true of drug testing: it may be useful and even necessary for determining liability in accidents, but it also threatens and undermines the right of privacy to which many Americans believe they are entitled. There are good reasons for requiring that such measures be used sparingly.

Equally disturbing are the increasingly vocal calls for people to inform not only on drug dealers but also on neighbors, friends, and even family members who use illicit drugs. Government calls on people not only to "just say no," but also to report those who have not heeded the message. Intolerance of illicit-drug use and users is heralded not only as an indispensable ingredient in the war against drugs, but also as a mark of good citizenship. Certainly every society requires citizens to assist in the enforcement of criminal laws. But societies—particularly democratic and pluralistic ones—also rely strongly on an ethic of tolerance toward those who are different but do no harm to others. Overzealous enforcement of the drug laws risks undermining that ethic, and encouraging the creation of a society of informants. This results in an immorality that is far more dangerous in its own way than that associated with the use of illicit drugs.

THE BENEFITS OF LEGALIZATION

Repealing the drug-prohibition laws promises tremendous advantages. Between reduced government expenditures on enforcing drug laws and new tax revenue from legal drug production and sales, public treasuries would enjoy a net benefit of at least ten billion dollars a year, and possibly much more. The quality of urban life would rise significantly. Homicide rates would decline. So would robbery and burglary rates. Organized criminal groups, particularly the newer ones that have yet to diversify out of drugs, would be dealt a devastating setback. The police, prosecutors, and courts would focus their resources on combating the types of crimes that people cannot walk away from. More ghetto residents would turn their backs on criminal careers and seek out legitimate opportunities instead. And the health and quality of life of many drug users—and even drug abusers—would improve significantly.

All the benefits of legalization would be for naught, however, if millions more Americans were to become drug abusers. Our experience with alcohol and tobacco provides ample warnings. Today, alcohol is consumed by 140 million Americans and tobacco by 50 million. All of the health costs associated with abuse of the illicit drugs pale in comparison with those resulting from tobacco and alcohol abuse. In 1986, for example, alcohol was identified as a contributing factor in 10 percent of work-related injuries, 40 percent of suicide attempts, and about 40 percent of the approximately 46,000 annual traffic deaths in 1983. An estimated eighteen million Americans are reported to be either alcoholics or alcohol abusers. The total cost of alcohol abuse to American society is estimated at over 100 billion dollars annually. Alcohol has been identified as the direct cause of 80,000 to 100,000 deaths annually, and as a contributing factor in an additional 100,000 deaths. The health costs of tobacco use are of similar magnitude. In the United States alone, an estimated 320,000 people die prematurely each year as a consequence of their consumption of tobacco. By comparison, the National Council on Alcoholism reported that only 3,562 people were known to have died in 1985 from use of all illegal drugs combined. Even if we assume that thousands more deaths were related in one way or another to illicit drug abuse but not reported as such, we are still left with the conclusion that all of the health costs of marijuana, cocaine, and heroin combined amount to only a small fraction of those caused by tobacco and alcohol.

Most Americans are just beginning to recognize the extensive costs of alcohol and tobacco abuse. At the same time, they seem to believe that there is something fundamentally different about alcohol and tobacco that supports the legal distinction between those two substances, on the one hand, and the illicit ones, on the other. The most common distinction is based on the assumption that the illicit drugs are more dangerous than the licit ones. Cocaine, heroin, the various hallucinogens, and (to a lesser extent) marijuana are widely perceived as, in the words of the President's Commission on Organized Crime, "inherently destructive to mind and body." They are also believed to be more addictive and more likely to cause dangerous and violent behavior than alcohol and tobacco. All use of illicit drugs is therefore thought to be abusive; in other words, the distinction between use and abuse of psychoactive substances that most people recognize with respect to alcohol is not acknowledged with respect to the illicit substances.

Most Americans make the fallacious assumption that the government would not criminalize certain psychoactive substances if they were not in fact dangerous. They then jump to the conclusion that any use of those substances is a form of abuse. The government, in its effort to discourage people from using illicit drugs, has encouraged and perpetuated these misconceptions—not only in its rhetoric but also in its purportedly educational materials. Only by reading between the lines can one discern the fact that the vast majority of Americans who have used illicit drugs have done so in moderation, that relatively few have suffered negative short-term consequences, and that few are likely to suffer long-term harm.

The evidence is most persuasive with respect to marijuana. U.S. drug-enforcement and health agencies do not even report figures on marijuana-related deaths, apparently because so few occur. Although there are good health reasons for children, pregnant women, and some others not to smoke marijuana, there still appears to be little evidence that occasional marijuana consumption does much harm. Certainly, it is not healthy to inhale marijuana smoke into one's lungs; indeed, the National Institute on Drug Abuse (NIDA) has declared that "marijuana smoke contains more cancer-causing agents than is found in tobacco smoke." On the other hand, the number of joints smoked by all but a very small percentage of marijuana smokers is a tiny fraction of the twenty cigarettes a day smoked by the average cigarette smoker; indeed, the average may be closer to one or two joints a week than one or two a day. Note that NIDA defines a "heavy" marijuana smoker as one who consumes at least two joints "daily." A heavy tobacco smoker, by contrast, smokes about forty cigarettes a day.

Nor is marijuana strongly identified as a dependence-causing substance. A 1982 survey of marijuana use by young adults (eighteen to twenty-five years old) found that 64 percent had tried marijuana at least once, that 42 percent had used it at least ten times, and that 27 percent had smoked in the last month. It also found that 21 percent had passed through a period during which they smoked "daily" (defined as twenty or more days per month), but that only one-third of those currently smoked "daily" and only one-fifth (about 4 percent of all young adults) could be described as heavy daily users (averaging two or more joints per day). This suggests that daily marijuana use is typically a phase through which people pass, after which their use becomes more moderate.

Marijuana has also been attacked as the "gateway drug" that leads people to the use of even more dangerous illegal drugs. It is true that people who have smoked marijuana are more likely than people who have not to try, use, and abuse other illicit substances. It is also true that people who have smoked tobacco or drunk alcohol are more likely than those who have not to experiment with illicit drugs and to become substance abusers. The reasons are obvious enough. Familiarity with smoking cigarettes, for instance, removes one of the major barriers to smoking marijuana, which is the experience of inhaling smoke into one's lungs. Similarly, familiarity with altering one's state of consciousness by consuming psychoactive substances such as alcohol or marijuana decreases the fear and increases the curiosity regarding other substances and "highs." But the evidence also indicates that there is nothing inevitable about the process. The great majority of people who have smoked marijuana do not become substance abusers of either legal or illegal substances. At the same time, it is certainly true that many of those who do become substance abusers after using marijuana would have become abusers even if they had never smoked a joint in their life.

DEALING WITH DRUGS' DANGERS

The dangers associated with cocaine, heroin, the hallucinogens, and other illicit substances are greater than those posed by marijuana, but not nearly so great as many people seem to think. Consider the case of cocaine. In 1986 NIDA reported that over 20 million Americans had tried cocaine, that 12.2 million had consumed it at least once during 1985, and that nearly 5.8 million had used it within the past month. Among those between the ages of eighteen and twenty-five, 8.2 million had tried cocaine, 5.3 million had used it within the past year, 2.5 million had used it within the past month, and 250,000 had used it weekly. Extrapolation might suggest that a quarter of a million young

Americans are potential problem users. But one could also conclude that only 3 percent of those between the ages of eighteen and twenty-five who had ever tried the drug fell into that category, and that only 10 percent of those who had used cocaine monthly were at risk. (The NIDA survey did not, it should be noted, include people residing in military or student dormitories, prison inmates, or the homeless.)

All of this is not to deny that cocaine is a potentially dangerous drug, especially when it is injected, smoked in the form of crack, or consumed in tandem with other powerful substances. Clearly, tens of thousands of Americans have suffered severely from their abuse of cocaine, and a tiny fraction have died. But there is also overwhelming evidence that most users of cocaine do not get into trouble with the drug. So much of the media attention has focused on the small percentage of cocaine users who become addicted that the popular perception of how most people use cocaine has become badly distorted. In one survey of high school seniors' drug use, the researchers questioned recent cocaine users, asking whether they had ever tried to stop using cocaine and found that they couldn't. Only 3.8 percent responded affirmatively, in contrast to the almost 7 percent of marijuana smokers who said they had tried to stop and found they couldn't, and the 18 percent of cigarette smokers who answered similarly. Although a similar survey of adult users would probably reveal a higher proportion of cocaine addicts, evidence such as this suggests that only a small percentage of people who use cocaine end up having a problem with it. In this respect, most people differ from monkeys, who have demonstrated in experiments that they will starve themselves to death if provided with unlimited cocaine.

With respect to the hallucinogens such as LSD and psilocybic mushrooms, their potential for addiction is virtually nil. The dangers arise primarily from using them irresponsibly on individual occasions. Although many of those who have used one or another of the hallucinogens have experienced "bad trips," others have reported positive experiences, and very few have suffered any long-term harm.

Perhaps no drugs are regarded with as much horror as the opiates, and in particular heroin, which is a concentrated form of morphine. As with most drugs, heroin can be eaten, snorted, smoked, or injected. Most Americans, unfortunately, prefer injection. There is no question that heroin is potentially highly addictive, perhaps as addictive as nicotine. But despite the popular association of heroin use with the most down-and-out inhabitants of urban ghettos, heroin causes relatively little physical harm to the human body. Consumed on an occasional or regular basis under sanitary conditions, its worst side effect, apart from addiction itself, is constipation. That is one reason why many doctors in early twentieth-century America saw opiate addiction as preferable to alcoholism, and prescribed the former as treatment for the latter when abstinence did not seem a realistic option.

It is important to think about the illicit drugs in the same way we think about alcohol and tobacco. Like tobacco, many of the illicit substances are highly addictive, but can be consumed on a regular basis for decades without any demonstrable harm. Like alcohol, most of the substances can be, and are, used by most consumers in moderation, with little in the way of harmful effects; but like alcohol, they also lend themselves to abuse by a minority of users who become addicted or otherwise harm themselves or others as a consequence. And as is the case with both the legal substances, the psychoactive effects of the various illegal drugs vary greatly from one person to another. To be sure, the pharmacology of the substance is important, as is its purity and the manner in which it is consumed. But much also depends upon not only the physiology and psychology of the consumer, but also his expectations regarding the drug, his social milieu, and the broader cultural environment—what Harvard University psychiatrist Norman Zinberg has called the "set and setting" of the drug. It is factors such as these that might change dramatically, albeit in indeterminate ways, were the illicit drugs made legally available.

CAN LEGALIZATION WORK?

It is thus impossible to predict whether legalization would lead to much greater levels of drug abuse, and exact costs comparable to those of alcohol and tobacco abuse. The lessons that can be drawn from other societies are mixed. China's experience with the British opium pushers of the nineteenth century, when millions became addicted to the drug, offers one worst-case scenario. The devastation of many native American tribes by alcohol presents another. On the other hand, the legal availability of opium and cannabis in many Asian societies did not result in large addict populations until recently. Indeed, in many countries U.S.-inspired opium bans imposed during the past few decades have paradoxically contributed to dramatic increases in heroin consumption among Asian youth. Within the United States, the decriminalization of marijuana by about a dozen states during the 1970s did not lead to increases in marijuana consumption. In the Netherlands, which went even further in decriminalizing cannabis during the 1970s, consumption has actually declined significantly. The policy has succeeded, as the government intended, in making drug use boring. Finally, late nineteenth-century America was a society in which there were almost no drug laws or even drug regulations—but levels of drug use then were about what they are today. Drug abuse was considered a serious problem, but the criminal-justice system was not regarded as part of the solution.

There are, however, reasons to believe that none of the currently illicit substances would become as popular as alcohol or tobacco, even if they were legalized. Alcohol has long been the principal intoxicant in most societies, including many in which other substances have been legally available. Presumably, its diverse properties account for its popularity—it quenches thirst, goes well with food, and promotes appetite as well as sociability. The popularity of tobacco probably stems not just from its powerful addictive qualities, but from the fact that its psychoactive effects are sufficiently subtle that cigarettes can be integrated with most other human activities. The illicit substances do not share these qualities to the same extent, nor is it likely that they would acquire them if they were legalized. Moreover, none of the illicit substances can compete with alcohol's special place in American culture and history.

An additional advantage of the illicit drugs is that none of them appears to be as insidious as either alcohol or tobacco. Consumed in their more benign forms, few of the illicit substances are as damaging to the human body over the long term as alcohol and tobacco, and none is as strongly linked with violent behavior as alcohol. On the other hand, much of the damage caused today by illegal drugs stems from their consumption in particularly dangerous ways. There is good reason to doubt that many Americans would inject cocaine or heroin into their veins even if given the chance to do so legally. And just as the dramatic growth in the heroin-consuming population during the 1960s leveled off for reasons apparently having little to do with law enforcement, so we can expect a leveling-off—which may already have begun—in the number of people smoking crack. The logic of legalization thus depends upon two assumptions: that most illegal drugs are not so dangerous as is commonly believed; and that the drugs and methods of consumption that are most risky are unlikely to prove appealing to many people, precisely because they are so obviously dangerous.

Perhaps the most reassuring reason for believing that repeal of the drug-prohibition laws will not lead to tremendous increases in drug-abuse levels is the fact that we have learned something from our past experiences with alcohol and tobacco abuse. We now know, for instance, that consumption taxes are an effective method of limiting consumption rates. We also know that restrictions and bans on advertising, as well as a campaign of negative advertising, can make a difference. The same is true of other government measures, including restrictions on time and place of sale, prohibition of consumption in public places, packaging requirements, mandated adjustments in insurance policies, crackdowns on driving while under the influence, and laws holding bartenders and hosts responsible for the drinking of customers and guests. There is even some evidence that government-sponsored education programs about the dangers of cigarette smoking have deterred many children from beginning to smoke.

Clearly it is possible to avoid repeating the mistakes of the past in designing an effective plan for legalization. We know more about the illegal drugs now than we knew about alcohol when Prohibition was repealed, or about tobacco when the anti-tobacco laws were repealed by many states in the early years of this century. Moreover, we can and must avoid having effective drug-control policies undermined by powerful lobbies like those that now protect the interests of alcohol and tobacco producers. We are also in a far better position than we were sixty years ago to prevent organized criminals from finding and creating new opportunities when their most lucrative source of income dries up.

It is important to stress what legalization is not. It is not a capitulation to the drug dealers—but rather a means to put them out of business. It is not an endorsement of drug use—but rather a recognition of the rights of adult Americans to make their own choices free of the fear of criminal sanctions. It is not a repudiation of the "just say no" approach—but rather an appeal to government to provide assistance and positive inducements, not criminal penalties and more repressive measures, in support of that approach. It is not even a call for the elimination of the criminal-justice system from drug regulation—but rather a proposal for the redirection of its efforts and attention.

There is no question that legalization is a risky policy, since it may lead to an increase in the number of people who abuse drugs. But that is a risk—not a certainty. At the same time, current drug-control policies are failing, and new proposals promise only to be more costly and more repressive. We know that repealing the drug-prohibition laws would eliminate or greatly reduce many of the ills that people commonly identify as part and parcel of the "drug problem." Yet legalization is repeatedly and vociferously dismissed, without any attempt to evaluate it openly and objectively. The past twenty years have demonstrated that a drug policy shaped by exaggerated rhetoric designed to arouse fear has only led to our current disaster. Unless we are willing to honestly evaluate our options, including various legalization strategies, we will run a still greater risk: we may never find the best solution for our drug problems.

ENDNOTES

1. The total number of state and federal prison inmates in 1975 was under 250,000; in 1980 it was 350,000; and in 1987 it was 575,000. The projected total for 2000 is one million.
2. It should be emphasized that the numbers cited do not include the many inmates sentenced for "drug-related" crimes such as acts of violence committed by drug dealers, typically against one another, and robberies committed to earn the money needed to pay for illegal drugs.

NO

Against the Legalization of Drugs

James Q. Wilson

In 1972, the President appointed me chairman of the National Advisory Council for Drug Abuse Prevention. Created by Congress, the Council was charged with providing guidance on how best to coordinate the national war on drugs. (Yes, we called it a war then, too.) In those days, the drug we were chiefly concerned with was heroin. When I took office, heroin use had been increasing dramatically. Everybody was worried that this increase would continue. Such phrases as "heroin epidemic" were commonplace.

The same year, the eminent economist Milton Friedman published an essay in *Newsweek* in which he called for legalizing heroin. His argument was on two grounds: as a matter of ethics, the government has no right to tell people not to use heroin (or to drink or to commit suicide); as a matter of economics, the prohibition of drug use imposes costs on society that far exceed the benefits. Others, such as the psychoanalyst Thomas Szasz, made the same argument.

We did not take Friedman's advice. (Government commissions rarely do.) I do not recall that we even discussed legalizing heroin, though we did discuss (but did not take action on) legalizing a drug, cocaine, that many people then argued was benign. Our marching orders were to figure out how to win the war on heroin, not to run up the white flag of surrender.

That was 1972. Today, we have the same number of heroin addicts that we had then—half a million, give or take a few thousand. Having that many heroin addicts is no trivial matter; these people deserve our attention. But not having had an increase in that number for over fifteen years is also something that deserves our attention. What happened to the "heroin epidemic" that many people once thought would overwhelm us?

The facts are clear: a more or less stable pool of heroin addicts has been getting older, with relatively few new recruits. In 1976 the average age of heroin users who appeared in hospital emergency rooms was about twenty-seven; ten years later it was thirty-two. More than two-thirds of all heroin users appearing in emergency rooms are now over the age of thirty. Back in the early 1970's, when heroin got onto the national political agenda, the typical heroin addict was much younger, often a teenager. Household surveys show the same thing—the rate of opiate use (which includes heroin) has been flat for the better part of two decades. More fine-grained studies of inner-city neighborhoods confirm this. John Boyle and Ann Brunswick found that the percentage of young blacks in Harlem who used heroin fell from 8 percent in 1970–71 to about 3 percent in 1975–76.

Why did heroin lose its appeal for young people? When the young blacks in Harlem were asked why they stopped, more than half mentioned "trouble with the law" or "high cost" (and high cost is, of course, directly the result of law enforcement). Two-thirds said that heroin hurt their health; nearly all said they had had a bad experience with it. We need not rely, however, simply on what they said. In New York City in 1973–75, the street price of heroin rose dramatically and its purity sharply declined, probably as a result of the heroin shortage caused by the success of the Turkish government in reducing the supply of opium base and of the French government in closing down heroin-processing laboratories located in and around Marseilles. These were short-lived gains for, just as Friedman predicted, alternative sources of supply—mostly in Mexico—quickly emerged. But the three-year heroin shortage interrupted the easy recruitment of new users.

Health and related problems were no doubt part of the reason for the reduced flow of recruits. Over the preceding years, Harlem youth had watched as more and more heroin users died of overdoses, were poisoned by adulterated doses, or acquired hepatitis from dirty needles. The word got around: heroin can kill you. By 1974 new hepatitis cases and drug-overdose deaths had dropped to a fraction of what they had been in 1970.

Alas, treatment did not seem to explain much of the cessation in drug use. Treatment programs can and do help heroin addicts, but treatment did not explain the drop in the number of *new* users (who by definition had never been in treatment) nor even much of the reduction in the number of experienced users.

No one knows how much of the decline to attribute to personal observation as opposed to high prices or reduced supply. But other evidence suggests strongly that price and supply played a large role. In 1972 the National Advisory Council was especially worried by the prospect that U.S. servicemen returning to this country from Vietnam would bring their heroin habits with them. Fortunately, a brilliant study by Lee Robins of Washington University in St. Louis put that fear to rest. She measured drug use of Vietnam veterans shortly after they had returned home. Though many had used heroin regularly while in Southeast Asia, most gave up the habit when back in the United States. The reason: here, heroin was less available and sanctions on its use were more pronounced. Of course, if a veteran had been willing to pay enough—which might have meant traveling to another city and would certainly have meant making an illegal contact with a disreputable dealer in a threatening neighborhood in order to acquire a (possibly) dangerous dose—he could have sustained his drug habit. Most veterans were unwilling to pay this price, and so their drug use declined or disappeared.

RELIVING THE PAST

Suppose we had taken Friedman's advice in 1972. What would have happened? We cannot be entirely certain, but at a minimum we would have placed the young heroin addicts (and, above all, the prospective addicts) in a very different position from the one in which they actually found themselves. Heroin would have been legal. Its price would have been reduced by 95 percent (minus whatever we chose to recover in taxes). Now that it could be sold by the same people who make aspirin, its quality would have been assured—no poisons, no adulterants. Sterile hypodermic needles would have been readily available at the neighborhood drugstore, probably at the same counter where the heroin was sold. No need to travel to big cities or unfamiliar neighborhoods—heroin could have been purchased anywhere, perhaps by mail order.

There would no longer have been any financial or medical reason to avoid heroin use. Anybody could have afforded it. We might have tried to prevent children from buying it, but as we have learned from our efforts to prevent minors from buying alcohol and tobacco, young people have a way of penetrating markets theoretically reserved for adults. Returning Vietnam veterans would have discovered that Omaha and Raleigh had been converted into the pharmaceutical equivalent of Saigon.

Under these circumstances, can we doubt for a moment that heroin use would have grown exponentially? Or that a vastly larger supply of new users would have been recruited? Professor Friedman is a Nobel Prize-winning economist whose understanding of market forces is profound. What did he think would happen to consumption under his legalized regime? Here are his works: "Legalizing drugs might increase the number of addicts, but it is not clear that it would. Forbidden fruit is attractive, particularly to the young."

Really? I suppose that we should expect no increase in Porsche sales if we cut the price by 95 percent, no increase in whiskey sales if we cut the price by a comparable amount—because young people only want fast cars and strong liquor when they are "forbidden." Perhaps Friedman's uncharacteristic lapse from the obvious implications of price theory can be explained by a misunderstanding of how drug users are recruited. In his 1972 essay he said that "drug addicts are deliberately made by pushers, who give likely prospects their first few doses free." If drugs were legal it would not pay anybody to produce addicts, because everybody would buy from the cheapest source. But as every drug expert knows, pushers do not produce addicts. Friends or acquaintances do. In fact, pushers are usually reluctant to deal with non-users because a non-user could be an undercover cop. Drug use spreads in the same way any fad or fashion spreads: somebody who is already a user urges his friends to try, or simply shows already-eager friends how to do it.

But we need not rely on speculation, however plausible, that lowered prices and more abundant supplies would have increased heroin usage. Great Britain once followed such a policy and with almost exactly those results. Until the mid-1960s, British physicians were allowed to prescribe heroin to certain classes of addicts. (Possessing these drugs without a doctor's prescription remained a criminal offense.) For many years this policy worked well enough because the addict patients were typically middle-class people who had become dependent on opiate painkillers while undergoing hospital treatment. There was no drug culture. The British system worked for many years, not because it prevented drug abuse, but because there was no problem of drug abuse that would test the system.

All that changed in the 1960's. A few unscrupulous doctors began passing out heroin in wholesale amounts. One doctor prescribed almost 600,000 heroin tablets—that is, over thirteen pounds—in just one year. A youthful drug culture emerged with a demand for drugs far different from that of the older addicts. As a result, the British government required doctors to refer users to government-run clinics to receive their heroin.

But the shift to clinics did not curtail the growth in heroin use. Throughout the 1960's the number of addicts increased—the late John Kaplan of Stanford estimated by fivefold—in part as a result of the diversion of heroin from clinic patients to new users on the streets. An addict would bargain with the clinic doctor over how big a dose he would receive. The patient wanted as much as he could get, the doctor wanted to give as little as was needed. The patient had an advantage in this conflict because the doctor could not be certain how much was really needed. Many patients would use some of their "maintenance" dose and sell the remaining part to friends, thereby recruiting new addicts. As the clinics learned of this, they began to shift their treatment away from heroin and toward methadone, an addictive drug that, when taken orally, does not produce a "high" but will block the withdrawal pains associated with heroin abstinence.

Whether what happened in England in the 1960's was a mini-epidemic or an epidemic depends on whether one looks at numbers or at rates of change. Compared to the United States, the numbers were small. In 1960 there were 68 heroin addicts known to the British government; by 1968 there were 2,000 in treatment and many more who refused treatment. (They would refuse in part because they did not want to get methadone at a clinic if they could get heroin on the street.) Richard Hartnoll estimates that the actual number of addicts in England is five times the number officially registered. At a minimum, the number of British addicts increased by thirtyfold in ten years; the actual increase may have been much larger.

In the early 1980's the numbers began to rise again, and this time nobody doubted that a real epidemic was at hand. The increase was estimated to be 40 percent a year. By 1982 there were thought to be 20,000 heroin users in London alone. Geoffrey Pearson reports that many cities—Glasgow, Liverpool, Manchester, and Sheffield among them—were now experiencing a drug problem that once had been largely confined to London. The problem, again, was supply. The country was being flooded with cheap, high-quality heroin, first from Iran and then from Southeast Asia.

The United States began the 1960's with a much larger number of heroin addicts and probably a bigger at-risk population than was the case in Great Britain. Even though it would be foolhardy to suppose that the British system, if installed here, would have worked the same way or with the same results, it would be equally foolhardy to suppose that a combination of heroin available from leaky clinics and from street dealers who faced only minimal law-enforcement risks would not have produced a much greater increase in heroin use than we actually experienced. My guess is that if we had allowed either doctors or clinics to prescribe heroin, we would have had far worse results than were produced in Britain, if for no other reason than the vastly larger number of addicts with which we began. We would have had to find some way to police thousands (not scores) of physicians and hundreds (not dozens) of clinics. If the British civil service found it difficult to keep heroin in the hands of addicts and out of the hands of recruits when it was dealing with a few hundred people, how well would the American civil service have accomplished the same tasks when dealing with tens of thousands of people?

BACK TO THE FUTURE

Now cocaine, especially in its potent form, crack, is the focus of attention. Now as in 1972 the government is trying to reduce its use. Now as then some people are advocating legalization. Is there any more reason to yield to those arguments today than there was almost two decades ago?*

I think not. If we had yielded in 1972 we almost certainly would have had today a permanent population of several million, not several hundred thousand, heroin addicts. If we yield now we will have a far more serious problem with cocaine.

Crack is worse than heroin by almost any measure. Heroin produces a pleasant drowsiness and, if hygienically administered, has only the physical side effects of constipation and sexual impotence. Regular heroin use incapacitates many users, especially poor ones, for any productive work or social responsibility. They will sit nodding on a street corner, helpless but at least harmless. By contrast, regular cocaine use leaves the user neither helpless nor harmless. When smoked (as with crack) or injected, cocaine produces instant, intense, and short-lived euphoria. The experience generates a powerful desire to repeat it. If the drug is readily available, repeat use will occur. Those people who progress to "bingeing" on cocaine become devoted to the drug and its effects to the exclusion of almost all other considerations—job, family, children, sleep, food, even sex. Dr. Frank Gawin at Yale and Dr. Everett Ellinwood at Duke report that a substantial percentage of all high-dose, binge users become uninhibited, impulsive, hypersexual, compulsive, irritable, and hyperactive. Their moods vacillate dramatically, leading at times to violence and homicide.

Women are much more likely to use crack than heroin, and if they are pregnant, the effects on their babies are tragic. Douglas Besharov, who has been following the effects of drugs on infants for twenty years, writes that nothing he learned about heroin prepared him for the devastation of cocaine. Cocaine harms the fetus and can lead to physical deformities or neurological damage. Some crack babies have for all practical purposes suffered a disabling stroke while still in the womb. The long-term consequences of this brain

---

* I do not here take up the question of marijuana. For a variety of reasons—its widespread use and its lesser tendency to addict—it presents a different problem from cocaine or heroin.

damage are lowered cognitive ability and the onset of mood disorders. Besharov estimates that about 30,000 to 50,000 such babies are born every year, about 7,000 in New York City alone. There may be ways to treat such infants, but from everything we now know the treatment will be long, difficult, and expensive. Worse, the mothers who are most likely to produce crack babies are precisely the ones who, because of poverty or temperament, are least able and willing to obtain such treatment. In fact, anecdotal evidence suggests that crack mothers are likely to abuse their infants.

The notion that abusing drugs such as cocaine is a "victimless crime" is not only absurd but dangerous. Even ignoring the fetal drug syndrome, crack-dependent people are, like heroin addicts, individuals who regularly victimize their children by neglect, their spouses by improvidence, their employers by lethargy, and their co-workers by carelessness. Society is not and could never be a collection of autonomous individuals. We all have a stake in ensuring that each of us displays a minimal level of dignity, responsibility, and empathy. We cannot, of course, coerce people into goodness, but we can and should insist that some standards must be met if society itself—on which the very existence of the human personality depends—is to persist. Drawing the line that defines those standards is difficult and contentious, but if crack and heroin use do not fall below it, what does?

The advocates of legalization will respond by suggesting that my picture is overdrawn. Ethan Nadelmann of Princeton argues that the risk of legalization is less than most people suppose. Over 20 million Americans between the ages of eighteen and twenty-five have tried cocaine (according to a government survey), but only a quarter million use it daily. From this Nadelmann concludes that at most 3 percent of all young people who try cocaine develop a problem with it. The implication is clear: make the drug legal and we only have to worry about 3 percent of our youth.

The implication rests on a logical fallacy and a factual error. The fallacy is this: the percentage of occasional cocaine users who become binge users *when the drug is illegal* (and thus expensive and hard to find) tells us nothing about the percentage who will become dependent when the drug is legal (and thus cheap and abundant). Drs. Gawin and Ellinwood report, in common with several other researchers, that controlled or occasional use of cocaine changes to compulsive and frequent use "when access to the drug increases" or when the user switches from snorting to smoking. More cocaine more potently administered alters, perhaps sharply, the proportion of "controlled" users who become heavy users.

The factual error is this: the federal survey Nadelmann quotes was done in 1985, *before* crack had become common. Thus the probability of becoming dependent on cocaine was derived from the responses of users who snorted the drug. The speed and potency of cocaine's action increase dramatically when it is smoked. We do not yet know how greatly the advent of crack increases the risk of dependency, but all the clinical evidence suggests that the increase is likely to be large.

It is possible that some people will not become heavy users even when the drug is readily available in its most potent form. So far there are no scientific grounds for predicting who will and who will not become dependent. Neither socioeconomic background nor personality traits differentiate between casual and intensive users. Thus, the only way to settle the question of who is correct about the effect of easy availability on drug use, Nadelmann or Gawin and Ellinwood, is to try it and see. But that social experiment is so risky as to be no experiment at all, for if cocaine is legalized and if the rate of its abusive use increases dramatically, there is no way to put the genie back in the bottle, and it is not a kindly genie.

HAVE WE LOST?

Many people who agree that there are risks in legalizing cocaine or heroin still favor it because, they think, we have lost the war on drugs. "Nothing we have done has worked" and the current federal policy is just "more of the same." Whatever the costs of greater drug use, surely they would be less than the costs of our present, failed efforts.

That is exactly what I was told in 1972—and heroin is not quite as bad a drug as cocaine. We did not surrender and we did not lose. We did not win, either. What the nation accomplished then was what most efforts to save people from themselves accomplish: the problem was contained and the number of victims minimized, all at a considerable cost in law enforcement and increased crime. Was the cost worth it? I think so, but others may disagree. What are the lives of would-be addicts worth? I recall some people saying to me then, "Let them kill themselves." I was appalled. Happily, such views did not prevail.

Have we lost today? Not at all. High-rate cocaine use is not commonplace. The National Institute of Drug Abuse (NIDA) reports that less than 5 percent of high-school seniors used cocaine within the last thirty days. Of course this survey misses young people who have dropped out of school and miscounts those who lie on the questionnaire, but even if we inflate the NIDA estimate by some plausible percentage, it is still not much above 5 percent. Medical examiners reported in 1987 that about 1,500 died from cocaine use; hospital emergency rooms reported about 30,000 admissions related to cocaine abuse.

These are not small numbers, but neither are they evidence of a nationwide plague that threatens to engulf us all. Moreover, cities vary greatly in the proportion of people who are involved with cocaine. To get city-level data we need to turn to drug tests carried out on arrested persons, who obviously are more likely to be drug users than the average citizen. The National Institute of Justice, through its Drug Use Forecasting (DUF) project, collects urinalysis data on arrestees in 22 cities. As we have already seen, opiate (chiefly heroin) use has been flat or declining in most of these cities over the last decade. Cocaine use has gone up sharply, but with great variation among cities. New York, Philadelphia, and Washington, D.C., all report that two-thirds or more of their arrestees tested positive for cocaine, but in Portland, San Antonio, and Indianapolis the percentage was one-third or less.

In some neighborhoods, of course, matters have reached crisis proportions. Gangs control the streets, shootings terrorize residents, and drug-dealing occurs in plain view. The police seem barely able to contain matters. But in these neighborhoods—unlike at Palo Alto cocktail parties—the people are not calling for legalization, they are calling for help. And often not much help has come. Many cities are willing to do almost anything about the drug problem except spend more money on it. The federal government cannot change that; only local voters and politicians can. It is not clear that they will.

It took about ten years to contain heroin. We have had experience with crack for only about three or four years. Each year we spend perhaps $11 billion on law enforcement (and some of that goes to deal with marijuana) and perhaps $2 billion on treatment. Large sums, but not sums that should lead anyone to say, "We just can't afford this any more."

The illegality of drugs increases crime, partly because some users turn to crime to pay for their habits, partly because some users are stimulated by certain drugs (such as crack or PCP) to act more violently or ruthlessly than they otherwise would, and partly because criminal organizations seeking to control drug supplies use force to manage their markets. These also are serious costs, but no one knows how much they would be reduced if drugs were legalized. Addicts would no longer steal to pay black-market prices for drugs, a real gain. But some, perhaps a great deal, of that gain would be offset by the great increase in the number of addicts. These people, nodding on heroin or living in the delusion-ridden high of cocaine, would hardly be ideal employees. Many would steal simply to support themselves, since snatch-and-grab, opportunistic crime can be managed even by people unable to hold a regular job or plan an elaborate crime. Those British addicts who get their supplies from government clinics are not models of law-abiding decency. Most are in crime, and though their per-capita rate of cirminality may be lower thanks to the cheapness of their drugs, the total volume of crime they produce may be quite large. Of course, society could decide to support all unemployable addicts on welfare, but that would mean that gains from lowered rates of crime would have to be offset by large increases in welfare budgets.

Proponents of legalization claim that the costs of having more addicts around would be largely if not entirely offset by having more money available with which to treat and care for them. The money would come from taxes levied on the sale of heroin and cocaine.

To obtain this fiscal dividend, however, legalization's supporters must first solve an economic dilemma. If they want to raise a lot of money to pay for welfare and treatment, the tax rate on the drugs will have to be quite high. Even if they themselves do not want a high rate, the politicians' love of "sin taxes" would probably guarantee that it would be high anyway. But the higher the tax, the higher the price of the drug, and the higher the price the greater the likelihood that addicts will turn to crime to find the money for it and that criminal organizations will be formed to sell tax-free drugs at below-market rates. If we managed to keep taxes (and thus prices) low, we would get that much less money to pay for welfare and treatment and more people could afford to become addicts. There may be an optimal tax rate for drugs that maximizes revenue while minimizing crime, bootlegging, and the recruitment of new addicts, but our experience with alcohol does not suggest that we know how to find it.

THE BENEFITS OF ILLEGALITY

The advocates of legalization find nothing to be said in favor of the current system except, possibly, that it keeps the number of addicts smaller than it would otherwise be. In fact, the benefits are more substantial than that.

First, treatment. All the talk about providing "treatment on demand" implies that there is a demand for treatment. That is not quite right. There are some drug-dependent people who genuinely want treatment and will remain in it if offered; they should receive it. But there are far more who want only short-term help after a bad crash; once stabilized and bathed, they are back on the street again, hustling. And even many of the addicts who enroll in a program honestly wanting help drop out after a short while when they discover that help takes time and commitment. Drug-dependent people have very short time horizons and a weak capacity for commitment. These two groups—those looking for a quick fix and those unable to stick with a long-term fix—are not easily helped. Even if we increase the number of treatment slots—as we should—we would have to do something to make treatment more effective.

One thing that can often make it more effective is compulsion. Douglas Anglin of UCLA, in common with many other researchers, has found that the longer one stays in a treatment program, the better the chances of a reduction in drug dependency. But he, again like most other researchers, has found that drop-out rates are high. He has also found, however, that patients who enter treatment under legal compulsion stay in the program longer than those not subject to such pressure. His research on the California civil-commitment program, for example, found that heroin users involved with its required drug-testing program had over the long term a lower rate of heroin use than similar addicts who were free of such constraints. If for many addicts compulsion is a useful component of treatment, it is not clear how compulsion could be achieved in a society in which purchasing, possessing, and using the drug were legal. It could be managed, I suppose, but I would not want to have to answer the challenge from the American Civil Liberties Union that it is wrong to compel a person to undergo treatment for consuming a legal commodity.

Next, education. We are now investing substantially in drug-education programs in the schools. Though we do not yet know for certain what will work, there are some promising leads. But I wonder how credible such programs would be if they were aimed at dissuading children from doing something perfectly legal. We could, of course, treat drug education like smoking education: inhaling crack and inhaling tobacco are both legal, but you should not do it because it is bad for you. That tobacco is bad for you is easily shown; the Surgeon General has seen to that. But what do we say about crack? It is pleasurable, but devoting yourself to so much pleasure is not a good idea (though perfectly legal)? Unlike tobacco, cocaine will not give you cancer or emphysema, but it will lead you to neglect your duties to family, job, and neighborhood? Everybody is doing cocaine, but you should not?

Again, it might be possible under a legalized regime to have effective drug-prevention programs, but their effectiveness would depend heavily, I think, on first having decided that cocaine use, like tobacco use, is purely a matter of practical consequences; no fundamental moral significance attaches to either. But if we believe—as I do—that dependency on certain mind-altering drugs *is* a moral issue and that their illegality rests in part on their immorality, then legalizing them undercuts, if it does not eliminate altogether, the moral message.

That message is at the root of the distinction we now make between nicotine and cocaine. Both are highly addictive; both have harmful physical effects. But we treat the two drugs differently, not simply because nicotine is so widely used as to be beyond the reach of effective prohibition, but because its use does not destroy the user's essential humanity. Tobacco shortens one's life, cocaine debases it. Nicotine alters one's habits, cocaine alters one's soul. The heavy use of crack, unlike the heavy use of tobacco, corrodes those natural sentiments of sympathy and duty that constitute our human nature and make possible our social life. To say, as does Nadelmann, that distinguishing morally between tobacco and cocaine is "little more than a transient prejudice" is close to saying that morality itself is but a prejudice.

THE ALCOHOL PROBLEM

Now we have arrived where many arguments about legalizing drugs begin: is there any reason to treat heroin and cocaine differently from the way we treat alcohol?

There is no easy answer to that question because, as with so many human problems, one cannot decide simply on the basis either of moral principles or of individual consequences; one has to temper any policy by a common-sense judgment of what is possible. Alcohol, like heroin, cocaine, PCP, and marijuana, is a drug—that is, a mood-altering substance—and consumed to excess it certainly has harmful consequences: auto accidents, barroom fights, bedroom shootings. It is also, for some people, addictive. We cannot confidently compare the addictive powers of these drugs, but the best evidence suggests that crack and heroin are much more addictive than alcohol.

Many people, Nadelmann included, argue that since the health and financial costs of alcohol abuse are so much higher than those of cocaine or heroin abuse, it is hypocritical folly to devote our efforts to preventing cocaine or drug use. But as Mark Kleiman of Harvard has pointed out, this comparison is quite misleading. What Nadelmann is doing is showing that a *legalized* drug (alcohol) produces greater social harm than *illegal* ones (cocaine and heroin). But of course. Suppose that in the 1920's we had made heroin and cocaine legal and alcohol illegal. Can anyone doubt that Nadelmann would now be writing that it is folly to continue our ban on alcohol because cocaine and heroin are so much more harmful?

And let there be no doubt about it—widespread heroin and cocaine use are associated with all manner of ills. Thomas Bewley found that the mortality rate of British heroin addicts in 1968 was 28 times as high as the death rate of the same age group of non-addicts, even though in England at the time an addict could obtain free or low-cost heroin and clean needles from British clinics. Perform the following mental experiment: suppose we legalized heroin and cocaine in this country. In what proportion of auto fatalities would the state police report that the driver was nodding off on heroin or recklessly driving on a coke high? In what proportion of spouse-assault and child-abuse cases would the local police report that crack was involved? In what proportion of industrial accidents would safety investigators report that the forklift or drill-press operator was in a drug-induced stupor or frenzy? We do not know exactly what the proportion would be, but anyone who asserts that it would not be much higher than it is now would have to believe that these drugs have little appeal except when they are illegal. And that is nonsense.

An advocate of legalization might concede that social harm—perhaps harm equivalent to that already produced by alcohol—would follow from making cocaine and heroin generally available. But at least, he might add, we would have the problem "out in the open" where it could be treated as a matter of "public health." That is well and good, *if* we knew how to treat—that is, cure—heroin and cocaine abuse. But we do not know how to do it for all the people who would need such help. We are having only limited success in coping with chronic alcoholics. Addictive behavior is immensely difficult to change, and the best methods for changing it—living in drug-free therapeutic communities, becoming faithful members of Alcoholics Anonymous or Narcotics Anonymous—require great personal commitment, a quality that is, alas, in short supply among the very persons—young people, disadvantaged people—who are often most at risk for addiction.

Suppose that today we had, not 15 million alcohol abusers, but half a million. Suppose that we already knew what we have learned from our long experience with the widespread use of alcohol. Would we make whiskey illegal? I do not know, but I suspect there would be a lively debate. The Surgeon General would remind us of the risks alcohol poses to pregnant women. The National Highway Traffic Safety Administration would point to the likelihood of more highway fatalities caused by drunk drivers. The Food and Drug Administration might find that there is a nontrivial increase in cancer associated with alcohol consumption. At the same time the police would report great difficulty in keeping illegal whiskey out of our cities, officers being corrupted by bootleggers, and alcohol addicts often resorting to crime to feed their habit. Libertarians, for their part, would argue that every citizen has a right to drink anything he wishes and that drinking is, in any event, a "victimless crime."

However the debate might turn out, the central fact would be that the problem was still, at that point, a small one. The government cannot legislate away the addictive tendencies in all of us, nor can it remove completely even the most dangerous addictive substances. But it can cope with harms when the harms are still manageable.

SCIENCE AND ADDICTION

One advantage of containing a problem while it is still containable is that it buys time for science to learn more about it and perhaps to discover a cure. Almost unnoticed in the current debate over legalizing drugs is that basic science has made rapid strides in identifying the underlying neurological processes involved in some forms of addiction. Stimulants such as cocaine and amphetamines alter the way certain brain cells communicate with one another. That alteration is complex and not entirely understood, but in simplified form it involves modifying the way in which a neurotransmitter called dopamine sends signals from one cell to another.

When dopamine crosses the synapse between two cells, it is in effect carrying a message from the first cell to activate the second one. In certain parts of the brain that message is experienced as pleasure. After the message is delivered, the dopamine returns to the first cell. Cocaine apparently blocks this return, or "reuptake," so that the excited cell and others nearby continue to send pleasure messages. When the exaggerated high produced by cocaine-influenced dopamine finally ends, the brain cells may (in ways that are still a matter of dispute) suffer from an extreme lack of dopamine, thereby making the individual unable to experience any pleasure at all. This would explain why cocaine users often feel so depressed after enjoying the drug. Stimulants may also affect the way in which other neurotransmitters, such as serotonin and noradrenaline, operate.

Whatever the exact mechanism may be, once it is identified it becomes possible to use drugs to block either the effect of cocaine or its tendency to produce dependency. There have already been experiments using desipramine, imipramine, bromocriptine, carbamazepine, and other chemicals. There are some promising results.

Tragically, we spend very little on such research, and the agencies funding it have not in the past occupied very influential or visible posts in the federal bureaucracy. If there is one aspect of the "war on drugs" metaphor that I dislike, it is its tendency to focus attention almost exclusively on the troops in the trenches, whether engaged in enforcement or treatment, and away from the research-and-development efforts back on the home front where the war may ultimately be decided.

I believe that the prospects of scientists in controlling addiction will be strongly influenced by the size and character of the problem they face. If the problem is a few hundred thousand chronic, high-dose users of an illegal product, the chances of making a difference at a reasonable cost will be much greater than if the problem is a few million chronic users of legal substances. Once a drug is legal, not only will its use increase but many of those who then use it will prefer the drug to the treatment: they will want the pleasure, whatever the cost to themselves or their families, and they will resist—probably successfully—any effort to wean them away from experiencing the high that comes from inhaling a legal substance.

IF I AM WRONG . . .

No one can know what our society would be like if we changed the law to make access to cocaine, heroin, and PCP easier. I believe, for reasons given, that the result would be a sharp increase in use, a more widespread degradation of the human personality, and a greater rate of accidents and violence.

I may be wrong. If I am, then we will needlessly have incurred heavy costs in law enforcement and some forms of criminality. But if I am right, and the legalizers prevail anyway, then we will have consigned millions of people, hundreds of thousands of infants, and hundreds of neighborhoods to a life of oblivion and disease. To the lives and families destroyed by alcohol we will have added countless more destroyed by cocaine, heroin, PCP, and whatever else a basement scientist can invent.

Human character is formed by society; indeed, human character is inconceivable without society, and good character is less likely in a bad society. Will we, in the name of an abstract doctrine of radical individualism, and with the false comfort of suspect predictions, decide to take the chance that somehow individual decency can survive amid a more general level of degradation?

I think not. The American people are too wise for that, whatever the academic essayists and cocktail-party pundits may say. But if Americans today are less wise than I suppose, then Americans at some future time will look back on us now and wonder, what kind of people were they that they could have done such a thing?

Letters from Readers

To the Editor of Commentary:

James Q. Wilson's article, "Against the Legalization of Drugs" [February], perpetuates several myths about drug use and drug legalization. Moreover, the substance of his empirical arguments—that the drug war has curtailed drug use and that legalization would result in significant increases in drug abuse—is open to serious dispute. Finally, his philosophical argument—that a specific category of drugs is immoral—is based on misrepresentation of the effects of the drugs in question and a narrow conceptualization of morality.

At the outset, Mr. Wilson suggests that legalization is akin to raising the white flag of surrender. This is an oft-repeated but inaccurate piece of rhetoric. Proponents of drug legalization do not suggest that we "give in" to drug use. Most proponents view legalization as having two beneficial consequences: first, legalization would remove the drug trade from the hands of organized crime and children, thereby eliminating much of the attendant violence; and second, legalization would enable us to focus our attention on education (as we have done with nicotine) regarding the health and other hazards of drug use.

Mr. Wilson then moves on to suggest that the drug war caused the decline, or at least stabilization, that we have seen in the use of heroin. He points to price increases for heroin in the 70's as evidence that prohibition worked—that it led to price hikes with the result that would-be addicts stayed away from heroin. Mr. Wilson has some of his facts right. Heroin use did stabilize in the early 1980's (though it may be climbing). However, it is difficult to attribute this to the drug war, since, in fact, the price of heroin declined in the 80's by 20 percent, while purity rose some 33 percent. Clearly, factors other than the drug war and its price effects were at work here. Moreover, while heroin use stabilized, the use of cocaine climbed during the 80's, to peak in the mid-80's. Over the past several years, cocaine use has declined despite rapidly falling prices and more plentiful supplies. . . . In other words, drug use—whether of heroin or cocaine—has fluctuated under a regime of prohibition in patterns apparently unrelated to price or illegality. . . .

Mr. Wilson's own arguments undermine some of his assertions. Many proponents of legalization argue that most drug users, despite popular conceptions to the contrary, exhibit controlled consumption, whether of heroin, cocaine, or marijuana. And those who curtail consumption report that they do so primarily for health reasons and not because of fear of the law or of rising prices. Mr. Wilson himself notes a survey that showed that two-thirds of a group of blacks in Harlem claimed that they stopped their drug use for health reasons. A survey of high-school students nationwide showed that 21 percent stopped their use of cocaine for health reasons, 12 percent due to pressure from family and friends, 12 percent due to cost, and *none* due to fear of law enforcement. These surveys bode well for a scenario of legalization, since they suggest that an educational campaign about the health effects of drugs accompanying legalization can, as education has done with nicotine, help to curtail use. . . .

After dismissing the health effects of cocaine as grounds neither for supporting nor opposing prohibition, Mr. Wilson gets to the real heart of his argument. He believes that certain categories of drugs are immoral. They are immoral because they are mind-altering, and this, he says, is why nicotine is legal and cocaine, heroin, and marijuana are not.

First, the facts. While heroin, cocaine, marijuana, and other illicit drugs have varying impacts on the body and brain, this does not mean that their use necessarily impairs one's ability to lead a successful life. Indeed, the vast majority of individuals who use marijuana on a casual basis are productive citizens with healthy emotional lives. The same is true for the recreational users of cocaine and even heroin. Dr. Arnold Trebach of the Drug Policy Foundation and others have amply documented that casual use does not necessarily lead to mental, emotional, or physical impairment. . . . Mr. Wilson's characterization of drug use in general is simply false. . . .

Mr. Wilson is correct that for some users cocaine, heroin, or marijuana, like alcohol, can be highly debilitating (though, incidentally, on this score Mr. Wilson overplays the differences between legal drugs like nicotine and illegal ones). Most proponents of legalization share Mr. Wilson's concern over this debility. But to acknowledge that some individuals suffer enormously from their drug addiction and do harm to others as a result does not lead automatically to the conclusion that all drug users manifest immoral, inhumane, unsympathetic behavior. In short, drug use does not, as Mr. Wilson contends, "destroy the drug user's essential humanity." This being the case, Mr. Wilson's moral argument falls apart. . . .

Mr. Wilson writes that "human character is inconceivable without society, and good character is less likely in a bad society." But what is a bad society? Here, Mr.

Wilson overlooks the enormous harm to basic principles of due process of law now being wrought by the drug war. These principles, which are designed to protect us against arbitrary authority, serve as the foundation for a society based on responsible and free individuals. Such a foundation allows for a pluralistic climate in which families, churches, and social groups can prosper. That, I would argue, is what makes a "good society."

A genuine concern about legalization is that it would lead to significant increases in the numbers of people using (or abusing) drugs. Mr. Wilson, with little but gut feelings to back his views, firmly insists that drug use would increase. While any discussion of the effects of legalization on use is necessarily speculative, one can point to evidence that suggests Mr. Wilson is wrong. For example, decriminalization of marijuana in the Netherlands and in a number of U.S. states has not been accompanied by increased use; in fact, use has declined in these areas. And in Finland, too, there was no increase in the use of alcohol after prohibition was repealed, to the accompaniment of a public-education campaign.

Mr. Wilson's description of the British system of drug regulation is also misleading. For forty years that system worked without entailing increases in heroin use. The increases in use since the 60's are very likely attributable at least in part to changes in the system. At the very least, one can conclude that legalization *per se* did not lead to increased use, since increased heroin use did not occur during the first four decades that the system was in place.

We cannot know for certain what the effects of legalization would be on use. But we can direct our policy efforts toward implementing legalization measures that attempt to address this risk through education, restrictions on use by minors, and so on. Before we can construct such policies, however, we need to discard the kind of moralistic arguments set forth by Mr. Wilson that are largely based on hyperbole about drug use, drug abuse, and the human soul.

—*Lynn Scarlett*
Reason Foundation
Santa Monica, California

To the Editor of Commentary:
It would take an article of equal length to correct the outright lies, half-truths, and misrepresentations made by James Q. Wilson in his article, "Against the Legalization of Drugs." . . .

A few short points are worth making:
The British system has not failed; it has managed drug abuse better than we have and has limited crime better than our system has. If given a choice between the U.S. and Great Britain in terms both of heroin use and crime, most Americans would choose Britain. The British themselves have chosen to continue their system; in fact, with the onset of AIDS, they have become even more humane in their treatment of addicts.

Mr. Wilson was cowardly to avoid mentioning marijuana, but he had no choice. Marijuana legalization makes so much sense that even a rabid prohibitionist like Mr. Wilson could not distort the facts enough to make a credible argument. Marijuana is too important for prohibitionists to ignore. According to the FBI it accounts for more than one-third of all drug arrests and is the most valuable farm crop in the United States. In fact, in 1982 the National Academy of Sciences issued a report entitled "An Analysis of Marijuana Policy" which urged immediate decriminalization of possession and personal cultivation of marijuana, and advocated experimentation with regulated sales.

In regard to currently legal drugs, Mr. Wilson certainly does not advocate the prohibition of nicotine and alcohol, even though he highlights the failures of our policies in connection with these drugs. (By the way, legislation to prohibit tobacco has been introduced in Hawaii.) It is more important to highlight the successes: the use of alcohol and tobacco, as well as caffeine, is being reduced. Both drugs are becoming safer, with the introduction of low-tar, low-nicotine cigarettes and "lite" beers and wine coolers. We are having more success with legal drugs than we are with illegal drugs and we are doing it without gang warfare on the streets, smugglers fighting interdictors on the high seas, assassinations in Colombia, corrupted public officials, the expansion of organized crime, the loss of civil liberties, and the overburdening of our criminal-justice system.

The war on drugs has been given more of a chance to succeed than it deserves. During the 1980's the drug war met all of its goals: a record increase in incarcerations; one million drug arrests last year; record seizures; a well-funded antidrug publicity campaign; and an ocean of urine tested for drugs. Before the "Reagan war" we did not have crack, had never heard of ice, and our President could enter Colombia without having to hide. The world is not safer or healthier after the successes of the last decade, and there is no reason to think it will be so in the 1990's.

—*Kevin B. Zeese*
Drug Policy Foundation
Washington, D.C.

To the Editor of Commentary:

James Q. Wilson's defense of current drug policies is the most cogent . . . I have yet read, but it still fails to carry the burden of persuasion. And that burden is his, not the legalizers', to carry. This is so for two reasons.

First, the private consensual behavior of adults (which is the only thing that legalizers intend to make legal) is normally beyond the effective reach of democratic government. . . . When our government seeks to impose drastic penal sanctions on such conduct, whether it is abortion, gambling, pornography, or dope, we must recognize it as the extreme . . . intrusion that it is, and require compelling proof of necessity before getting on board.

Secondly, Mr. Wilson writes as though severe penal laws against drugs were something brand-new, and that we should extend to them the kind of benefit of the doubt that we normally extend to bold and well-intended social experiments, as though the imposition of such laws on consenting adults were just another Head Start program. But the fact is that we have been enforcing penal drug laws of ever-increasing severity for seventy-five years, and what do we have to show for it? Ever-increasing quantities of drugs of ever-increasing potency available to wider and wider audiences of users; drugs whose contents are neither labeled nor controlled, and whose patterns of underworld distribution guarantee violent street wars, corrupt police, and demoralized neighborhoods. These are not statistical extrapolations, but real-life facts. The drug laws are no longer in their experimental phase, and one would think that after seventy-five years we would insist that our government show us—with a clear and palpable demonstration of its successes—why we should allow this costly and destructive experiment to continue. . . .

Mr. Wilson barely mentions, let alone discusses, the hideous consequences of current policy, and gives no real evidence showing either that more of the same will reduce these consequences or that more of the same is demonstrably better than legalization. Instead, he offers some nebulous, albeit uplifting, notions of "morality" and "character" as worthy justifications for staying the penal course, bolstered by statistically extrapolated predictions of increased drug usage. . . .

To summarize: while the legalizers can point to longstanding . . . measurable negative consequences from current policy, James Q. Wilson and the other drug warriors offer only abstract hypotheses—what Mr. Wilson himself calls "the false comfort of suspect predictions"—to justify a continuation of that policy, one which has given us no palpable benefits in three-quarters of a century. . . .

—*Stanley Neustadter*
New York City

To the Editor of Commentary:

James Q. Wilson's argument in support of the drug war is essentially that, at least to a limited extent, it works. If we legalized drugs, he asserts, there would be far more usage than there is today, with attendant consequences that affect us all—like crack-addicted babies or drug-related traffic fatalities.

There are other solutions to such specific problems, however. Since the mother of a crack-addicted child has proven herself, at the outset, to be abusive and unfit, the child should be taken from her. To help pay for its care, she should be fined or held ineligible for any government assistance for the remainder of her life. . . .

Drivers on drugs could be treated the same way we treat drivers on alcohol, only more drastically. For repeat offenses, or for causing a serious accident, a driver on drugs might face prison (there would be more room, were the drug war ended) or even capital punishment, for his "reckless disregard of the lives of others." If punitive programs have been ineffective with alcohol, it is only because of weak penalties and enforcement. With random testing of drivers, we could easily solve this problem, if, again, we held people appropriately accountable for their actions.

The more general argument for the drug war is that users hurt themselves, and that the influx of millions of new users likely under legalization can only have a negative, if noncriminal, effect on society as a whole. . . . I am not at all sure of the dire consequences legalization is supposed to bring, but if it does, then so be it. Better to die as a free people than live like slaves. I rather think, though, that this is not really the choice before us anyway. If we are such idiots as to need protection from labeled substances in bottles, I suspect we are doomed anyway. . . .

—*R. T. Peterson*
Chicago, Illinois

To the Editor of Commentary:

James Q. Wilson presents two alternate views of the nature of morality and drugs. When it comes to cocaine and certain other "mind-altering drugs," he tells us that their "illegality rests in part on their immorality." And cocaine is immoral because it "alters one's soul, . . . [and] corrodes those natural sentiments of sympathy and duty that constitute our human nature and make possible our social life." By telling us that he thinks Ethan Nadelmann's pro-legalization position "is close to saying that morality itself is but a prejudice," Mr. Wilson makes it clear that in relation to cocaine he regards the moral question as an absolute one.

But then, in the very next paragraph, he tells us that when it comes to alcohol the moral question is a relative one, because "one cannot decide [alcohol policy] on the basis of either moral principles or of individual consequences; one has to temper any policy by a common-sense judgment of what is possible." Now by any measure—deaths, number of problem users, violent behavior—alcohol use *per se* is a much more serious health and social problem than cocaine use *per se* (the illegal status of which does cause many serious social problems). But in the case of alcohol, Mr. Wilson tells us that we cannot apply an absolute moral standard. One must give him credit at least for fairly presenting the two opposing views or morality, the absolutist and the relativist. One would just like to know which one he subscribes to.

The real problem with all this moralism is that none of it solves the drug problem, which in this country begins with alcohol and tobacco. What is needed to replace the current, completely failed illegalization policy is a comprehensive public-health approach to combat the use of *all* drugs. . . .

—*Steven Jonas, M.D.*
Department of Preventive Medicine
School of Medicine-SUNY
Stony Brook, New York

To the Editor of Commentary:

James Q. Wilson's attempted refutation of calls for drug legalization is based on moral assumptions about what may happen in the future, and misunderstandings of what has already occurred in the past.

His interpretation of the opinions and behavior of American citizens is too narrow and limiting. In today's world, the threshold of abuse already exists. I can't imagine that many more citizens (if any at all) would choose to damage their lives and their families by becoming drug *abusers*.

It seems to me that the way we manage the harm done by drugs must be rooted in sound social, medical, and economic practices. This is surely preferable to the police-state mentality championed by politicians ranting about morality who pontificate about how "tough" they are in the drug war.

Our views on Vietnam matured when family members, neighbors, and friends came home in coffins and wheelchairs. Our views on the drug war will mature when we realize that family members, neighbors, and friends are being led off to jail, their lifelong possessions stolen from them under drug-forfeiture acts.

The imprisonment policy of the present drug czar only recycles dealers and abusers (and now casual users) into costly . . . penal compost heaps.

Mr. Wilson is mistaken if he thinks the policy of the past few decades has served as an effective containment model for drug abuse. He writes as though he has never met a casual user who otherwise productively serves the needs of family and society.

Michael R. Weddle
State Representative
House of Representatives
Concord, New Hampshire

To the Editor of Commentary:

As a former prosecutor, I have admired the . . . observations of James Q. Wilson and in particular his book, *Thinking About Crime*, which is both iconoclastic and refreshingly on target. But if Mr. Wilson's views on the criminal-justice system have been for the most part the essence of the practical and pragmatic, not so his article on drugs.

I believe Mr. Wilson has either disregarded, or failed to assess fully, the insignificance of the problems of 1972 as compared to those of 1990. . . . During the 70's I participated as a prosecutor in the criminal-justice system on the federal and county levels and I witnessed that system lumbering along like a pair of aging oxen under a barely manageable cartload. Even then, the "justice" of the system was as occasional as the production of oxen manure. In 1990, the load has been trebled and quadrupled, one of the oxen has since died, and at least two of the wheels of the cart have fallen off. It is not a pretty picture.

In my country, since 1972, the cost of inmate incarceration has risen 500 percent, and if we incarcerated everyone required under the drug-war rules, the prison population would *increase 400 percent*. The money cannot be printed fast enough to maintain the prisoners of war even in lousy conditions, never mind those the ACLU might find acceptable. When one chump hits the street, the taxpayer reaches into his pocket again to pay for the next one who follows close on his heels. And the next and the next and the next.

To extend the analogy, that last ox is about to cash in his chips, thanks to the factor of prison capacity, . . . which will defeat the war on drugs. More than 70 percent of the encaged are there for drug-related offenses. The issue is not so much one of getting Mr. Wilson's genie back into the bottle as it is of doing something about the masses of uneducated, helpless, and hopeless drugoids on their way into, or out of, jail. . . .

Mr. Wilson himself seems to indulge in the all-or-nothing-at-all verbiage which currently characterizes most of the Grand Drug Debate. I suggest there exists a middle ground between the war whoops of the "lock-'em-up" gang versus the "come-and-get-it" crowd. . . .

For starters, we should rethink the question of the decriminalization of marijuana. Among all my adventures in law enforcement, I found marijuana prosecutions to be the most unredeemedly useless. We should try methods of regional experimentation, look to the successes of Head Start, for example, and begin using some of those enforcement bucks to imprint children's minds. Or we should consider modern marketing techniques to dissuade, or think, perhaps, of the viability of medical oversight and certification of addiction. . . .

I, for one, am unwilling to assume that droves of educated and appropriately conditioned people will rush hell-bent for a line of legalized blow. In my county, as in any county with an urban center, the stuff is there for the asking, but the steady customers are still the city's losers in life. Given a diet other than one of despair and ghetto hopelessness, there has been significant resistance to the crack syndrome. That in and of itself says much about the potentially addicted.

What we are doing now flat out doesn't work, and it doesn't work on a level that rivals any previous government folly. The eloquence of James Q. Wilson notwithstanding, let us please try a different course.

—*Bill Mathesius*
County Executive
County of Mercer
Trenton, New Jersey

DISCUSSION QUESTIONS

1. What is a drug? Does your definition cover alcohol? Tobacco? Heroin? Marijuana? What are the important differences, if any?
2. If drugs were legalized, what steps should government take, if any at all, to ensure the health and safety of users?
3. If taxes were collected from the sale of drugs, should that revenue go toward treatment and prevention programs, or should it be concentrated on other societal problems? Why?
4. Should some currently legal drugs be made illegal?
5. What do you think are the main advantages of legalizing drugs? What are the principal disadvantages? Should any drugs be legal? Why?

6. Are there important policy reasons why tobacco should be treated differently from, say, marijuana? Heroin? LSD? Cocaine? Why?
7. Do you think that making certain drugs illegal denies important liberties to individuals? Why or why not?
8. What impact would legalizing drugs have on their price? How, in turn, would that affect drug-related crimes? How would it affect drug use? What evidence supports your position?
9. Where should government focus its efforts at drug control? At the federal level or states and localities? On the individual user or the supplier of drugs? On law enforcement or interdiction? Should there be a governmental effort at all? Why or why not?
10. Should strict minimum sentences be required for individuals caught distributing drugs? Using drugs?
11. Have you ever used an illegal drug? How, if at all, does that affect your position on the legalization debate?
12. What impact would drug legalization have on your use of drugs (or that of your friends), if any? Why?

ADDITIONAL READINGS

Benjamin, Daniel K., and Robert LeRoy Miller. *Undoing Drugs: Beyond Legalization* (New York: Basic Books, 1991).

Evans, Rod L., and Irwin M. Berent, eds. *Drug Legalization: For and Against* (LaSalle, Ill.: Open Court, 1992).

Husak, Douglas N. *Drugs and Rights* (Cambridge: Cambridge University Press, 1992).

Jacobs, James. "Imagining Drug Legalization." *The Public Interest* (Fall 1990).

Kaplan, John. "Taking Drugs Seriously." *The Public Interest* (Summer 1988).

Kleiman, Mark, and Aaron Saiger. *Drug Legalization: The Importance of Asking the Right Question* (Cambridge, Mass.: John F. Kennedy School of Government, Working Paper 89-01-16, 1989).

Krauss, Melvyn B., and Edward P. Lazear, eds. *Searching for Alternatives: Drug-Control Policy in the United States* (Stanford, Calif.: Hoover Institution Press, 1991).

Kwitny, Jonathan. *Acceptable Risks* (New York: Poseidon Press, 1992).

Nadelmann, Ethan A. "Drug Prohibition in the United States: Costs, Consequences, and Alternatives." *Science* (September 1, 1989).

Ostrowski, James. *Thinking About Drug Legalization* (Washington, D.C.: Cato Institute, 1989).

Perl, Raphael F., ed. *Drugs and Foreign Policy: A Critical Review* (Boulder, Colo.: Westview Press, 1994).

Reuter, Peter. "Can the Borders Be Sealed?" *The Public Interest* (Summer 1988).

Szasz, Thomas Stephen. *Our Right to Drugs: The Case for a Free Market* (New York: Praeger, 1992).

Trebach, Arnold S., and James A. Inciardi. *Legalize It?: Debating American Drug Policy* (Washington, D.C.: American University Press, 1993).

Vallance, Theodore R. *Prohibition's Second Failure: The Quest for a Rational and Humane Drug Policy* (Westport, Conn.: Praeger, 1993).

16
GUN CONTROL

"Should the Sale of Handguns Be More Strictly Controlled?"

The November 1993 passage of the so-called "Brady Bill" marked the first major gun-control legislation to be enacted at the federal level since 1968. In that year, the Gun Control Act prohibited the interstate sale or shipment of firearms and ammunition and required dealers to keep records of gun transactions. The act was passed in response to the sense of national crisis that followed the assassinations of Dr. Martin Luther King Jr. and Senator Robert F. Kennedy as well as the urban riots that swept across the country in that year. The Brady Bill institutes a mandatory five-day waiting period for the purchase of handguns, during which time a background check is conducted into the past criminal and psychiatric history of the purchaser. It furthermore makes funds available for the development of a centrally coordinated computerized system to allow for instantaneous checks and, ultimately, the elimination of the five-day waiting period.

Like the Gun Control Act of 1968, the Brady Bill legislation comes in response to a period of perceived crisis in the nation, albeit a more slowly evolving one. Federal officials estimate that Americans may own 200 million guns and are buying them at a rate of more than 4 million per year, around half of them handguns. The spring 1993 standoff at Waco, Texas between agents of the Bureau of Alcohol, Tobacco, and Firearms and the heavily armed religious cult leader David Koresh and his followers made clear the problem of the proliferation of assault weapons. The FBI reported that more than 55 percent of the 22,540 murders that occurred in 1992 were committed with a handgun. If other firearms, such as shotguns and assault rifles, are taken into account, the figure rises to over 68 percent of all murders.[1] In 1990, 94 out of every 100,000 Americans faced robbery at the point of a gun. This was up from 73 per 100,000 in 1985, but was still less than the rate of 101.3 per 100,000 in 1980.[2] In 1989, more than 26 percent of rapes and over 22 percent of aggravated assaults involved the use of a handgun.[3] Among African-American males age fifteen to thirty-four, firearm violence is the leading cause of death.[4] Compared to the portion of the population, it is startling that more African-American males were homicide victims in 1988 than white males.

Crime rates in the United States are exceptionally high when compared to those of the other industrial democracies. In 1990, there were 10,567 handgun murders in the United States, compared with 22 in Great Britain, 87 in Japan, and 68 in Canada.[5] Even when population differences are accounted for, the figures for these nations are drastically lower than the United States: The per-capita death rate from handgun violence was 1 per 391,000 residents of Canada, 1 per 1.4 million in Japan, and 1 per 2.5 million in Britain; the comparable figure for the United States was 1 for every 24,000 residents, or 16 times the rate in Canada and 104 times the rate in Britain. Aside from the human cost of gun violence, the financial cost alone is enormous. A 1989 study estimated the average lifetime cost of firearm fatalities due to medical expenses and lost productivity to be $487,700 (in 1992 dollars) for each incident; from that figure it was extrapolated that the cost of gunfire injury and death in the United States in 1985 amounted to some $14.4 billion dollars.[6] Incarceration rates, which have more than doubled in the last decade, now surpass three prisoners for every 1,000 people, one of the highest rates in the world.

But while the public perceives crime rates to be increasing, crime statistics indicate otherwise. Perhaps the most reliable measure, the homicide rate, has held at a relatively steady rate for the last two decades. Crime rates as a whole declined in 1991, 1992, and 1993. The FBI's Uniform Crime Reports Index, based on data from police reports, showed a slight decline over the past ten years; the Census Bureau's National Crime Survey, based on self-reported crimes, fell more significantly. Why, then, has the public perceived crime to be a more serious problem than statistics indicate?

Part of the explanation lies with news reports about crime that show not only increasingly random criminal acts, but also those perpetrated by teenagers. Late-night news is filled with graphic accounts of drive-by shootings, gang wars, innocent people caught in cross fire—all of which connote a sense of lawlessness that frightens many Americans. As criminologist James Q. Wilson notes, "People are not responding to the statistics, but what they hear reported. . . . It's the stranger-to-stranger nature of the crime, the youth of the offenders, and the level at which they're armed which alarms people."[7] Furthermore, while overall levels of crime have remained constant or fallen steadily, inner-city crime rates have increased and are substantially higher than crime rates in suburban and rural areas. Compared to a national rate of over 660 violent crimes per 100,000 people in 1989, cities such as Newark, Miami, St. Louis, and Atlanta had rates of over 3,000 per 100,000 persons (other cities such as Arlington, San Antonio, Honolulu, Austin, Virginia Beach, and Lexington had rates below the national average). Compared to a national rate of 8.7 murders per 100,000 people, the rates for Detroit and Atlanta hover near 60 and in dozens of other cities exceed 25 per 100,000 persons.

Visions of children passing through metal detectors on entering inner-city schools in an attempt to prohibit handguns brought the issue of gun control even greater attention. One study estimated that one in twenty-five high school students carried a gun in one month in 1990, and gunshot wounds are the leading cause of death for both white and minority teenage boys. Indeed, because of its pervasiveness in the lives of many inner-city residents, crime is increasingly being viewed as a public health issue by many prominent health officials, such as the head of the Centers for Disease Control, Walter R. Dowdle.

A final explanation for heightened public concern is that certain crimes have increased substantially over the past two decades. Rape, for example, has climbed from 18.7 per 100,000 population in 1970 to nearly 40 per 100,000 in 1990 (most of the increase was between 1970 and 1980), and the number and rate of other violent crimes have risen since 1980. While inner-city crime receives most of the media attention, the suburbs and rural areas are not immune. As the relative of a random shooting victim on a suburban train put it, "It could have happened to anyone. You think of the random shootings in the city [New York]; you feel somewhat isolated out here. Now, you feel there are no borders."[8]

Public response to these levels of violence has coalesced into significant public support for gun-control measures in the United States. A March 1993 Gallup poll showed that 70 percent of Americans favor tightening gun laws, with greater support among women and minorities.[9] Support for gun control has increased, beginning at 59 percent in 1983 and reaching a peak of 78 percent in 1990; support then fell to 68 percent in 1991 but had returned to the 70 percent figure above by 1993. The same March poll found that 88 percent of Americans favored passage of the Brady Bill, down from a peak level of 95 percent in 1990, while 66 percent favored banning semiautomatic rifles. Only when the question turned to one of a total ban on the possession of handguns except by police and other authorized persons did support fall below 50 percent. However, those who favored an outright ban made up a significant minority (42 percent) compared with 54 percent opposed to the ban, and the percentage favoring the ban has grown since its 1980 level of 31 percent. Another poll showed that even among gun owners, fully 84 percent supported a seven-day waiting period for purchasing handguns.[10]

With these levels of public support, it would seem that gun-control legislation would be easily forthcoming. However, the issue of gun control is highly controversial and involves powerful political interests. The relatively unrestricted possession of firearms has a long tradition in the United States and is tightly intertwined with constitutional protections. While the Second Amendment to the U.S. Constitution is often put forward as a limitation on governmental restriction on the ownership of firearms, it is unclear which rights are indeed guaranteed.[11] The courts have many times upheld state and local restrictions on the possession of firearms as well as national laws such as the 1934 National Firearms Act, which set restrictions on weapons such as sawed-off shotguns.[12] As a result, interest groups like the National Rifle Association (NRA) have hesitated in using litigation to fight gun-control measures, preferring instead to concentrate their significant political clout in federal and state legislatures.

With over three million members, the NRA uses varying strategies in its effort to preserve the right to possess firearms with a minimum of restrictions. The organization spent some $1.7 million on the 1992 congressional campaign.[13] What is more, it has the capability of putting its 3.3 million members to good use through a sophisticated grass-roots mobilization system; few politicians wish to be targeted by the NRA.[14] The NRA opposed the waiting period of the Brady Bill, but does favor an instantaneous background check when the technology and the funds become available. It also opposes any attempt to ban or limit the possession of semiautomatic assault rifles as well as other restrictive measures, such as taxing ammunition. The NRA is particularly strong in southern and western states; it is estimated that 60 percent of families own at least one gun in the South, compared with under 30 percent in eastern states. Gun-control opponents found political support from Presidents Reagan and Bush. President Reagan expressed his disapproval of gun-control measures in 1986 in a manner consistent with the NRA's position: "As long as there are guns, the individual that wants a gun for a crime is going to have one and going to get it. The only person who's going to be penalized and have difficulty is the law-abiding citizen, who then cannot have [it] if he wants protection—the protection of a weapon in his home, for home protection."

With the election of President Clinton in 1992, the NRA lost one of its most valued tools, the presidential veto. Since the Gun Control Act of 1968, the NRA has been able to rely on the threat of the presidential veto as a hedge against gun-control legislation. George Bush, a lifetime member of the NRA, blocked the Brady Bill with the veto threat throughout his term in office. However, President Clinton announced his intention of signing the Brady Bill and other gun-control legislation, such as the assault rifle ban, during his campaign and made good on that promise in the eleventh month of his presidency. Many states already have a waiting period for handgun purchases, frequently longer than the five days required in the Brady Bill, so its impact on crime may not be large. Supporters view its success as the first of many possible restrictions on handgun purchases. Other proposals include taxing ammunition, banning assault rifles, and instituting more gun "buy-back" programs and other measures to reduce crimes committed using guns.

But the NRA is not the only obstacle to gun-control laws. There is substantial uncertainty over what impact various forms of gun control would have, largely because little scientific research has been conducted. Instead, the debate is too often based on conjectures and speculation rather than evidence. One of the central issues over gun control is whether fewer people would die or be injured from violent encounters and whether there would be fewer of them. The answer is presently unclear. In robberies, where most gun-related deaths occur, the presence of a gun reduces the chance of victim injury, but where injuries result from robberies, guns are (not surprisingly) far more deadly than knives and other weapons.[15] Frequently ignored is the effect of gun control on noncriminal violence such as accidents and suicide. Gun-control advocates argue that fewer guns mean less gun violence. The opposition counters that "guns don't kill; people do" (to which Senator Daniel Moynihan has responded, in pushing for a tax on ammunition, "guns don't kill; bullets do"). Little hard evidence supports either gun-control position, however.

In the articles below William Greider of Rolling Stone magazine argues that not only should the Brady Bill be passed, but that handguns should be banned completely from private ownership. He gives his solid support to Republican Senator John Chafee's bill to do just that. Only an action such as this, he feels, would stop the gun violence wracking the nation. David B.

Kopel, the director of the Second Amendment Project, responds that there is no evidence that gun-control measures would result in lower levels of violence or other crime. Instead he argues for increased punishment of criminals and for a greater emphasis on handgun safety education.

Endnotes

1. U.S. Department of Justice, Federal Bureau of Investigation, *Unified Crime Reports of the United States, 1992* (Washington, D.C.: U.S. Government Printing Office, 1993).
2. U.S. Department of Commerce, Bureau of the Census, *Statistical Abstract of the United States, 1992* (Washington, D.C.: U.S. Government Printing Office, 1992), Table 294.
3. Ibid., Table 298.
4. L. A. Fingerhut, advanced data from *Vital and Health Statistics*, no. 231, National Center for Health Statistics, 1993, cited in "As Easy as Buying a Toothbrush" (editorial), *Lancet* 431 (May 29, 1993), pp. 1375–1376.
5. Handgun Control Inc., "Firearm Facts" (October 1993) (Washington, D.C.).
6. *Lancet*, "As Easy as Buying a Toothbrush."
7. Quoted in Neil A. Lewis, "Crime: Falling Rates but Rising Fear," *New York Times* (December 8, 1993), p. B6.
8. Quoted in Peter Marks, "5 Everyday People, by Chance or Ritual, Riding in Car No. 3," *New York Times* (December 9, 1993), p. 1.
9. George Gallup Jr., *The Gallup Poll Monthly*, no. 330 (March 1993), pp. 2–5.
10. New York Times/CBS poll of March 28–31, 1993, reported in the *New York Times* (August 15, 1993), Section 4, p. 4.
11. The Second Amendment reads: "A well regulated Militia, being necessary to the security of a free State, the right of the people to keep and bear Arms, shall not be infringed."
12. H. Idelson, "Gun Rights and Restrictions: The Territory Reconfigured," *Congressional Quarterly* (April 24, 1993), p. 1022.
13. Ibid., p. 1023.
14. Ibid.
15. Franklin E. Zimring, "Firearms, Violence, and Public Policy," *Scientific American* (November 1991), p. 51.

YES

A Pistol-Whipped Nation

William Greider

In politics, as in everyday life, the ultimate curse may be to get what you wish for. The proponents of gun control are about to experience that dispiriting turn of events. After a decade of uphill struggle, they are actually going to win. Their trophy will be passage of the Brady bill, named in honor of Jim Brady, Ronald Reagan's press secretary, who was severely wounded when John Hinckley shot the president outside the Washington Hilton in 1981. Brady's wife, Sarah, subsequently took up the cause as the chair of Handgun Control Inc., the leading reform organization, and the couple has campaigned energetically for gun control ever since.

Both the House and Senate passed versions of the Brady bill in 1991, but it was included in a larger crime bill that never made it out of Congress, a bill that in any event George Bush had promised to veto. Now there is a president who has endorsed the Brady bill and promised to sign it when it reaches his desk. In other words, it's greased for success, either this fall or early next year.

But when the cheering subsides, the victory will seem much smaller than advertised. The plain fact is that the United States is now hostage to a harrowing epidemic of gun violence, and the Brady bill won't do much to change that. The National Rifle Association has been saying this all along, and the NRA is right. The measure simply requires a five-working-day waiting period for handgun purchases. That means licensed gun dealers must check with law-enforcement authorities to see if the buyer is certifiably a dangerous character. That's it. Once a nationwide "instant" felon-identification system is up and running, even the five-day delay would be eliminated. The dealer would simply telephone the computer registry of felons, then make the sale.

This character check might—theoretically—make it harder for bad guys to get a handgun, but it won't do a thing to stop the extraordinary arms buildup among other citizens. There are something like 60 million or 70 million handguns in circulation—nobody knows the exact number—and 2 million new ones are sold every year. As Josh Sugarmann of the Violence Policy Center has reported, the nation now has more gun dealers than gas stations. The Brady bill won't do a thing to affect that number.

The NRA has also argued that a waiting period won't prevent criminals from getting guns. And it's right about that, too. In 1991, the Justice Department surveyed state prison inmates. Of those who had owned handguns, only 27 percent had bought their guns legally. Thirty-one percent had got them from family or friends; 28 percent had bought them on the black market; and 9 percent had stolen them. In other words, two-thirds of the guns were already illegal or beyond the reach of the Brady bill.

Enactment of the Brady bill will, however, represent a victory of some political significance—a visible defeat for the tenacious lobbying power of the NRA. For decades, the gun owners' organization has successfully terrorized politicians with its ability to raise money and target voter wrath against anyone who supported even the most innocuous forms of regulation. According to the NRA, any measure designed to control any kind of gun will ultimately lead to government confiscation of all weapons, disarming Americans against the gun-toting criminals trying to break into their homes.

Thus the limited scope of the Brady bill was justified as a necessary first step toward breaking the NRA's power—a way to demonstrate that politicians could support a moderate version of control and survive. This was a plausible strategy a decade ago, especially when conservative Republicans held the White House, but it has been overtaken by events. For one thing, the violence has escalated. Handgun murders have been increasing every year since 1987. There were nearly 12,000 murders in 1991, and more than 24,000 handgun deaths in all. The horror of drive-by shootings or random cross fire that claims innocent victims is now commonplace in cities.

Supported by rising public alarm, some brave politicians have tested the climate and discovered that the NRA's hammerlock is weakening, even without the passage of the Brady bill. In Virginia, Gov. Douglas Wilder went head-to-head with the gun lobby this year and prevailed on a measure to limit gun purchases to one per month. Virginia was embarrassed by its reputation as a favorite one-stop shopping mall for out-of-state drug dealers. Also this year, New Jersey Gov. Jim Florio held off Republican attempts to repeal a ban on assault weapons. In Congress, members like Rep. Mike Synar of Oklahoma have withstood withering assaults from the NRA during elections. And Bill Clinton won the White House while defying the gun nuts.

But even if finally passing the Brady bill will prove the NRA is waning, it will nevertheless create a dilemma for reformers. Though the law won't change much, it might close the subject for a number of years. Politicians could duck the issue by saying, "Let's wait and see what the Brady bill accomplishes." Citizens might eventually conclude that gun control is impotent, since gun violence will continue unabated. The NRA will say, "We told you so."

These circumstances call for a brave new politics, a bold and honest campaign that takes aim at the real problem: the guns themselves. Now is the time to ban handguns.

Sen. John H. Chafee of Rhode Island is a middle-of-the-road Republican with liberal views on social issues, which puts him in a minority within the minority. That lonely position requires stamina and patience, since it means losing often. But it also provides a certain kind of freedom—the freedom to think independently. Chafee came to the gun issue by way of health-care reform. His study of the complexities of that topic led him to a radical conclusion on guns: The only genuine way to end the public-health threat of handguns is to ban their private ownership.

"A radical proposal? Hardly," the senator wrote in a *Washington Post* Op-Ed. "What I would call radical is allowing the terrible status quo to continue."

After Chafee introduced his handgun prohibition bill last year, the NRA naturally added him to its hit list, as did right-wing radio and TV talk shows. "Send Chafee back to Cuba," among other cries, was soon heard. "We're getting the crap beat out of us," a Chafee aide observed.

For a senator up for re-election next year, this is most impolitic behavior. "They will probably target me, but they should be careful about doing that because I fully intend to win that election," Chafee ways. "The NRA likes to scare the daylights out of people, but if they target me and they lose, that will hurt them, not me."

Rhode Island, after all, is not exactly the Wild West. "I have to acknowledge my state isn't Montana or Wyoming," the senator says. "That might be another matter. I talk to my people, and while this thing isn't a political plus, it's not hurting me like it might in, say, Colorado."

Chafee's purpose is to push the gun-control debate past the NRA's scare tactics to confront the fundamentals. "This may not happen in my lifetime," he's told his staff, "but I'm going to keep putting it on the table and try to force a real debate on the issue."

Many of his Senate colleagues have expressed admiration for his courageous position—in private conversations. But Chafee's bill, reintroduced in May, attracted only one co-sponsor. "Many important voyages start with only a few travelers," Chafee says.

Politicians are wary because the senator does not hedge on the implications of what he is proposing: a flat prohibition on the manufacturing, sale and possession of handguns and handgun ammunition. His bill allows common-sense exceptions. The military, law-enforcement officers, licensed security guards, antique-gun collectors and target-shooting clubs would be exempt.

Everyone else would be required to turn in their handguns. Chafee proposes a six-month grace period, in which gun owners would be compensated at fair-market value for their weapons. After that, owners who voluntarily surrendered their handguns would escape criminal prosecution but might be subject to a civil fine. Anyone caught with a handgun could face hard time.

A one-time buyout of 60 million to 70 million handguns would be very expensive, Chafee concedes, but still cheap compared with the full costs of the warfare now under way. In any case, even with strong public cooperation, it would probably take years, perhaps a generation or more, to eradicate the guns in circulation.

In the meantime, the NRA would continue to inflame the public with raw appeals. That is the core of what makes Chafee's prohibition bill so provocative—it challenges the conventional presumptions that have surrounded the gun-control debate for decades. The gun problem, Chafee argues, is not just about criminals. It is about everyone who owns guns. Guns are not primarily an issue of criminal justice. Guns constitute a large and expensive threat to public health as well as to public education.

The facts support him, of course, though that does not necessarily convince scared citizens. "The downside of the pressure for gun control is that many people say the answer to guns is that they want one, too," the senator acknowledges. "If we were starting out fresh and there were none available, no one would say let's have handguns. But if we try to put a ban on them now, that makes some people nervous, and I understand that.

"But you've got to turn off this spigot sometime," Chafee says. "I just feel very strongly that we can get handguns under control if we start now. We'll get all those handguns from the bad guys. We may not get them all right away, but by God, we'll get them. And we will save lots of lives by doing so."

In terms of society's most dangerous objects, guns rank second only to cars and trucks—and are closing fast. If present trends continue, it's conceivable that in a few years guns will surpass motor vehicles as the leading cause of fatalities. In 1990, Louisiana and Texas both had a death rate from firearms hither than the death rate from auto accidents. In 1991, accidental deaths dropped in most categories, including autos; firearms, however, increased by 8 percent.

Criminals do their share. For instance, 70 percent of the police officers killed in the line of duty in 1991 were shot with handguns. In the inner cities, the proliferation of drug commerce and enhanced firepower has changed the mortality statistics of black teenage boys. "For an entire generation of black males, guns are the leading cause of death," Chafee says. "These young men are being wiped out—obliterated—by guns."

But here is the unpleasant truth that many people (especially scared white suburbanites) find difficult to accept: The mere presence of guns in abundant numbers is by itself the leading killer, not just crime and habitual criminals. The NRA likes to say that guns don't kill people, people kill people. Right. But guns make the killing a lot easier.

According to Justice Department statistics, nearly half of all handgun murders are committed during an argument among friends or family. As Chafee points out: "Handguns are far, far more likely to kill a loved one than an intruder."

Likewise, suicides are made easier—especially for young people—by the easy availability of guns in homes. Handguns are the weapon of choice in 12,600 suicides every year. "Teens are particularly susceptible to impulse suicide," the senator notes, "and the odds that a suicidal teen will kill him- or herself more than double if a gun is available in the home."

Finally, children are among the major victims of handguns—usually killed by other children. A study of 266 accidental handgun shootings of children found that nearly 90 percent took place in the child's own home or a friend's home. In a little over half the cases, the shooters were other children.

Beyond these facts, there is the extraordinary cost. The annual health-care bill for treating gunshot wounds has been estimated at $4 billion—most of it borne by taxpayers. A study by University of California at Davis researchers calculated the average cost of hospital treatment for gunshot victims at $13,200, with individual cases ranging as high as $495,000. Spinal-cord injuries and paralysis, often associated with gun violence, are especially expensive. Three months of therapy at a rehab center typically costs $135,000.

"The type and severity of the trauma now seen in our hospitals is so similar to that seen on the battlefield," says Chafee, "that Navy and Army physicians are doing rotations at urban trauma centers as training for military combat."

The country, in other words, is at war with itself, and the guns are winning.

No one should imagine that Clinton or a majority of either the House or the Senate will soon rush to Chafee's cause. But it is possible to imagine that the senator's courage constitutes a turning point in the long, frustrating debate over violence. At the very least, it should blow away some of the pretense and wishful thinking that have surrounded gun control and start people arguing over the right questions.

Chafee's careful legal research has demolished a favorite red herring of the NRA's—the claim that the Second Amendment would prohibit his legislation. On the contrary, as a half-century of Supreme Court precedents makes clear, the Second Amendment does not proscribe a prohibition of handguns. "One thing we've accomplished," Chafee says, "is that we've blown away the Second Amendment argument. They've backed away from peddling that scam anymore."

Other gun measures are now being put forward in Congress that fall somewhere between the Brady bill's waiting period and Chafee's flat-out prohibition. Having carried the banner for moderate reform measures for so many years, Handgun Control Inc. cannot quite deal with Chafee's provocative departure. "Prohibition has not been shown to work," says Cheryl Brolin, a spokesperson for HCI. "There are certain valid reasons people have to own guns. We don't believe Sen. Chafee's bill is realistically addressing the situation. We're trying to pursue more middle-ground proposals—one where gun owners and antigun people can find some common ground."

But the violent reality of American life has moved beyond such sweet compromises. Right now, it's time for a healthy, fundamental argument among the reformers themselves. This will be hastened, I think, as other groups representing public health concerns, children and law enforcement come forward to redefine gun control in broader terms, just as Chafee is doing.

In the meantime, timid politicians still reluctant to take on the NRA, still afraid to pursue genuine solutions, should take note of public opinion. This summer, a Harris Poll found that for the first time ever, a majority of Americans—52 percent—actually favor the radical step of banning the private ownership of handguns. Once again, it seems, the folks are a step or two ahead of Washington.

NO

Hold Your Fire: Gun Control Won't Stop Rising Violence

David B. Kopel

As deaths from rampant gun violence mount, and city-dwellers from Boston to Los Angeles learn to distinguish the pop of a Smith & Wesson pistol from the blast of a Winchester shotgun, Americans insist on action to combat the national crime epidemic.

Although the per-capital murder rate remains below the record set in 1980, the actual number of homicides reached an all-time high of 24,703 in 1991; most of these murders were committed with guns. Most disturbing of all is the rise in violent crimes committed by gun-wielding teenagers. Able to acquire illegal weapons with ease, in spite of a nationwide prohibition on firearms sales to minors, teenage thugs display a disregard for human life that would have shocked the criminals of earlier generations. The latest urban terror, "carjacking," is the seizure at gunpoint of automobiles from their drivers, usually women.

As armed gangs settle turf disputes over drug-selling territory through mortal combat, they kill not only each other, but also innocent bystanders caught in the crossfire. Firearms violence, once thought to be the problem of the inner city, is spreading into the suburbs and beyond. And with depressing frequency, newspapers report stories of children dying in senseless gun accidents. In Louisiana last October, a Japanese exchange student was mistakenly shot when he entered the wrong house on the way to a Halloween party, and, not understanding the warning, continued to advance toward the homeowner despite an order to "Freeze!"

To some well-meaning Americans, the antidote to gun crime is gun control. Senator John Chafee (R–RI) calls for the confiscation of all handguns. Other voices, such as Handgun Control, Inc.'s Sarah Brady, urge a national waiting period on handgun purchases, and a ban on assault weapons. The national media's insistent message is that we must "do something" about guns.

Meanwhile, the National Rifle Association adds tens of thousands of members every month—membership is at a record three million—and continues to stymie gun control at nearly every turn. Although the 99th, 100th, and 101st Congresses passed some minor gun controls, the 102nd Congress went home without enacting any new gun-control measures. The New Jersey legislature is ready to overturn its assault-weapon ban the moment the legislative leadership schedules a vote on the issue.

Critics of gun control believe that it violates the right to keep and bear arms guaranteed by the Second Amendment of the United States Constitution and by 43 state constitutions. In the American political tradition, the right to own a gun is seen as intimately related to the natural right of self-defense, to what John Locke described as the natural right to control and protect one's body and property. Millions of Americans consider an armed citizenry to be one of the principal safeguards against possible tyranny by the state.

The constitutional argument against laws that infringe on gun ownership was strengthened by the 1990 Supreme Court decision in *United States* v. *Verdugo-Urquidez*. There, Chief Justice Rehnquist observed that the phrase "right of the people" occurs several times in the Bill of Rights, specifically the Second Amendment's "right of the people to keep and bear arms," the First Amendment's "right of the people peaceably to assemble," and the Fourth Amendment's "right of the people to be secure in their persons, houses, papers and effects against unreasonable searches and seizures." In all cases, the Court said, the phrase "right of the people" was used as a "term of art" that referred to individual Americans.

But critics of gun control do not base their opposition on political principles alone. They also cite a large body of recent social science research, much of which has been produced by scholars who formerly believed that gun control was an obvious solution to crime.

JIMMY CARTER'S SHOCKER

When gun control first became an important national issue in the 1960s, there was almost no research worth noting on the subject. Partisans on both sides of the debate had hardly more ammunition than intuitions and bumper-sticker slogans.

The man most responsible for the change in the intellectual terms of the gun debate was Jimmy Carter, or, more precisely, the grant-review team that Carter appointed to the National Institute of Justice. Intending to build the case for comprehensive federal gun restrictions, the Carter administration handed out a major gun-control research grant in 1978 to sociology professor James D. Wright and his colleagues Peter Rossi and Kathleen Daly. Wright was already on record as favoring much stricter controls, and he and his colleagues were highly regarded sociologists. Rossi, a University of Massachusetts professor, would later become president of the American Sociology Association. Wright, who formerly served as director of the Social and Demographic Research Institute at the University of Massachusetts, now teaches at Tulane. Daly is now at the University of Michigan.

Wright and his colleagues were asked to survey the state of research regarding the efficacy of gun control, presumably to show that gun control worked and that America needed more of it. But when the researchers produced their report for the National Institute of Justice in 1982, they delivered a document quite different from the one they had expected to write. Carefully reviewing all existing research, the three scholars found no persuasive scholarly evidence that America's 20,000 gun-control laws had reduced criminal violence. For example, the federal Gun Control Act of 1968, which banned most interstate gun sales, had no discernible impact on the criminal acquisition of guns from other states. Washington, D.C.'s ban on the ownership of handguns that had not already been registered in the District was not linked to any reduction in gun crime. Even Detroit's law providing mandatory sentences for felonies committed with a gun was found to have no effect on gun-crime patterns, in part because judges would often reduce the sentence for the underlying offense in order to balance out the mandatory two-year extra sentence for use of a gun.

WHAT CRIMINALS SAY ABOUT GUN CONTROL

The most thorough subsequent study of the efficacy of gun control has been performed by Florida State University's Gary Kleck, who analyzed data for all 170 U.S. cities with a population over 100,000, testing for the impact of 19 different types of gun controls, and looking for the controls' effects on suicides, accidents, and five different crimes. Kleck, a liberal Democrat and ACLU member, found that gun controls did reduce gun suicide, but not the overall suicide rate. The only control that reduced crime was a strict penalty for carrying an illegal gun, which seemed to lower the robbery rate. Waiting periods, various licensing systems, and registration appeared to have no statistically discernible impact. Kleck's analysis was based on data for the years 1979–1981, and is included in his recent book, *Point Blank*, which contains the best single-volume overview of gun-control research.

Wright and Rossi produced another study for the National Institute of Justice, this one involving the habits of America's felons. Interviewing felony prisoners in 10 state correctional systems in 1981, Wright and Rossi found that gun-control laws had no effect on criminals' ability to obtain guns. Only 12 percent of criminals, and only 7 percent of the criminals specializing in handgun crime, had acquired their last crime handgun at a gun store. Of those, about one quarter had stolen the gun from a store; a large number of the rest, Wright and Rossi suggested, had probably procured the gun through a legal surrogate buyer, such as a girlfriend with a clean record. For the few remaining felons who actually did buy their own guns, the purchase might have been lawful because the purchaser as yet had no felony record.

The survey further indicated that 56 percent of the prisoners said that a criminal would not attack a potential victim who was known to be armed. Seventy-four percent agreed with the statement that "One reason burglars avoid houses where people are at home is that they fear being shot during the crime." Thirty-nine percent of the felons had personally decided not to commit a crime because they thought the victim might have a gun, and 8 percent said the experience had occurred "many times." Criminals in states with higher civilian gun-ownership rates worried the most about armed victims.

Since criminals can never be entirely sure which burglary targets may or may not contain a homeowner with a gun, or which potential robbery or rape victims may be carrying a concealed firearm, the ownership of firearms by half of American households provides a general deterrent to crime that benefits the entire population.

HOW GUNS PREVENT CRIME

Consistent with the reports of criminals, ordinary citizens also report that gun ownership plays an important role in preventing crime. Professor Kleck estimates that handguns are used approximately 645,000 times for defense against an attacker every year in the United States.

The figure, ironically, is based on data from a survey conducted on behalf of the pro-control National Alliance Against Violence (NAAV). NAAV hired Peter Hart, a leading Democratic pollster, to survey Americans on guns, asking, among other things: "Within the past five years, have you yourself or another member of your household used a handgun, even if it was not fired, for self-protection or protection of property at home, work, or elsewhere, excluding military service or police work?" Six percent answered "yes." Follow-up questions revealed that 3 percent of the respondents had used the handgun against a person, 2 percent against an animal, and 1 percent against both. That 4 percent said "yes" to defensive gun use against persons meant that about 18 percent of households where a handgun was owned for protection had actually used the handgun for protection.

Kleck's analysis started with the 4-percent "yes" from Hart's data. Kleck made the conservative assumption that each "yes" related to only one gun usage in the last five years—that no household used a firearm for self-defense two or more times in the five years. Thus, 3,224,880 households reported self-defense usage. Kleck then divided by five (since the question had asked about usage in the last five years) to arrive at an estimate for the annual number of uses of a handgun for self-defense: 644,976—or roughly once every 48 seconds.

Since Kleck's estimate is based on responses to a pollster, it should be emphasized that the 645,000 figure is necessarily imprecise. The original question posed by Peter Hart could have elicited a "yes" answer from an insecure gun owner who had perceived a criminal threat that did not in fact exist. Kleck partly controlled self-defense inflation from false "yes" answers by assuming that no "yes" answer related to more than one defensive use. In addition, the 645,000 estimate applies only to handguns; the original question did not ask about defensive use of rifles or shotguns.

In 1990, Professor Gary Mauser, of Canada's Simon Fraser University, asked Americans about use of a handgun or a long gun for self-defense; the responses suggested approximately 691,000 annual defensive uses of guns of all types. Accordingly, we may conclude that guns are used defensively at least half a million times a year.

Of course, the fact that a gun is used for defense does not mean that a shot is fired, or an attacker wounded or killed. About 95 percent of self-defense usage, says Kleck, involves merely the brandishing of a weapon to deter a perceived attack.

While the majority of defensive handgun use is simply brandishing a weapon to frighten away an attacker, Kleck suggests that 1,700 to 3,100 homicides a year are actually justifiable homicides committed by citizens using a firearm to defend themselves or another person against violent attack.

ONE BULLET AT A TIME

While most Americans believe they have a right to own a gun, and believe that guns can be protective, even many gun owners are baffled at the gun lobby's apparent intransigence in its refusal to accept a ban on so-called assault weapons or a waiting period on gun purchases.

The assault-weapon issue, however, turns out to involve much less than meets the eye. First of all, it should be emphasized that most people who own semiautomatics support strong controls on actual machine guns. Ever since the National Firearms Act of 1934, acquisition of real machine guns—guns that continue to fire bullets repeatedly as long as the trigger is held down—has required a difficult-to-obtain federal license. The NRA did not oppose the restrictive machine gun law when it was enacted, and has never indicated any desire to repeal the law.

While machine guns do have a unique capacity for rapid fire, what we know as assault weapons do not. Although most of the public believes that assault weapons are machine guns, the guns in question simply look like military weapons. Appearances notwithstanding, the guns fire just as every common American gun does: squeezing the trigger fires one, and only one, bullet. According to Martin Fackler, former director of the Letterman Army Institute of Research, assault weapons are actually less lethal than many firearms commonly associated with hunting, such as an old-fashioned 12-gauge Winchester shotgun. The Bureau of Alcohol, Tobacco, and Firearms states that no guns available for sale to the public can be easily converted to fire automatically.

HARD TO CONVERT

The fact that semiautomatic assault weapons differ from other guns only cosmetically is one reason why legislative bodies have had so much trouble defining them. Since the guns do not fire faster than other guns, legislative definitions sometimes focus on extraneous features, such as the presence of a bayonet lug—as if we were suffering from a rash of criminals bayonetting people.

Other definitions are merely a list of particular guns with a military appearance. Among the guns targeted by assault-weapons legislation are the M1 Carbine; the AKS Rifle; the Uzi Pistol and Carbine, the Colt AR-15 H-Bar Rifle; the Springfield Armory 4800 Rifle; the M10 Pistol and Carbine; and the AK-56 rifle. Yet some of these guns are in no way distinguishable from many other guns not on the lists, such as the popular hunting rifles made by Winchester, Remington, and Ruger. As former Attorney General Richard Thornburgh noted, the main characteristic of an assault weapon seems to be that it has a black plastic stock rather than a brown wooden stock.

In practical terms, the legislative definition of assault weapon amounts to "the largest number of guns that a given legislature can be convinced to ban." The New Jersey assault-weapon prohibition even outlaws BB guns.

While assault weapons have been claimed to be the "weapon of choice" of criminals, such guns constitute a very small number of the crime guns seized by the police. The Florida Assault Weapons Commission's 1990 report found that assault weapons were used in 17 of 7,500 gun crimes in the years 1986–1989. The Washington, D.C., director of the police firearms section stated in early 1989 that not one of the more than 3,000 weapons the Washington police confiscated in 1988 was a semiautomatic assault rifle.

While some gun-prohibition advocates have claimed that a record number of police are being murdered by assault weapons, police-officer deaths in the line of duty are at their lowest level since 1968. The percentage of police homicides perpetrated with assault weapons is about 4 percent, a figure that has stayed constant over the last decade. The FBI's Uniform Crime Reporting Program, which collects extensive data on all murders of police officers, reports no instance of a drug dealer ever killing a police officer with an Uzi.

That assault weapons should appear so rarely as crime guns seized makes sense. Street criminals need concealable weapons, and a Colt or a Kalashnikov rifle is pretty difficult to stick in a pocket. Indeed, rifles of all types constitute a tiny percentage of crime guns. According to the Washington, D.C., Metropolitan Police Department, rifles are used in less than one-tenth of 1 percent of armed robberies in the District. Nationally, only about 4 percent of the weapons used in homicides are rifles.

Occasionally, so-called assault weapons are used in gruesome mass murders. In Stockton, California in January 1991, Patrick Purdy used a Kalashnikov-type semiautomatic rifle to fire 105 shots in about four minutes at a schoolyard full of Cambodian immigrant children. Thirty-five people were wounded, six of whom died. Purdy's rate of fire could have been duplicated by anyone with an old-fashioned bolt-action rifle or simple revolver, and autopsies of the victims showed that the wounds were approximately equal in severity to wounds associated with a medium-sized handgun, which explains why 29 of the 35 people who were shot survived.

Thus, Purdy could have committed the same crime using many other types of guns. But the national media incorrectly told the American public that Purdy had used an automatic AK-47 rifle, and that such guns could be bought over the counter.

Lost in the media frenzy over Purdy's gun was Purdy himself, who committed suicide with a pistol at the end of his spree. Purdy perpetrated his crime after he had told a state mental-health worker that he thought about committing a mass murder with a gun or a bomb, and even though a parole report called him "a danger to himself and others."

Purdy had a lengthy history of crime and arrests, including a robbery in which a 55-year-old woman was seriously injured, receipt of stolen property, criminal conspiracy, possession of illegal weapons, and assault of a police officer, all reduced to misdemeanor charges. His crime career began when he was 14 years old and continued unabated for the next decade, until he killed himself at Stockton. Not one of Purdy's two-dozen encounters with the law ever led to more than a few weeks in prison. The media's hysterical focus on Purdy's gun enabled California's decrepit criminal-justice bureaucracy to escape public censure for allowing Purdy to roam the streets, free to commit his final, horrible crime.

"COOLING OFF"

The waiting period, like the assault-weapon ban, becomes considerably less attractive when examined carefully. While the waiting-period initiative is often called the "Brady Bill," it would not have prevented John Hinckley from shooting Ronald Reagan and Jim Brady. When Hinckley bought two hand-guns in October 1980, he had no felony record, and no public record of mental illness. The simple police and mental-health records check proposed by the Brady Bill would not have turned up anything on him. And since Hinckley bought the guns more than five months in advance, a one-week wait would not have made any difference to him.

Indeed, a "cooling-off" period for handgun purchases requires a number of unlikely assumptions in order to work. First, the potential murderer—denied a handgun immediately—must then decide not to buy a rifle or a shotgun, which the Brady Bill would allow him to do. Then, he must not know how to buy a handgun on the black market, or how to obtain one from friends, relatives, or acquaintances. In addition, the type of murder he intends must not be one for which readily available alternative weapons, such as knives, automobiles, or bare hands, will work. Finally, the person who was literally ready to commit a murder on day one of the waiting period must calm down by day seven, and stay calm from that day forward.

This scenario, while implausible, is not impossible; it is at least theoretically imaginable that a waiting period could "save at least one life." But a waiting period can cost lives, too.

"I'LL BE DEAD BY THEN"

Even a short waiting period will inevitably prevent people from protecting themselves against criminal attack during the wait. When Los Angeles citizens went to gun stores to buy firearms to protect life and property during the recent riots, they were told to come back 15 days later, to comply with California's waiting period on all guns.

After Hurricane Andrew, Florida's looters did considerably less damage than their California counterparts, in part because Florida has only a three-day handgun waiting period, and no wait at all on long guns.

Nor are waiting period victimizations confined only to periods of civil disorder. In September 1990, a mail carrier named Catherine Latta of Charlotte, North Carolina, went to the police to obtain permission to buy a handgun. Her ex-boyfriend had previously robbed her, assaulted her several times, and raped her. The clerk at the sheriff's office informed her the gun permit would take two to four weeks. "I told her I'd be dead by then," Latta later recalled. That afternoon, she bought an illegal $20 semiautomatic pistol on the street. Five hours later, her ex-boyfriend attacked her outside her house, and she shot him dead. The county prosecutor decided not to prosecute Latta for either the self-defense homicide or the illegal gun.

A Wisconsin woman, Bonnie Elmasri, was not so lucky. On March 5, 1991 she called a firearms instructor, worried that her husband—who was subject to a restraining order to stay away from her—had been threatening her and her children. When she asked the instructor about getting a handgun, the instructor explained that Wisconsin has a 48-hour waiting period. Elmasri and her two children were murdered by her husband 24 hours later.

Waiting periods that appear reasonable in a legislative chamber may become unreasonable through administrative abuse. Although New Jersey law requires that the authorities act on gun license applications within 30 days, delays of 90 days are routine; some applications are delayed for years for no valid reason. In Maryland, where an appeals process exists, the police are overruled on 78 percent of the denials that are appealed.

INSTANT RECORDS CHECK

If it is determined that the way to keep criminals from getting guns is to impose background checks on retail handgun sales—a questionable determination—a mandatory instant records check makes sense. The same technology that allows a store to receive verification of credit card validity within a few minutes can also allow firearms dealers to dial a state government registry and verify that a gun buyer has no felony record.

Polling data suggest that most Americans prefer the instant check to the waiting period, particularly when presented with the choice of mandatory immediate check (the NRA proposal) versus a waiting period with no requirement that any check be conducted (the Brady Bill). In recent years, many states have made major progress in bringing their criminal-records histories online. Thus, an instant check should become feasible in the near future.

And if records are not sufficiently accurate to support an instant check, they are also not sufficient to support a check with a one-week wait. Former Attorney General Thornburgh's task force found that even if there were no improvement in state criminal records, an instant check would be just as accurate as a check that could be completed in one week.

Unfortunately, if adequate safeguards are not in place, the instant check, like the waiting period, can be misused by police departments to create a registry of gun owners. In 1991, California admitted that it had used the state's handgun waiting period to create a list of handgun owners, even though nothing in California law authorizes the compilation of such a list.

Although the federal gun-control debate talks almost exclusively about retail handgun sales and the Brady Bill, the most effective method to deal with criminals obtaining guns might be to focus on the major source of criminal guns: the black market. A sensible first step in dealing with the black market would be to increase penalties for fencing a gun known to be stolen. In some states, theft and sale of a $75 gun amounts only to petty larceny. Selling a "hot" $75 pistol ought to be a more serious offense than selling a "hot" $75 toaster-oven.

NRA'S REFORM PROPOSAL

While Congress has spent most of its gun-control effort debating new restrictions on gun acquisition, the discussion in many state legislatures has shifted to the carrying of firearms. The Second Amendment refers to a right "to keep and bear arms," and if the text is read consistently with original intent and judicial interpretations of the following century, the government cannot require that citizens ask for permission to carry an unconcealed gun in public.

But in many states, the right to carry has been obliterated by laws that require a police license to carry, and by police administrators who give out carry licenses only to the political elite. In New York City, crime victims who will testify at a forthcoming trial, and who are receiving death threats from the criminal's friends, are denied carry permits—while politically powerful citizens are routinely granted them. While New York's abuse of licensing discretion is notorious, the licensing systems in many other cities are also skewed against people without some kind of clout.

Based on a literalist reading of the Constitution, Second-Amendment advocates should lobby for repeal of all laws requiring a license to carry a gun. But instead, the NRA suggests only reform of easily abused gun licensing systems.

The NRA proposal requires that applicants for a permit to carry a protective firearm must undergo safety training and must submit to a police background check. Then, if the applicant passes the safety class and background check, he or she is to be granted a license to carry. The bureaucratic discretion to deny permits to qualified citizens simply because the bureaucrat does not like guns would be removed.

PROGRESS IN THE GUNSHINE STATE

Carry reform was first enacted in Florida in 1987, amidst vociferous cries from gun-control supporters in the legislature that blood would run in the streets as Floridians shot each other while jostling in line at fast-food restaurants. Florida would become the "Gunshine State," it was warned.

Today, those same critics have admitted that they were wrong, and that they regret the harm done to Florida's reputation by the histrionic campaign against carry reform. Indeed, while the murder rate has risen 14 percent nationally from 1986 to 1991, it has fallen 20 percent in Florida. The state's total murder rate was 36 percent higher than the U.S. murder rate in 1986, and is now 4 percent below the national average. In the same period, robbery rose 9 percent in Florida, and 21 percent nationally.

There has been no research proving that Florida's carry reform was part of the reason for Florida's relative improvement in recent years. But the experience of Florida, and of other carry-reform states such as Oregon, Montana, Mississippi, and Pennsylvania, demonstrates that people who are already good citizens and who are willing to pass through a licensing process do not suddenly turn into murderous psychopaths when granted a permit to carry a firearm for protection.

INTERRUPTING A MASS MURDER

While tragic mass murders are frequently used by the pro-control lobby to push restrictive laws, evidence suggests that laws prohibiting firearms carrying may be costing innocent lives.

In October 1991 in Killeen, Texas, a psychopath named George Hennard rammed his pickup truck through the plate glass window of a Luby's cafeteria. Using a pair of ordinary pistols, he murdered 23 people in 10 minutes, stopping only when the police arrived.

Dr. Suzanna Gratia, a cafeteria patron, had a gun in her car, but, in conformity to Texas law, she did not carry the gun; Texas, despite its Wild-West image, has the most severe law in the country against carrying firearms. Carry-reform legislation had almost passed the state legislature, but had been stopped in House Rules Committee by the gun-control lobby.

Gratia later testified that if she had been carrying her gun, she could have shot at Hennard: "I know what a lot of people think, they think, 'Oh, my God, then you would have had a gunfight and then more people would have been killed.' Unhunh, no. I was down on the floor; this guy is standing up; everybody else is down on the floor. I had a perfect shot at him. It would have been clear. I had a place to prop my hand. The guy was not even aware of what we were doing. I'm not saying that I could have saved anybody in there, but I would have had a chance." Hennard reloaded five times, and had to throw away one pistol because it jammed, so there was plenty of opportunity for someone to fire at him.

Even if Gratia hadn't killed or wounded Hennard, he would have had to dodge hostile gunfire, and wouldn't have been able methodically to finish off his victims as they lay wounded on the floor. The hypothetical risks of a stray bullet from Gratia would have been rather small compared with the actual risks of Hennard not facing any resistance. But because of the Texas law, Gratia had left her gun in the car and couldn't take a shot at Hennard. Instead, she watched him murder both her parents.

Two months later, a pair of criminals with stolen pistols herded 20 customers and employees into the walk-in refrigerator of a Shoney's restaurant in Anniston, Alabama. Hiding under the table in the restaurant was Thomas Glenn Terry, armed with the .45 semiautomatic pistol he carried legally under Alabama law. One of the robbers discovered Terry, but Terry killed him with five shots in the chest. The second robber, who had been holding the manager hostage, shot at Terry and grazed him. Terry returned fire, and mortally wounded the robber.

Twenty-three people died in Killeen, where carrying a gun for self-defense was illegal. Twenty lives were saved, and only the two criminals died in Anniston, where self-defense permits are legal. Yet while Anniston never made the network news, Killeen did, and is used to this day as supposed proof of the need for severe gun controls. Precisely because lives are saved, instances of citizens using firearms carried on their persons to defend themselves and others rarely make the national news, even though such defensive acts occur with great frequency, as the research of Professors Kleck and Mauser demonstrates.

EMPHASIS ON GUN SAFETY

Gun control, properly conceived, is not simply a matter of passing laws, or adding to the paperwork involved in retail gun purchases. Gun control needs to involve people control, or more precisely, helping people take control of their own actions. In this regard, the NRA's gun safety programs rank as America's most successful gun-control efforts.

The National Rifle Association was founded in 1871 by Union Army generals dismayed at the poor marksmanship displayed by Union forces during the recent war. The NRA always has placed heavy emphasis on its mission to train American citizens in responsible and effective firearms handling.

Happily, the fatal gun accident rate is now at an all-time low. In 1945, for every million Americans, there were about 350,000 firearms and 18 fatal gun accidents. Today, the per-million rate is 850,000 and 6 accidents. As the gun supply per capita more than doubled, fatal accidents fell by two-thirds.

NRA safety programs implemented by the 32,000 instructors and coaches who have earned NRA Instructor certification have played an important role in the accident drop, and will become even more important in coming years as more and more women choose to own handguns. Since women gun owners are more likely to own for protection, and less likely to have been initiated in sport shooting by an older male relative, safety training for these new gun owners is especially worthwhile, and the NRA has, accordingly, set up a program offering free safety training to women.

The number of fatal firearm accidents for children aged 0–14 has fallen from 550 in 1975 to 250 in 1988. While the NRA always has had junior shooting and hunting programs that emphasize the development of safe sporting gun use under adult supervision, in 1988 the organization launched a safety campaign aimed at the millions of children who never have any exposure to the shooting sports.

The NRA's Eddie Eagle Elementary Gun Safety Education Program is geared for children in pre-school through sixth grade. Using teacher-tested materials such as an animated video, cartoon workbooks, role-playing, and fun safety activities, Eddie Eagle teaches the simple lesson: "If you see a gun: Stop! Don't Touch. Leave the Area. Tell an Adult."

To date, the Eddie Eagle program has reached almost 4 million children and their parents through schools, law-enforcement programs, and a variety of youth programs. Unfortunately, it has been excluded from some urban schools by administrators who refuse to allow pupils to contact anything related to the NRA, even though the Eddie Eagle curriculum does not discuss political issues.

CONTROLLING CRIMINALS, NOT GUNS

The NRA's most controversial recent effort is the organization's CrimeStrike program, which takes aim at aspects of the criminal justice system that the NRA considers too lenient. In pushing for laws allowing greater pretrial detention of violent repeat offenders, the NRA adheres to its conservative roots, to the chagrin of some its libertarian supporters, who are unwilling to protect the Second Amendment by weakening the Eighth Amendment right to bail.

Other aspects of CrimeStrike, such as support for victims' rights laws, cause no dissent within the pro-Second Amendment coalition, and offer an opportunity to improve a criminal justice bureaucracy that sometimes lets the desire to process cases overshadow the necessity to do justice to the criminal *and* the victim.

NRA CrimeStrike strategies, like NRA lobbying, rely heavily on grassroots pressure. In a recent Texas case, Charles Edward Bruton had been sentenced to two 10-year terms for shooting at a woman and for committing a heinous sexual assault against her 11-year-old daughter. Having served only three years, Bruton was up for parole last September. After the shooting victim asked CrimeStrike for assistance, NRA members were notified through NRA magazines destined for Texas; the Texas Board of Pardons and Appeals was flooded with calls and letters; the parole was denied.

CrimeStrike will not single-handedly fix the criminal justice system, nor will safety education eliminate all accidents, nor will carry reform wipe out all street crime. But each of these efforts will improve public safety for all citizens, whether they own guns or not. Everyone benefits from a prison system that keeps violent felons off the streets; everyone benefits from reduced risks of gun accidents; and everyone benefits from street criminals facing increased odds of victims resisting successfully.

Today, rather than merely opposing poorly conceived gun-control legislation, right-to-keep-and-bear-arms supporters are working in positive ways. These efforts will enhance not only the rights of the 50 percent of American families who own guns, but also the safety of the 50 percent who do not.

DISCUSSION QUESTIONS

1. Do you think restricting access to firearms would reduce gun-related injuries and crimes? Are there other considerations relevant for public policy decisions? What are they?
2. How do you think the framers of the Constitution would respond to the rise in gun violence? Why?
3. Given the level of popular support for gun-control measures, why do you think such legislation has had difficulty passing?
4. Should gun-control measures be enacted at the federal level, or should such legislation be reserved for states and localities? Why?
5. Should gun-control legislation be focused on the owners of guns or on those who manufacture and sell such weapons? Why?
6. Would a tax on ammunition be effective in reducing violence (or have other beneficial characteristics)? What do you see as advantages and disadvantages of such a proposal?
7. What impact do gun buy-back programs have? Who are most likely to sell their guns? How effective would you expect such programs to be in reducing crime?
8. What impact do you think fewer guns would have on deaths from accidents and suicides? Or would accidental deaths and suicides merely occur by other means?
9. Is it appropriate to view violence as a public health issue, or are there important distinctions between public health and crime? Why?

ADDITIONAL READINGS

Bogus, Carl T. "The Strong Case for Gun Control." *The American Prospect* (Summer 1992).

Congressional Digest (June–July 1991) on Brady Bill.

Cozic, Charles P., ed. *Gun Control* (San Diego, Calif.: Greenhaven Press, 1992).

Davidson, Osha Gray. *Under Fire: The NRA and the Battle for Gun Control* (New York: Henry Holt, 1993).

Halbrook, Stephen P. "What the Framers Intended: A Linguistic Analysis of the Right to 'Bear Arms.'" *Law and Contemporary Problems* (Winter 1986).

Kates, Don B., Jr. "Gun Control: Can It Work?" *National Review* (May 15, 1981).

Kates, Don B., Jr., ed. *Firearms and Violence: Issues of Public Policy* (San Francisco, Calif.: Pacific Institute for Public Policy Research, 1984).

Kleck, Gary. "Policy Lessons from Recent Gun Control Research." *Law and Contemporary Problems* (Winter 1986).

Kleck, Gary. *Point Blank: Guns and Violence in America* (New York: A. de Gruyter, 1991).

Larson, Erik. *Lethal Passage: How the Travels of a Single Handgun Expose the Roots of America's Gun Crisis* (New York: Crown Publishers, 1994).

Leddy, Edward F. *Magnum Force Lobby: The National Rifle Association Fights Gun Control* (Lanham, Md.: University Press of America, 1987).

Long, Robert Emmet, ed. *Gun Control* (New York: H.W. Wilson, 1989).

Nisbet, Lee, ed. *The Gun Control Debate: You Decide* (Buffalo, N.Y.: Prometheus Books, 1990).

Stell, Lance K. "Close Encounters of the Lethal Kind: The Use of Deadly Force in Self-Defense." *Law and Contemporary Problems* (Winter 1986).

Wright, James D. "Second Thoughts About Gun Control." *The Public Interest* (Spring 1988).

Wright, James D., Peter H. Rossi, and Kathleen Daly. *Under the Gun: Weapons, Crime, and Violence in America* (New York: Aldine Publishing Co., 1983).

Zimring, Franklin E. "Firearms, Violence, and Public Policy." *Scientific American* (November 1991).

Zimring, Franklin E., and Gordon Hawkins. *The Citizen's Guide to Gun Control* (New York: Macmillan, 1987).

17

ABORTION POLICY

"Should the Federal Government Provide Funding for Abortions through Medicaid?"

The politics of the abortion debate is one of the most polarized and divisive in our nation. There appears to be little common political ground between the advocate factions of the so-called "pro-life" and "pro-choice" movements. Televised scenes of pro-life protesters blocking access to abortion clinics and the murder of doctors who perform abortions are indicative of the vitriol displayed in this intense confrontation. One sign at a "right-to-life" convention read: "Auschwitz, Dachau, and Margaret Sanger: Three of a Kind." The debates between these groups have consistently been framed in ways that make the question of abortion one of complete and unrestricted availability, as embodied in the Freedom of Choice Act,* versus the opposing position favoring the introduction of a constitutional amendment banning all abortions.† Furthermore, this issue has been strongly identified with party politics for more than a decade; indeed, in many political campaigns, particularly during the 1980s, the abortion debate has been featured prominently. Although it was less true of the 1992 race for the White House, the issue has been near the forefront of the most recent presidential campaigns and particularly on the appointment of several Supreme Court justices. Alan Guttmacher's 1972 observation, "The ironic fact is that those who favor legalization of abortion share a common goal with those who don't—the elimination of all abortions," seems to have been lost on the contemporary abortion debate.

Indeed, it has been in the courts that abortion policy has seen some of its most rancorous debates. Although the liberalization of abortion laws began in state legislatures in 1967, and many states permitted abortions with varying restrictions on availability, the origins of the modern abortion debate are most often traced to the *Roe* v. *Wade* decision of 1973. The *Roe* decision ruled unconstitutional—and a violation of the right to privacy of a woman's reproductive choice implied in the Ninth Amendment—nearly all laws forbidding abortion in the first trimester of gestation. As Justice Blackmun wrote in the opinion, "The states are not free, under the guise of protecting maternal health or potential life, to intimidate women into continuing pregnancies." It did,

---

* This is a bill introduced into Congress in recent years that would through statute guarantee a woman's right to abortion.

† This was in the Republican Party platform of the 1992 Republican national convention.

however, allow for regulation in order to protect the mother's health in the second trimester and further regulation protecting the interests of the fetus in the third trimester when it was presumed the fetus was viable outside the mother's womb. The companion case to the *Roe* decision, *Doe* v. *Bolton*, further prohibited state laws that created obstacles to obtaining abortions, such as residency restrictions, which were ruled as violations of a woman's rights.

With the *Roe* decision, the abortion controversy shifted from states to national center stage. Nominations to the Supreme Court and the lower courts made by Republican administrations (President Carter did not appoint a Supreme Court justice) led to an ever-expanding conservative tilt to Court decisions. Debate in the Congress focused on the introduction of constitutional amendments ranging from extensions of due process and equal protection to individuals at the moment of conception to specific bans on abortion. None have passed.

The fundamental right to an abortion has not been threatened in the more than twenty years since *Roe*, although restrictions on the availability of abortion have been successfully enacted. The Hyde amendment banning federal funding for abortion, except in circumstances of rape, incest, or where the life of the mother is threatened, was successfully attached to the fiscal year 1977 Labor–HEW (Health, Education, and Welfare) appropriation bill and has remained intact ever since. It was challenged before and constitutionally upheld by the U.S. Supreme Court in *Harris* v. *McCrae* in 1980.[1] State restrictions on the availability of abortion, such as requirements for the testing of fetal viability, banning public facilities and employees from being involved in abortion, and mandatory abortion counseling and waiting periods, have been upheld in the recent decisions of *Webster* v. *Reproductive Health Services* and *Planned Parenthood* v. *Casey*.[2] The appointment of pro-choice Justice Ruth Bader Ginsburg to the Court by President Clinton in 1993 strengthens the likelihood that the basic right to an abortion will be protected into the foreseeable future.

In Europe the availability of abortion varies greatly from country to country. Both Northern Ireland and the Republic of Ireland impose a total prohibition on abortions, while in the Netherlands abortion on demand is available through the first twenty-four weeks of pregnancy.[3] Belgium in 1990 partly relaxed its prohibition against abortion, and Spain in 1985 began allowing abortion in the first twelve weeks of gestation in cases of rape, twenty-two weeks for genetic reasons, and with no limitation when the mother's life or health is threatened.[4] One of the more interesting cases has been that of Germany, where reunification brought together two nations with very different abortion laws. West Germany had a restrictive abortion law that allowed for abortion in the first three months only if a doctor found a valid medical reason for it,[5] while East Germany allowed abortion on demand through the first trimester.[6] A compromise had to be arranged between the two nations in order to complete the unification contract. It was agreed that each nation would retain its own abortion laws until the end of 1992 when a new abortion law was put into effect.[7]

Polling data for the years since the "legalizing" decision of Roe v. Wade in 1973 consistently show that a majority of Americans support the availability of abortion concurrent with strong state regulation designed to discourage the number of abortions. A Gallup poll conducted in January 1992 showed that in a national sample, 53 percent favored legal abortion under certain circumstances, 31 percent thought that abortion should be legal in all cases, and 14 percent thought that abortion should never be legal. The opinions of males and females differed only slightly: An equivalent percentage of males and females (33 percent) felt that abortion should be legal under all circumstances, 55 percent of males and 50 percent of females thought that it should be legal under certain circumstances, and 13 percent of males and 15 percent of females felt that it should never be legal. There was, however, a strong correlation between educational attainment and occupational income and attitudes on abortion: Those with higher levels of education and income favored more liberalized abortion laws.[8] The cleavages of the national debate do not seem to extend to the general voter, who favors some middle ground of legalized abortion with some restrictions.

However, while the question of abortion has been debated, the practice of abortion has continued unabated throughout the last quarter century. In 1990, the Centers for Disease Control estimated that over 1.4 million legal abortions were performed in the United States. Indeed, there have been almost 27 million legal abortions in the United States since abortion-law liberalization in 1967. The abortion rate per 1,000 women of child-bearing age (fifteen to forty-four years) jumped after the Roe decision from thirteen in 1972 to twenty-one in 1976. The rate held relatively constant at approximately twenty-four abortions per 1,000 women throughout the 1980s, and this trend continued into 1990.[9] Statistics show that 89 percent of abortions take place in the first trimester and that less than 1 percent take place in the third trimester, the great majority of which are necessary to preserve the life of the mother or are performed for anencephaly in the fetus.[10] Women below age fifteen, who obtain only 1 percent of abortions, have the highest abortion-to-birth ratio of any age group: 886 abortions for every 1,000 live births. This is compared to an abortion ratio of 187 abortions per 1,000 live births for women between the ages of thirty and thirty-four.[11] Of those women obtaining an abortion in 1990, over 55 percent were less than twenty-five years of age, with over 22 percent of that number being under age nineteen.[12]

Twenty-one states currently require parental involvement in abortions for minors.[13] Most of these states, however, provide the option of obtaining a court order that allows for a bypass of parental involvement. Sixty-one percent of minors obtaining an abortion do so with the knowledge of a parent; this percentage decreases the older the minor.[14] Teenagers having an abortion give lack of financial resources as a motivating decision 75 percent of the time, while 66 percent believe they are too immature to raise a child.[15] Older women having abortions cite reasons such as interference with work, school, and other responsibilities; no desire to be a single parent; and wishing to avoid problems with their husbands or partners.[16] However, as with other groups, financial resources are a primary motivating factor as well. The Alan Guttmacher Institute has shown that poor women are almost three times more likely to obtain an abortion than women who are financially better off.[17]

While many of the arguments for and against abortion are familiar, the issue here combines not only whether abortion is appropriate, and under what conditions, but also whether federal funding ought to be used to subsidize abortion. Critics claim that by subsidizing abortion, the federal government is encouraging it. Abortion rights opponents argue that "Legalized abortion is the first 'giant step' being taken in this new campaign which promotes death as a solution to solve social problems"; another intones that "We don't eliminate the problems that people have simply by eliminating the people."

Abortion rights supporters claim that poor women should not be denied the right to an abortion simply because of their financial status. Margaret Sanger wrote in 1917, "I found that the women of the working class had emphatic views on the crime of bringing children into the world to die of hunger. They would rather risk their lives through abortion than give birth to little ones they could not feed and care for." But the abortion issue involves not only class differences but also the perception of the unequal power women have in American politics. As one woman said, "If men could get pregnant, abortion would be a sacrament."

The following statements from the *Congressional Record* were made in the House and Senate in June 1976 over the controversial Hyde amendment. The statements for federal funding of abortion (against the Hyde amendment) are from Senators Robert Packwood and William Hathaway and Representatives Patricia Schroeder and Daniel Flood. Opponents of federal abortion funding (for the Hyde amendment) include Representatives Robert Bauman, Henry Hyde, and Ron Paul.

Endnotes

1. A. M. Pearson and P. M. Kurtz, "The Abortion Controversy: A Study in Law and Politics," in J. D. Butler and D. F. Walbert, eds., *Abortion, Medicine, and the Law* (New York: Facts on File Publications, 1986), pp. 107–135.
2. J. Rovner, "Abortion Ruling Slows Momentum of Freedom of Choice Act," *Congressional Quarterly Weekly Report* (July 4, 1992), pp. 1951–1954.
3. R. H. Nicholson, "Abortion Remains a Live Issue," *The Hastings Center Report* (September–October 1991), p. 5.
4. Ibid.
5. Annette Tuffs, *Germany: Abortion Ways and Means*, cited in *Lancet* (November 23, 1991), p. 1323.
6. Nicholson, "Abortion Remains a Live Issue."
7. Ibid.
8. *The Gallup Poll Monthly*, No. 316 (January 1992), pp. 8–9.
9. Centers for Disease Control, *Abortion Surveillance: Morbidity and Mortality Weekly Report*, Vol. 41, No. 50 (Atlanta: CDC).
10. Alan Guttmacher Institute, *Facts in Brief* (New York: Alan Guttmacher, January 4, 1993).

11. Centers for Disease Control, *Abortion Surveillance: Morbidity and Mortality Weekly Report*, Vol. 41, No. SS-5 (Atlanta: September 4, 1992).

12. CDC, *Abortion Surveillance: Morbidity and Mortality Weekly Report*, Vol. 41, No. 50.

13. Alan Guttmacher Institute, *Facts in Brief*.

14. Ibid.

15. Ibid.

16. Ibid.

17. Ibid.

YES

Comments by
Senators Robert W. Packwood and
William D. Hathaway and
Representatives Patricia Schroeder
and Daniel Flood

SEN. PACKWOOD: [The Hyde Amendment] is the same old chestnut we have had for the past few years, on this bill or in other efforts on this floor, to write into law, or in one case to write into the U.S. Constitution, a provision to prohibit abortions, sometimes prohibiting them under any circumstances and sometimes under limited circumstances.

In this particular case it is the most odious of all amendments, because the amendment put into the bill by the House would prohibit any Federal money—and bear in mind, this is HEW appropriations, covering community hospitals, medical schools, medicaid, and so forth—from being used for certain kinds of population planning under family planning programs or for therapeutic abortions of any kind. Thus, abortions to save the life of the mother, abortions because the child is likely to be born deformed, abortions of any kind would be prohibited if any Federal dollars were involved. . . .

There have been no less than 10 cases in which the courts have considered the attempt to limit the use of medicaid funds for abortion; and in every instance the Federal district courts have found the issue unconstitutional. In every case which has involved a State denial of medicaid benefits for the performance of an abortion, the lower Federal courts have consistently held that under *Roe* and *Doe*—those were the two principal Supreme Court cases—a woman's constitutional guaranteed right to privacy includes her fundamental right to abort a pregnancy. Any State action interfering with that right must be justified by a compelling State interest. However, no Federal court which has addressed this constitutional issue—and as mentioned there have been at least 10 such cases according to the American Law Division of the Library of Congress—has sustained a State's claim to compelling interest in this area.

Courts have reasoned that once a State chooses to pay for medical services providing prenatal care for poor women, it cannot refuse to pay for abortion services unless there is a legitimate, compelling State interest. Courts, including the Supreme Court, have held that moral disapproval, cost, desire to discourage, and administrative convenience are not sufficiently compelling to allow a State to restrict a constructional right. . . .

Two years ago, Dr. Louis Hellman of the Department of Health, Education, and Welfare stated some facts to the conference committee that was considering the bill which contained the Bartlett amendment.

This was 2 years ago, bear in mind.

What he said was this:

First—

Most of the women denied medicaid for abortions would be forced to carry unwanted pregnancies to term. The cost to the Government for the first year alone after birth for medical care and public assistance would be between $450 million and $565 million.

That figure represents just those who receive medicaid service for abortions because they are too poor to afford abortions of their own. If they do not have Government-assisted abortions, they will carry their pregnancies to term.

Thus, make no mistake about what the provision in this bill does. The amendment that is now in the House bill does not prohibit abortions. It prohibits abortions for poor people. The rich can still have their abortions. The rich still will have their abortions. They will go to whatever State permits them, whatever State does them with ease, or whatever country does them with ease, and we will simply force the poor back to the situation that existed prior to the Supreme Court decision in the *Roe* and *Doe* cases. . . .

Let us talk about whose lives we are concerned with. Again we are not going to stop abortions by retaining passing this House language. What we are going to do is put them back into the butcher shop and backroom, with coat hanger abortionists, and we are going to have many women dying immediately from badly performed abortions or dying very soon afterward from infections resulting from improperly performed abortions.

So if we are talking about sympathy and empathy, the desire to save lives, we are not going to do it by the inclusion of this provision in the bill. In addition to the 125 to 250 who will die, up to 25,000 cases involving serious medical complications from self-induced abortions would result. The hospital costs involved, and again, this is the estimate by Dr. Hellman 2 years ago, would be anywhere from $375 to $2,000 per patient. . . .

Senator . . . Helms, when we were considering his constitutional amendment several months ago, or at least considering the motion to consider it, indicated that abortion was really a moral issue. I am inclined to agree that it is. It is not a financial issue. It is not really a legal issue. It is a moral issue. The moral issue is, Should this Congress in one form or another attempt to impose upon the whole country a law or a constitutional amendment, if it could be passed, that would prohibit abortions—prohibit them in all cases, prohibit them in some cases, or whatever, but prohibit abortions? That is one view, that that is the function of Congress. That view is held very sincerely, very honestly, and in many cases very religiously by people who oppose abortion.

I have seldom seen in my now almost quarter century, in one form or another, of public life, an issue whose adherents on both sides more passionately felt that they are right. But just as there are those who want to prohibit abortions and are convinced, for whatever reasons, moral, religious, or others, that they are right, there are an equal number on the other side equally convinced that whether or not a woman chooses to have an abortion is not the business of this Congress, this Government, or of anyone else, but a private decision to be made between the woman and her physician. They feel that just as passionately. . . .

. . . Any group we might think of that has stature in this country, whether it be a group concerned with medical practices or with the law or with moral concern, has endorsed legalized abortion. These are not groups unconcerned with the sanctity of life. These are not barbaric, anti-Judeo-Christian, anti-Western civilization mores. These are groups concerned with the sacredness of the unborn and with the sacredness of women as anybody else.

We are a pluralistic society. We wisely wrote into our Constitution, especially in the Bill of Rights, severe restrictions on the Government's desire to impose on a majority of its citizens a particular point of view.

In this particular case, if the normal polls, such as those by Lou Harris, Dr. Gallup, and others, are to be believed on the issue of legalized abortion, a majority of Americans support the Supreme Court, and that has been a consistent position in polling for the last few years.

So in this case, it is not an effort by a well-intentioned majority to impose its wishes on a minority. It is an effort by a well-intentioned, sincere, zealous minority—minority—to impose on everyone in this country that minority's view of law, that minority's view of medicine, that minority's view of morality. I think it is a mistake. . . .

. . . If I might respond to the Senator from Rhode Island, what he says is that he is opposed to using tax money for something that is either controversial or has morality involved on both sides. It is something he is opposed to morally.

There were thousands, maybe millions, of people in this country who were morally opposed to the Vietnam war. We used public funds to prosecute that war. Many people opposing the war went to jail. They refused to pay their taxes. They said it was immoral. We said in a democracy the majority has the right to govern and the fact that the minority does not like the expenditure of funds . . .

What is the difference in using somebody's money to carry out a war that many people thought was immoral—using their money to carry out something they thought was immoral? . . .

All I am saying to the Senator from Rhode Island is that the history of this country is replete with expenditures by the Federal Government and by State governments for purposes that sometimes a few and sometimes many people thought were wrong and immoral. . . .

. . . The arguments can be well summarized by the proponents and opponents of this amendment. Perhaps the most telling point is the Draconian effect this is going to have on everyone in this country who has any interest in having an abortion and is poor. This is not a half-way amendment. This is a total, absolute prohibition. It says that no matter what the circumstances, no matter how dire the medical circumstance, no matter how endangered the life of the woman, there will be no Federal funds used for abortion, despite the fact that the Constitution now guarantees that women in this country shall have a choice as to whether or not they want an abortion.

We are going to make sure, unless my amendment passes, that that constitutional right to abortion is going to be effectively denied to a large group of citizens in this country.

Yes; the Supreme Court has passed on this type of issue before. They have said there were certain kinds of constitutional rights that cannot be taken away because somebody is too poor to take advantage of them. One is the right to counsel in a trial. For years we have said if a person has a constitutional right to defend himself in a court, he cannot be denied that right because he is too poor to afford it.

Now the Supreme Court has said that everyone has a constitutional right to decide for themselves, and I emphasize to decide for themselves, whether or not they want an abortion.

I think it would be immoral for this Congress to say, "Yes, the Constitution guarantees you the right to decide for yourself whether or not to have an abortion, but we are going to effectively take away that right for those who cannot afford it."

I know the frustration of those who say there have not been hearings in the Finance Committee, or adequate hearings elsewhere. In 1970 I proposed a bill which would have legalized abortion nationally. This was before the Supreme Court decision legalized it. I could not get any hearings. Although the Senator from Oklahoma and the Senator from North Carolina who individually support their particular position were not here at the time, many Senators who are here now were very opposed to my having any hearing on that amendment.

Many of the very same organizations in this country who are complaining they have not had a hearing, including the Right to Life group, were vehemently opposed to giving me any hearing when the law was on their side.

So let us call a spade a spade. The law has changed. The law is now on the side of those who want to have an abortion. Those who were so vehemently opposed to hearings before, when the law was on their side, now are turning the argument and complaining that the very argument they made is being used against them. When indeed it has not been used against them.

When I introduced my amendments there was not a single hearing in this entire Congress on the issue. There was not a single vote on the floor on this issue. Now we have had vote after vote after vote, and we have had hearings, more hearings than any normal bill or constitutional amendment gets.

If we are going to adopt the standard that the Federal Government or the State governments will not spend money on something that a bare minority of its citizens are passionately or morally opposed to, then we are not going to spend money for much of anything. A representative form of government cannot work if a minority at any particular stage will say, "Wait, we feel strongly about that so we are not going to spend any money."

We have a system in this country which says, within the limits of the Constitution, the majority shall have the right to rule consonant with the protection of minority rights guaranteed by the Constitution.

We cannot allow a determined minority to attempt to impose upon all of the majority a view that that minority alone holds.

All I am asking when we finally vote in a few moments to table this amendment is to consider whether or not we want to keep a provision in this bill which is not neutral, but a discriminatory provision that says to everyone in this country who has been guaranteed a right to obtain an abortion by the Constitution and is poor, "Forget it"; and to everyone in this country who has been guaranteed a right by the Constitution and who is rich, "Pay for it to preserve it."

If we have come to the place where the preservation of critical constitutional rights is dependent upon wealth, and wealth alone, then we have reached a very sorry passel in this country. . . .

Senator [Helms] makes the argument—or claims that I made the argument—that it is cheaper to have abortions than to have women bear pregnancies to term and then to take care of the children in a variety of ways if they happen to be poor or welfare cases. That is not why I am opposed to the Hyde amendment, any more than I support capital punishment because it might be cheaper to execute criminals than to imprison them for life. I do support capital punishment, but not on the basis of fiscal conservatism.

I think the woman is entitled to determine for herself whether or not she wants to terminate an unwanted pregnancy. It is not the business of the Senator from North Carolina nor me nor the U.S. Government, nor anybody else. It is a decision for that woman to make.

To try to draw analogies to other countries—and the Senator from North Carolina made reference to Nazi Germany—does no good. Actually, the situation was that under the Weimar Republic, abortions were legal in Germany. When Hitler came to power, the Government of the Third Reich made abortions in Germany illegal, because there was a manpower shortage in Germany. I do not know what that proves.

Japan has had legal abortion since 1947. Japan is a perfectly civilized, mature country, able, when they have scandals in their government, to put their own house in order. What does that prove about abortions? That abortions are all right because Japan is a democratic government, or that abortions are bad because some government we do not like allows them? I do not think it proves anything at all. It is a non sequitur.

Abortion is a moral issue. It is one of the most evenly divided issues that this country has faced in this century. Although the position on abortion throughout history has changed from time to time—just look at the common law, forgetting for the moment the rest of Europe. By and large, under common law, until 1800 in England, abortions were legal, not a crime, and they were legal in this country under common law. It was not until the early and mid-1800's that laws were passed against abortions.

Part of the reason for the change was moral. People began to think that abortions were bad. Part of it was medical; abortions were a very unsafe procedure. Many, many more women died from abortions than died from carrying pregnancies to term. So, for a variety of reasons, starting roughly in the 1830's and 1840's, we began in this country to see States passing laws prohibiting abortions.

Then, starting in the early and mid-1960's, we began to see States again changing their laws on abortion. The State of Colorado was a forerunner in passing what was regarded then as a modern abortion statute. The State of New York, in its legislature, passed a statute legalizing abortion in that State. The State of Washington had the issue on the ballot; the State of Washington voted for legalized abortion. Some States have had it on the ballot and have turned it down.

All I am using these illustrations for is to prove that there has been a cycle of opinion about abortion. Never, in our history, either in terms of religious annals or in terms of legal annals, has there been an irrevocable time when everybody said, "It is right" or "It is wrong." Never has there been a 100-percent agreement on the subject of abortion. But we can say that in 200 years, we have gone full circle, in terms of at least a majority opinion, from legal to illegal and back to legal again.

I maintain that God did not talk to any of us at any time in that complete circle and say, "At this point in time, we have reached the final decision on abortion: it is right, it is just, it is moral;" or, "It is awful, it is illegal, it is immoral."

If anything, it is a personal decision, a very, very personal decision, and one that should be left to a woman and her physician to determine whether or not that abortion is going to be performed.

The argument of morality is brought into this so often that each time we have this argument, I want to read the list of just religious organizations—not the dozens of others, just the religious organizations—that are on record in favor of legalized abortion.

The religious organizations which have endorsed abortion rights are:

[A long list of organizations followed.]

That only takes the religious list through the last few months of 1975. It does not include religious organizations that, in 1976, have endorsed legalized abortion. I cite that list simply to say that there is a religious division in this country as to whether or not we should have legalized abortion: a very significant portion of religious leadership in this country says yes, and a very significant portion says no. Under those circumstances, we should not, in this country, attempt to intervene on one side or the other in what is essentially a moral dispute.

Let us make no mistake about it: We are not going to stop abortions by passing the Hyde amendment. Rich women will have safe abortions. Poor women will either bear their pregnancies to term, whether they want to or not, or they will have illegal abortions and, in many cases, they will die from infection and the other aftereffects of cheap, backroom, butcher shop abortions.

We are not going to stop it. What we are going to do is make a distinction between the rich and the poor. If that is what this Congress wants to do, if this Congress wants to weigh in on one side of a very personal, moral issue, then let them know full well that they are not weighing in to stop abortions; they are weighing in to stop abortions for a small slice of this country that is so poor, so barren of any economic resources, that unless they have Government help for medical assistance, they get no medical assistance. In this case, they would get no medical assistance for abortion.

I hope that will not be the position of this Congress, because if that is the position of this Congress, then we are being hypocritical in the sense of thinking that we are going to stop abortions, and we are sentencing many women to death who will try to have abortions that will be badly, unscientifically performed, and who will die as a result of those abortions. . . .

SEN. HATHAWAY: . . . The constitutional nature of this particular issue is clear, and this amendment clearly runs counter to existing constitutional law. Three years ago, in Roe against Wade and Doe against Bolton, the Supreme Court held that every woman has a qualified right to terminate her pregnancy, based on her constitutional right to privacy. In the face of that decision, opponents of that right have quite correctly realized that nothing short of a constitutional amendment would be sufficient to alter that decision. Supporters of such an amendment brought it to the floor of the Senate this past April 28, despite the fact that the amendment had not been reported by the Committee on the Judiciary, which is charged with its consideration. The Senate voted at that time to table that amendment, by a vote of 47 to 40. I believe that vote should stand for the time being as a Senate rejection of the very heart of the antiabortion argument, that it should be unconstitutional to perform one.

Finally, since the Senate has refused to accept the argument that abortions should be outlawed in the U.S. Constitution, and since the Supreme Court has held that the Constitution guarantees at least a qualified right to an abortion, an amendment such as the one currently before us would clearly violate other constitutional rights, such as the 14th amendment right of poor and indigent women to equal protection under the health laws of this country.

If Federal funds can be provided for maternal care under our health laws, and abortion has been held to be both legal and constitutional, it would be blatant discrimination to deny such legal medical procedures to women who need them. This is especially true with regard to the totally unqualified restriction in the House amendment. . . .

. . . In my opinion, this amendment which the House adopted, prohibiting any funds for purposes of abortion, is in direct contravention of the 14th amendment to the Constitution, the equal protection amendment, particularly and perhaps only with respect to medicaid funds.

The situation we are setting up by denying States the right to spend money for abortion purposes under the medicaid program is this: We are saying, in effect, that the poor or indigent woman who is pregnant can get money under medicaid only if she intends to go through or is medically able to go through with a full-term pregnancy. If that is not her intention, however, and she wishes or needs to exercise her right, guaranteed by the Supreme Court under the Constitution of the United States, to have an abortion, we are denying her those funds. That is clearly a violation of the equal protection provision, because we are discriminating within a class of people who are entitled to Federal funds. Please note this is not a "rich against poor" argument, but rather the setting up of discrimination classes among the poor.

Second, and I suppose this is the most important, is the public policy argument. Are we going on record, as a Congress, saying we are going to deny Federal funds for certain individuals, those who want or need to have an abortion, or those who have been advised by a physician to have an abortion? Are we going on record saying that they will be deprived of Federal funds for this purpose? Aside from the 14th amendment argument, should it be the policy of Congress to undercut any right that belongs to the people under the Constitution, such as the right interpreted by the Supreme Court in Roe against Wade and in Doe against Bolton.

I think this is an extremely important issue. It does not really make any difference whether you are on the side of abortion or whether you are against abortion. It is our responsibility to uphold the Constitution of the United States as interpreted by the Supreme Court. Our only recourse in that regard is to amend the Constitution. Of course, there have been efforts in regard to amending the Constitution with respect to abortion. At the present time they have not seen fruition, but perhaps some day that will be the subject of debate in the Senate.

In the meantime, the Constitution as interpreted by the Supreme Court remains. We certainly are obligated not to discourage people from exercising their right under the Constitution by depriving them of funds so they can so exercise that right.

. . . I have heard a lot of arguments with respect to the morality of abortion. I think we all know that morality is an individual question. There may be people who have moral feelings about the Supreme Court's ruling. There may be people who have moral feelings about other provisions in the Constitution—the right to bear arms, for example. I suppose there are some people who are pacifists who do not think that provision of the Constitution should be there.

I think it is highly necessary in this society that we have, each of us, strong moral principles to which we adhere. But we have all agreed that the Constitution, as interpreted by the Supreme Court, is the fundamental law of the land, and that each of our own moral feelings or holdings do not override that Constitution. Although we may disagree with the Constitution and the laws because of our moral precepts, nevertheless we are committed to obeying those laws and to adhering to the basic principles of the Constitution.

As I mentioned earlier, if we care to either change those laws or amend the Constitution we are certainly free to do so. But as long as there is a constitutional right remaining which allows women to have an abortion under certain circumstances, we certainly should not discourage them from using that right by the tactic that has been employed by the House. . . .

REP. SCHROEDER . . . The Hyde amendment is the most far-reaching antiabortion rider ever passed by Congress. Let us note, however, that it will not stop abortions. This amendment will only limit the availability of safe abortions to poor women.

It is ironic that the Hyde amendment violates the very purpose of this Labor-HEW appropriations bill—that of providing services for all Americans regardless of their economic status. The issue at hand is a health service—determined by a patient and her physician. The Hyde amendment will interfere with that medical decision as it affects low-income women only. Those who can pay will have no trouble obtaining the services.

This is a harsh amendment, which cruelly hits the young, since teenage abortions account for one-third of all the abortions performed, according to Government sources.

The April 1976 report of HEW's abortion surveillance unit, the Center for Disease Control on Abortion, states that there are 205,000 teenage abortions annually. Their statistics indicate that the abortion age distribution has remained unchanged for 3 years. One-third of all abortions are teenage, one-third between the ages 20 and 24, and the remaining third, 25 years and older.

The report goes on to say that more pregnant women below the age of 15 underwent abortion than had a live birth in 1974. In summary, this Government report said that women obtaining legal abortion tended to be young, white, unmarried, pregnant for the first time, and early in pregnancy.

The Subcommittee on Census and Population, which I chair, has been holding oversight hearings on the issue of population. We have been confronted time and again with the magnitude of the teenage pregnancy problem. In 1973, of 3.1 million births, 407,000 were born out of wedlock, with 55 percent or 216,000 born to teenagers.

A nationwide survey in 1971 showed that four-fifths of the sexually experienced, unmarried teenagers did not use contraception when engaging in sexual intercourse. The major reasons cited for failing to use contraception were inaccurate knowledge about the risk of pregnancy or difficulty in obtaining contraception. One witness illustrated the extent of the problem of teenage pregnancies this way: If present rates continue, the 2 million girls who reached their 14th birthdays in 1975 will bear nearly one quarter of a million children out-of-wedlock before they reach their 20th birthdays in 1981. The consequences of these unwanted pregnancies among teenagers are tragic and costly—for the individual, for the unborn child, and for society.

When I asked the American Public Health Association for their position on the Hyde amendment, they warned that—

> The public health community would definitely predict a rise in maternal and infant mortality and morbidity in the United States as a result of these restrictions.

HEW Under Secretary Marjarie Lynch last month underscored the health risks from teenage births. She indicated that young mothers were more apt to bear low-birth-weight babies with greater risks of birth defects, retardation, and death.

My colleagues, I ask you to consider carefully the decision you make today. The consequences of the adoption of the Hyde amendment are disastrous. Such consequences include illegal or self-induced abortions, unwanted or mistimed births, out-of-wedlock births, school drop-outs, suicides, and precipitous marriages, not to mention the other health and social problems.

We cannot ignore the staggering costs of this amendment. Dr. Louis Hellman, in an official HEW impact statement on the Hyde amendment, reports that while medicaid reimbursement for abortions amounts to $50 million annually, the implementation of this amendment, forcing poor women to carry unwanted pregnancies to term, will cost the Government from $450 to $565 million for medical care and public assistance for the first year after birth.

The Colorado Department of Health has put together some interesting statistics on the costs of unwanted pregnancies. They estimate that for every $1 spent on family planning services in Colorado, $12 are saved in State, local, and Federal money. The department arrived at this figure by adding up the savings to the State in social services and medicaid payments, payments to Colorado General Hospital, sales tax revenues from the earnings of women who might have been prevented from working due to child-bearing, the costs in general and special education programs, and the costs of community centers and facilities for mentally handicapped individuals who would have been born.

Each of our States will suffer the consequences of the action we take here today—a burden they can ill afford.

In addition, retention of the Hyde amendment would interfere with existing State statutes on use of public funds for abortions. Forty-seven States and the District of Columbia now permit medicaid reimbursement for abortions, but the Hyde amendment would prevent them from following their own State laws and guidelines. The result would be administrative chaos and increased litigation.

This amendment is clearly discriminatory and violates the equal protection clause of the 5th and 14th amendments and the right to privacy as interpreted by the U.S. Supreme Court in Roe against Wade, which was reaffirmed by the High Court's July 1 ruling that outlawed State laws requiring spousal or parental consent for abortions.

Adoption of this amendment would be untimely indeed. Only recently the Supreme Court announced that it would hear arguments during this fall session on two cases involving use of medicaid funds for abortions. It would be inappropriate for Congress to enact into law at this time a measure which may well be ruled unconstitutional this year.

I recently received a letter from the Religious Coalition for Abortion Rights about the Hyde amendment. The letter from the coalition said that—

> While the 23 diverse religious groups have differing views on when abortion is morally justifiable, all agreed that every woman, regardless of economic status, should have the legal choice with respect to abortion, consistent with sound medical practice and in accordance with her conscience.

It added that the Hyde amendment would deny constitutionally guaranteed rights of conscience and freedom to follow one's own religious teachings on abortion by imposing on poor women a religious doctrine which is not shared by all people.

. . . I ask that the House of Representatives have respect for our Constitution and compassion for the poor—those who can very often least afford to bear unwanted or unplanned children. Denial to poor women of the rights granted in the Supreme Court decisions is clearly discriminatory. . . .

REP. FLOOD: . . . I oppose this amendment, and I will tell you why. Listen. This is blatantly discriminatory; that is why.

The Members do not like that? Of course they do not. It does not prohibit abortion. No, it does not prohibit abortion. It prohibits abortion for poor people. That is what it does. That is a horse of a different rolling stone. That is what it does. It does not require any change in the practice of the middle-income and the upper-income people. Oh, no. They are able to go to their private practitioners and get the service done for a fee. But, it does take away the option from those of our citizens who must rely on medicaid—and other public programs for medical care.

Now abortion, Mr. Chairman, abortion is not an economic issue; not at all. The morality—all right, the morality of abortion is no different for a poor family—the morality of abortion is no different for a poor family than it is for a rich family. Is that right? Of course: a standard of morality is a standard.

To accept—now, this is coming from me—to accept this amendment, the right of this country to impose on its poor citizens, impose on them a morality which it is not willing to impose on the rich as well, we would not dare do that. That is what this amendment does. To me, the choice is clear. Listen: A vote for this amendment is not a vote against abortion. It is a vote against poor people. That is what it is, as plain as the nose on your face. . . .

NO

Comments by Representatives Robert E. Bauman, Henry J. Hyde, and Ron Paul

REP. BAUMAN: . . . [Rep. Flood] objects to using an appropriation bill for the purpose of making public policy, but no question was raised against the form of this amendment, and none could be, because it is a legitimate limit on the expenditure of Federal funds.

[Rep. Flood] raises an interesting . . . point . . . that this would discriminate against poor people. The answer is that we have not been able to pass a constitutional amendment that would permit the right to life, regardless of poverty or wealth. But I do not understand that the child of a poor parent has any less right to live than the child of a rich parent. If we could protect the right to life for all children, we would do it. But the fact of the matter is, under medicaid and other programs that are financed in this bill, the Federal Government has been paying for more than 300,000 abortions annually at a cost of $40 to $50 million.

I think the unborn children whose lives are being snuffed out, even though they may not be adults, have a right to live, too, regardless of the mistaken and immoral Supreme Court decision. I do not think the taxpayers of the United States have any obligation to permit their money to be used in this manner for federally financed abortions. That is the only issue here today.

. . . This is indeed a vote on whether or not we are for the right to life for millions of people who are not being permitted to be born. And they are people. The vote we cast on this will show whether or not we are for the right to live. Let us permit, those who are children of the poor to live, and then let us go on and hold up our action as an example. Let the House act on this fundamental issue, so that perhaps one day soon all unborn people in the United States can be permitted to live.

This is the most fundamental issue that this House will ever address; it involves a precious right once accorded to every Member at some time in the past, the right to live. Let us not deny it to others. . . .

REP. HYDE: . . . This amendment may stimulate a lot of debate—but it need not—because I believe most Members know how they will vote on this issue.

Nevertheless, there are those of us who believe it is to the everlasting shame of this country that in 1973 approximately 800,000 legal abortions were performed in this country—and so it is fair to assume that this year over a million human lives will be destroyed because they are inconvenient to someone.

The unborn child facing an abortion can best be classified as a member of the innocently inconvenient and since the pernicious doctrine that some lives are more important than others seems to be persuasive with the pro-abortion forces, we who seek to protect that most defenseless and innocent of human lives, the unborn—seek to inhibit the use of Federal funds to pay for and thus encourage abortion as an answer to the human and compelling problem of an unwanted child.

We are all exercised at the wanton killing of the porpoise, the baby seal. We urge big game hunters to save the tiger, but we somehow turn away at the specter of a million human beings being violently destroyed because this great society does not want them.

And make no mistake, an abortion is violent.

I think in the final analysis, you must determine whether or not the unborn person is human. If you think it is animal or vegetable then, of course, it is disposable like an empty beer can to be crushed and thrown out with the rest of the trash.

But medicine, biology, embryology, say that growing living organism is not animal or vegetable or mineral—but it is a human life.

And if you believe that human life is deserving of due process of law—of equal protection of the laws, then you cannot in logic and conscience help fund the execution of these innocent defenseless human lives.

If we are to order our lives by the precepts of animal husbandry, then I guess abortion is an acceptable answer. If we human beings are not of a higher order than animals then let us save our pretentious aspirations for a better and more just world and recognize this is an anthill we inhabit and there are no such things as ideals or justice or morality.

Once conception has occurred a new and unique genetic package has been created, not a potential human being, but a human being with potential. For 9 months the mother provides nourishment and shelter, and birth is no substantial change, it is merely a change of address.

We are told that bringing an unwanted child into the world is an obscene act. Unwanted by whom? Is it too subtle a notion to understand it is more important to be a loving person than to be one who is loved? We need more people who are capable of projecting love.

We hear the claim that the poor are denied a right available to other women if we do not use tax money to fund abortions.

Well, make a list of all the things society denies poor women and let them make the choice of what we will give them.

Don't say "poor women, go destroy your young, and we will pay for it."

An innocent, defenseless human life, in a caring and humane society deserves better than to be flushed down a toilet or burned in an incinerator.

The promise of America is that life is not just for the privileged, the planned, or the perfect. . . .

There are three major objections raised by opponents of the so-called Hyde amendment. The first is: "If permitted to stand it will prevent abortions to save the life of the mother."

Let me make it crystal clear that this amendment is not intended to prohibit any abortion deemed necessary to save the life of the mother. Such operations do not even fall within the medical terminology of abortion. They are called removal of a diseased uterus, or removal of an ectopic pregnancy, or some similar terms. Also, the medical indications for so-called therapeutics abortions today are almost zero due to advances in medical science and technology.

But nevertheless, let there be no doubt about the legislative intent of this amendment: It does not apply to those abortions necessary to save the life of the mother nor is it intended to apply to the IUD, the intrauterine device, nor to the so-called "morning after" pills.

The next inaccurate claim is that this amendment may even have "a restrictive impact upon those federally funded medical schools where abortion is taught as a medical procedure."

This is not the intent of this amendment at all. All we intend to do is to deny the use of taxpayers' funds to pay for the actual abortion procedure and to forbid the use of Federal funds to promote or encourage anyone to have an abortion. We are all to familiar with those instances where the social worker makes the decision, not the distressed pregnant woman.

Lastly, the most emotional appeal is made that this amendment denies to a poor woman a right to an abortion which a rich woman can enjoy. To accept the argument that this amendment denies the right to an abortion to a poor woman, we have to accept the argument that an abortion is a desirable thing. I reject that completely. Abortion is violence.

The gentleman from Maryland asked if we had ever seen a coathanger abortion. Take a look at any abortion and tell me that that is not violence.

Abortion is an inhuman solution to a very human problem. The only virtue to abortion is that it is a final solution. Believe me, it is a final solution, especially to the unborn child.

Let the poor women of America make a list of those things that society denies them and which are enjoyed by rich women. Decent housing, decent education, decent food, decent income, and then say to them, "Now, those will take second place. But we will encourage you to kill your unborn young children. Besides, there are too many of you anyway."

If rich women want to enjoy their high-priced vices, that is their responsibility. They can get the finest heroin in the world that is not available on the street. They can get a face lift. They can fly to Las Vegas and gamble. That is fine, but not at the taxpayers' expense. . . .

. . . To kill an unborn child is to deny to the most defenseless of human beings the most basic right of all, the right to life. What good are the rest of our cherished freedoms, the right to free speech, freedom of the press, freedom of worship; yes, even of privacy, if we are not alive to enjoy them.

Thank God our parents did not believe in abortion or I would be talking to an empty hall.

I submit the preborn child is not a set of diseased tonsils. It is not a diseased appendix to be excised and flushed away. It is a human being.

Yes, a woman has a right not to become pregnant, but once a human life has been created, a new set of rights and duties arises, and to kill this life because it is innocently inconvenient, to say that some lives are worthwhile and some are socially expendable, is to totally reject the words of our forefathers that "All men are created equal," not born equal, created equal.

All of us should have a particular sensitivity to the concept of the word genocide. In New York City, last year for every 1,000 minority births, there were 1,304 minority abortions. That is one way to get rid of the poverty problem, get rid of poor people. Let us call that pooricide.

Jesse Jackson says:

You just can't kill poor people who are in your way.

Dick Gregory says:

I know a man in Chicago who wipes out 125 black babies a day in one of those abortion clinics. You say a poor black woman has as much right to an abortion as a rich white one. Well, then, give her the right to a Cadillac, a mink, and a trip to Paris.

The fact that the Supreme Court has "legalized" abortion in no way sanctifies nor enshrines this procedure. Justice Holmes called wiretapping a "dirty business." The wholesale slaughter of the innocently inconvenient in this country could well be called a "bloody business" and one that must make Herod's biblical slaughter of the innocents seem almost benign.

It is estimated in this country today that there are about 1 million abortions each year in America. This is almost twice as many as the number of people we lost in all the wars of this century; World War I, World War II, Korea and Vietnam, all put together.

Last year 275,000 abortions were paid for by tax money at a cost of $50 million.

But as to the Supreme Court sanction, let me remind everyone that that Court once found Dred Scott to be a chattel, a thing.

I say whenever human life is cheapened, devalued, whenever it becomes a disposable commodity, a thing, then we truly inhabit an anthill. . . .

No one, least of all myself, denies the hardship and even in some cases tragedy that can result from an unwanted pregnancy. The issue, however, is whether the avoidance of this hardship is worth the killing of a human life. The issue is the nature of the sacrifice to avoid this hardship.

The word "kill" is a harsh word—the preferred word among abortionists is "terminate." Can you imagine anyone saying "I'm going to terminate these mosquitoes or cockroaches or crabgrass"? No, you "kill" these pests but you "terminate" the human life of an unwanted and innocent pregnancy through abortion. The use of terminate instead of kill is a triumph of esthetics over intractable reality.

George Will, in the current issue of *Newsweek* in an editorial entitled "Discretionary Killing," tells us that last year there were a million abortions in the United States and 50 million worldwide. He characterizes the killing of the unborn on this scale "a revolution against the judgment of generations."

An article in the *Chicago Tribune* of August 20 by columnist Joan Beck states:

A sad irony now confronts the feminists who fought so hard and so long to make abortion on demand legally available: Abortion is increasingly being used to end the life of healthy unborn infants just because they are not of the sex their parents prefer. And almost all of the unborn babies being aborted for no reason except that they are of an unwanted sex, are female.

This ultimate discrimination against females is expected to increase rapidly in the next few years. Cheap and highly accurate methods of learning the sex of unborn infants early in pregnancy will become widely available in one or two years. These methods will replace the complex and expensive techniques now required for the purpose. Couples willing to resort to abortion will then find it easy to produce only sons or daughters in the precise order they desire.

Justice William O. Douglas is esteemed by many Americans as a man of limitless sensitivity and compassion. In a lengthy dissent in the 1972 case of *Sierra Club* vs. *Morton* (405 U.S. 727), he urged that in cases concerning the environment—

Environmental issues should be tendered by the inanimate object itself. Then there will be assurances that all of the forms of life which it represents will stand before the Court—the pileated woodpecker as well as the coyote and bear, the lemming as well as the trout in the streams. Those inarticulate members of the ecological group cannot speak. But those people who have so frequented the place as to know its values and wonders will be able to speak for the entire ecological community.

He also said:

The ordinary corporation is a "person" for purposes of the adjudication process whether it represents proprietary, spiritual, esthetic or charitable causes. So it should be as respects valleys, Alpine meadows, rivers, lakes, estuaries, beaches, ridges, groves of trees, swampland or even air, that feel the destructive pressures of modern technology and modern life.

I have difficulty in reconciling these views with those holding the unborn to have no standing in court or in their mother's womb. The unborn possess this distinction—they are human and, if not killed by some physician, then life and thought, emotion and choice, love and reason, will go on inside them.

I do support this amendment, not because it is perfect, but because it is the best attainable. Many human lives will be saved, and this is no small achievement.

This language says that human beings are not mere commodities to be manipulated, exploited, or thrown away. This language tells the social and biological engineers that this Congress still believes that human life is unique in creation and possessed of dignity.

REP. PAUL   . . . Abortion and its ramifications [are] probably the most complex, controversial, social, legal, religious, medical issue[s] of all times. There is no simple answer to satisfy all persons involved. Those who believe there is an easy solution are kidding themselves. Sincere deliberation with the hope and intention of reducing the subjective emotional response to objective reasoning is of the utmost importance if the social antagonism that has arisen over this issue is to be alleviated. Those who would belittle its importance fail to see the significance of the impact that Presidential aspirant Ellen McCormick has made this past 6 months. What other single social issue since slavery has prompted such political activism. . . .

Up until April of 1976 I had been practicing obstetrics and gynecology. I have been involved in medicine for 19 years. After medical school the specialty training that I received took 5 years. In other words, I have treated thousands of obstetrical cases and delivered an estimated 4,000 babies. During this period of time I never saw one case which required therapeutic abortion in order to preserve the life of the mother. The issue of "the 'threat' to the mother" is not realistic since it is so rare. This is emotionally concocted and does not do justice to those who use this as the reason for legislation.

When it does exist the Hyde amendment would not prevent treatment to the mother. Today we do not need to abort women for heart disease and diabetes; that is for the medical illnesses. The conditions that require treatment for the mother in order to save her life are today limited to cancer. This amendment would not prevent this treatment and the loss of fetal life would be incidental to the radiation treatment or the hysterectomy, if required. One other item—there are many examples of some chronic illnesses improving with pregnancy when at one time the medical community believed pregnancy increased the severity of the disease.

Many use as the justification to abort, the potential birth of a malformed child. This to me is the worst reason conceivable. This literally justifies the elimination of newborn defective life and those who are apparently useless. Most would classify this as murder and even many of the pro-abortionists would agree. However, there are many who reason that the decisionmaking should extend up to 1 year of life. The question you must be forced to ask then is, What about defective and useless ideas that disrupt society. History shows that others have justified this also and destroyed life for causes such as religious and political beliefs.

I did not always draw rather stringent lines on abortion until I was forced as a young physician to face up to the problem. I was called to assist one day as many young residents are in an operation performed by a staff member. It turned out to be a hysterotomy, a type of caesarian section with the removal of a 2-pound infant that cried and breathed. The infant was put in the trash and left to die. At that time it was even in defiance of all current laws. We as physicians can now save many infants that are born weighing 2 pounds. The Supreme Court now permits abortion up to 6 months of gestation and later under special circumstances. Frequently this will involve infants weighing as much as 3 pounds. Following this experience I reconsidered my position of "necessary abortion" and came up with an entirely different perspective. One physician who ran an abortion clinic for years and supervised thousands of abortions has recently joined me in reassessing his position and now opposes abortion due to the callousness with which it is administered. Young people came to my office asking for an abortion as if it were requesting an aspirin for a headache. This lack of concern for human life is an omnious sign of a decaying culture. We as a Congress must not contribute to this decay.

Civil libertarians must oppose tax dollars for abortion if they choose to be consistent. The use of tax dollars for abortion flaunts the first amendment protection of religious liberty. The advice I give to the pro-abortionists is "Do not use the dollar of citizens with devout religious beliefs against abortion to carry out this procedure." This is like waving a red flag in front of a bull and providing an incentive for the antiabortionist to organize and rally with great strength. Just remember how the antiwar groups rallied and changed a bad situation in the 1960's when kids were forced to serve and die and taxpayers forced to pay for an undeclared illegal war pursued by an ill-advised administration.

The 14th amendment protects depriving any person of life. Government exists to protect life, not to destroy it. Those of you who still believe that life is not involved need to visit more operating rooms and possibly you would be converted like I was.

Legally there is good historic precedent to establish the rights of the unborn and to recognize their legal existence. Right of inheritance is recognized for the conceived but unborn infants when the death of the father occurs prior to the birth. The right of suit by the unborn is recognized in accidents that kill or injure an unborn. The right of suit by the unborn is recognized in injury that harms the unborn in such cases as drug injury. The injured unborn can sue MD's after birth for malpractice if we as physicians injure the infant with bad medical judgment. From day one in medical school we are taught two lives are involved and the responsibility is ominous, in that we need to give deep concern for the new life to be and protect it in the best way possible so that it can enter its new environment free of injury since its more vulnerable predelivered state is so precarious and needs specific help, assistance, protection, and consideration.

The sickest argument for abortion is that the poor black population needs to be reduced. Keep them off the welfare rolls some conservatives argue. Even liberals have argued with me that since I oppose the welfare state this would fit into my desire. I am for reducing the welfare state but certainly not this way. The welfare state will be reduced when the welfare ethic of materialistic redistribution by force is challenged and changed.

Frequently abortion is performed at the desire of an aggressive social worker who fears food may become scarce and for various other personal prejudices. Teenage abortion now is done with specific exclusion of parental consent, if the Government so chooses; another attack on religious convictions regarding the sanctity of the family. Opposite to this is the abortion for the mother of the pregnant girl "to save face." In the private practice I had, this was the strongest motivating factor for abortion. The pregnant girl usually had a great psychological need and desire to be pregnant and deliver a baby. A symbol to her of something that represented love and affection. Abortion carelessly given, financed by the Government, hardly will settle this deep psychological problem.

My entire political philosophy is built on the firm conviction of the absolute right to one's life and property but precludes all violent activity. Some challenge my position on abortion as saying that I violate the mother's right to her life by preventing abortion. Since the key lies in whether or not one or two lives exist my decision is based on my medical knowledge that life does exist prior to birth and after conception. If the mother can reject that same life in her body because it just happens to be there she could reject that same life in her house. Besides a strong argument exists that the mother's rights are violated by a newborn, screaming, hungry, naked infant much more so than by the inconvenience of an innocent, silent, warm, contented unborn. The newborn demands a much greater amount of care, concern, time, and effort, and therefore is a so-called violation of the mother's rights and yet we recognize caring for a child as a responsibility both legal and moral once birth occurs.

DISCUSSION QUESTIONS

1. Are the reproductive rights of women absolute? Do you think any restrictions should be placed on the availability of abortion?
2. Abortion in some countries is used to favor the birth of male children. Do you think the possibility exists that abortion could be used in the United States to select children with certain characteristics deemed advantageous by the parents? Is there any problem with this?
3. How have other nations dealt with the abortion issue? Has the issue been as divisive in other nations as it has in the United States? Why or why not?
4. What is the governmental role in ensuring equity in the availability of abortion? Does it have a role at all? Why or why not?
5. What role should men play, if any, in deciding whether an abortion is appropriate?
6. Do you know anyone who has had an abortion? Describe her experience (as best you know it), and compare it with various stereotypes of women having abortions. Are the experiences similar or different? Why?
7. Do you think that subsidizing the cost of abortions would increase the number of abortions performed? Why or why not? How does this conclusion affect your argument to the debate question of this chapter?
8. Should minors be required to have parental permission in order to have an abortion? Why or why not?
9. What impact do you think a Supreme Court ruling that denied women the right to an abortion would actually have?

ADDITIONAL READINGS

Bonavoglia, Angela, ed. *The Choices We Made: Twenty-Five Women Speak Out About Abortion* (New York: Random House, 1991).

Brodie, M. Janine, Shelley A. M. Gavigan, and Jane Jenson. *The Politics of Abortion* (Toronto: Oxford University Press, 1992).

Campbell, Dennis, ed. *Abortion Law and Public Policy* (Dordrecht, Holland: Martinus Nijhoff, 1984).

Connery, John. *Abortion: The Development of the Roman Catholic Perspective* (Chicago: Loyola University Press, 1977).

Craig, Barbara Hinkson, and David M. O'Brien. *Abortion and American Politics* (Chatham, N.J.: Chatham House, 1993).

Dellinger, Walter. "Should We Compromise on Abortion?" *The American Prospect* (Summer 1990).

Feldman, Dr. David. *Birth Control in Jewish Law* (New York: New York University Press, 1968).

Glendon, Mary Ann. *Abortion and Divorce in Western Law* (Cambridge, Mass.: Harvard University Press, 1987).

Glendon, Mary Ann. *Rights Talk: The Impoverishment of Political Discourse* (New York: Free Press, 1991).

Grisez, Germain. *Abortion: The Myths, the Realities, and the Arguments* (New York: Corpus Books, 1970).

Jacobson, Jodi L. *The Global Politics of Abortion* (Washington, D.C.: Worldwatch Institute, 1990).

Luker, Kristin. *Abortion and the Politics of Motherhood* (Berkeley: University of California Press, 1984).

Mohr, James C. *Abortion in America: The Origins and Evolution of National Policy, 1800–1900* (New York: Oxford University Press, 1978).

Morowitz, Harold J., and James S. Trefil. *The Facts of Life: Science and the Abortion Controversy* (New York: Oxford University Press, 1992).

Noonan, John, ed. *The Morality of Abortion: Legal and Historical Perspectives* (Cambridge, Mass.: Harvard University Press, 1970).

Rosenblatt, Roger. *Life Itself: Abortion in the American Mind* (New York: Random House, 1992).

Tribe, Laurence H. "The Abortion Funding Conundrum: Inalienable Rights, Affirmative Duties, and the Dilemma of Independence." *Harvard Law Review* (November 1985).

Tribe, Laurence H. *Abortion: The Clash of Absolutes* (New York: Norton, 1990).

Wills, Garry. *Under God: Religion and American Politics* (New York: Simon & Schuster, 1960).

Wishner, Jane B., ed. *Abortion and the States: Political Change and Future Regulation* (Chicago: American Bar Association, 1993).

Credits *(continued from page iv)*

ABOUT THE AUTHOR

John A. Hird teaches public policy and environmental policy in the Department of Political Science at the University of Massachusetts at Amherst. He received his Ph.D. in public policy from the University of California at Berkeley, and has served as Research Fellow at the Brookings Institution and as an economist with the President's Council of Economic Advisers. In 1992 he received the first annual Miriam Mills Award, given to an outstanding contributor in policy studies under the age of 35, from the Policy Studies Organization. He is the author of *Superfund: The Political Economy of Environmental Risk* (Johns Hopkins University Press, 1994).